"Fliers," "first-of-Mays," "web girls" train long hours under Big Top at Winter Quarters

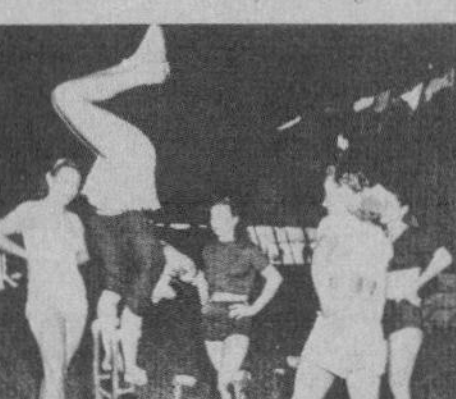

Girl practices handstand on the ground until she is adept enough to try it 60 feet up. In circus parlance aerialists are "fliers," newcomers are "first-of-Mays" and "web girls" are the ones who work the ropes, trapezes.

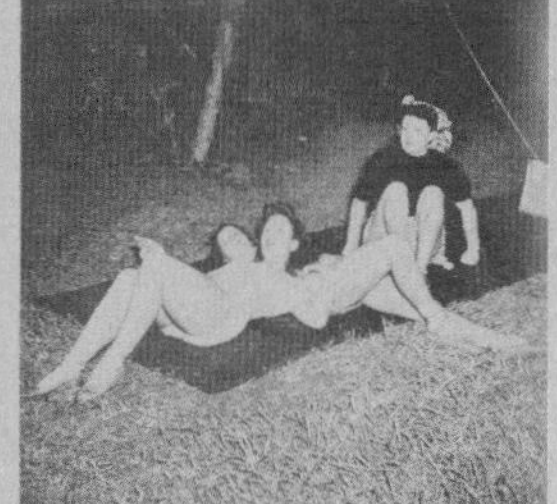

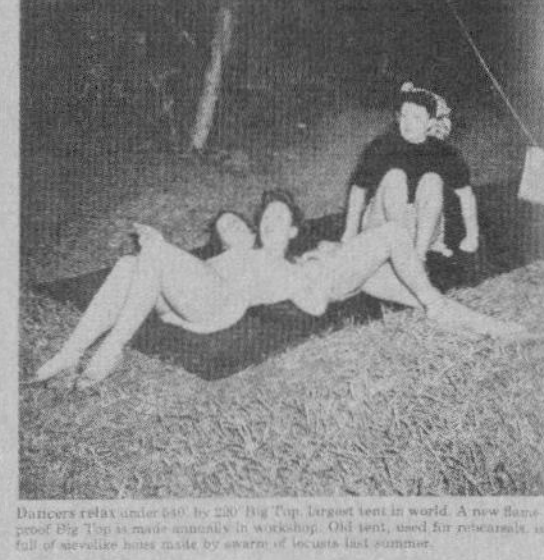

Dancers relax under 540- by 220' Big Top, largest tent in world. A new flame-proof Big Top is made annually in workshop. Old tent, used for rehearsals, is full of sievelike holes made by swarm of locusts last summer.

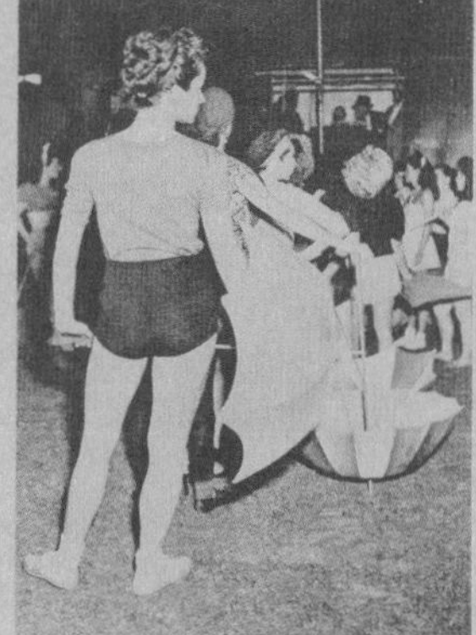

Girls in "Dixie" number wait to go on. Model Jean Rockwell, foreground, is a "first-of-May," gets $60 a week, all her meals, $20 extra for "web work." She sleeps in a converted hospital railroad car with 40 other girls.

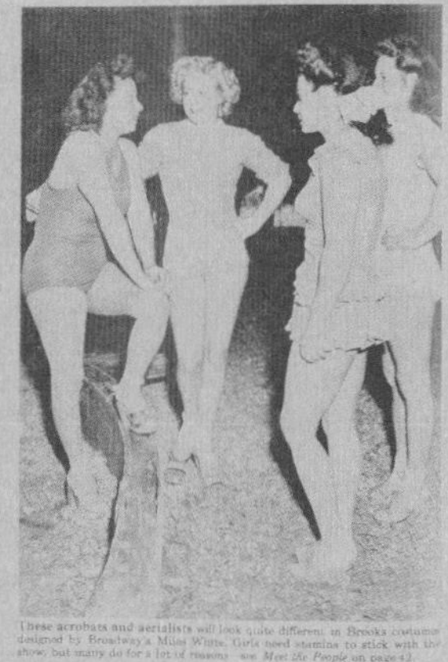

These acrobats and aerialists will look quite different in Brooks costumes designed by Broadway's Miles White. Girls need stamina to stick with the show, but many do for a lot of reasons—see *Meet the People* on page 42.

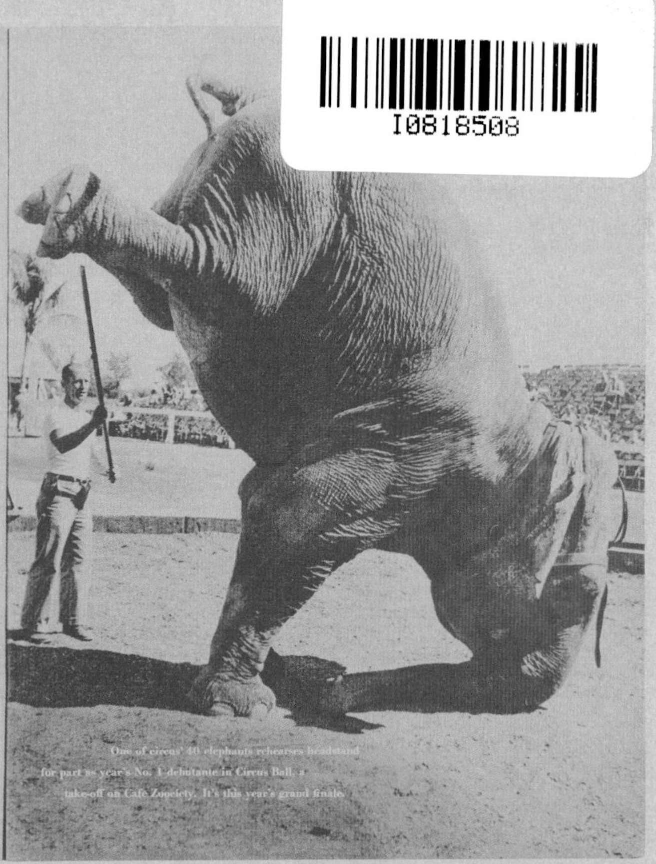

One of circus' 40 elephants rehearses headstand for part as year's No. 1 debutante in Circus Ball, a take-off on Café Zoociety. It's this year's grand finale.

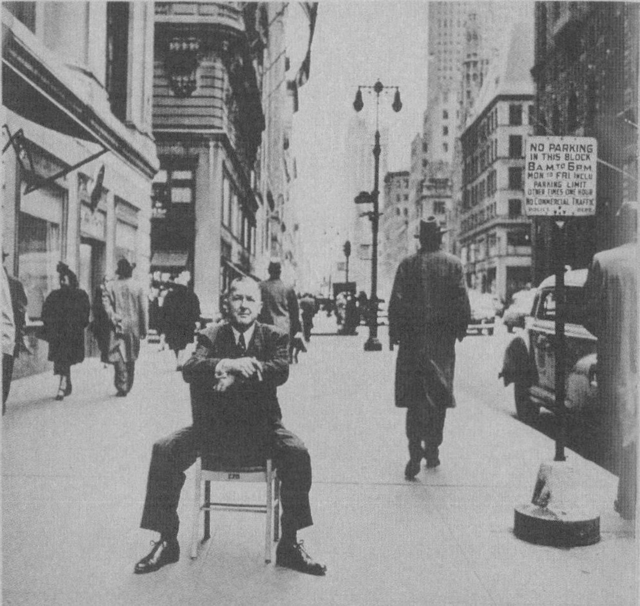

George Grosz, famous Berlin painter who chose New York in 1932 when Hitler menace loomed, straddles chair on Fifth Avenue sidewalk and symbolizes world artists who find stimulation and peace to work in New York. Unaware passersby typify public oblivious that city is now world art center.

NEW YORK

WORLD ART CENTER

Unknown to most of New York City's millions, their town has become the art center of the world. Its art activity has grown from a handful of galleries at the turn of the century to over 300 art showplaces that present up to 60 opening exhibitions a week. Art patronage has expanded from a few wealthy collectors and cognoscenti to include multitudes who merely like to look at pictures and who frequently buy. Most important, New York has become the city chosen by artists all over the world as the best place to find excitement in the work of others and solitude in which to worry out their own aesthetic problems. New York leaves them alone.

As artists once went to Paris for stimulation and freedom, they now turn to New York, where many thousands of men and women are practising painting and sculpture creatively. Their choice of place-to-work is no mystery to those who frequent studios like those shown on the following page, where artists say to each other, "It used to be Paris, now it's here."

Artists who choose New York for freedom and stimulation

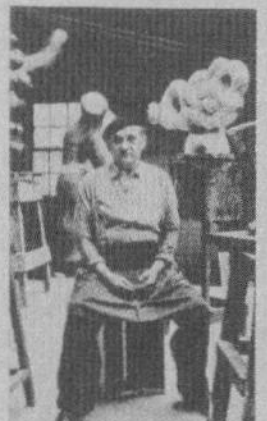

Jacques Lipchitz came from France in 1940, says, "There is something in the air here that is good for work."

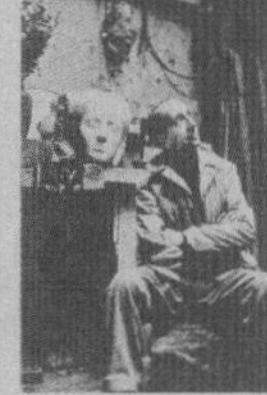

Spanish-born José de Creeft agrees New York's art life has expanded immensely since his arrival in 1929.

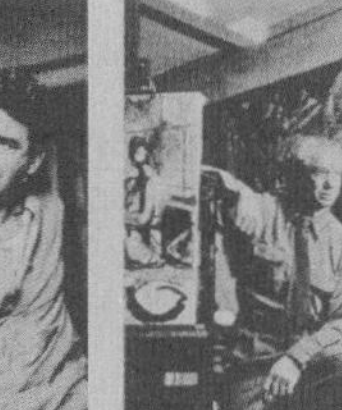

"New York is where I want to be. It is very close to me," says Abraham Rattner after two decades in Paris.

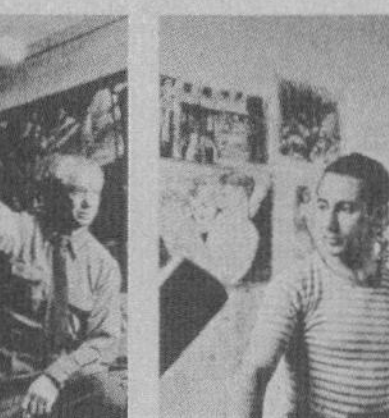

Sigmund Menkes left Paris in 1939, says he can find in New York "peace of mind to follow through an idea."

Viennese Henry Koerner left Austria in 1939, served in U.S. Army, chose New York to follow career as artist.

New York's beauty, dynamism have excitement for Italian-born Enrico Donati. He came from Paris in 1940.

An artist's life in Paris posed many problems for Joseph Floch, who sought New York's stability in 1941.

Reuben Tam left his native Hawaii to seek artistic stimulation, company of other young artists in New York.

END

CONTINUED FROM PAGE 52

Listed below are additional cities in which replicas of Mr. Blandings' Dream House are now being built. The names of the builders and stores follow:

Bakersfield, California
Denver, Colorado
Houston, Texas
Oklahoma City, Oklahoma
Philadelphia, Pennsylvania
Portland, Oregon
Providence, Rhode Island
Rochester, New York
Sacramento, California
South Bend, Indiana
Springfield, Massachusetts
Tarrytown, New York

Watch your local newspapers for further announcements regarding Mr. Blandings and his Dream Houses.

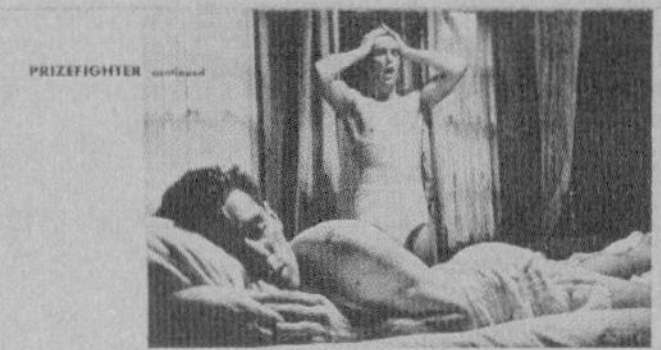

Walter sleeps until 9:30 on a day he's going to fight. In training, he gets up at 5:30, runs four miles. Twin brother Vincent sleeps on.

Vince helps train Walter, serves him breakfast of orange juice, three soft-boiled eggs, toast and coffee. Their Aunt Eva oversees the meal.

THE DAY OF A FIGHT

Cartier sleeps late, eats carefully, gets a physical check-up —and goes to church.

On way to fight, Walter stops at church, prays that he escape serious injury.

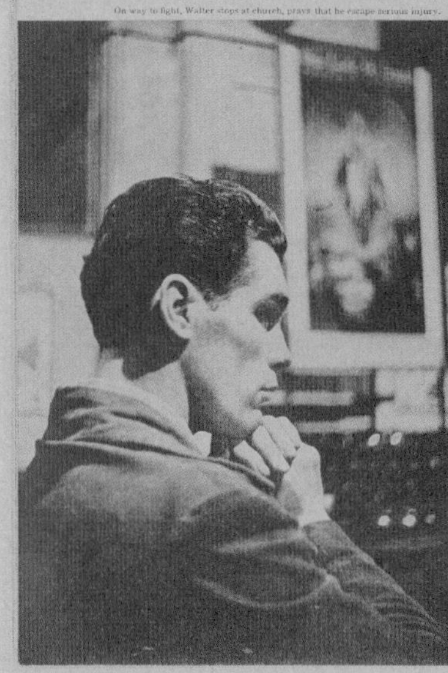

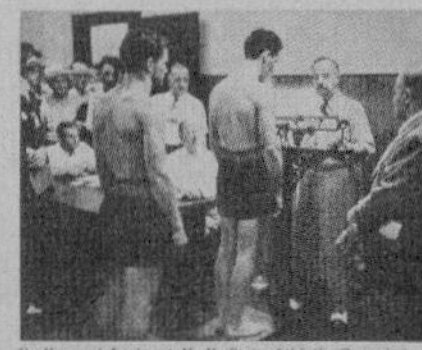

Cartier weighs in at N. Y. State Athletic Commission around noon. An official checks him on the scales.

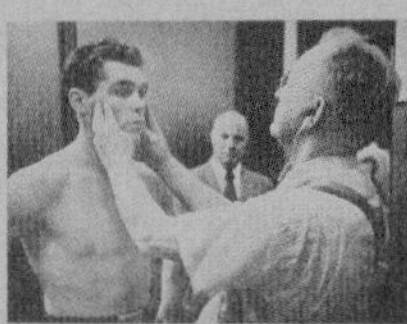

Doctor carefully examines eyes. Eye cuts, an occupational hazard, often impair vision, sometimes bring blindness.

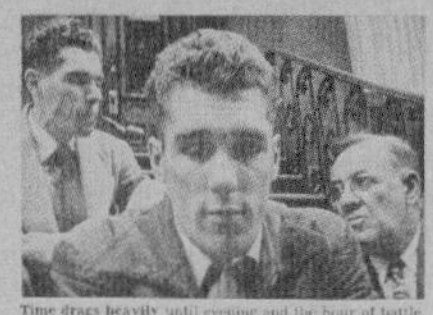

Time drags heavily until evening and the hour of battle. Walter sits it out on front steps with brother, neighbor.

The fight. Walter carries attack to Tony D'Amico at Jerome Stadium, drives spittle from Tony's mouth. He led until head butt cut his right eye, gave Tony technical KO.

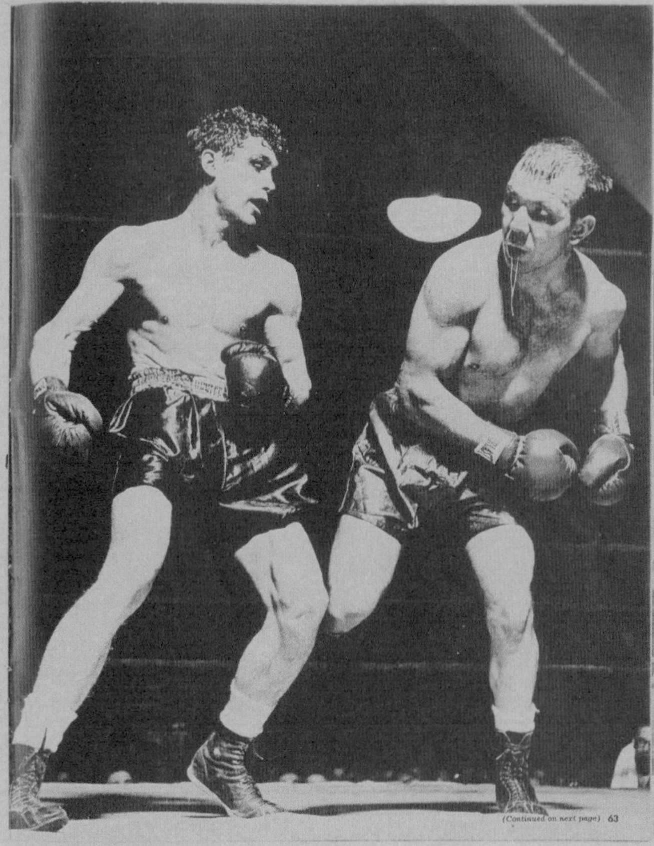

(Continued on next page)

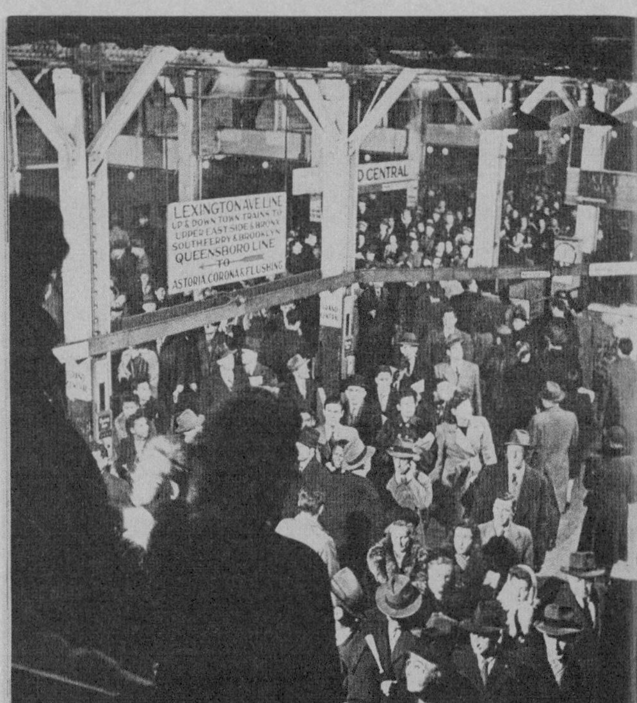

The shuttle at Grand Central Station. This picture was taken at the peak of the afternoon rush hour as thousands jammed through the underground passages in the daily struggle to get home. On an average day almost 8,000,000 fares are collected by the subways. Record of 9,374,910 was set Dec. 23, 1946.

Life and Love on the New York Subway

New York's subway trains are a reading room on wheels, a lover's lane and, after 11 p.m., a flophouse. And they give the city's 8,000,000 subway riders the noisiest and biggest nickel's worth of transportation in the world. The average New Yorker spends more than an hour a day packed into the subway. He's called a sardine — for obvious reasons. These pictures show that practically everything and anything can happen in a subway train. And subway riders are not surprised.

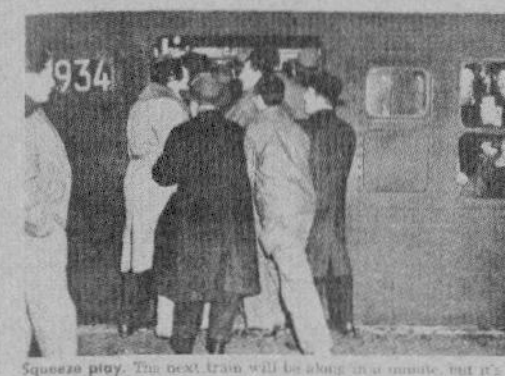

Squeeze play. The next train will be along in a minute, but it's a matter of pride to prove there's always room for one more dozen.

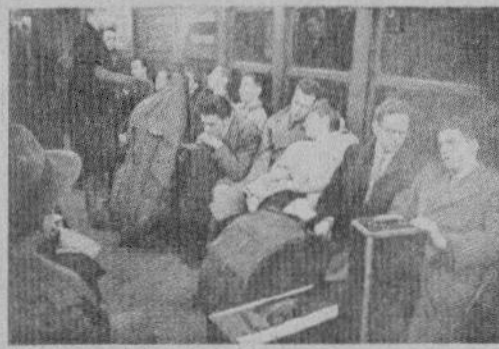

It's not so crowded later in day. So this 15-piece orchestra, complete with instruments and girl vocalist, travels by subway to a late show.

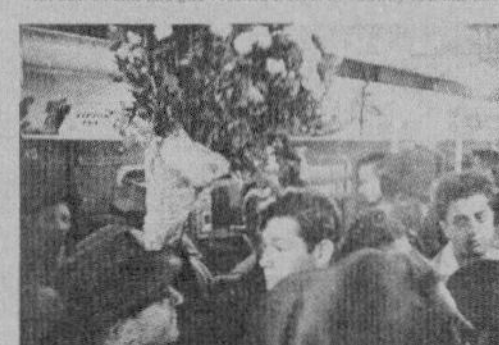

Flowers for my lady. They may be a bit battered by the time they reach her, but this lad's doing his best to keep them above the crowd.

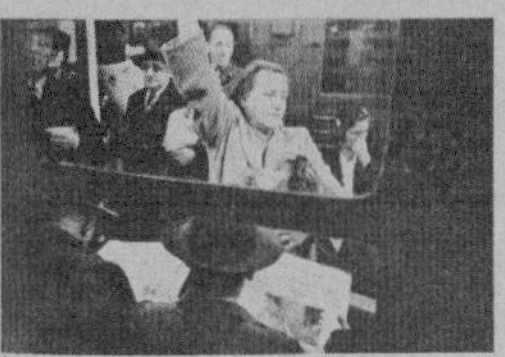

Subway etiquette. When should a gentleman give a lady his seat? Not, as picture shows, when he can hide his face behind a newspaper.

(Continued on page 62)

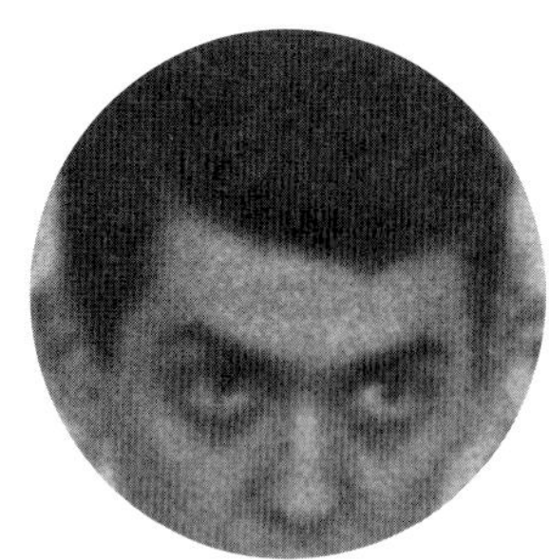

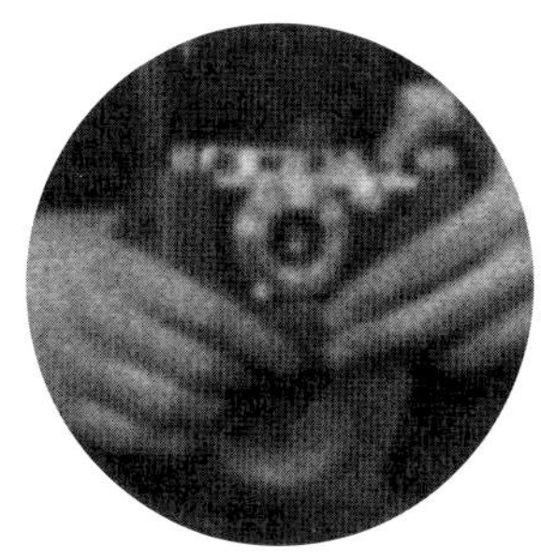

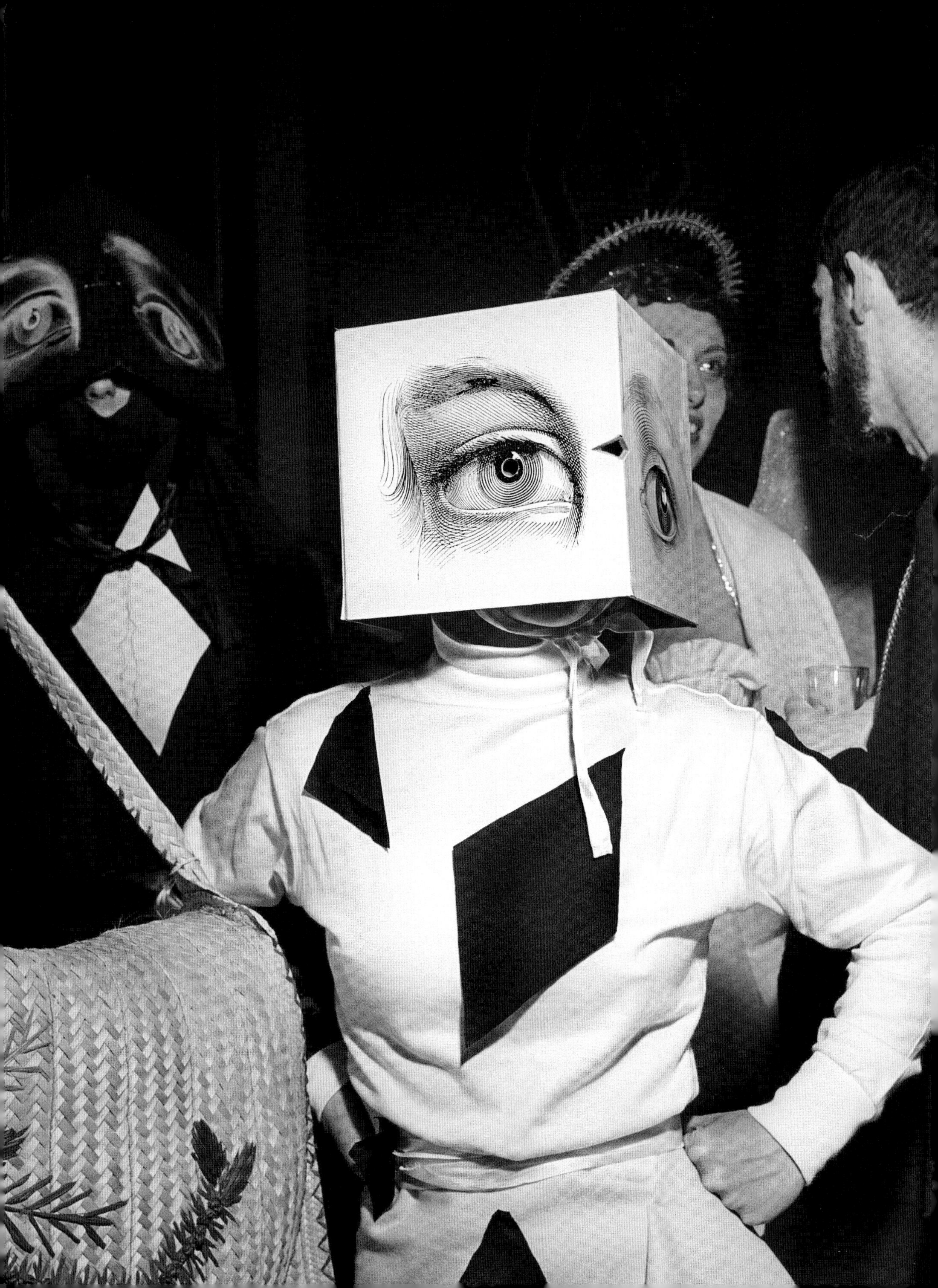

DONALD ALBRECHT
SEAN CORCORAN
EDITORS

THROUGH A DIFFERENT LENS: STANLEY KUBRICK PHOTOGRAPHS

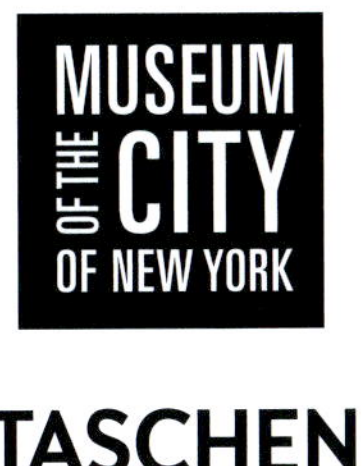

TASCHEN

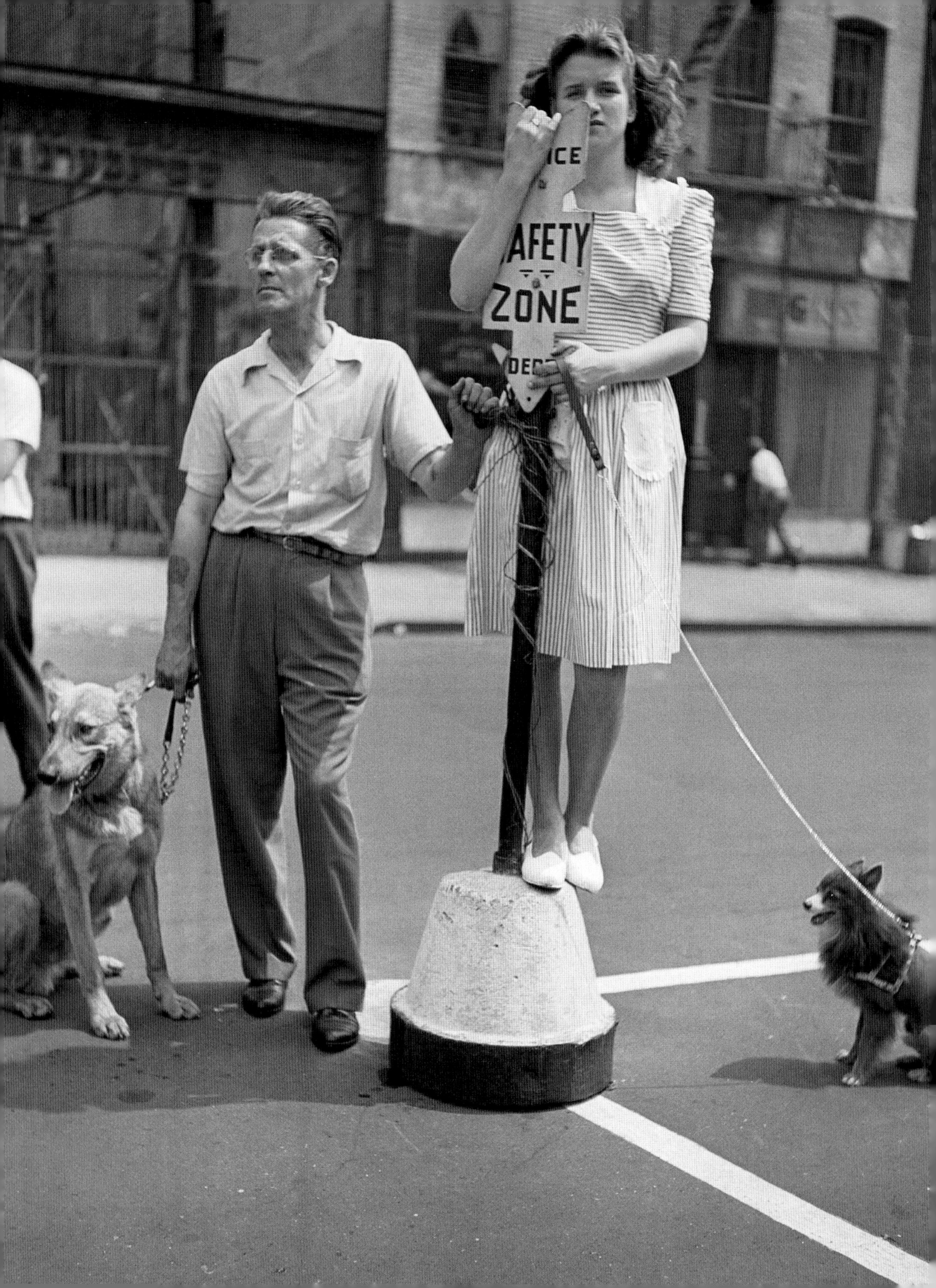
ZONE

CONTENTS

PAGE 6
PREFACE
WHITNEY W. DONHAUSER

PAGE 8
THROUGH A DIFFERENT LENS: STANLEY KUBRICK PHOTOGRAPHS
DONALD ALBRECHT
SEAN CORCORAN

PAGE 16
STANLEY KUBRICK: LEARNING TO LOOK
LUCY SANTE

PORTFOLIO:

PAGE 24
1946

PAGE 46
1947

PAGE 100
1948

PAGE 160
1949

PAGE 248
1950

PAGE 295
ADDITIONAL ASSIGNMENTS 1946–1950

PAGE 327
FILMOGRAPHY
BIBLIOGRAPHY

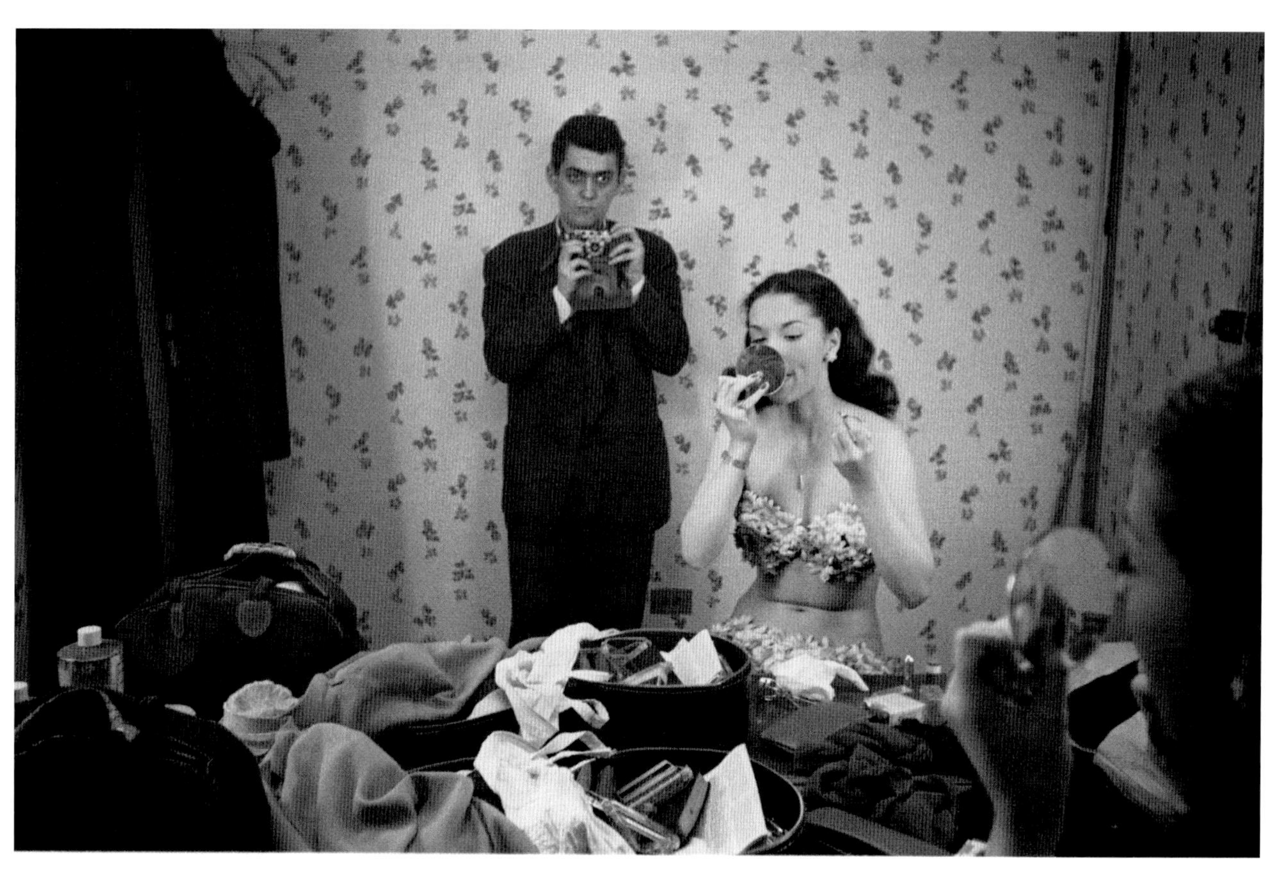

Stanley Kubrick and Rosemary Williams,
from an unpublished 1949 assignment

PREFACE

Photographs taken for *Look* magazine, one of the nation's premier 20th-century newsmagazines, are a highlight of the extraordinary collections at the Museum of the City of New York. Including most of the New York assignments made between the magazine's founding in the late 1930s and 1961, this collection numbers approximately 200,000 images—negatives, contact sheets, transparencies, and prints—that were donated by *Look*'s parent company, Cowles Magazine, Inc., beginning in the 1950s.

Selected from this huge collection, *Through a Different Lens: Stanley Kubrick Photographs* focuses on images created by the then-teenage photographer between 1945 and 1950 before he turned to a career in film that brought him international renown. During his five years with the magazine, Kubrick was prolific, contributing images to more than 135 articles in *Look* and two for Cowles's short-lived culture magazine, *Flair*. The Museum of the City of New York's *Look* archive includes 129 of Kubrick's assignments and more than 12,000 of his contact prints and negatives and is the sole source material for this publication. The Library of Congress, which acquired the remainder of the *Look* archive when the magazine folded in 1971, holds a similar number of Kubrick's contact sheets and negatives. While much of the material included in this volume was originally published in the pages of *Look* magazine, this book includes many unpublished images. Additionally, the book showcases several of Kubrick's exceptional unpublished assignments, such as "Shoeshine Boy," "Naked City," and "Rosemary Williams—Showgirl." The images were selected with the intention of complementing the published articles while trying to expand the notion of photographic style and sensibility unique to Stanley Kubrick.

This publication would not have been possible without the cooperation of the Stanley Kubrick Film Archive, and I specifically want to thank Christiane Kubrick, Jan Harlan, Philip Grosz, and Jonathan Cameron. Digitization of the Stanley Kubrick photographs from the *Look* magazine collection was made possible in part by the Charina Endowment Fund, Bloomberg Philanthropies, and other generous donors. I also want to acknowledge the efforts of Donald Albrecht, the Museum's curator of architecture and design, and Sean Corcoran, its curator of prints and photographs, who edited and contributed to the book and organized the accompanying exhibition. An excellent essay by Lucy Sante adds immeasurably not only to this book, but also to our understanding of Kubrick as a photographer. Donald and Sean were ably assisted by Susan Johnson, director of publications. Sarah Henry, the Museum's deputy director and chief curator, supervised the project. Natalie Shivers provided excellent editorial guidance, and Kristina Feliciano wrote the book's captions. The Kubrick archive has been photographed, scanned, and retouched by Victoria Martens, Mia Moffett, and Allyson Ross. Over the years several interns have been invaluable to this project, including Dawn Boldizsar, Max Carol, Heather Rigg, and Daphne Yuen. This book is the first time the Museum has worked with TASCHEN. I want to thank the publisher Benedikt Taschen and the editor Reuel Golden. Finally, the design firm Pure+Applied has created a book in sync with the flair and style of both Stanley Kubrick's photographs and his New York City of the late 1940s.

WHITNEY W. DONHAUSER
Ronay Menschel Director and President
Museum of the City of New York

56 Pictures- Roosevelt—From Boy to President
Inauguration of Harry S. Truman
TRUMAN TAKES OFFICE
Roosevelt Rites Tomorrow
5¢
Journal American
LATEST NEWS
Vows to Give All to War
PM Daily
Roosevelt Dead
Daily Mirror
F.D.R. DEAD
End Comes at Warm Springs
Truman Sworn as President
9TH FAR PAST ELBE. TANKS MAY REACH BERLIN TODA

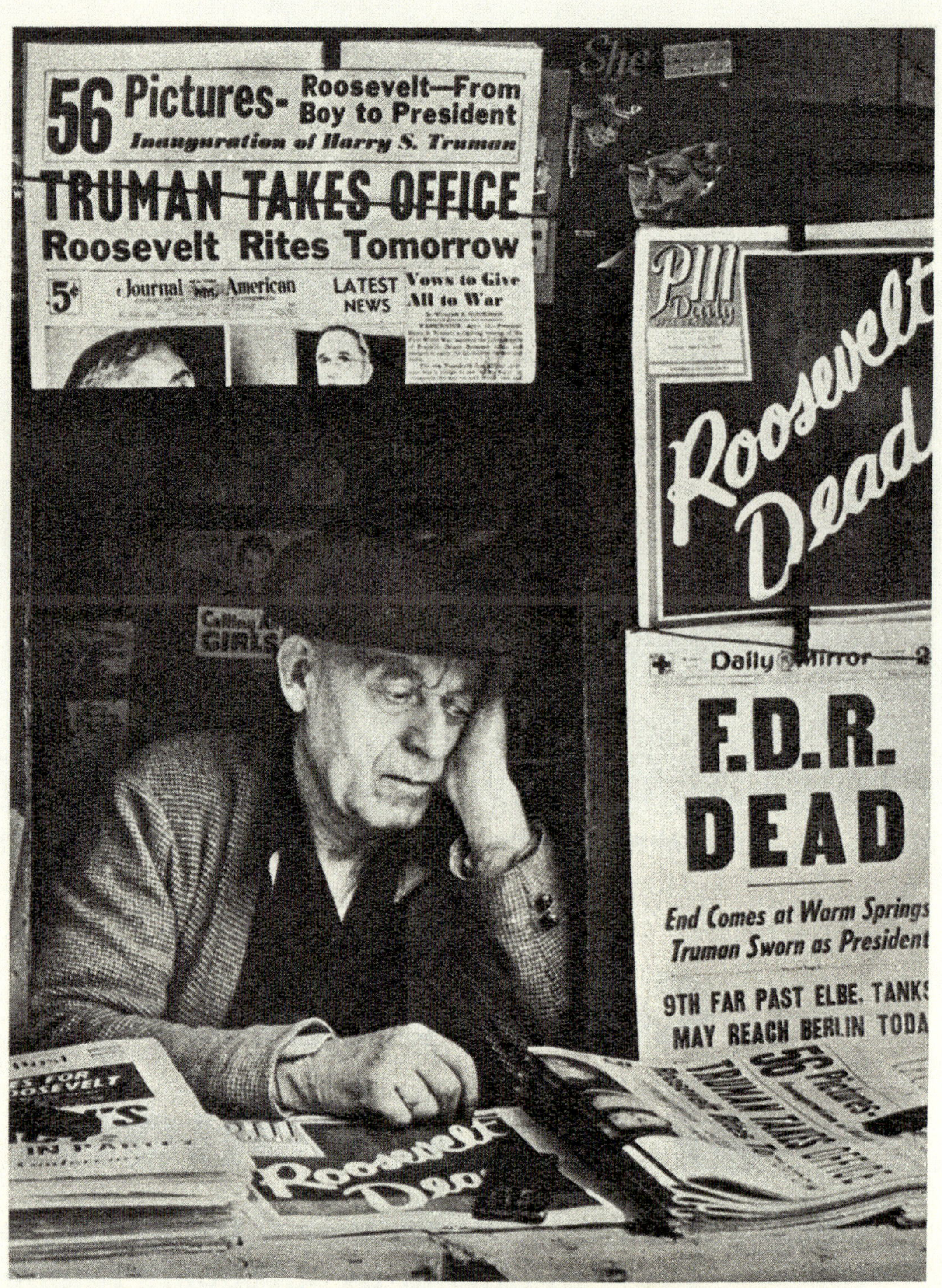

APRIL, 1945

DONALD ALBRECHT & SEAN CORCORAN

THROUGH A DIFFERENT LENS: STANLEY KUBRICK PHOTOGRAPHS

Stanley Kubrick's early career as a photojournalist for *Look* magazine is a revelation for most people who know him as a filmmaker. Between 1945 and 1950, before he was Stanley Kubrick, the internationally famous director of such films as *Dr. Strangelove*, *2001: A Space Odyssey*, and *A Clockwork Orange*, he was just Stanley, the teenager from New York City with an uncanny photographic sensibility, scouting human-interest stories for *Look* magazine.

Born in 1928 in the Bronx, Kubrick was less interested in formal education—he was a poor student who barely made it out of high school—than in lessons of the real world. For Kubrick, the Manhattan offices of *Look* proved to be his college, its editors and fellow photographers his professors, and New York City his field of study. "By the time I was 21 I had four years of seeing how things worked in the world," Kubrick later said of his time at *Look*. "I think if I had gone to college I would never have become a director."[1] Turning his camera on his native city, and occasionally further afield, Kubrick was inspired by New York's dramatic personae. The celebrities, the eccentrics, and the shoeshine boys who populated its streets caught his eye, and the nightclubs and sports arenas captured his attention. He memorialized New Yorkers in images that expressed the pathos of ordinary life in ways that belied his youth—and pointed toward his future as one of the 20th-century's great artists.[2]

A passion for photography (and chess) was instilled in Kubrick by his father, a doctor and serious amateur photographer, who gave Stanley a professional Graflex camera for his 13th birthday, irrevocably setting him on his career path. In the 1940s there was no better place to be a burgeoning photographer than *Look*, which had been founded by Gardner Cowles Jr. in early 1937 with the goal to provide "reader interest for yourself, for your wife, for your private secretary, for your office boy."[3] While the magazine's writers and photographers scoured the world for stories on a wide range of subjects, *Look*'s own backyard proved to be a favorite arena for its articles. The magazine portrayed New York City with drama, humor, and wit, stressing human interest and interaction, and drawing larger messages about society from the actions of individuals.

While *Look* and *Life* magazines were famous rivals for the public's attention, each had its own distinctive approach to depicting contemporary life and events, with *Look*, in Cowles's view, seeking "a lower, broader field" than its competitor.[4] *Life*, which was founded by Henry Luce in 1936, had a more grandiose mission than *Look*: "to see life; to see the world; to eyewitness great events; to watch the faces of the poor and the gestures of the proud."[5] Because *Look* was a biweekly, its staff did not need to cover breaking news and could be more freewheeling in their search for human-interest stories than *Life*'s team driven by their magazine's weekly publication imperative. *Look*'s articles, as

TRUMAN IS A NEW DEALER, TOO
AUTHOR: **RICHARD WILSON**
PUBLISHED: **JUNE 26, 1945**

Kubrick's first published photograph for *Look* depicted a dejected newsstand employee surrounded by newspapers announcing President Franklin Delano Roosevelt's death. The photograph appeared in a double-page spread of photographs chronicling the careers of Roosevelt and his successor, Harry S. Truman.

described by historian Mary Panzer, seemed "to record a slightly foreign civilization, a quirky, alternative universe ... *Look* often probed what its genteel critics scorned as 'the seamier side of American life.' In fact, *Look* was full of dark stories on unemployment, alcoholism, juvenile delinquency, divorce—topics that *Life* readers seemed to see less frequently, and then, quite often, with a silver lining."[6]

Panzer also noted that *Life* operated as a well-oiled, hierarchical assembly line, whereas *Look* functioned as teams of people that varied from assignment to assignment: "they decided how to best tell the story. It made for an uneven and often surprising magazine."[7] This looser approach may have been generated by the magazine's editor Daniel D. Mich, who worked in a variety of executive positions between the magazine's founding in 1937 and his death in 1965. Mich fostered a work environment that produced a plethora of story ideas, generated by staff as well as freelancers. Ultimately, the decision to publish an article belonged to Mich, who assessed its timeliness and its relevance to *Look*'s audience. (Many assignments did not meet these criteria and were never published.) Throughout this process, successful photographers learned that it was advantageous to shoot liberally, in order to give the magazine's art department a wide range of choices for story layouts.

Kubrick's tenure at *Look* began in 1945, when the magazine published his photograph of a despondent newspaper vendor the day after Franklin Delano Roosevelt's death. Kubrick later admitted he urged the salesman to look more depressed than he was for dramatic effect—an early example of his ability to elicit a performance and stage a scene. This opportunity transformed Kubrick from an amateur photographer into a professional. In the spring of 1946, Helen O'Brian, *Look*'s picture editor, who had purchased several of his photographs (including the one of the newspaper vendor), suggested that the magazine hire Kubrick for an apprenticeship. Although this was not typical practice for *Look*, Kubrick was about to graduate from William Howard Taft High School, and the staff recognized the talent and ambition of the young man. Kubrick was by far the magazine's youngest photographer (just 17 at the time), but with a paycheck of $50 per week, the magazine could afford to take the chance.

In his early years at *Look*, Kubrick was assigned small features consisting of a handful of photographs accompanied by brief texts. "How a Monkey Looks to People . . . How People Look to a Monkey" (published August 20, 1946) and "Bronx Street Scene" (published November 26, 1946) demonstrated his keen sense of observation and fascination with human relationships. His images caught intimate moments between New Yorkers shared in full public view, from two families enjoying the sights at the Bronx Zoo to friends engaged in deep conversation. Through his dramatic compositions he imbued these ordinary and mundane moments with tension or humor. While Kubrick was often assigned stories, he also pitched his own photo essays to his editors. "Teacher Puts 'Ham' in Hamlet" (published April 2, 1946) consisted of a series of images of his high-school English teacher, Aaron Traister, acting out *Hamlet*. For each of these assignments, Kubrick created a flowing and forceful narrative. His gift for storytelling was recognized by his employers, and he was taken on as a staff photographer in October 1946.

The teenage novice formally joined an illustrious group of photojournalists, including Arthur Rothstein, the magazine's technical director, and John Vachon. Both had been photographers for the Farm Security Administration, established by Franklin D. Roosevelt to document the living conditions of the rural poor during the Great Depression. This sensibility also characterized their work at *Look* and influenced the young Kubrick as he labored alongside them and other seasoned photojournalists on occasional assignments, such as "Fight Night at the Garden" with Rothstein and Vachon (published February 15, 1949) and the unpublished assignment "Advertising Sign Painters at Work" with Frank Bauman and Tom Weber (filed September 3, 1947). *Look*'s senior photographers also mentored Kubrick in his personal life, forming a "Bringing Up Stanley Club" to help the teenager navigate the adult workplace and world. Kubrick's clothes proved a major hurdle that was successfully overcome: "Once given to wearing teenage trademarks—saddle shoes, lounge jackets and sports shirts—Stanley now leans toward glen plaid business suits and white shirts."[8]

A veteran photographer at 19, Stanley Kubrick makes up for youth with zeal

THE DISTINGUISHED faculty members and officials at Columbia University weren't used to being pushed around. So what did this rank teen-ager mean, telling them what to do?

Like any experienced photographer, Stanley Kubrick knew exactly what he wanted. The impatient mutterings of dignitaries had long since failed to ruffle this quiet, brown-eyed youngster. For two weeks, Stanley stuck to the job on the university campus and got the excellent pictorial story of Columbia that appears with Don Wharton's article, on pages 25–33.

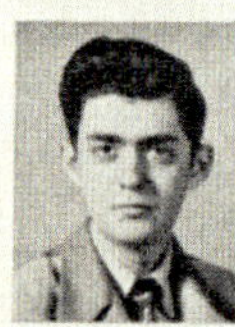

At 19, Stanley is a two-year veteran on the LOOK photographic staff. And even before he was graduated from high school in the Bronx, in 1946, he sold his candidly shot pictures to LOOK.

When Stanley joined the staff, his fellow photographers were quick to observe his intense preoccupation with his work. In a spirit of friendly co-operation, they formed a "Bringing Up Stanley Club," dedicated to reminding Stanley not to forget his keys, glasses, overshoes and other miscellaneous trivia.

The subtle influence of this loosely organized advisory group has also brought an apparent change in the young man's clothing tastes. Once given to wearing teen-age trade-marks—saddle shoes, lounge jackets and sports shirts—Stanley now leans toward glen plaid business suits and white shirts.

But his preoccupation with photography is unchanged. In his spare time, Stanley experiments with cinematography and dreams of the day when he can make documentary films.

The young fellow may go on forgetting his keys. But photographically, Stanley doesn't need any help in bringing himself up.

A VETERAN PHOTOGRAPHER AT 19, STANLEY KUBRICK MAKES UP FOR YOUTH WITH ZEAL
PUBLISHED: **MAY 11, 1948**

Promoting the teenage Kubrick as a wunderkind, this short article appeared alongside the table of contents in the same issue as an extensive essay on Columbia University illustrated exclusively with Kubrick's photographs.

TEACHER PUTS 'HAM' IN HAMLET
PUBLISHED: **APRIL 2, 1946**

Kubrick's photographs for this article recorded his high-school English teacher, Aaron Traister, acting out scenes from Shakespeare's play.

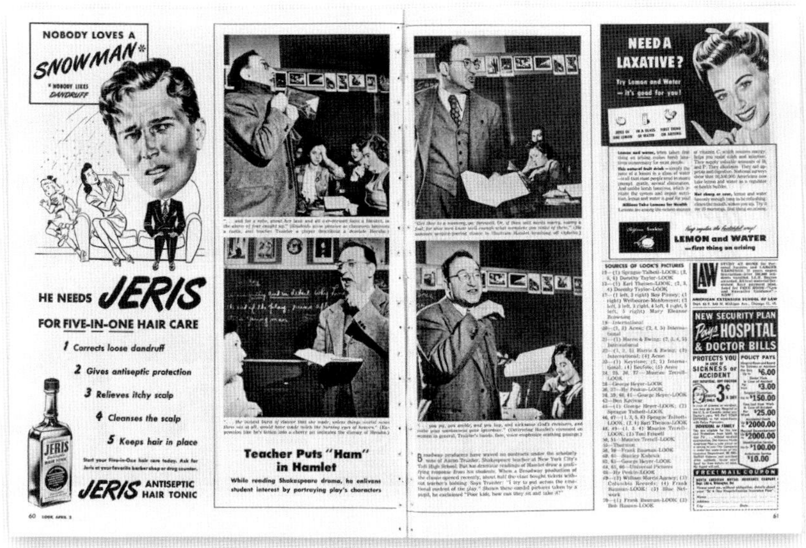
NOBODY LOVES A SNOWMAN*

* NOBODY LIKES DANDRUFF

HE NEEDS JERIS

FOR FIVE-IN-ONE HAIR CARE

1 Corrects loose dandruff

2 Gives antiseptic protection

3 Relieves itchy scalp

4 Cleanses the scalp

5 Keeps hair in place

JERIS ANTISEPTIC HAIR TONIC

Teacher Puts "Ham" in Hamlet

While reading Shakespeare drama, he enlivens student interest by portraying play's characters

NEED A LAXATIVE?

Try Lemon and Water — it's good for you!

LEMON and WATER

— first thing on arising

NEW SECURITY PLAN

HOSPITAL & DOCTOR BILLS

Kubrick's name finally appeared on the magazine's masthead on January 7, 1947. His first extended assignment, "Life and Love on the New York Subway," was published two months later, in the March 4 issue. In preparation for the story, he had spent two weeks riding the subways, a camera around his neck with a wire running down his sleeve to a shutter release in his pocket, concealing his effort to photograph ordinary citizens. He sometimes used a collaborator to stage images that were needed to tell the story—an unexceptional practice in photojournalism at the time. In the 29 photographs published in the article, Kubrick was able to illustrate what the author called "the nosiest and biggest nickel's worth of transportation in the world."[9] Kubrick recorded weary commuters, drunks, lovers, and lonely individuals in their daily lives.

In the fall of 1947, Kubrick began working on more extended narrative-based assignments. One of the earliest stories, "Shoeshine Boy" (filed October 6, 1947), was a day-in-the-life portrait of Mickey, a New York adolescent who went to school, played sports, gambled with his friends, kept a pigeon coop, and earned money for his family shining shoes on the streets of New York. In the unpublished article, Kubrick, who was about seven years older than his subject, highlighted the contrasts between Mickey's adult-like work ethic and his exuberant, childish hijinks. By the spring of 1948, Kubrick's ability to create long-form narrative photo essays had matured with a quick succession of extended assignments. "Columbia University" (published May 11, 1948) examined the then commonly held faith in American progress and scientific advancement represented by an elite American university. "How the Circus Gets Set" (published May 25, 1948), a portrayal of the Ringling Bros. circus that mined the odd setting for humorous juxtapositions, emphasized Kubrick's interest in eccentric and absurd subjects. Those photo essays were quickly followed by two assignments outside of New York City: "Mooseheart—The Child City" (published June 8, 1948), focusing on an orphanage about 40 miles west of Chicago, and "Holiday in Portugal" (published August 3, 1948), which followed a young American couple on a European holiday.

Of the topics Kubrick covered for *Look*, however, none aligned more closely with his burgeoning interest in film than the explorations of entertainment and media, even then key aspects of New York City's economy and identity. Stories about radio and television personalities demonstrated Kubrick's transition from a novice learning his trade to a more mature artist pushing the boundaries of powerful and humanistic photojournalism. His ability to translate an individual's complex psychological life into visual form was apparent in profiles of composer and conductor Leonard Bernstein, boxer Walter Cartier, television personality Faye Emerson, theater actor Betsy von Furstenberg, and showgirl Rosemary Williams. In each profile Kubrick explored the public and private lives of these

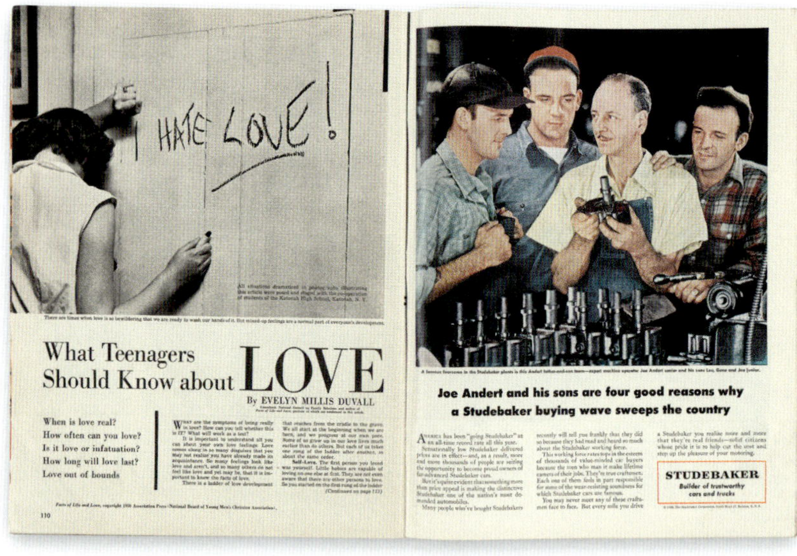
I HATE LOVE!

What Teenagers Should Know about LOVE

By EVELYN MILLIS DUVALL

When is love real?
How often can you love?
Is it love or infatuation?
How long will love last?
Love out of bounds

110

Joe Andert and his sons are four good reasons why a Studebaker buying wave sweeps the country

STUDEBAKER
Builder of trustworthy cars and trucks

WHAT TEENAGERS SHOULD KNOW ABOUT LOVE
AUTHOR: **EVELYN MILLIS DUVALL**
PUBLISHED: **OCTOBER 10, 1950**

This essay explored "a ladder of love development that reaches from the cradle to the grave." Like the article on dating published earlier the same year, this one featured staged images involving suburban high-school students. Kubrick's photographs chronicled phases of teenage love, from "bewilderment"—depicted by a distraught teenager scrawling the words "I HATE LOVE!" in lipstick on a door—to "love for father," "love for an older man," and "teen-age crushes."

individuals. In some portraits—Emerson and von Furstenberg, for example—Kubrick's images suggested that the public and private personas were one and the same, while others, such as his depiction of Williams, underscored the disconnect between her glamorous on-stage persona and her hard-scrabble backstage reality.

Radio was still the dominant form of home entertainment at the time, and Kubrick contributed to *Look*'s profiles of popular radio personalities like Vaughn Monroe (published August 16, 1949) and Arthur Godfrey (published February 1, 1949). While television was still in its adolescence in these years, *Look* focused on familiarizing its readers with the medium. (Ironically, within the next decade, the small screen superseded magazines as the nation's most popular form of communication, culminating in *Look*'s closure in 1971.) In its January 7, 1947, issue, for example, *Look*, as part of a series on new trends in entertainment, featured Kubrick's photograph of a typical television studio overlaid with descriptions of each production component to help *Look*'s audience understand the new medium. Several years later, Kubrick was assigned to take pictures on the set of *The Howdy Doody Show*, with Bob Smith as the character Buffalo Bob and the puppet Howdy Doody (published December 20, 1949), and to create an in-depth profile of Faye Emerson, a Hollywood actress who transitioned to television talk-show host in the late 1940s (published August 15, 1950). Kubrick saw firsthand the ways that celebrities crafted their public personas and was regularly behind the scenes and on the set, seeing the production process up close.

The clearest premonition of Kubrick's film career can be seen in his unpublished photographs taken on the set of the Academy Award–winning film The *Naked City* (1948), one of Hollywood's first productions to revive on-location filmmaking. It must have been a thrilling experience for an avid consumer of popular film noir at the city's commercial theaters, as well as more artistic fare at the Museum of Modern Art. Kubrick spent many hours on the set watching director Jules Dassin and cinematographer William H. Daniels film the dark police procedural on the streets of New York City. While it is unknown if this was the seminal experience that got Kubrick interested in filmmaking, it surely had an impact on the young man. "In his spare time, Stanley experiments with cinematography," *Look* magazine noted in May of 1948, "and dreams of the day when he can make documentary films."[10]

In 1950, near the end of his tenure at *Look*, Kubrick explored themes of teenage love, teenage dating, and marital jealousy in three assignments, effectively directing the stories, for which he posed high-school students "starring" in the teenage stories, and actors in the marital story. As foundational as these assignments were, however, it was the story "Prizefighter" (published January 18, 1949) about Walter Cartier that formally

JEALOUSY: A THREAT TO MARRIAGE
AUTHOR: **JACQUES BACAL**
PUBLISHED: **OCTOBER 24, 1950**

Lawyer Jacques Bacal, who coauthored (with Louise Sloane) the book *ABC of Divorce* (1947), wrote this article about case studies of marriages that were damaged, and often destroyed, by jealousy. Some of Bacal's examples of violent rages were especially lurid: a wife who stabbed her husband and left him under the Christmas tree; a man who drove over his wife's beloved dog. Rather than illustrate these particular stories, Kubrick staged and photographed a series of images that depicted situations that could trigger jealousy or manifest it. These proto-cinematic photographs bridged Kubrick's transition from photojournalist to filmmaker.

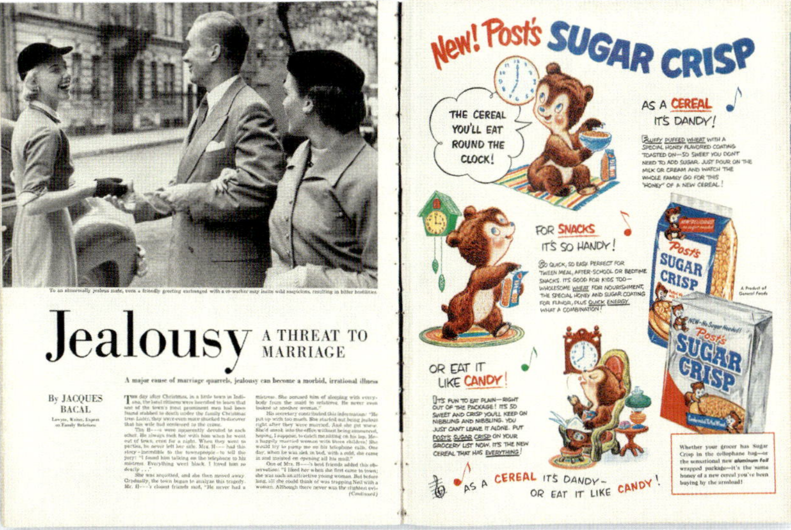

launched Kubrick's filmmaking career. Kubrick went on to feature Cartier as the subject of his first independently produced documentary, *Day of the Fight*, a 16-minute film that premiered in 1951 and went into worldwide distribution.

After completing several short films without making a profit, however, Kubrick realized that he would need to direct features if he was to make a career in cinema. He quit his job at *Look* in August 1950 and began work on his first full-length film, *Fear and Desire* (1953), an abstract exploration of the relationships between soldiers and an unnamed girl involved in a war between unidentified countries. Kubrick's next two movies, *Killer's Kiss* (1955) and *The Killing* (1956), shared the dark, film noir aesthetic of some of his most distinctive work at *Look*, particularly those assignments exploring the lives of noirish urban characters such as boxers and showgirls.

Kubrick's five-year tenure at *Look* proved formative. There he participated in the process of making art in a collaborative setting, not unlike filmmaking. He learned to tell stories through images in dynamic narrative sequences and to focus on subtle human interactions. He mastered how to frame, compose, and light compelling images, many of which have the dispassionate view of life he would adopt in many of his films. Reviewing Kubrick's early career at *Look*, it is possible to regard that experience as the start of his celebrated career as an artist and filmmaker—a time when he honed his skills as both a storyteller and an image maker, albeit through a different lens.

FOLLOWING SPREAD
WHAT EVERY TEENAGER SHOULD KNOW ABOUT DATING
AUTHOR: **EVELYN MILLIS DUVALL**
PUBLISHED: **AUGUST 1, 1950**

Kubrick's photographs of teenagers in myriad romantic situations accompanied an article by Evelyn Millis Duvall, an American author and teacher who specialized in dating, parenting, and family life. Condensing parts of Duvall's 1950 book *Facts of Life and Love*, the article comprised short segments on subjects from "dressing for a date" to "pick-ups are risky." Making the assignment especially valuable to Kubrick as a budding filmmaker, its situations were "dramatized," as *Look*'s editors stated in the magazine, and its photographs were "posed and staged" with the cooperation of students from a suburban New York high school.

ENDNOTES

1 Stanley Kubrick, quoted in Paul D. Zimmerman, "Kubrick's Brilliant Vision," *Newsweek*, January 3, 1972, 31.
2 For some of this essay's background information on *Look* magazine, we have drawn from the essay "Only in New York," written by Donald Albrecht and Thomas Mellins in their book *Only in New York: Photographs from* Look *Magazine*, co-published by the Museum of the City of New York and The Monacelli Press in 2009. For Kubrick's tenure at *Look* magazine, an invaluable resource was *Stanley Kubrick at* Look *Magazine: Authorship and Genre in Photojournalism and Film*, written by Philippe Mather and published by Intellect in 2013.
3 Gardner Cowles Jr., quoted in "Look Out," *Time*, January 11, 1937, 25.
4 Gardner Cowles Jr., quoted in "Look Out," *Time*, January 11, 1937, 25.
5 *Life* magazine mission statement, quoted on the website of the Beinecke Rare Book & Manuscript Library, https://brbl-dl.library.yale.edu/vufind/Author?author=Life+magazine&type=Author&page=2, accessed December 4, 2017.
6 Mary Panzer, "Eyes Wide Open," *Vanity Fair*, March 2005, 410–42.
7 Mary Panzer, "Eyes Wide Open," *Vanity Fair*, March 2005, 442.
8 "A veteran photographer at 19, Stanley Kubrick makes up for youth with zeal," *Look*, May 11, 1948, 2.
9 "Life and Love on the New York Subway," *Look*, March 4, 1947, 60.
10 "A veteran photographer at 19, Stanley Kubrick makes up for youth with zeal," *Look*, May 11, 1948, 2.

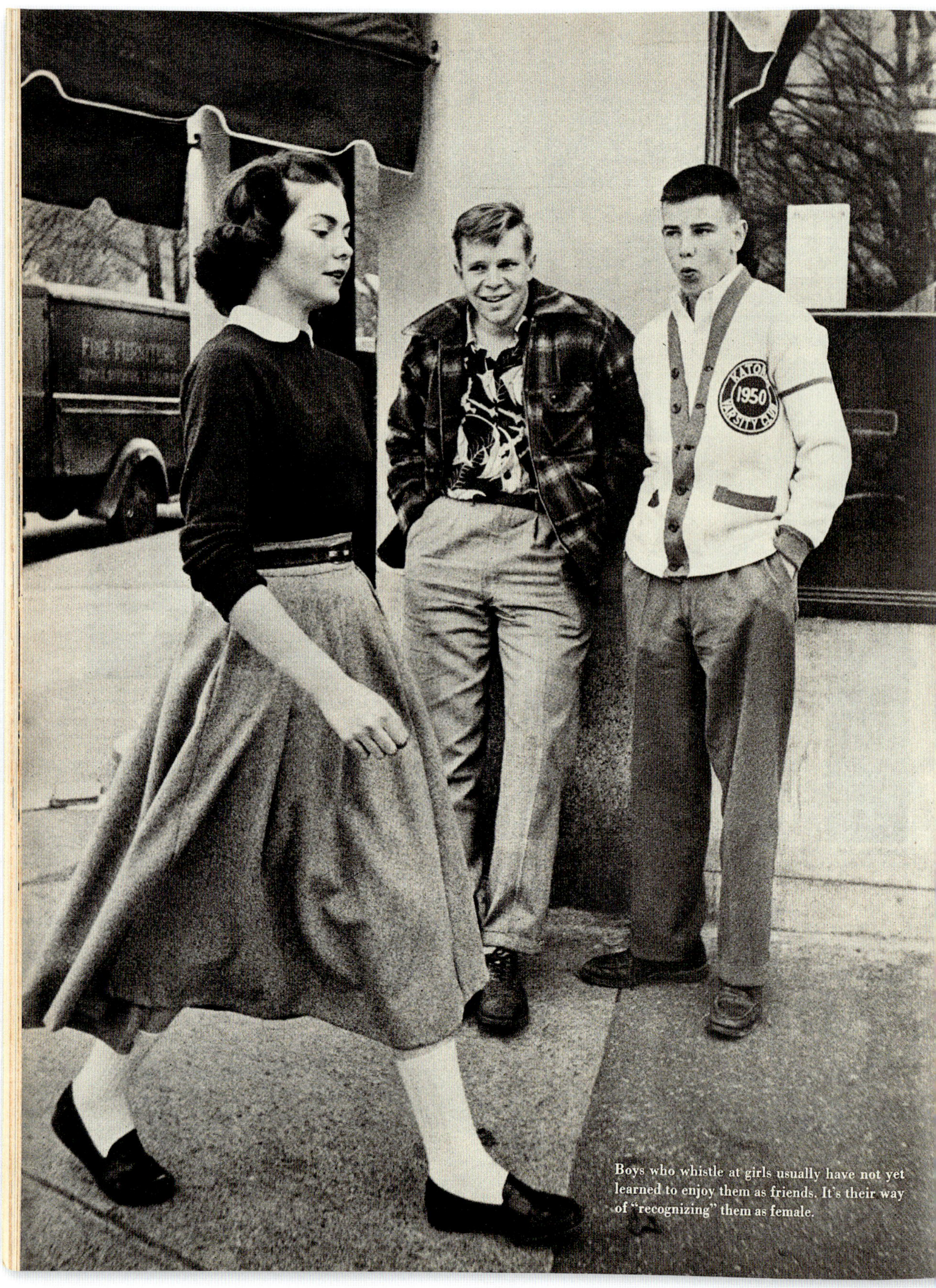

Boys who whistle at girls usually have not yet learned to enjoy them as friends. It's their way of "recognizing" them as female.

What every Teenager should know about Dating

A guide to the do's and don'ts of youth's early friendships that will answer many tough questions for boys and girls—and for their parents as well

By EVELYN MILLIS DUVALL

Consultant, National Council on Family Relations and author of *Facts of Life and Love*, portions of which are condensed in this article.

"WHAT is the matter with me?" you may wonder if you don't have dates. Everybody around you seems to be talking about their good times—what he said and what she said, and then what they did. You may get to thinking that there is something wrong with you that keeps you from going places and doing things with the other sex. You may put on a big act and pretend that you have special friends and admirers (as many of the others do too). But deep down inside you may be puzzled about what it takes to make friends and to get a date. You wonder why some people seem to do it all so easily while others have to work so hard at it. How you get started in dating, why some people start when they are so young and others only when they are much older, and what you can do about getting the hang of it yourself are some of the questions that this article takes up.

Your age is only one piece in the puzzle of your readiness for dating. Many other influences are at work. There are, of course, such obvious assets as looks, grooming, good clothes and money. But even more important is the attitude of your parents. Some parents are eager for their sons and daughters to start dating and make it easy for them to meet young people by giving parties in their homes. Other parents try to delay the age at which their sons and daughters begin dating; some say flatly that their daughters cannot have dates until they are 16. Then there are some who expect, and perhaps need, so much help around the house that they discourage any outside social life for their children. Still other parents take a middle ground of neither resisting nor encouraging the dating of their children. If an elder son or daughter proves by his behavior that dates do not bring trouble, then these parents tend to relax and allow younger brothers and sisters more freedom.

Finally, it is important for you to recognize that girls tend

(Continued on next page)

All situations dramatized in photographs illustrating this article were posed and staged with the co-operation of students of the Katonah High School, Katonah, N. Y.

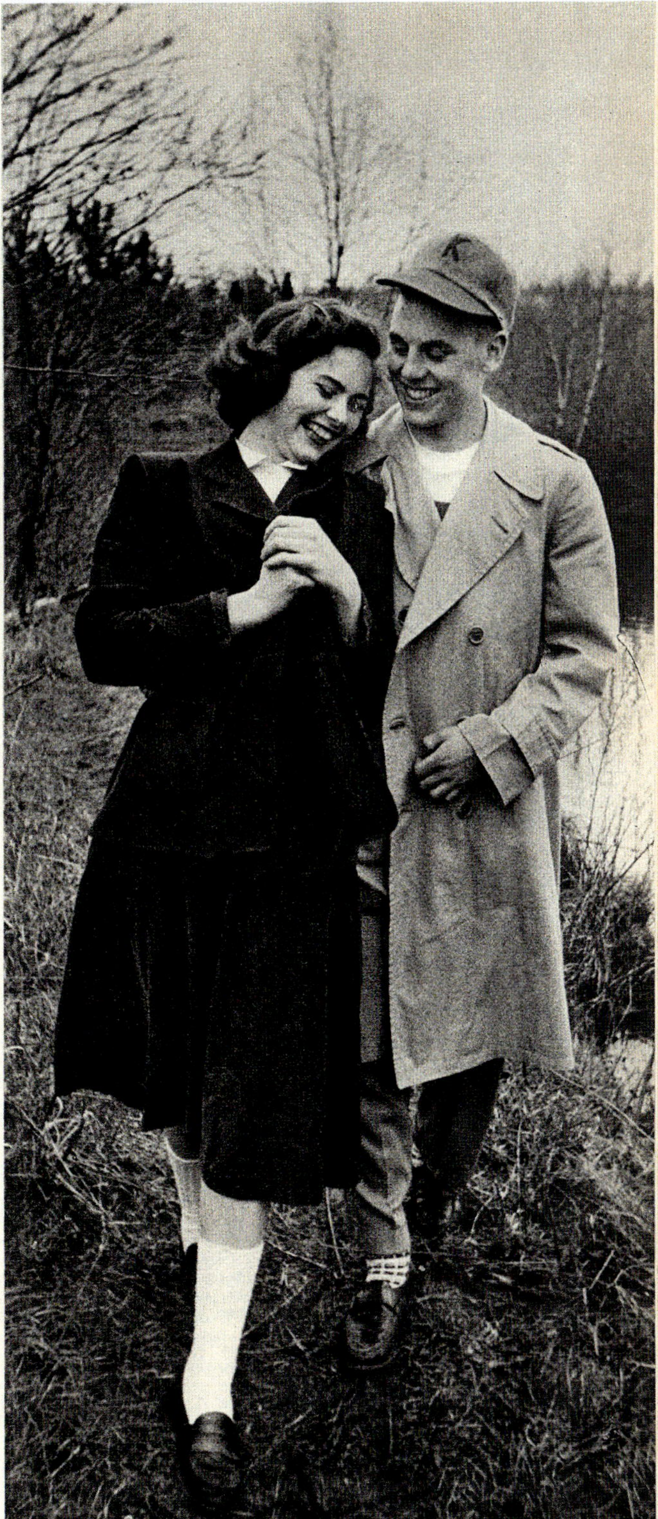

Things to do on a date vary with people. It may be simple as a stroll.

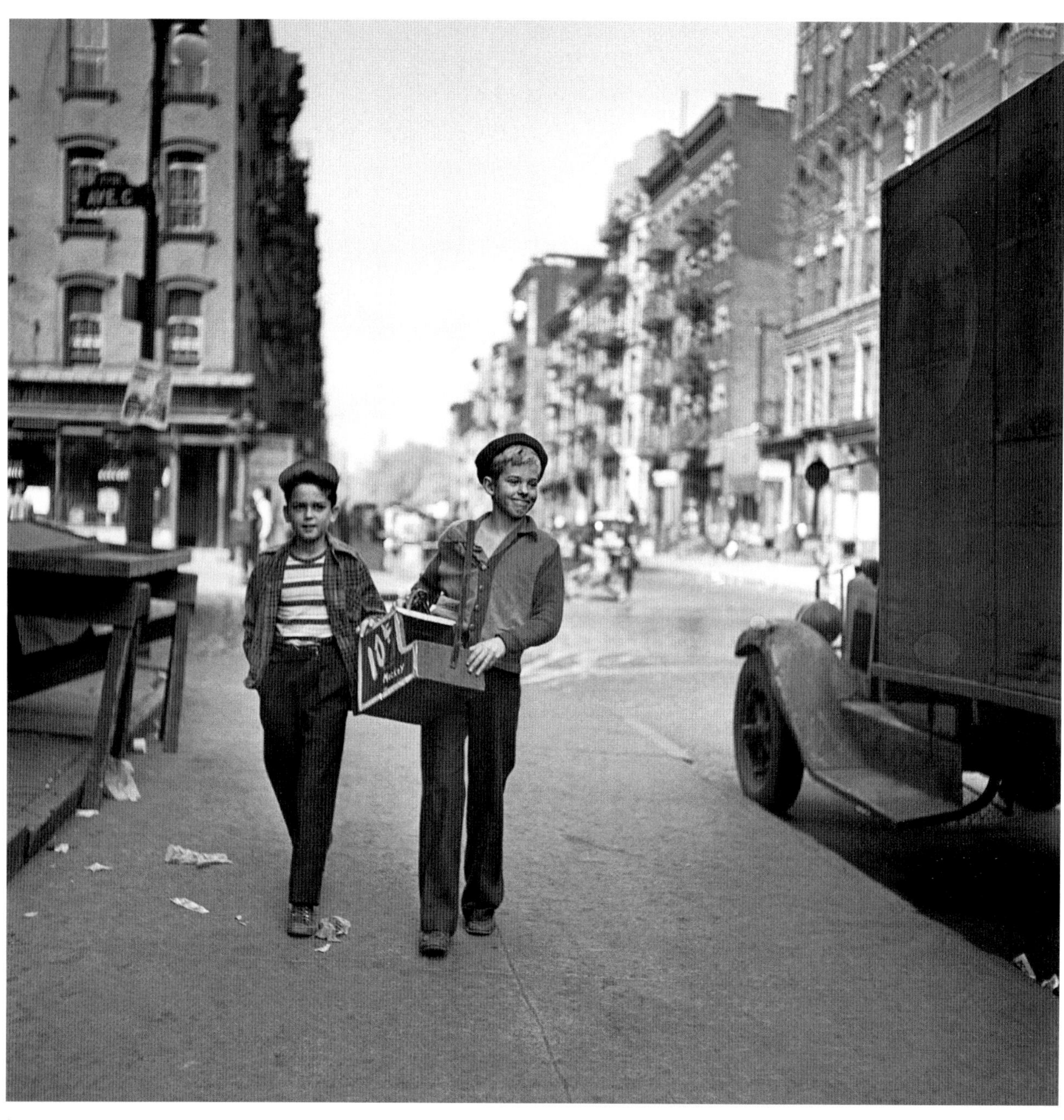

Mickey, a shoeshine boy, with his friend on the streets of New York, from an unpublished 1947 assignment. Photo by Stanley Kubrick

LUCY SANTE

STANLEY KUBRICK: LEARNING TO LOOK

"Stanley always acted like he knew something you didn't know," wrote the author and journalist Michael Herr, quoting an acquaintance of Kubrick's youth.[1] It will surprise no one to learn that Stanley Kubrick, the nonpareil director of *Dr. Strangelove*, *2001: A Space Odyssey*, *Barry Lyndon*, and 10 other enduring and fanatically controlled feature films, was something of a prodigy. Not a child prodigy, mind you, but very nearly. Before he was out of high school he had sold two pictures to *Look* magazine, and not long after graduation was hired as a staff photographer, a job he would hold until he was 22. He covered all sorts of subjects, in New York City and beyond, producing celebrity profiles, extended essays, human-interest stories, man-on-the-street spots, hidden-camera probes, and shot sequences, laid out in tight horizontal formats, that presaged his future cinematic career.

The late 1940s were a good time to become a photographer. The war was over, people had money to spend the way they hadn't had in a decade and a half, and every newsstand was overflowing with illustrated magazines. Following the course laid out in the late '30s by *Life* and *Look*, not to mention *Fortune*, *Vogue*, and *Harper's Bazaar*, there were now dozens of photographically illustrated general-interest periodicals pitched to various income levels and ranges of literacy; specialized journals formerly reliant on line art began stuffing their pages with photographs as well. And New York City was the single best place in the world to practice the craft. In addition to being the seat of the magazine trade, the city was at its all-time peak as a carnival of contrasts. Seemingly every sort of person could be found on its streets; any corner at any hour could provide some tableau, some human spectacle, some chance collision of wildly disparate elements. What Paris had been in the 1920s—when it had birthed dozens of important photographic careers—New York now claimed for itself, and enterprising youngsters from the five boroughs and beyond were not slow to seize the occasion.

Kubrick falls chronologically near the middle of a passel of New York photographers who worked the streets: Ted Croner and Louis Stettner, born 1922; Diane Arbus and Saul Leiter, born 1923; Robert Frank and Jerome Liebling, born 1924; Simpson Kalisher, born 1926; Garry Winogrand, William Klein, and Elliott Erwitt, born 1928; Bruce Davidson, born 1933; and Lee Friedlander, born 1934. It is instructive to compare Kubrick to his exact contemporary Winogrand, who likewise was raised in the Bronx and likewise forewent a college education in favor of photography. Winogrand had a much harder time of it, freelancing for many years and seldom able to crack the prestige market, the bulk of his early photographs appearing in places like *Collier's*, *Pageant*, and *Redbook*. But freelancing had certain advantages. While the two men's early magazine work could sometimes be mistaken for one another's—for example, Winogrand's study of a young boxer, "What Makes Nick Run?" (*Pageant*, May 1955),[2] is tonally very close to Kubrick's

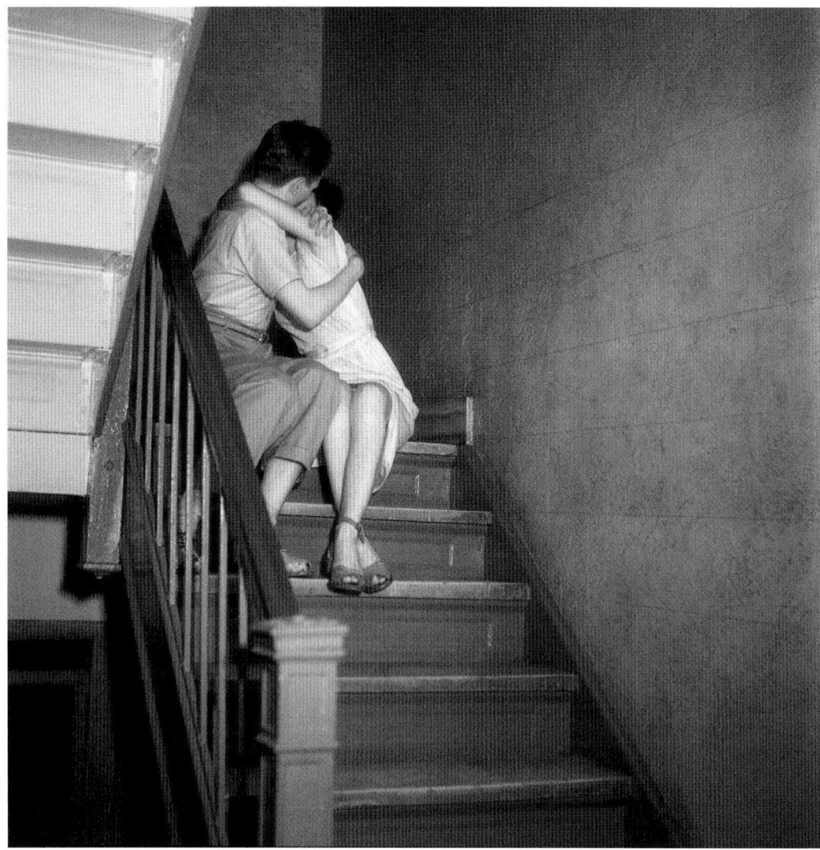

A couple caught in an embrace with infrared photography, from an unpublished 1946 assignment. Photo by Stanley Kubrick

work on similar subjects—Winogrand also had the downtime necessary to start building a radical style of his own, with his trademark tilted horizons and chaotic welter of visual information showing up very early in his portfolio. Kubrick, by contrast, was learning all the skills while tethered to a specific mandate; clarity and coverage were uppermost, and self-expression secondary at best.

Kubrick began his career at *Look* with subjects that were close to him, environmentally and emotionally as well as literally. The only teacher at Taft High School he felt much rapport with was Aaron Traister, who was known for his enthusiastic performance in English classes; in 1946 *Look* published a four-picture story by Kubrick showing the teacher, in class, acting out *Hamlet*. That same year the magazine ran a spread of 18 photos of people waiting outside a dentist's office, in attitudes ranging from boredom to serious pain; the pictures were all by Kubrick and the dentist was his own. He also made several series of sequential photographs of people on Bronx streets, gossiping and gesticulating and giving one another the hairy eyeball. At that point Kubrick was still very much a fledgling. His pictures were clear and effective, but lacked something in the way of personality. Perhaps that is why so many of those early pictures ran as assemblages of vignettes; the more of them there were, the stronger the impression. You could also make a case that Kubrick was already beginning to think in cinematic terms, that his shooting ratios were so large because he was more interested in capturing continuity of action than in any single image crowded with meaning.

You get a strong sense of New York City in the late 1940s from Kubrick's photos: rowdy, threadbare, optimistic, opinionated, moody, theatrical, democratic. It was the capital of its time, more important than it had ever been, leading the world in image production via art and advertising, with new glass-and-steel construction reshaping Midtown (including *Look*'s offices at 488 Madison Avenue, completed in 1950), while at the same time it was still a populist and heterogeneous port city, striated with vigorous

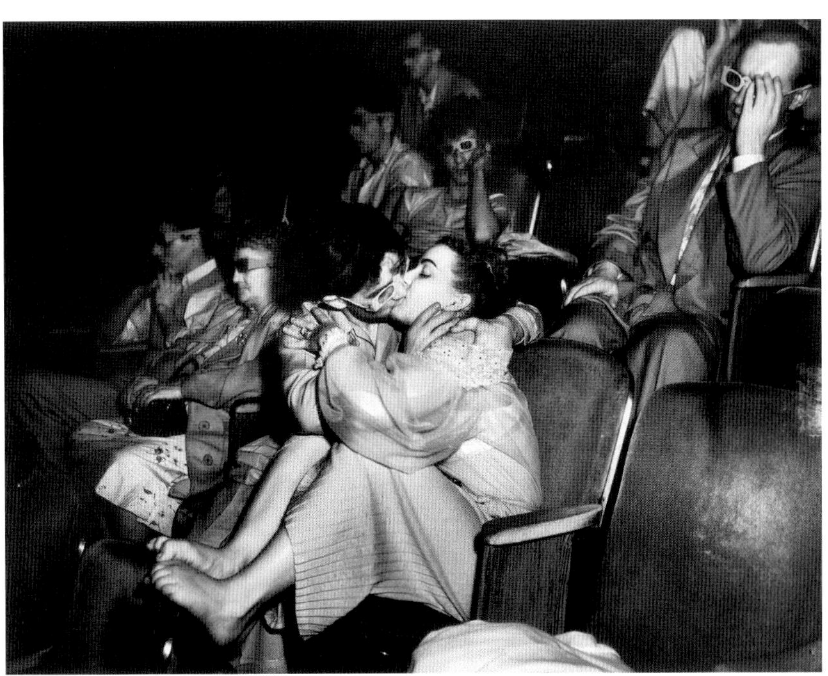

Lovers at the Palace Theatre, ca. 1953. Photo by Weegee

working-class ethnic neighborhoods, few of their inhabitants yet having made the exodus to the suburbs.

There were class distinctions, but everybody shared the same streets and often drank at the same bars and ate at the same lunch counters. Even a swell like the *New Yorker* cartoonist Peter Arno, squiring a girl half his age to an evening's entertainment, stops for a beer at the kind of unpretentious establishment that today would be labeled a "dive." The great expatriate German artist George Grosz is portrayed straddling a chair on a Fifth Avenue sidewalk, looking like the president of a travel agency—this to illustrate a spread on New York as the capital of the arts that otherwise featured more conventional pictures by other photographers. Quite unlike *Life* but rather like its later stablemate *People*, *Look* favored profiles that showed celebrities at work and at play, miming telephone conversations and busying themselves in their kitchens. Thus the ingenue actress Betsy von Furstenberg is seen being filmed, being measured for clothes, adjusting her makeup, reading a script in her apartment, emoting in her agent's office, sashaying around on a bicycle, disporting herself at a stuffy party with a nervous young man in evening dress, and peeling a banana with another at some white-tablecloth joint. The profiles were glamorized lifestyle fantasies, loosely based on their subjects' actual activities but rendered as a series of sculpted poses, compiled into *fumetti*-like miniature biopics that Kubrick can probably be said to have directed as well as photographed.

He had to come up with some sort of shooting script, ensuring a sufficient number of activities to make for an impression of continuity, not to mention a constant whirl of celebrity action, ideally structured around the course of one typically vigorous day. He got more cooperation from some personalities than others. Leonard Bernstein appears to have insisted he be primarily shown peering godlike into the far distance, in different settings, while Guy Lombardo was willing to do little more than show off various possessions, including a swarm of small dogs. And then there is Montgomery Clift, photographed to coincide with the release of his third film, on the edge of stardom but already seeming like a sure thing. He wears a torn T-shirt, looks melancholy and contemplative, drinks coffee, and smokes. He is a gay man, deeply closeted by necessity, who lives alone and does his socializing out of camera range. It is virtually impossible to construct a romantic lifestyle fantasy around him without an inordinate amount of contrivance, so he and Kubrick resort to a visit with his friend Kevin McCarthy's family, where Clift gamely if uncertainly plays horsey with their young son. Note by contrast that

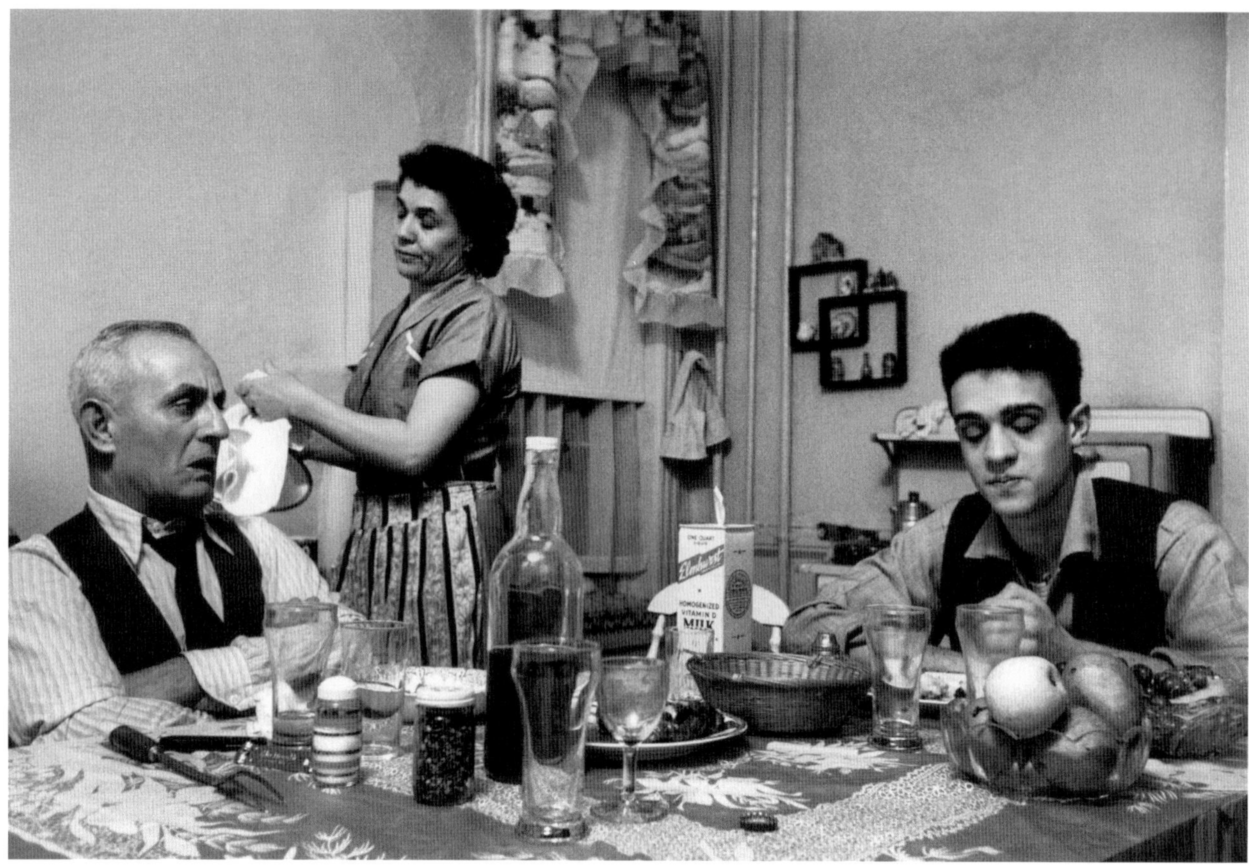

New York, 1954.
Photo by Garry Winogrand

Arno's open and undisguised harvesting of a very young woman is presented without comment, as simply an ordinary perquisite in the life of an aging man-about-town.

A showgirl named Rosemary Williams provides a particularly vivid and raffish New York narrative, on the edge of film noir, filled with contrasts and characters. Interestingly, what must have made her daily routine appear ideal for exploitation is possibly also the reason the story was never published. Williams came to the city with theatrical ambitions, but jobs being insufficient on what was called the "legitimate" stage, she paid the rent with her work as a showgirl, which means that in the course of her day she shows a lot of flesh—too much, maybe, for a family magazine. Her life cannot have been exactly easy—despite her wardrobe, she was living on the margins as much as any bohemian—but we see it filtered through the lens of male delectation; it is fitting that Kubrick himself appears reflected in her makeup mirror, looking reedy, his eyes black with concentration. Except backstage at the theater, where she plays cards *en déshabillé* with her colleagues, Williams is everywhere seen making nice with men: her manager, her lunch date, a fellow actor on a legit job, the male half of an older couple she accompanies to a depressing nightclub. Appropriately, she is pictured under a Times Square marquee advertising *The Set-Up* (which, as a boxing picture, may have signified something different for Kubrick).

All of Kubrick's profile subjects, no matter how café-society their lives, palpably exist in the same city as the shoeshine boy, who might have stepped out of the pages of Horatio Alger. Wearing a hat like Huntz Hall of the Bowery Boys, he drags his stand around and drums up business, gambles for bottle caps with his friends, peers at movie marquees—but also studies, picks up the family laundry, tends to his pigeons on the roof, and poses with his many brothers and sisters outside their tenement façade, covered with chalk graffiti. From our distant viewpoint the series looks almost too good to be true, but it could fit neatly into a selection of works by the Photo League, a socially conscious

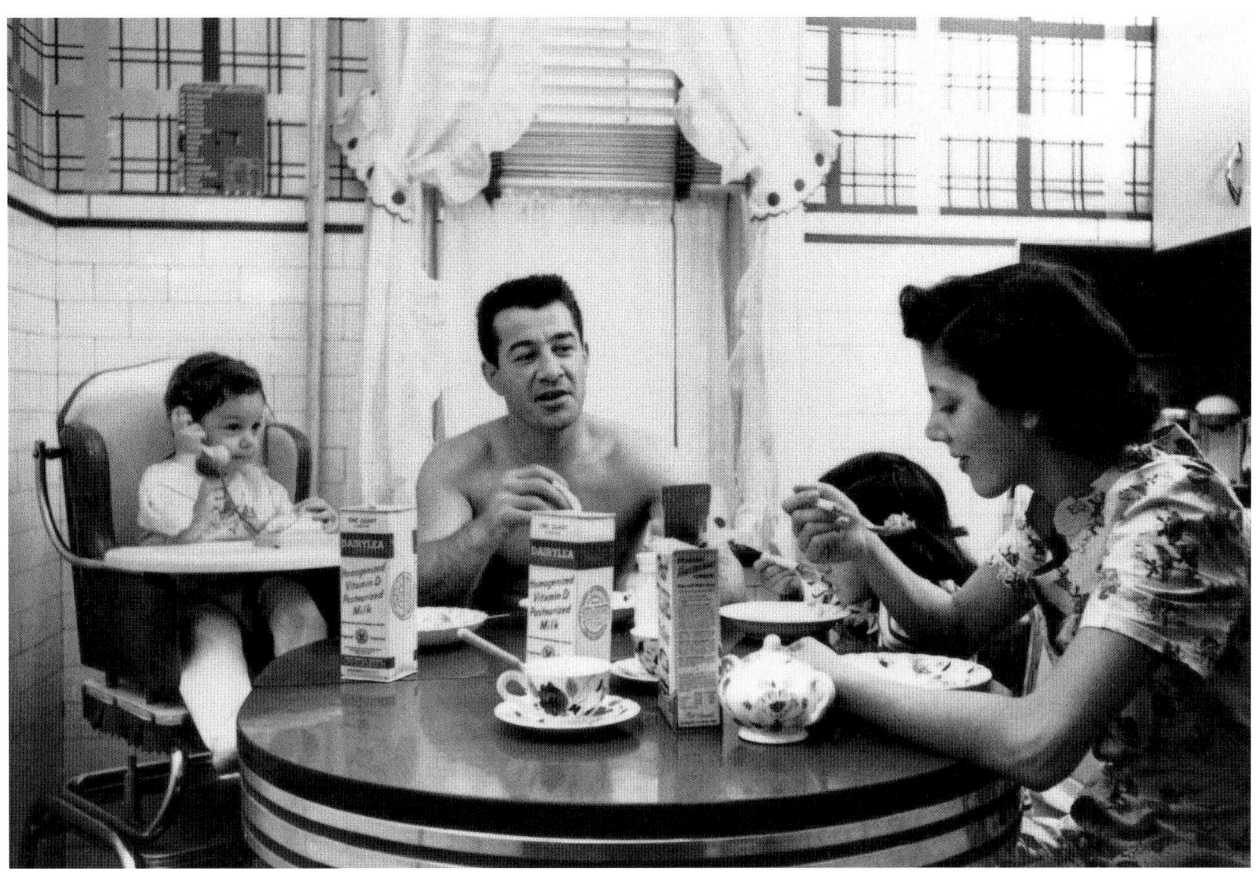

Rocky Graziano having breakfast with his family, from the 1950 article "Rocky Graziano: He's A Good Boy Now." Photo by Stanley Kubrick

photographers' cooperative, extant from 1936 until it was killed by McCarthyism in 1951, in which most New York street photographers of the generation just before Kubrick's were active at one time or another. The story differs chiefly from typical Photo League fare, with its extensive documentation of children's street games and scrappy, unbowed protagonists, in featuring a lad as blond as any farm boy in the middle of the country whose family might subscribe to *Look*.

The citizens of Kubrick's democratic city relaxed on the weekend by taking the ferry across the Hudson to Palisades Amusement Park. Kubrick shot a feature there in 1946, while still in his novitiate, and the piece allowed him to focus on an aspect of the craft he hadn't so far had a chance to explore. It turned out he really liked to compose shots, and while Manhattan and the Bronx didn't afford that many opportunities to do so, the amusement park—not too crowded and with a fair amount of open space around dramatically tall rides—proved ideal. It gave Kubrick opportunities for low-angle shots contrasting youngsters with the towering attractions—a variation on the heroic-worker poses, silhouetted against the sky, made in the 1930s by Dorothea Lange, Robert Capa, and Aleksandr Rodchenko. He was able to indulge that tendency again when he photographed the Ringling Bros. circus in 1948, the *Look* spread leading off with his highly confected photo of owner John Ringling North, in three-quarter low angle, miming a yell with a cupped hand while aerial acrobats ride the wire above and to the left—a postwar leisure-time version of a Constructivist poster shot.

That people, and especially children, were outdoors seemingly all the time in the city then is demonstrated by a series of pictures Kubrick took, for an unpublished feature, of the shooting of *The Naked City* in 1947. It was a rare Hollywood production for the time to be shot in part on location, on Delancey Street and the Manhattan Bridge on the Lower East Side, and the entire population of the neighborhood seems to have turned out, sprawling on cars, surrounding the camera truck, bellying up to the line in every set-up.

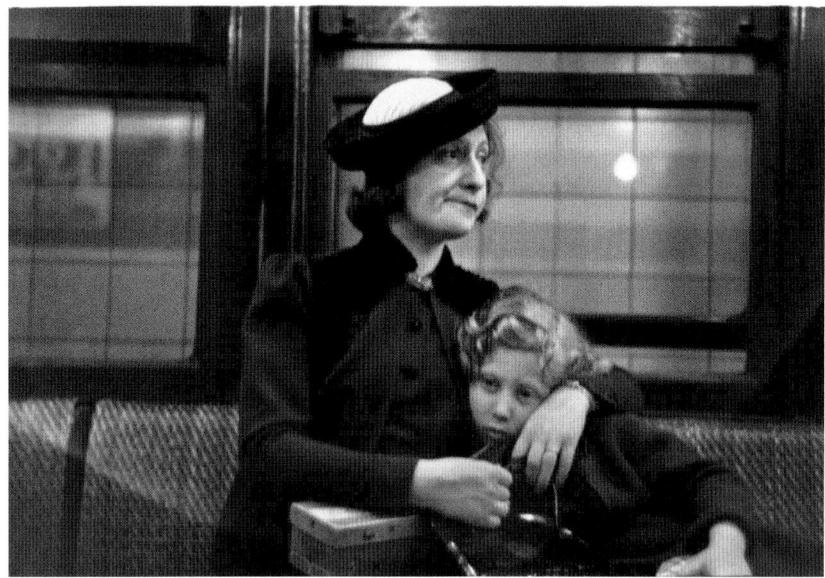

Subway Portrait, 1938.
Photo by Walker Evans

Kubrick's pictures are reminiscent of Weegee's crowds, and Kubrick also caught a shot or two of the man himself, since he had sold his title for the movie and served as technical adviser. Weegee by then was a celebrity and no longer a photographer for the daily press, but he remained a primary influence on every street photographer in the city and beyond, for decades afterward. The most obvious trace of Weegee in Kubrick's work is a series of voyeuristic ultraviolet shots of friends and classmates in romantic clinches in the dark, although the master of crowds and ballyhoo haunts his pictures of rubberneckers and stunts, such as the woman toting a sandwich-board advertisement. Fifteen years later Kubrick hired Weegee as special-effects consultant and still photographer on *Dr. Strangelove*; his photos provide the only surviving visual evidence of the pie fight originally intended as the movie's last sequence.

Weegee's influence also pervades Kubrick's subway story, the first multi-page feature he published. Spending entire days and nights in the system, Kubrick produced a portrait of the city that was romantic, alienated, mysterious, and workaday by turns. His individual portraits of riders are eerily similar to Walker Evans's, although he couldn't possibly have seen them (Evans took the pictures included in *Many Are Called* by 1941, but none was published until the 1960s). The pictures include romantic interludes, both obviously concocted (the couple in the 81st Street IND station, a derelict sprawled on the ground behind them) and probably authentic (the couple folded together on one of the rattan seats). A pencil-mustached man in evening clothes with his arm around his sleeping son suggests a ventriloquist toting his dummy. The long escalator at Grand Central, with its low, sloping ceiling, is shot looking down, so that its two triangles seem to point toward a far distant vortex, to our eyes recalling the deep-space effects in *2001: A Space Odyssey*.

His study of Aqueduct Racetrack, in 1947, may be the point at which we truly begin to recognize the emergence of Kubrick the filmmaker. In part that is because the pictures recall the racetrack scenes in *The Killing* (1956), his third feature, but also, more generally, because the horseplayers seem like recognizably Kubrick characters. Each figure is distinctive, whether pictured solo or backed by a crowd, and each suggests a complex life story: the respectable old lady with her Gibson Girl hat and chignon, marking up her *Racing Form*; the retired tough guy, possibly a longshoreman or boxing-ring cut-man, who gives one last look at his sheet before pitching it into the bin. These people palpably stirred Kubrick's imagination and sympathy in ways few subjects had previously. They certainly aren't celebrities, but they refuse to blend into the crowd—they become players on a stage. By now Kubrick is aware that his camera is not simply a

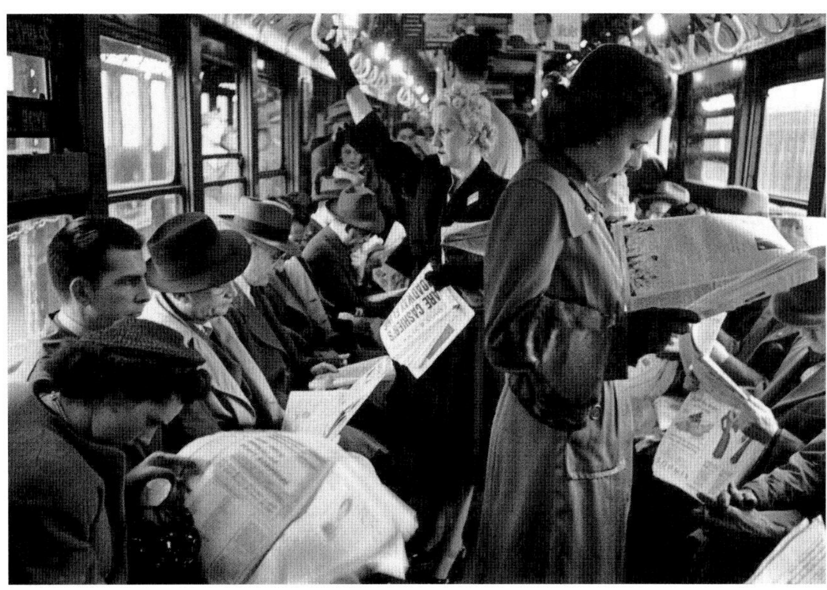

Subway passengers from the 1947 article "Life and Love on the New York Subway." Photo by Stanley Kubrick

mechanical contrivance, but a weirdly sensitive instrument that responds to the most fleeting emotions of its operator.

Boxing was an essential component of city life then, a spectator sport attended by thousands, a dramatic means by which poor kids could rise from the slums and become stars. Kubrick published four boxing stories in *Look*, including two fight-night features and a profile of the troubled but charismatic Rocky Graziano, who would go on to a minor show-business career. The most emblematic story, however, was that of Walter Cartier, a humble and introspective man of matinee-idol looks, furthermore eerily endowed with an identical twin brother, Vincent, a lawyer. Kubrick followed Walter through his fight day, including a visit to his church, a session with his trainer, and silent contemplation in the rubdown room before stepping into the ring. The fight scenes are dark and explosive, conveying action in flashing bursts. A year later Kubrick chose Cartier as the subject for his first film, a 16-minute documentary called *Day of the Fight* (1951), with the same story line as the *Look* feature. The film was bought by RKO Pictures for either $100 more or $100 less than it cost to make (accounts vary), but it did launch Kubrick on his future track. A few months later he made another documentary short, *Flying Padre* (1951), about a priest in the Southwest traveling to his widely scattered Native American parishes in his own small plane, after which Kubrick quit *Look* and began planning his first film feature.

Kubrick's work at *Look* is valuable in its own right. As a portrait of New York City at a crucial point—just after the war and just before everyone owned a TV set—when it was at its motley and innocent peak, and as a first-rate collection of photographs by an up-and-coming documentary photographer, perhaps not yet entirely formed but poised to strike out on a highly individual path, the lineaments of which can perhaps be dimly discerned. As the embryonic work of a major film director it offers almost too many clues, both psychological and aesthetic, to what lies ahead. You can see the beginnings of Kubrick's chiaroscuro moods, his deep-space compositions, his restless toggling between the micro and the macro. The viewer can also appreciate his fanatical attention to detail and his insistence on employing the world as a vast studio in which no nuance goes overlooked and nothing is left to mere chance. Stanley Kubrick was fortunate in his first place of employment—it is there that he learned to look.

ENDNOTES

1 Michael Herr, *Kubrick* (New York: Grove Press, 2000), 4.
2 Leo Rubinfien, *Garry Winogrand* (New Haven: Yale University Press, 2013), 18.

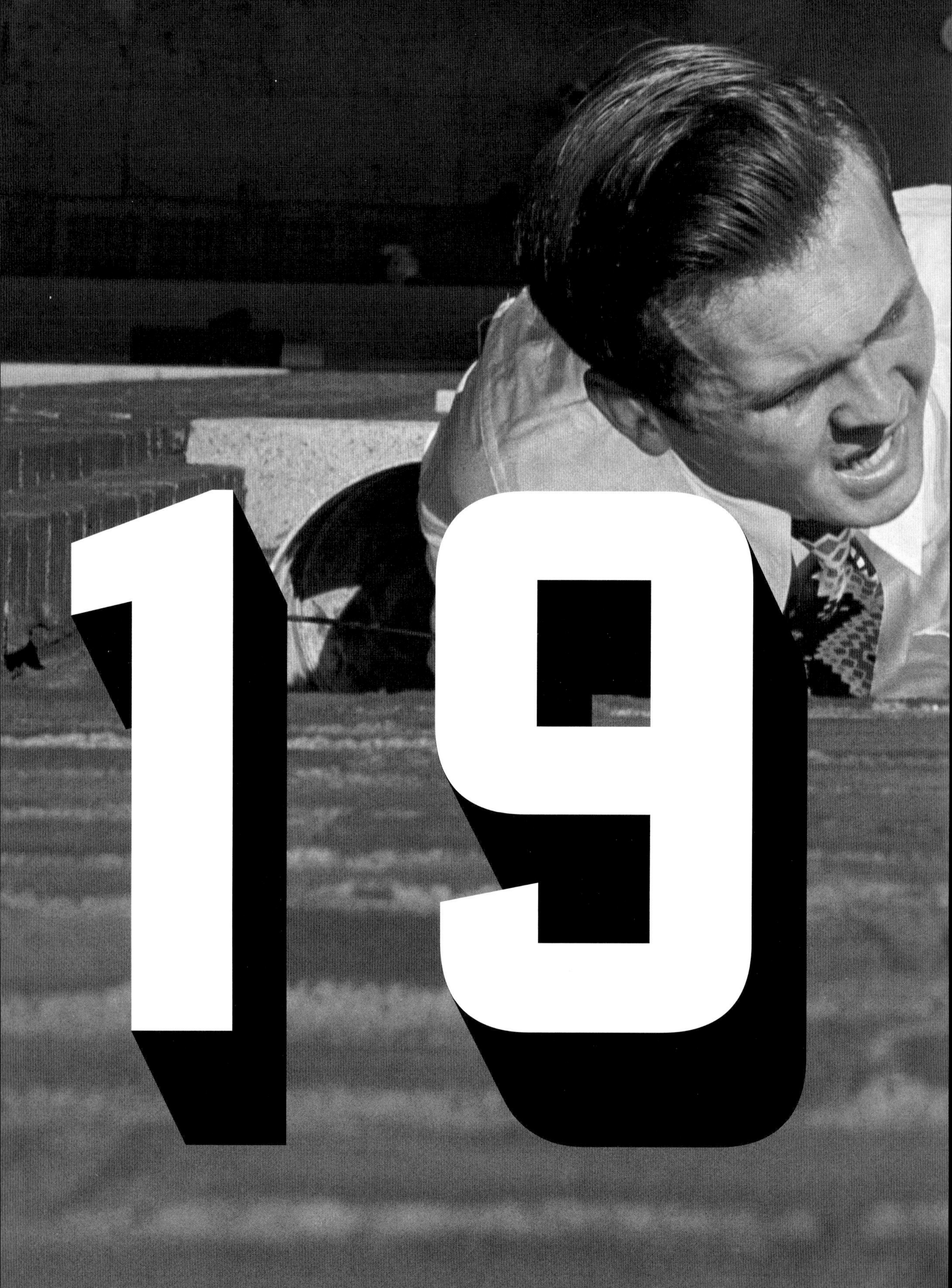
19

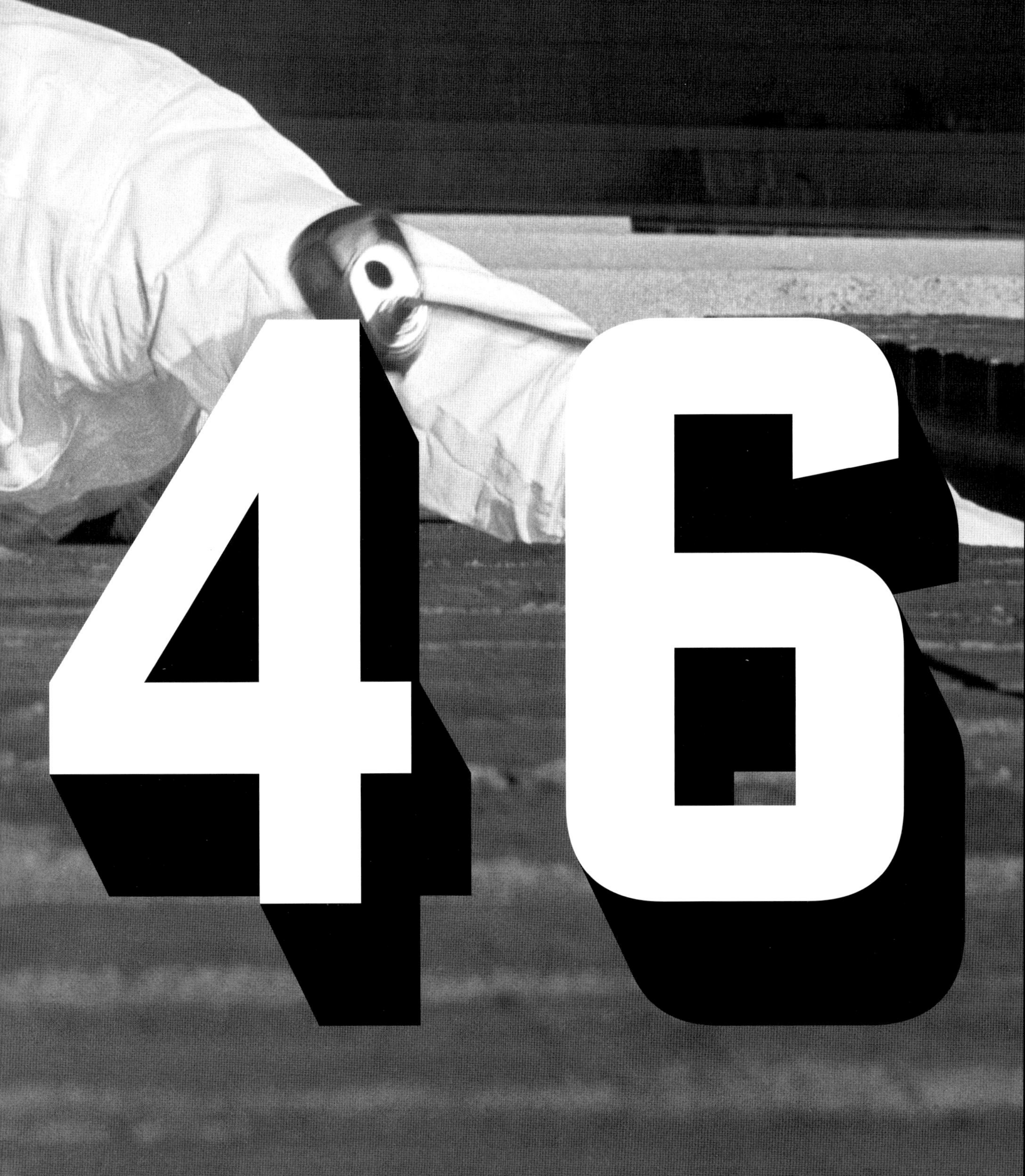
46

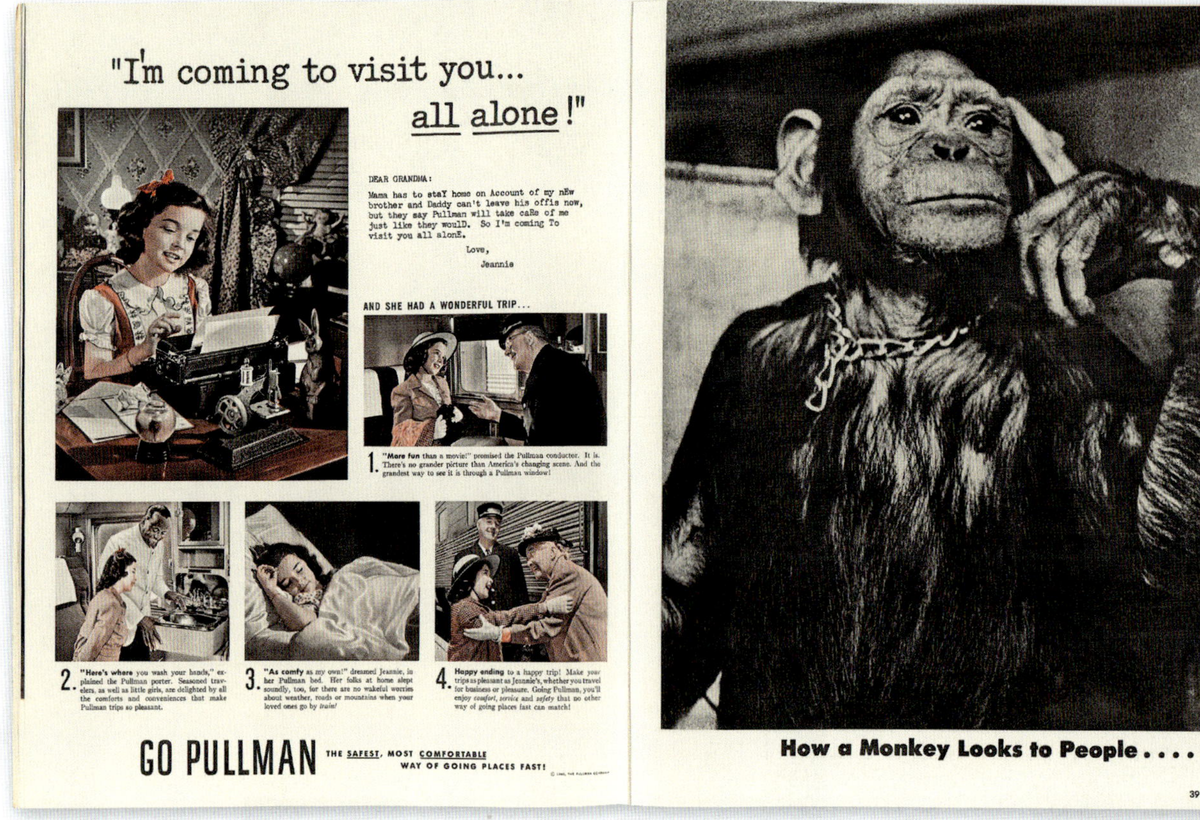

"I'm coming to visit you... all alone!"

DEAR GRANDMA:

Mama has to staY home on Account of my nEw brother and Daddy can't leave his offis now, but they say Pullman will take caRe of me just like they woulD. So I'm coming To visit you all alonE.

Love,
Jeannie

AND SHE HAD A WONDERFUL TRIP...

1. **"More fun** than a movie!" promised the Pullman conductor. It is. There's no grander picture than America's changing scene. And the grandest way to see it is through a Pullman window!

2. **"Here's where** you wash your hands," explained the Pullman porter. Seasoned travelers, as well as little girls, are delighted by all the comforts and conveniences that make Pullman trips so pleasant.

3. **"As comfy** as my own!" dreamed Jeannie, in her Pullman bed. Her folks at home slept soundly, too, for there are no wakeful worries about weather, roads or mountains when your loved ones go by *train!*

4. **Happy ending** to a happy trip! Make your trips as pleasant as Jeannie's, whether you travel for business or pleasure. Going Pullman, you'll enjoy *comfort*, *service* and *safety* that no other way of going places fast can match!

GO PULLMAN THE SAFEST, MOST COMFORTABLE WAY OF GOING PLACES FAST!

How a Monkey Looks to People.......

39

PUBLISHED AS

HOW A MONKEY LOOKS TO PEOPLE... HOW PEOPLE LOOK TO A MONKEY

DATE

AUGUST 20, 1946

Published early in Kubrick's career at *Look*, this story laid the groundwork for a recurring motif—observing people looking—that characterized many of his later assignments for the magazine and anticipated his interest in moviemaking. The published piece opened with a photograph of a pensive chimpanzee taken by noted animal photographer Ylla. Below the photograph, text with an ellipsis led readers to turn the page to see three cropped Kubrick photographs of people seemingly taken from the chimp's point of view within its cage.

OPPOSITE **While most of Kubrick's photographs for this article included both the caged monkeys and the zoo's visitors, *Look* cropped the published versions to eliminate the monkeys and focus on the spectators' faces.**

The title of each article cited in this portfolio corresponds to how it was listed in the magazine's table of contents.

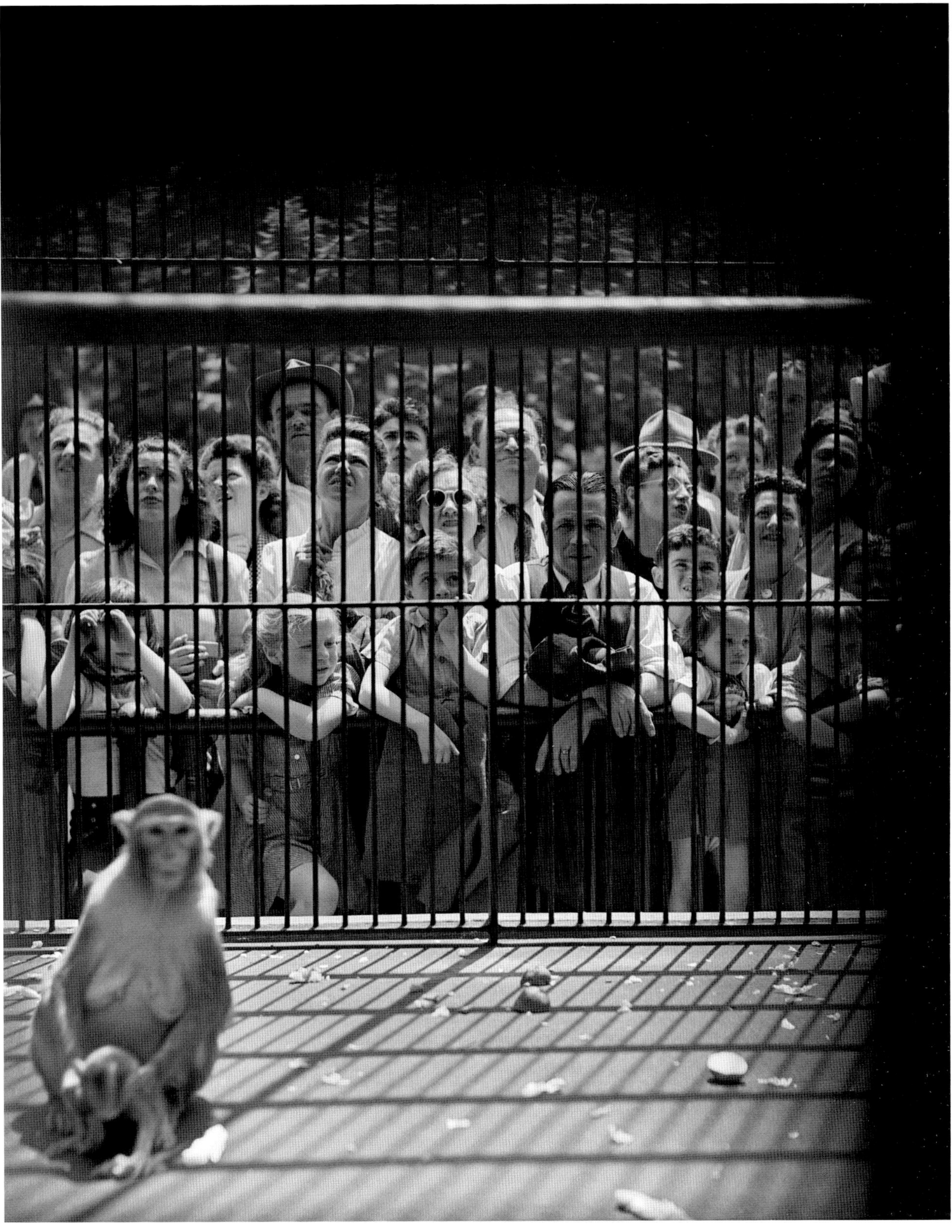

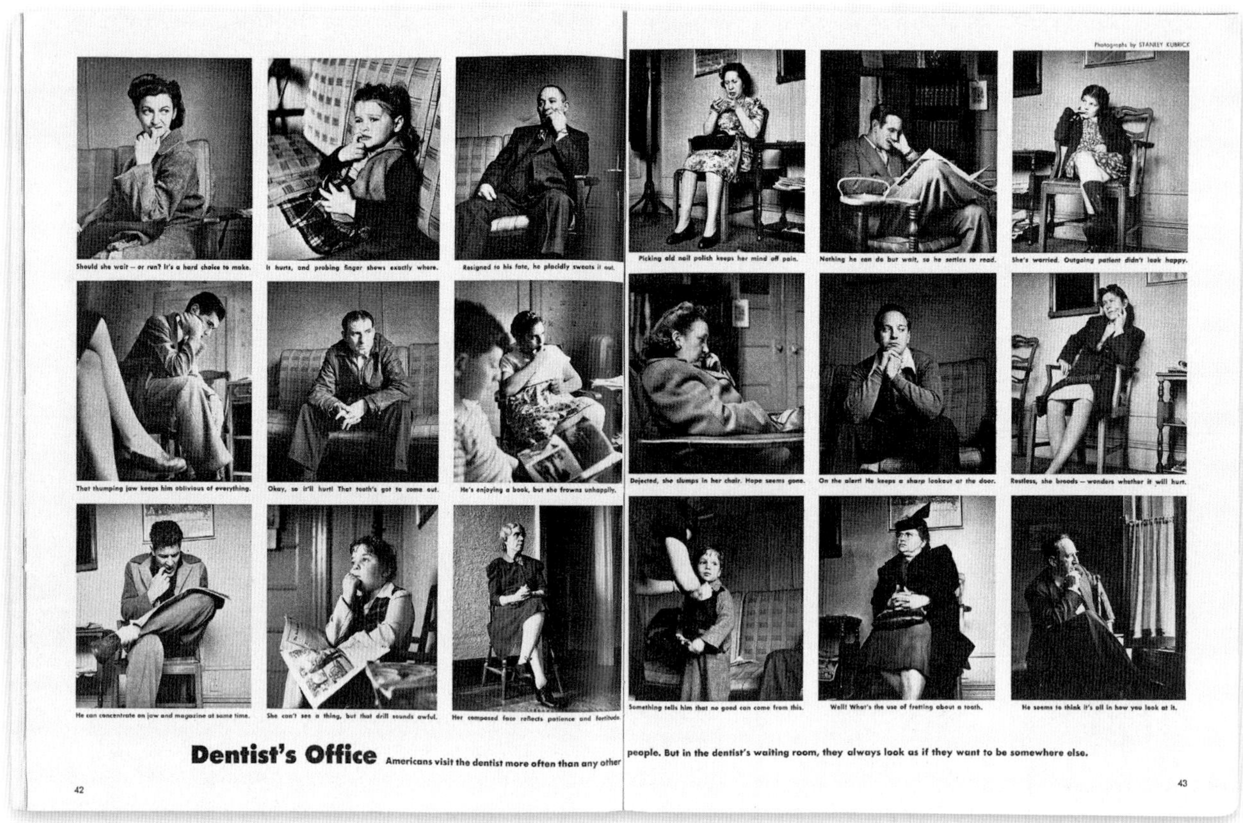

Photographs by STANLEY KUBRICK

Should she wait—or run? It's a hard choice to make.

It hurts, and probing finger shows exactly where.

Resigned to his fate, he placidly sweats it out.

Picking old nail polish keeps her mind off pain.

Nothing he can do but wait, so he settles to read.

She's worried. Outgoing patient didn't look happy.

That thumping jaw keeps him oblivious of everything.

Okay, so it'll hurt! That tooth's got to come out.

He's enjoying a book, but she frowns unhappily.

Dejected, she slumps in her chair. Hope seems gone.

On the alert! He keeps a sharp lookout at the door.

Restless, she broods—wonders whether it will hurt.

He can concentrate on jaw and magazine at same time.

She can't see a thing, but that drill sounds awful.

Her composed face reflects patience and fortitude.

Something tells him that no good can come from this.

Well! What's the use of fretting about a tooth.

He seems to think it's all in how you look at it.

Dentist's Office Americans visit the dentist more often than any other people. But in the dentist's waiting room, they always look as if they want to be somewhere else.

42

43

PUBLISHED AS

DENTIST'S OFFICE: AMERICANS ARE DUTIFUL BUT NERVOUS DENTAL PATIENTS

DATE

OCTOBER 1, 1946

Depicting people waiting for dental appointments—some with anxiety, others with fortitude, resignation, or patience—this article described their expressions with clever captions. "Should she wait—or run?" one read. "It's a hard choice to make." Another noted, "On the alert! He keeps a sharp lookout at the door." The published article was a single spread, featuring a grid of 18 photographs that offered readers a myriad of reactions in a glance.

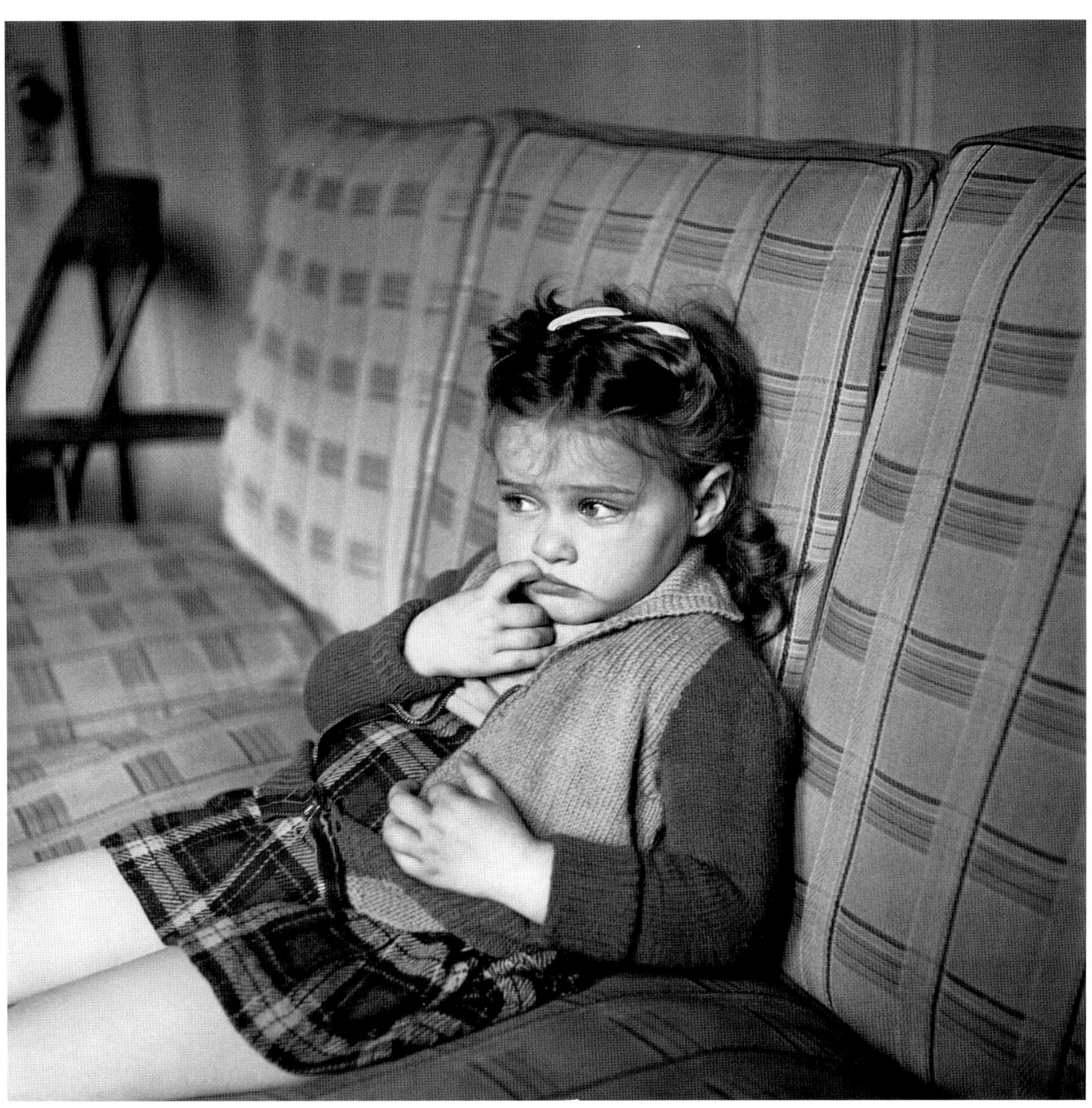

Anxiously waiting for the dentist

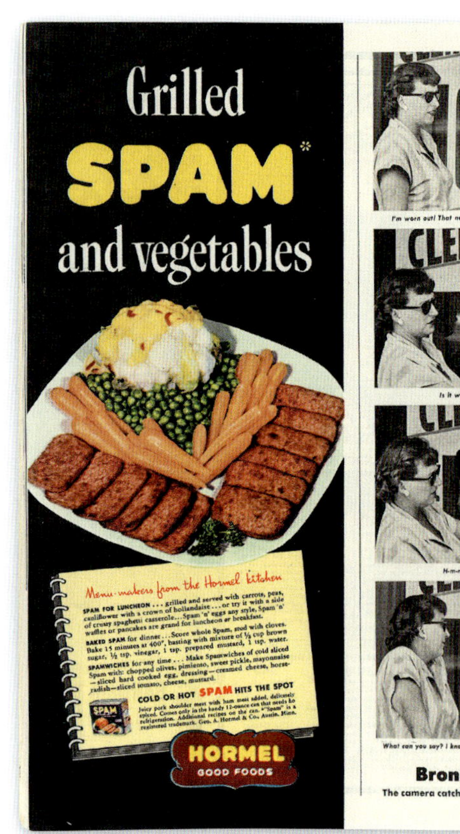

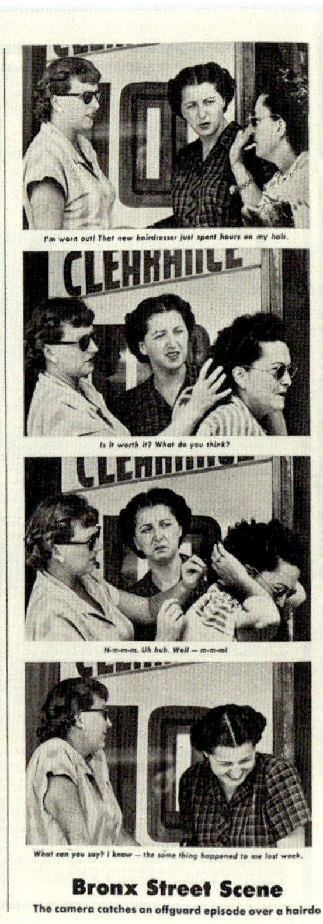
I'm worn out! That new hairdresser just spent hours on my hair.

Is it worth it? What do you think?

H-m-m-m. Uh huh. Well — m-m-m!

What can you say? I know — the same thing happened to me last week.

Bronx Street Scene

The camera catches an offguard episode over a hairdo

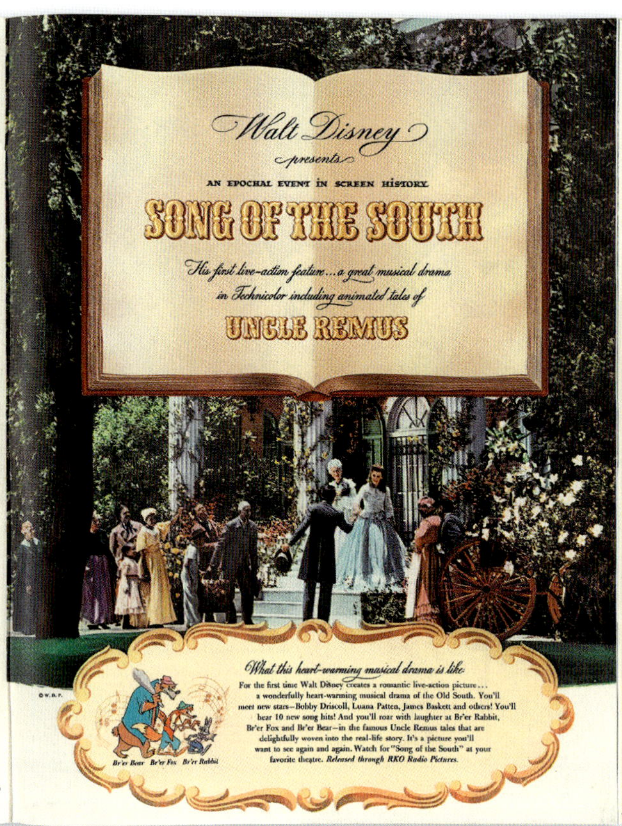

PUBLISHED AS

BRONX STREET SCENE: THE CAMERA CATCHES AN OFFGUARD EPISODE OVER A HAIRDO

DATE

NOVEMBER 26, 1946

After Kubrick photographed numerous people having conversations on New York City streets, the magazine chose to publish a four-image sequence in which his camera seemingly caught "an offguard episode over a hairdo." The assignment was photographed with a 35 mm camera, possibly with a telephoto lens, which allowed Kubrick enough distance from his subjects to remain unseen. The assignment's files contain photographic sequences of additional street interactions, some likely taken in Manhattan.

OPPOSITE **Kubrick shot from afar to photograph these three women discussing a hairdo.**

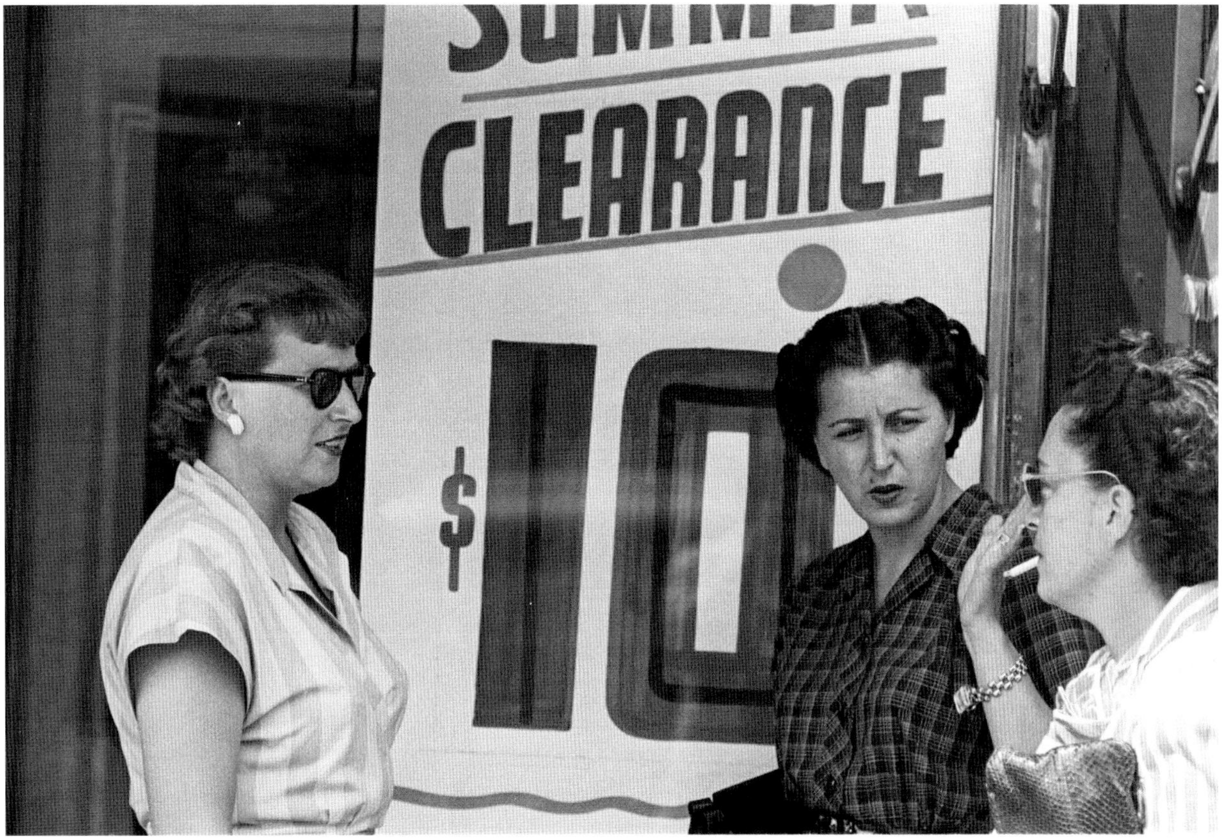
CLEARANCE
$10

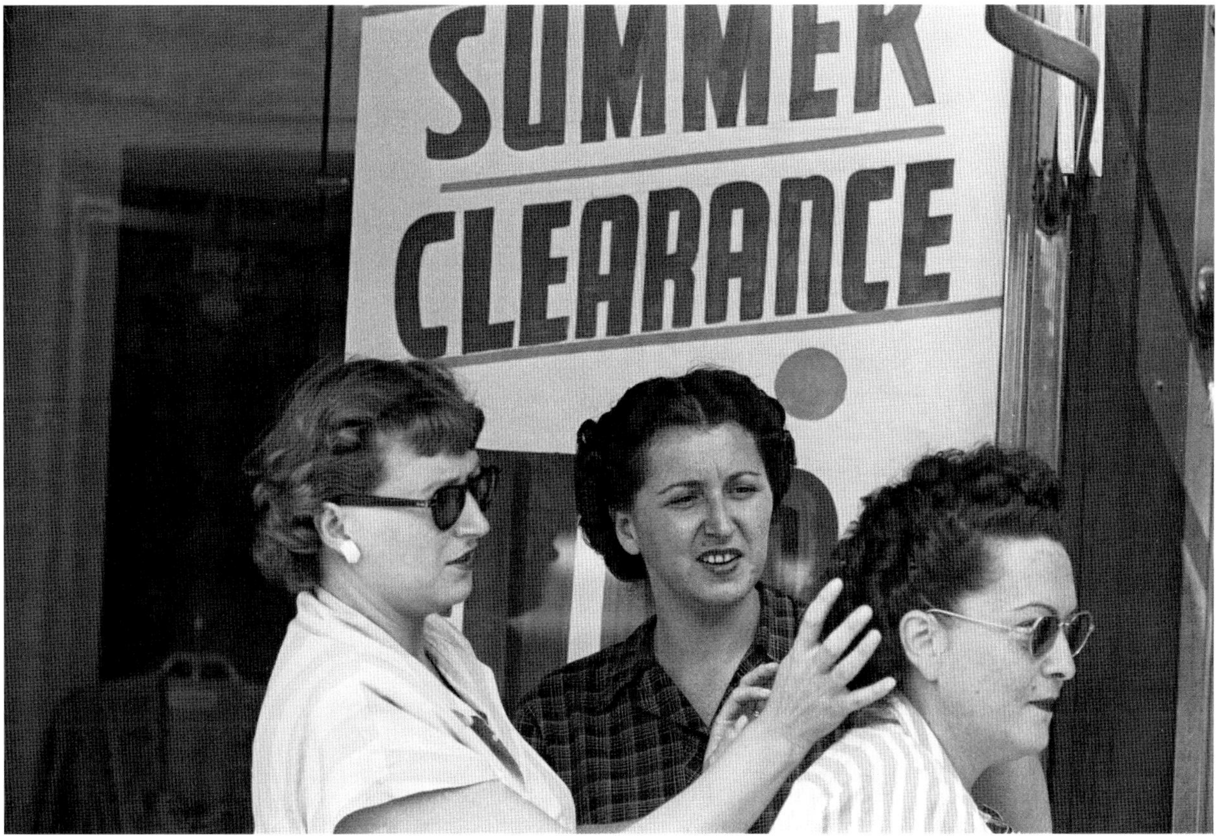
SUMMER
CLEARANCE

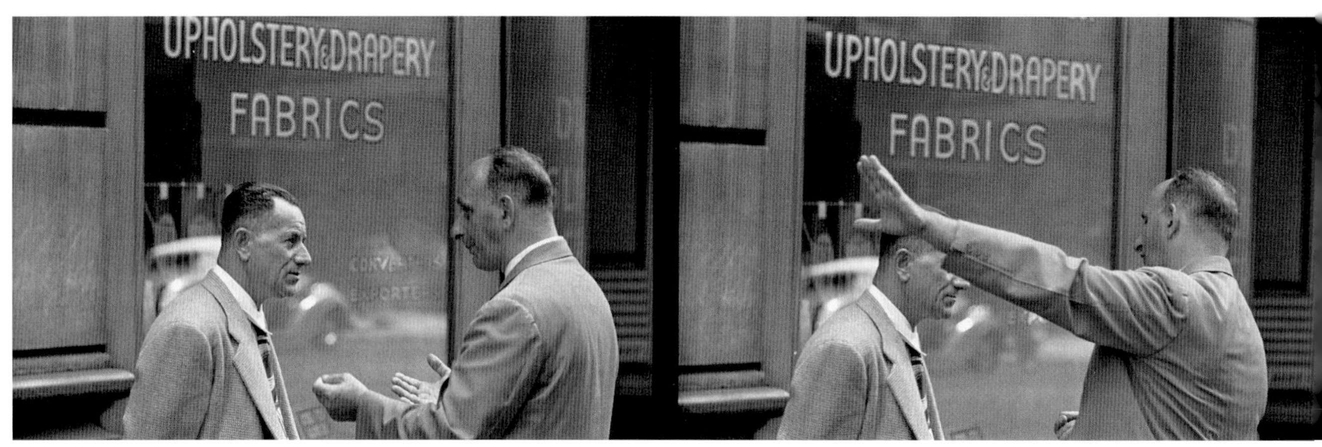

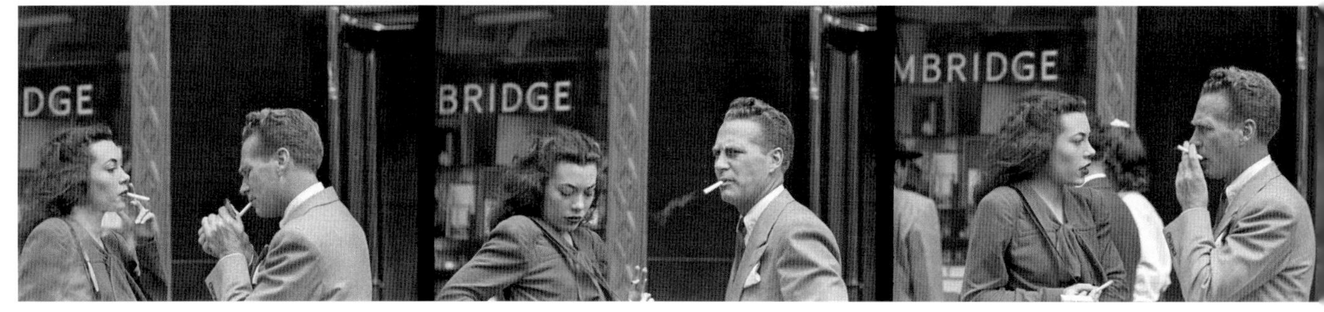

Unpublished contact strips depicting people conversing on the street

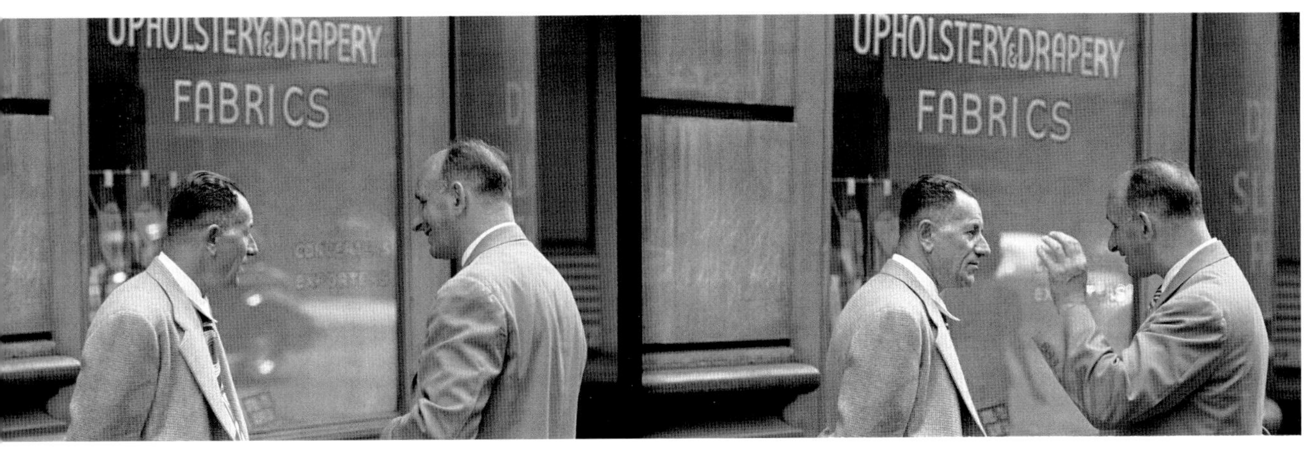
UPHOLSTERY&DRAPERY
FABRICS
UPHOLSTERY&DRAPERY
FABRICS

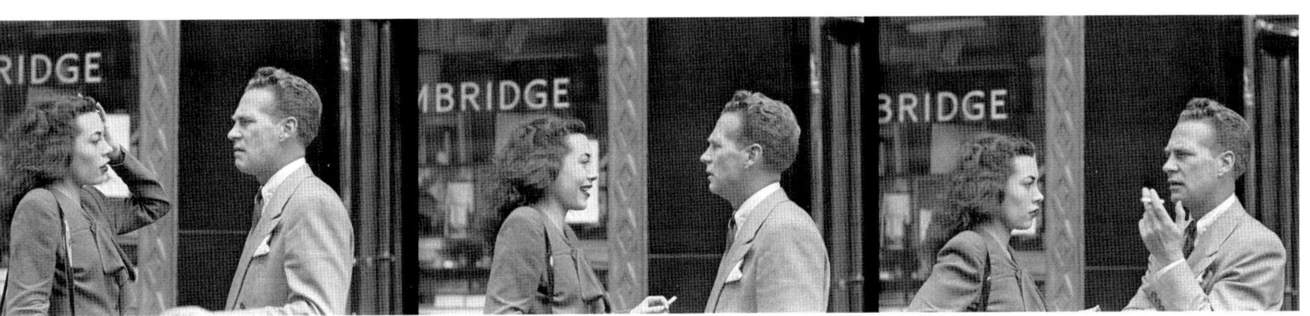
RIDGE
MBRIDGE
BRIDGE

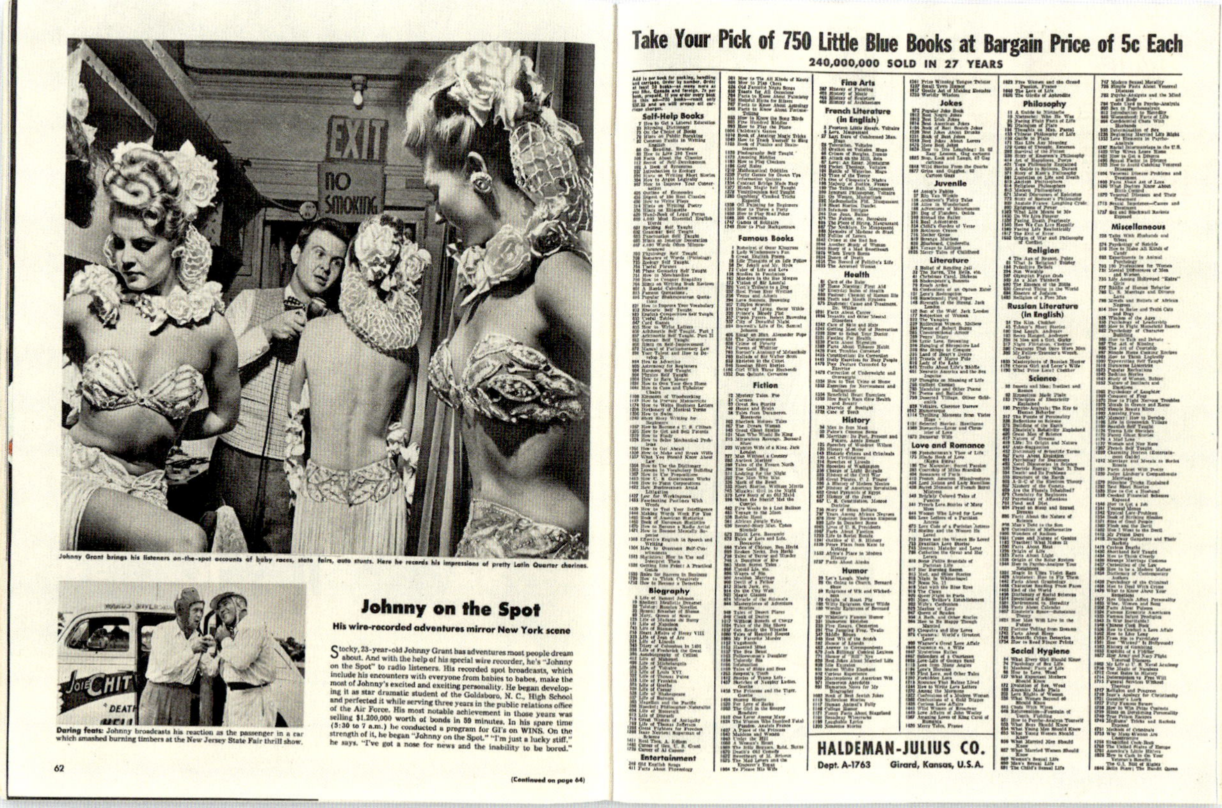

Johnny Grant brings his listeners on-the-spot accounts of baby races, state fairs, auto stunts. Here he records his impressions of pretty Latin Quarter chorines.

During feats: Johnny broadcasts his reaction as the passenger in a car which smashed burning timbers at the New Jersey State Fair thrill show.

Johnny on the Spot

His wire-recorded adventures mirror New York scene

Stocky, 23-year-old Johnny Grant has adventures most people dream about. And with the help of his special wire recorder, he's "Johnny on the Spot" to radio listeners. His recorded spot broadcasts, which include his encounters with everyone from babies to babes, make the most of Johnny's excited and exciting personality. He began developing it as star dramatic student of the Goldsboro, N. C., High School and perfected it while serving three years in the public relations office of the Air Force. His most notable achievement in those years was selling $1,200,000 worth of bonds in 59 minutes. In his spare time (5:30 to 7 a.m.) he conducted a program for GI's on WINS. On the strength of it, he began "Johnny on the Spot." "I'm just a lucky stiff," he says. "I've got a nose for news and the inability to be bored."

62

(Continued on page 64)

PUBLISHED AS

JOHNNY ON THE SPOT: HIS RECORDED ADVENTURES MIRROR THE NEW YORK SCENE

DATE

NOVEMBER 26, 1946

Johnny on the Spot was a New York radio program hosted by 23-year-old Johnny Grant, who did of-the-moment interviews with showgirls, celebrities, and even animals. "I'm just a lucky stiff," he noted in the article. "I've got a nose for news and the inability to be bored." In this early assignment, Kubrick created photographs that experimented with different, often dramatic, camera angles. These included a worm's-eye view of babies, which was published, and an unpublished high-angle, vertigo-inducing perspective of Grant hanging from a windowsill many stories above the street.

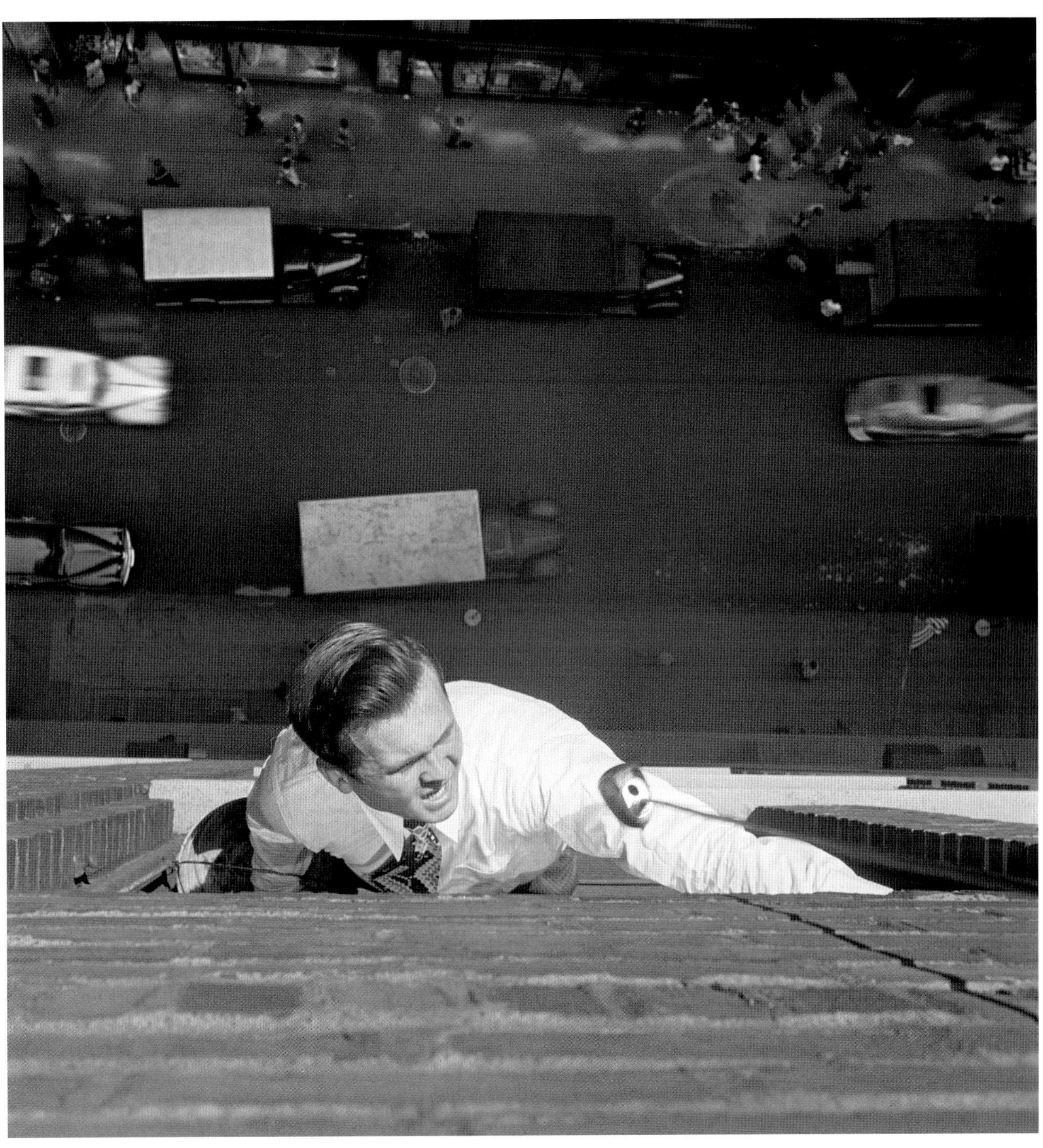

Unpublished portrait of the radio host, microphone at the ready, on a windowsill high above the city

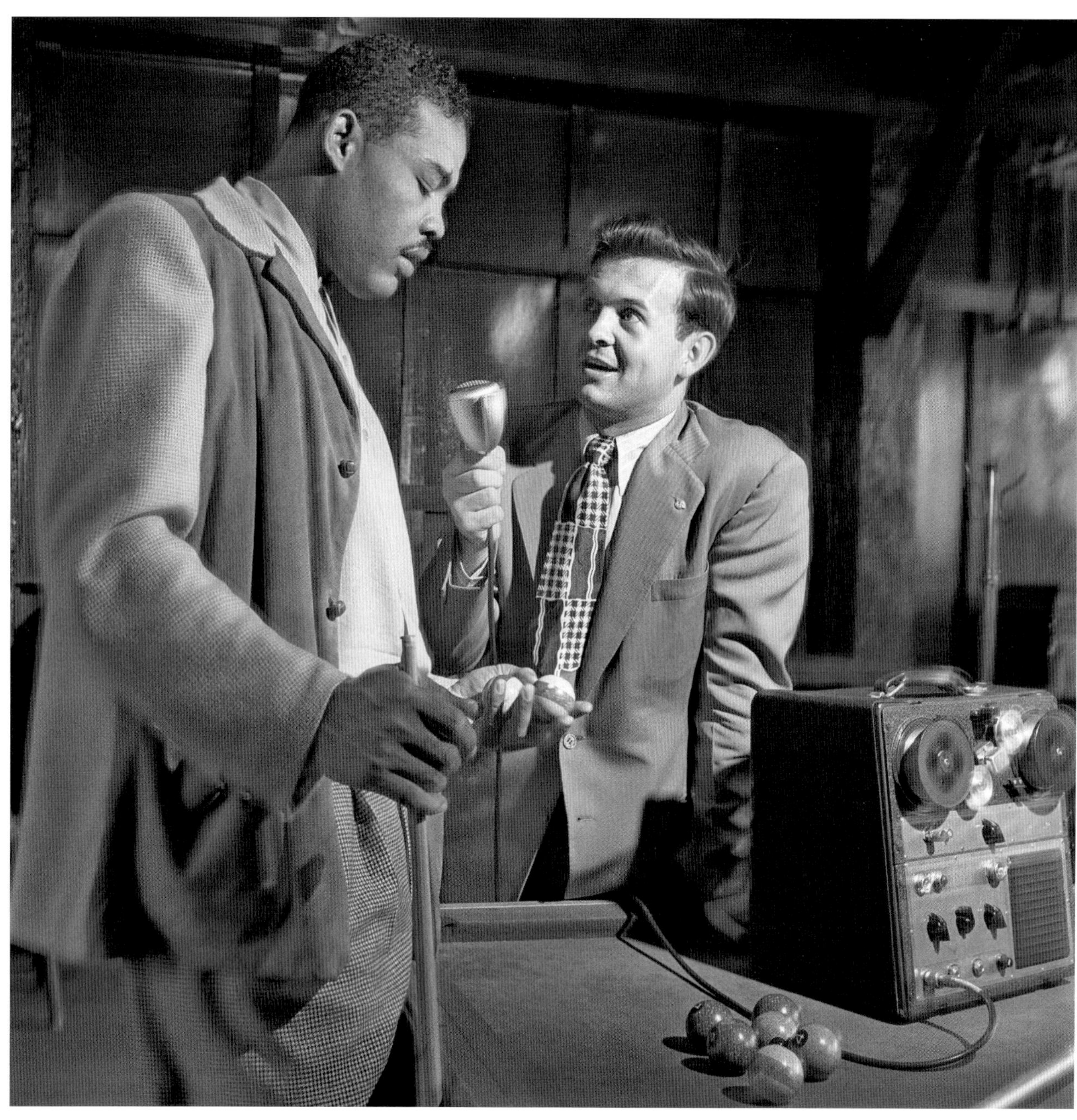

"Nothing excites Johnny more than meeting a celebrity," read the caption for this image of the host interviewing boxer Joe Louis in a pool hall.

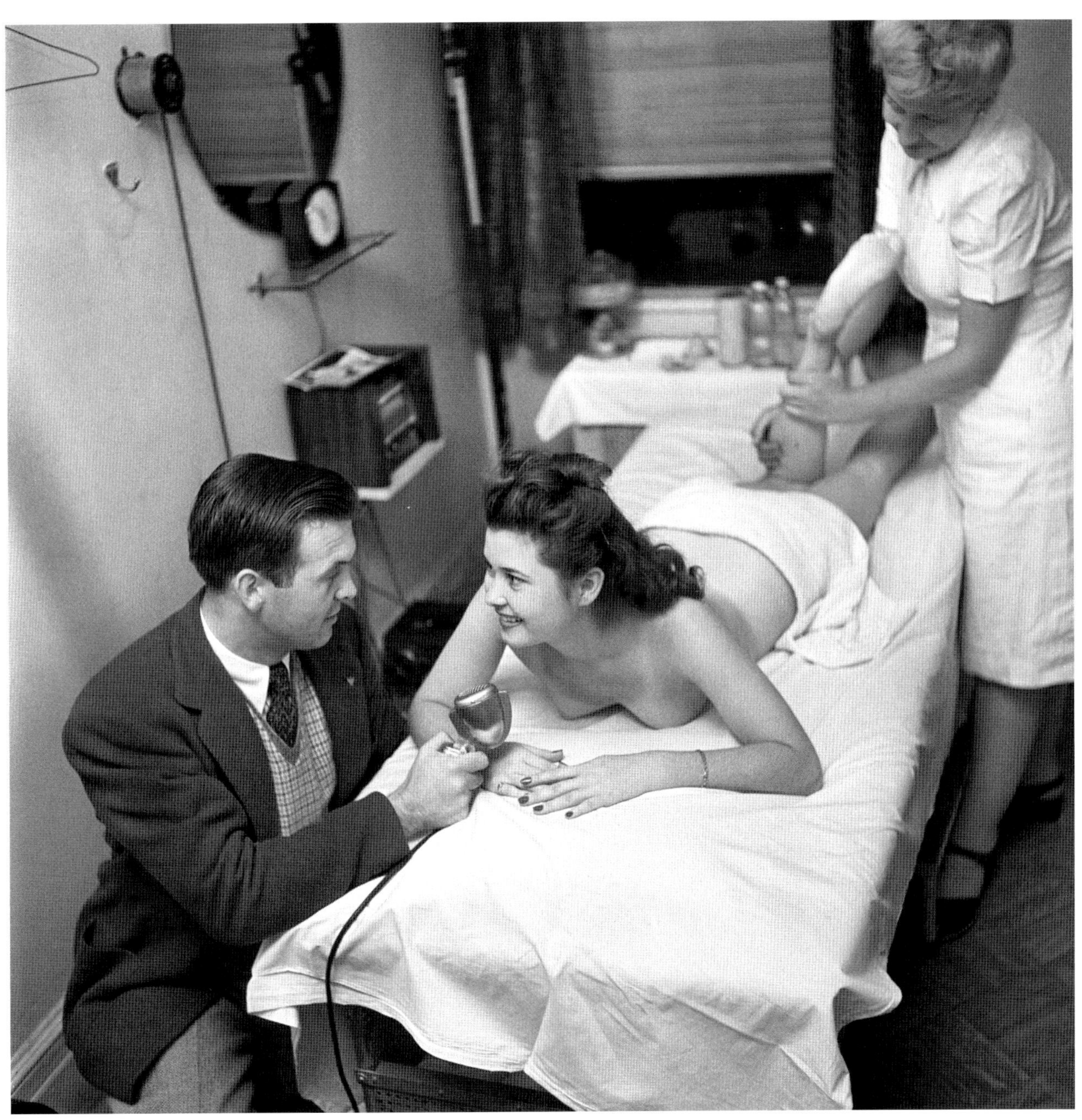

Johnny's radio adventures took him to behind-closed-door locations.

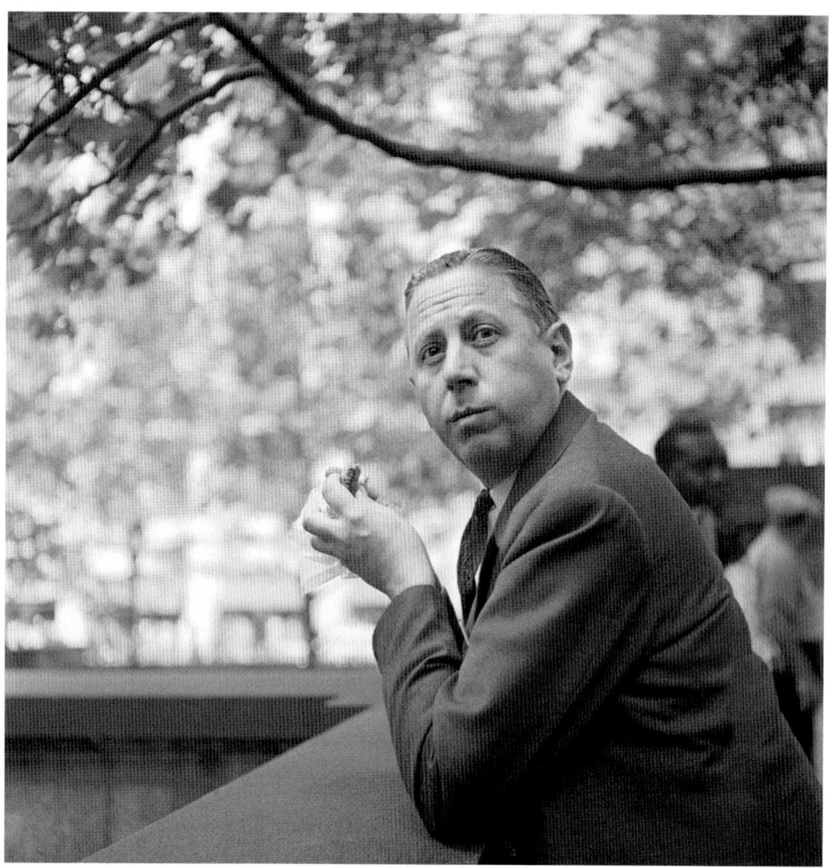

[UNPUBLISHED]

PEOPLE MUGGING

[FILED DATE]

NOVEMBER 12, 1946

Kubrick's photographs for this assignment recorded the theatrical facial expressions of New Yorkers on the city's streets. Some of his subjects seemed aware of his camera, some not. The inspiration and intention behind this unpublished assignment remain unknown.

Dining *alfresco*

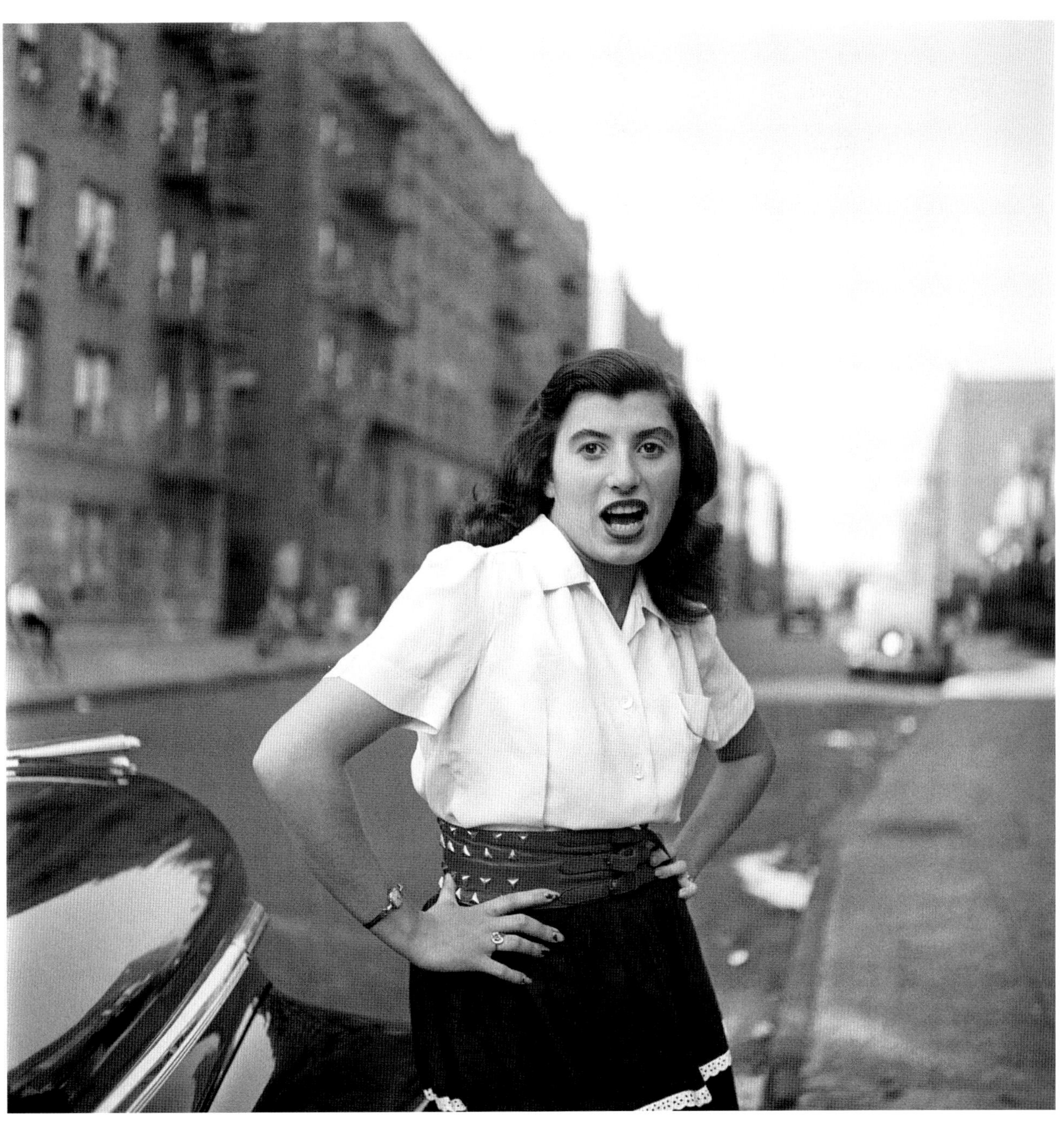

A fashionable young woman posing

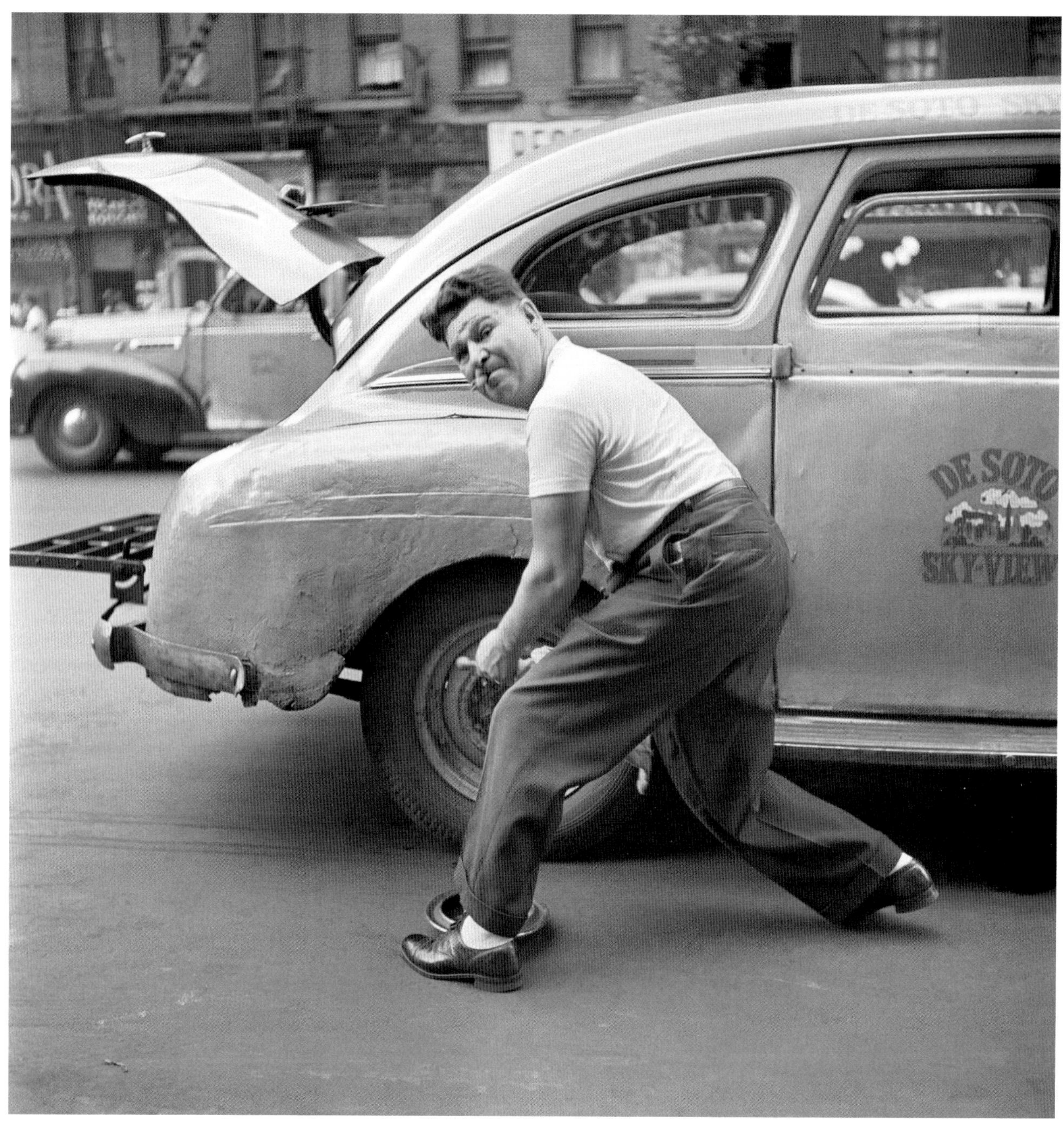

Changing a tire on the street

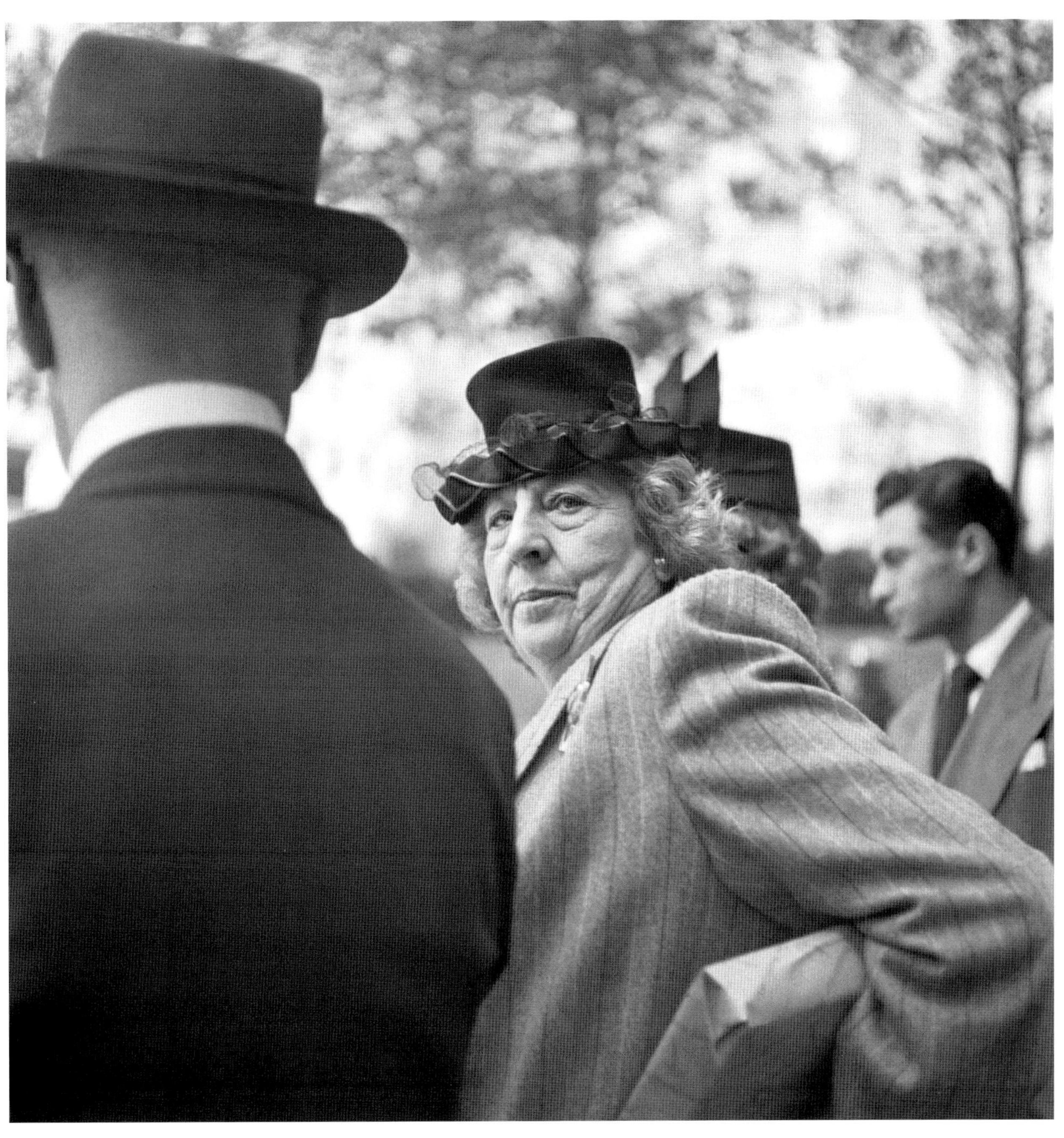

A smartly dressed woman responding
to Kubrick's camera

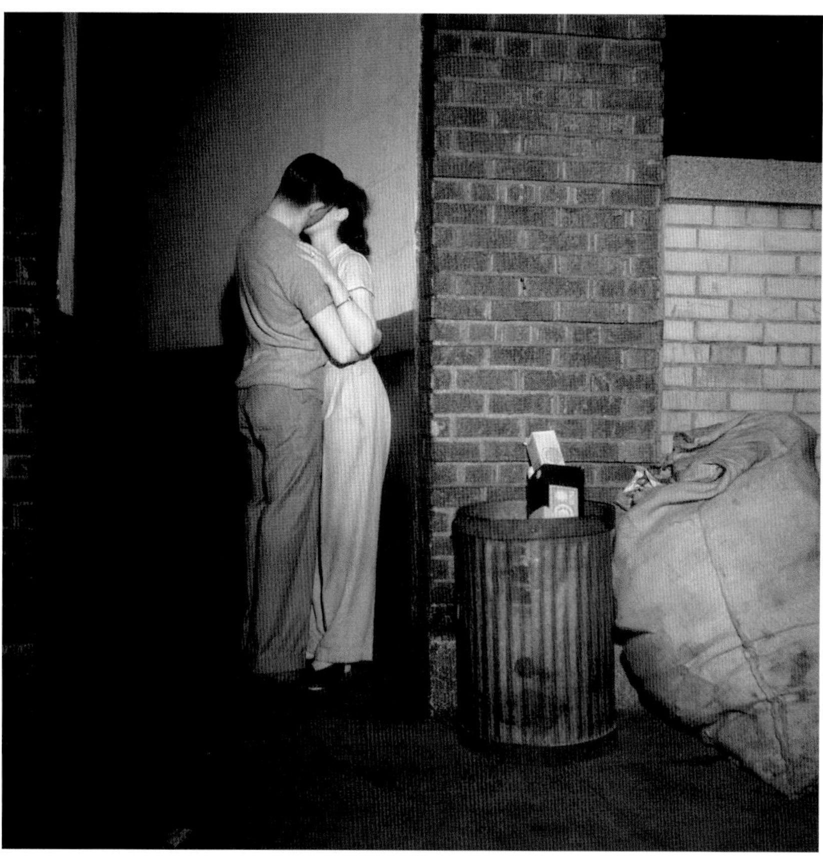

[UNPUBLISHED]

PARK BENCHES: LOVE IS EVERYWHERE

[FILED DATE]

MAY 1, 1946

Among Kubrick's most voyeuristic work for *Look*, these photographs captured New Yorkers, sometimes unaware of his camera, in romantic situations on park benches, fire escapes, and other locations. Several images from this assignment were probably taken with infrared film and flash, which allowed Kubrick to photograph in the dark. This technology was rarely used by magazine photographers at the time. Kubrick likely learned of it from the celebrated tabloid photographer Weegee, who had used the technology in the early 1940s to photograph seemingly unaware patrons at movie theaters.

Shooting with infrared film enabled Kubrick to expose secret moments.

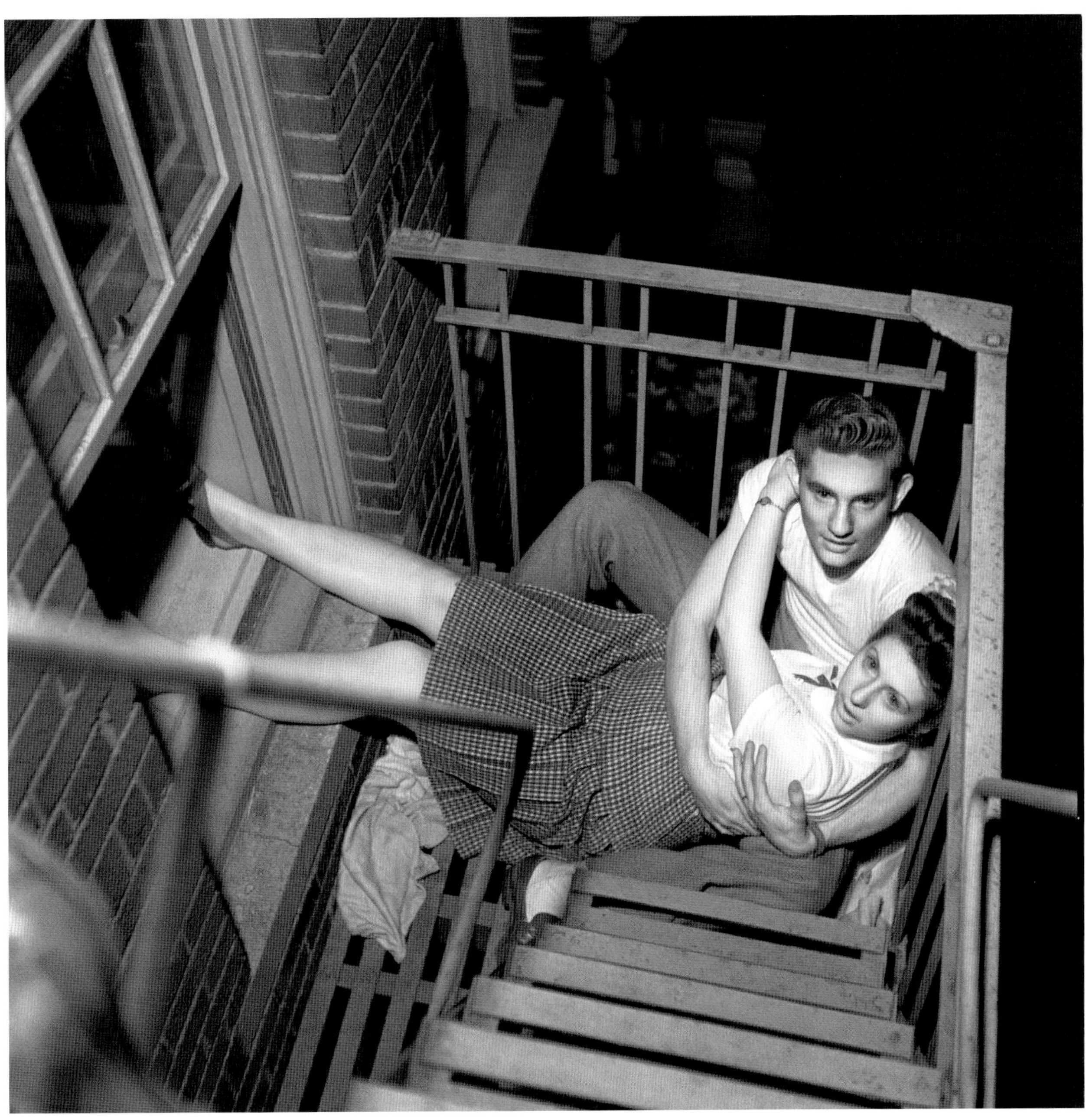

A couple embracing on a fire escape

FOLLOWING SPREAD **Four people on a bench in Bryant Park, two of them lovers sharing a kiss**

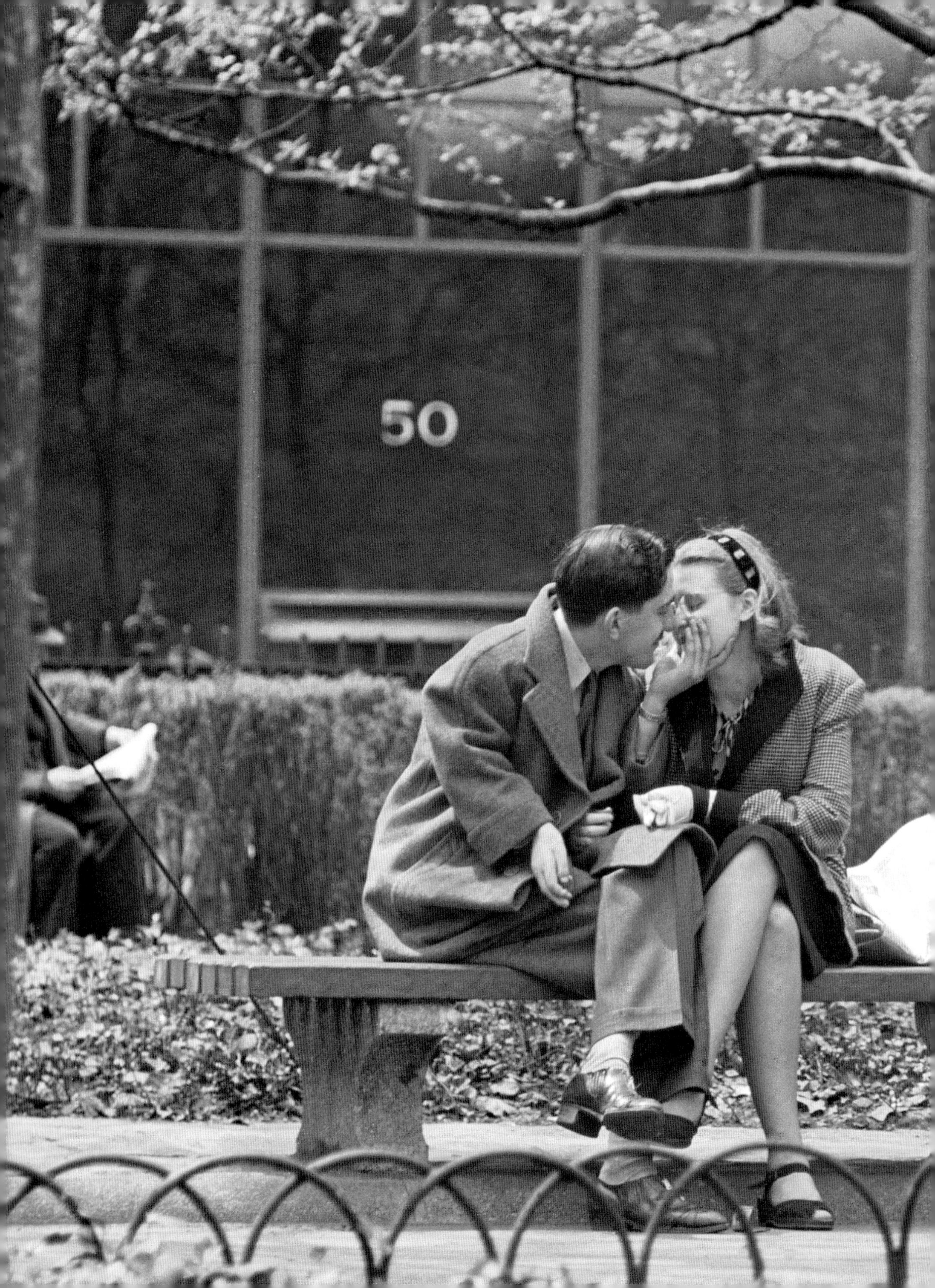
50

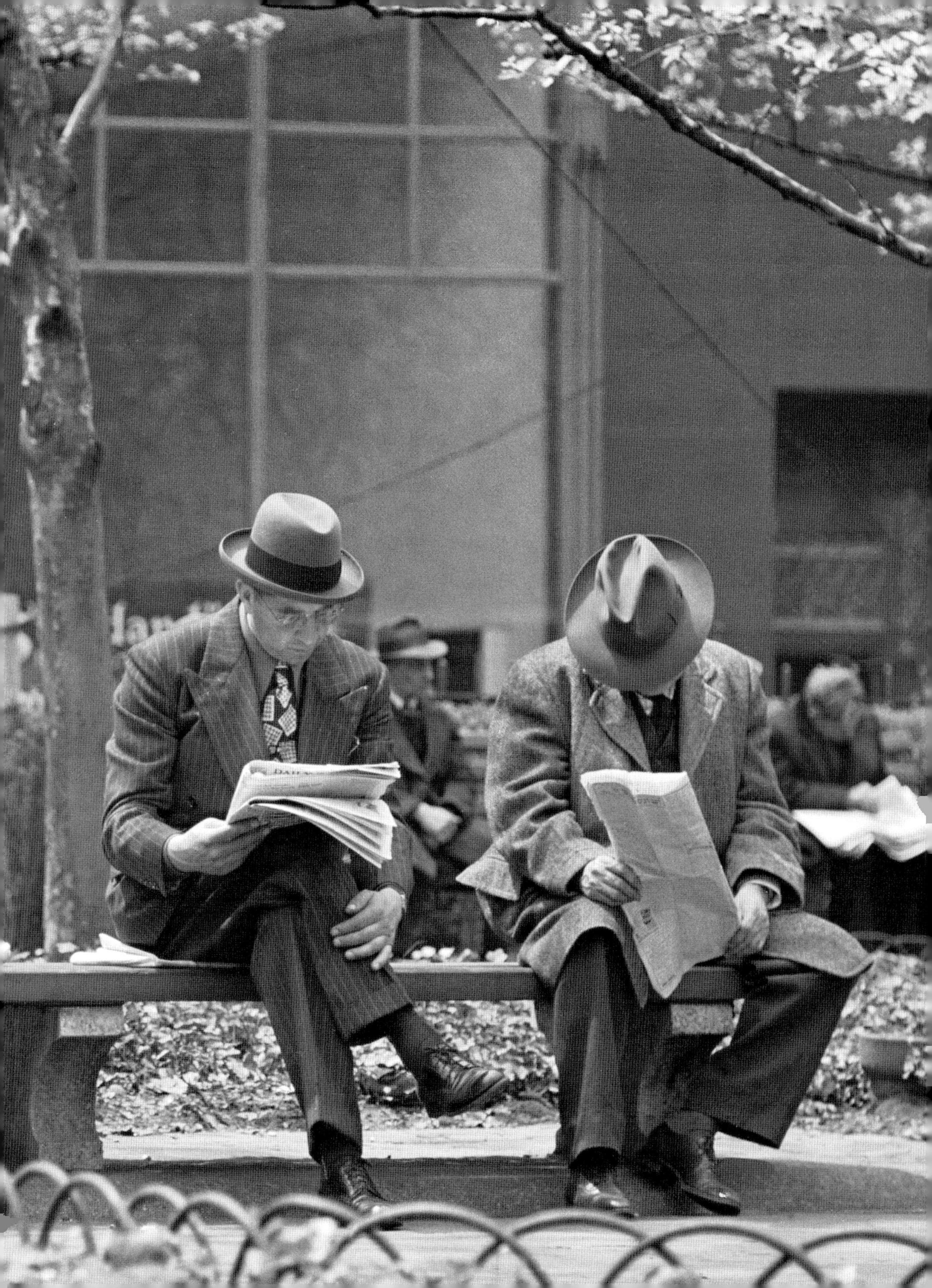

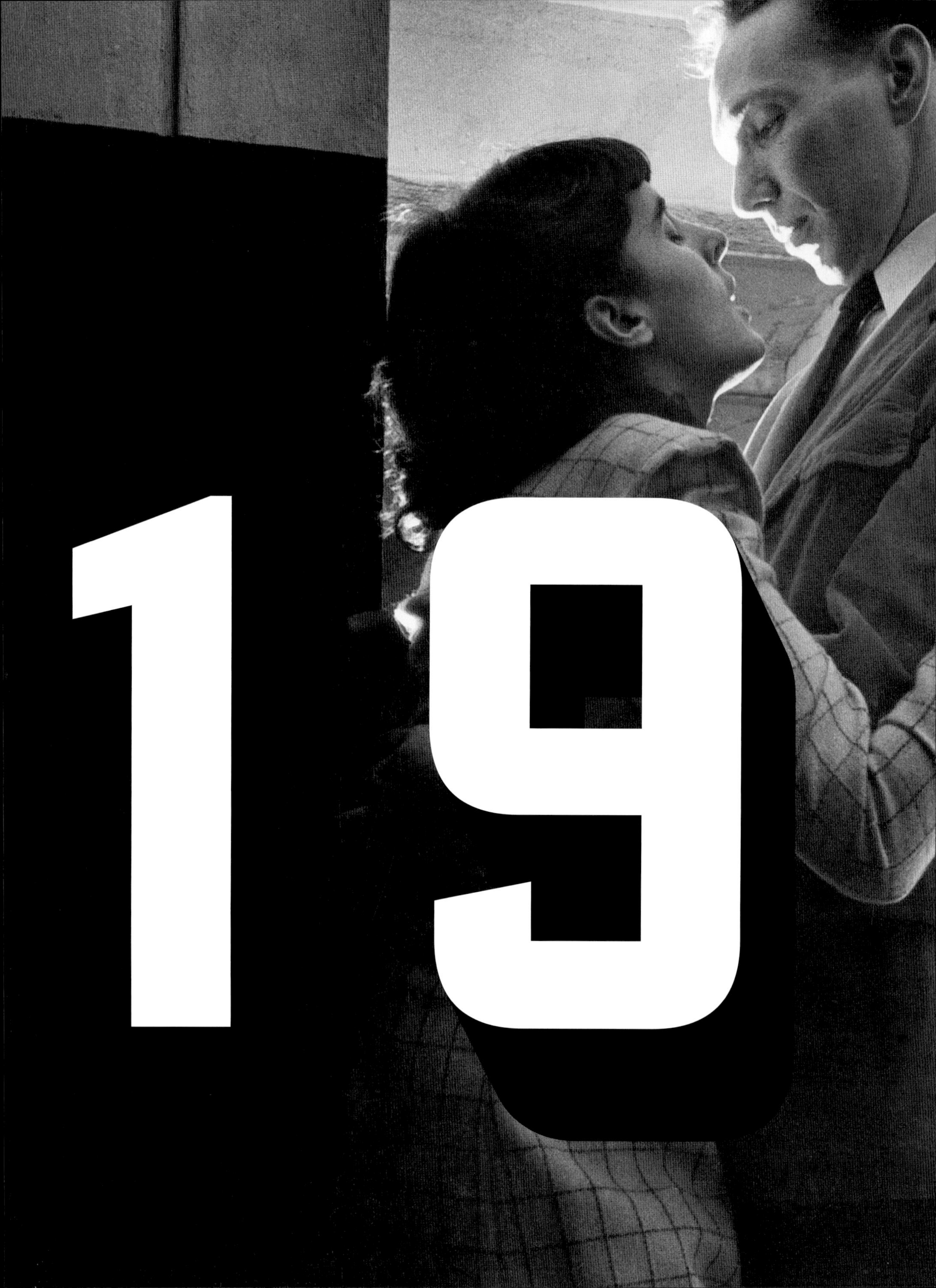
19

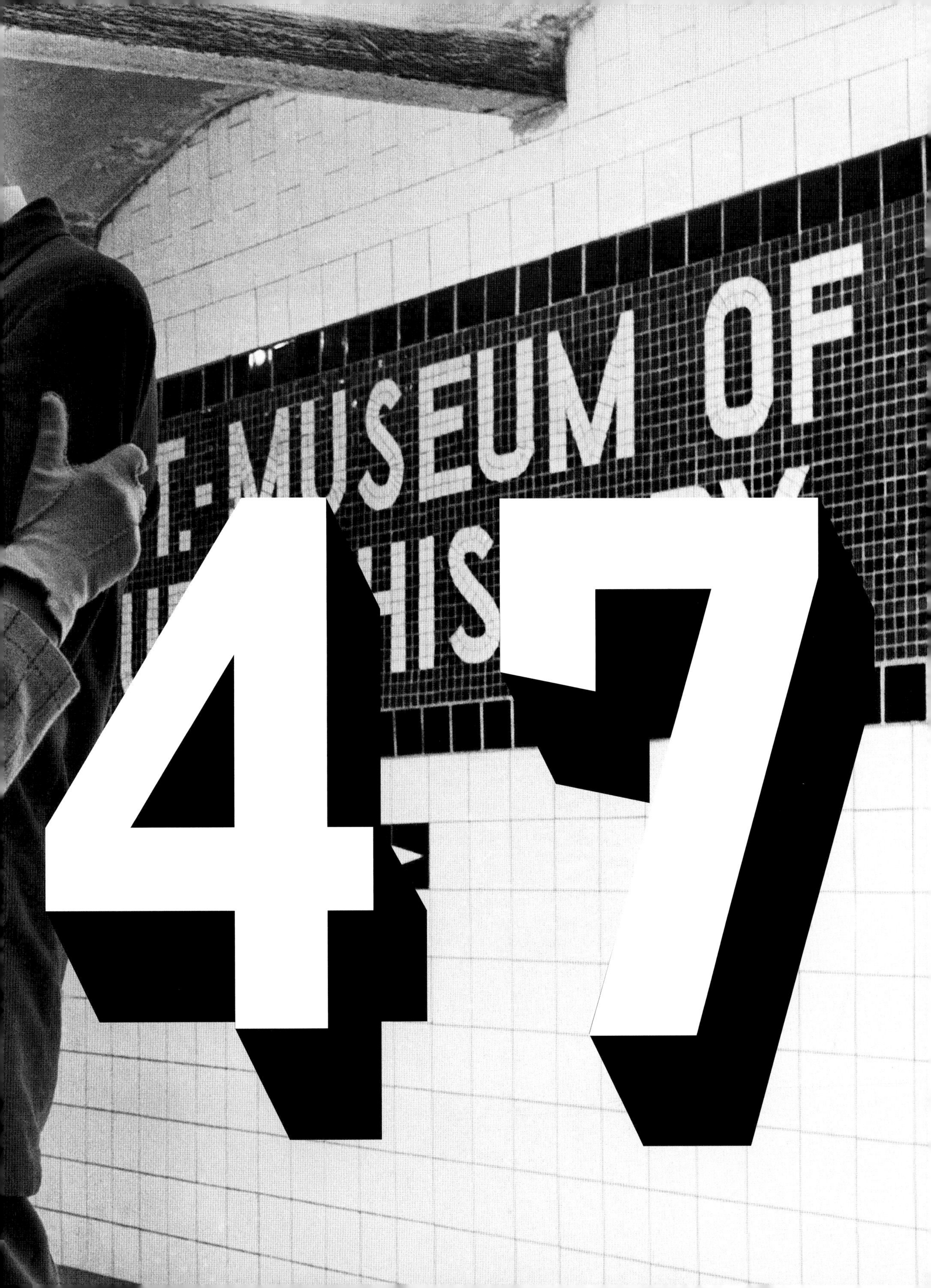
T.-MUSEUM OF
HIS
47

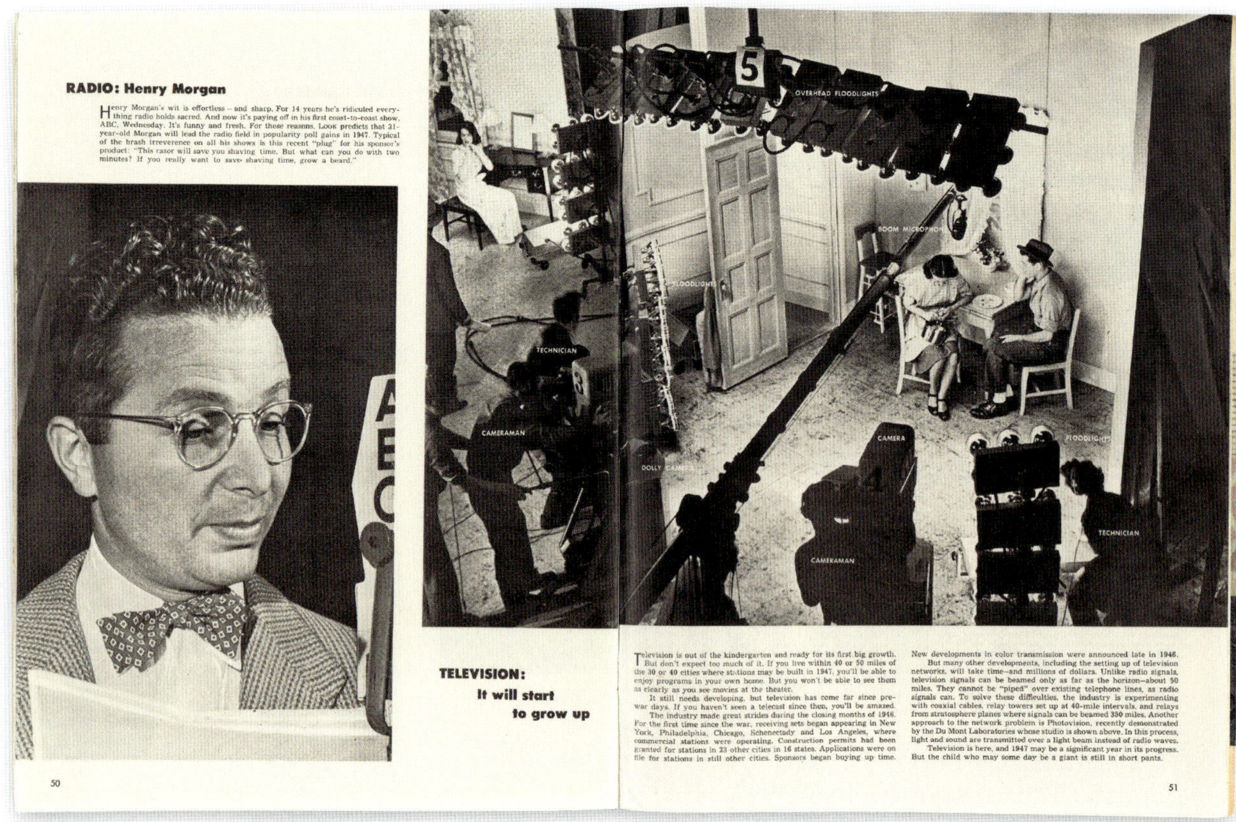

RADIO: Henry Morgan

Henry Morgan's wit is effortless – and sharp. For 14 years he's ridiculed everything radio holds sacred. And now it's paying off in his first coast-to-coast show, ABC, Wednesday. It's funny and fresh. For these reasons, LOOK predicts that 31-year-old Morgan will lead the radio field in popularity poll gains in 1947. Typical of the brash irreverence on all his shows is this recent "plug" for his sponsor's product: "This razor will save you shaving time. But what can you do with two minutes? If you really want to save shaving time, grow a beard."

TELEVISION: It will start to grow up

Television is out of the kindergarten and ready for its first big growth. But don't expect too much of it. If you live within 40 or 50 miles of the 30 or 40 cities where stations may be built in 1947, you'll be able to enjoy programs in your own home. But you won't be able to see them as clearly as you see movies at the theater.

It still needs developing, but television has come far since pre-war days. If you haven't seen a telecast since then, you'll be amazed.

The industry made great strides during the closing months of 1946. For the first time since the war, receiving sets began appearing in New York, Philadelphia, Chicago, Schenectady and Los Angeles, where commercial stations were operating. Construction permits had been granted for stations in 23 other cities in 16 states. Applications were on file for stations in still other cities. Sponsors began buying up time. New developments in color transmission were announced late in 1946.

But many other developments, including the setting up of television networks, will take time—and millions of dollars. Unlike radio signals, television signals can be beamed only as far as the horizon—about 50 miles. They cannot be "piped" over existing telephone lines, as radio signals can. To solve these difficulties, the industry is experimenting with coaxial cables, relay towers set up at 40-mile intervals, and relays from stratosphere planes where signals can be beamed 350 miles. Another approach to the network problem is Photovision, recently demonstrated by the Du Mont Laboratories whose studio is shown above. In this process, light and sound are transmitted over a light beam instead of radio waves.

Television is here, and 1947 may be a significant year in its progress. But the child who may some day be a giant is still in short pants.

50 51

PUBLISHED AS

TELEVISION: IT WILL START TO GROW UP

DATE

JANUARY 7, 1947

"We've polished up our crystal ball again," *Look*'s editors promised at the start of this issue devoted to predictions for 1947, from fashion to food, science to labor strikes. A section on movies and entertainment included one of Kubrick's pictures documenting the new medium of television. To explain how television worked, the magazine labeled the photograph, identifying crew and equipment on a set for a television show at the DuMont Laboratories in New Jersey. The article stressed television's infancy: "The child who may someday be a giant is still in short pants."

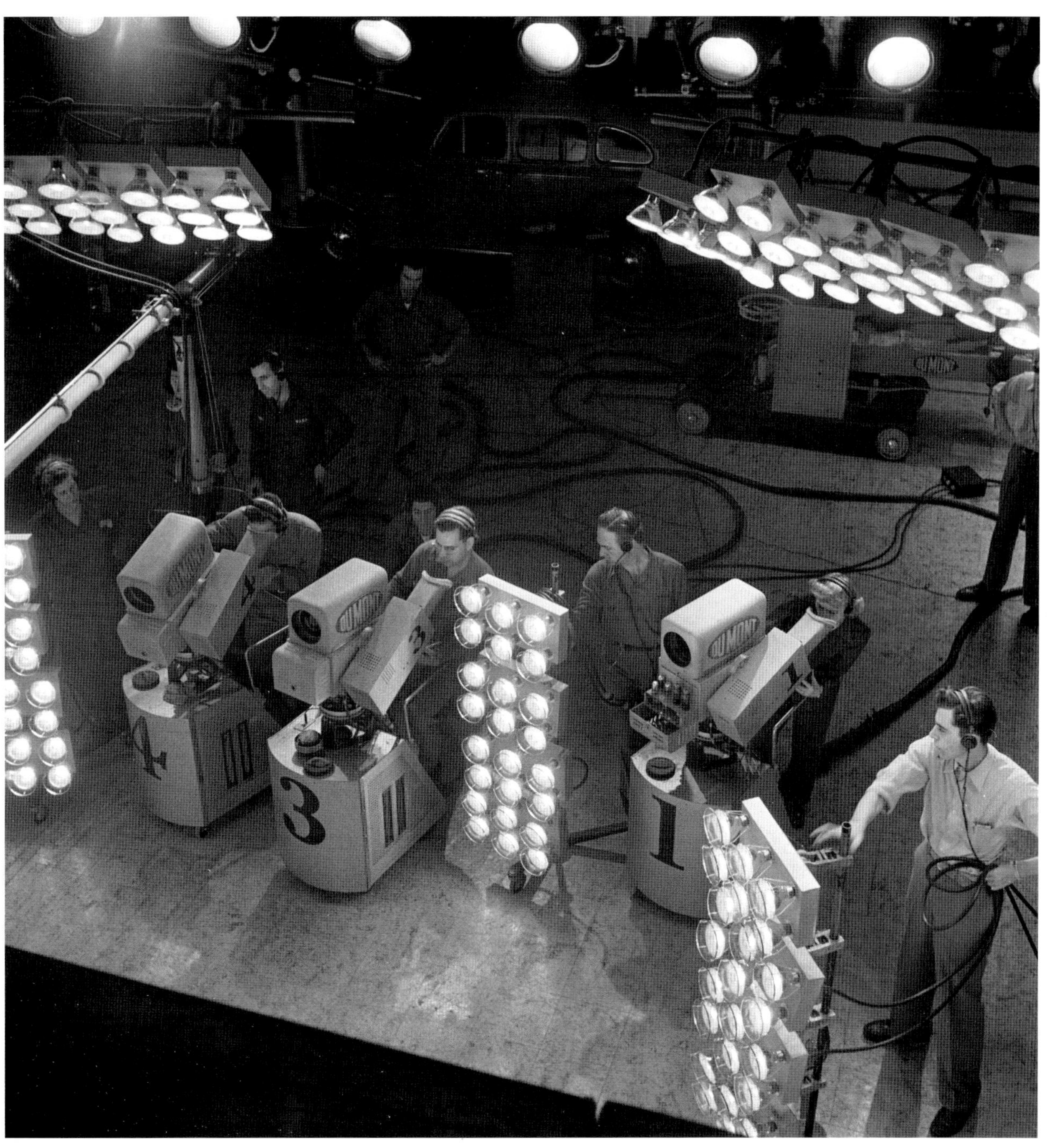

On the set of a television production

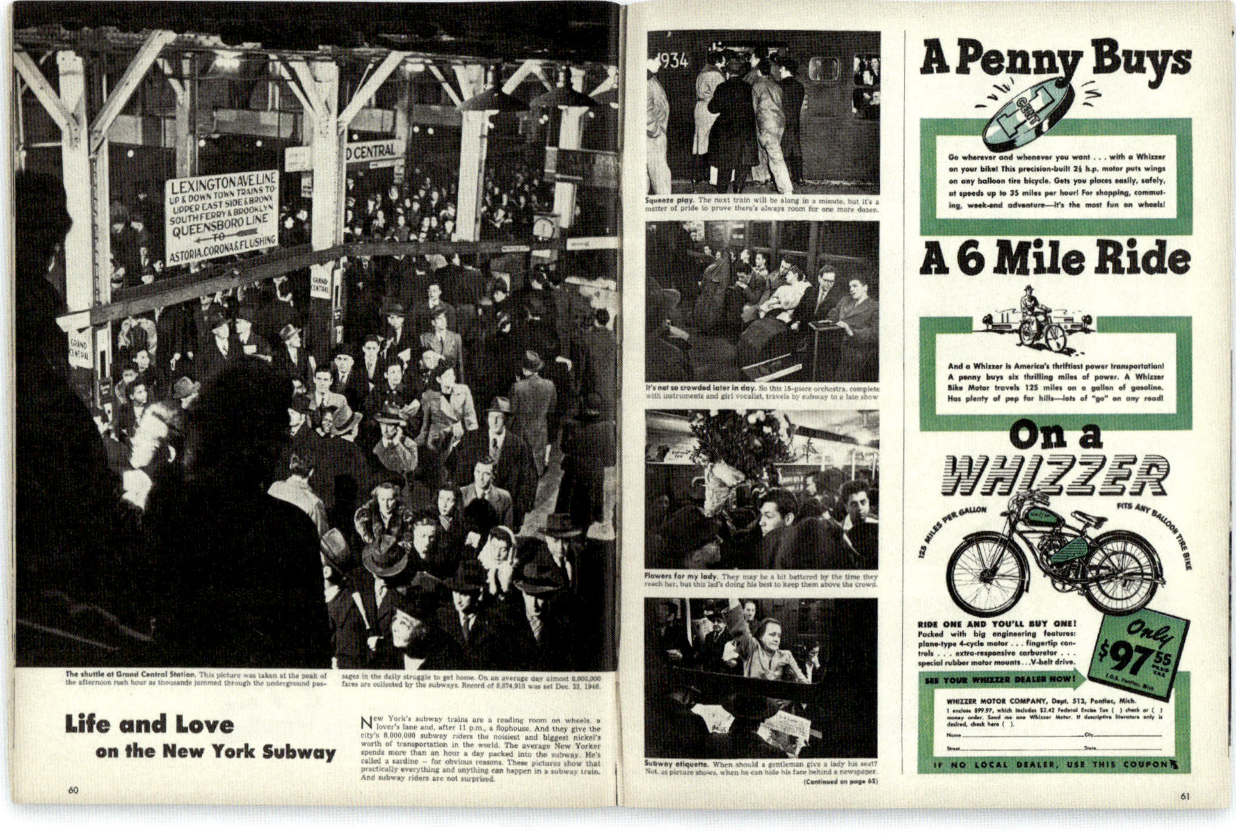

The shuttle at Grand Central Station. This picture was taken at the peak of the afternoon rush hour as thousands jammed through the underground passages in the daily struggle to get home. On an average day almost 8,000,000 fares are collected by the subways. Record of 8,874,910 was set Dec. 23, 1946.

Life and Love on the New York Subway

New York's subway trains are a reading room on wheels, a lover's lane and, after 11 p.m., a flophouse. And they give the city's 8,000,000 subway riders the noisiest and biggest nickel's worth of transportation in the world. The average New Yorker spends more than an hour a day packed into the subway. He's called a sardine – for obvious reasons. These pictures show that practically everything and anything can happen in a subway train. And subway riders are not surprised.

60

Squeeze play. The next train will be along in a minute, but it's a matter of pride to prove there's always room for one more dozen.

It's not so crowded later in day. So this 15-piece orchestra, complete with instruments and girl vocalist, travels by subway to a late show

Flowers for my lady. They may be a bit battered by the time they reach her, but this lad's doing his best to keep them above the crowd.

Subway etiquette. When should a gentleman give a lady his seat? Not, as picture shows, when he can hide his face behind a newspaper.

(Continued on page 62)

A Penny Buys

Go wherever and whenever you want . . . with a Whizzer on your bike! This precision-built 2½ h.p. motor puts wings on any balloon tire bicycle. Gets you places easily, safely, at speeds up to 35 miles per hour! For shopping, commuting, week-end adventure—it's the most fun on wheels!

A 6 Mile Ride

And a Whizzer is America's thriftiest power transportation! A penny buys six thrilling miles of power. A Whizzer Bike Motor travels 125 miles on a gallon of gasoline. Has plenty of pep for hills—lots of "go" on any road!

On a WHIZZER

125 MILES PER GALLON

FITS ANY BALLOON TIRE BIKE

RIDE ONE AND YOU'LL BUY ONE! Packed with big engineering features: plane-type 4-cycle motor . . . fingertip controls . . . extra-responsive carburetor . . . special rubber motor mounts . . . V-belt drive.

Only $97.55 PLUS TAX F.O.B. Pontiac, Mich.

SEE YOUR WHIZZER DEALER NOW!

WHIZZER MOTOR COMPANY, Dept. 513, Pontiac, Mich.
I enclose $99.97, which includes $2.42 Federal Excise Tax ( ) check or ( ) money order. Send me one Whizzer Motor. If descriptive literature only is desired, check here ( ).
Name ______ City ______
Street ______ State ______

IF NO LOCAL DEALER, USE THIS COUPON

61

PUBLISHED AS

LIFE AND LOVE ON THE NEW YORK SUBWAY

DATE

MARCH 4, 1947

"New York's subway trains are a reading room on wheels, a lover's lane and, after 11 p.m., a flophouse," began this six-page article with 29 photographs by Kubrick. The photographer's first long-form essay for *Look*, the article combined staged and candid photographs, as well as images taken surreptitiously with a hidden camera. All were photographed in natural light. The article provided a kaleidoscopic view of New York's subway system, where almost eight million fares were collected every day, and "practically everything and anything can happen… And subway riders are not surprised." Celebrated photographer Walker Evans had taken images of people in the New York subway during the Great Depression, but they were not published until Evans and author James Agee collaborated on the book *Many Are Called* (1966).

PAGE 52 **Kubrick photographed the subway system using dramatic angles and graphic compositions.**

PAGE 53 **Subway commuters passing the time by reading and sleeping**

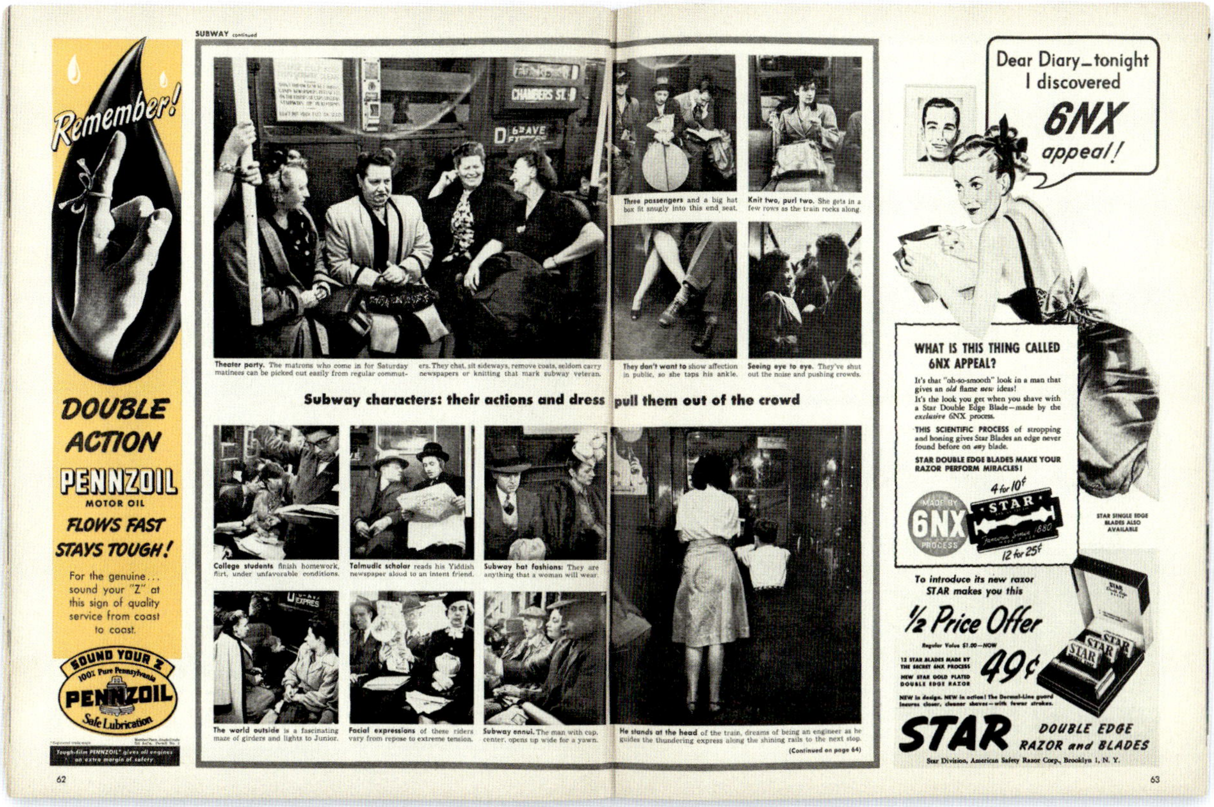

Remember!

DOUBLE ACTION PENNZOIL MOTOR OIL

FLOWS FAST STAYS TOUGH!

For the genuine... sound your "Z" at this sign of quality service from coast to coast.

SOUND YOUR Z
100% Pure Pennsylvania
PENNZOIL
Safe Lubrication

Tough-film PENNZOIL gives all engines an extra margin of safety.

Theater party. The matrons who come in for Saturday matinees can be picked out easily from regular commuters. They chat, sit sideways, remove coats, seldom carry newspapers or knitting that mark subway veteran.

Three passengers and a big hat box fit snugly into this end seat.

Knit two, purl two. She gets in a few rows as the train rocks along.

They don't want to show affection in public, so she taps his ankle.

Seeing eye to eye. They've shut out the noise and pushing crowds.

Subway characters: their actions and dress pull them out of the crowd

College students finish homework, flirt, under unfavorable conditions.

Talmudic scholar reads his Yiddish newspaper aloud to an intent friend.

Subway hat fashions: They are anything that a woman will wear.

The world outside is a fascinating maze of girders and lights to Junior.

Facial expressions of these riders vary from repose to extreme tension.

Subway ennui. The man with cap, center, opens up wide for a yawn.

He stands at the head of the train, dreams of being an engineer as he guides the thundering express along the shining rails to the next stop.

(Continued on page 64)

Dear Diary—tonight I discovered 6NX appeal!

WHAT IS THIS THING CALLED 6NX APPEAL?

It's that "oh-so-smooth" look in a man that gives an *old* flame *new* ideas!

It's the look you get when you shave with a Star Double Edge Blade—made by the *exclusive* 6NX process.

THIS SCIENTIFIC PROCESS of stropping and honing gives Star Blades an edge never found before on *any* blade.

STAR DOUBLE EDGE BLADES MAKE YOUR RAZOR PERFORM MIRACLES!

MADE BY 6NX PROCESS — STAR — 4 for 10¢ — 12 for 25¢

STAR SINGLE EDGE BLADES ALSO AVAILABLE

To introduce its new razor STAR makes you this ½ Price Offer

Regular Value $1.00—NOW 49¢

12 STAR BLADES MADE BY THE SECRET 6NX PROCESS
NEW STAR GOLD PLATED DOUBLE EDGE RAZOR

NEW in design. NEW in action! The Dermal-Line guard insures closer, cleaner shaves—with fewer strokes.

STAR DOUBLE EDGE RAZOR and BLADES

Star Division, American Safety Razor Corp., Brooklyn 1, N. Y.

62 63

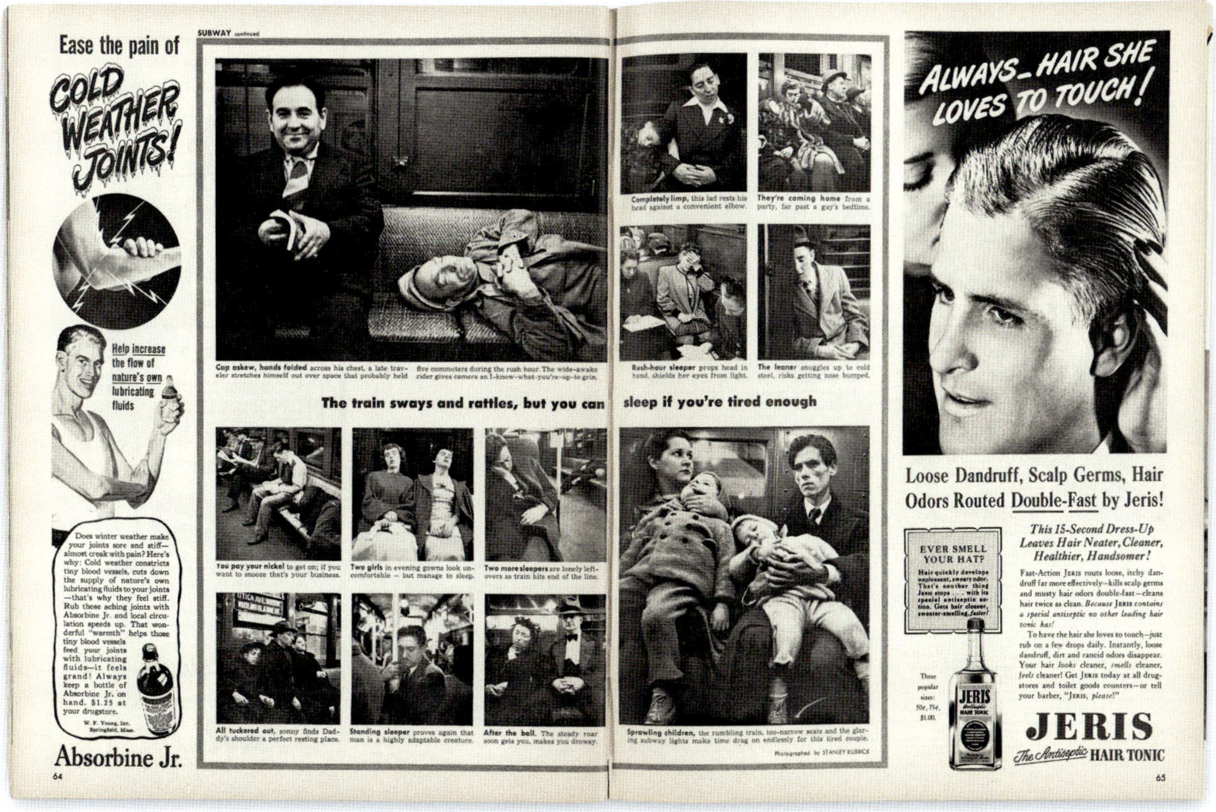

Ease the pain of COLD WEATHER JOINTS!

Help increase the flow of nature's own lubricating fluids

Does winter weather make your joints sore and stiff—almost creak with pain? Here's why: Cold weather constricts tiny blood vessels, cuts down the supply of nature's own lubricating fluids to your joints—that's why they feel stiff. Rub those aching joints with Absorbine Jr. and local circulation speeds up. That wonderful "warmth" helps those tiny blood vessels feed your joints with lubricating fluids—it feels grand! Always keep a bottle of Absorbine Jr. on hand. $1.25 at your drugstore.

W. F. Young, Inc. Springfield, Mass.

Absorbine Jr.

Cap askew, hands folded across his chest, a late traveler stretches himself out over space that probably held five commuters during the rush hour. The wide-awake rider gives camera an I-know-what-you're-up-to grin.

Completely limp, this lad rests his head against a convenient elbow.

They're coming home from a party, far past a guy's bedtime.

Rush-hour sleeper props head in hand, shields her eyes from light.

The leaner snuggles up to cold steel, risks getting nose bumped.

The train sways and rattles, but you can sleep if you're tired enough

You pay your nickel to get on; if you want to snooze that's your business.

Two girls in evening gowns look uncomfortable – but manage to sleep.

Two more sleepers are lonely leftovers as train hits end of the line.

All tuckered out, sonny finds Daddy's shoulder a perfect resting place.

Standing sleeper proves again that man is a highly adaptable creature.

After the ball. The steady roar soon gets you, makes you drowsy.

Sprawling children, the rumbling train, too-narrow seats and the glaring subway lights make time drag on endlessly for this tired couple.

Photographed by STANLEY KUBRICK

ALWAYS—HAIR SHE LOVES TO TOUCH!

Loose Dandruff, Scalp Germs, Hair Odors Routed Double-Fast by Jeris!

This 15-Second Dress-Up Leaves Hair Neater, Cleaner, Healthier, Handsomer!

EVER SMELL YOUR HAT?

Hair quickly develops unpleasant, sweaty odor. That's another thing Jeris stops . . . with its special antiseptic action. Gets hair cleaner, sweeter-smelling, *faster!*

Fast-Action JERIS routs loose, itchy dandruff far more effectively—kills scalp germs and musty hair odors double-fast—cleans hair twice as clean. *Because* JERIS *contains a special antiseptic no other leading hair tonic has!*

To have the hair she loves to touch—just rub on a few drops daily. Instantly, loose dandruff, dirt and rancid odors disappear. Your hair *looks* cleaner, *smells* cleaner, *feels* cleaner! Get JERIS today at all drugstores and toilet goods counters—or tell your barber, "JERIS, *please!*"

Three popular sizes: 50¢, 75¢, $1.00.

JERIS
The Antiseptic HAIR TONIC

64 65

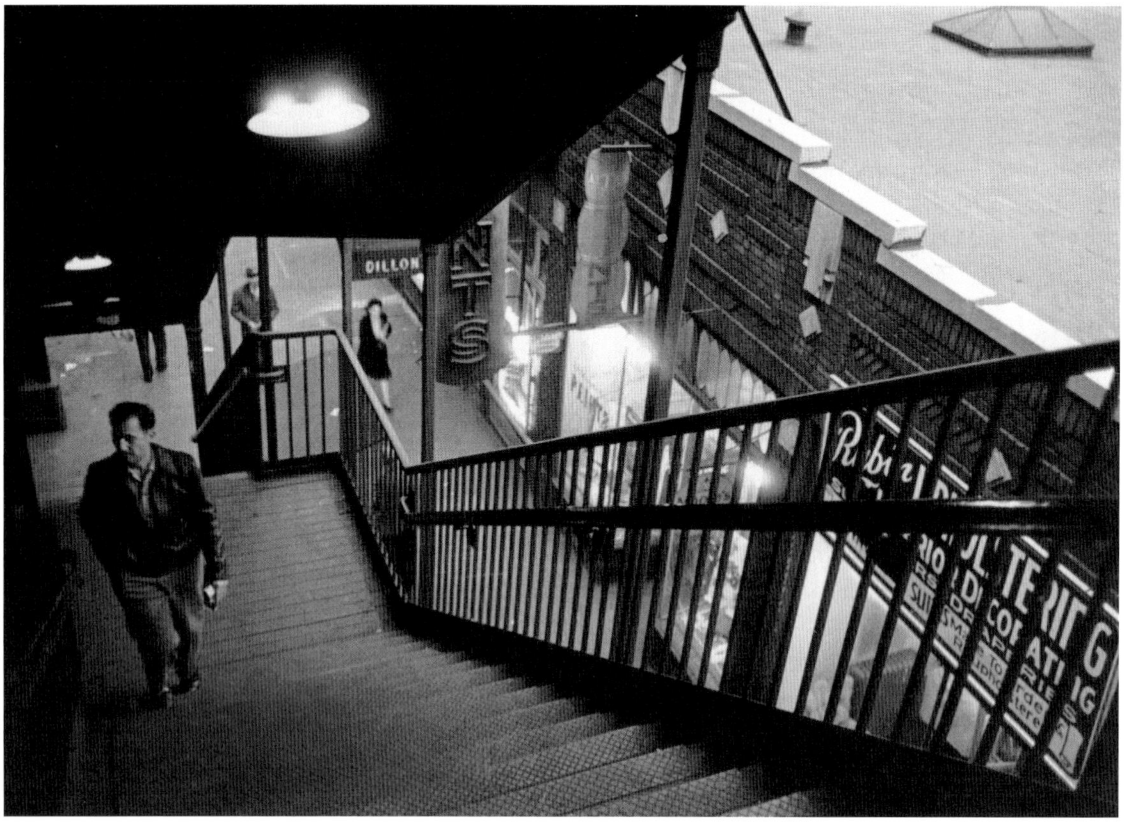

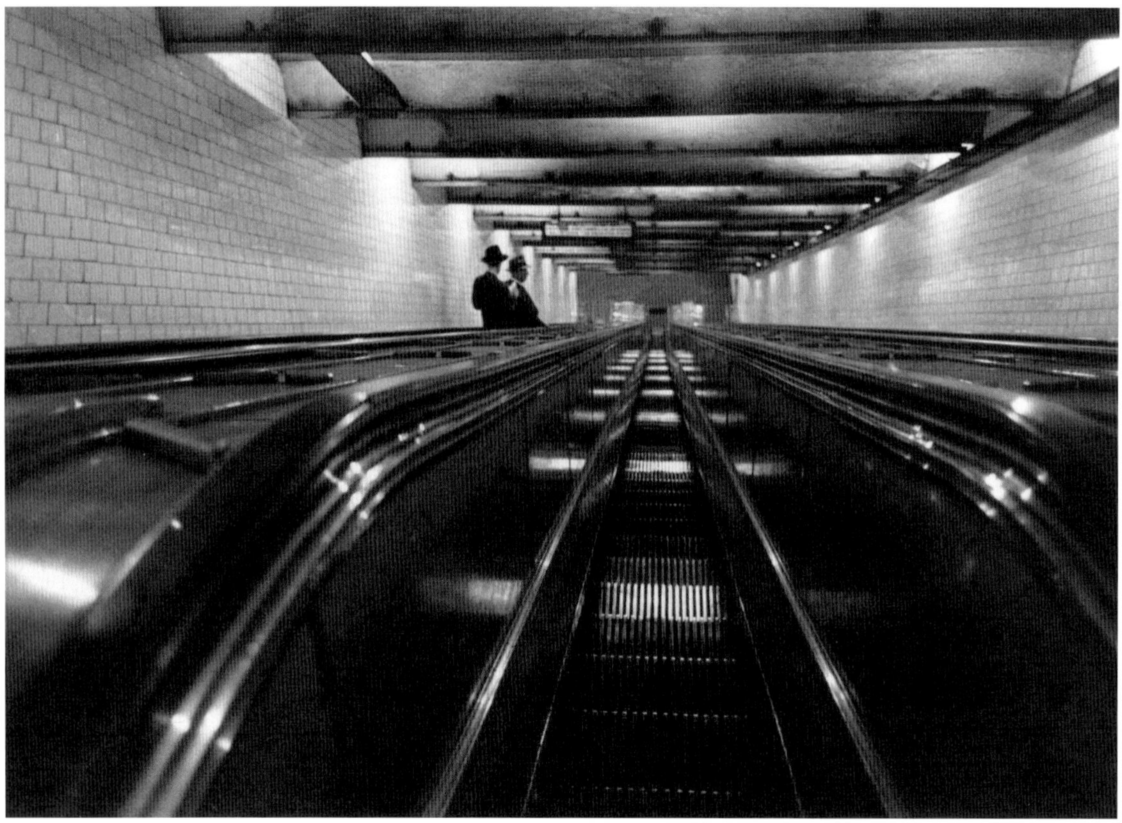

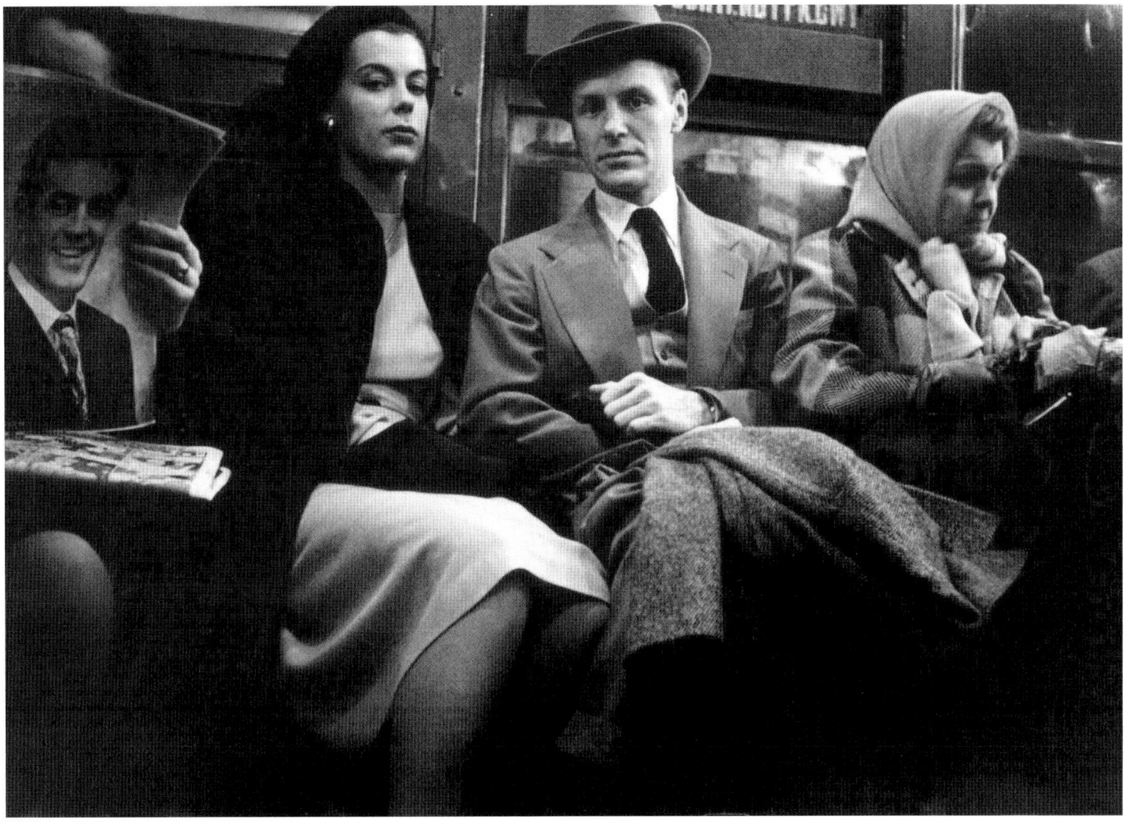

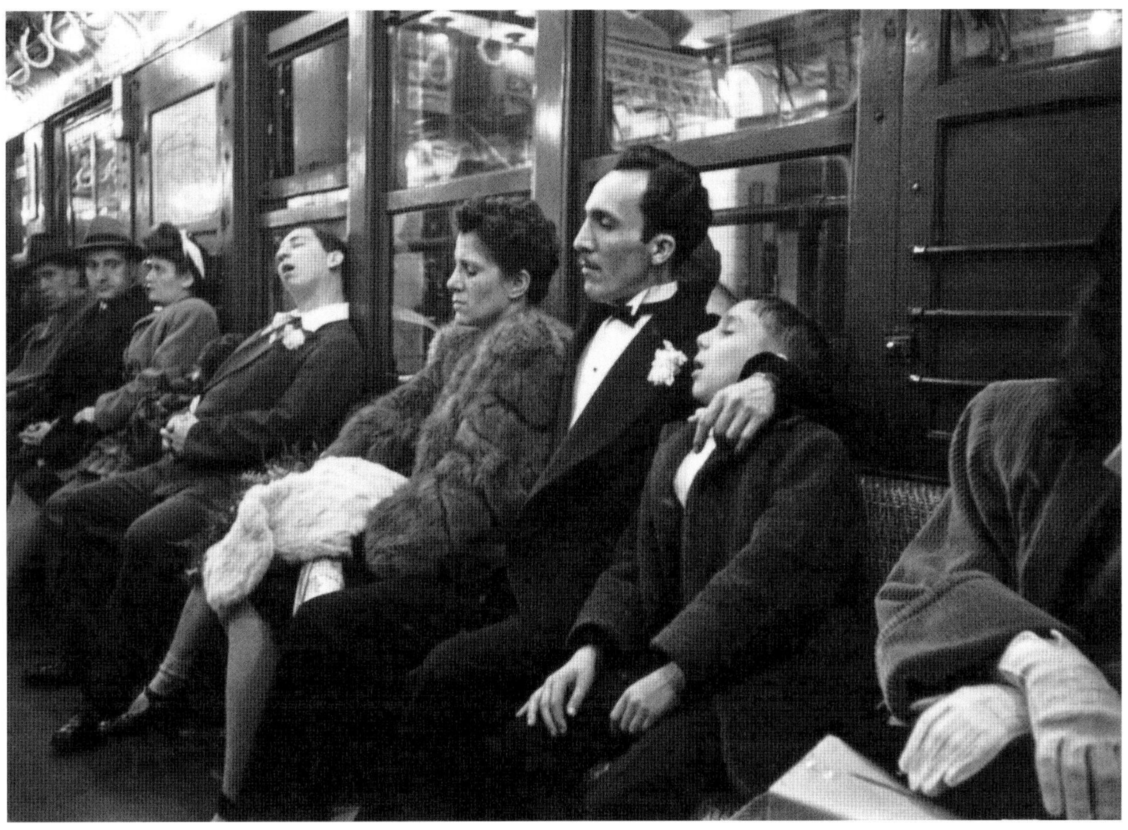

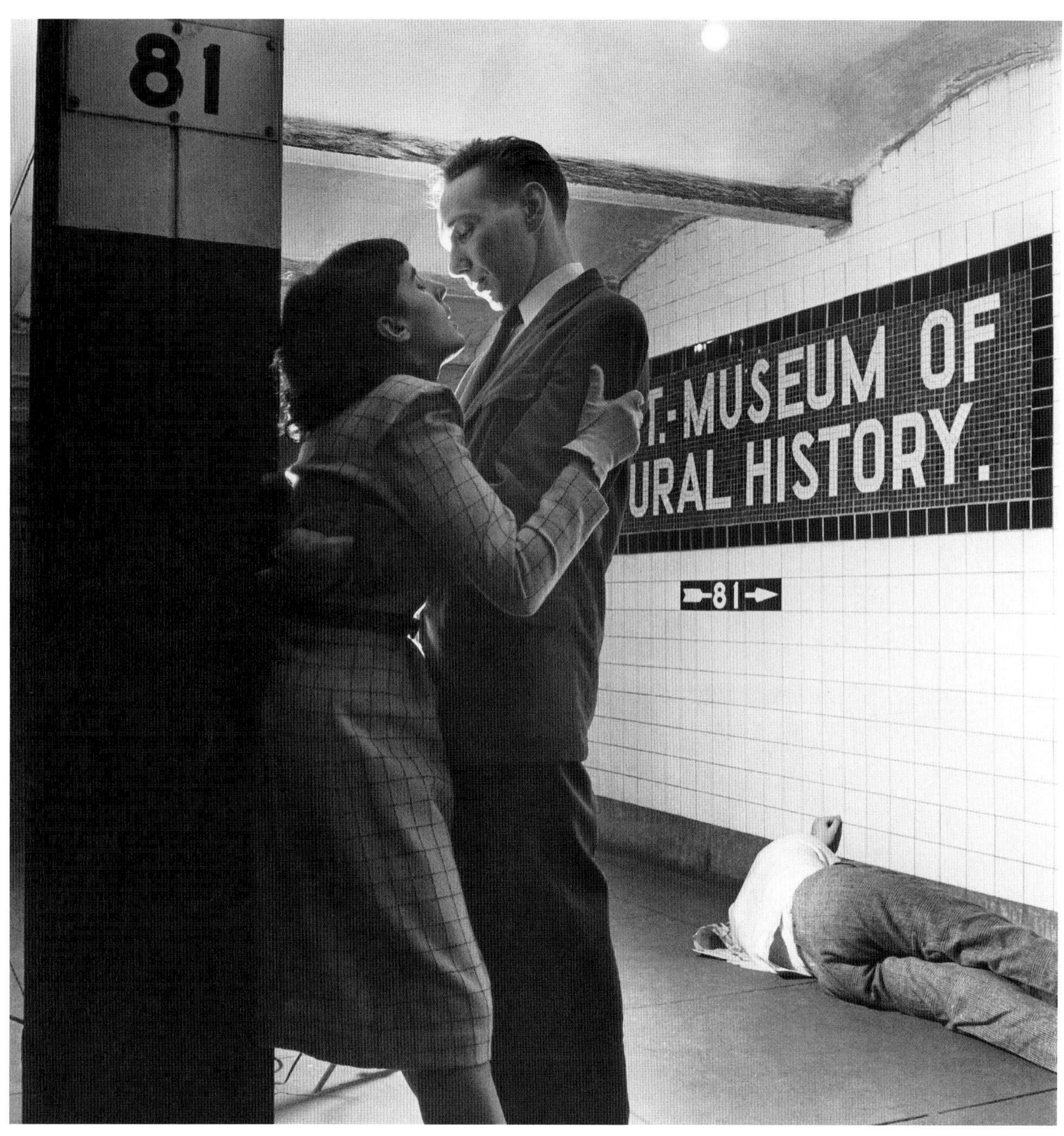

A staged scene on the West 81st Street subway platform

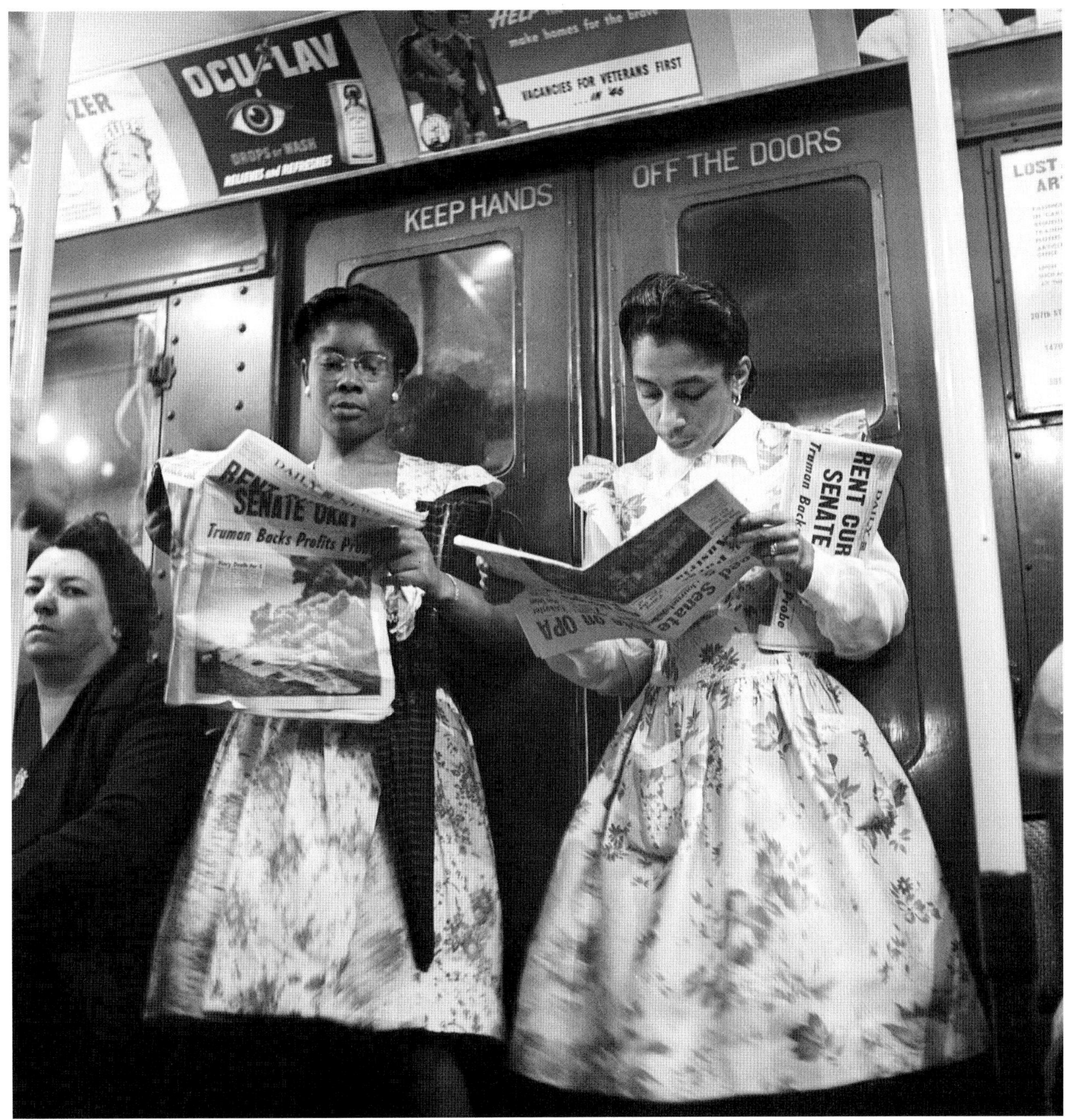

Kubrick tried to be invisible to fellow subway passengers, with varying degrees of success.

FOLLOWING SPREAD **Kubrick staged this intimate moment between two subway passengers.**

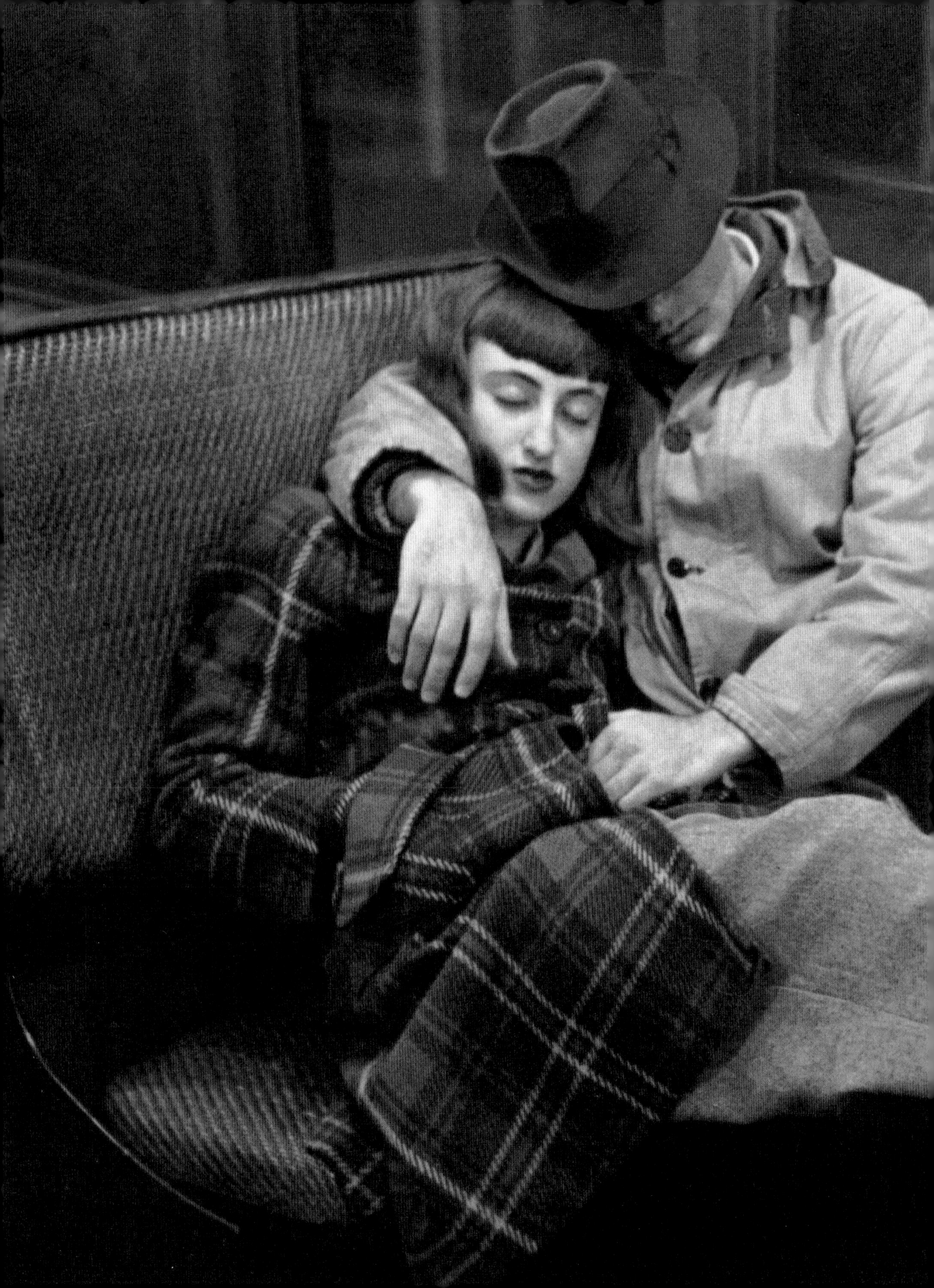

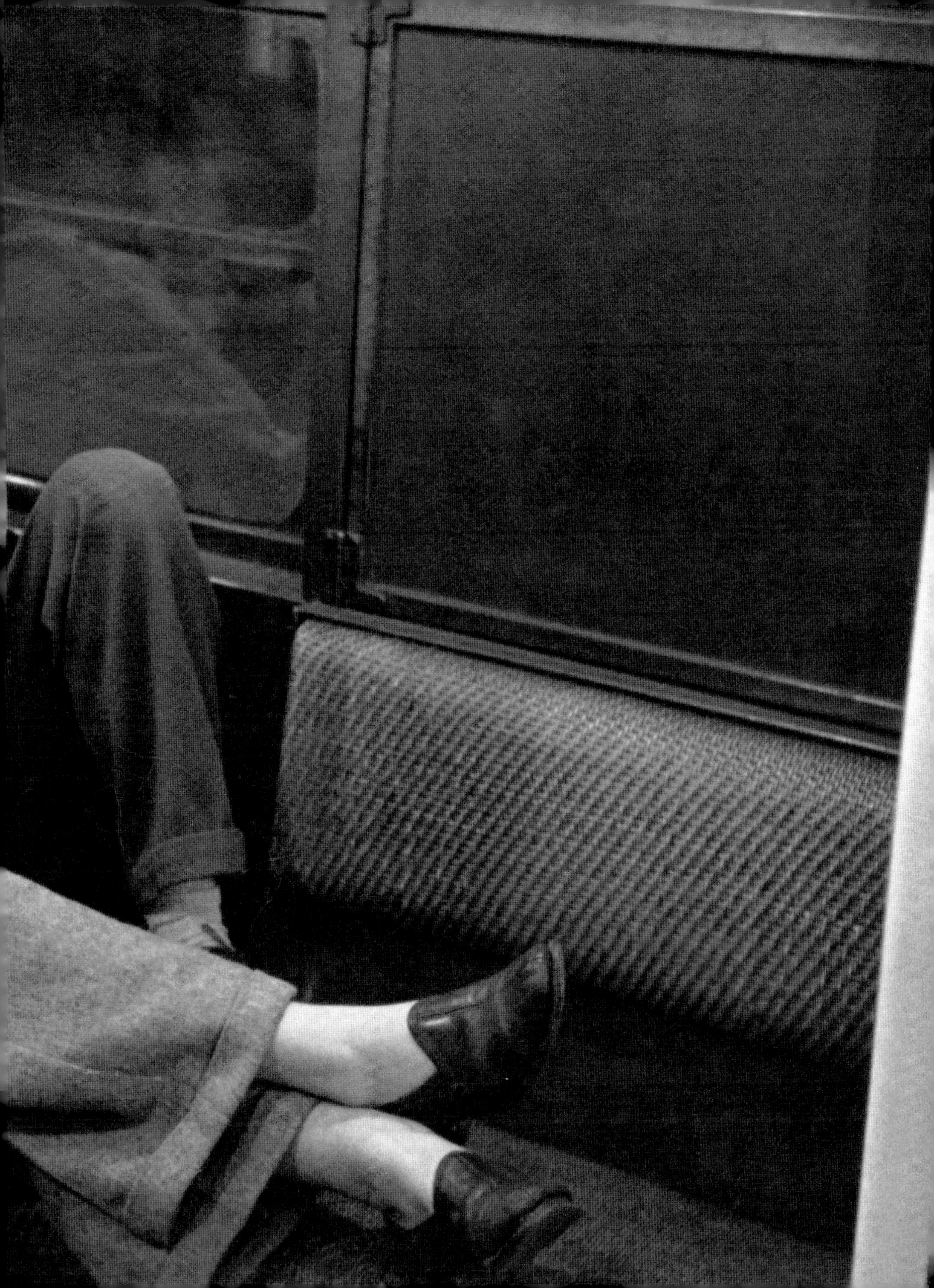

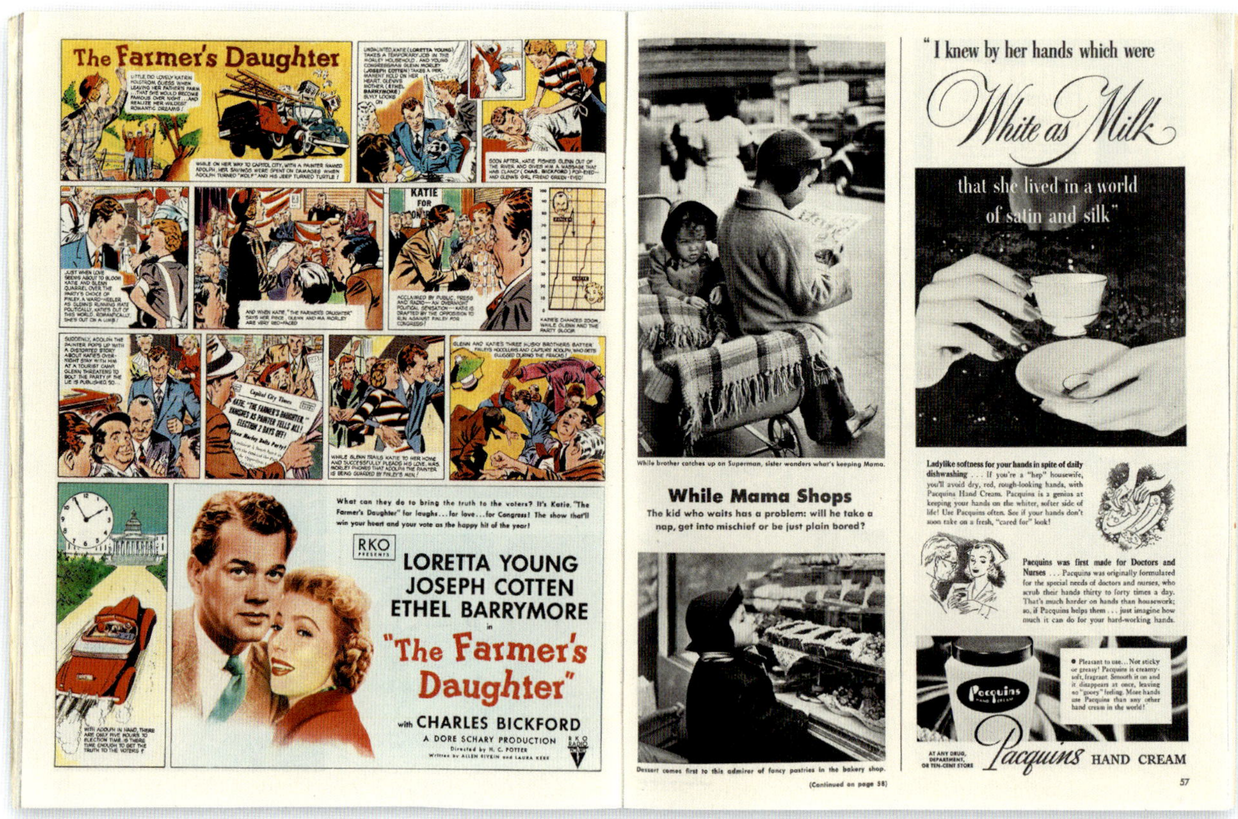

While brother catches up on Superman, sister wonders what's keeping Mama.

While Mama Shops

The kid who waits has a problem: will he take a nap, get into mischief or be just plain bored?

Dessert comes first to this admirer of fancy pastries in the bakery shop.

(Continued on page 58)

57

PUBLISHED AS

WHILE MAMA SHOPS: KIDS ARE BORED, GET INTO MISCHIEF WHILE MOM'S AWAY

DATE

MARCH 18, 1947

Post–World War II consumerism and people's body language and facial expressions while engaged in everyday activities were recurring subjects of Kubrick's photographs for *Look*. This article illustrated children waiting for their mothers to finish shopping. Some got bored, some caught up on their comics, while others played with whatever they could find on the street.

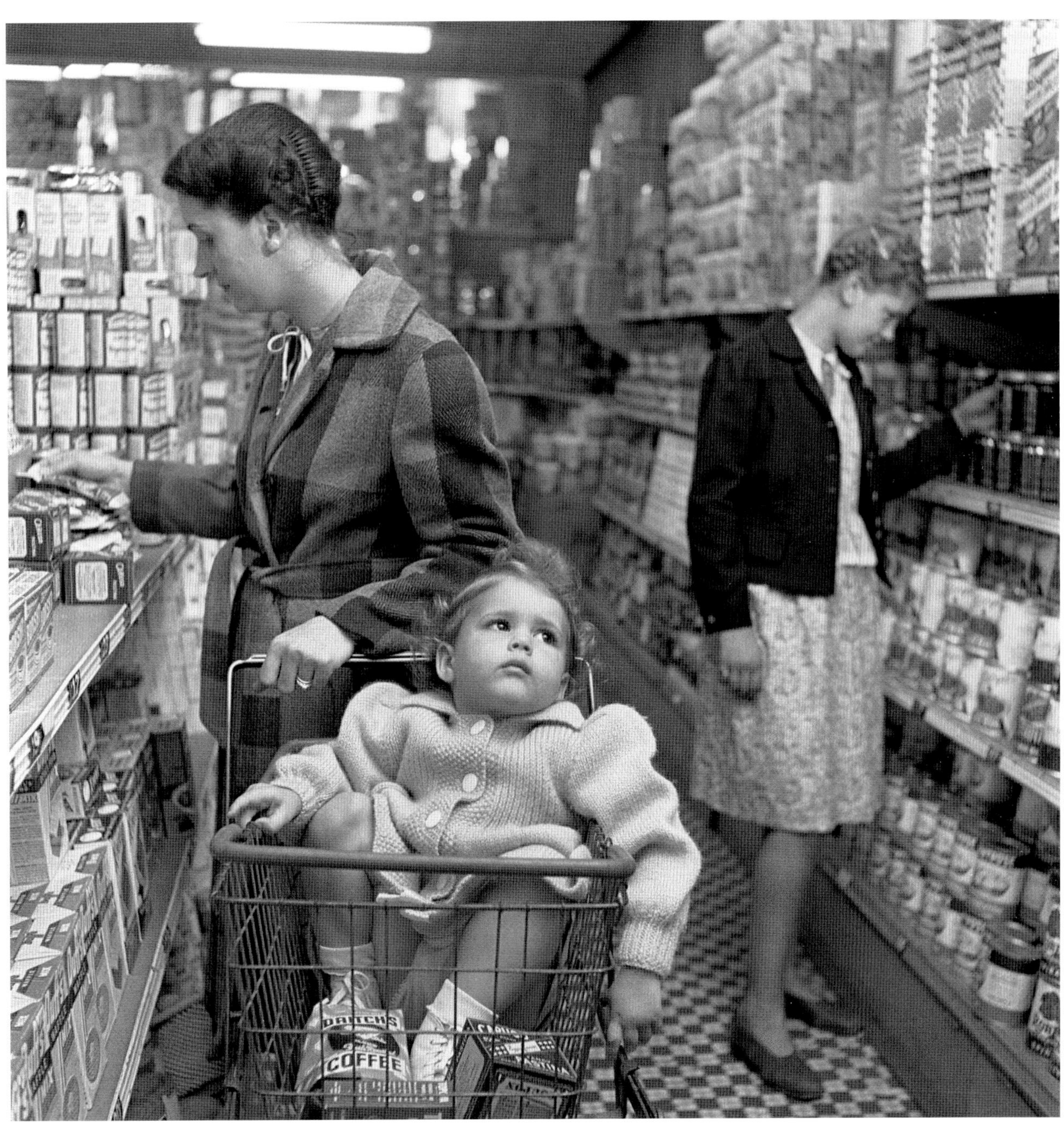

"After so many trips up the aisles in a shopping cart," the caption to this picture noted, "the novelty is gone."

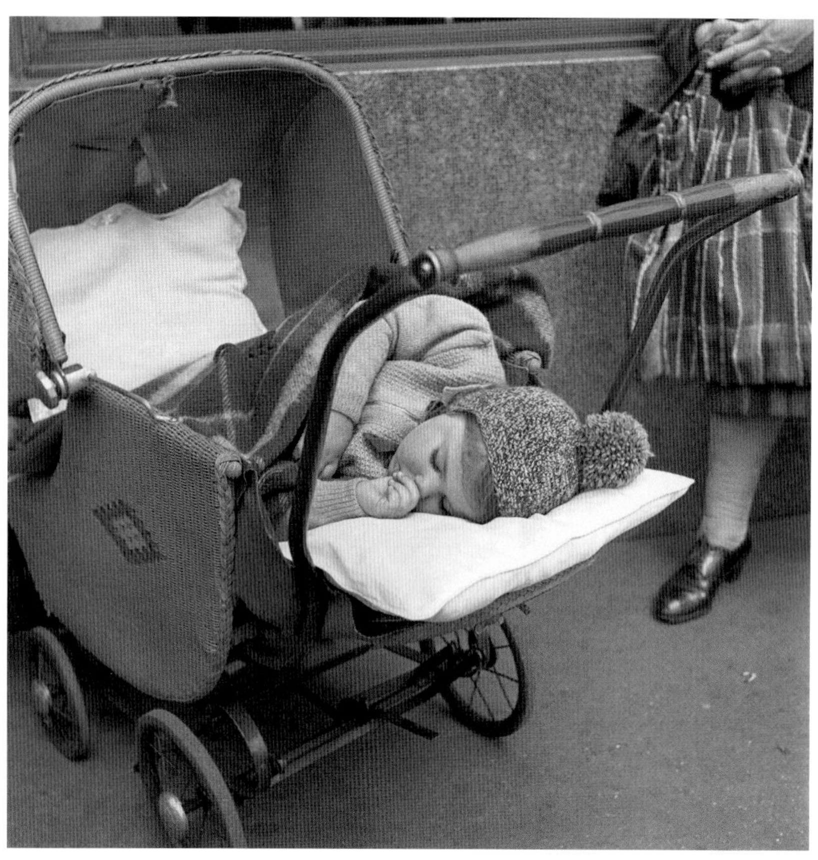

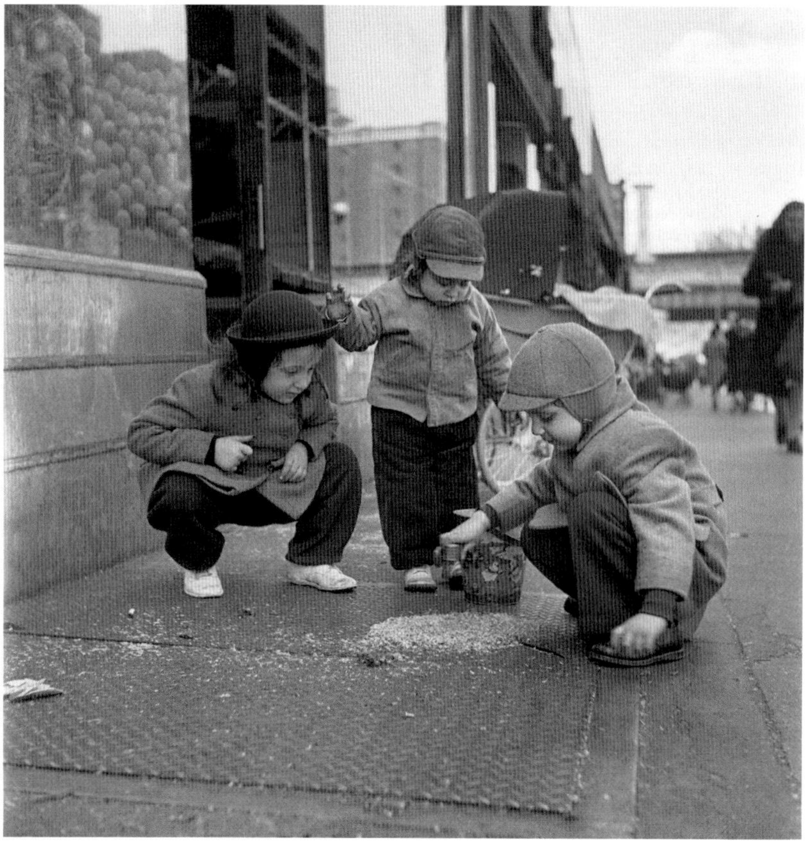

"The kid who waits has a problem," reported this essay's text. "Will he take a nap, get into mischief or be just plain bored?"

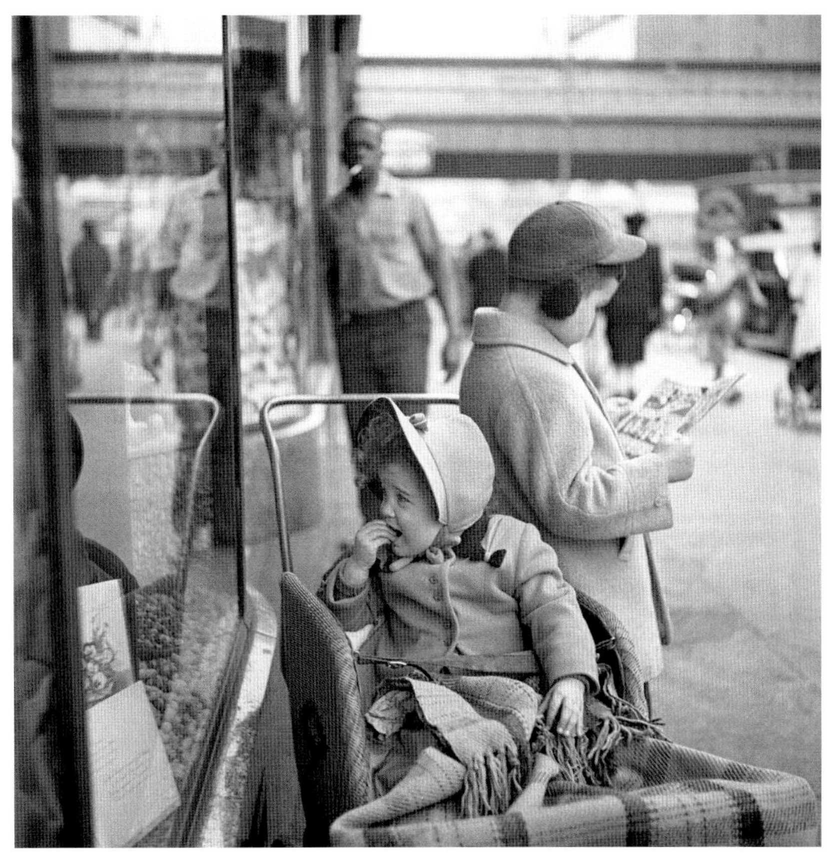

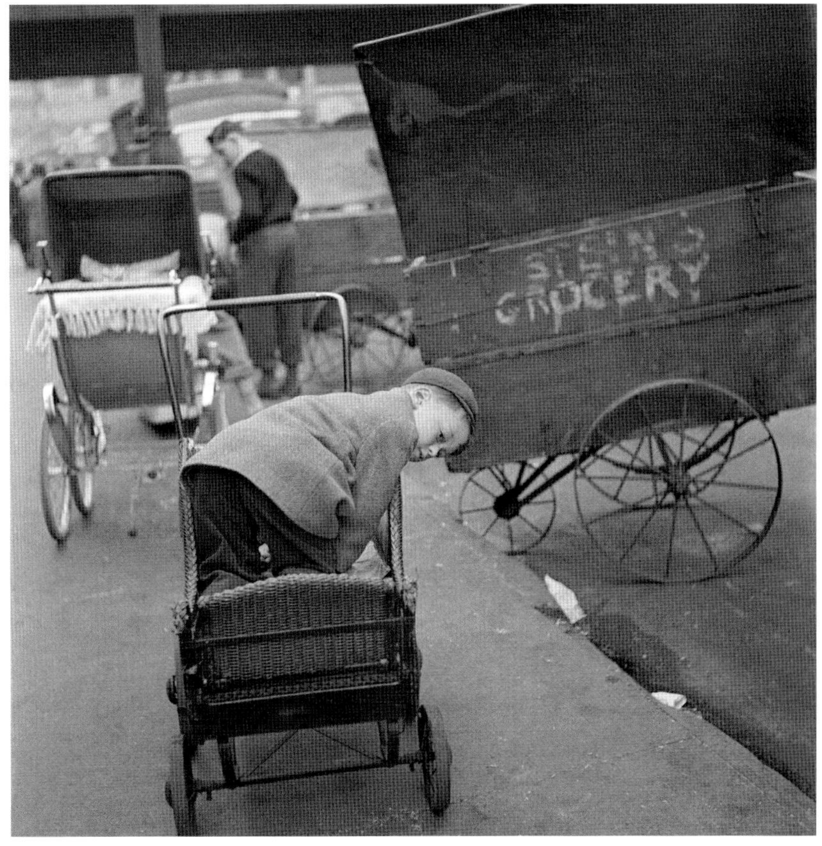
GROCERY

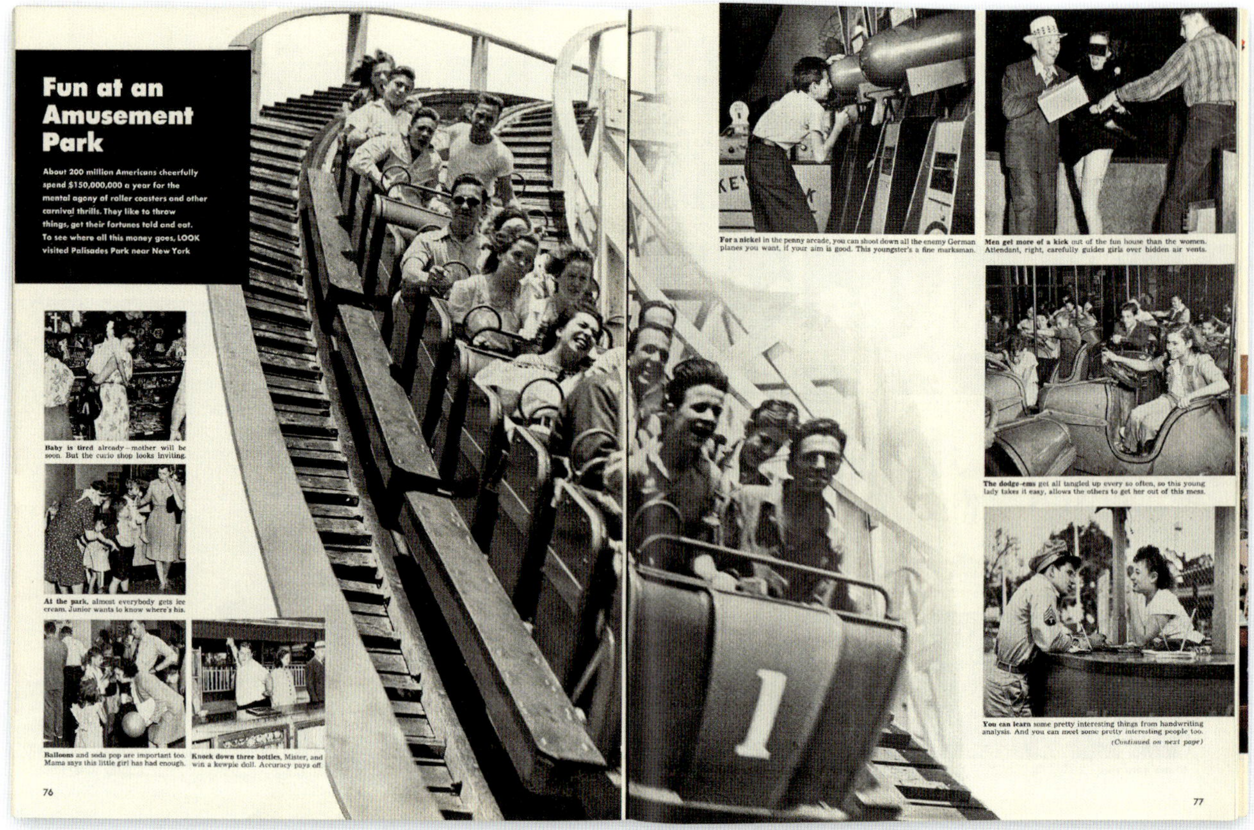

Fun at an Amusement Park

About 200 million Americans cheerfully spend $150,000,000 a year for the mental agony of roller coasters and other carnival thrills. They like to throw things, get their fortunes told and eat. To see where all this money goes, LOOK visited Palisades Park near New York

Baby is tired already—mother will be soon. But the curio shop looks inviting.

At the park, almost everybody gets ice cream. Junior wants to know where's his.

Balloons and soda pop are important too. Mama says this little girl has had enough.

Knock down three bottles, Mister, and win a kewpie doll. Accuracy pays off.

76

For a nickel in the penny arcade, you can shoot down all the enemy German planes you want, if your aim is good. This youngster's a fine marksman.

Men get more of a kick out of the fun house than the women. Attendant, right, carefully guides girls over hidden air vents.

The dodge-ems get all tangled up every so often, so this young lady takes it easy, allows the others to get her out of this mess.

You can learn some pretty interesting things from handwriting analysis. And you can meet some pretty interesting people too.

(Continued on next page)

77

PUBLISHED AS

FUN AT AN AMUSEMENT PARK: *LOOK* VISITS PALISADES PARK

DATE

JUNE 24, 1947

"About 200 million Americans cheerfully spend $150,000,000 a year," this article noted, "for the mental agony of roller coasters and other carnival thrills." To see how all of this money was spent, *Look* sent Kubrick to photograph Palisades Amusement Park near New York City. The article's 26 photographs combining posed and candid shots, some arranged in narrative sequence, captured the animated actions of park-goers guessing each other's weight, showing off their strength, and having their fortunes told, among other activities.

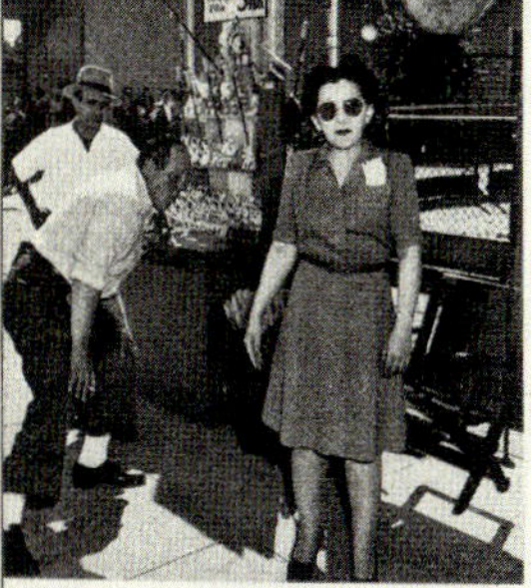

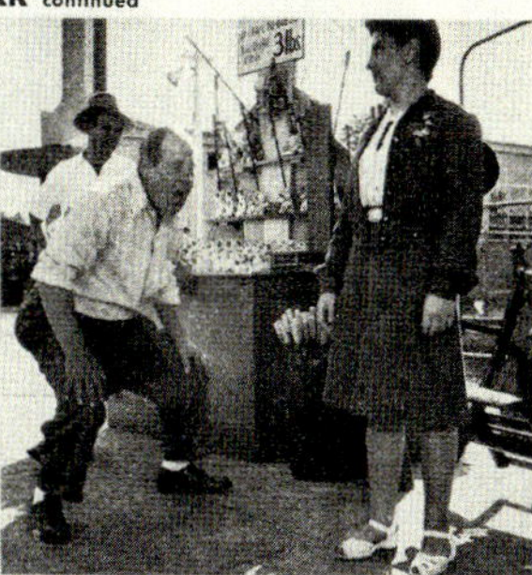

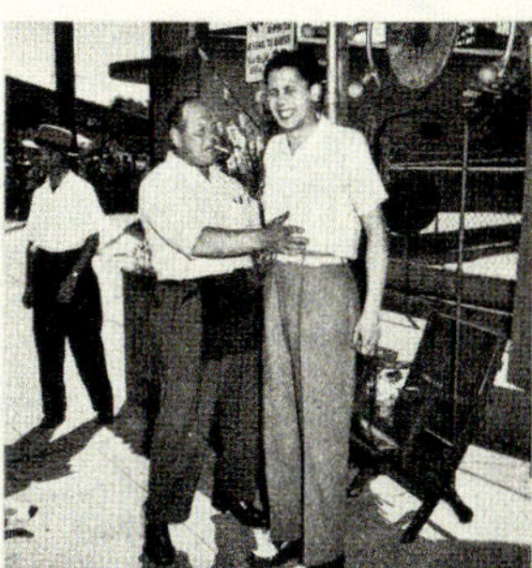

Guess your weight

For ten cents, this man will guess your weight, comment on your figure, hop around like a kangaroo and even tickle you. He'll tell a fat man to lay off the doughnuts, but he's more delicate in his advice to women. All his customers get prizes.

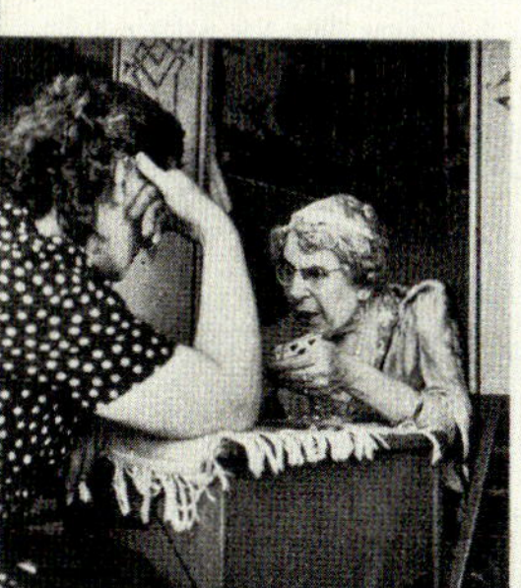

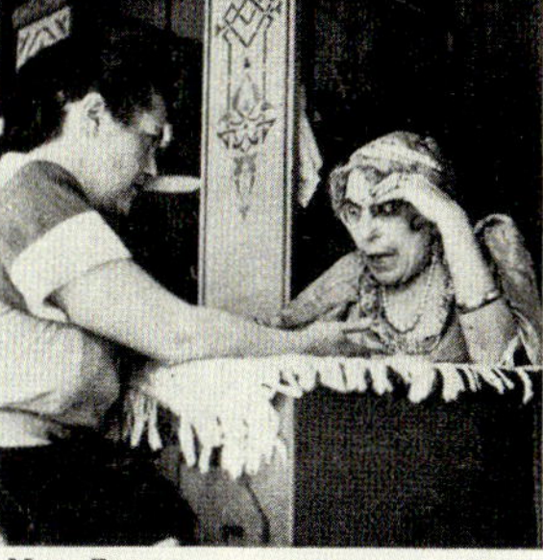

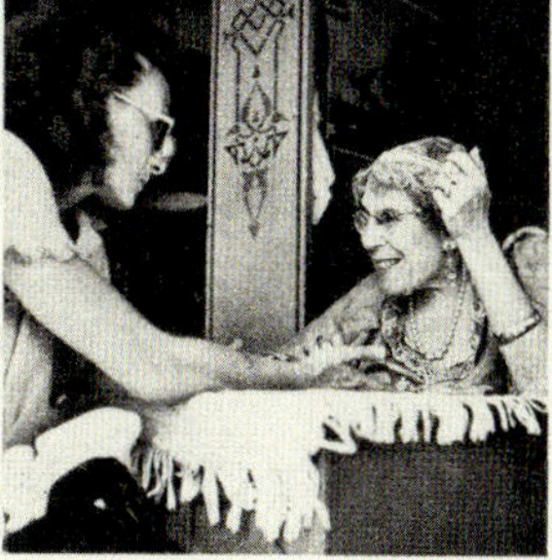

Tell your fortune

Mme. Zara, the fortune teller, has been at Palisades Park for 22 years, has clients who will not make a major decision without first asking her advice. An expert on love, marriage or success, she reads from the cards or from the palm of your hand.

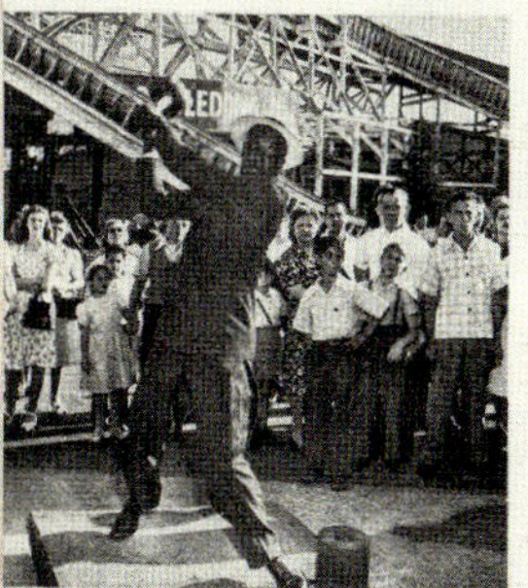

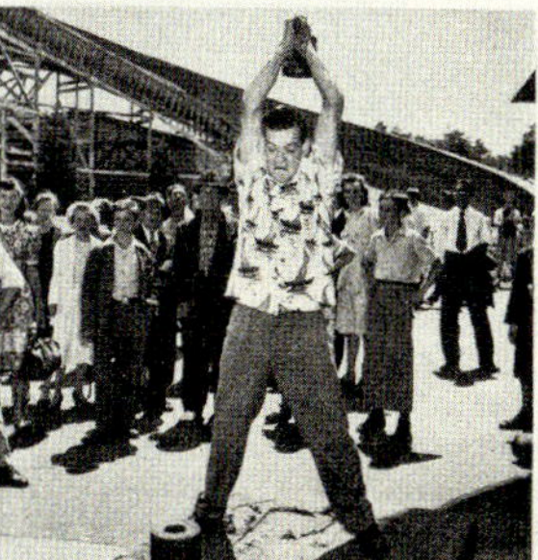

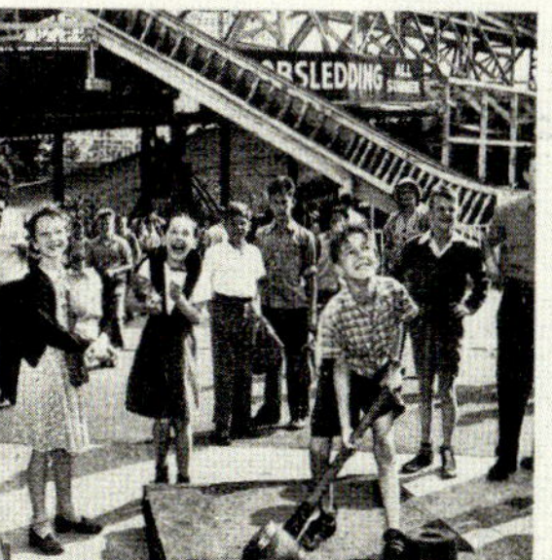

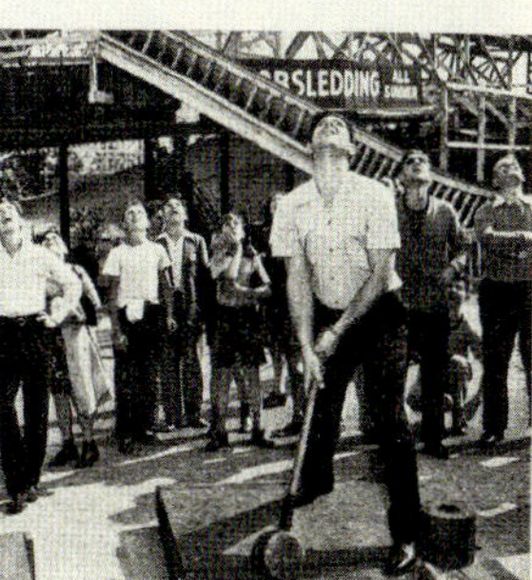

Ring the bell

Showing off his strength is a man's weakness, a fact that has consistently made money for amusement parks. If the hammer lands hard enough on the stump in foreground, a bell rings at top of a thermometer-like structure, and crowd howls approval.

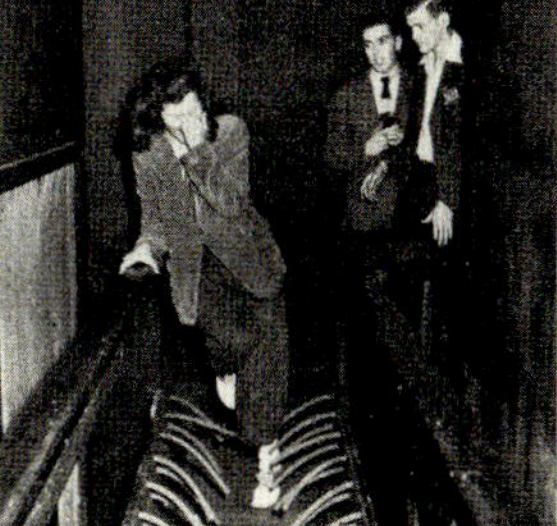

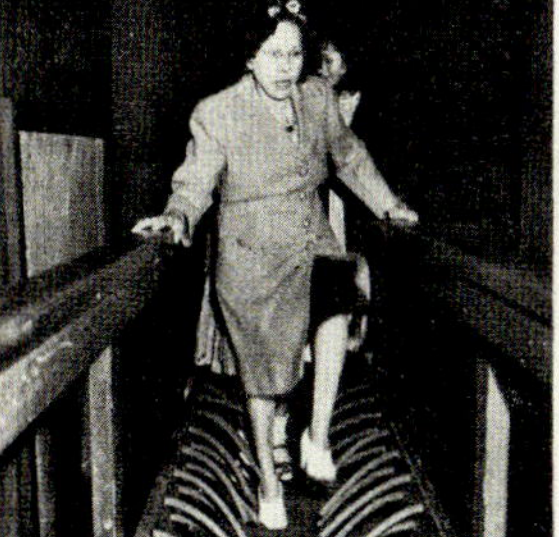

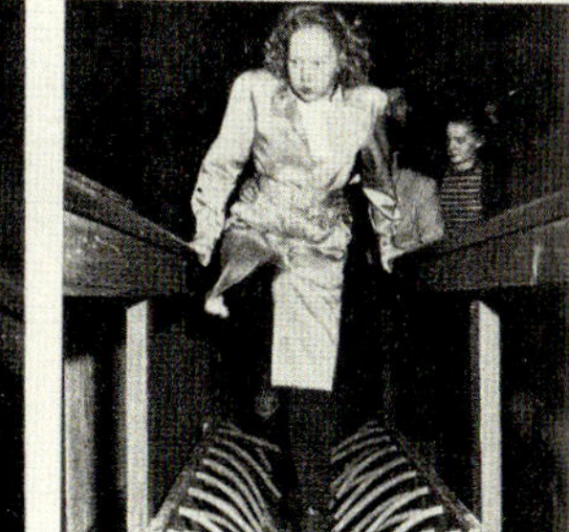

Watch your step

It's dark in this passageway, and all you can see is a too-realistic pair of rubber mice, playing mechanically in the distance. The rubber tubes that scrape your ankles could be mice too, and that's why these young women look so scared.

You'c

Photographed by STANLEY KUBRICK

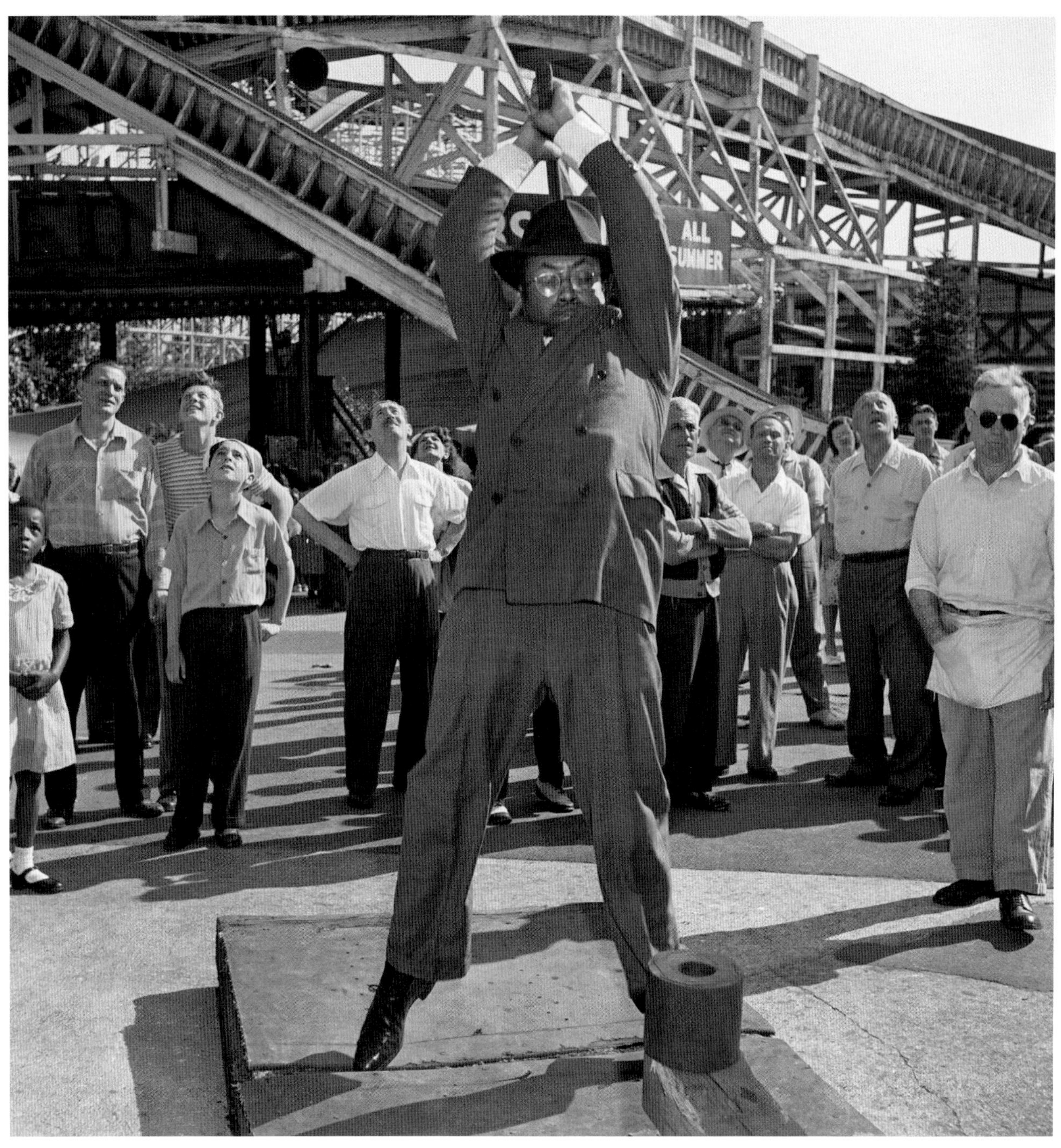

"Showing off his strength is a man's weakness," observed the caption for a series depicting men playing the game of Ring the Bell, "a fact that has consistently made money for amusement parks."

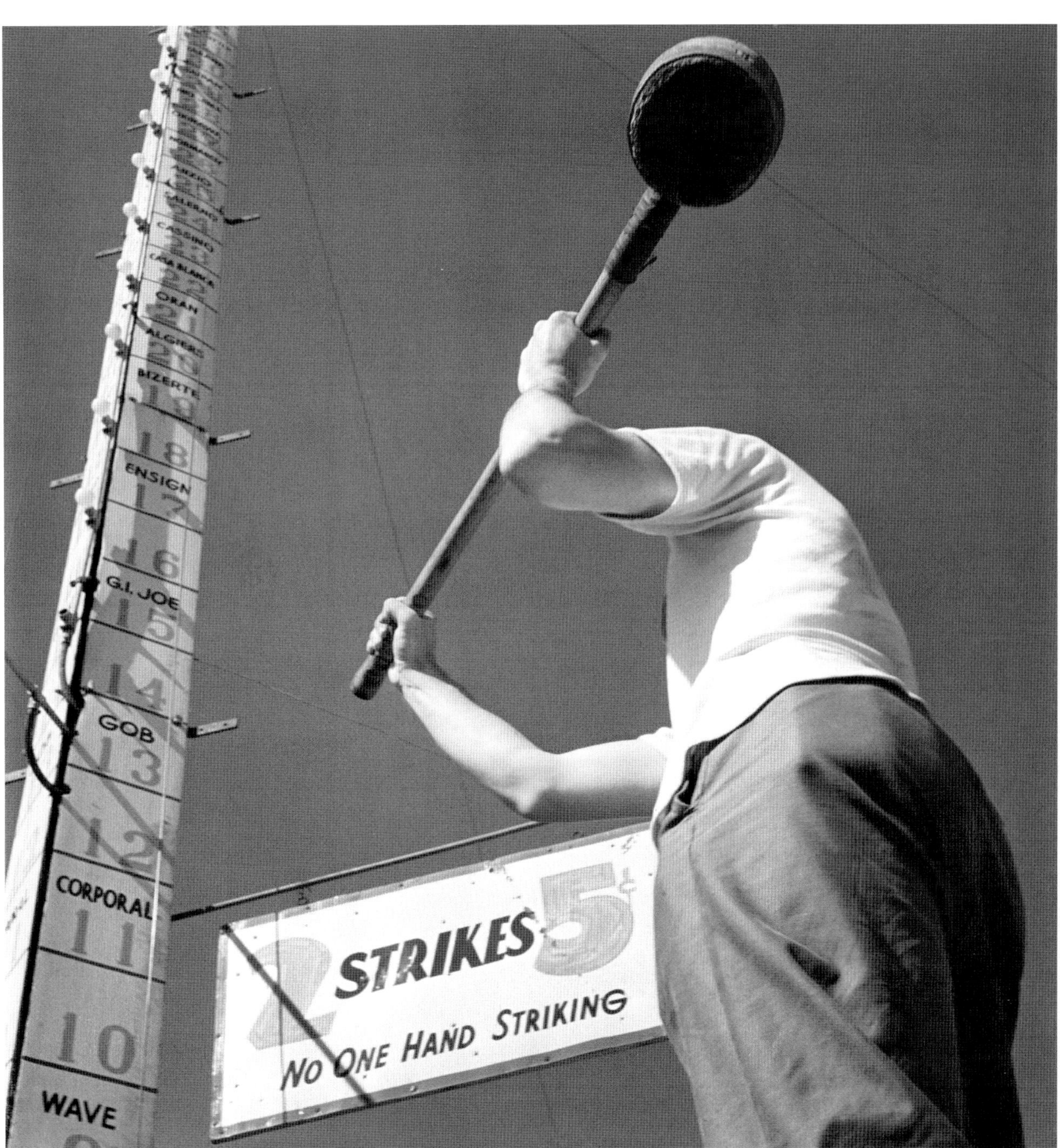
BIZERTE
18
ENSIGN
17
16
G.I. JOE
15
14
GOB
13
12
CORPORAL
11
10
WAVE
2 STRIKES 5¢
NO ONE HAND STRIKING

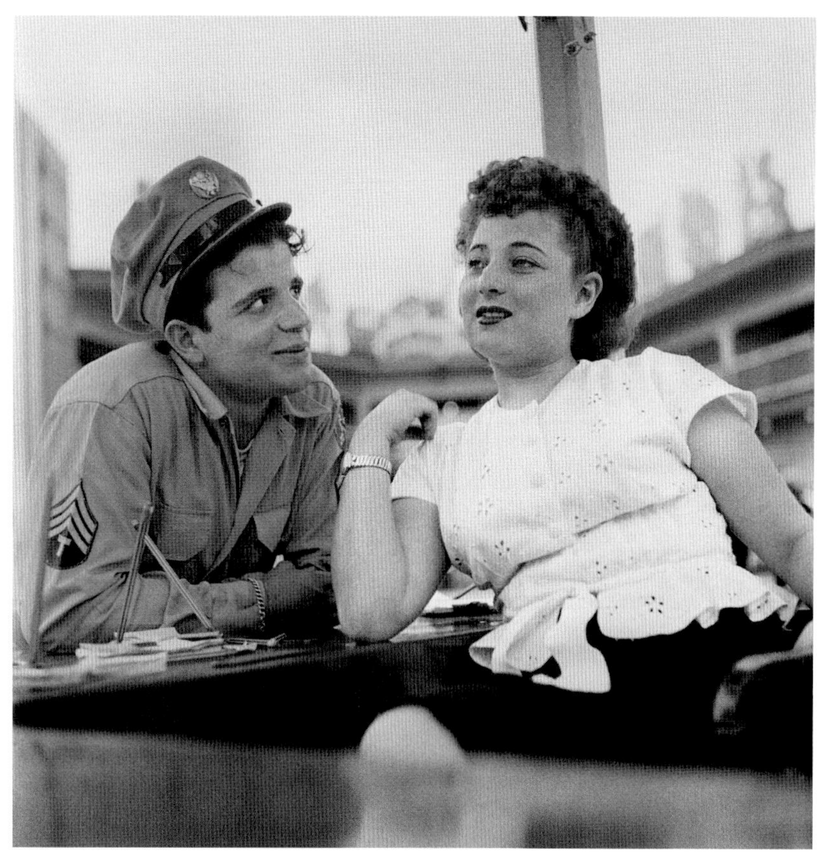

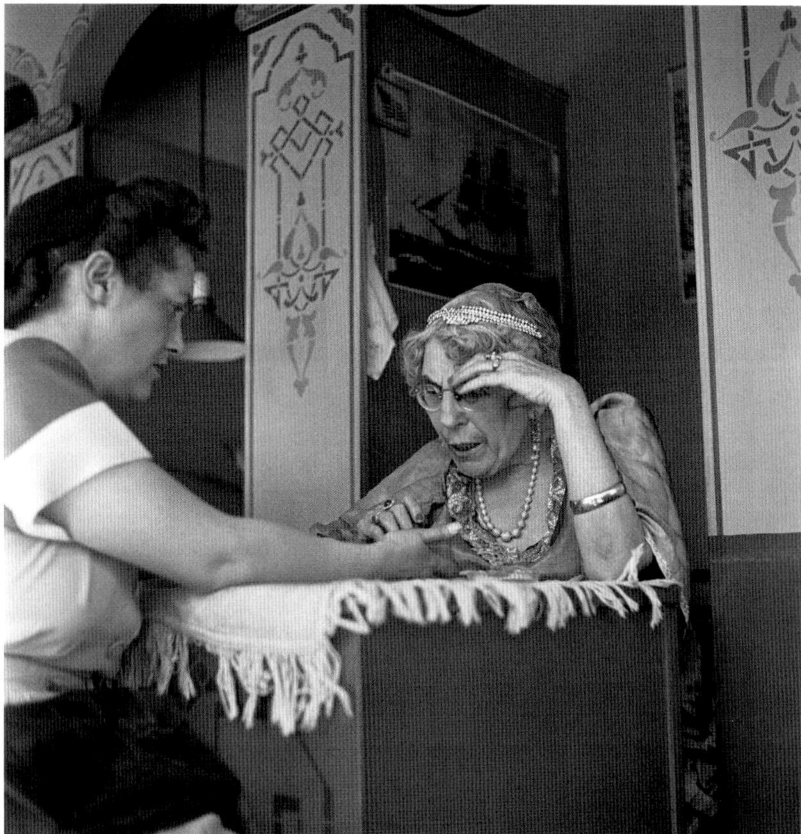

ABOVE **A serviceman passing the time at a handwriting-analysis booth**

LEFT **Fortune teller Madame Zara, a Palisades Amusement Park veteran of 22 years**

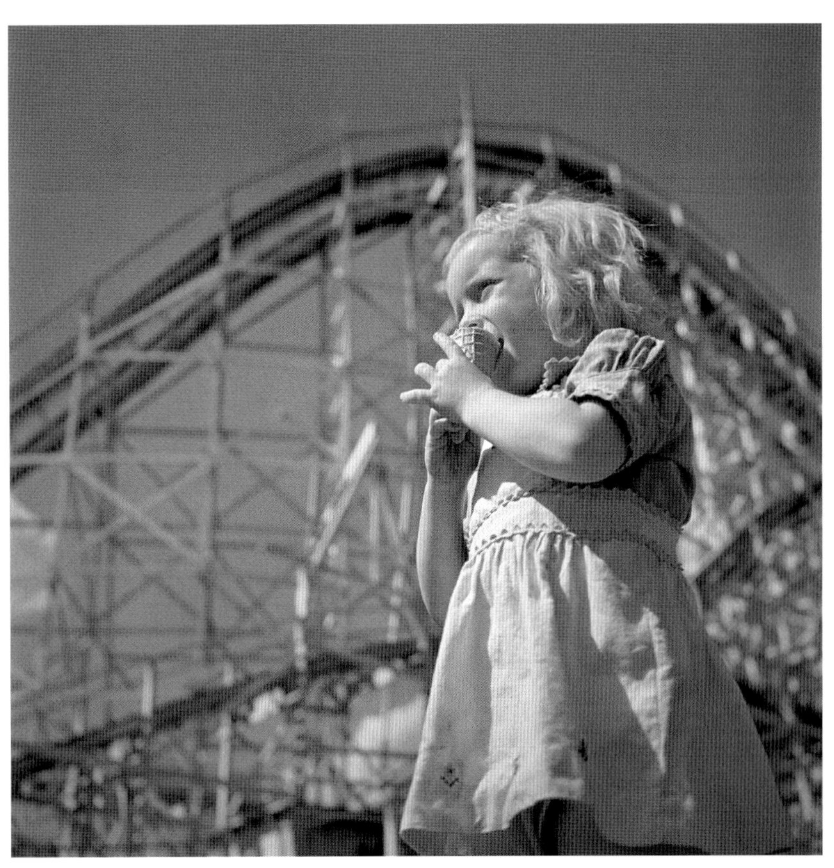

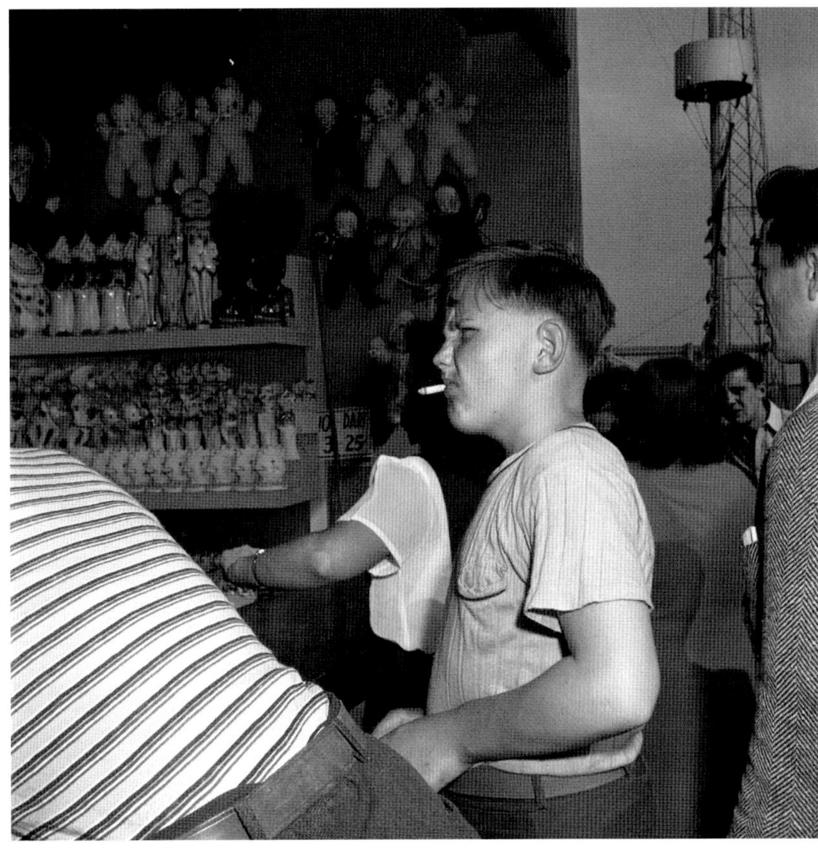

ABOVE **A girl enjoying an ice cream cone**

RIGHT **A young tough playing a game**

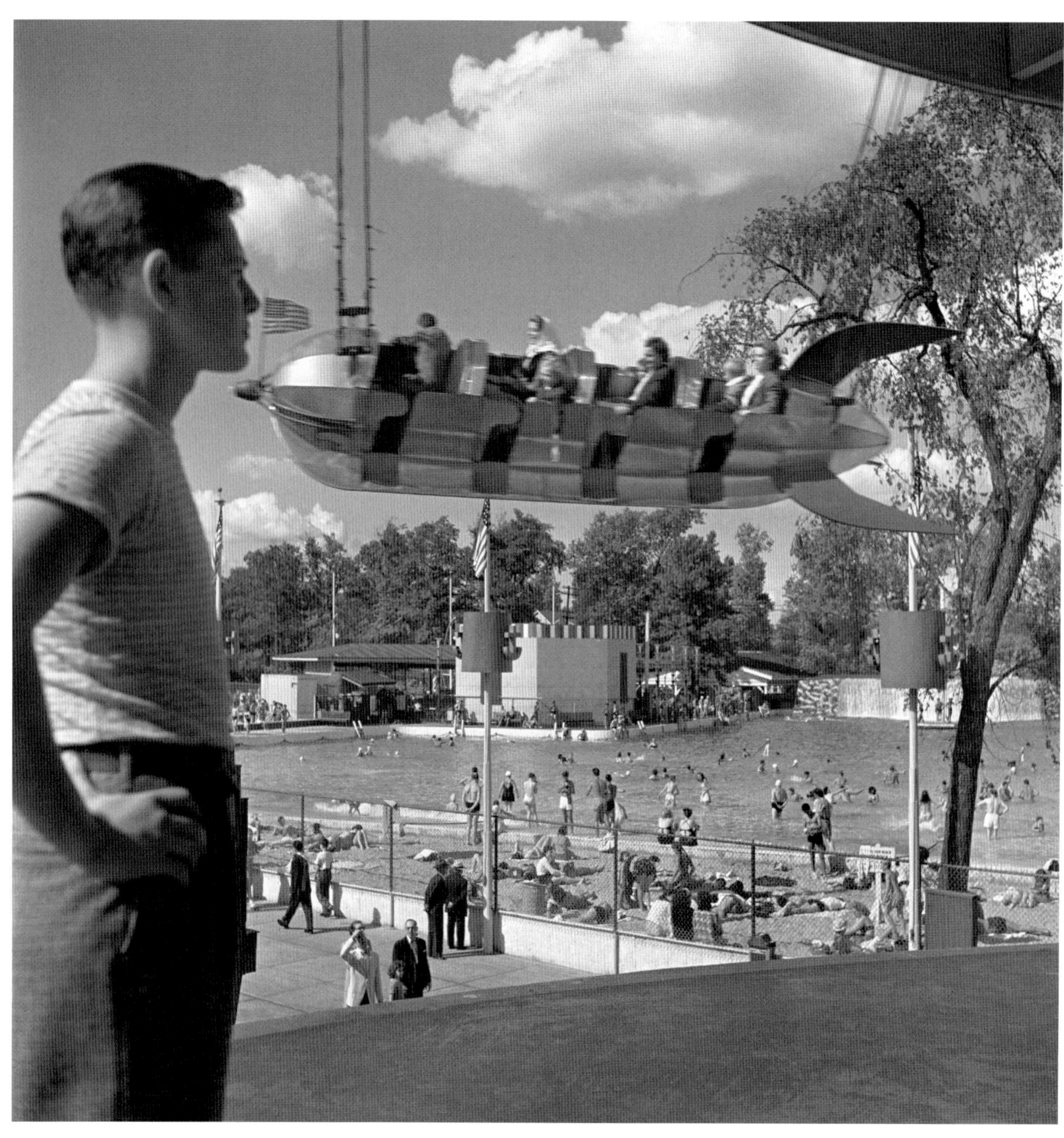

Swimming at the park

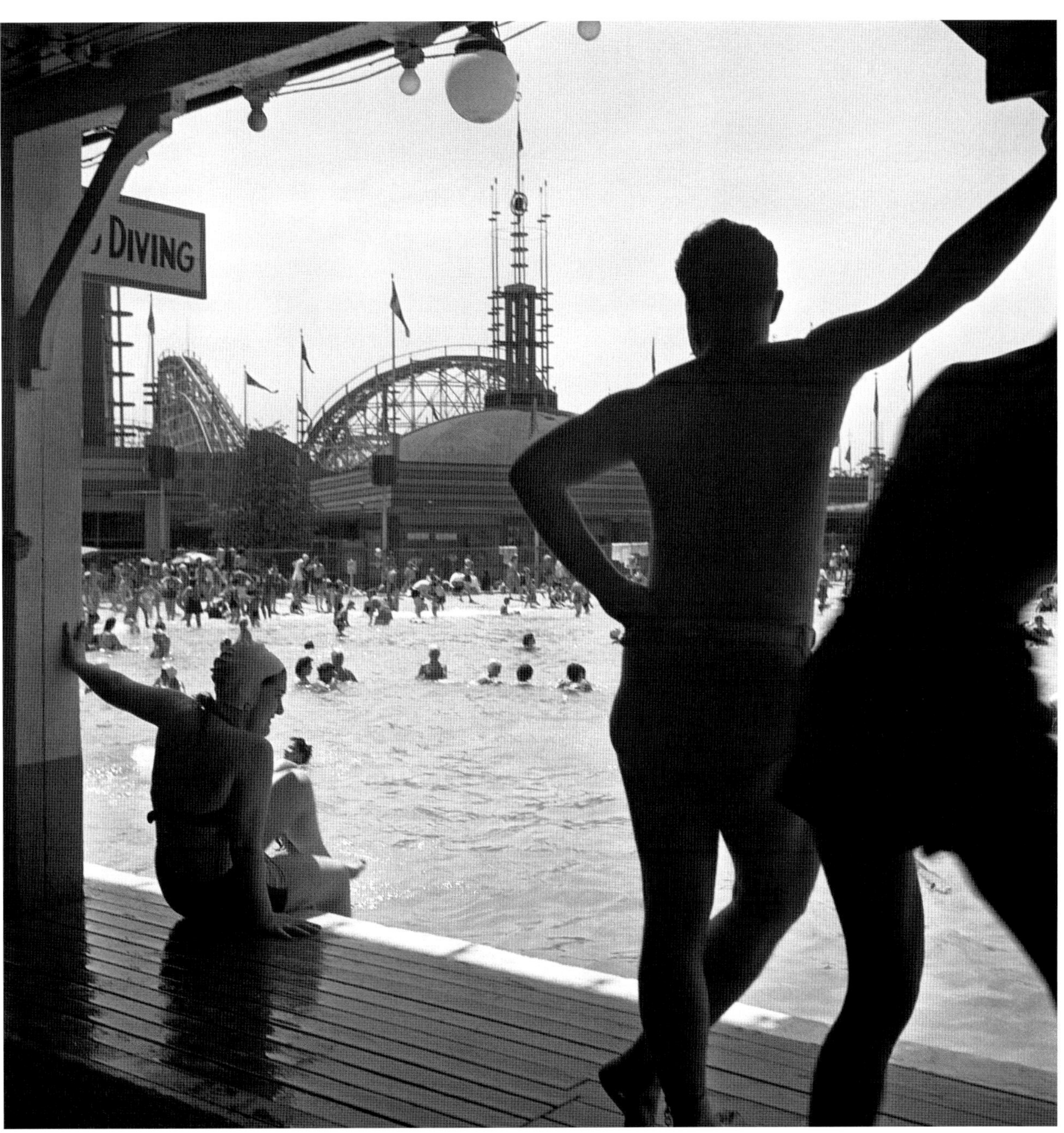
DIVING

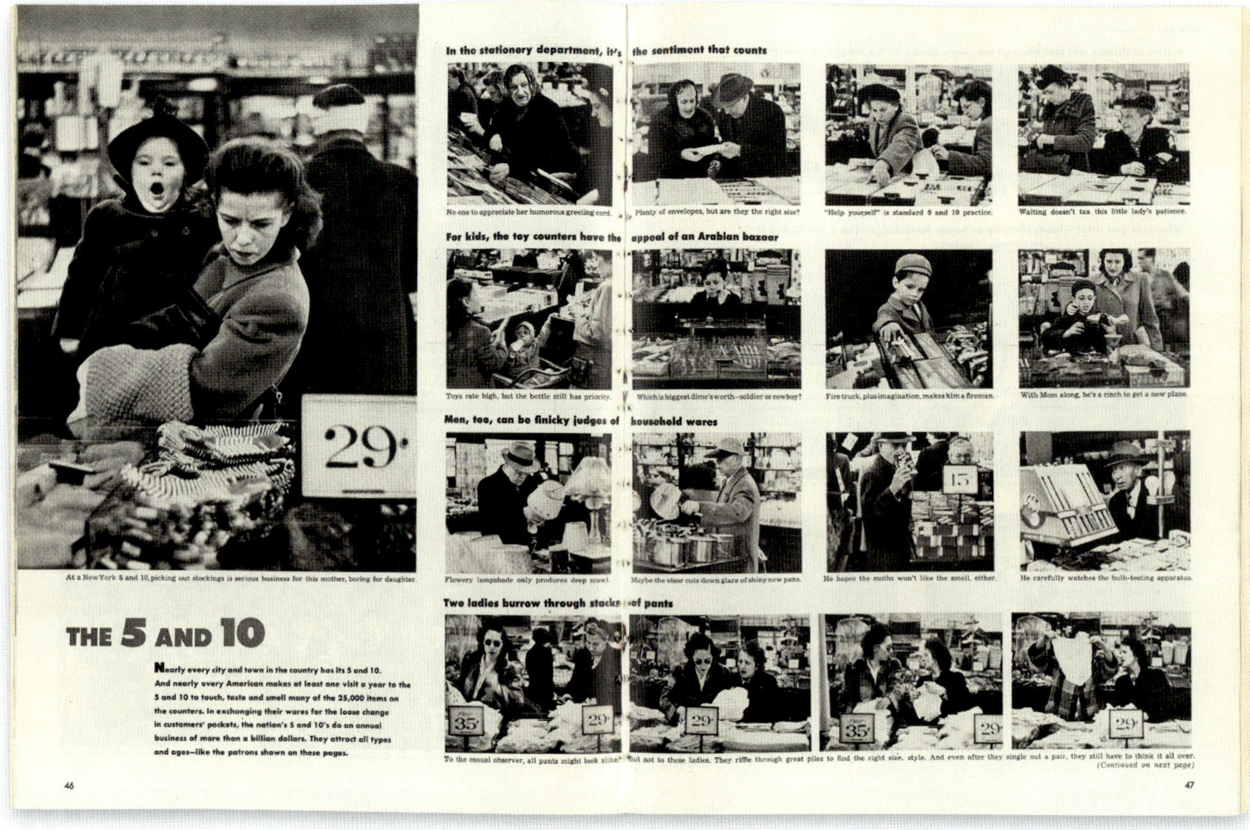

At a New York 5 and 10, picking out stockings is serious business for this mother, boring for daughter.

THE 5 AND 10

Nearly every city and town in the country has its 5 and 10. And nearly every American makes at least one visit a year to the 5 and 10 to touch, taste and smell many of the 25,000 items on the counters. In exchanging their wares for the loose change in customers' pockets, the nation's 5 and 10's do an annual business of more than a billion dollars. They attract all types and ages—like the patrons shown on these pages.

46

In the stationery department, it's the sentiment that counts

No one to appreciate her humorous greeting card. Plenty of envelopes, but are they the right size? "Help yourself" is standard 5 and 10 practice. Waiting doesn't tax this little lady's patience.

For kids, the toy counters have the appeal of an Arabian bazaar

Toys rate high, but the bottle still has priority. Which is biggest dime's worth—soldier or cowboy? Fire truck, plus imagination, makes him a fireman. With Mom along, he's a cinch to get a new plane.

Men, too, can be finicky judges of household wares

Flowery lampshade only produces deep scowl. Maybe the visor cuts down glare of shiny new pans. He hopes the moths won't like the smell, either. He carefully watches the bulb-testing apparatus.

Two ladies burrow through stacks of pants

To the casual observer, all pants might look alike. But not to these ladies. They riffle through great piles to find the right size, style. And even after they single out a pair, they still have to think it all over.

(Continued on next page)

47

PUBLISHED AS

THE 5 AND 10: IT ATTRACTS ALL TYPES AND AGES

DATE

SEPTEMBER 2, 1947

This exploration of a New York City 5 and 10 store, so named because its inexpensive wares could be bought for nickels and dimes, featured 32 images, all by Kubrick, that focused on the varied expressions of children and adults as they shopped for toys, stockings, stationery, and household items. The images were generally laid out in narrative sequences. The longest, at eight images, showed a little girl at the comic-book counter. "While she follows the adventures of Donald Duck and the Katzenjammer Kids, this young 5 and 10 customer absentmindedly munches a foot-long piece of licorice. As long as the candy holds out, she stands by her comic-book heroes through thick and thin. Like any reader, she smiles when her story has a happy ending."

OPPOSITE **A woman considering an array of pots and pans**

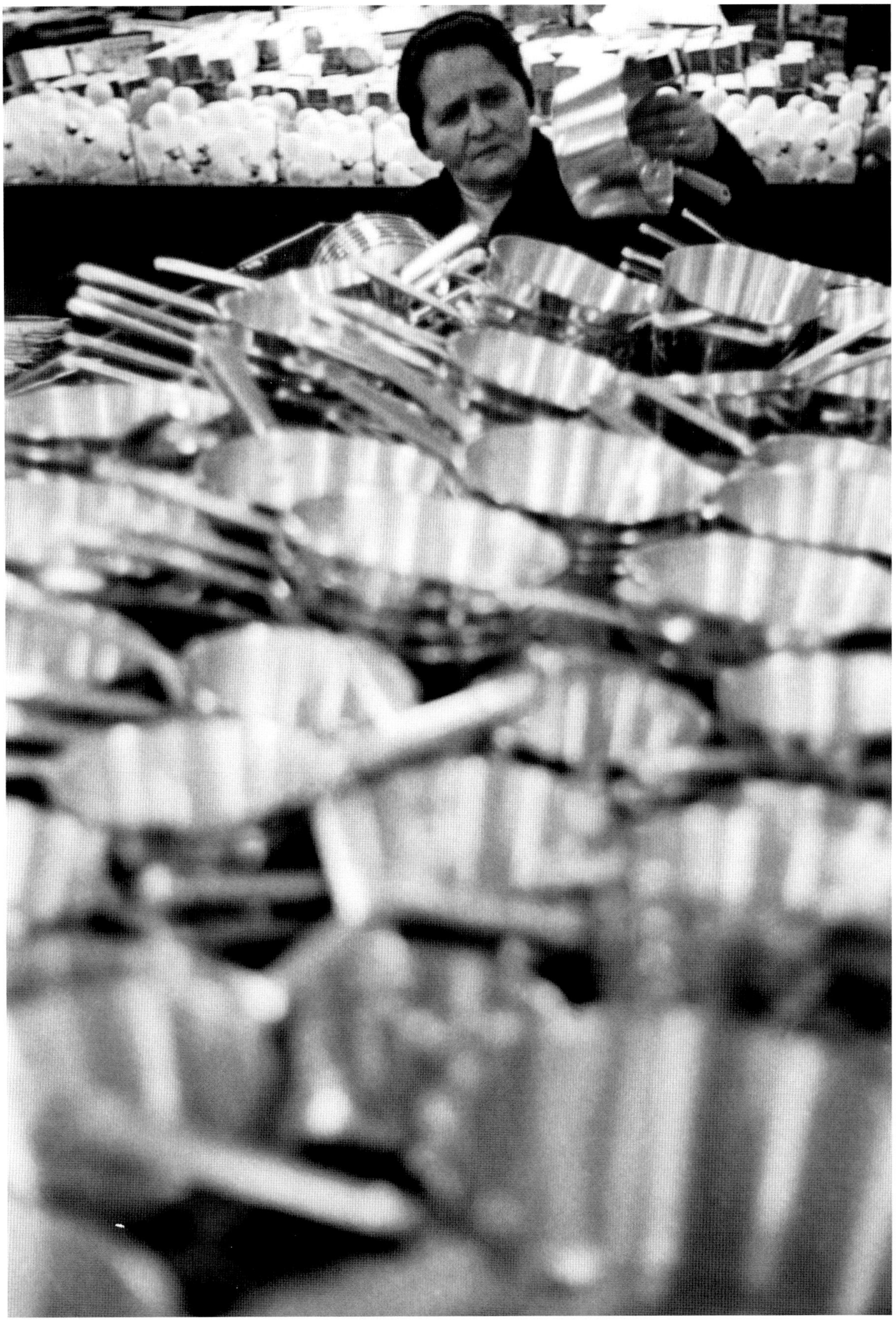

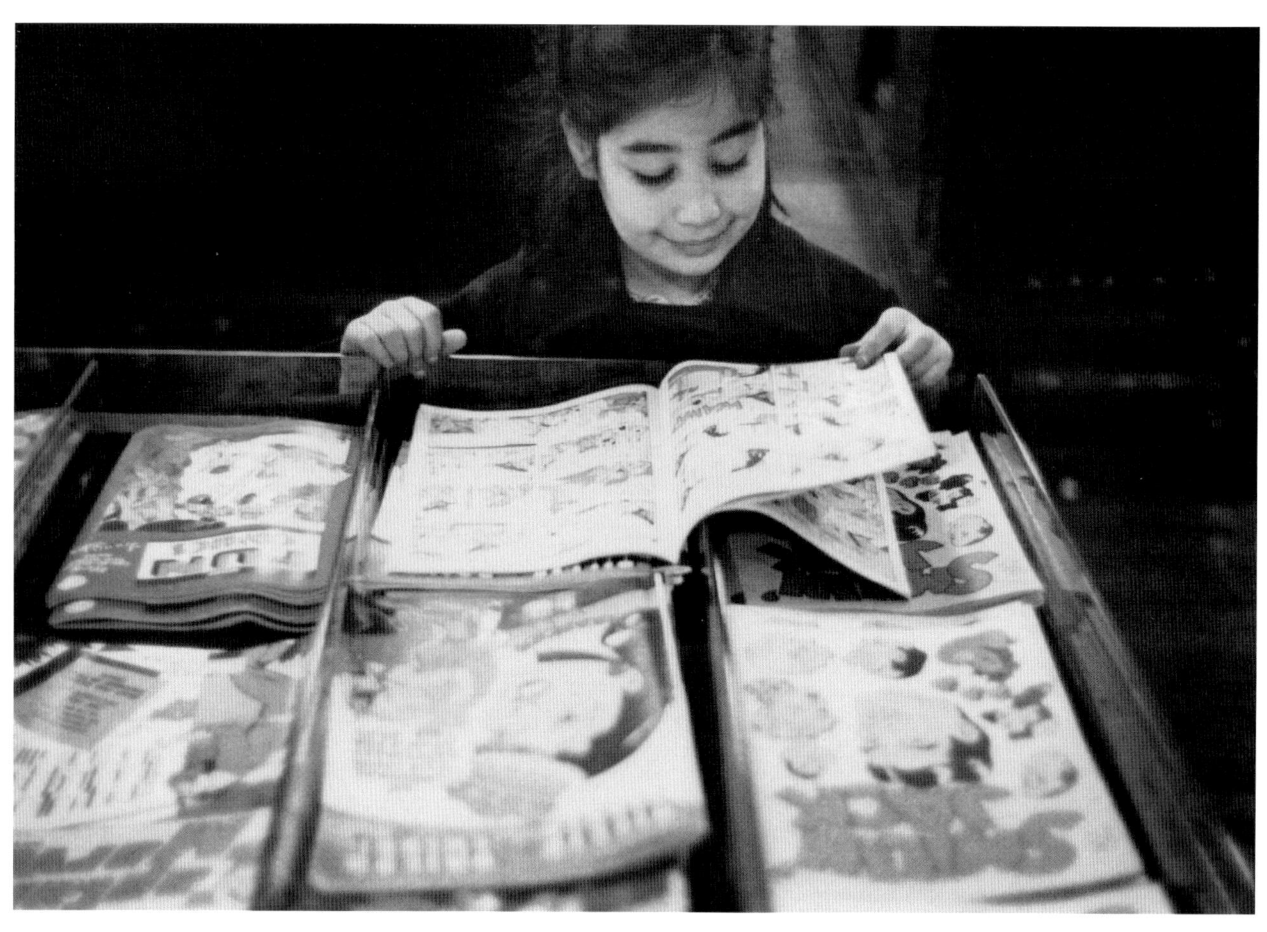

A little girl enjoying a comic book

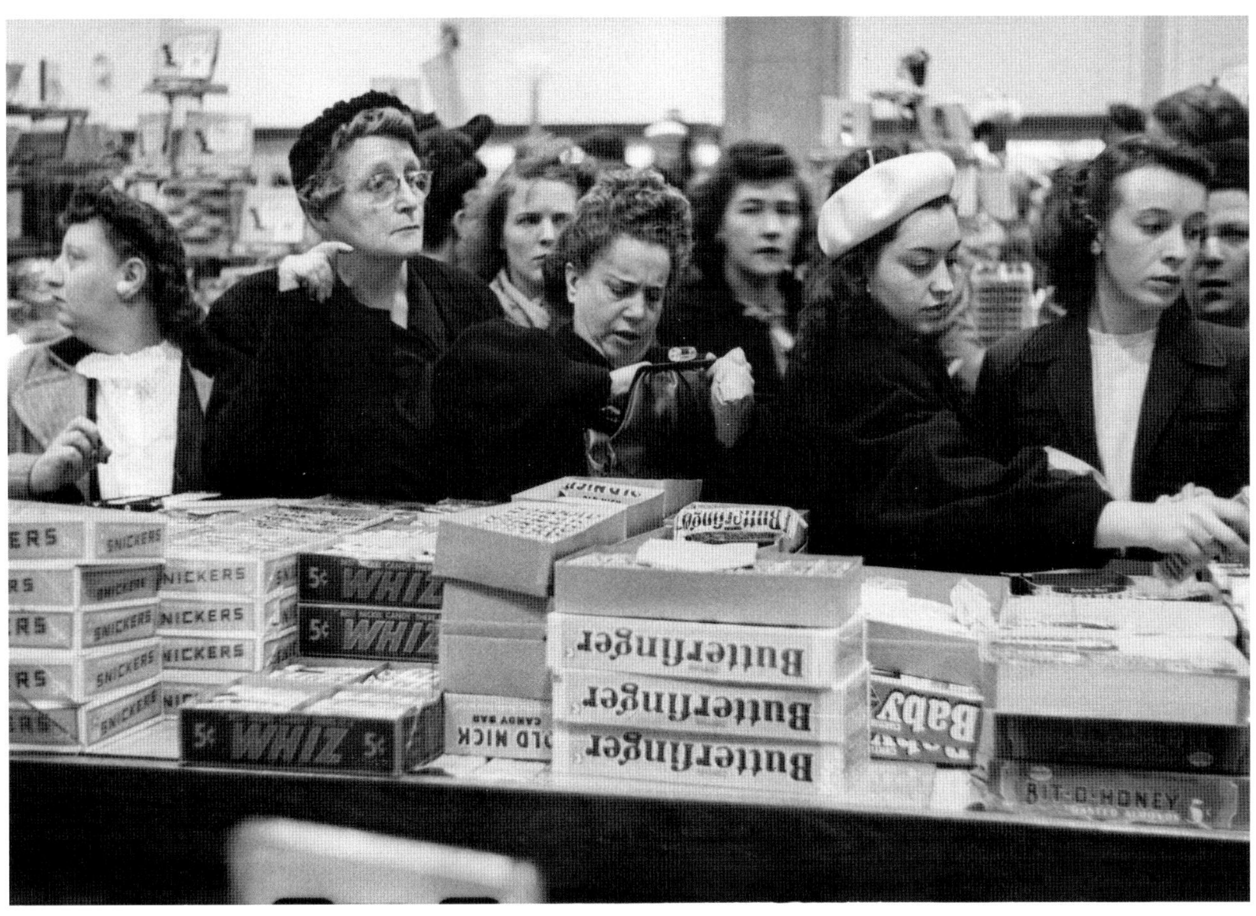

"Now that lots of candy is back on the counters," observed this photograph's caption, "customers line up two-deep."

FOLLOWING SPREAD **Women browsing at the perfume counter**

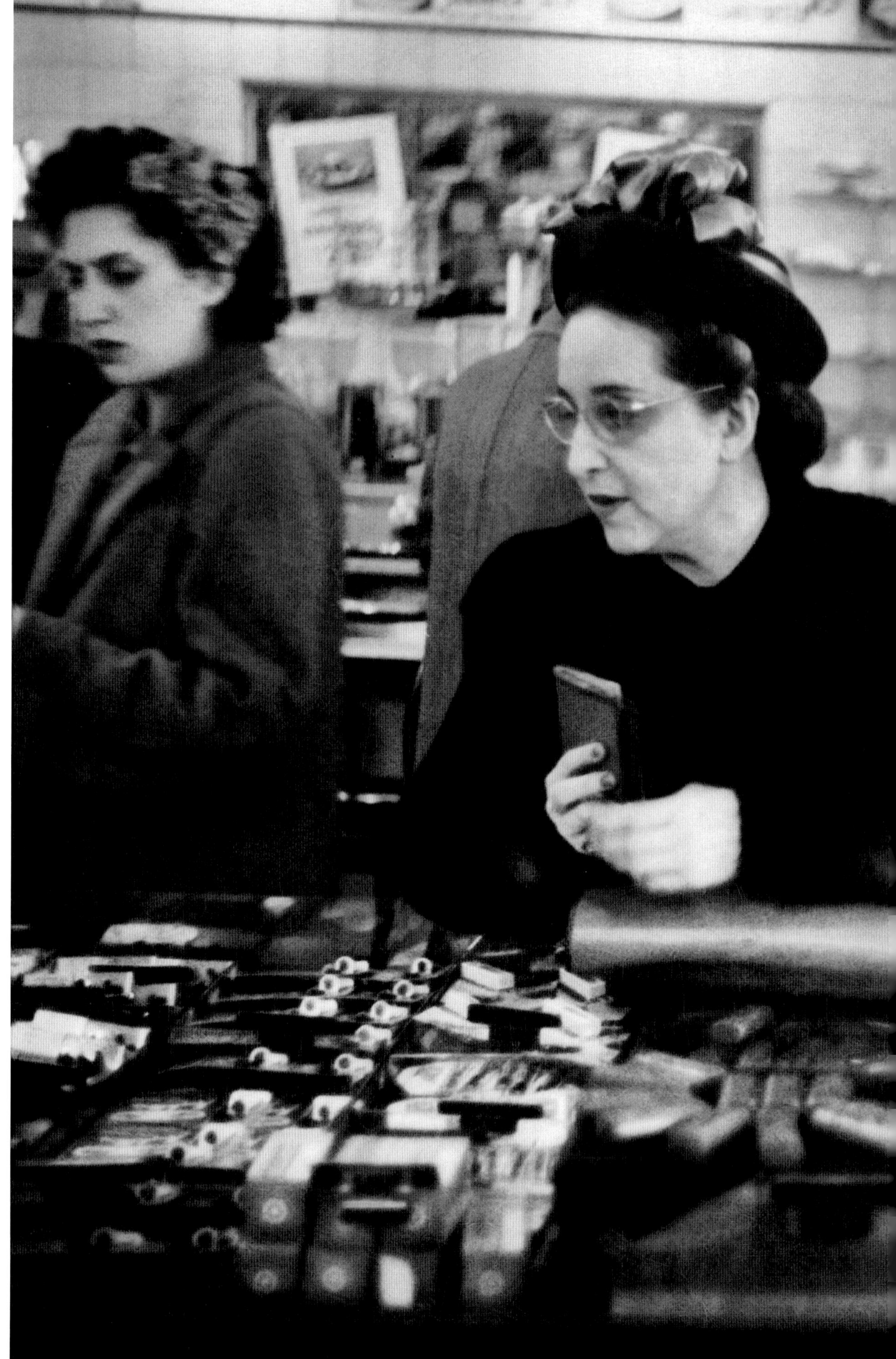

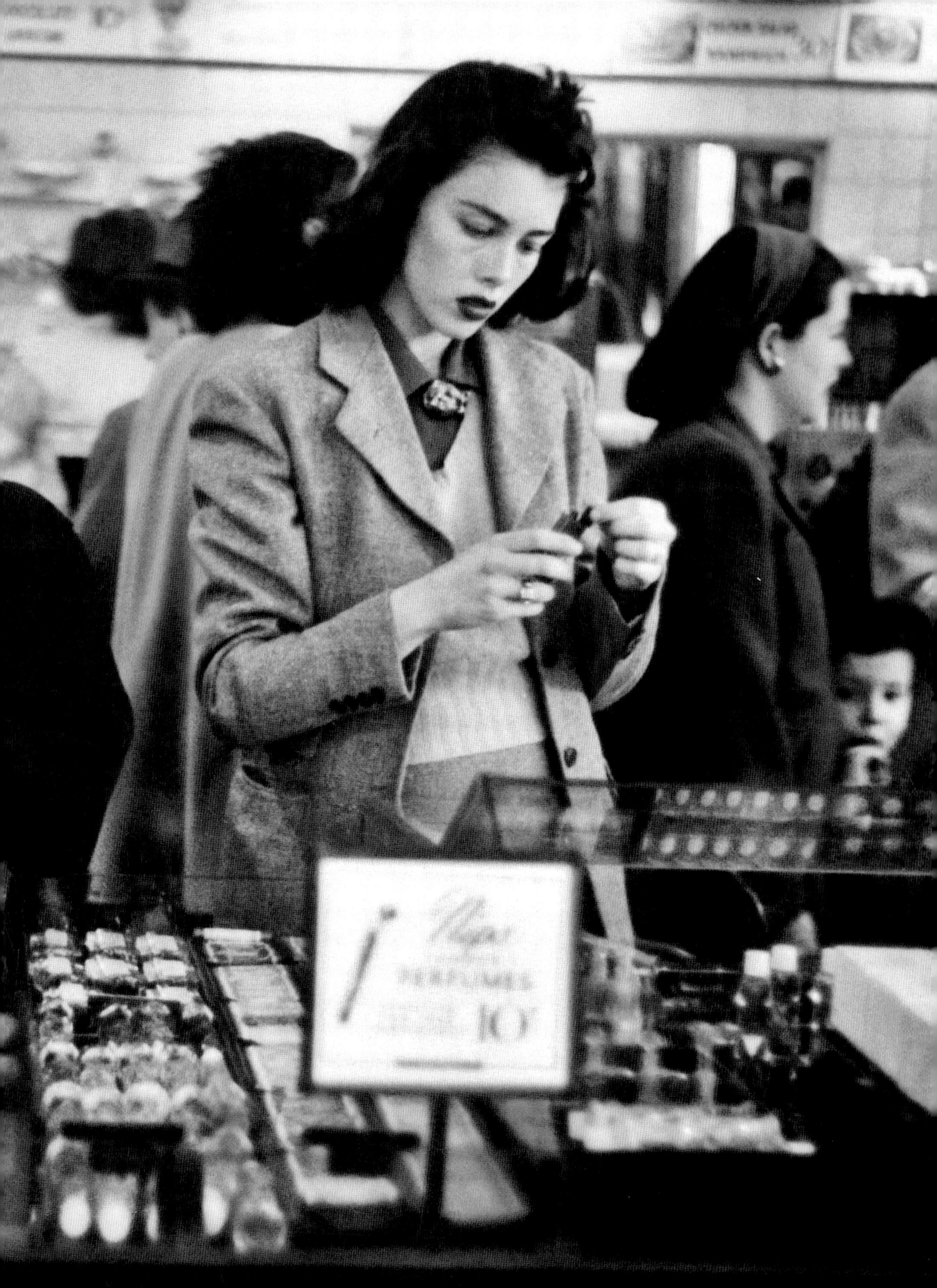
PERFUMES
10¢

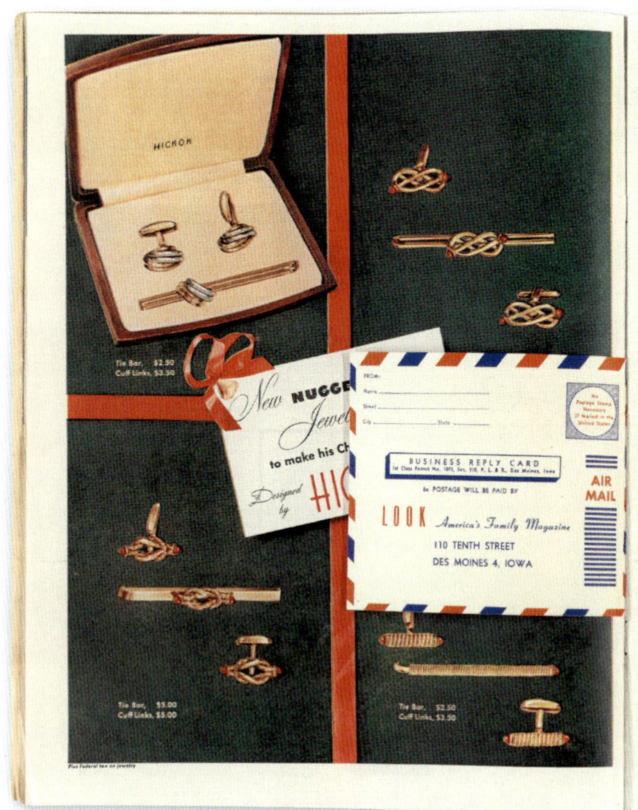

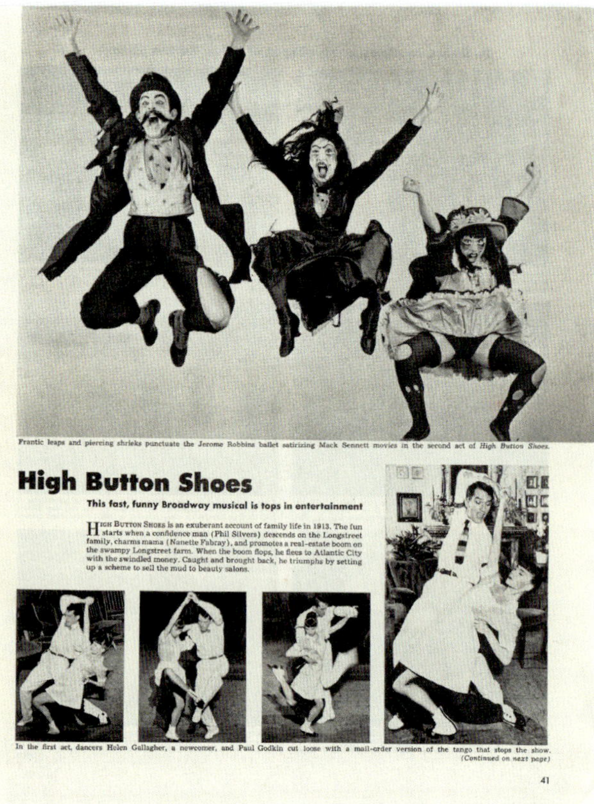

Frantic leaps and piercing shrieks punctuate the Jerome Robbins ballet satirizing Mack Sennett movies in the second act of *High Button Shoes.*

High Button Shoes

This fast, funny Broadway musical is tops in entertainment

HIGH BUTTON SHOES is an exuberant account of family life in 1913. The fun starts when a confidence man (Phil Silvers) descends on the Longstreet family, charms mama (Nanette Fabray), and promotes a real-estate boom on the swampy Longstreet farm. When the boom flops, he flees to Atlantic City with the swindled money. Caught and brought back, he triumphs by setting up a scheme to sell the mud to beauty salons.

In the first act, dancers Helen Gallagher, a newcomer, and Paul Godkin cut loose with a mail-order version of the tango that stops the show.

(Continued on next page)

41

PUBLISHED AS

HIGH BUTTON SHOES: FAST, FUNNY MUSICAL IS TOP ENTERTAINMENT

DATE

DECEMBER 9, 1947

Kubrick contributed the lead photograph to this article about the new Broadway musical *High Button Shoes*. Shot in a studio, the photograph depicted dancers performing a frantic ballet, choreographed by Jerome Robbins, that satirized the films of Mack Sennett. *Look*'s Bob Hansen took the article's photographs of the cast on stage.

OPPOSITE **Performers posing as they mimed the musical's second-act dance routine**

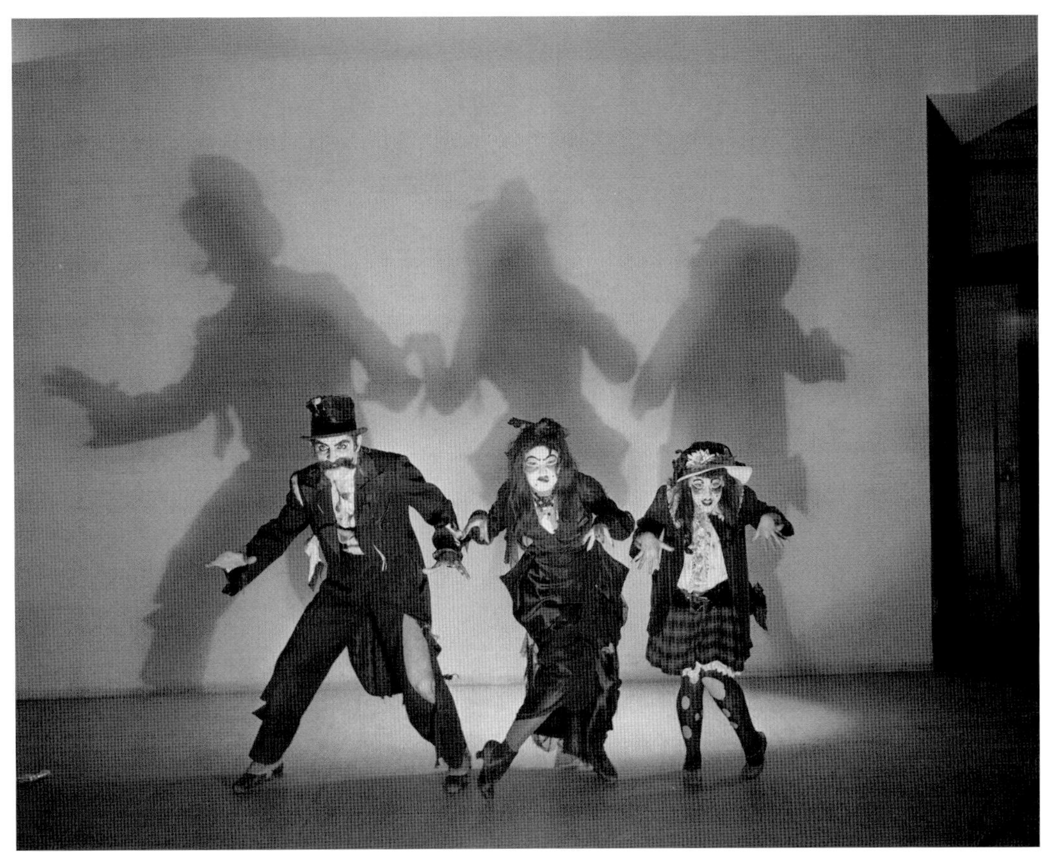

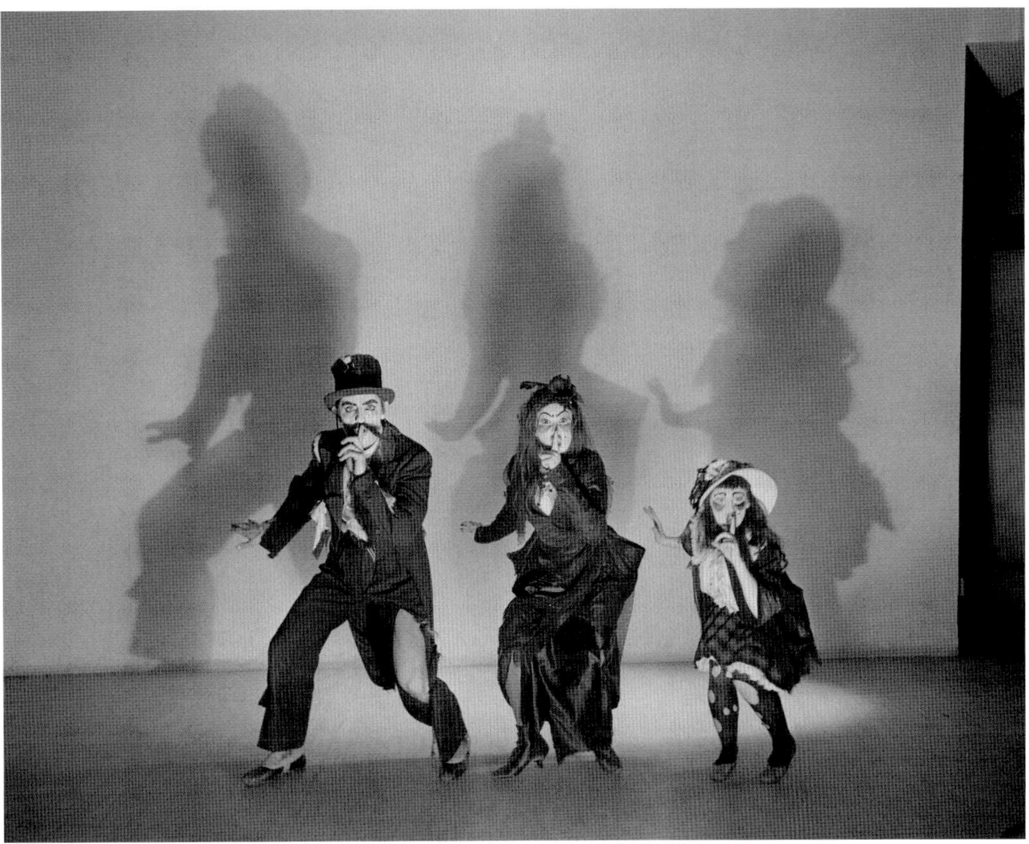

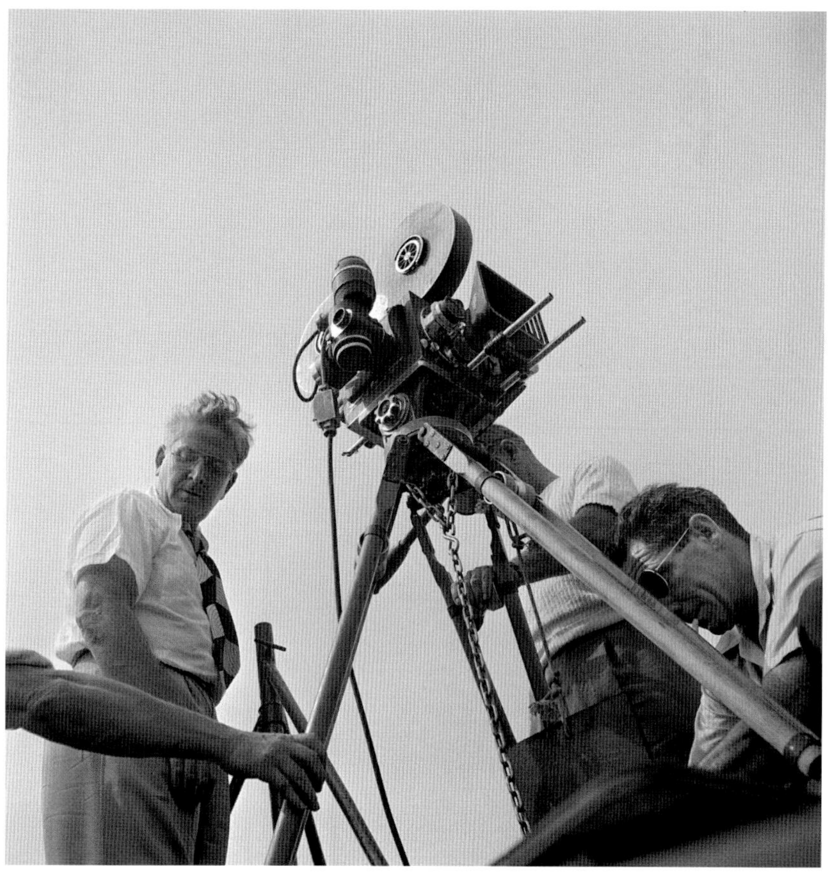

[UNPUBLISHED]

NAKED CITY

[FILED DATE]

JULY 31, 1947

No Kubrick assignment for *Look* so perfectly synchronized his personal and professional interests as this project, shot outdoors on the set of the 1948 Hollywood crime thriller The *Naked City*. The film's aesthetic was inspired by the gritty tabloid photographs of Weegee, a photographer Kubrick greatly admired, who served as a consultant to the filmmakers. Weegee's sensationalist book of New York street photographs, *Naked City* (1945), also provided the film's title. Directed by Jules Dassin, The *Naked City* was the first major American movie shot mostly on real locations in many decades. Infatuated with contemporary film noirs like The *Naked City*, Kubrick later made two films, *Killer's Kiss* (1955) and *The Killing* (1956), in that dark, stylized aesthetic.

Cinematographer William H. Daniels (left) preparing to film a scene

OPPOSITE **New Yorkers watching the filming on location, a novelty in 1947**

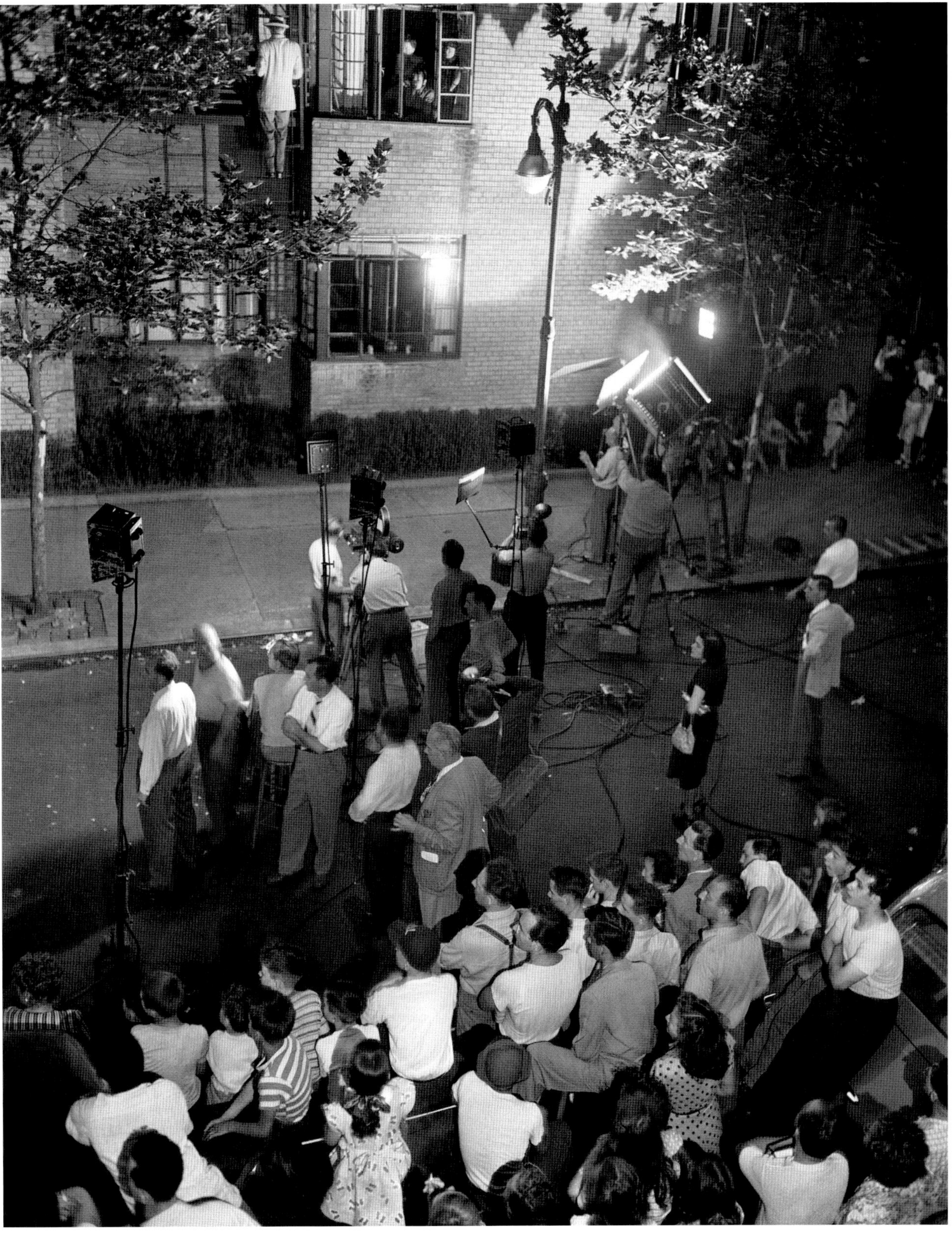

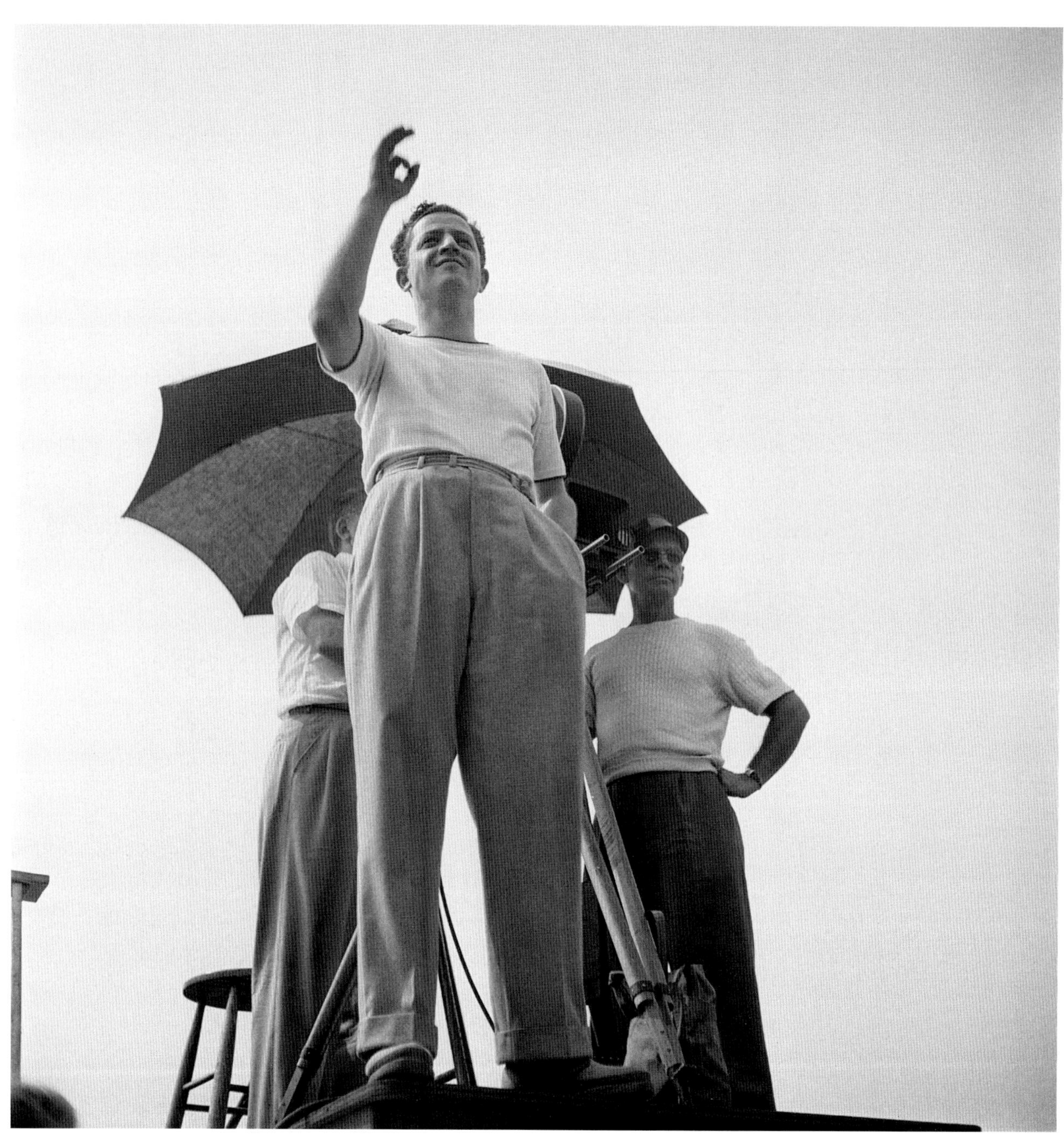

Director Jules Dassin giving the OK

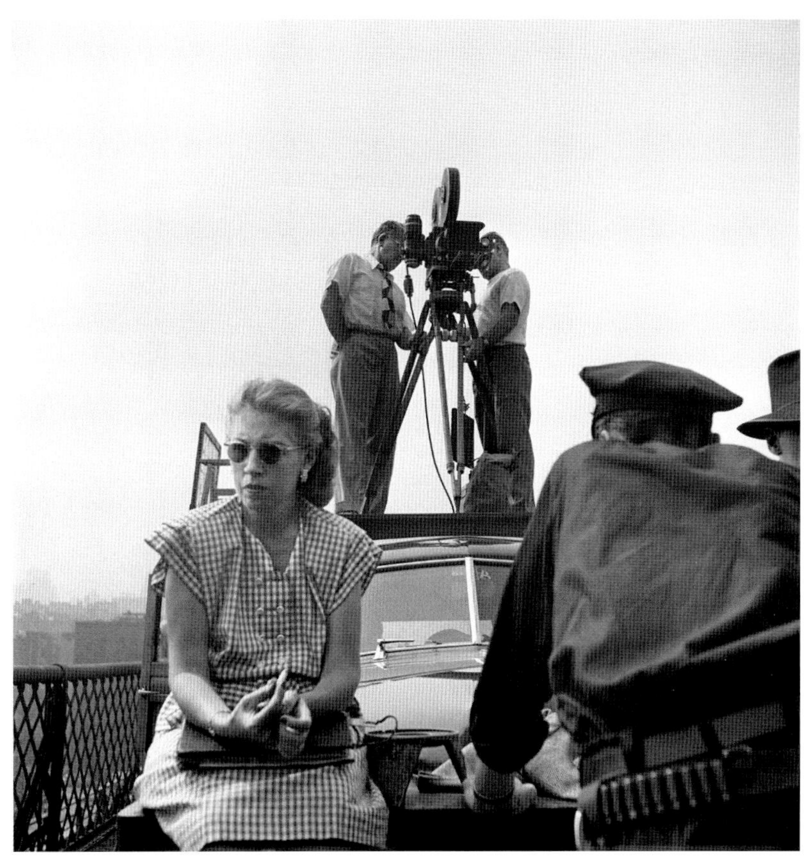

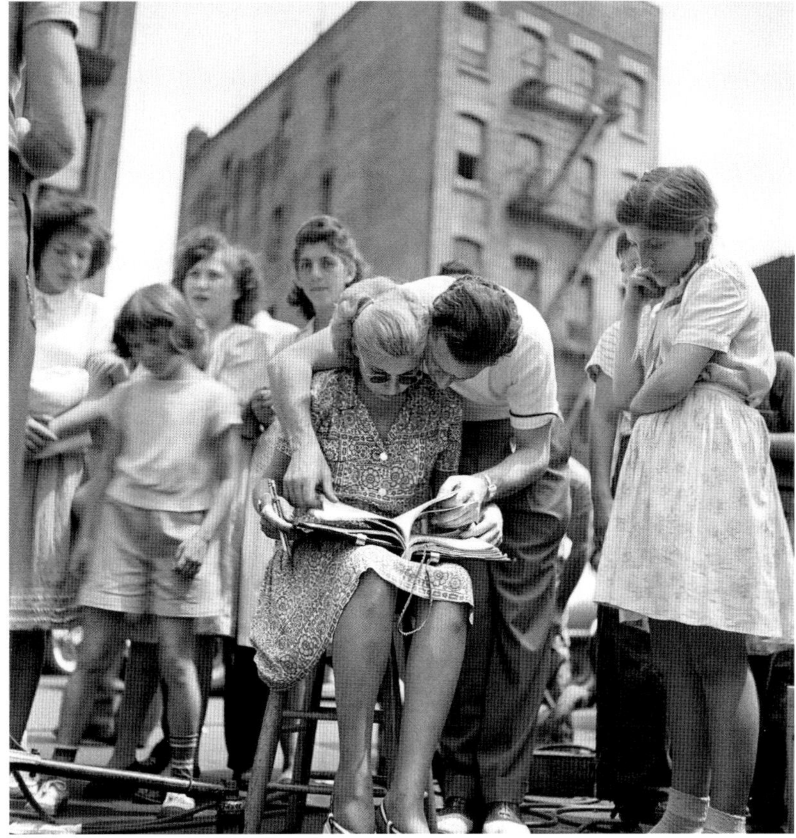

On the set

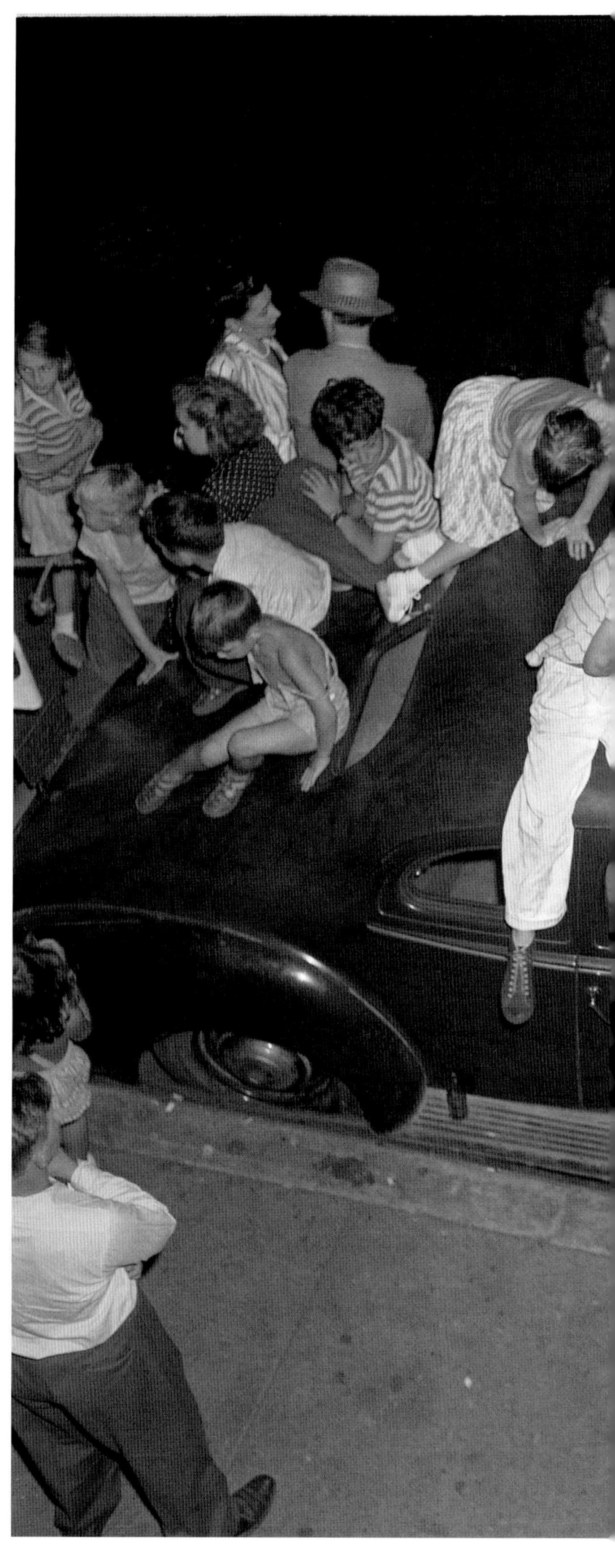

New Yorkers climbing on a car to get a better view of the action

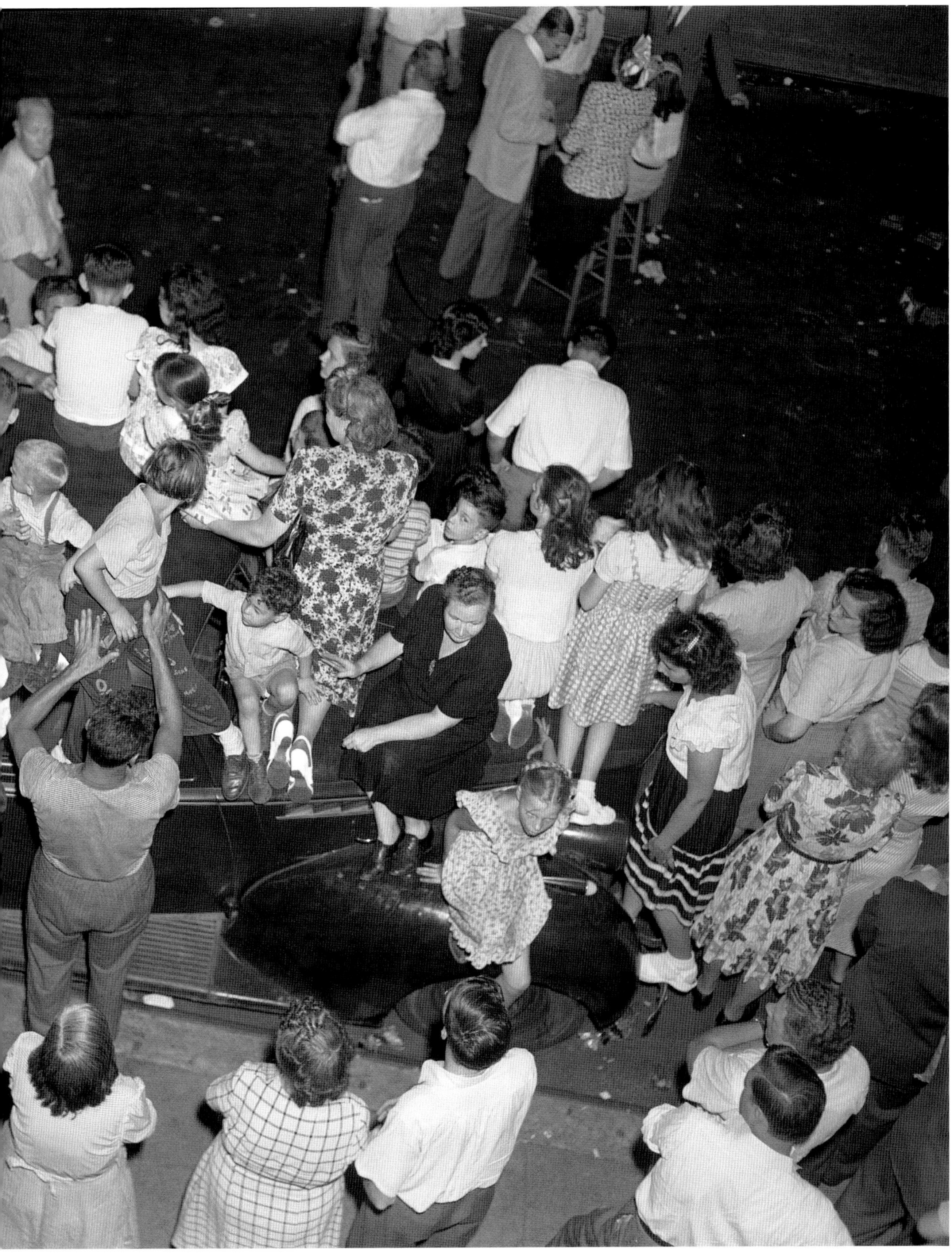

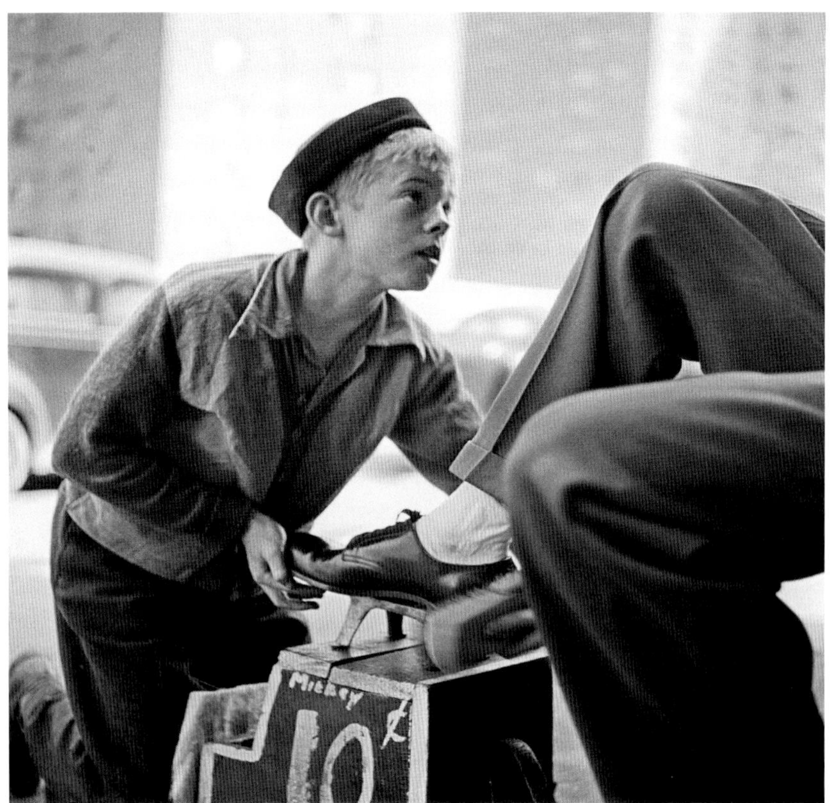

[UNPUBLISHED]

SHOESHINE BOY

[FILED DATE]

OCTOBER 6, 1947

One of the earliest narrative assignments Kubrick created for *Look* magazine was this series of photographs of Mickey, a shoeshine boy. Kubrick shot more than 250 photographs that closely followed Mickey through the course of a day: Mickey at school, doing chores, and on the streets hustling for business. He was also shown engaged in the typical activities of a child his age: playing sports, hanging around with friends, and raising pigeons on his roof. By photographing Mickey with his many brothers and sisters, Kubrick provided the context for why the boy worked so hard. The collection of images, which weren't published at the time, presented a complex portrait of a young man balancing adult responsibilities and childhood pleasures.

Mickey at work

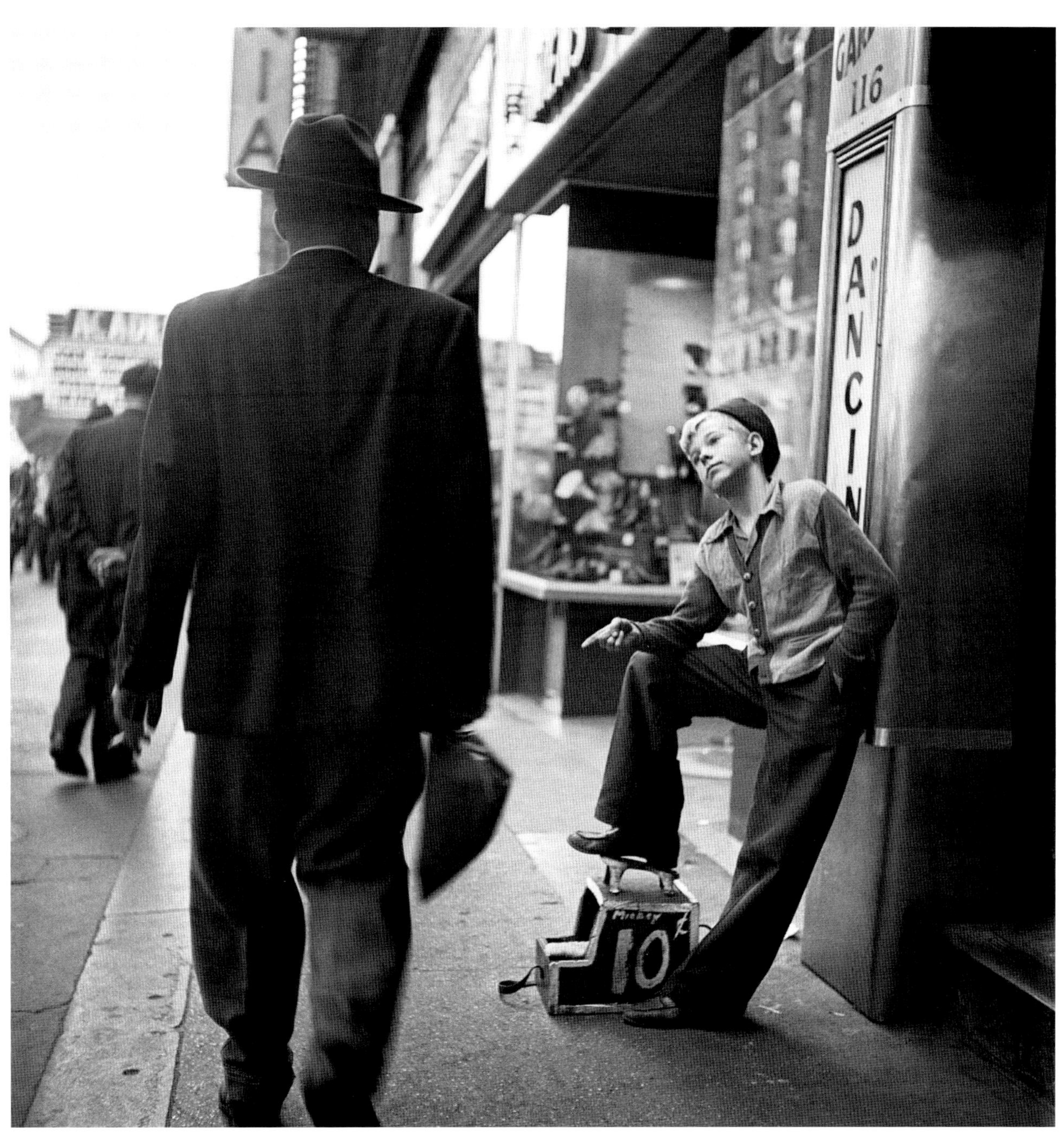

Mickey trying to drum up business

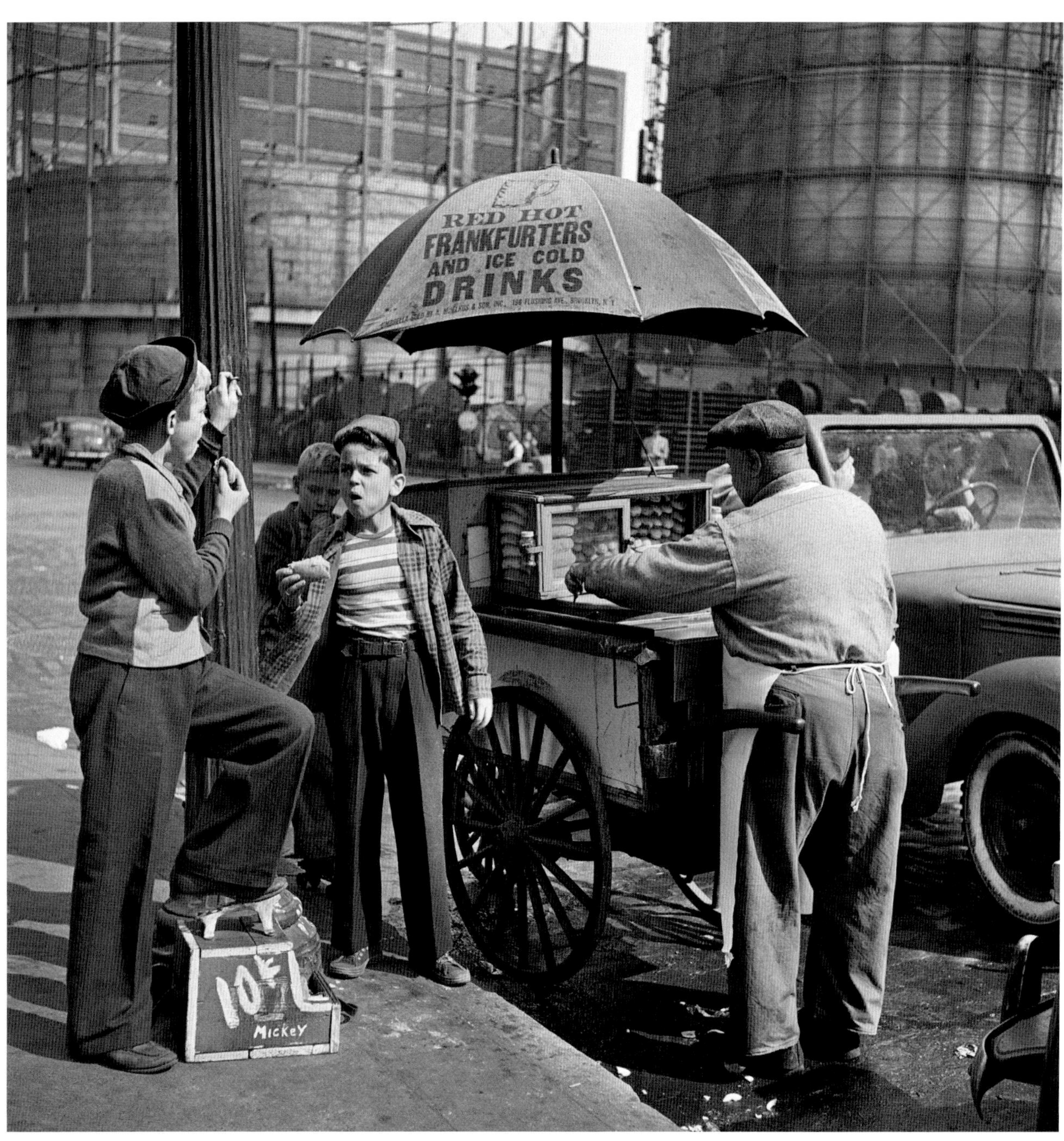

Mickey hanging out with friends

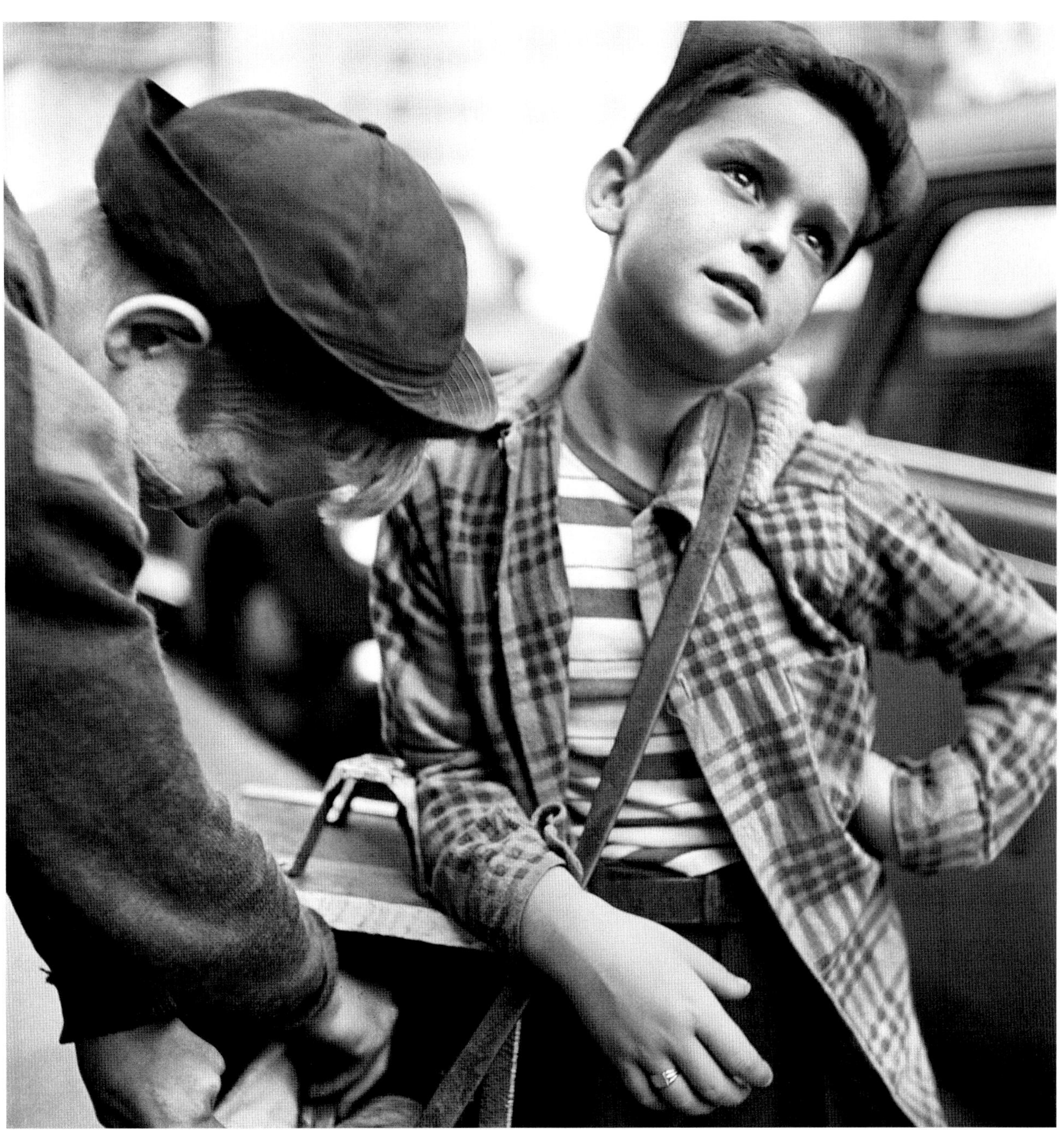

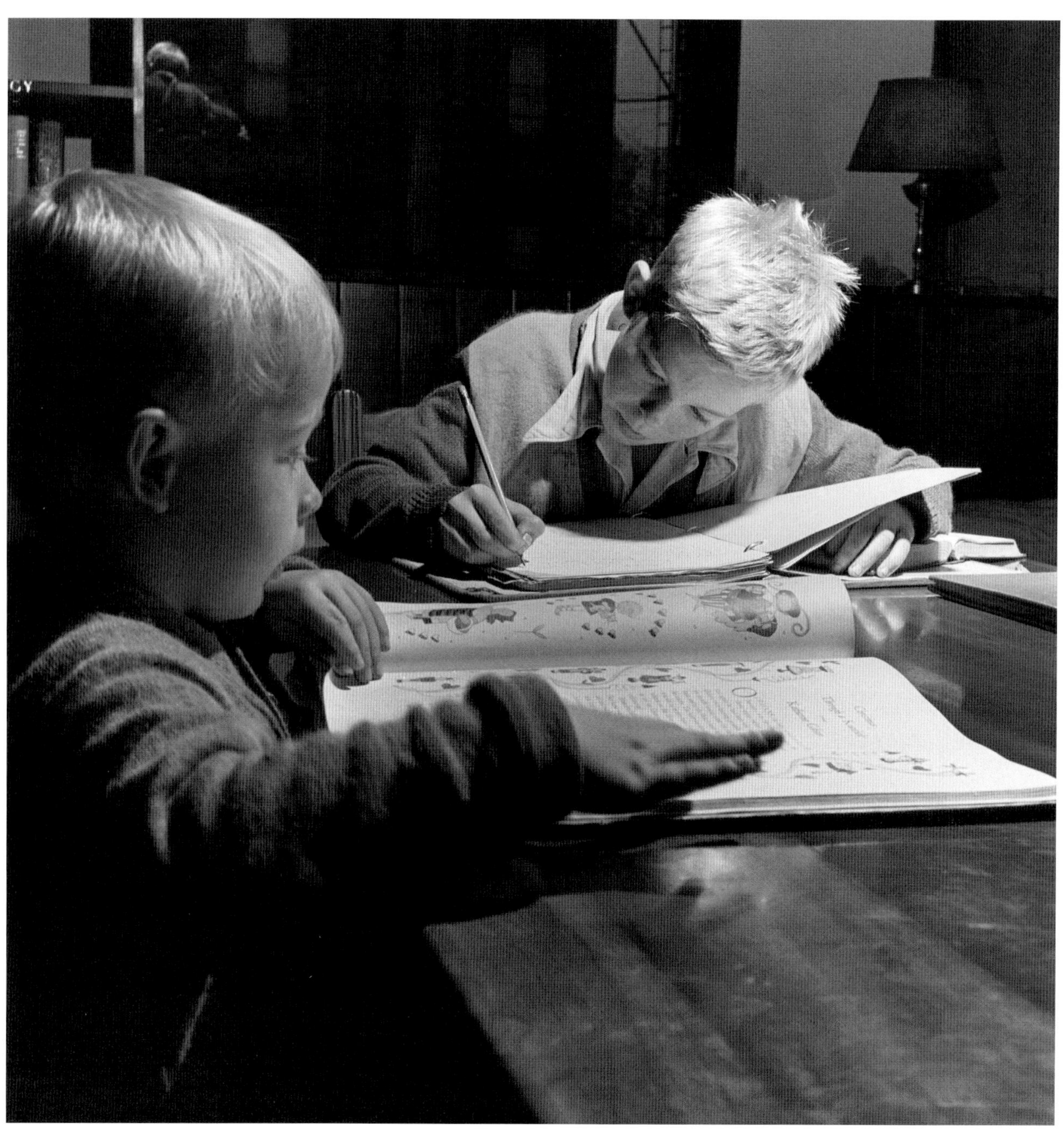

Mickey doing his homework

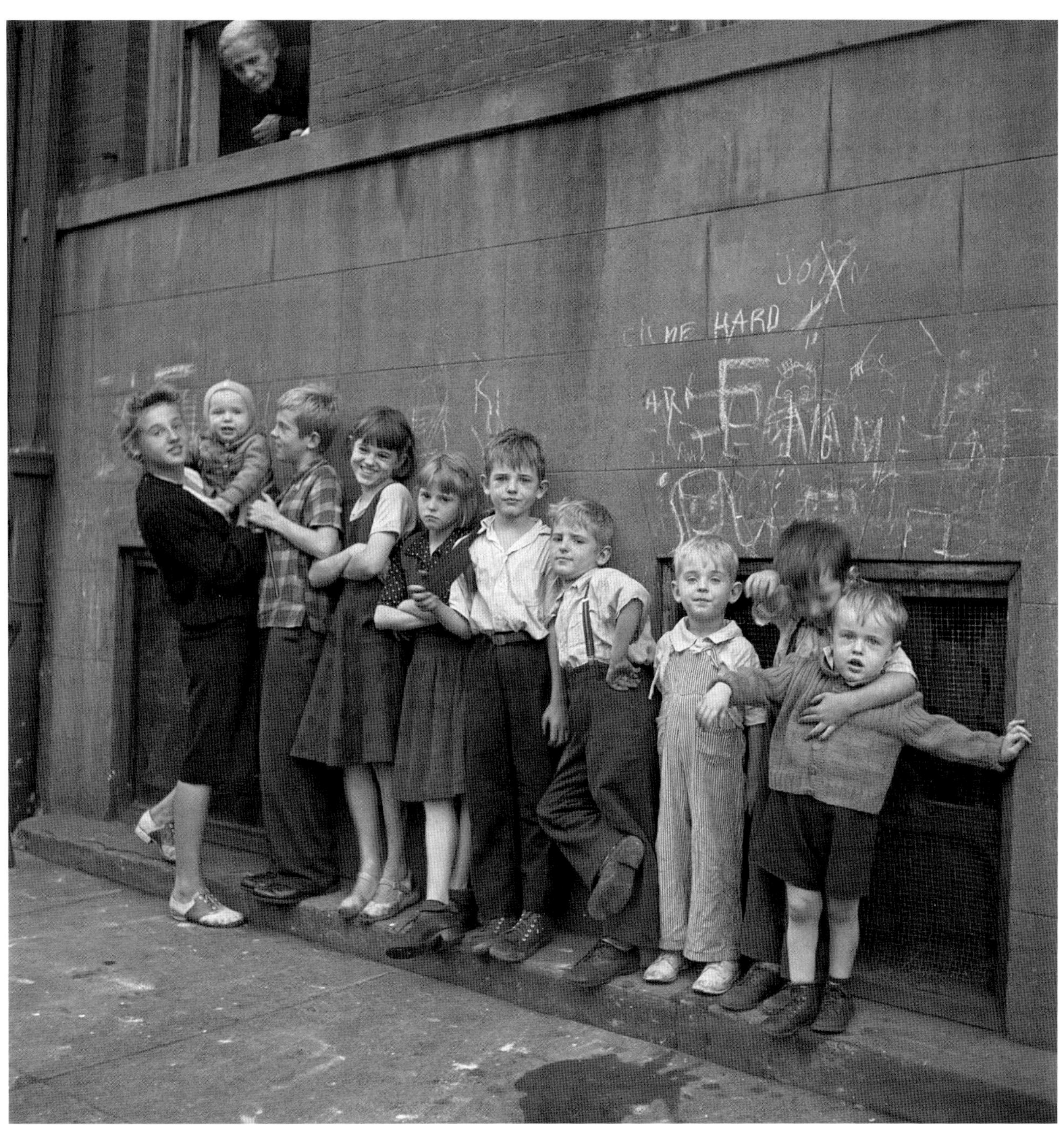

Mickey posing with his family

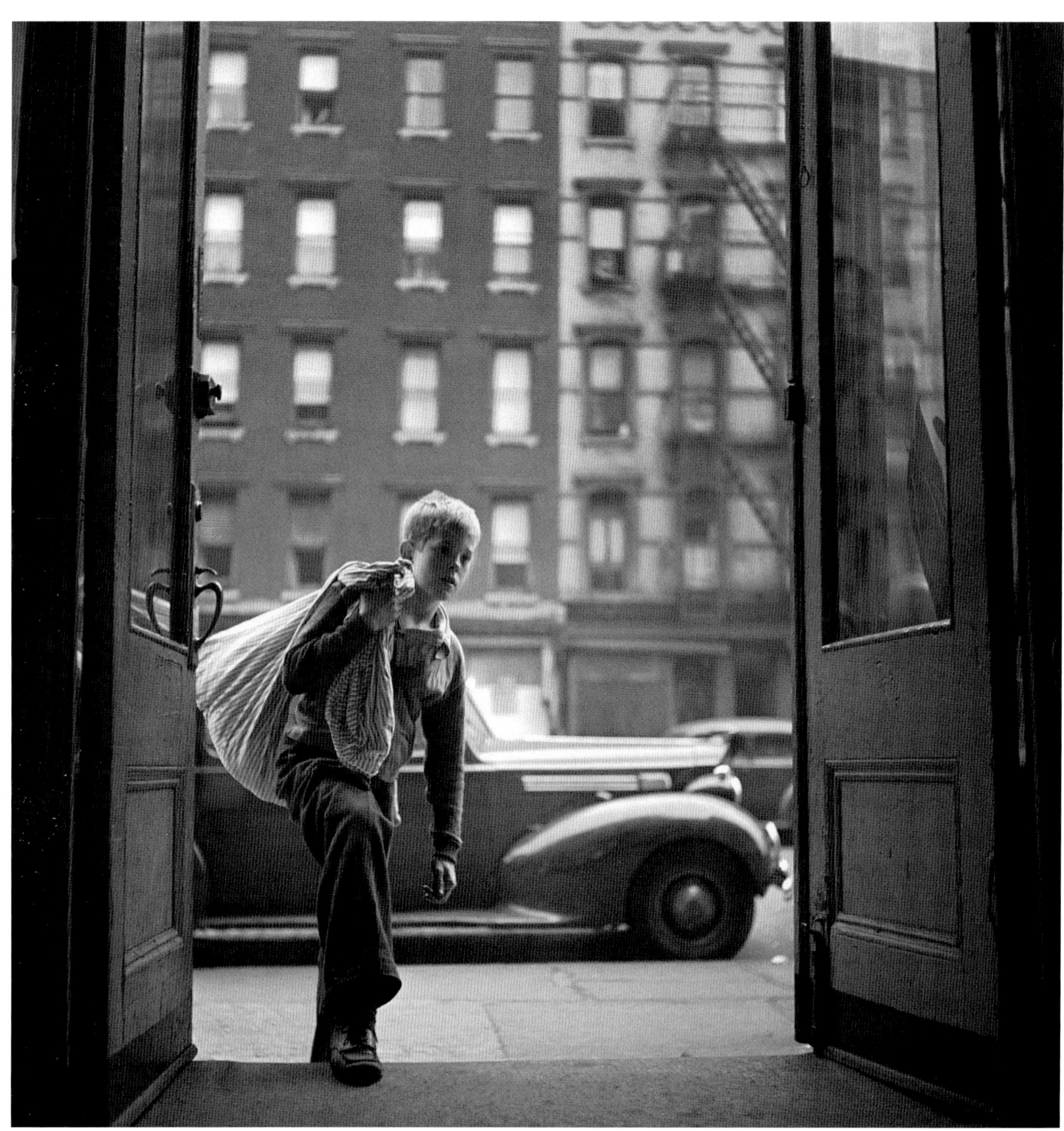

Mickey going to the laundry

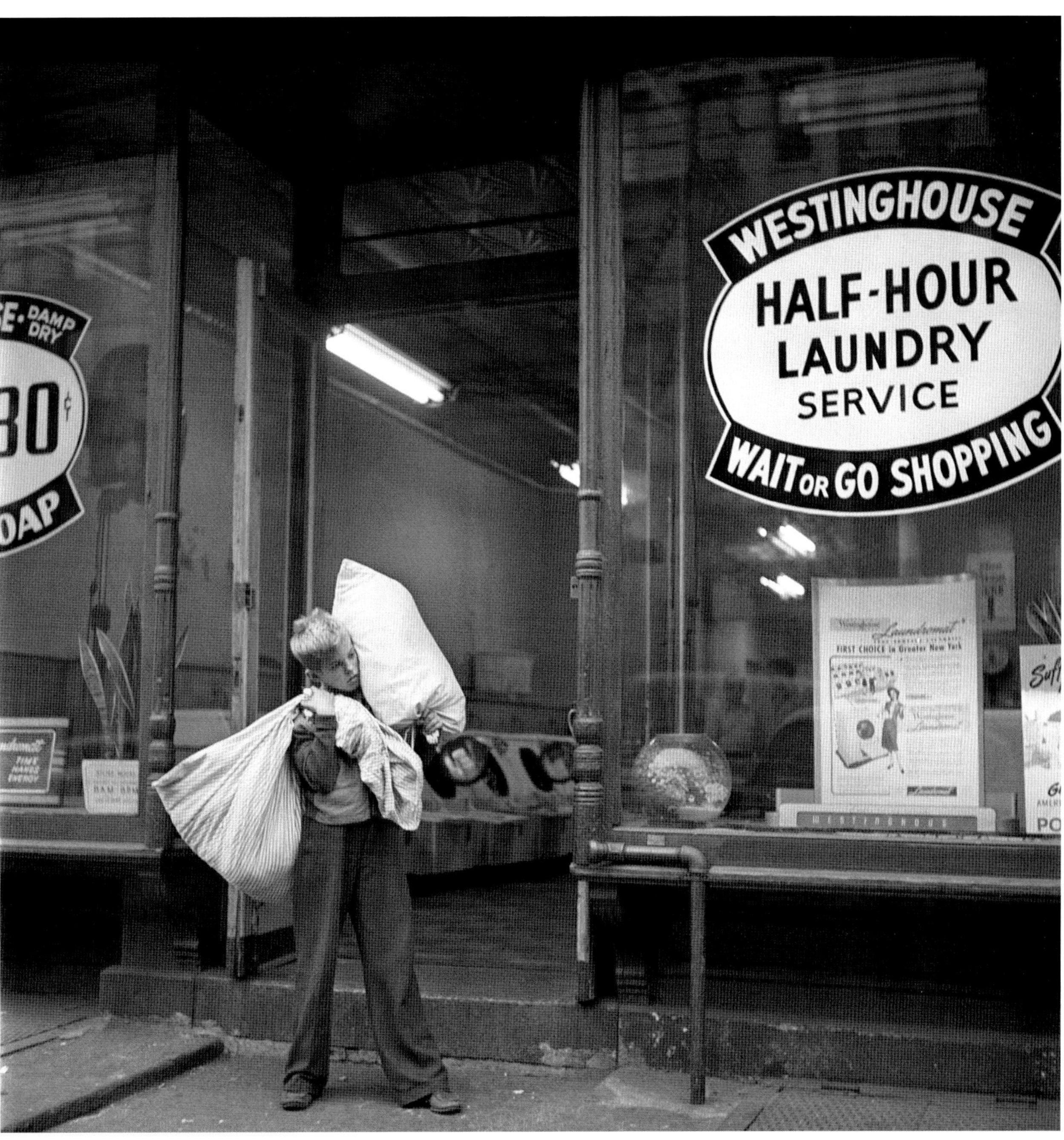
WESTINGHOUSE
HALF-HOUR
LAUNDRY
SERVICE
WAIT OR GO SHOPPING
FIRST CHOICE in Greater New York

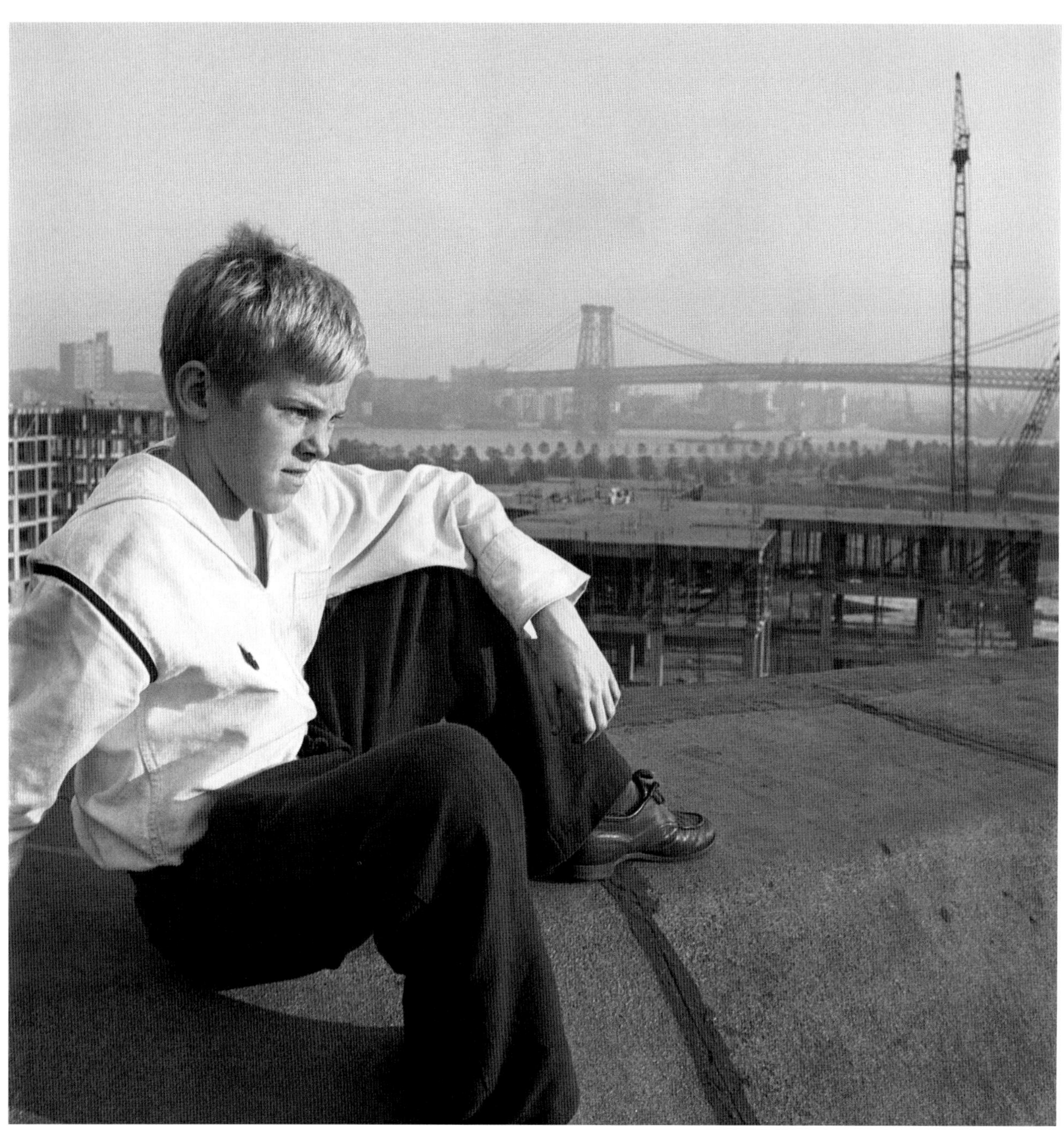

Mickey posing on the roof of his building, where he raises pigeons

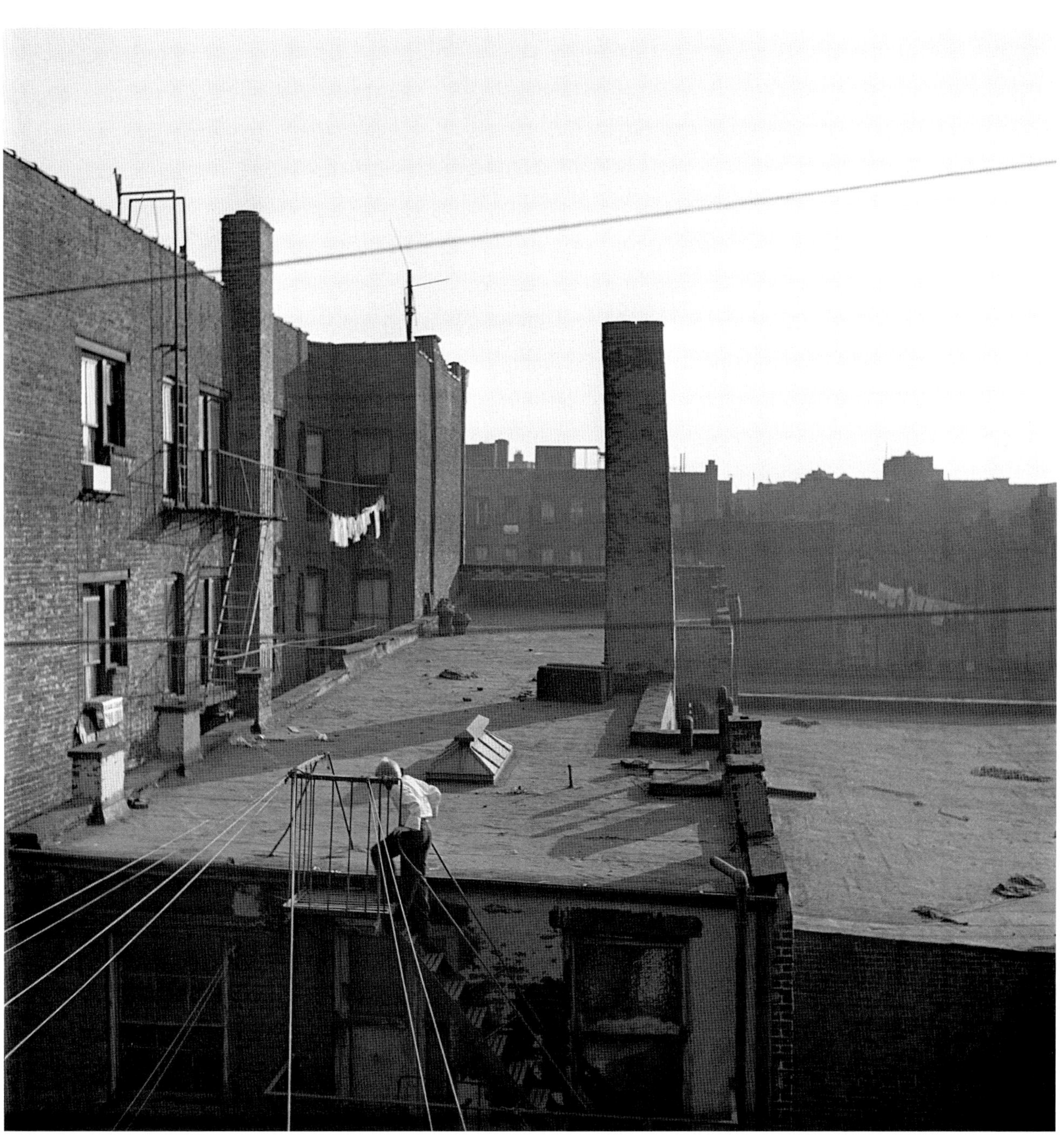

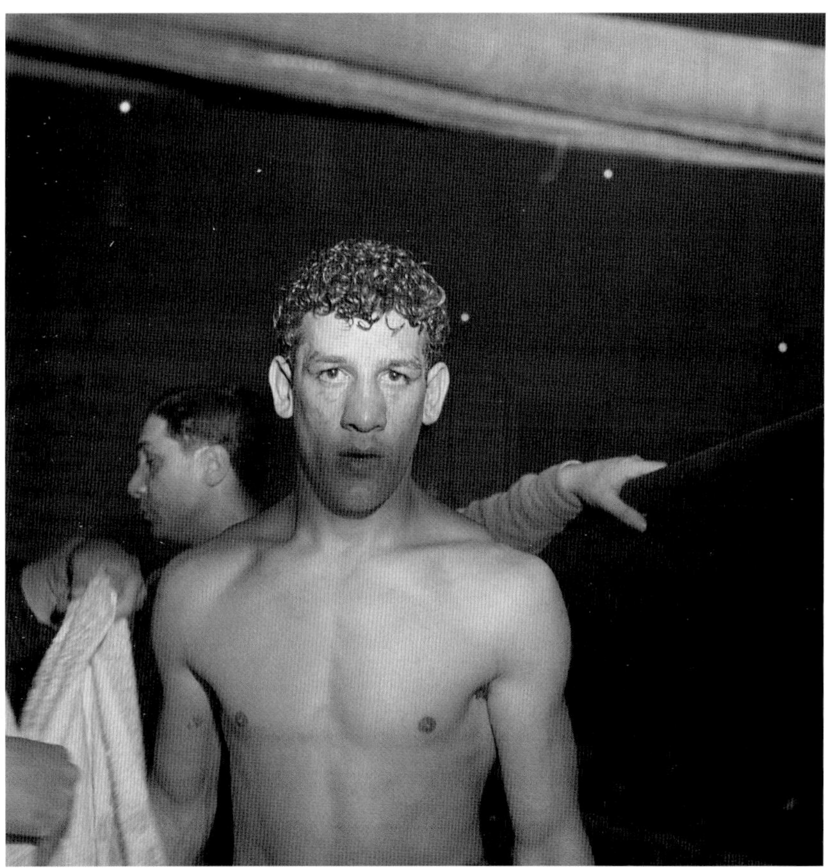

[UNPUBLISHED]

BOBBY RUFFIN AND WILLIE BELTRAM

[FILED DATE]

OCTOBER/NOVEMBER 1947

In late fall 1947, lightweight boxers Bobby Ruffin and Willie Beltram had two fights in quick succession. Beltram took the first bout at St. Nicholas Arena in Manhattan on November 4, but lost the follow-up match the pair headlined on December 1 at the Eastern Parkway Arena in Brownsville, Brooklyn. These images of the battered pugilists were Kubrick's first experience photographing boxers, but they would continue to be a subject of interest in his work at *Look* and in his early filmmaking.

Unpublished portraits of Willie Beltram, among Kubrick's earliest photographs of boxers

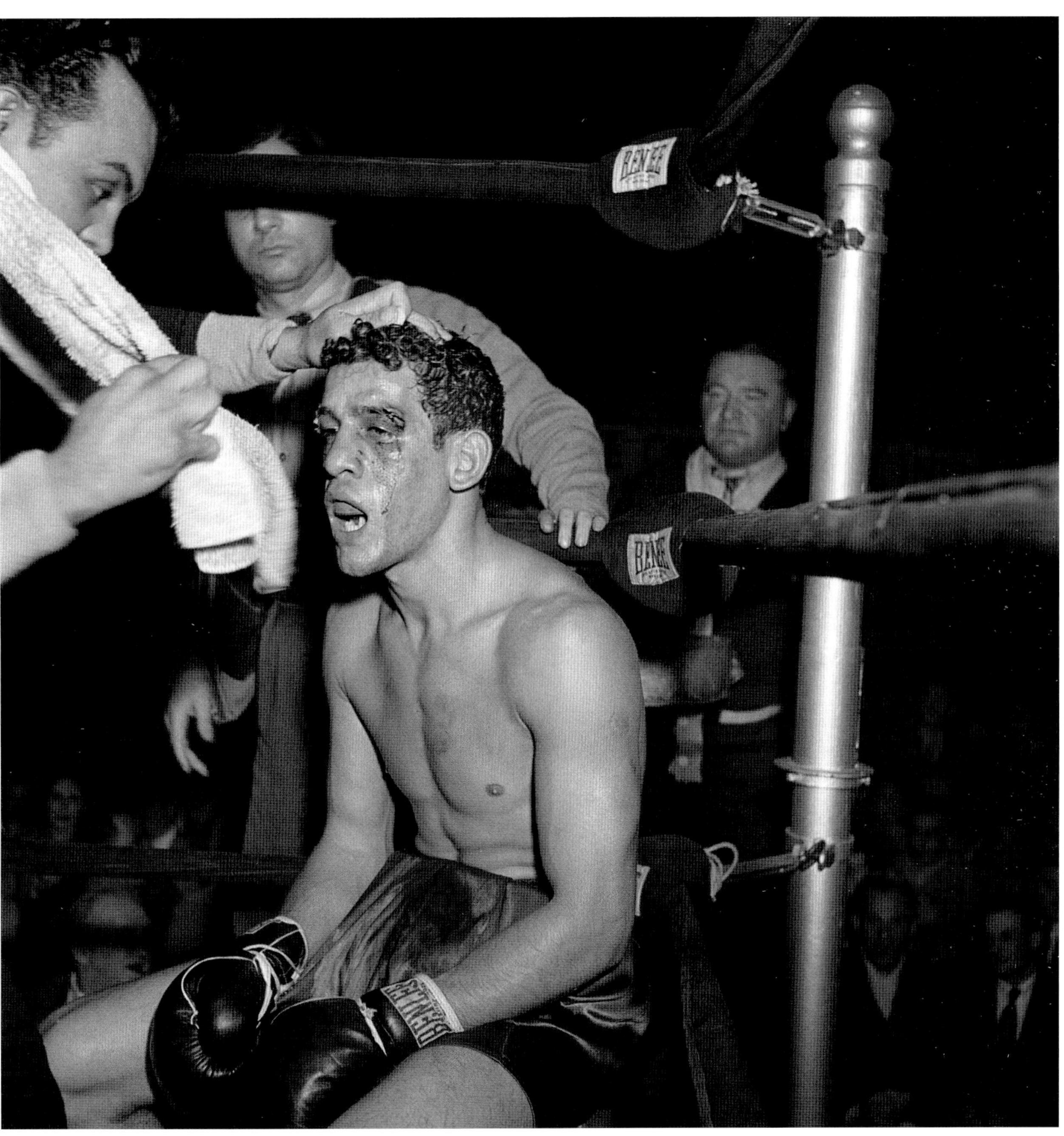

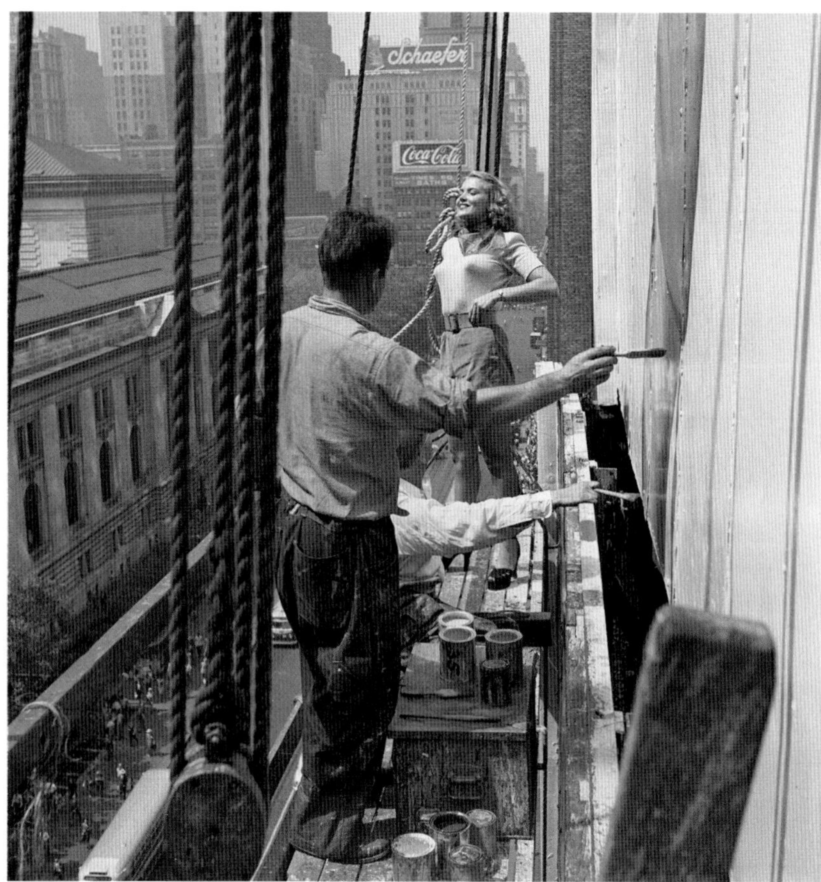

[UNPUBLISHED]

ADVERTISING SIGN PAINTERS AT WORK

[FILED DATE]

SEPTEMBER 3, 1947

Kubrick shared this unpublished assignment with two other photographers, Frank Bauman and Tom Weber. The photographers documented a publicity stunt performed by sign painters and a live female model as they created a billboard for a Peter Pan bra advertisement high above the corner of Fifth Avenue and 42nd Street. Kubrick shot close-ups of pedestrians on the street watching the event with responses ranging from befuddlement to amusement; Bauman captured the model and painters from the billboard scaffolding; and Weber, standing on the street, photographed the impromptu urban spectacle from a distance.

Look's **Frank Bauman photographed the billboard painters and live model at work above 42nd Street and Fifth Avenue.**

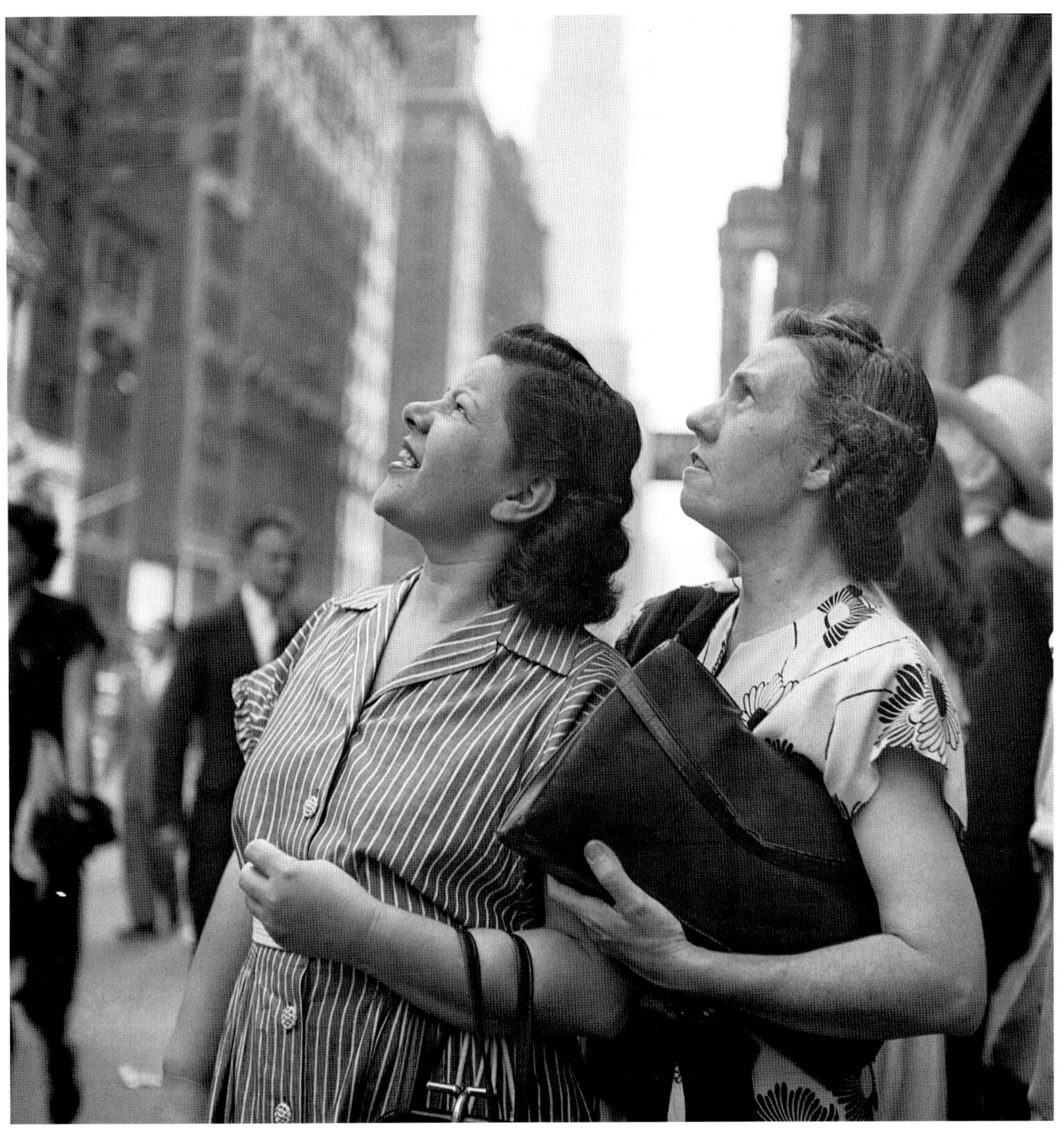

ABOVE AND FOLLOWING SPREAD
For this assignment, Kubrick contributed photographs of onlookers' reactions to the spectacle above.

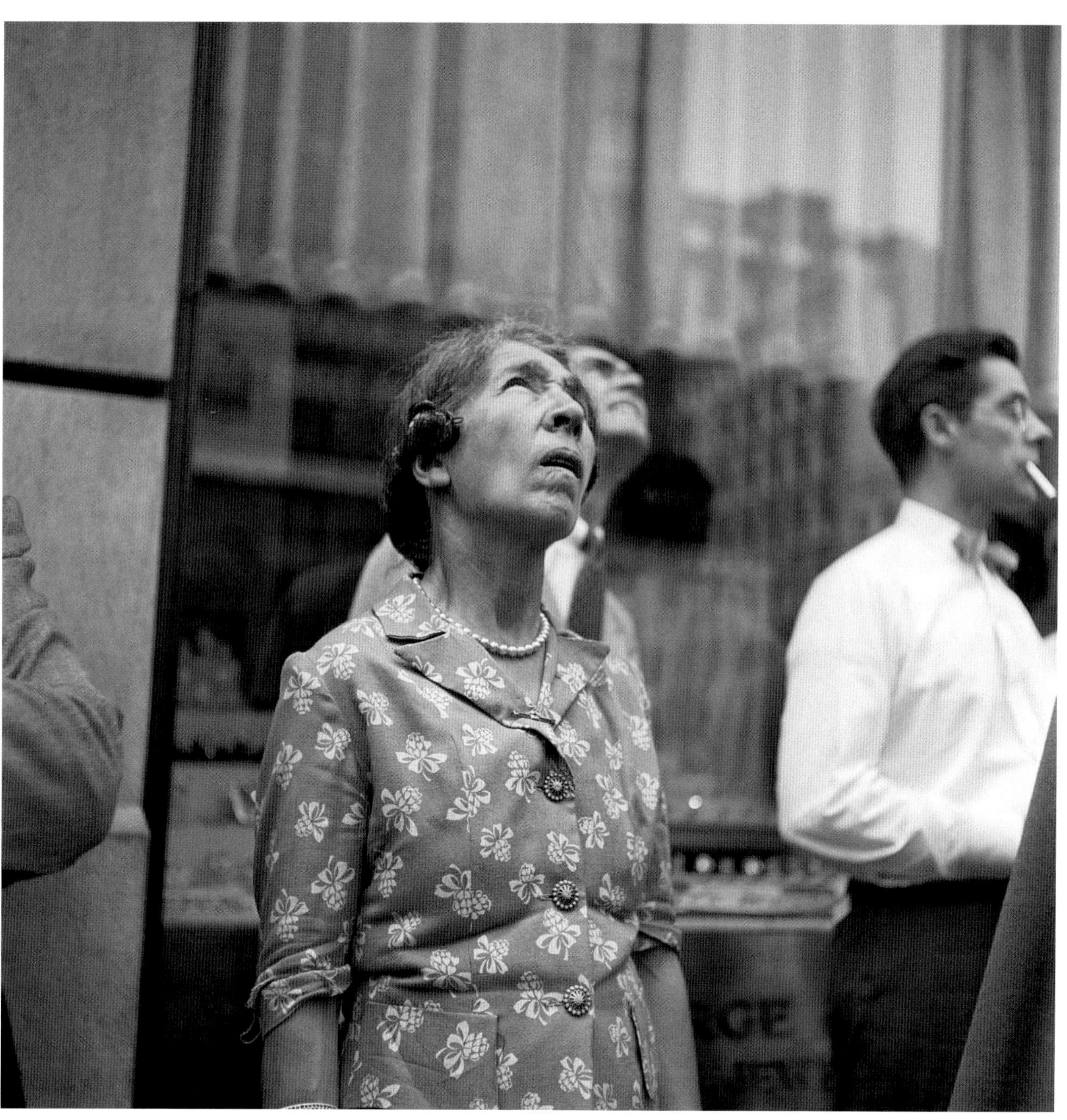

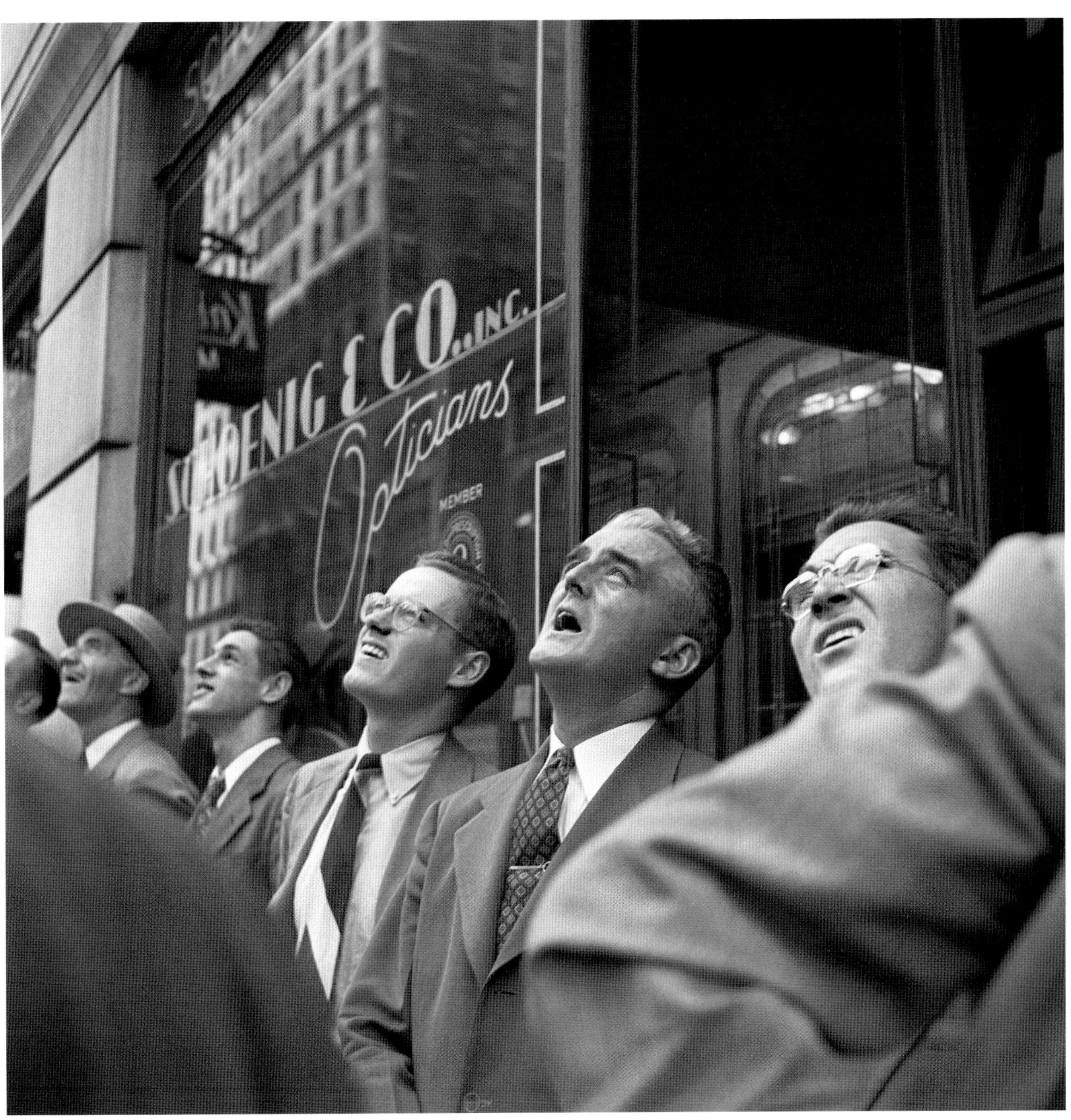
OENIG & CO., INC.
Opticians
MEMBER

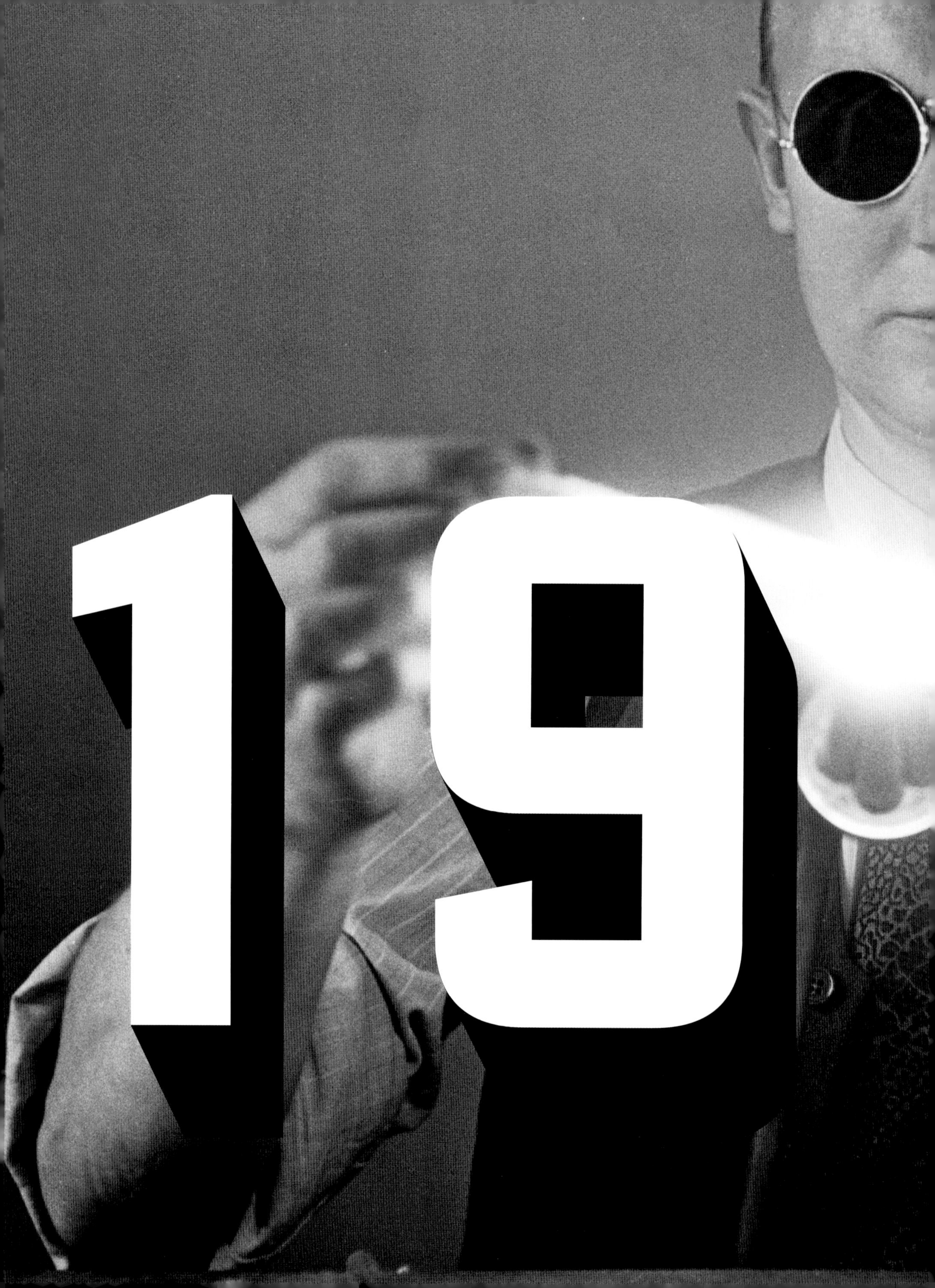
19

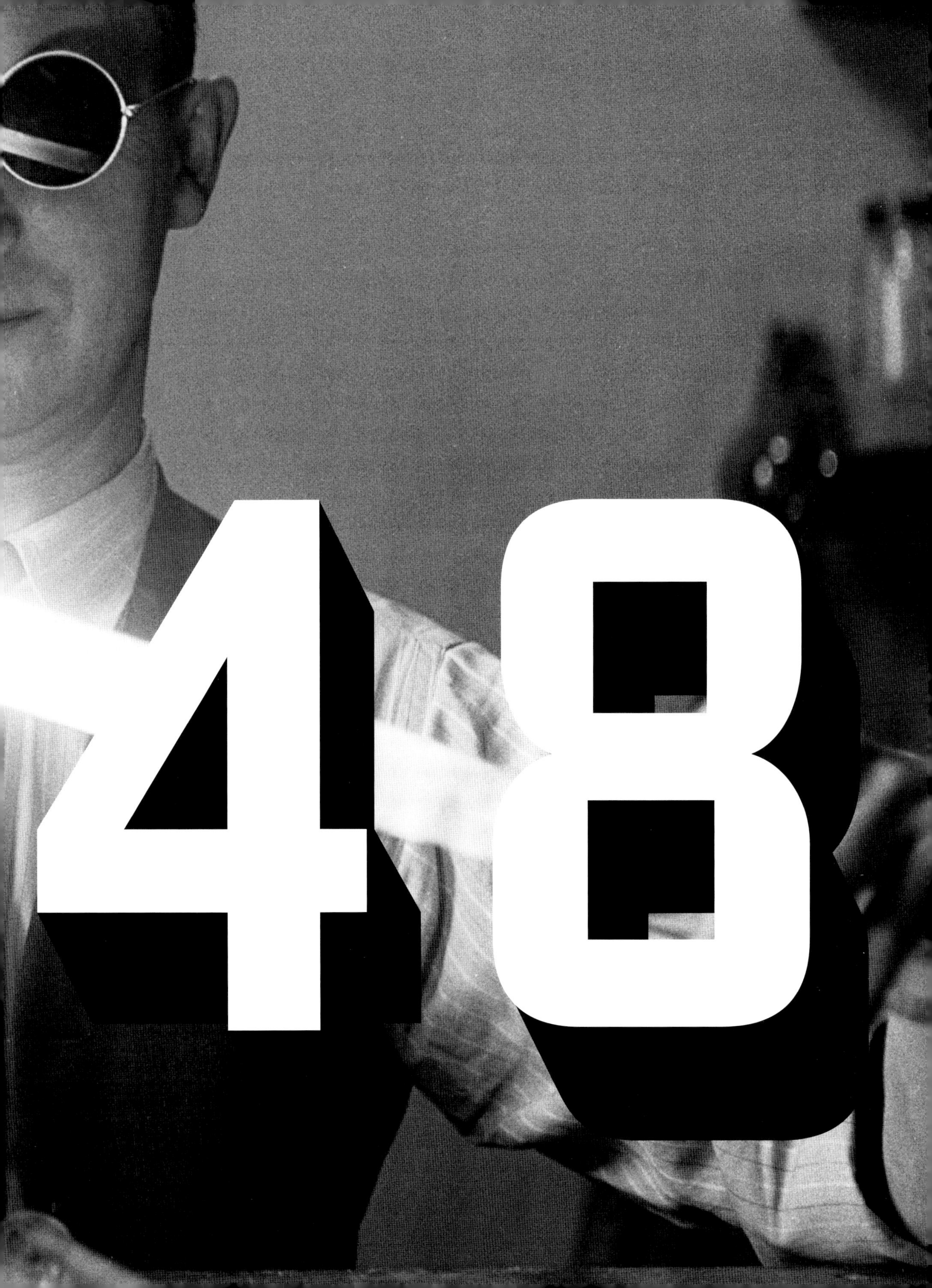
48

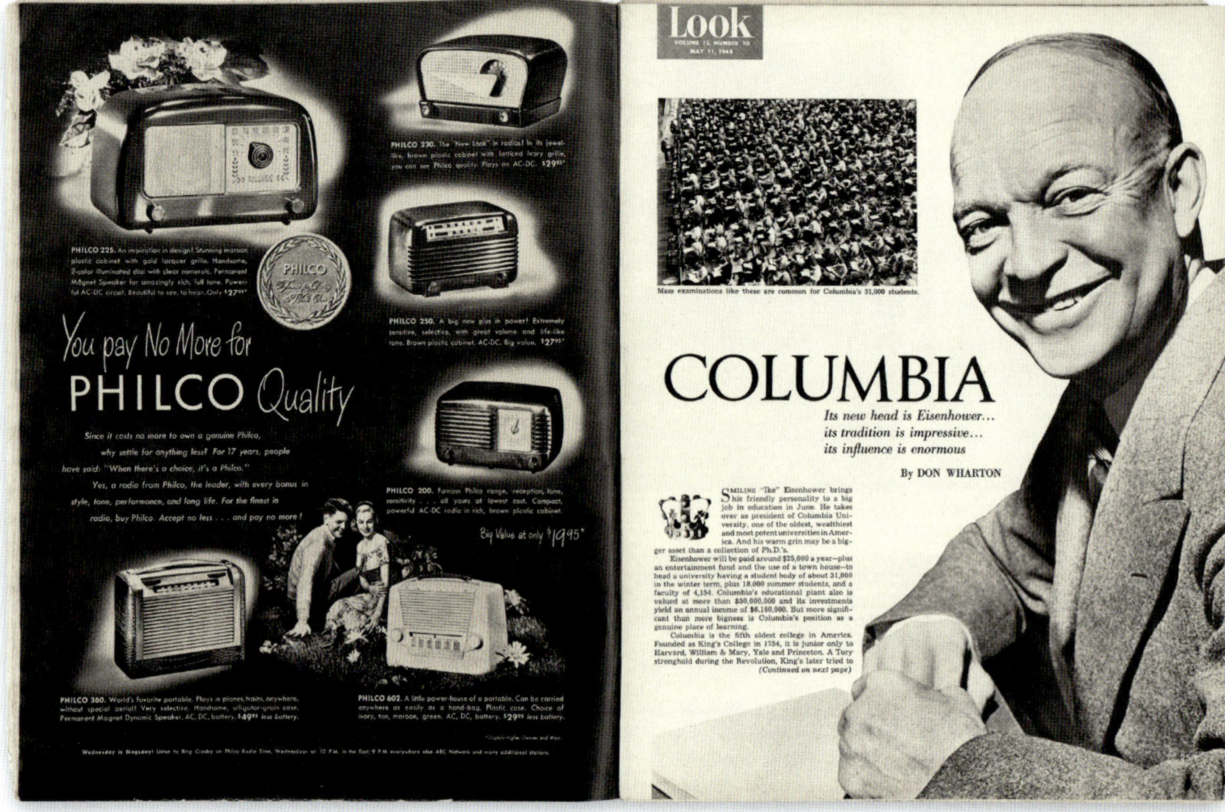

Look
VOLUME 12, NUMBER 10
MAY 11, 1948

Mass examinations like these are common for Columbia's 31,000 students.

COLUMBIA

Its new head is Eisenhower... its tradition is impressive... its influence is enormous

By DON WHARTON

Smiling "Ike" Eisenhower brings his friendly personality to a big job in education in June. He takes over as president of Columbia University, one of the oldest, wealthiest and most potent universities in America. And his warm grin may be a bigger asset than a collection of Ph.D.'s.

Eisenhower will be paid around $25,000 a year—plus an entertainment fund and the use of a town house—to head a university having a student body of about 31,000 in the winter term, plus 18,000 summer students, and a faculty of 4,154. Columbia's educational plant also is valued at more than $50,000,000 and its investments yield an annual income of $6,180,000. But more significant than mere bigness is Columbia's position as a genuine place of learning.

Columbia is the fifth oldest college in America. Founded as King's College in 1754, it is junior only to Harvard, William & Mary, Yale and Princeton. A Tory stronghold during the Revolution, King's later tried to

(Continued on next page)

PUBLISHED AS

COLUMBIA UNIVERSITY

DATE

MAY 11, 1948

AUTHOR

DON WHARTON

Written on the occasion of Dwight D. Eisenhower's assumption of Columbia University's presidency, this story opened with Kubrick's portrait of the World War II general and war hero, followed by an extensive essay by Don Wharton about the academic and social life on the Columbia campus. The article was illustrated with photographs of students in their dormitories and recreation centers, in art classes drawing nude models, and sitting in lecture halls. It also featured scientific research being conducted on campus (including aspects of the Manhattan Project), along with the medical and law schools. Kubrick, who was roughly the same age as many of the students, documented a complex education institution. Kubrick returned to this subject in "Mooseheart—The Child City" (published June 8, 1948) and "University of Michigan" (published May 10, 1949) in a compelling way that captured personal, sometimes intimate, moments within the institutional setting.

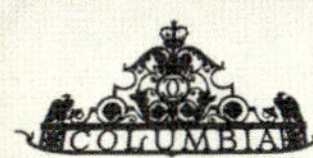

Columbia's faculty likes to say "the best in brains are here"

bia's courses are tough and the remarkable job the college does in picking its students is shown by what happened last fall: Out of 650 freshmen, only 19 had their pictures flashed on the screen; and, after study, only ten of these had to be put on probation. A mere 1½ per cent.

Last year, 250 out of 500 seniors had grades that made them eligible for Phi Beta Kappa. Three out of four Columbia graduates continue their studies in professional or graduate schools. Fraternities exist at Columbia but mean little. A student can't get too excited about dragging a girl to a fraternity house when, if he has the money, he can take her to the Stork Club or a Broadway hit. Girls aren't imported from the Smiths and Vassars for dances. As one football player puts it: "New York's got plenty of girls." Athletics are taken in stride and rarely does the Joe College spirit rear its head. Exceptions include Columbia's one Rose Bowl victory in 1934 when Columbia students wrecked an establishment or two on upper Broadway.

In the early years, prominent alumni were abundant: Alexander Hamilton, John Jay, Robert Livingston, DeWitt Clinton, John Stevens, Gouverneur Morris. Then came a century of inconspicuous alumni. Finally, in the 1880's, Columbia again began producing some outstanding men: Benjamin Cardozo, Michael Pupin and Butler himself.

Around two miles from the Columbia campus is one of New York's largest groups of related buildings: the Columbia-Presbyterian Medical Center. Here are joined in unique combination Presbyterian Hospital, with resources of more than $66,000,000, and the Columbia Faculty of Medicine. This faculty operates not simply a medical college but what might better be termed a medical university. One part is the famed College of Physicians and Surgeons; other parts include dental and oral surgery, public health and nursing. The work is for both graduates and undergraduates, and all the facilities are integrated under one faculty—at the faculty rather than the administrative level.

Its Medical School Is Small

It is ironical that, while Columbia is derided for being so large, its medical school is criticized for being so small. Many medical schools in the United States are much larger. But it is doubtful if any is better. Each year P & S admits 110 students who, by graduation time four years later, are reduced to a neat 100. The job of picking these 110 is one of the toughest in educational selection. For years, more than 1,500 men have applied annually. Last year 2,200 applied and today the applications for the next first-year class already total over 4,000. P & S gets the job done by first weeding out the unqualified and then weeding out the ones whose academic standings aren't high enough to be attractive. This reduces 2,200 to 500—picked men, though actually only about one in five of them can get in. The final 110 are picked from this group, by interview, with primary consideration not given to grades but to personality, character and resourcefulness.

Students in School of General Studies art class study elementary anatomy and figure drawing from life.

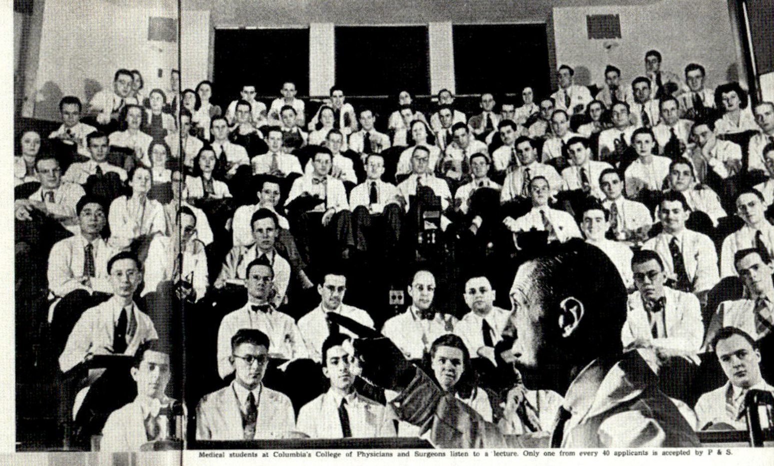

Medical students at Columbia's College of Physicians and Surgeons listen to a lecture. Only one from every 40 applicants is accepted by P & S.

Each of the lucky 110 receives what amounts to a $10,000 gift—the amount P & S pours into each man's education above and beyond what he pays in fees. Only the medical schools of Harvard, Yale and Johns Hopkins pour anything like that into a student's education. Last year, about one out of twelve New York City boys who applied were admitted, one out of thirteen New York State boys and one out of sixteen from other states.

Law School Trains Statesmen

The prestige of P & S hardly exceeds that of Columbia's Law School, certainly one of the half-dozen best in the country. Two law school alumni have become President of the United States (Theodore and Franklin Roosevelt), and two more have become Chief Justice (Hughes and Harlan Stone). Neither Roosevelt was graduated, Theodore leaving after a year and a half, Franklin failing on a course his last year. In the last 11 Presidential elections, Columbia Law School men have been nominees on eight tickets—this includes TR's Bull Moose ticket in 1912. In 1944, the Republican and Democratic tickets were headed by Columbia Law School men: Dewey and Roosevelt. At one time four members of the Supreme Court were Columbia Law School alumni: Hughes, Stone, Cardozo and Reed.

Altogether, Columbia University alumni include two presidents, two vice-presidents, three chief justices, four justices of the Supreme Court, three secretaries of state, two secretaries of the treasury and one attorney general.

About one in ten Ph.D.'s conferred in America are conferred by Columbia. This year more than 3,000 men and nearly 1,200 women are enrolled in Columbia's Graduate Faculties. This doesn't count the ones in the professional schools or the graduate students at Teachers College.

The Atomic Bomb and Columbia

The huge totals recall the day when Columbia was called "a Ph.D. factory," but that era

(Continued on next page)

Capt. Eisenhower (uniform), new president's son, attends class, will teach at West Point.

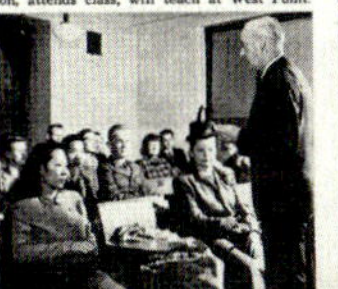

Josh Wheeler, Dallas, Texas (left), rehearses aria from *La Boheme* in Opera Workshop.

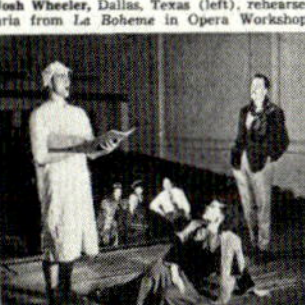

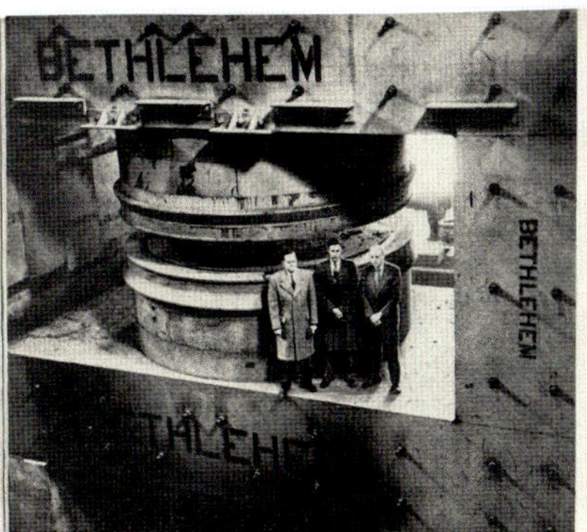

Prof. E. T. Booth (left), executive director Columbia's nuclear physics research center, stands with two other engineers on the partly finished 2,500-ton, 400-million-volt cyclotron for atom research.

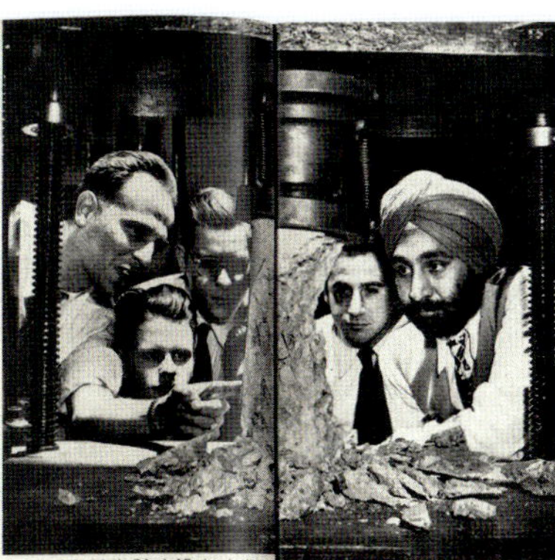

First year students in the School of Engineering listen to Instructor Nelson Fisk (left) explain what's happening in elementary compression test on block of concrete. Most technical classes at Columbia are small.

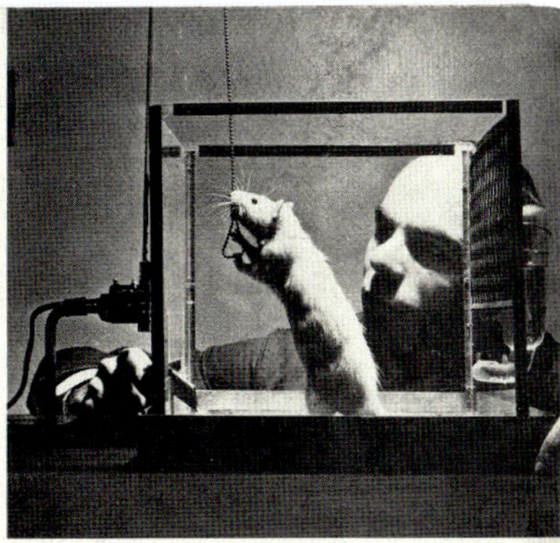

David Anderson, Columbia psychology lecturer, tries simple experiment with rat to teach it to pull chain and get food. Hundreds of men on Columbia's faculty are in some kind of research.

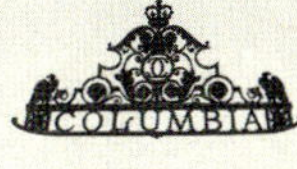

Scientific research thrives at Columbia, a center of early atomic bomb experiments

ended with the atomic bomb. Laymen, thinking of the universities' part in the bomb, are apt to think of the University of Chicago. There, at Stagg Field, Enrico Fermi and associates operated the first chain reaction pile of uranium and graphite.

But what most laymen do not realize is that Fermi was a Columbia professor; that many of his associates were Columbia professors; that they began this project at Columbia; and that they moved to Chicago because of lack of space. Space was lacking at Columbia because, there, Urey and Dunning were doing the work which led to the successful separation by gaseous diffusion of U-235 from its mixture with U-238.

But there was more. Early in 1939, Niels Bohr arrived in America with important nuclear news. In nine days, Dunning had demonstrated in Columbia's Pupin Hall the fissionable qualities of U-235. A few weeks later, Dean Pegram phoned Washington and arranged for Fermi to talk with the Navy Department. Later it was Pegram and Urey whom the government sent to England, and it was their report which stated that, if the Allies were to beat Germany to the bomb, the U. S. would have to do it. Columbia, on the scientific side, was the key university in the American development of the bomb.

Year round, the largest unit at Columbia is Teachers College. In the summer, when some 18,000 students pour onto Morningside Heights, about 12,000 of them matriculate at Teachers College. In the winter term it has more than 3,000 men and nearly 5,000 women. 90 per cent of them graduate students. No other unit has so many matriculated students. There are 9,597 in the university's School of General Studies but 8,355 of them are non-matriculated students—persons taking a course or two not for a degree but simply to add to their knowledge. This night school (also afternoon and Saturday) is one place in America where any qualified veteran can get in and get a degree.

As for Teachers College, there is nothing comparable to it in this or any other land. It not only teaches teachers to teach school and college students but also teaches teachers to teach teachers. It has courses for school superintendents, teachers of nurses and even deans of colleges. Several months ago, an employer heard a noise in a corridor. One man was complaining about not getting the proper attention. "I'm the dean of —— College," he stormed—without impressing anyone.

TC Graduates Are Everywhere

Today seven state commissioners of education are TC graduates. So are the presidents of 33 teachers colleges and the superintendents of schools in New York, Chicago, Philadelphia, Cleveland, San Francisco, Baltimore and hundreds of lesser cities. A check of six state teachers colleges shows one out of five faculty members are TC graduates. A TC professor, the late Patty Smith Hill, wrote the only song sung every day in every American state, *Happy Birthday to You.*

Across Broadway from Columbia is Barnard College, the university's school for undergraduate women. Columbia boys like to call the Barnard girls "the hens in the barnyard." But at a Columbia College dance, the "hens" usually outnumber the girls from any other college.

Barnard's academic standards are the same as those of Columbia College—high. Its girls may go to Columbia for undergraduate work in their senior year and graduate work. Some of them become well-known in the academic world—for instance, Margaret Mead, the anthropologist. But despite all Barnard's seriousness (it has no sororities, "only clubs with a purpose"), the school is perhaps best known for its movie and stage stars: Jane Wyatt, Aline MacMahon, Helen Gahagan Douglas (now Rep. from Cal.).

Of Barnard's 1,200 students, around a third come from New York City, a third from New York State, and a third from the rest of the country. It is more local than Columbia's other units. One third of the girls live in Barnard's dormitories, two thirds with relatives or friends in New York and surrounding suburbs.

Barnard, established in 1889, was one of the first girls' colleges to permit students to smoke and to give them a course in sex hygiene. Its students may stay out at night until 1:30 a.m. Today, almost every time a Barnard girl lights a cigaret she helps Barnard's treasury: The school investment portfolio includes common stock in both Reynolds (Camels) and Liggett & Myers (Chesterfields).

Columbia men are frequently asked, "Why,

(Continued on next page)

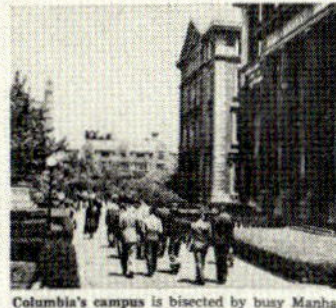

Columbia's campus is bisected by busy Manhattan streets and there are few trees. But it has some quiet walks which make it an oasis in the city.

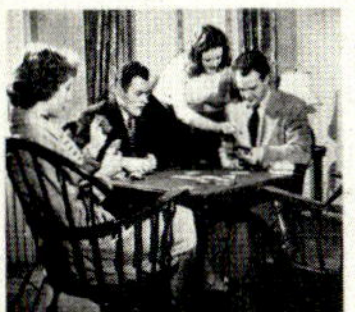

Bridge is favorite recreation for Barnard students and Columbia dates from across street. One third of Barnard's 1,200 students are New Yorkers.

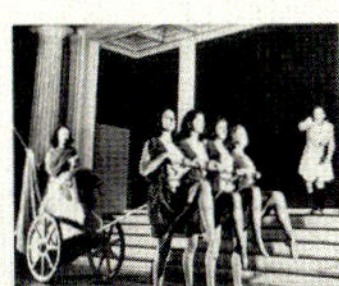

Barnard's unique "Greek Games" are 46-year-old tradition. Freshmen and sophomores compete. Games have been called "mad, comic, lovely."

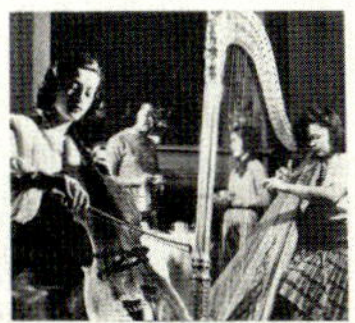

Music plays part in Barnard College scheme where academic and social standards are high. Barnard girls are sometimes called "hens in the barnyard."

30

31

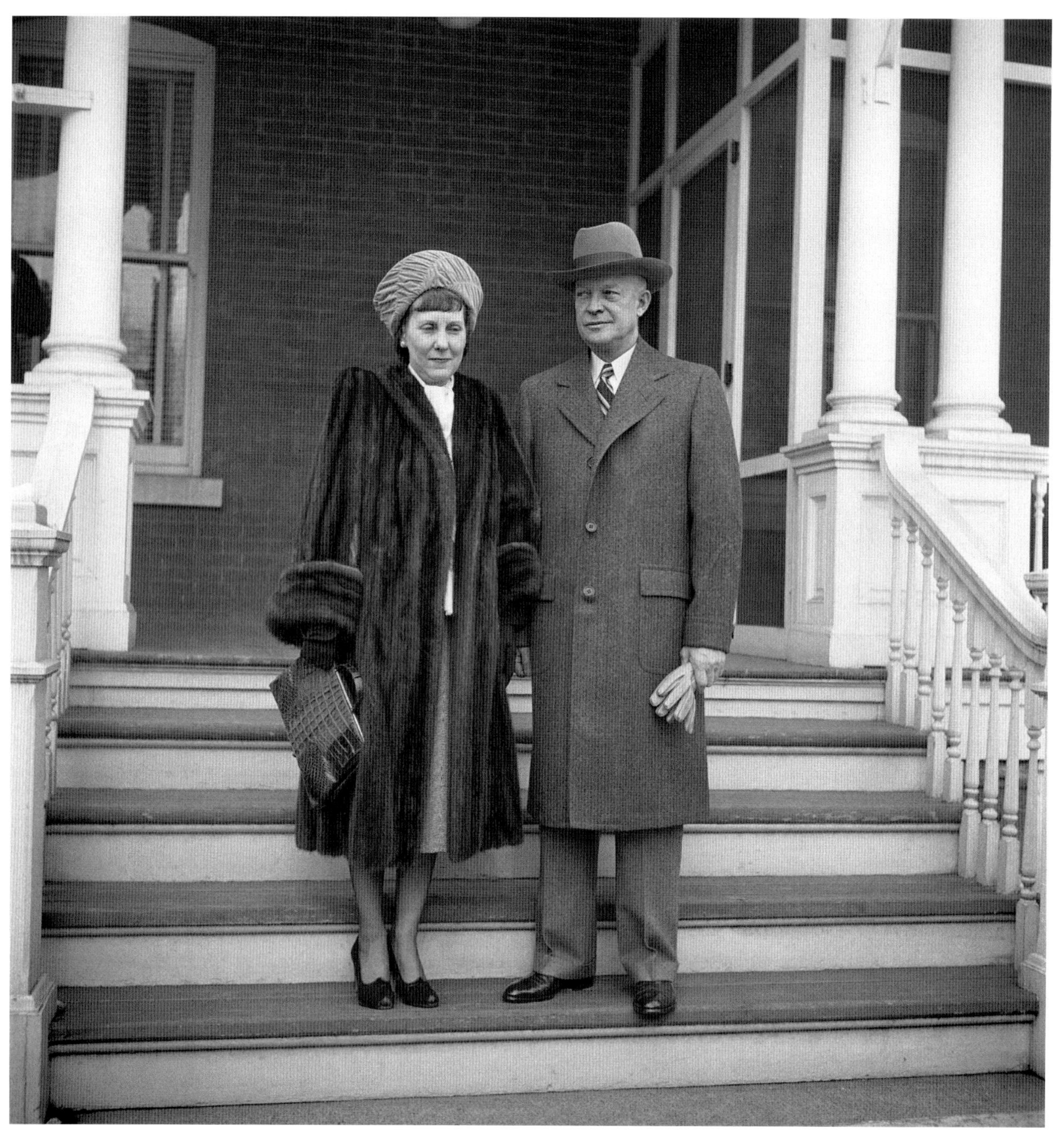

Dwight D. Eisenhower with his wife, Mamie

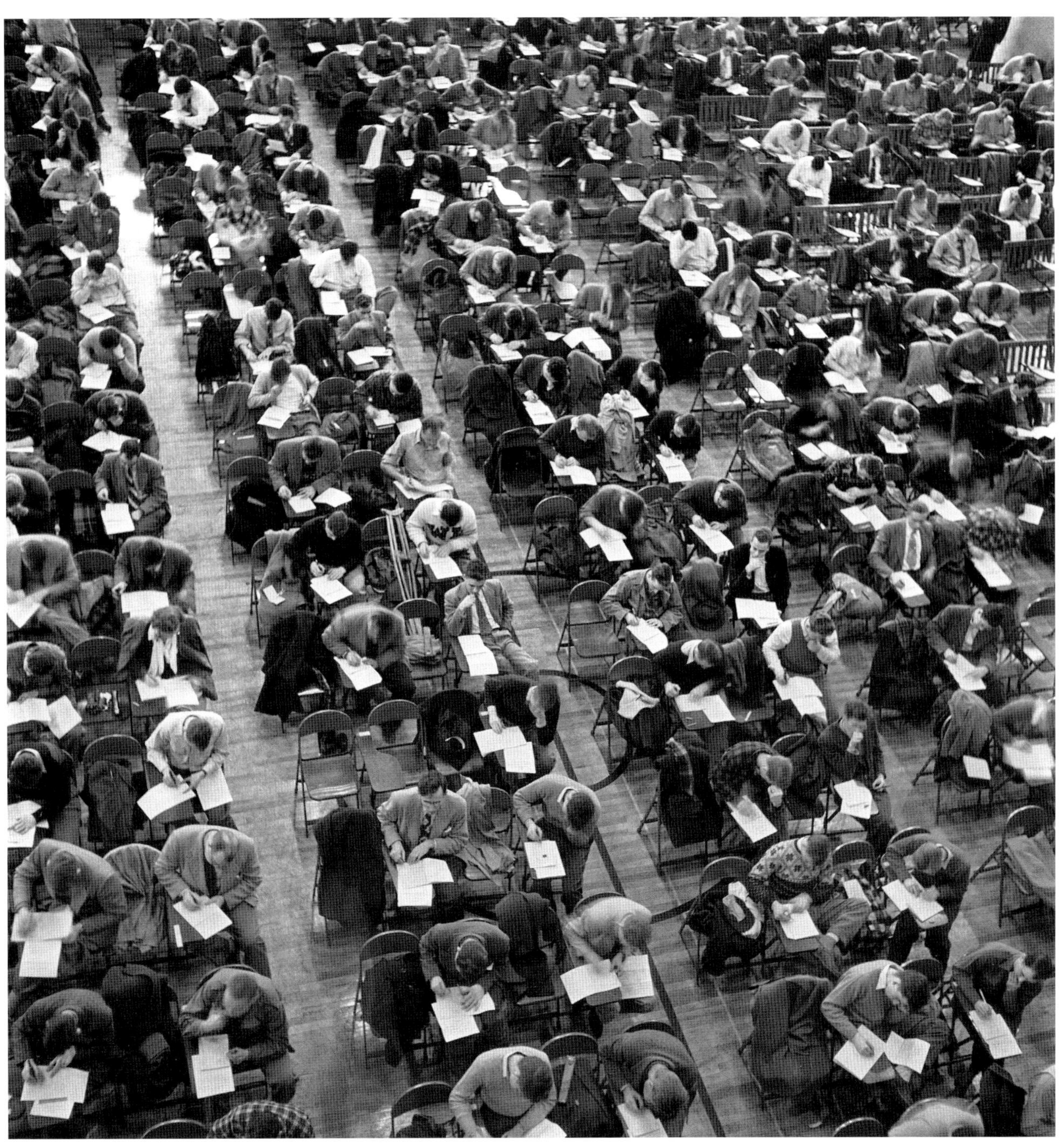

Students taking a test *en masse*

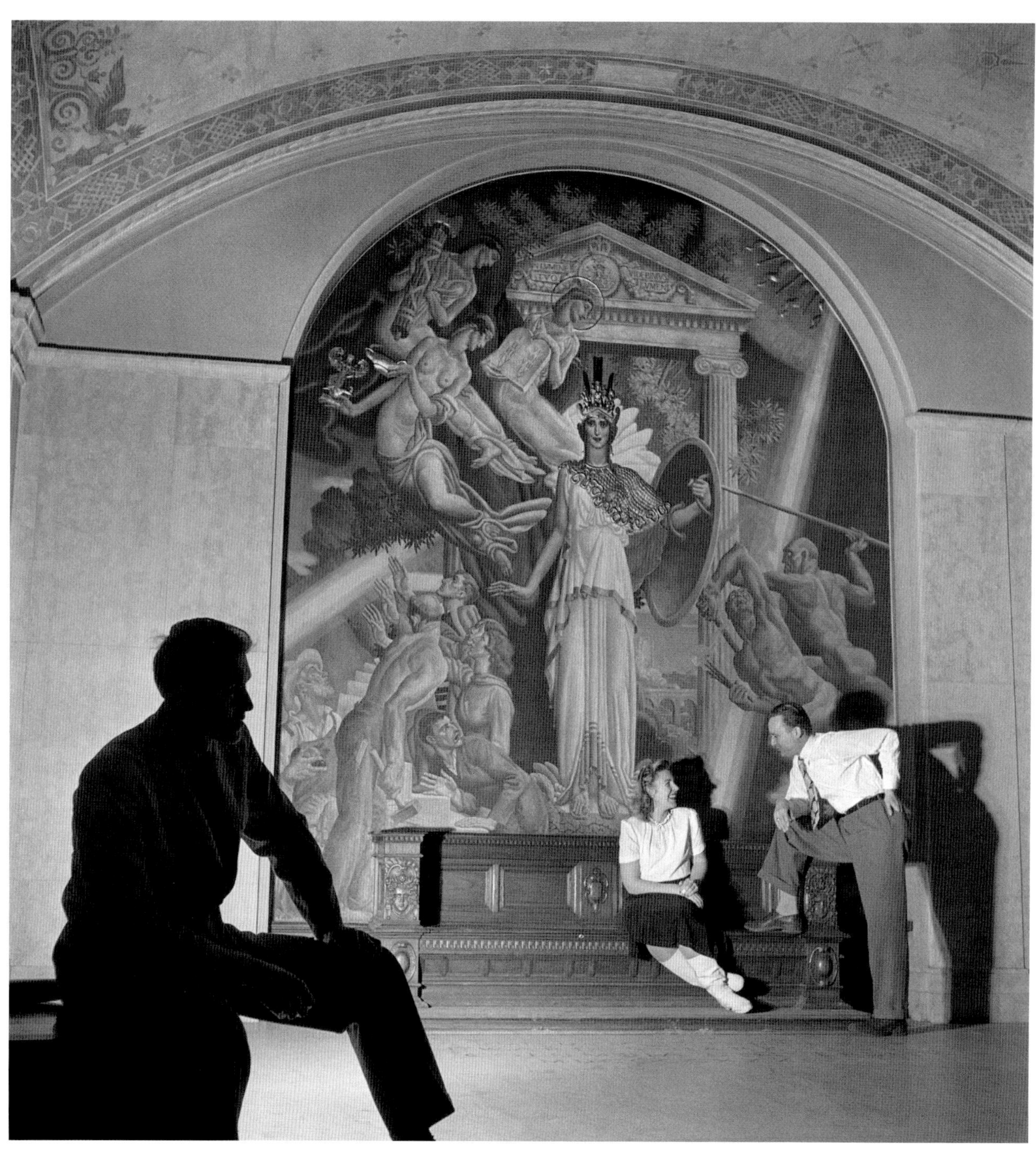

Deep shadows in the foreground and background added drama to a campus interaction.

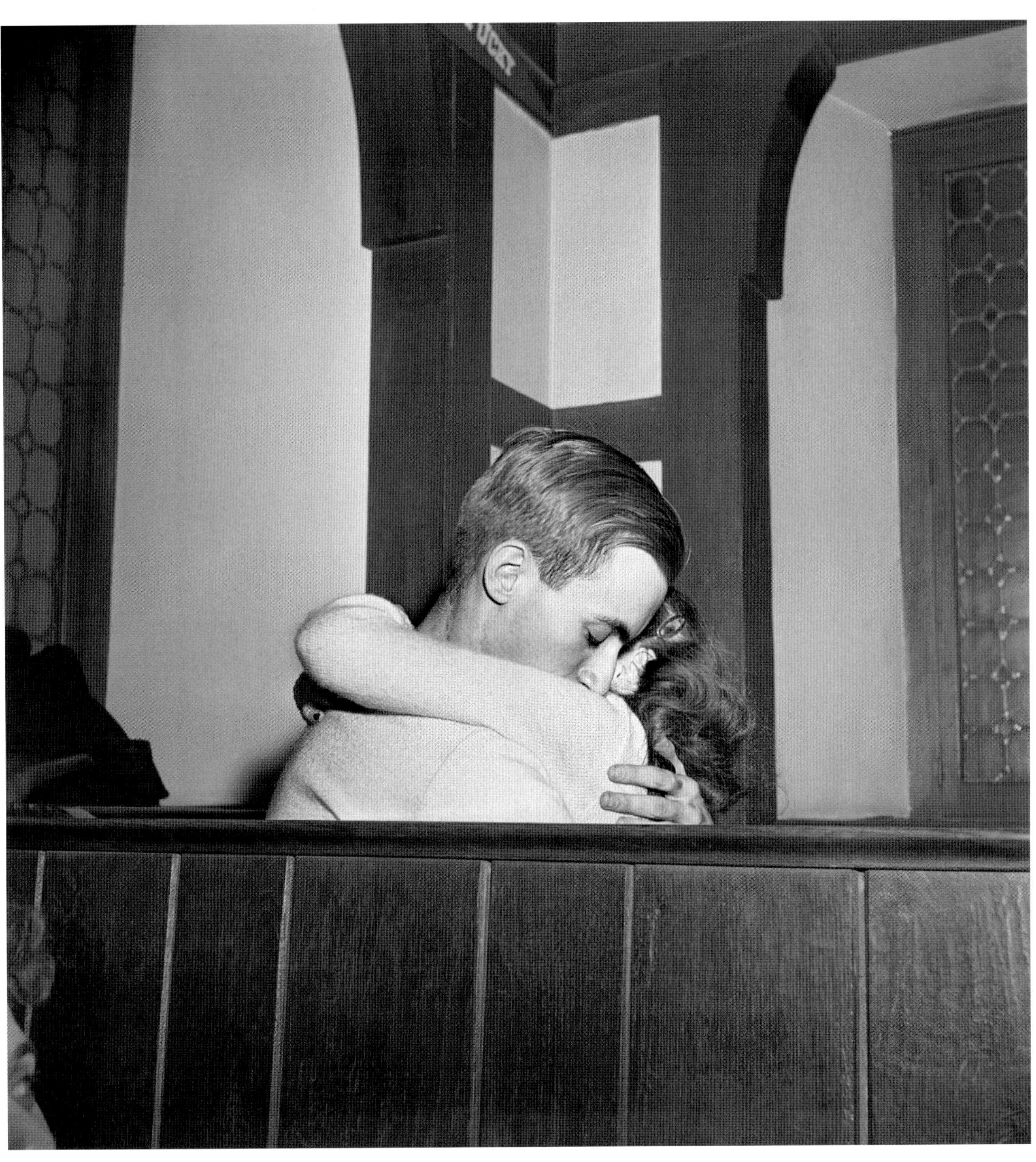

Kubrick captured private moments on campus.

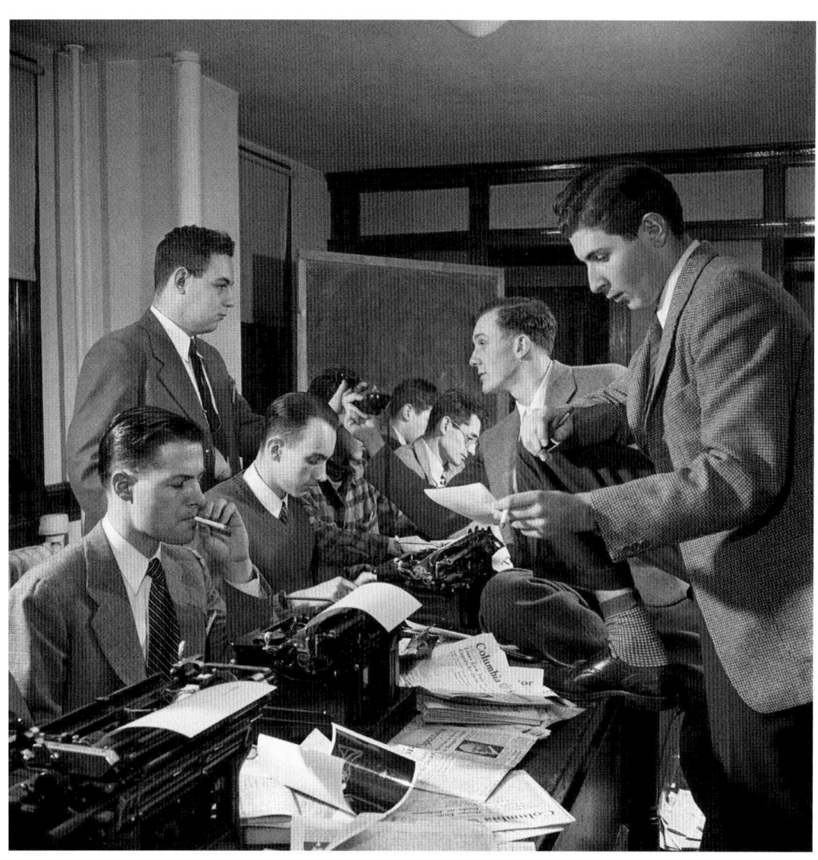

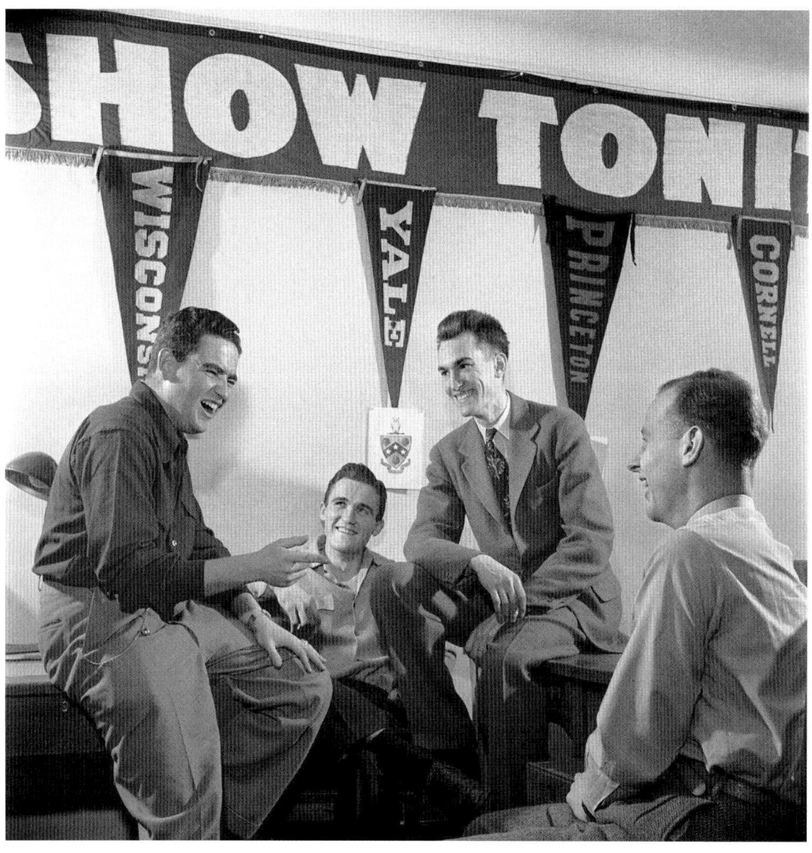

ABOVE **Journalism students at work**

LEFT **Students chatting in Hartley Hall**

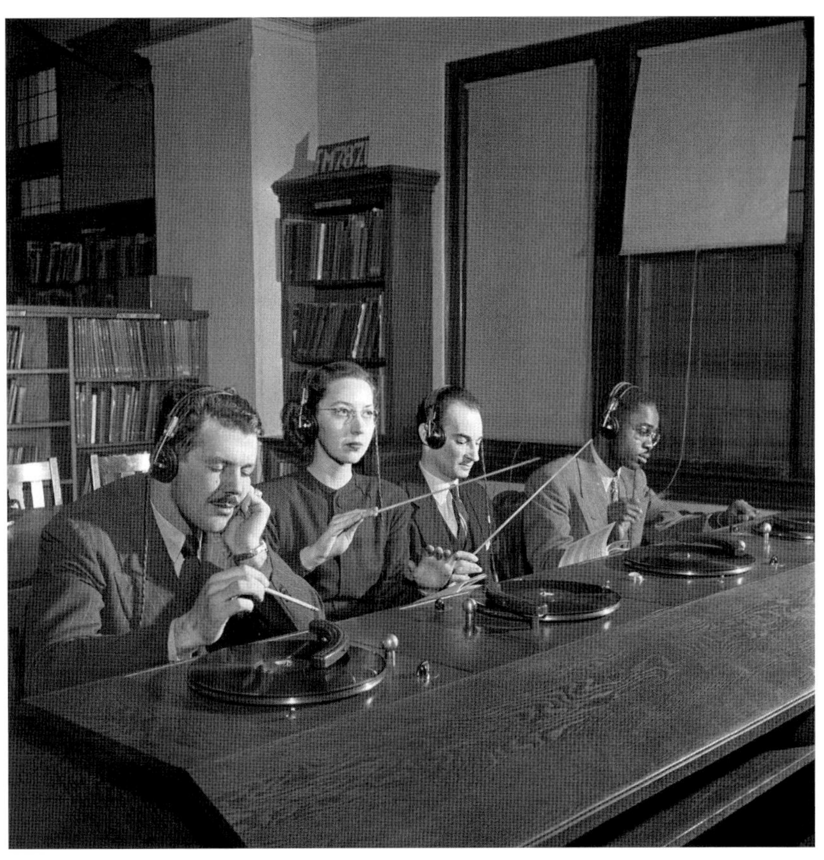

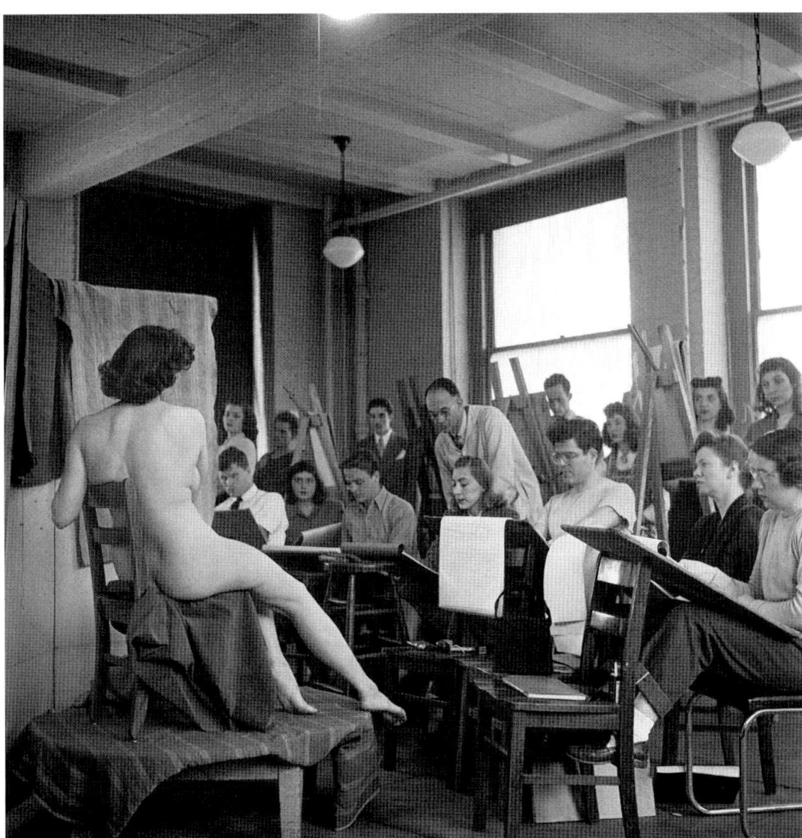

ABOVE **Music students conducting while listening to records**

RIGHT **Students drawing a model in a School of General Studies art class**

FOLLOWING SPREAD **Professor lecturing to medical students at Columbia's College of Physicians and Surgeons**

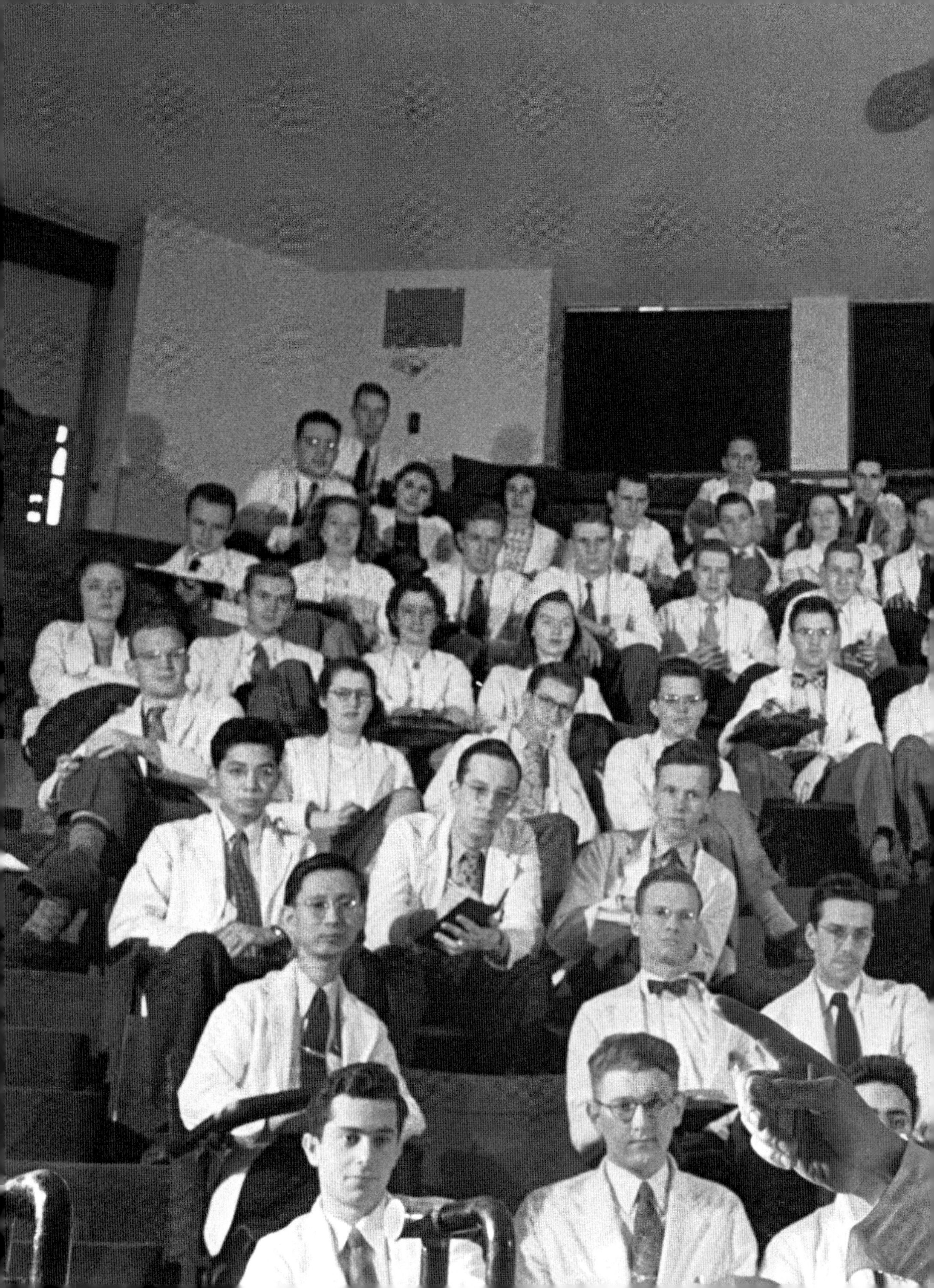

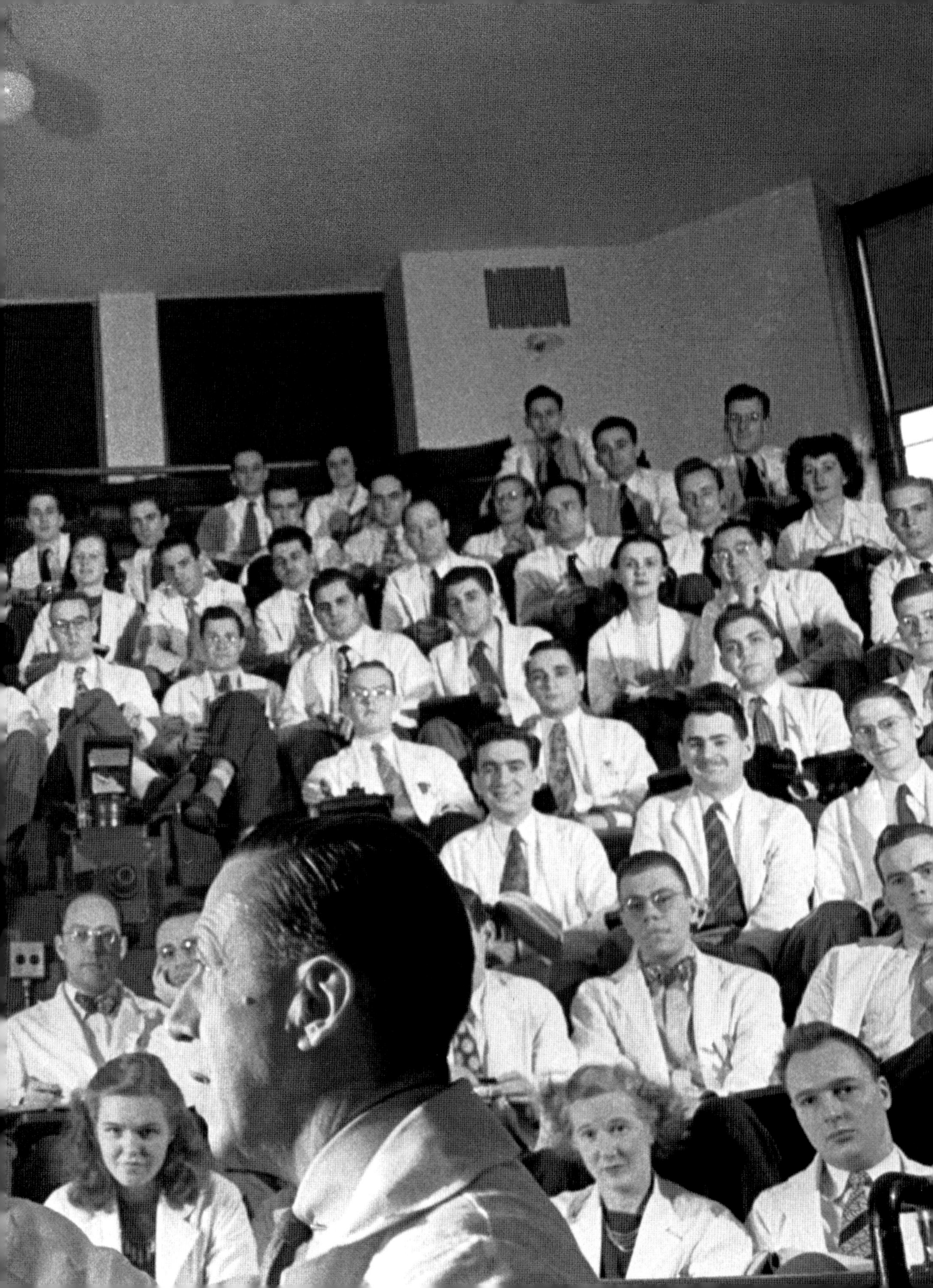

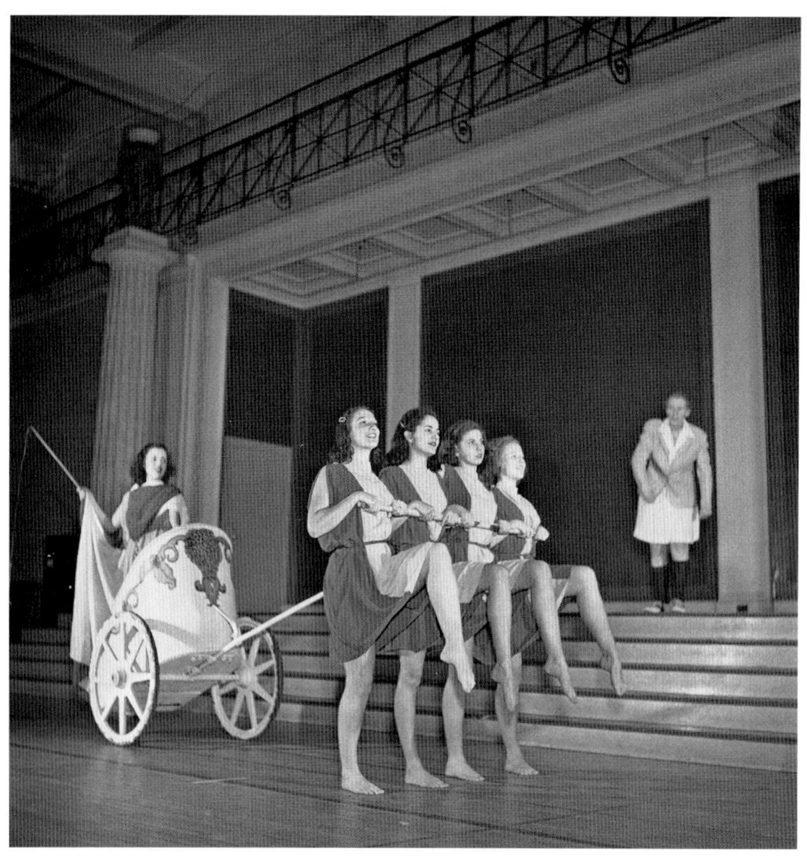

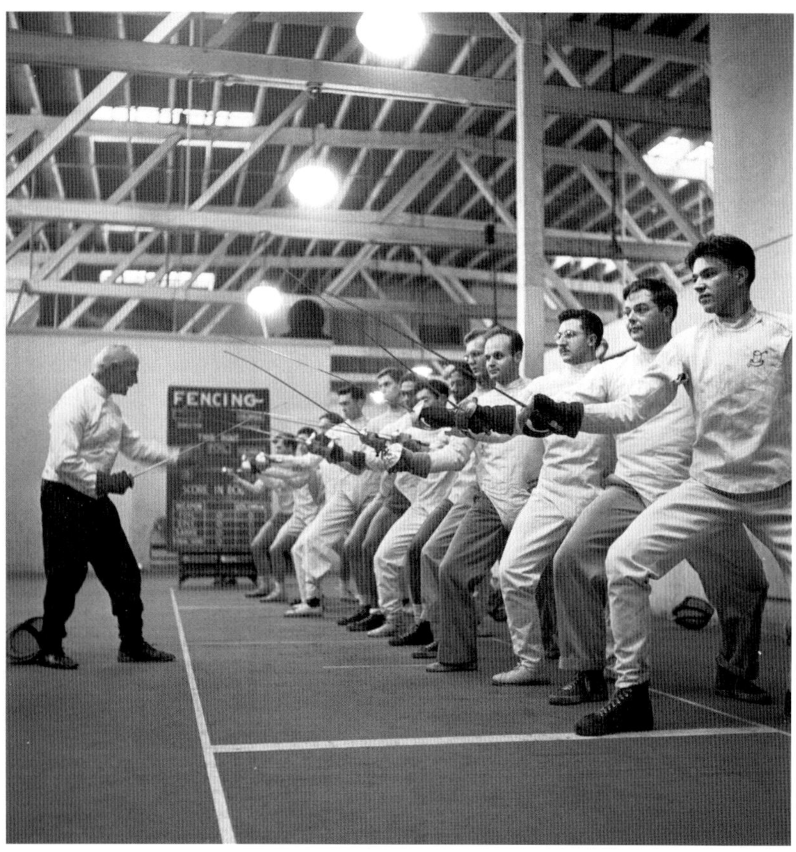

ABOVE **"Greek Games," a 46-year-old tradition performed at Barnard College, a Columbia University affiliate**

LEFT **Fencers practicing**

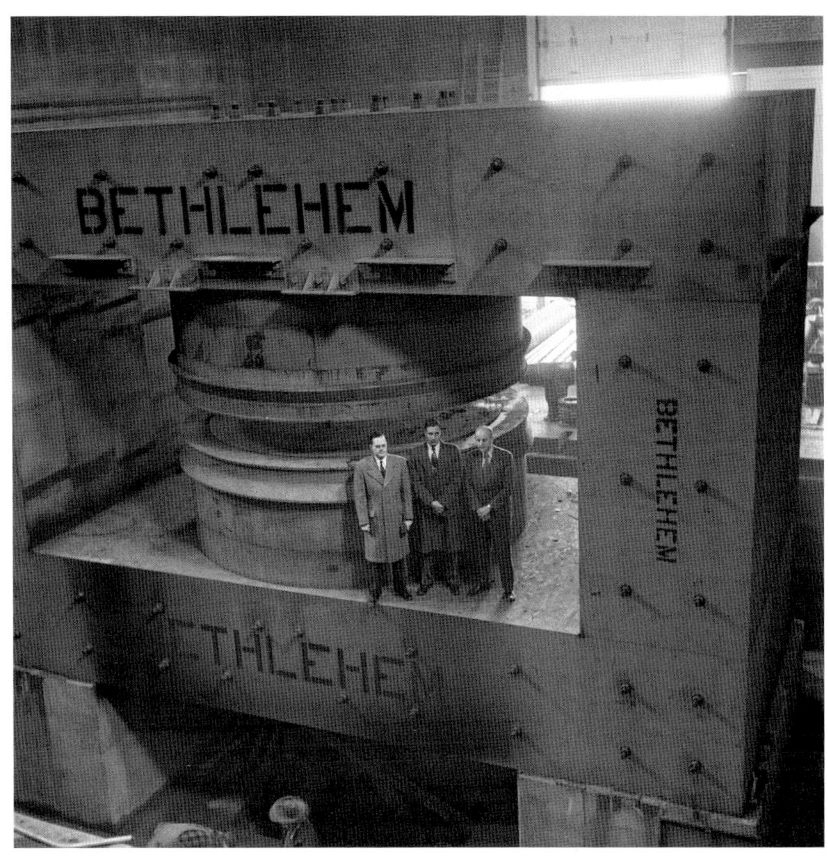

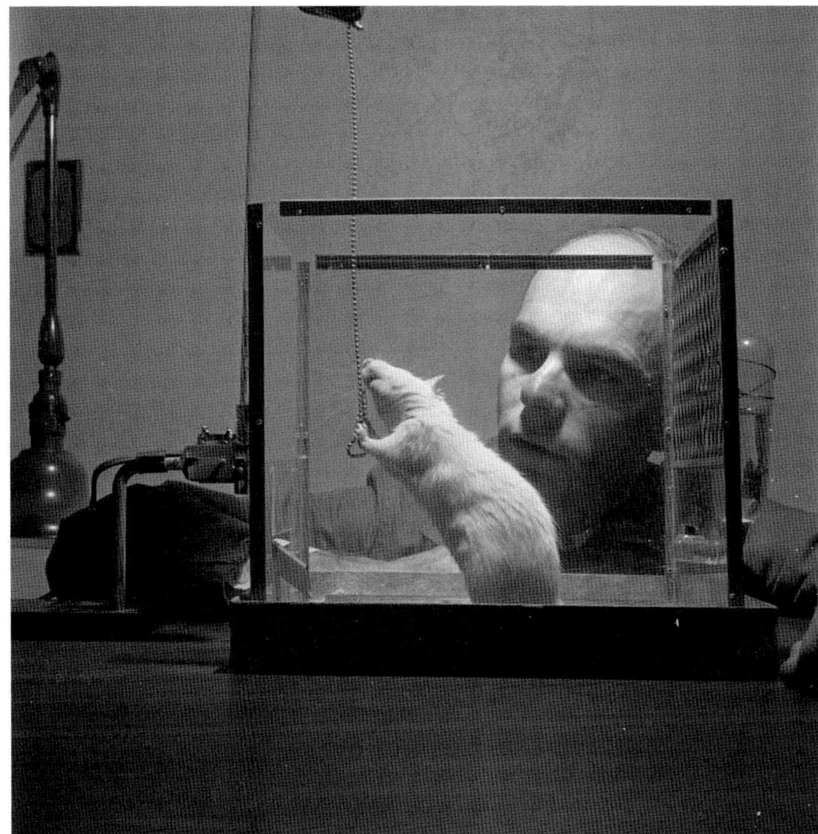

ABOVE **Professor Eugene T. Booth (left), executive director of the university's nuclear physics research center, posing with fellow engineers on the partly finished cyclotron to be used for atom research**

RIGHT **A psychology lecturer teaching a rat to pull a chain for food**

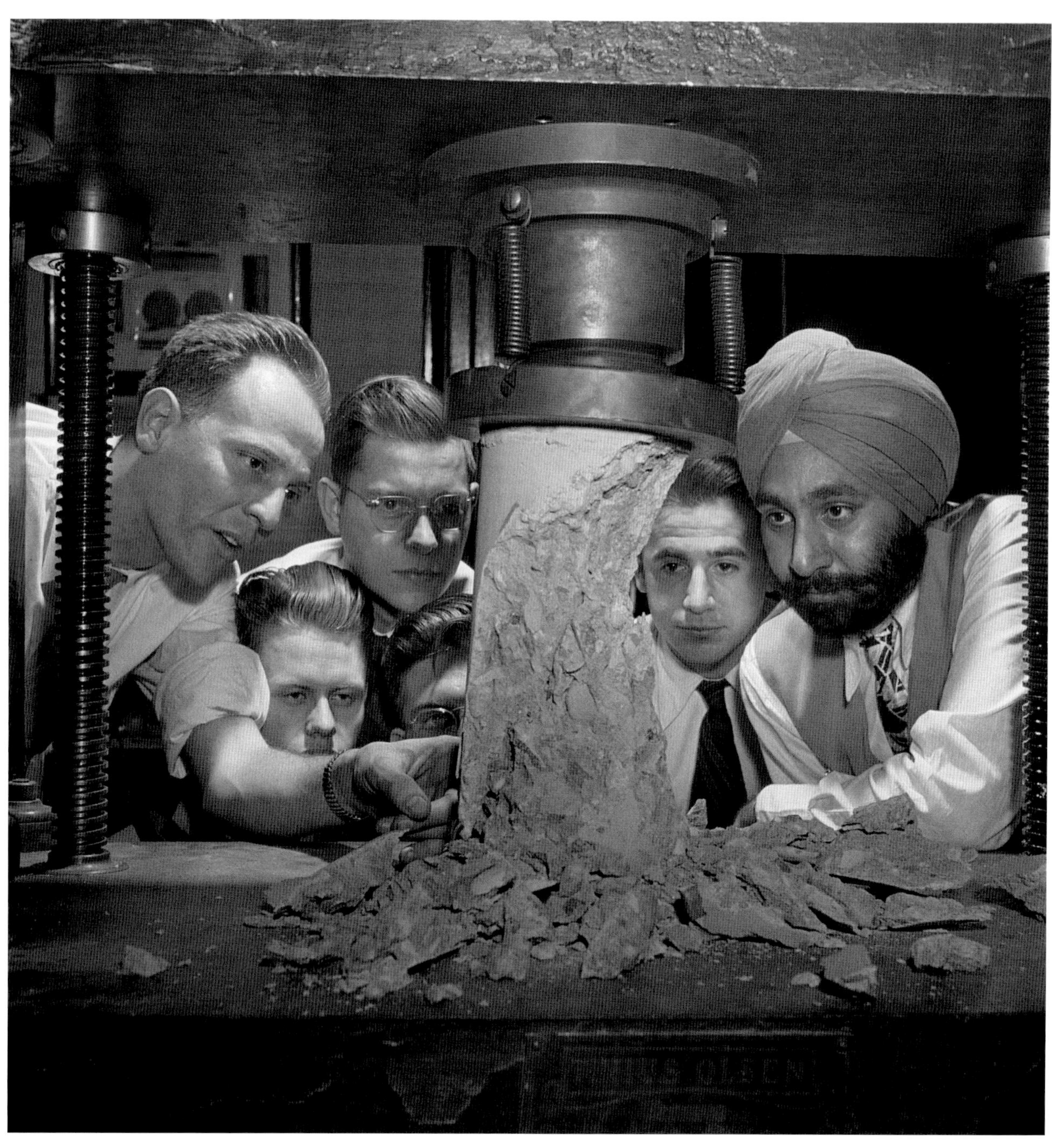

Engineering students listening to an instructor (left) explaining concrete compression

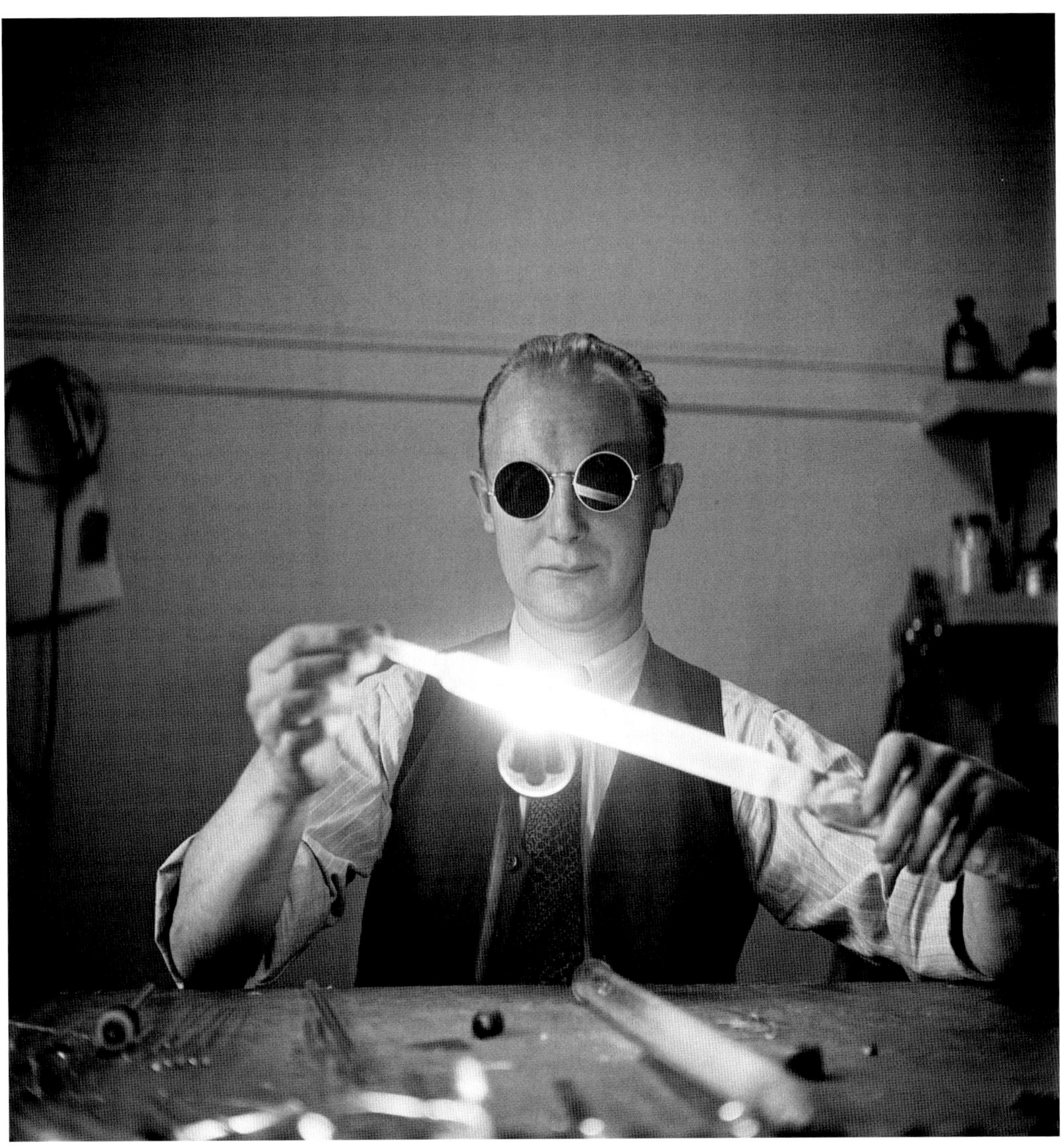

"Hundreds of men on Columbia's faculty are in some kind of research," reported the magazine.

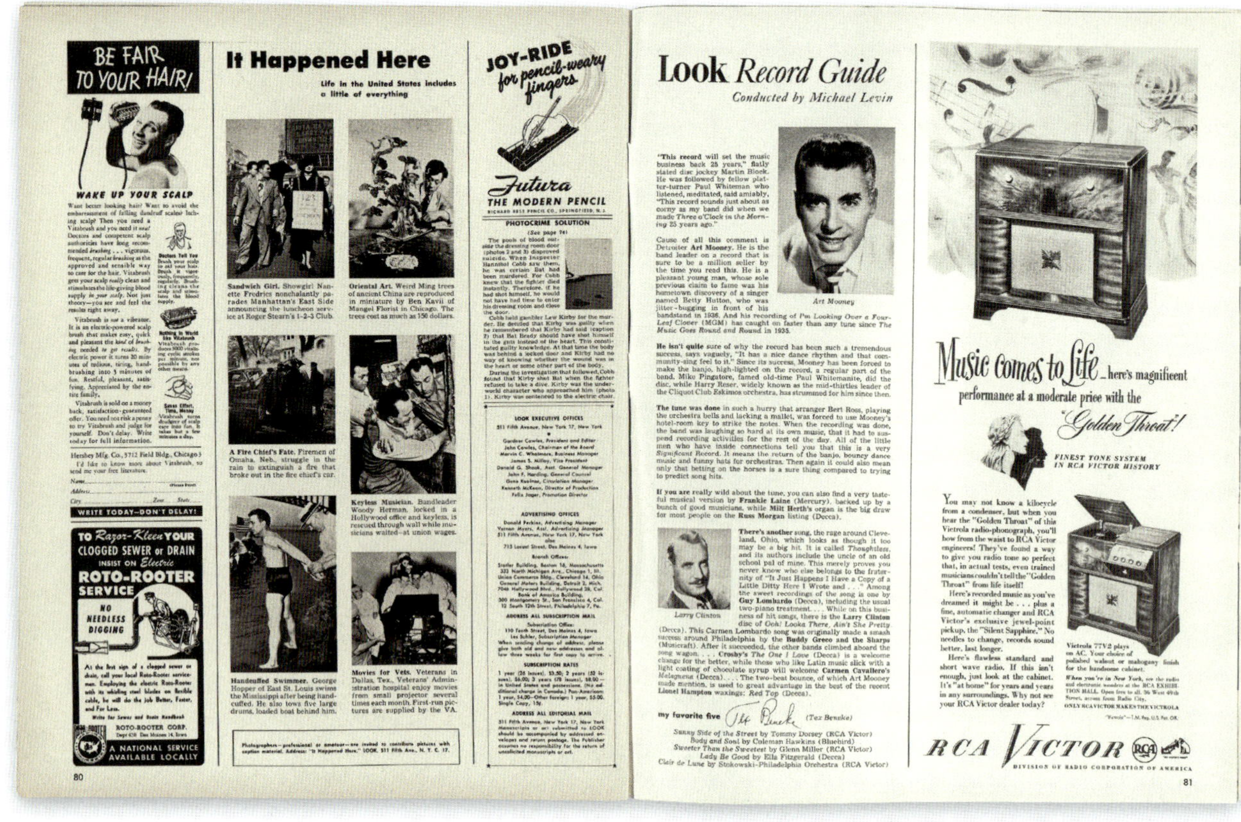

It Happened Here

Life in the United States includes a little of everything

Sandwich Girl. Showgirl Nanette Fredrics nonchalantly parades Manhattan's East Side announcing the luncheon service at Roger Stearn's 1-2-3 Club.

Oriental Art. Weird Ming trees of ancient China are reproduced in miniature by Ben Kavil of Mangel Florist in Chicago. The trees cost as much as 150 dollars.

A Fire Chief's Fate. Firemen of Omaha, Neb., struggle in the rain to extinguish a fire that broke out in the fire chief's car.

Keyless Musician. Bandleader Woody Herman, locked in a Hollywood office and keyless, is rescued through wall while musicians waited—at union wages.

Handcuffed Swimmer. George Hopper of East St. Louis swims the Mississippi after being handcuffed. He also tows five large drums, loaded boat behind him.

Movies for Vets. Veterans in Dallas, Tex., Veterans' Administration hospital enjoy movies from small projector several times each month. First-run pictures are supplied by the VA.

Photographers—professional or amateur—are invited to contribute pictures with caption material. Address: "It Happened Here," LOOK, 511 Fifth Ave., N. Y. C. 17.

80

Look *Record Guide*

Conducted by Michael Levin

"This record will set the music business back 25 years," flatly stated disc jockey Martin Block. He was followed by fellow platter-turner Paul Whiteman who listened, meditated, said amiably, "This record sounds just about as corny as my band did when we made *Three o'Clock in the Morning* 25 years ago."

Cause of all this comment is Detroiter **Art Mooney.** He is the band leader on a record that is sure to be a million seller by the time you read this. He is a pleasant young man, whose sole previous claim to fame was his hometown discovery of a singer named Betty Hutton, who was jitter-bugging in front of his bandstand in 1936. And his recording of *I'm Looking Over a Four-Leaf Clover* (MGM) has caught on faster than any tune since *The Music Goes Round and Round* in 1935.

Art Mooney

He isn't quite sure of why the record has been such a tremendous success, says vaguely, "It has a nice dance rhythm and that community-sing feel to it." Since its success, Mooney has been forced to make the banjo, high-lighted on the record, a regular part of the band. Mike Pingatore, famed old-time Paul Whitemanite, did the disc, while Harry Reser, widely known as the mid-thirties leader of the Cliquot Club Eskimos orchestra, has strummed for him since then.

The tune was done in such a hurry that arranger Bert Ross, playing the orchestra bells and lacking a mallet, was forced to use Mooney's hotel-room key to strike the notes. When the recording was done, the band was laughing so hard at its own music, that it had to suspend recording activities for the rest of the day. All of the little men who have inside connections tell you that this is a very *Significant Record.* It means the return of the banjo, bouncy dance music and funny hats for orchestras. Then again it could also mean only that betting on the horses is a sure thing compared to trying to predict song hits.

If you are really wild about the tune, you can also find a very tasteful musical version by **Frankie Laine** (Mercury), backed up by a bunch of good musicians, while **Milt Herth's organ** is the big draw for most people on the **Russ Morgan** listing (Decca).

Larry Clinton

There's another song, the rage around Cleveland, Ohio, which looks as though it too may be a big hit. It is called *Thoughtless,* and its authors include the uncle of an old school pal of mine. This merely proves you never know who else belongs to the fraternity of "It Just Happens I Have a Copy of a Little Ditty Here I Wrote and . . ." Among the sweet recordings of the song is one by **Guy Lombardo** (Decca), including the usual two-piano treatment. . . . While on this business of hit songs, there is the **Larry Clinton** disc of *Ooh! Looka There, Ain't She Pretty* (Decca). This Carmen Lombardo song was originally made a smash success around Philadelphia by the **Buddy Greco and the Sharps** (Musicraft). After it succeeded, the other bands climbed aboard the song wagon. . . . **Crosby's** *The One I Love* (Decca) is a welcome change for the better, while those who like Latin music slick with a light coating of chocolate syrup will welcome **Carmen Cavallero's** *Malaguena* (Decca). . . . The two-beat bounce, of which Art Mooney made mention, is used to great advantage in the best of the recent **Lionel Hampton** waxings: *Red Top* (Decca).

my favorite five (Tex Beneke)

Sunny Side of the Street by Tommy Dorsey (RCA Victor)
Body and Soul by Coleman Hawkins (Bluebird)
Sweeter Than the Sweetest by Glenn Miller (RCA Victor)
Lady Be Good by Ella Fitzgerald (Decca)
Clair de Lune by Stokowski-Philadelphia Orchestra (RCA Victor)

81

PUBLISHED AS

IT HAPPENED HERE: LIFE IN THE U.S. HAS A LITTLE OF EVERYTHING

DATE

MARCH 2, 1948

Kubrick's photograph, captioned "Sandwich Girl," depicted showgirl Nanette Fredrics on Manhattan's East Side, advertising luncheon service for the 1-2-3 Club. The often-humorous interactions between Fredrics and passing pedestrians were the visual punch lines of the published photograph and related outtakes.

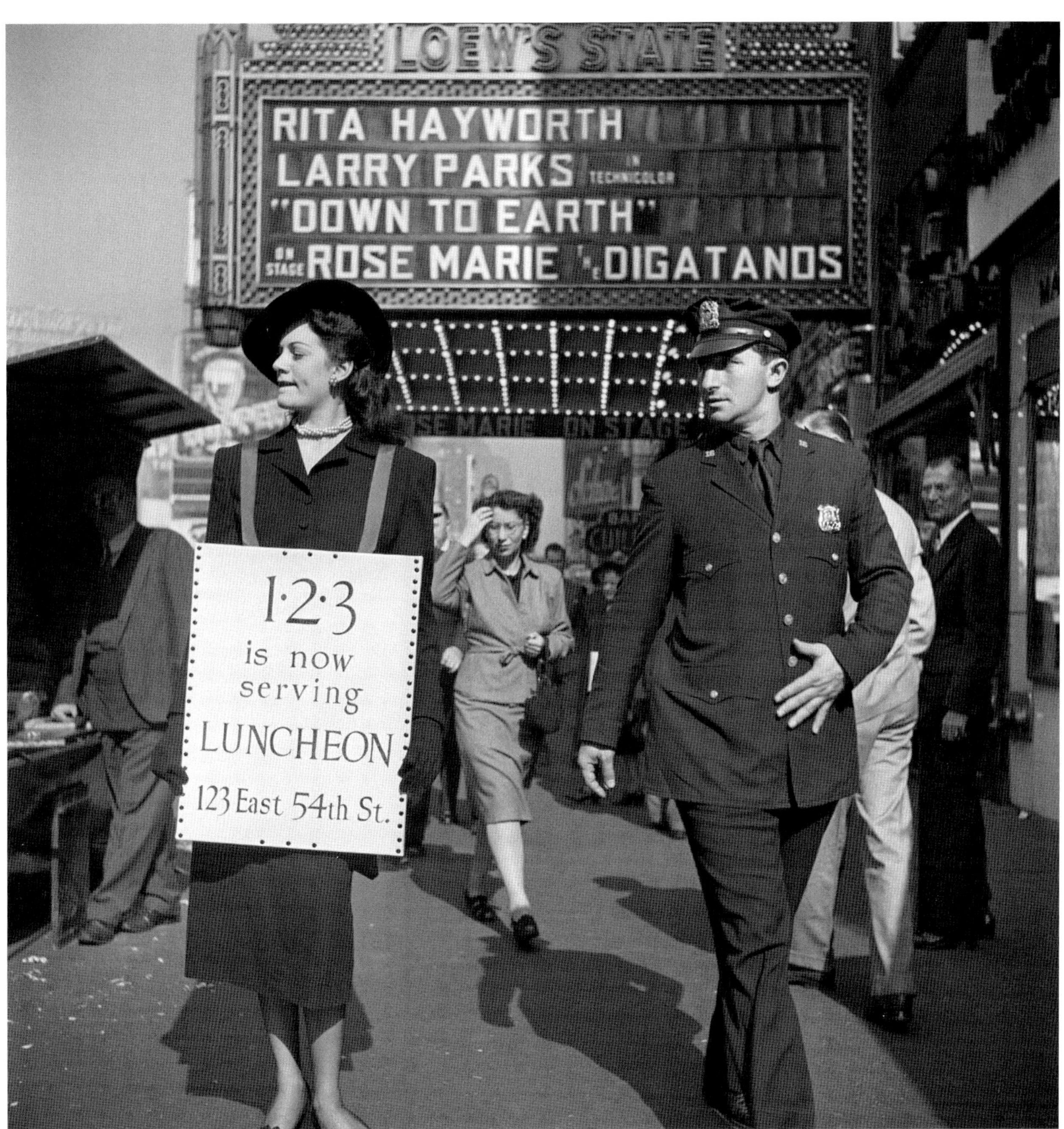

Showgirl Nanette Fredrics advertising a lunch spot

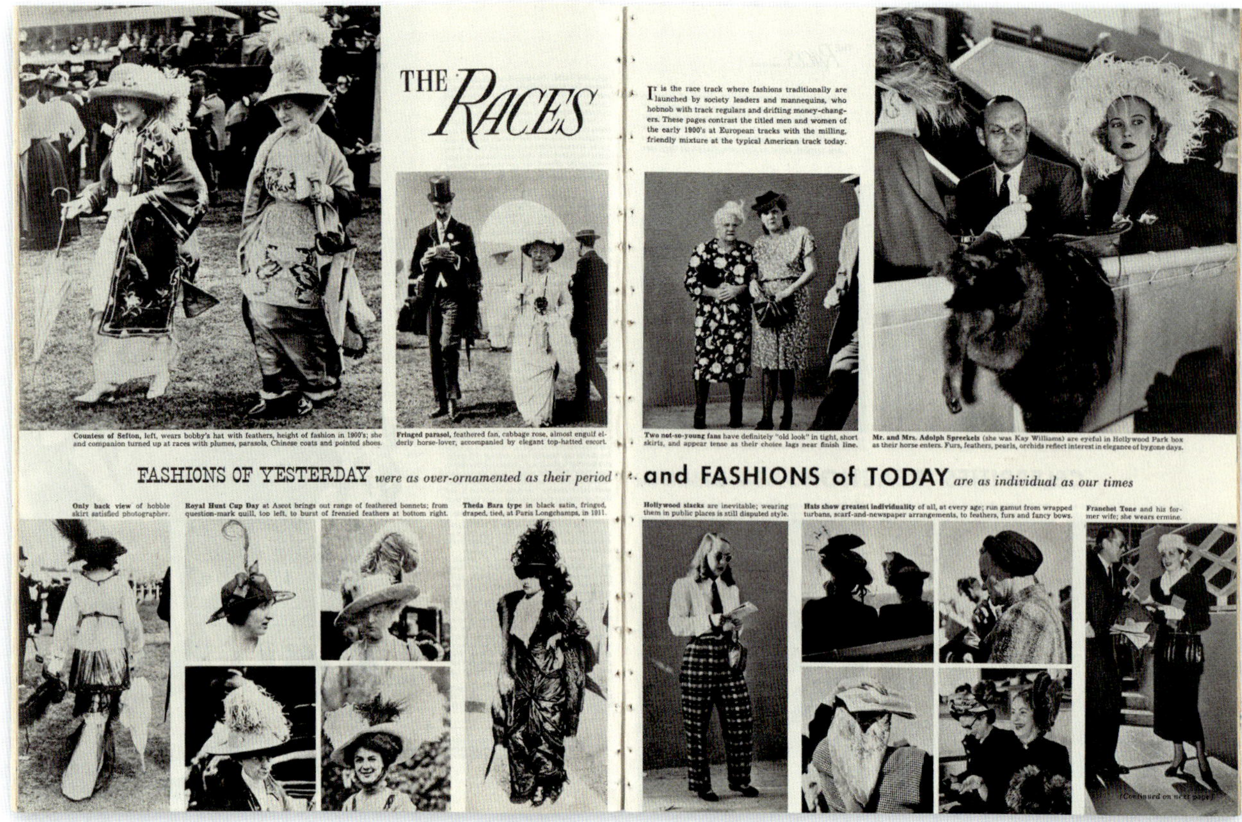

THE RACES

It is the race track where fashions traditionally are launched by society leaders and mannequins, who hobnob with track regulars and drifting money-changers. These pages contrast the titled men and women of the early 1900's at European tracks with the milling, friendly mixture at the typical American track today.

Countess of Sefton, left, wears bobby's hat with feathers, height of fashion in 1900's; she and companion turned up at races with plumes, parasols, Chinese coats and pointed shoes.

Fringed parasol, feathered fan, cabbage rose, almost engulf elderly horse-lover, accompanied by elegant top-hatted escort.

Two not-so-young fans have definitely "old look" in tight, short skirts, and appear tense as their choice lags near finish line.

Mr. and Mrs. Adolph Spreckels (she was Kay Williams) are eyeful in Hollywood Park box as their horse enters. Furs, feathers, pearls, orchids reflect interest in elegance of bygone days.

FASHIONS OF YESTERDAY *were as over-ornamented as their period* and FASHIONS of TODAY *are as individual as our times*

Only back view of hobble skirt satisfied photographer.

Royal Hunt Cup Day at Ascot brings out range of feathered bonnets; from question-mark quill, top left, to burst of frenzied feathers at bottom right.

Theda Bara type in black satin, fringed, draped, tied, at Paris Longchamps, in 1911.

Hollywood slacks are inevitable; wearing them in public places is still disputed style.

Hats show greatest individuality of all, at every age; run gamut from wrapped turbans, scarf-and-newspaper arrangements, to feathers, furs and fancy bows.

Franchot Tone and his former wife; she wears ermine.

(Continued on next page)

PUBLISHED AS

THE RACES: FASHIONS OF YESTERDAY WERE AS OVER-ORNAMENTED AS THEIR PERIOD; FASHIONS OF TODAY ARE AS INDIVIDUAL AS OUR TIMES

DATE

DECEMBER 7, 1948

Some of Kubrick's photographs of the Aqueduct Racetrack in Queens, New York, appeared in this photo essay, which followed a more extensive article about the Santa Anita Park racetrack outside Los Angeles. Kubrick's downbeat images of the track—such as one depicting a lone man wandering amid post-race debris—were not included in the more upbeat published story focusing on fashion.

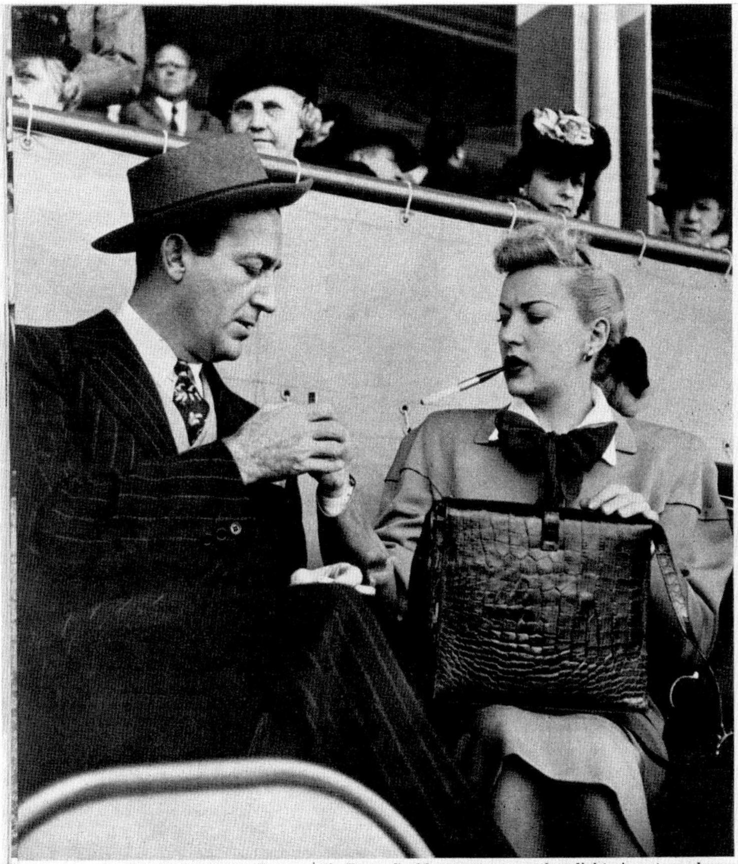

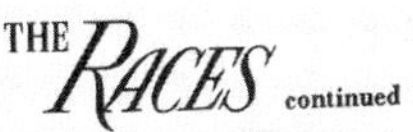

CELEBRITIES and unknowns rub elbows, all intent on selecting right horse in each race. Bets range from $2 to $100 for each ticket (though some bets run to the thousands). Faces, caught by LOOK cameraman, tell race results, indicate tenseness of spectators while horses are running, relief as they win, disgust as they lose.

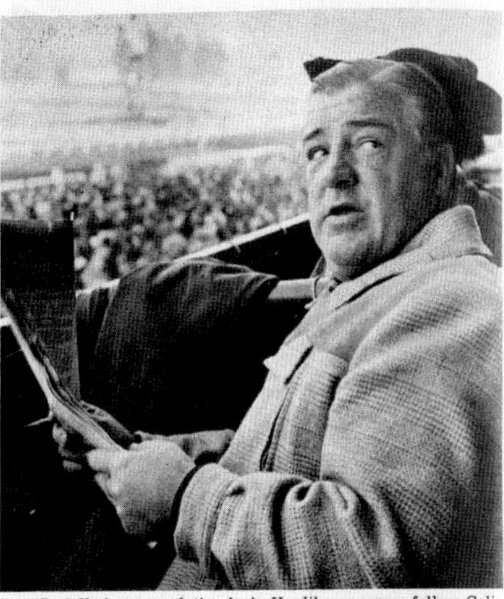

Bandleader Harry James, wife Betty Grable, are tense as they light cigarets; as horse owners, they are regulars at California's Santa Anita and Hollywood Park race tracks.

Lou Costello has speculative look. He, like so many fellow Californians, wears sport jacket of loud racing checks to race track.

CELEBRITIES' REACTIONS *are barometer of betting . . .*

Bud Abbott chews cigaret holder until horses cross the finish line.

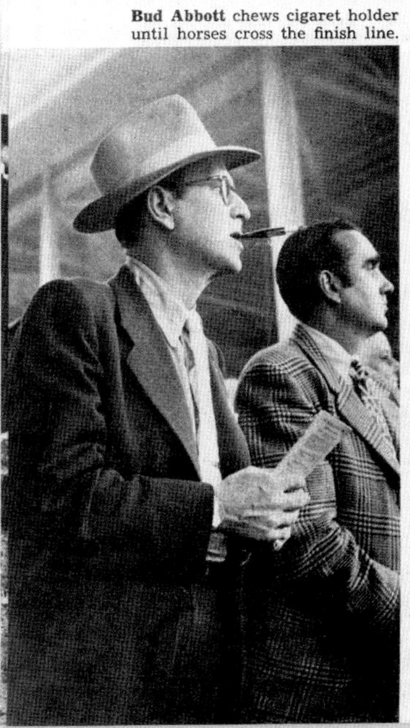

"Prince" Mike Romanoff, Hollywood restaurateur, checks tote-board for odds on next race.

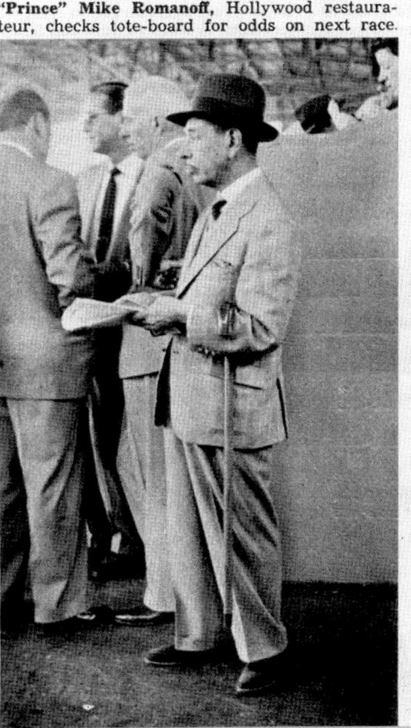

Two New Yorkers, dressed to the hilt, wear feathered hats, elaborate corsages and jewelry; one sports ubiquitous dark glasses.

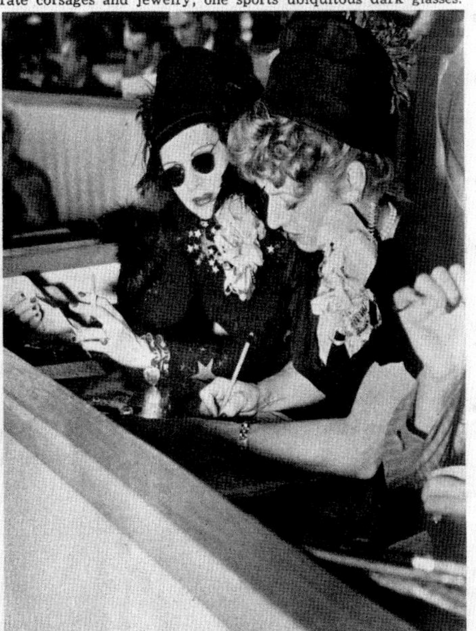

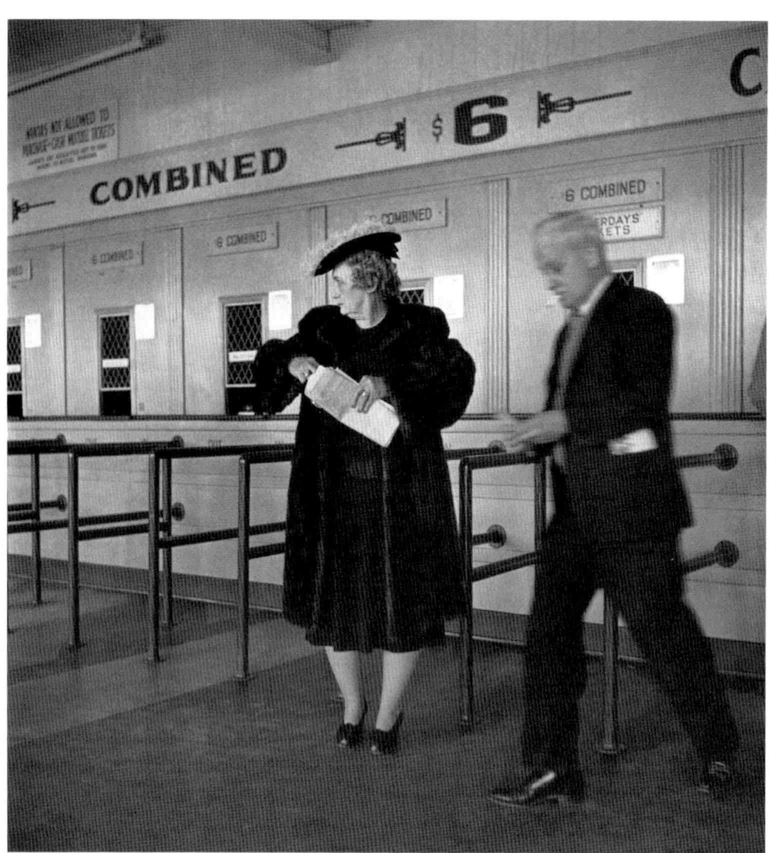

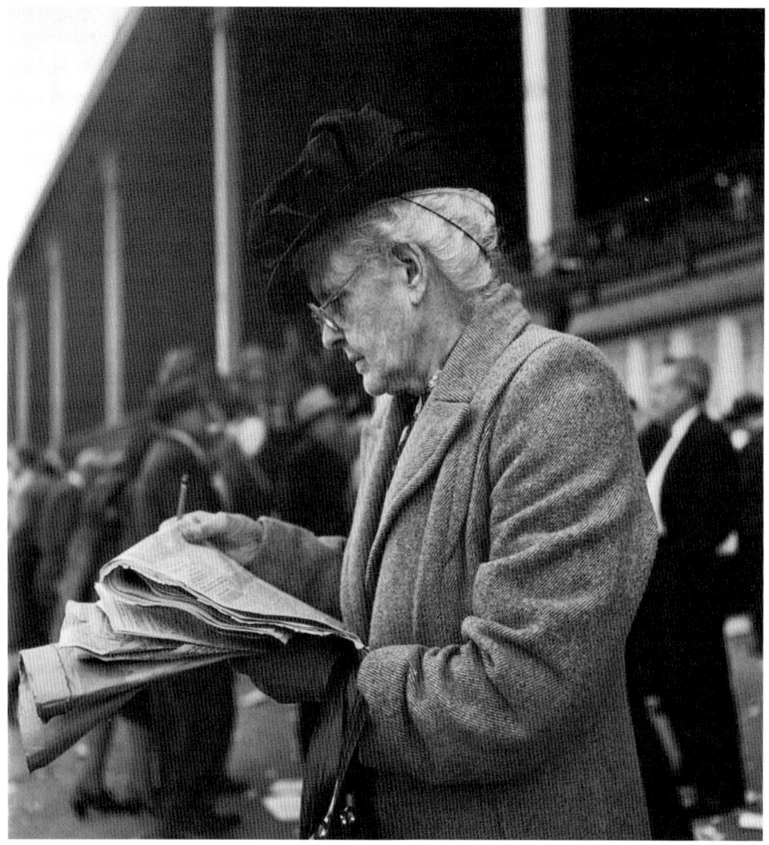

"Older matrons" found horse racing "a time-killer," noted this article.

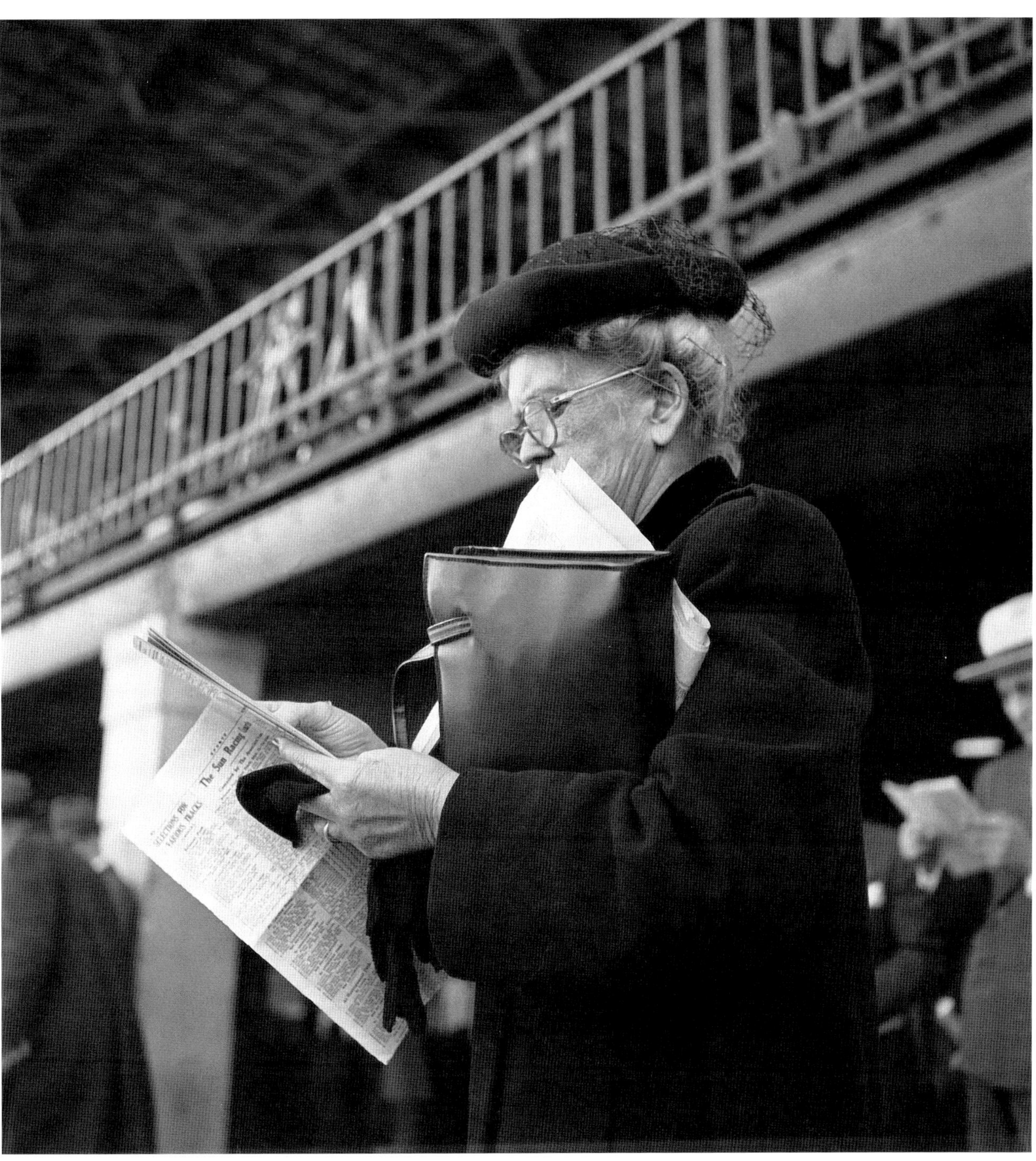
SELECTIONS FOR VARIOUS TRACKS
The Sun Racing

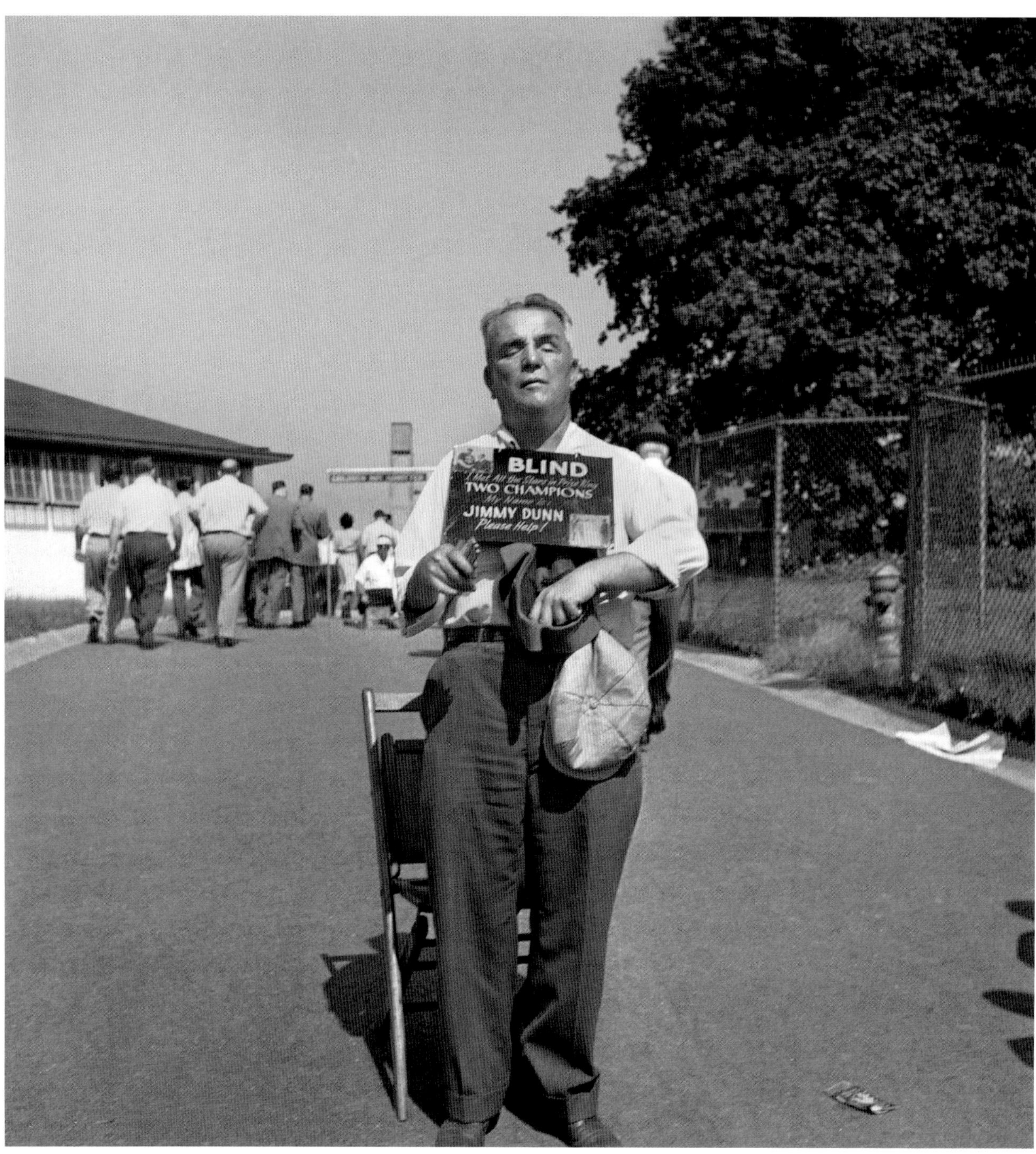

Disquieting images such as this one of a blind panhandler were not included in the published article, which focused on racetrack fashions.

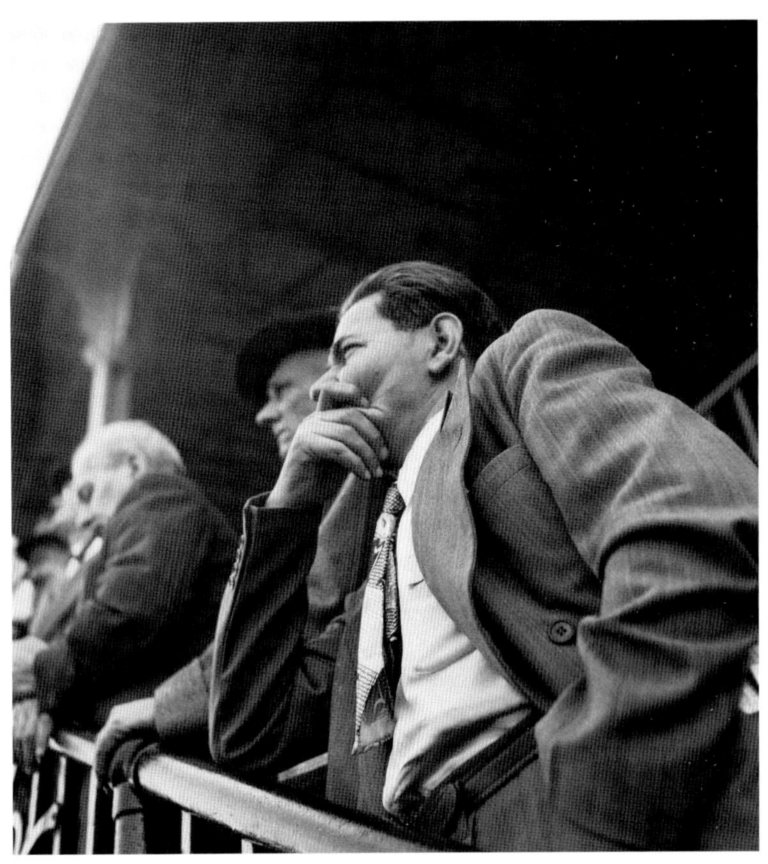

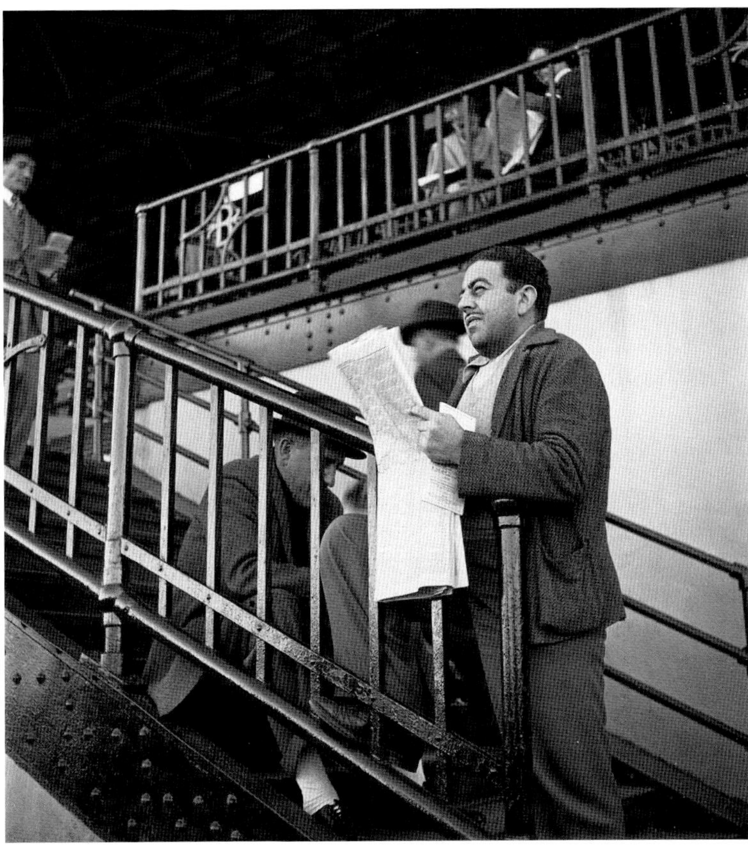

Spectators watching the action intently

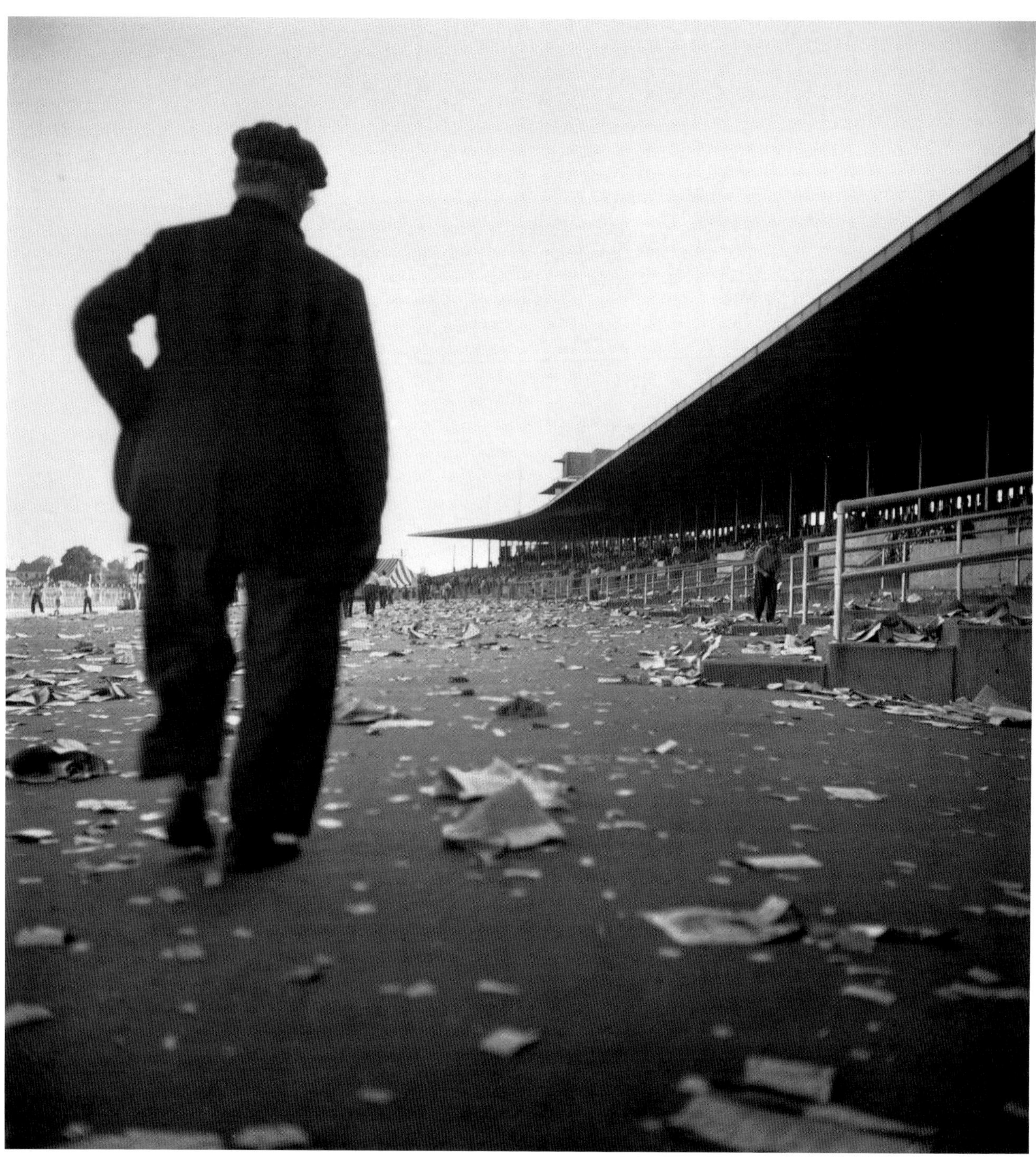

These unpublished images explored
the grittier side of racetrack gambling.

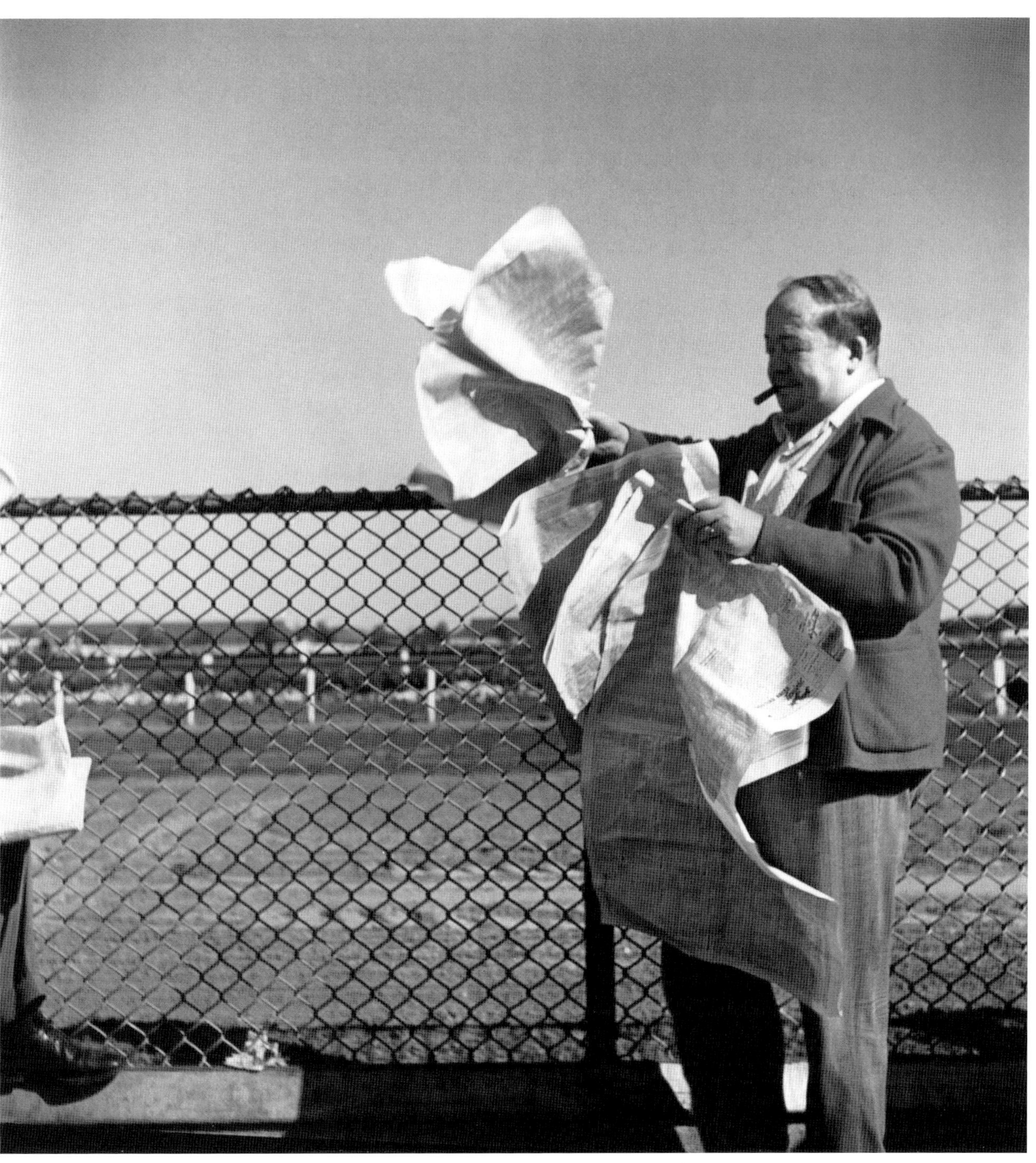

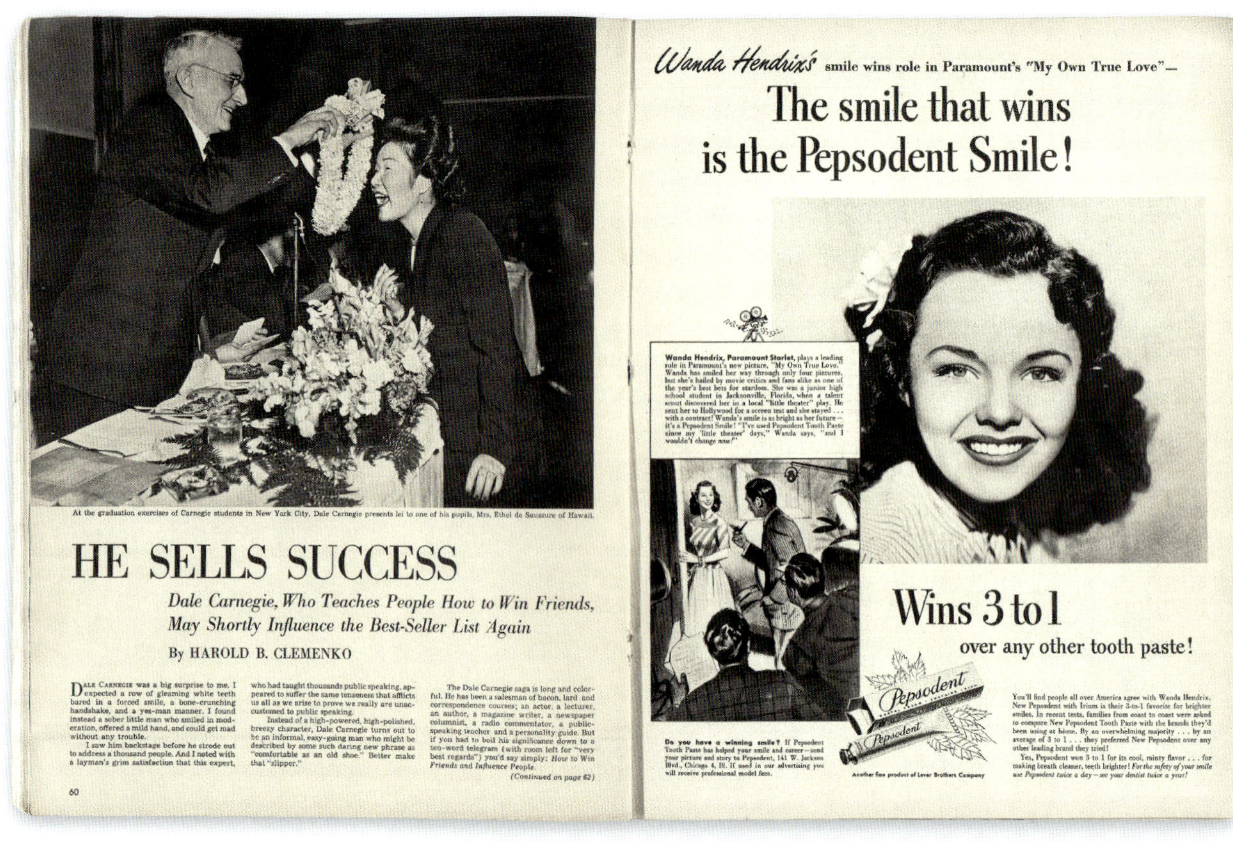

At the graduation exercises of Carnegie students in New York City, Dale Carnegie presents lei to one of his pupils, Mrs. Ethel de Saussure of Hawaii.

HE SELLS SUCCESS

Dale Carnegie, Who Teaches People How to Win Friends, May Shortly Influence the Best-Seller List Again

By HAROLD B. CLEMENKO

Dale Carnegie was a big surprise to me. I expected a row of gleaming white teeth bared in a forced smile, a bone-crunching handshake, and a yes-man manner. I found instead a sober little man who smiled in moderation, offered a mild hand, and could get mad without any trouble.

I saw him backstage before he strode out to address a thousand people. And I noted with a layman's grim satisfaction that this expert, who had taught thousands public speaking, appeared to suffer the same tenseness that afflicts us all as we arise to prove we really are unaccustomed to public speaking.

Instead of a high-powered, high-polished, breezy character, Dale Carnegie turns out to be an informal, easy-going man who might be described by some such daring new phrase as "comfortable as an old shoe." Better make that "slipper."

The Dale Carnegie saga is long and colorful. He has been a salesman of bacon, lard and correspondence courses; an actor, a lecturer, an author, a magazine writer, a newspaper columnist, a radio commentator, a public-speaking teacher and a personality guide. But if you had to boil his significance down to a ten-word telegram (with room left for "very best regards") you'd say simply: *How to Win Friends and Influence People.*

(Continued on page 62)

60

PUBLISHED AS

DALE CARNEGIE: HE SELLS SUCCESS

DATE

MAY 25, 1948

AUTHOR

HAROLD B. CLEMENKO

Published to coincide with the release of author and self-help guru Dale Carnegie's book *How to Stop Worrying and Start Living*, this long article explored the biography, philosophy, and teaching methods of the man best known for the inspirational best seller *How to Win Friends and Influence People*. Kubrick's photographs depicted Carnegie in action—cajoling, orating, and judging students attending his 17-week course in New York.

"I'm one of the luckiest men alive," Carnegie told *Look*. "If I owned Missouri with a hog-tight fence around it, I'd still continue my work!"

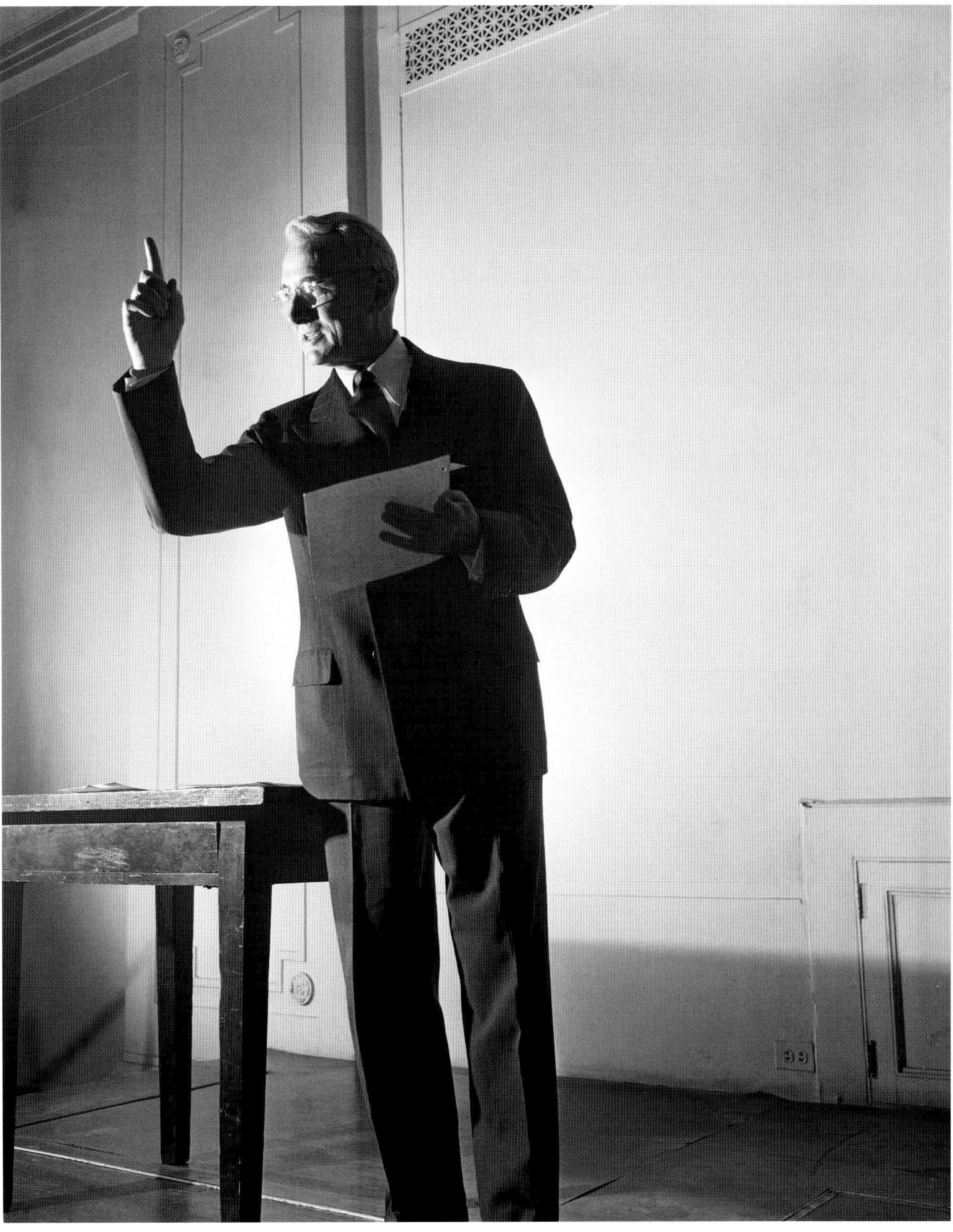

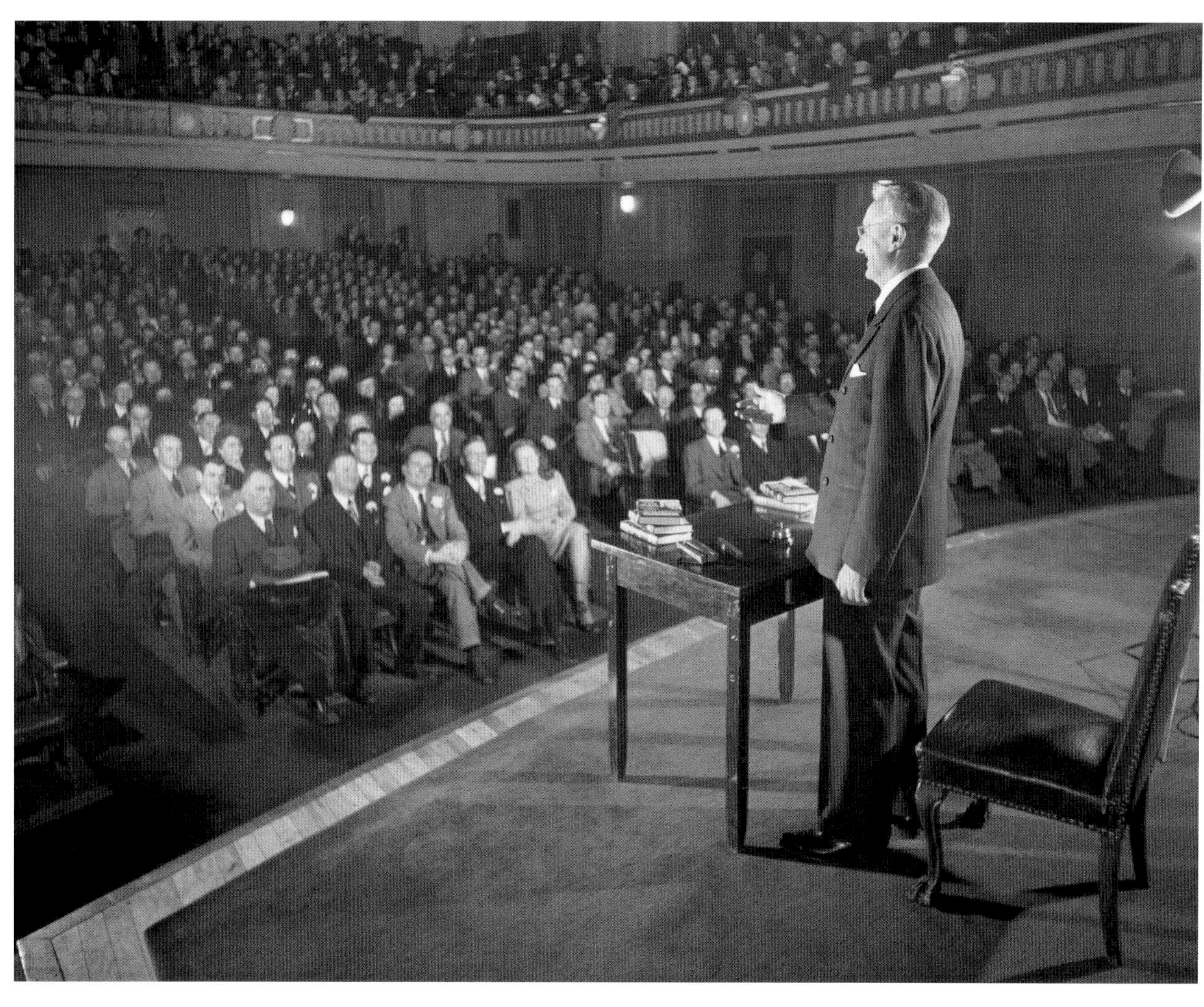

Carnegie lecturing to students taking his 17-week course

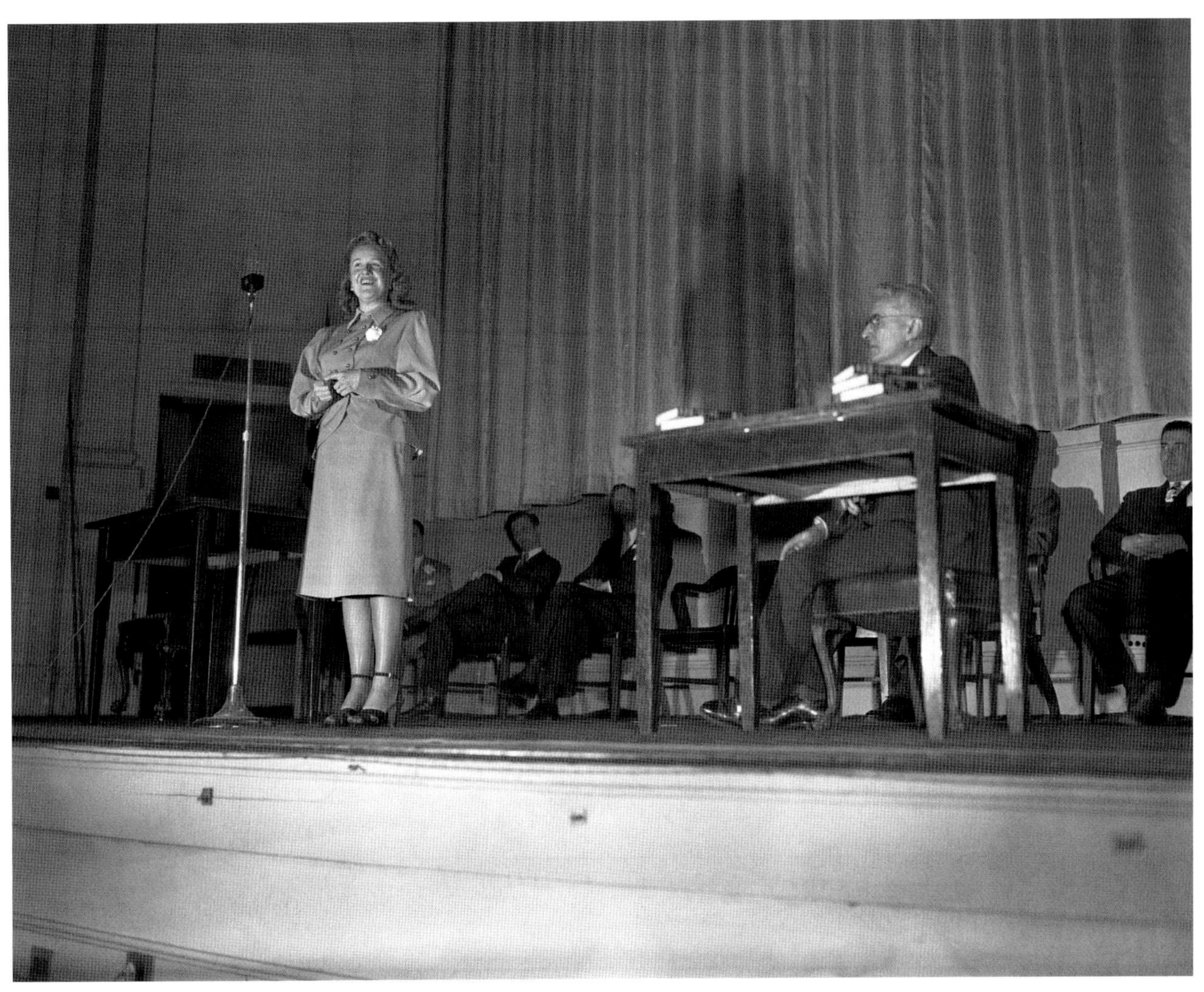

"This housewife smilingly tells how she urged her husband to take the course," the caption to this picture reported, " then found she needed it herself."

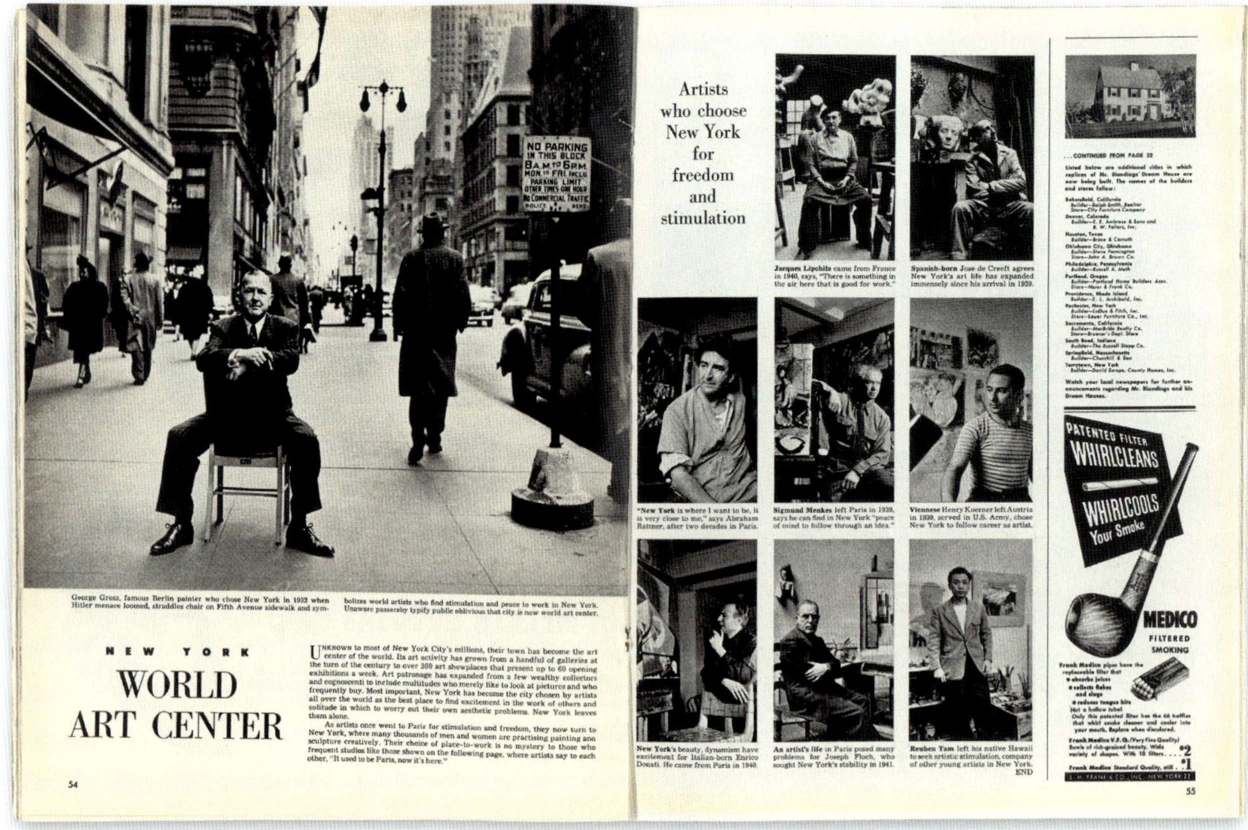

George Grosz, famous Berlin painter who chose New York in 1932 when Hitler menace loomed, straddles chair on Fifth Avenue sidewalk and symbolizes world artists who find stimulation and peace to work in New York. Unaware passersby typify public oblivious that city is now world art center.

NEW YORK

WORLD ART CENTER

Unknown to most of New York City's millions, their town has become the art center of the world. Its art activity has grown from a handful of galleries at the turn of the century to over 300 art showplaces that present up to 60 opening exhibitions a week. Art patronage has expanded from a few wealthy collectors and cognoscenti to include multitudes who merely like to look at pictures and who frequently buy. Most important, New York has become the city chosen by artists all over the world as the best place to find excitement in the work of others and solitude in which to worry out their own aesthetic problems. New York leaves them alone.

As artists once went to Paris for stimulation and freedom, they now turn to New York, where many thousands of men and women are practising painting and sculpture creatively. Their choice of place-to-work is no mystery to those who frequent studios like those shown on the following page, where artists say to each other, "It used to be Paris, now it's here."

54

Artists who choose New York for freedom and stimulation

Jacques Lipchitz came from France in 1940, says, "There is something in the air here that is good for work."

Spanish-born Jose de Creeft agrees New York's art life has expanded immensely since his arrival in 1929.

"New York is where I want to be, it is very close to me," says Abraham Rattner, after two decades in Paris.

Sigmund Menkes left Paris in 1939, says he can find in New York "peace of mind to follow through an idea."

Viennese Henry Koerner left Austria in 1939, served in U.S. Army, chose New York to follow career as artist.

New York's beauty, dynamism have excitement for Italian-born Enrico Donati. He came from Paris in 1940.

An artist's life in Paris posed many problems for Joseph Floch, who sought New York's stability in 1941.

Reuben Tam left his native Hawaii to seek artistic stimulation, company of other young artists in New York.

END

55

PUBLISHED AS

NEW YORK—WORLD ART CENTER: NEW YORK REPLACES PARIS AS ARTISTS' FAVORITE WORKSHOP

DATE

JUNE 8, 1948

Kubrick's photograph of Berlin painter George Grosz, who moved to New York in 1933 to escape the rise of Nazism, opened this photo essay about the city as "the art center of the world." Kubrick's image was the only one shot on the city's streets; all the other *Look* photographers worked in artists' studios. Sitting on an otherwise busy Fifth Avenue, Grosz "symbolizes world artists who find stimulation and peace to work in New York," while unaware passersby "typify public oblivious that city is now world art center." Kubrick and Grosz collaborated on the portrait's unusual Fifth Avenue setting, which the magazine described as "an artistic meeting of minds." Grosz followed up by complimenting Kubrick in a letter to the editor, published the following month (July 20, 1948).

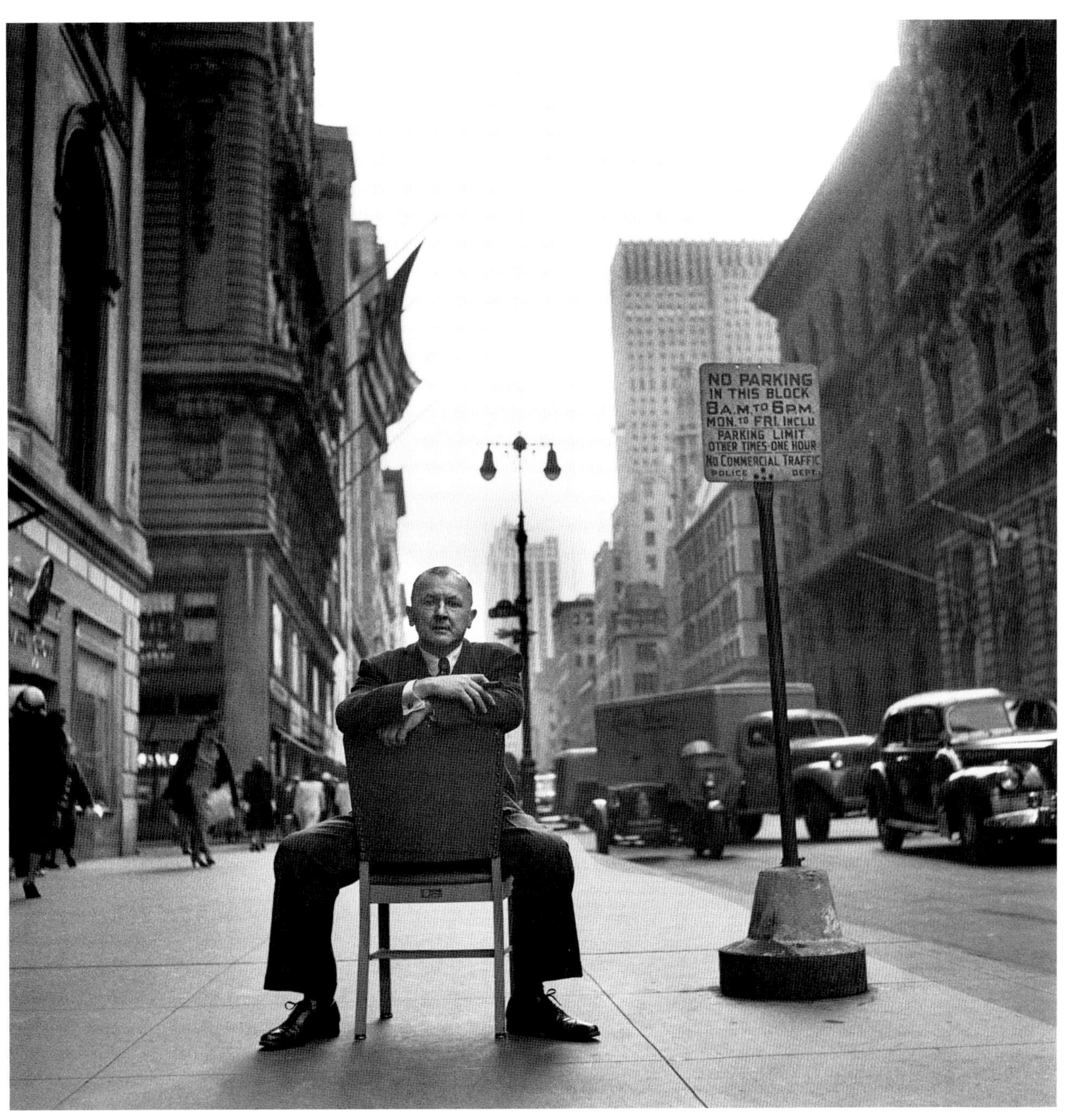

An outtake from Kubrick's portrait session with Grosz on Fifth Avenue, without the passing pedestrians who appeared in the published image

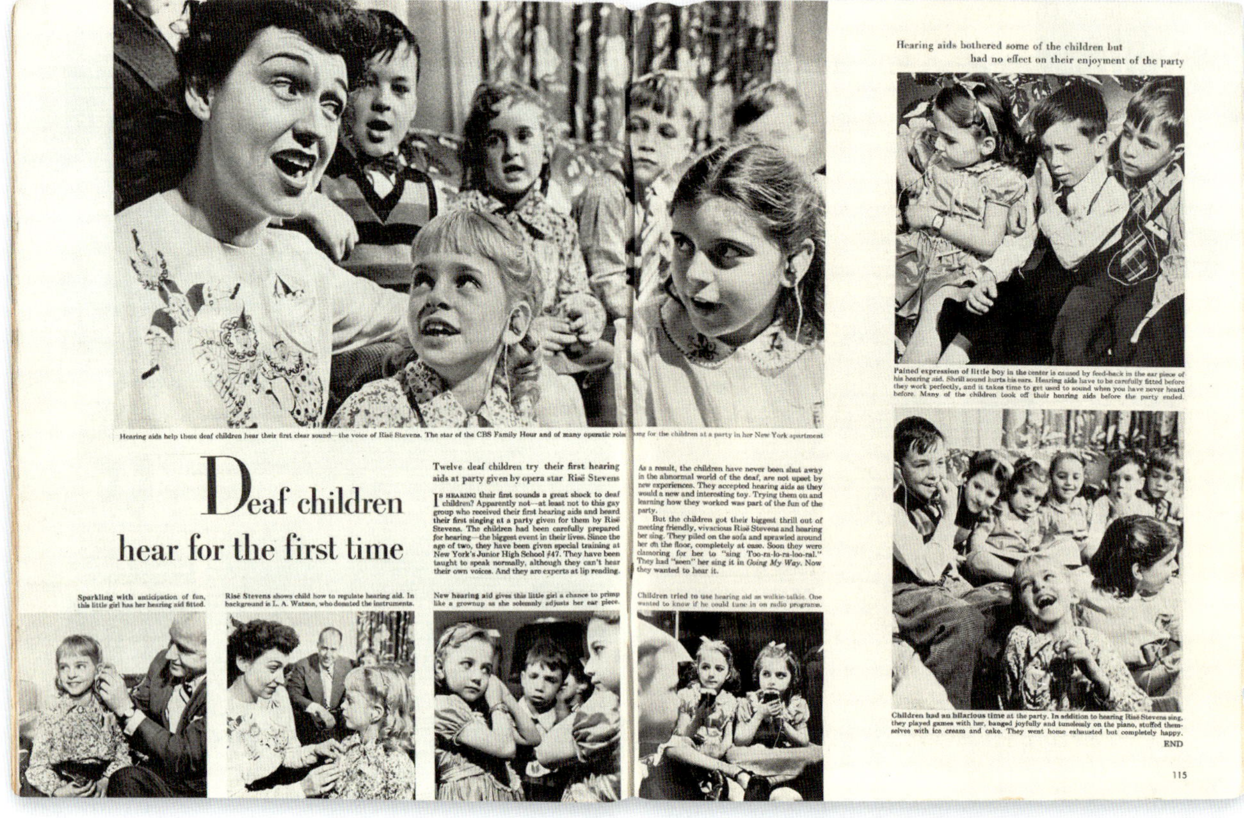

Hearing aids help these deaf children hear their first clear sound—the voice of Risë Stevens. The star of the CBS Family Hour and of many operatic roles sang for the children at a party in her New York apartment

Deaf children hear for the first time

Twelve deaf children try their first hearing aids at party given by opera star Risë Stevens

Is HEARING their first sounds a great shock to deaf children? Apparently not—at least not to this gay group who received their first hearing aids and heard their first singing at a party given for them by Risë Stevens. The children had been carefully prepared for hearing—the biggest event in their lives. Since the age of two, they have been given special training at New York's Junior High School #47. They have been taught to speak normally, although they can't hear their own voices. And they are experts at lip reading. As a result, the children have never been shut away in the abnormal world of the deaf, are not upset by new experiences. They accepted hearing aids as they would a new and interesting toy. Trying them on and learning how they worked was part of the fun of the party.

But the children got their biggest thrill out of meeting friendly, vivacious Risë Stevens and hearing her sing. They piled on the sofa and sprawled around her on the floor, completely at ease. Soon they were clamoring for her to "sing Too-ra-lo-ra-loo-ral." They had "seen" her sing it in *Going My Way*. Now they wanted to hear it.

Sparkling with anticipation of fun, this little girl has her hearing aid fitted.

Risë Stevens shows child how to regulate hearing aid. In background is L. A. Watson, who donated the instruments.

New hearing aid gives this little girl a chance to primp like a grownup as she solemnly adjusts her ear piece.

Children tried to use hearing aid as walkie-talkie. One wanted to know if he could tune in on radio programs.

Hearing aids bothered some of the children but had no effect on their enjoyment of the party

Pained expression of little boy in the center is caused by feed-back in the ear piece of his hearing aid. Shrill sound hurts his ears. Hearing aids have to be carefully fitted before they work perfectly, and it takes time to get used to sound when you have never heard before. Many of the children took off their hearing aids before the party ended.

Children had an hilarious time at the party. In addition to hearing Risë Stevens sing, they played games with her, banged joyfully and tunelessly on the piano, stuffed themselves with ice cream and cake. They went home exhausted but completely happy.

END

115

PUBLISHED AS

DEAF CHILDREN HEAR FOR THE FIRST TIME: RISË STEVENS ENTERTAINS THEM AT HER HOME

DATE

MAY 25, 1948

For this story Kubrick documented the visit of 12 deaf children to the New York apartment of opera singer and radio personality Risë Stevens. The children, who could speak and were expert at lipreading, used hearing aids to listen to Stevens sing. This experience was the first time they had heard a human voice.

The students embraced their hearing aids as they would "a new and interesting toy," commented the article.

FOLLOWING SPREAD **Young girls trying on their new hearing aids**

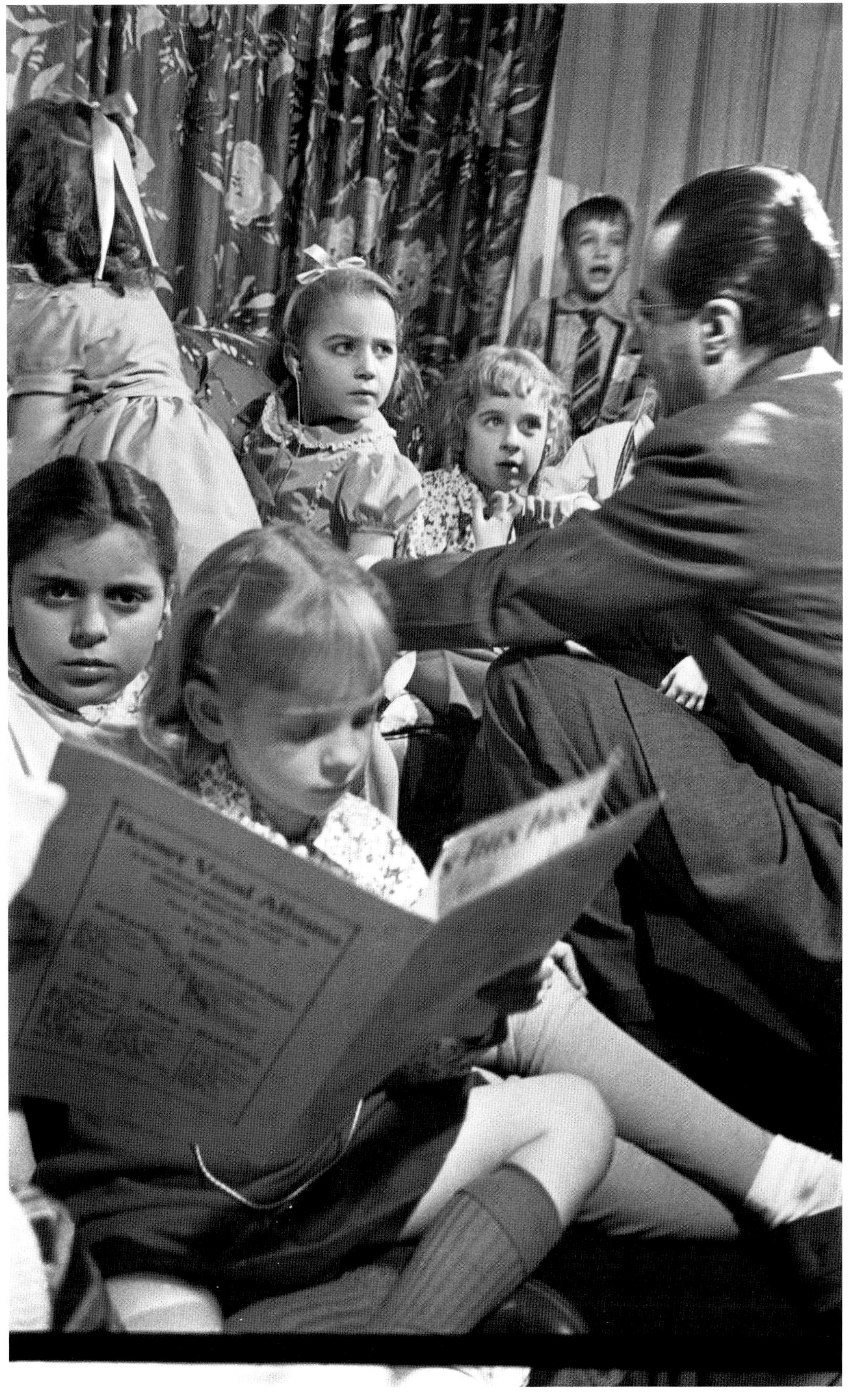

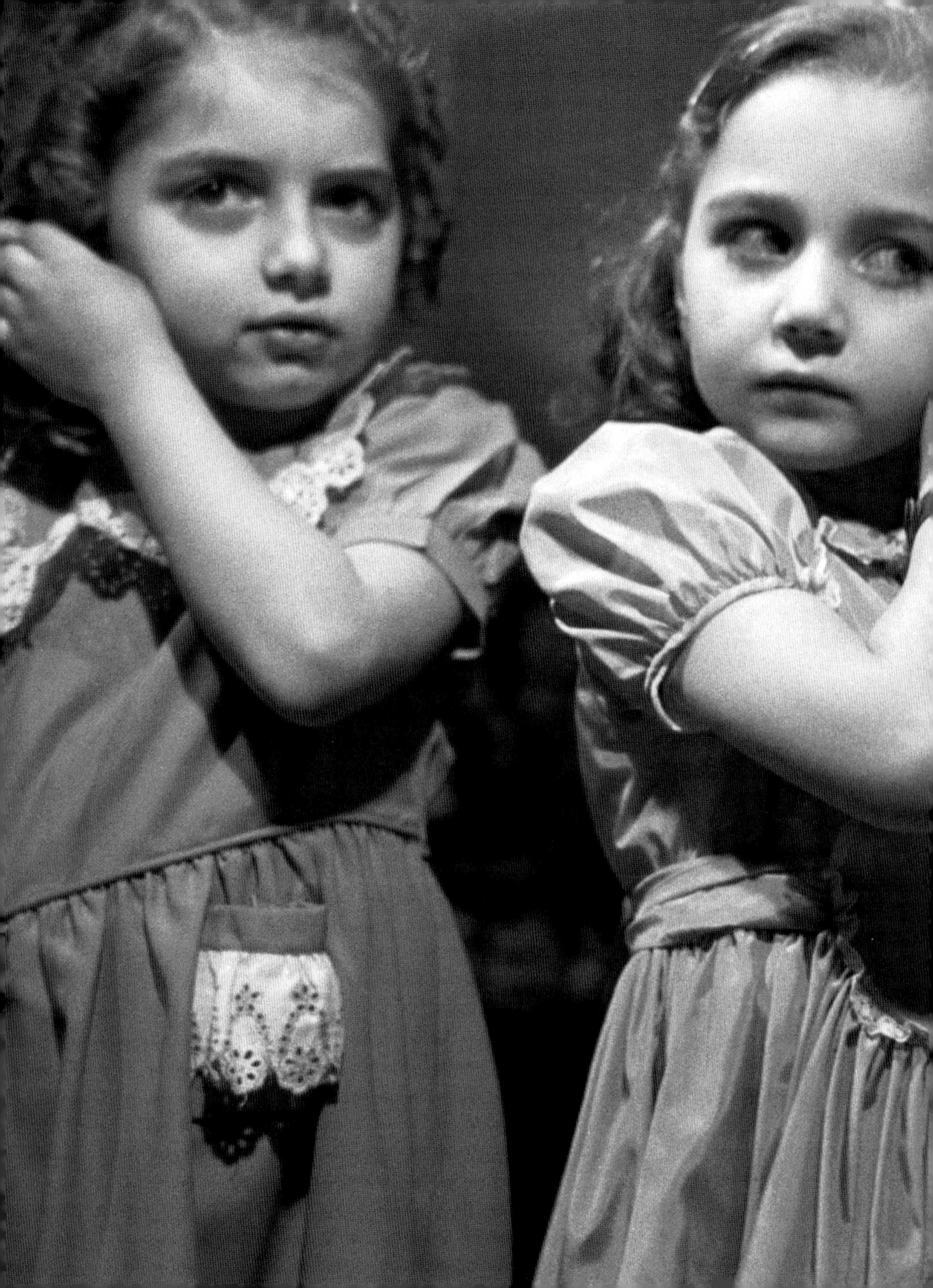

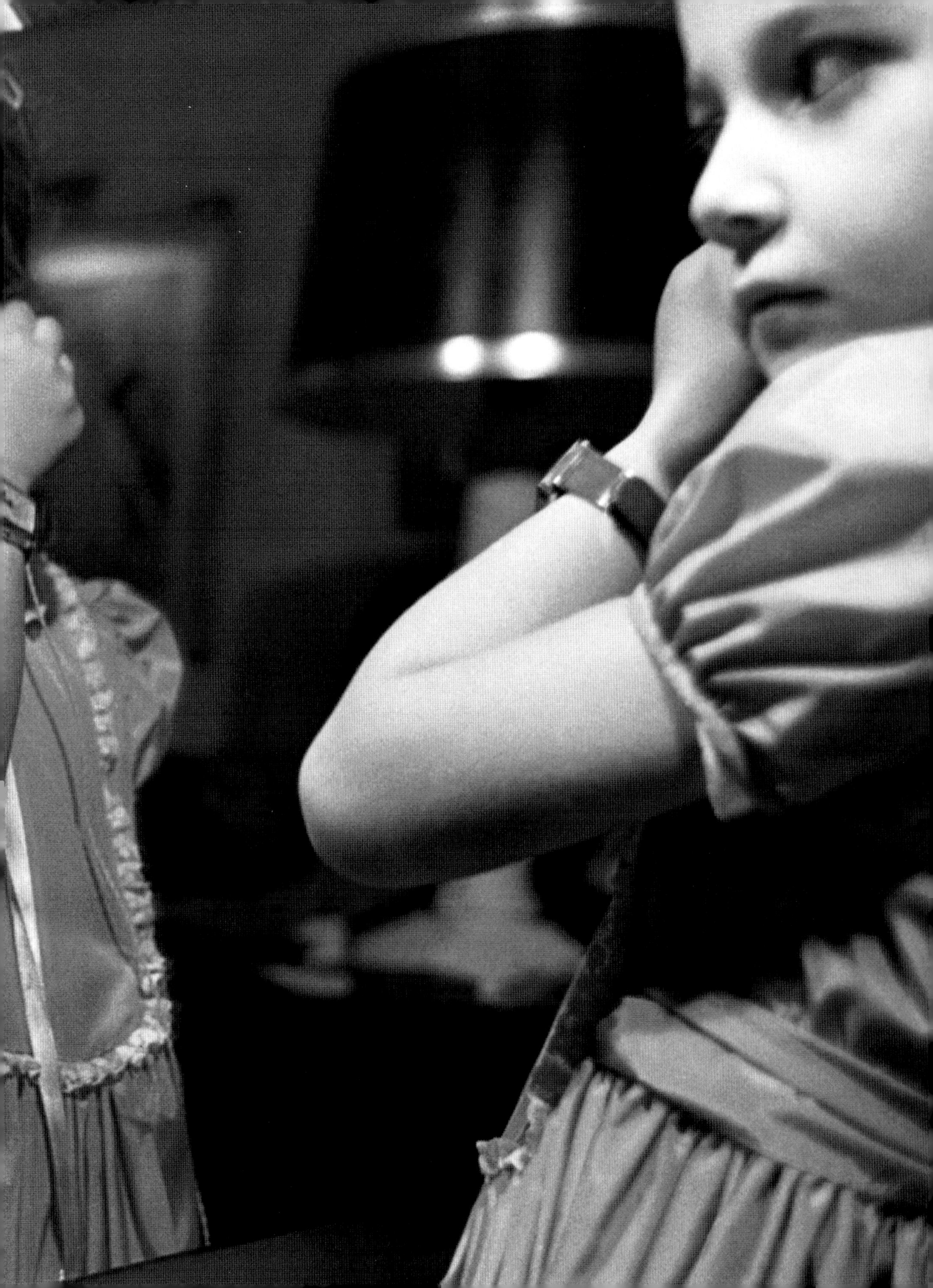

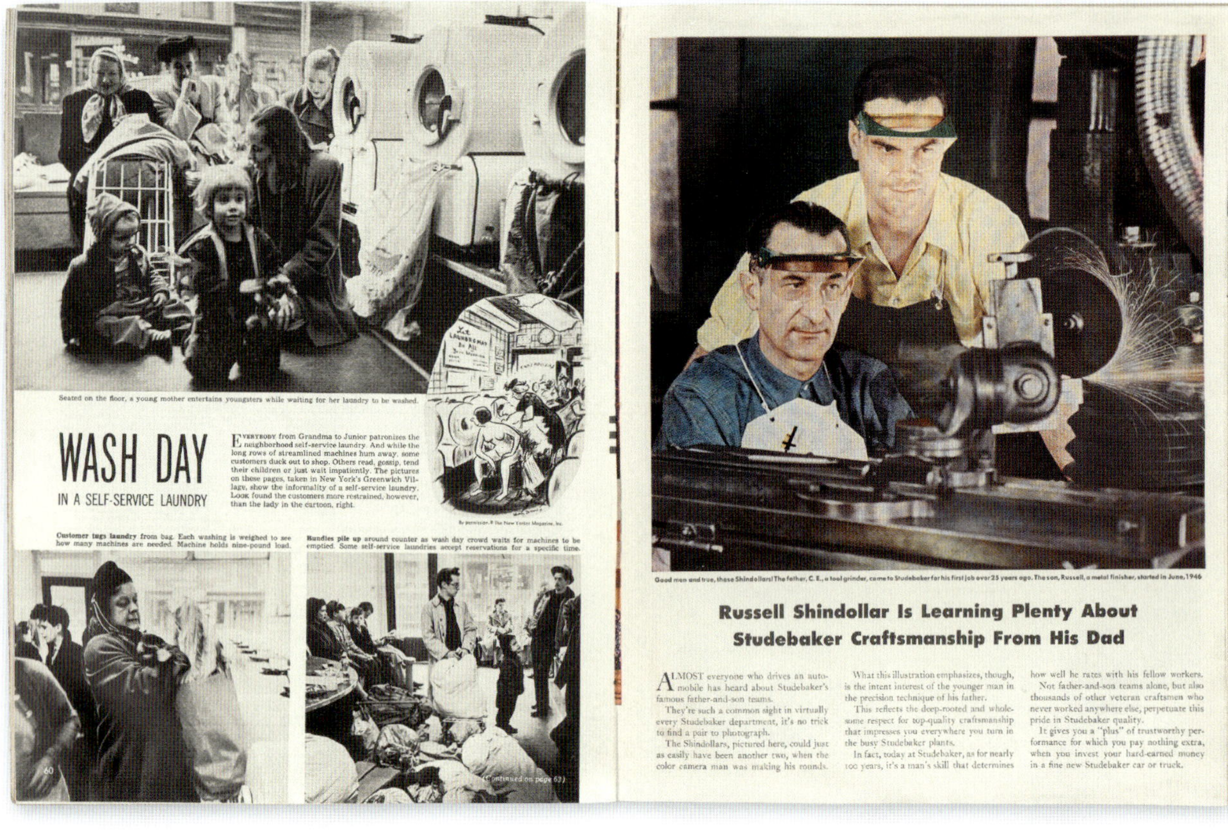

Seated on the floor, a young mother entertains youngsters while waiting for her laundry to be washed.

WASH DAY

IN A SELF-SERVICE LAUNDRY

EVERYBODY from Grandma to Junior patronizes the neighborhood self-service laundry. And while the long rows of streamlined machines hum away, some customers duck out to shop. Others read, gossip, tend their children or just wait impatiently. The pictures on these pages, taken in New York's Greenwich Village, show the informality of a self-service laundry. LOOK found the customers more restrained, however, than the lady in the cartoon, right.

By permission. © The New Yorker Magazine, Inc.

Customer tugs laundry from bag. Each washing is weighed to see how many machines are needed. Machine holds nine-pound load.

Bundles pile up around counter as wash day crowd waits for machines to be emptied. Some self-service laundries accept reservations for a specific time.

60

(continued on page 63)

Good men and true, these Shindollars! The father, C. E., a tool grinder, came to Studebaker for his first job over 25 years ago. The son, Russell, a metal finisher, started in June, 1946

Russell Shindollar Is Learning Plenty About Studebaker Craftsmanship From His Dad

ALMOST everyone who drives an automobile has heard about Studebaker's famous father-and-son teams.

They're such a common sight in virtually every Studebaker department, it's no trick to find a pair to photograph.

The Shindollars, pictured here, could just as easily have been another two, when the color camera man was making his rounds.

What this illustration emphasizes, though, is the intent interest of the younger man in the precision technique of his father.

This reflects the deep-rooted and wholesome respect for top-quality craftsmanship that impresses you everywhere you turn in the busy Studebaker plants.

In fact, today at Studebaker, as for nearly 100 years, it's a man's skill that determines how well he rates with his fellow workers.

Not father-and-son teams alone, but also thousands of other veteran craftsmen who never worked anywhere else, perpetuate this pride in Studebaker quality.

It gives you a "plus" of trustworthy performance for which you pay nothing extra, when you invest your hard-earned money in a fine new Studebaker car or truck.

PUBLISHED AS

WASH DAY: *LOOK* VISITS A GREENWICH VILLAGE SELF-SERVICE LAUNDRY

DATE

APRIL 27, 1948

Like Kubrick's story about people waiting to see their dentist, this article captured regular people engaged in everyday activities. This assignment illustrated what residents of New York's Greenwich Village did while washing their clothes in a self-service laundry. "And while the long rows of streamlined machines hum away," the article noted, "some customers duck out to shop. Others read, gossip, tend their children or just wait impatiently."

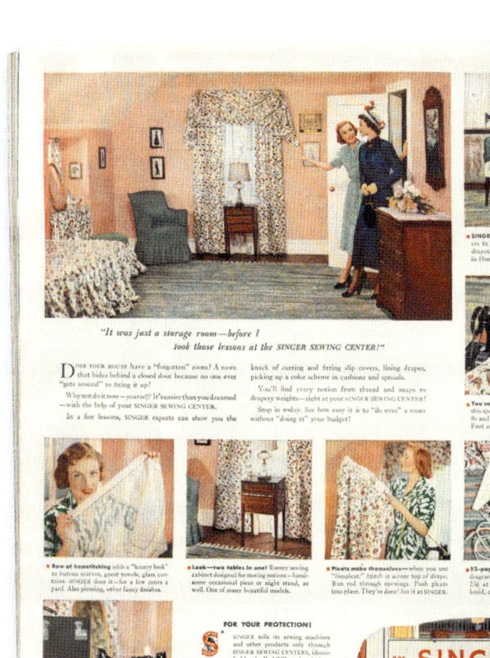

"It was just a storage room—before I took those lessons at the SINGER SEWING CENTER!"

FOR YOUR PROTECTION!

SINGER SEWING CENTERS

THERE'S ONE NEAR YOU TO SERVE YOU

WASH DAY continued

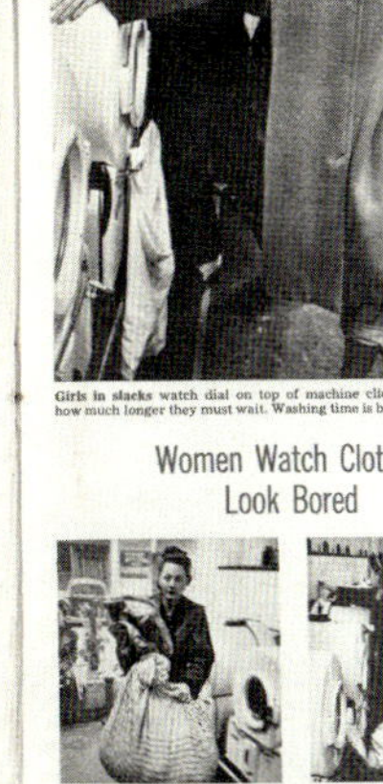

Girls in slacks watch dial on top of machine click around, indicating how much longer they must wait. Washing time is between 30-40 minutes.

Women Watch Clothes Look Bored

Package-laden woman gathers up her wash in chenille bedspread.

Time's up, and a customer scoops her laundry out of the machine.

Self-service patron waits impatiently for turn to stuff in clothes.

Yawning young woman passes time chatting with her bored companion.

(Continued on page 63)

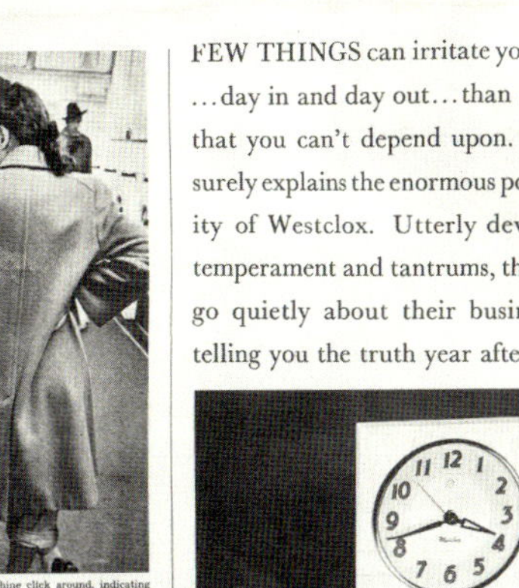

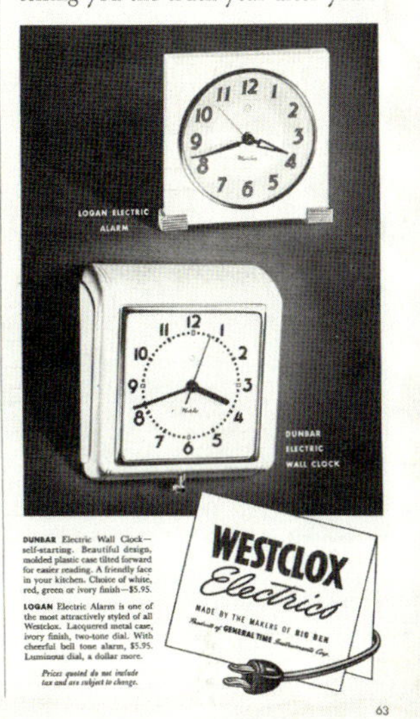

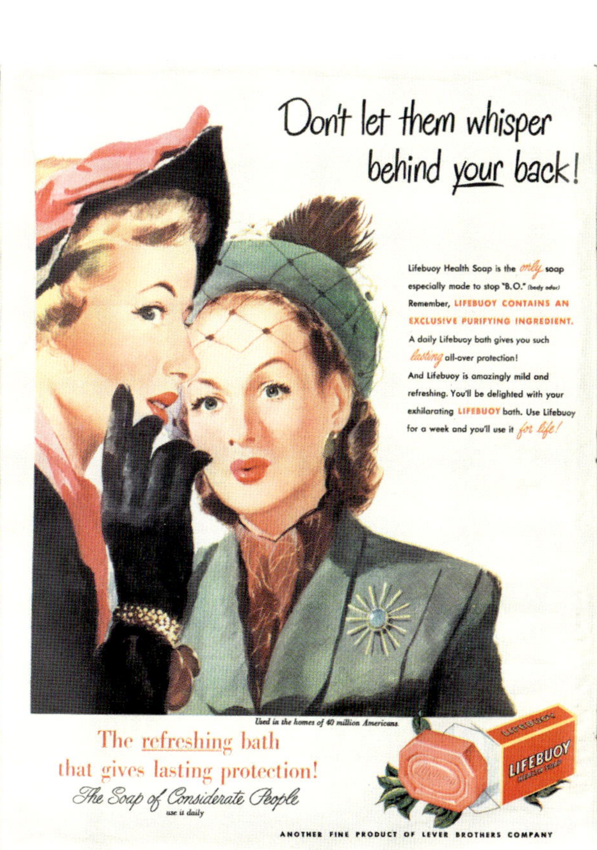

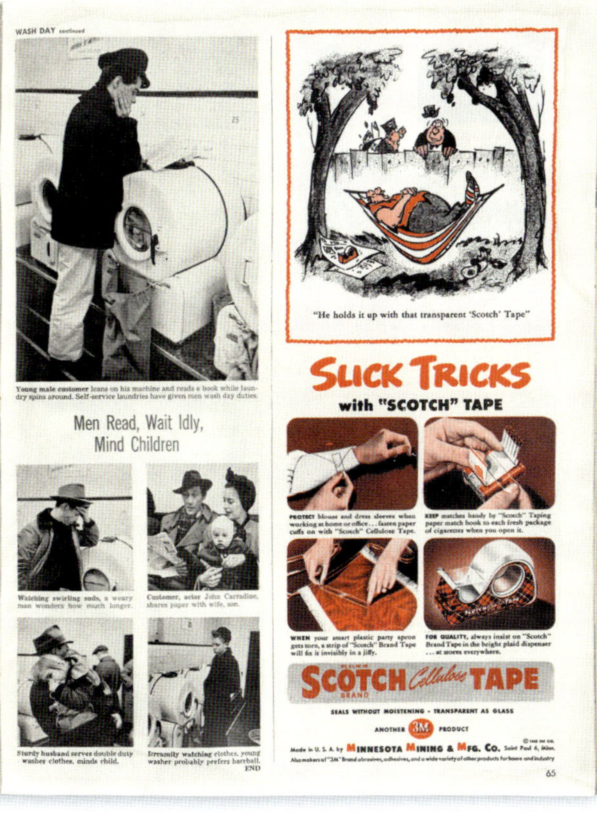

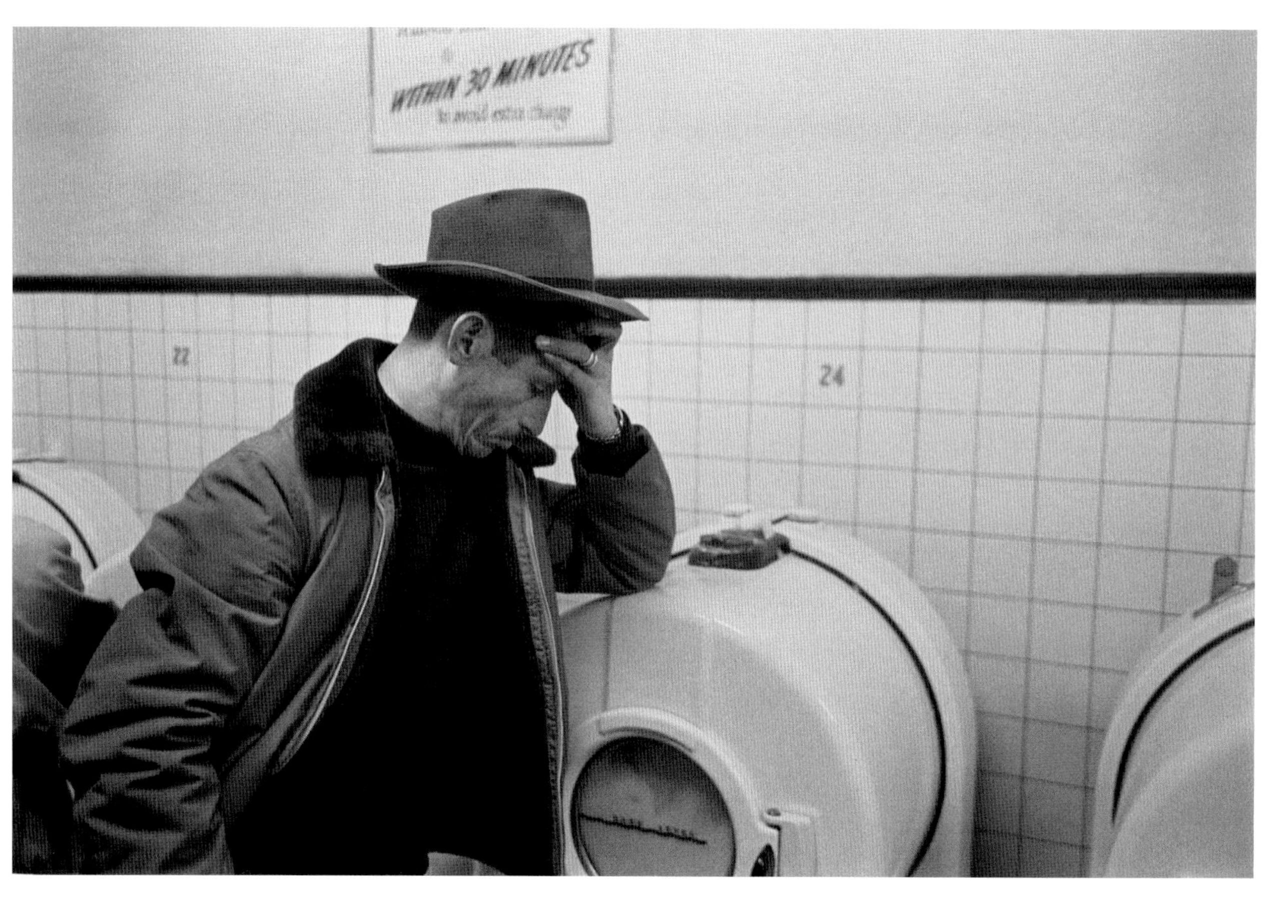

THIS SPREAD AND FOLLOWING
Greenwich Villagers patiently waiting for their laundry to finish

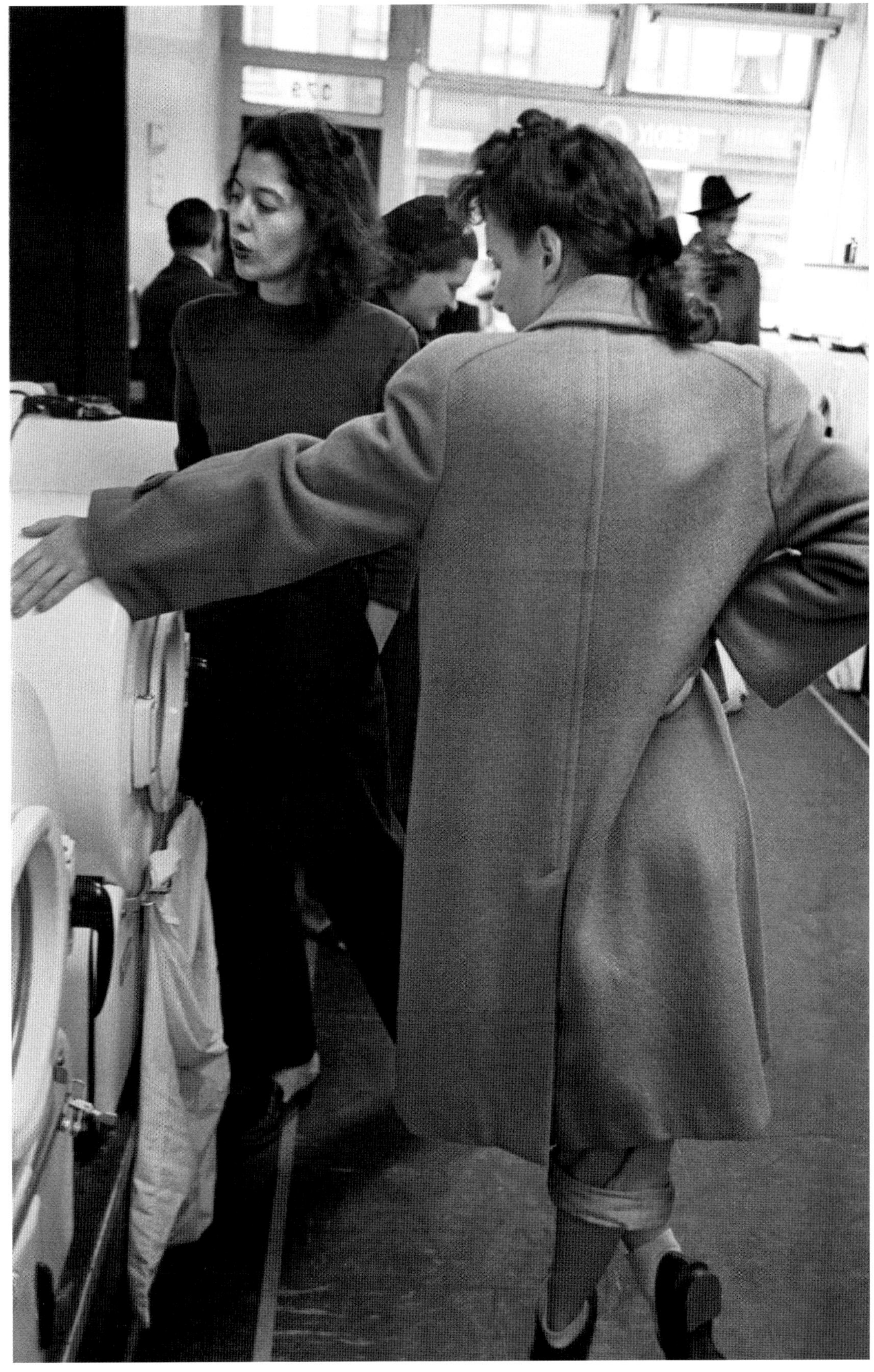

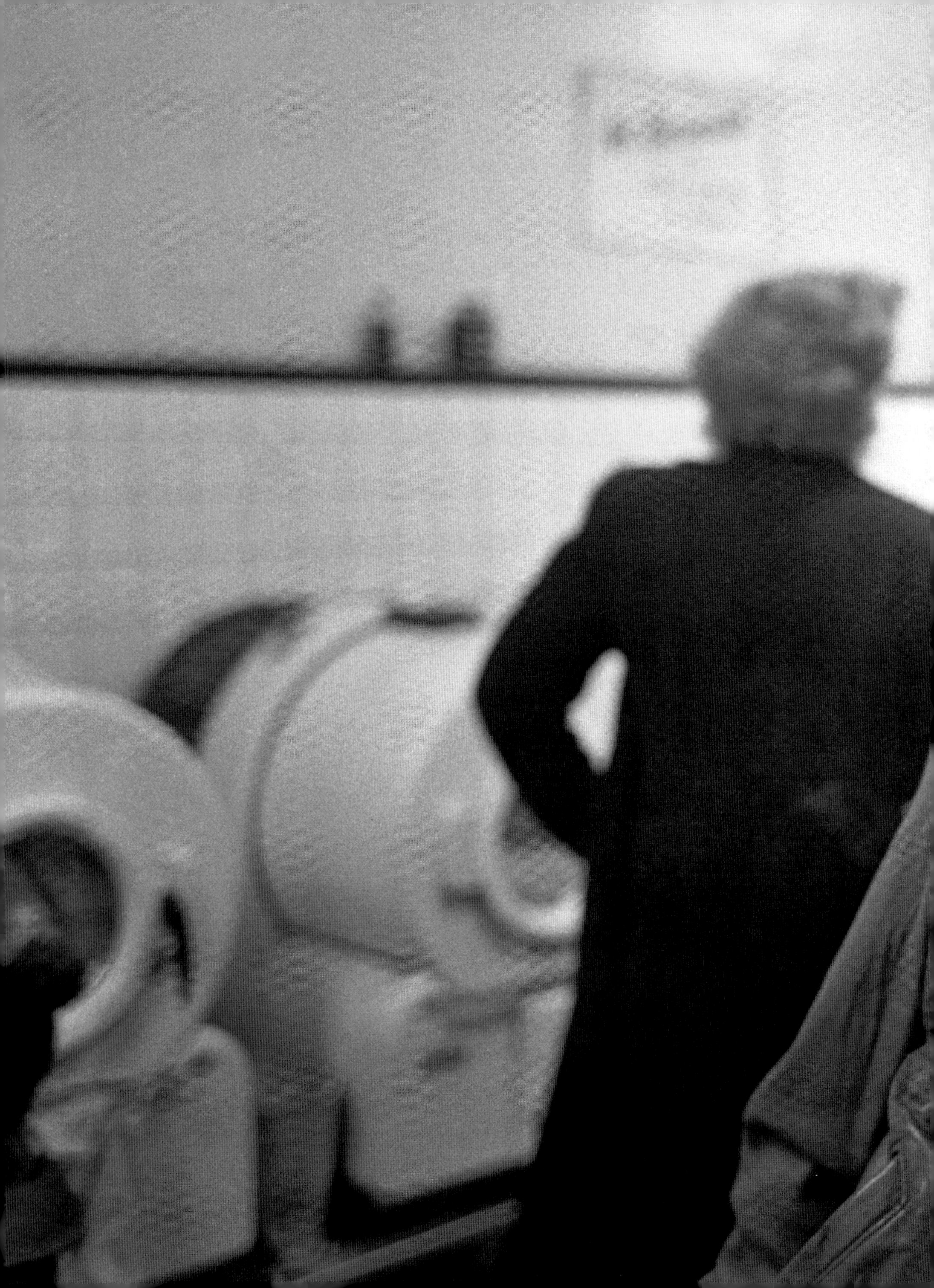

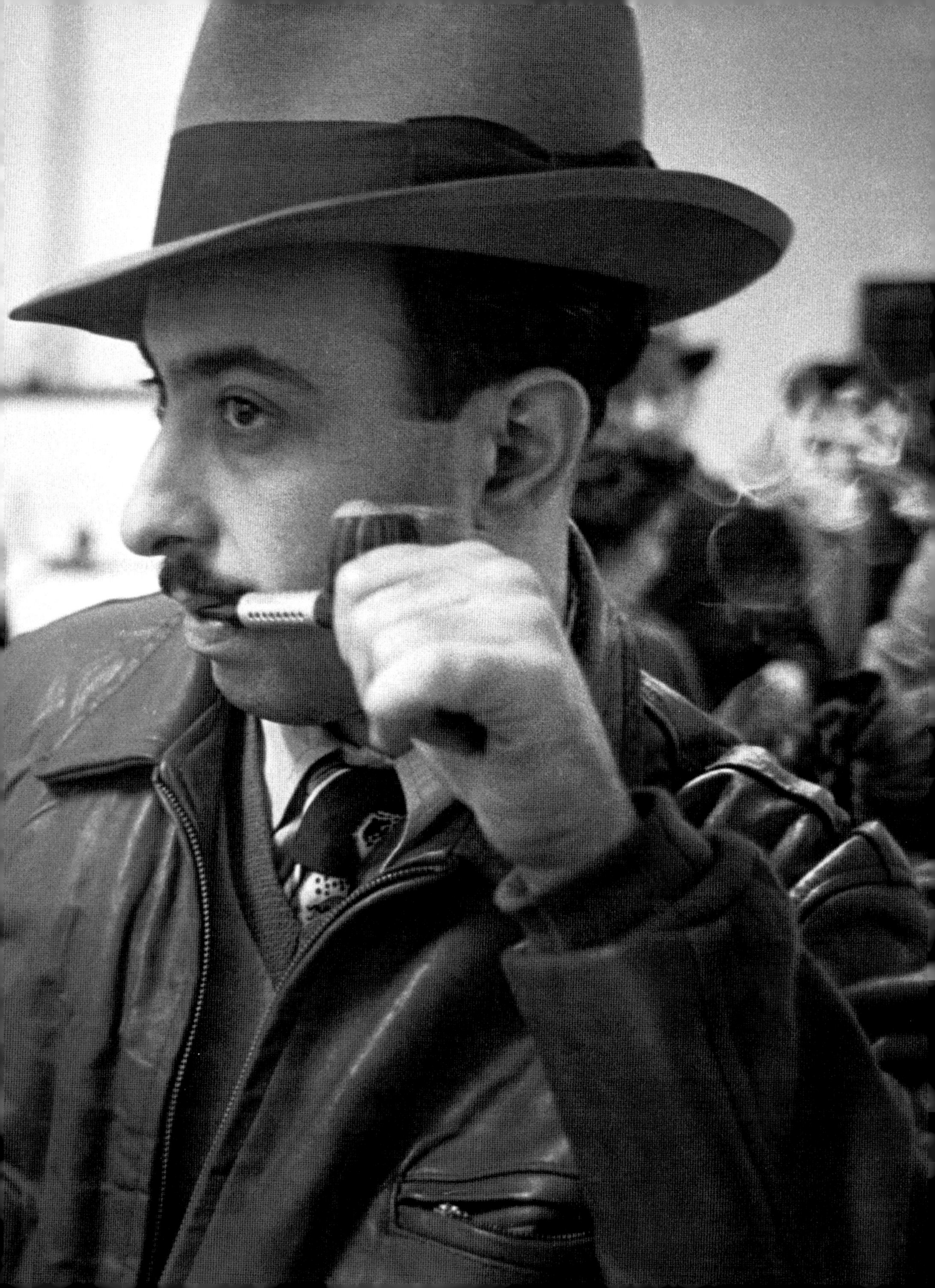

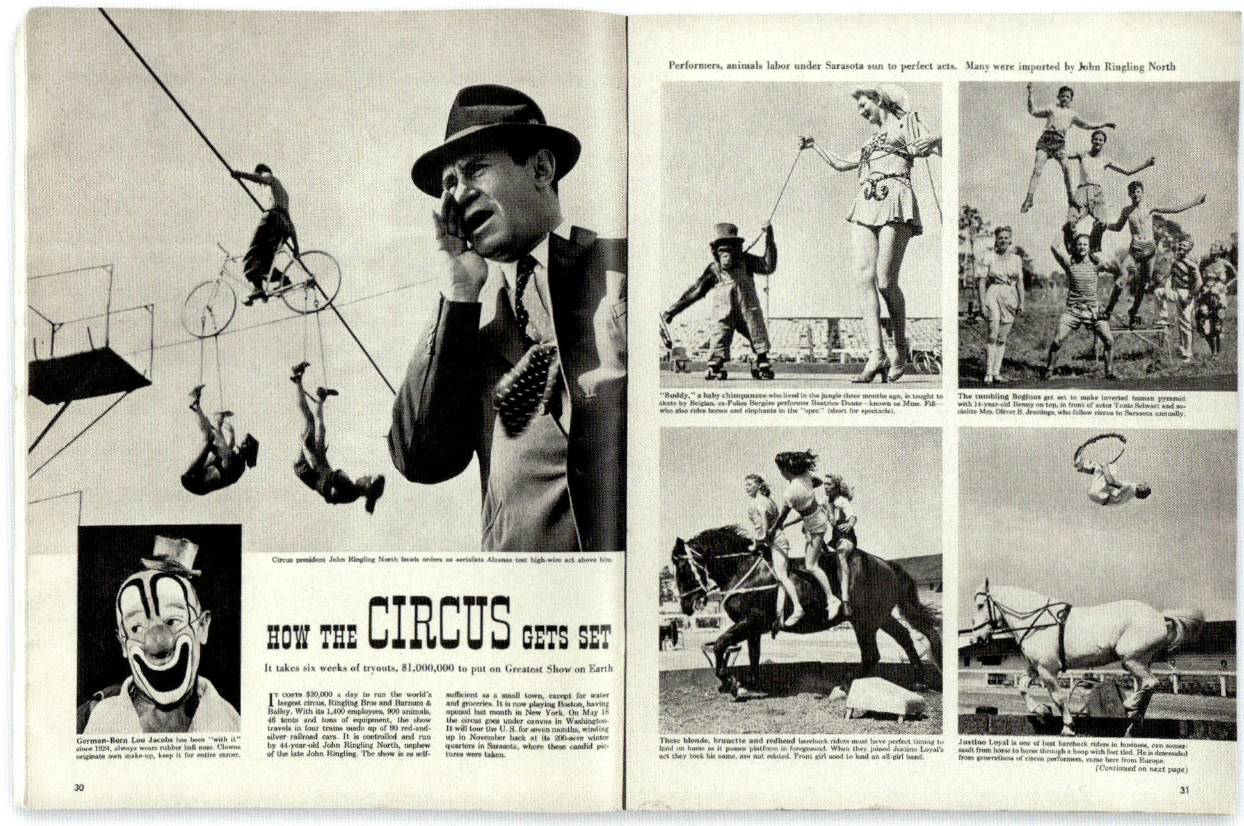

Circus president John Ringling North bawls orders as aerialists Alzanas test high-wire act above him.

HOW THE CIRCUS GETS SET

It takes six weeks of tryouts, $1,000,000 to put on Greatest Show on Earth

IT COSTS $20,000 a day to run the world's largest circus, Ringling Bros and Barnum & Bailey. With its 1,400 employees, 900 animals, 46 tents and tons of equipment, the show travels in four trains made up of 90 red-and-silver railroad cars. It is controlled and run by 44-year-old John Ringling North, nephew of the late John Ringling. The show is as self-sufficient as a small town, except for water and groceries. It is now playing Boston, having opened last month in New York. On May 18 the circus goes under canvas in Washington. It will tour the U. S. for seven months, winding up in November back at its 200-acre winter quarters in Sarasota, where these candid pictures were taken.

German-Born Lou Jacobs has been "with it" since 1924, always wears rubber ball nose. Clowns originate own make-up, keep it for entire career.

30

Performers, animals labor under Sarasota sun to perfect acts. Many were imported by John Ringling North

"Buddy," a baby chimpanzee who lived in the jungle three months ago, is taught to skate by Belgian, ex-Folies Bergère performer Beatrice Dante—known as Mme. Fifi—who also rides horses and elephants in the "spec" (short for spectacle).

The tumbling Boginos get set to make inverted human pyramid with 14-year-old Benny on top, in front of actor Tonio Selwart and socialite Mrs. Oliver B. Jennings, who follow circus to Sarasota annually.

These blonde, brunette and redhead bareback riders must have perfect timing to land on horse as it passes platform in foreground. When they joined Justino Loyal's act they took his name, are not related. Front girl used to lead an all-girl band.

Justino Loyal is one of best bareback riders in business, can somersault from horse to horse through a hoop with feet tied. He is descended from generations of circus performers, came here from Europe.

(Continued on next page)

31

PUBLISHED AS

HOW THE CIRCUS GETS SET

DATE

MAY 25, 1948

Kubrick's interest in eccentric and absurd subjects was represented in a portrayal of the Ringling Bros. and Barnum & Bailey circus. *Look*'s editors sent Kubrick to the circus's 200-acre winter headquarters in Sarasota, Florida, resulting in his first published long-form story set outside the New York City region. The article's images showed performers, aerialists, baby chimpanzees, and horse riders training to go on a seven-month national tour. "It takes six weeks of tryouts," the article stated, and "$1,000,000 to put on Greatest Show on Earth." While Kubrick also photographed the circus's opening night, these images were not included in the story. The issue's cover featured Kubrick's rare use of Kodachrome color film for a portrait of German-born clown Lou Jacobs.

"Fliers," "first-of-Mays," "web girls" train long hours under Big Top at Winter Quarters

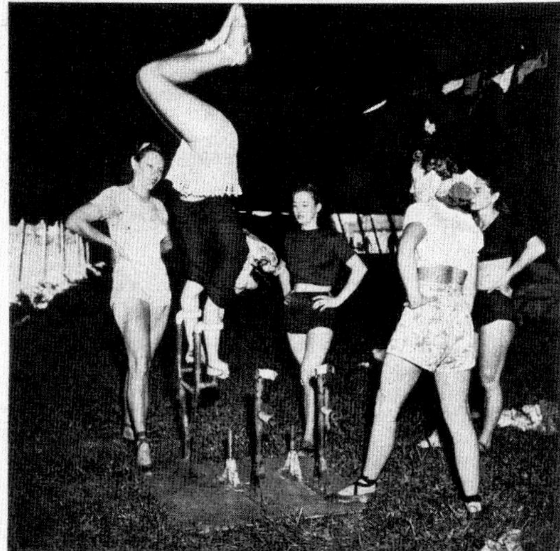

Girl practices handstand on the ground until she is adept enough to try it 60 feet up. In circus parlance aerialists are "fliers," newcomers are "first-of-Mays" and "web girls" are the ones who work the ropes, trapezes.

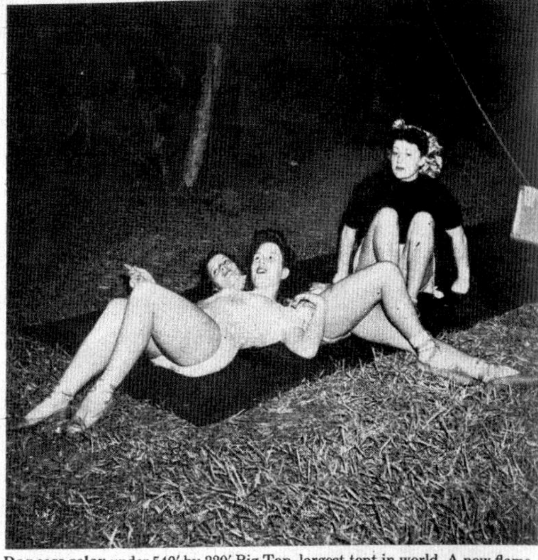

Dancers relax under 540′ by 220′ Big Top, largest tent in world. A new flameproof Big Top is made annually in workshop. Old tent, used for rehearsals, is full of sievelike holes made by swarm of locusts last summer.

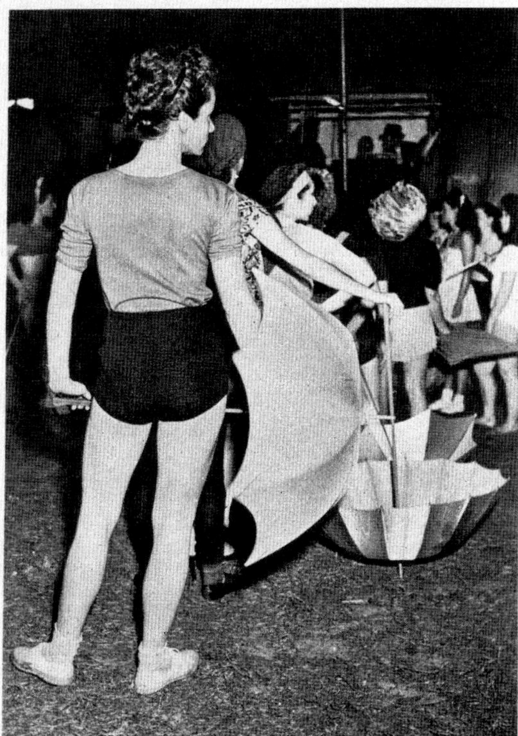

Girls in "Dixie" number wait to go on. Model Jean Rockwell, foreground, is a "first-of-May," gets $60 a week, all her meals, $20 extra for "web work." She sleeps in a converted hospital railroad car with 40 other girls.

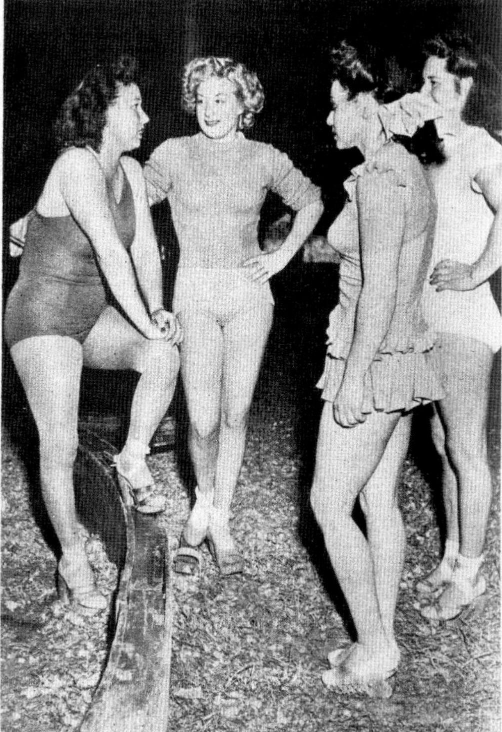

These acrobats and aerialists will look quite different in Brooks costumes designed by Broadway's Miles White. Girls need stamina to stick with the show, but many do for a lot of reasons—see *Meet the People* on page 42.

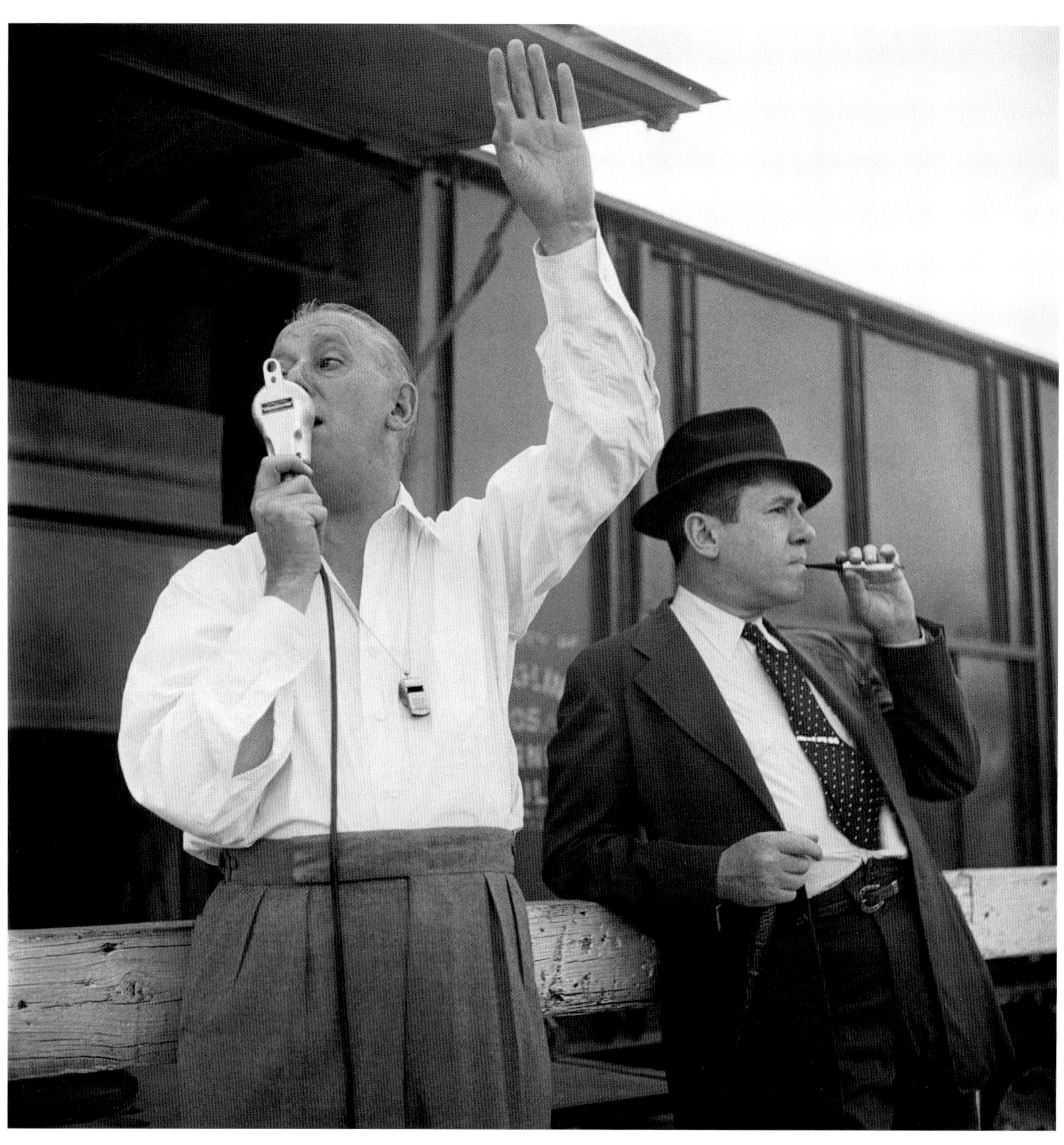

Circus president John Ringling North (right) intently watching tryouts

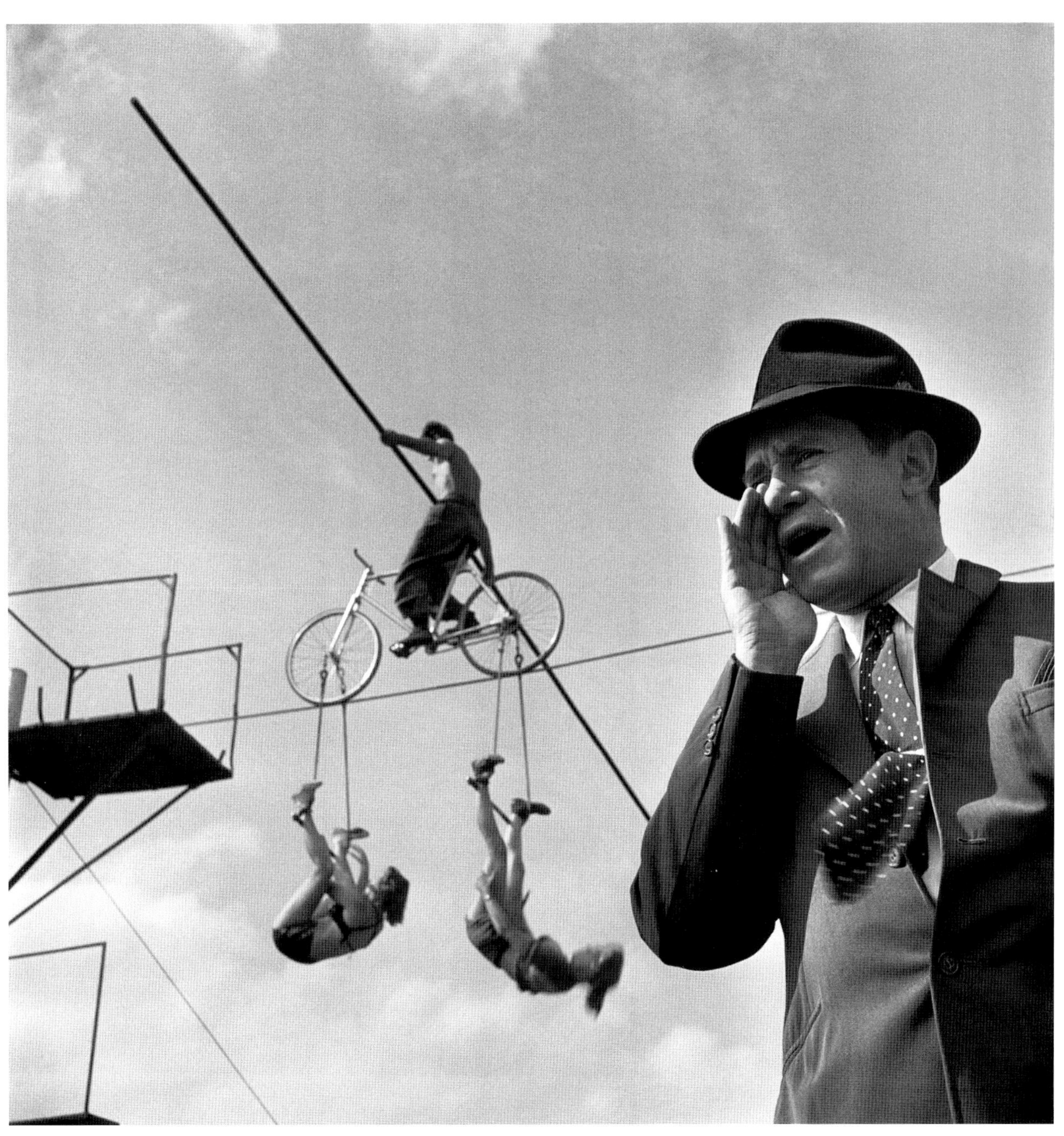

John Ringling North with the Alzanas perfecting their aerial act above

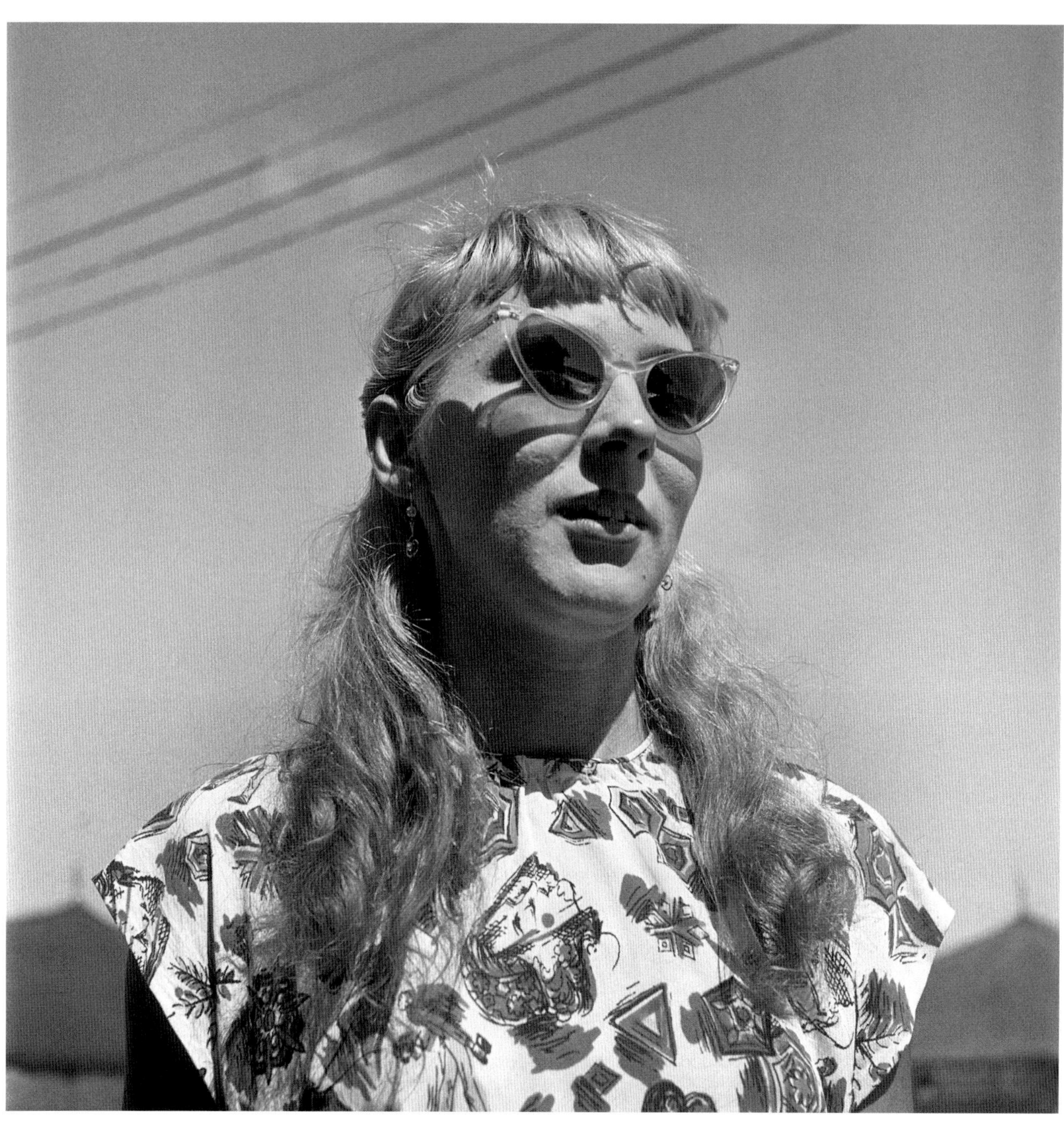

Performer Laurencia Klaja, orphaned New Yorker and ballet dancer, age 22

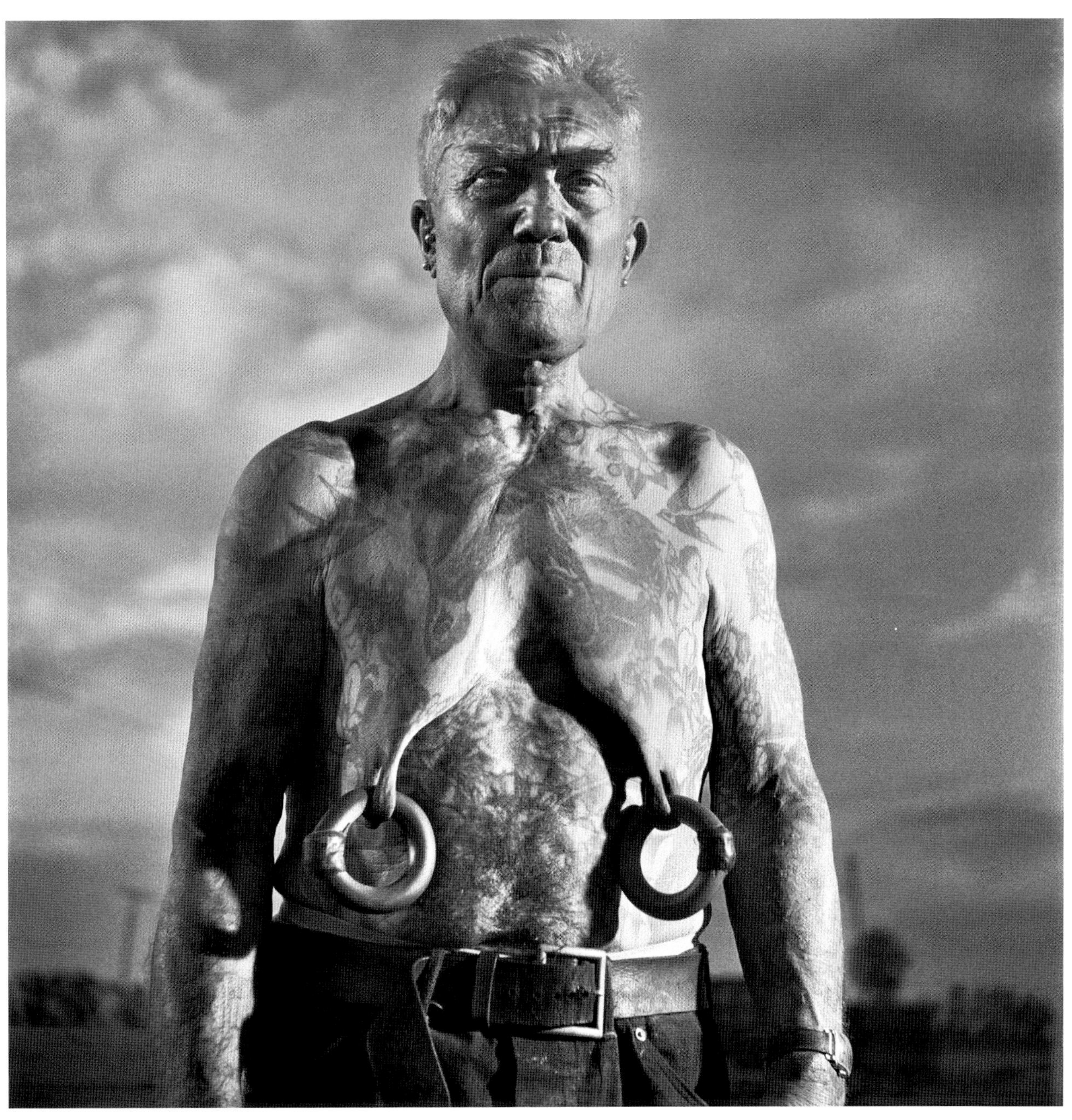

This photograph of a tattooed and pierced man may have been too grotesque for *Look* to publish.

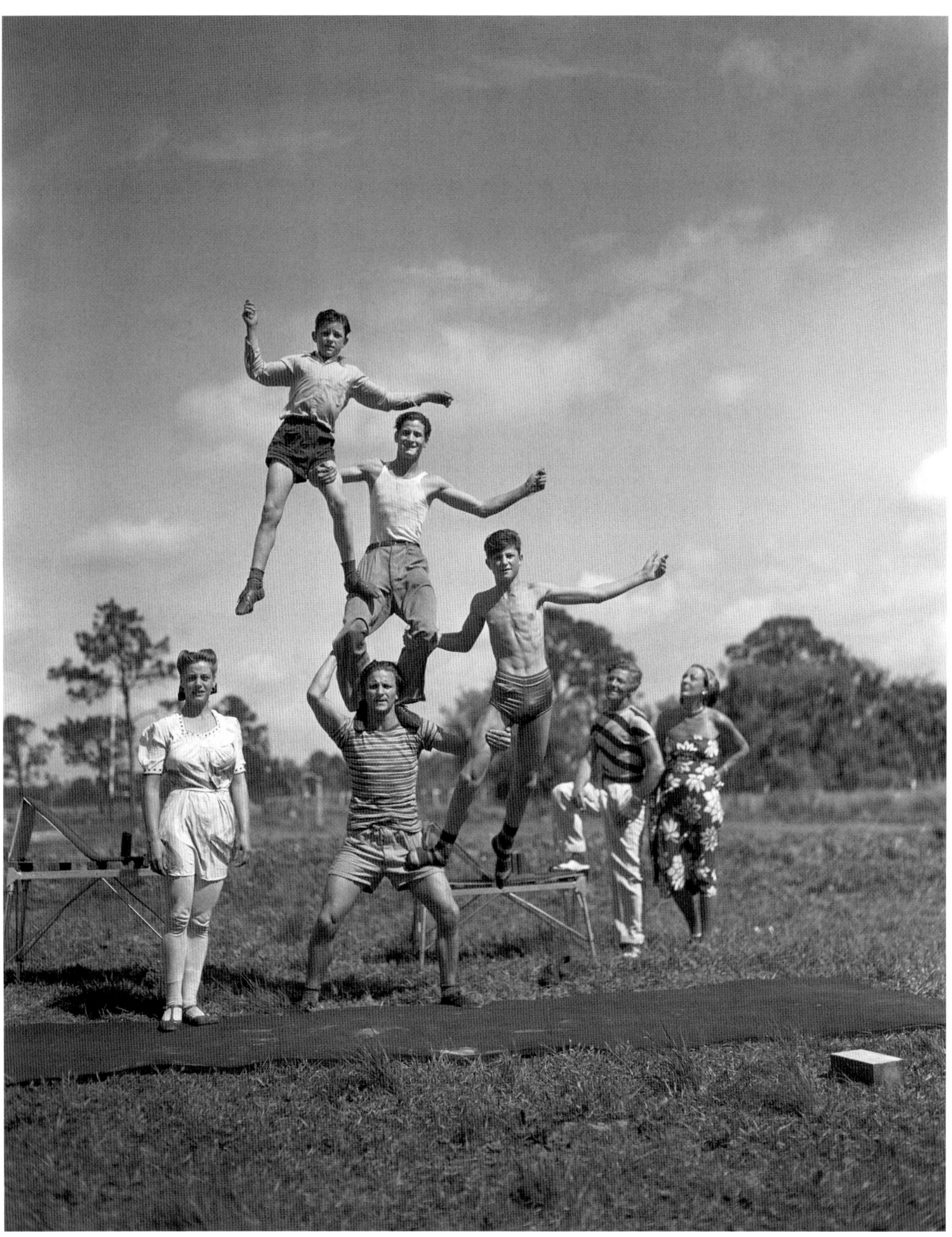

OPPOSITE **The Bogino family of acrobats in formation**

BELOW **An elephant practicing for the Circus Ball, the finale of the company's season**

FOLLOWING SPREAD **Justino Loyal, one of the best bareback riders in the business, practicing his act**

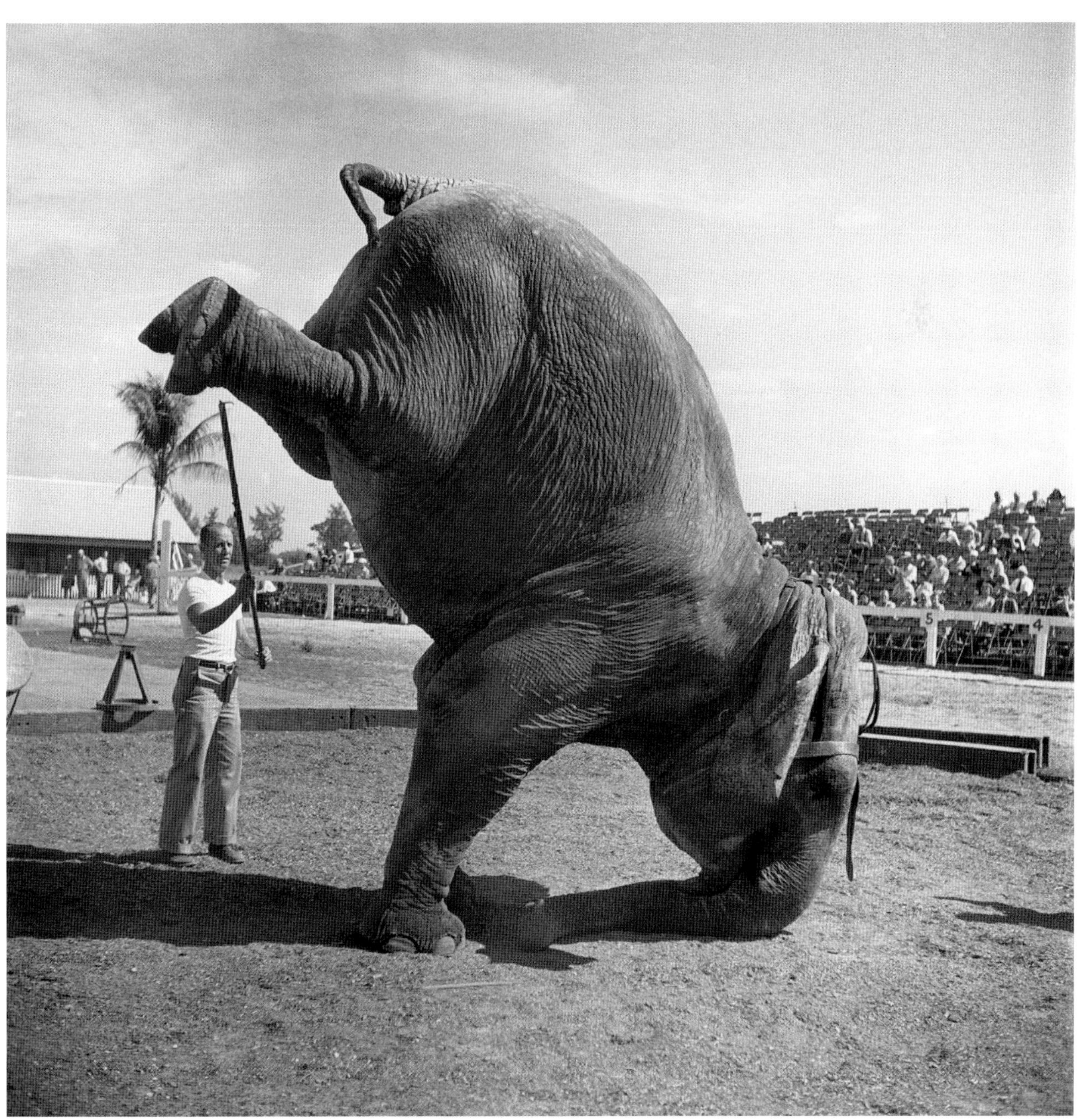

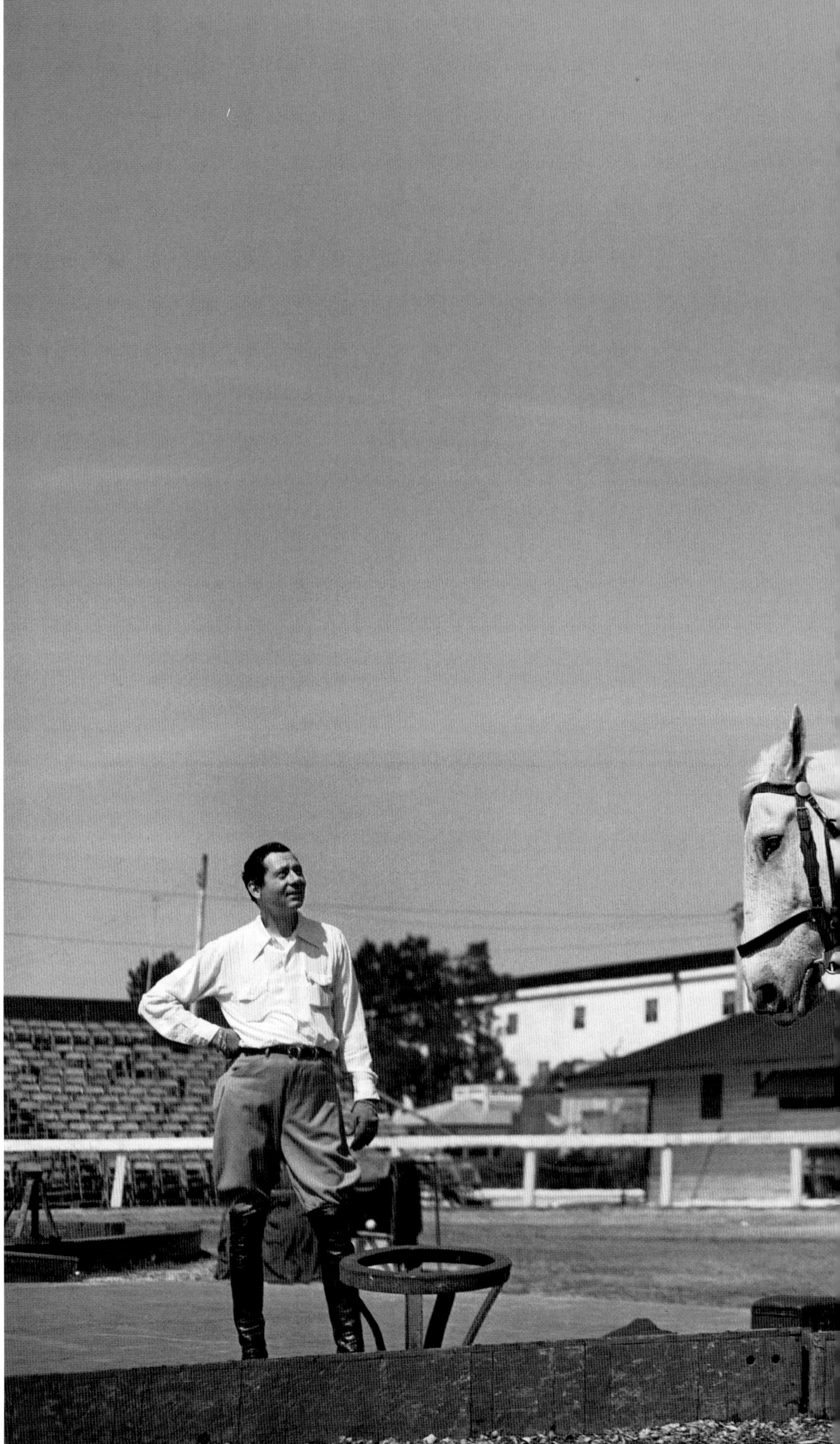

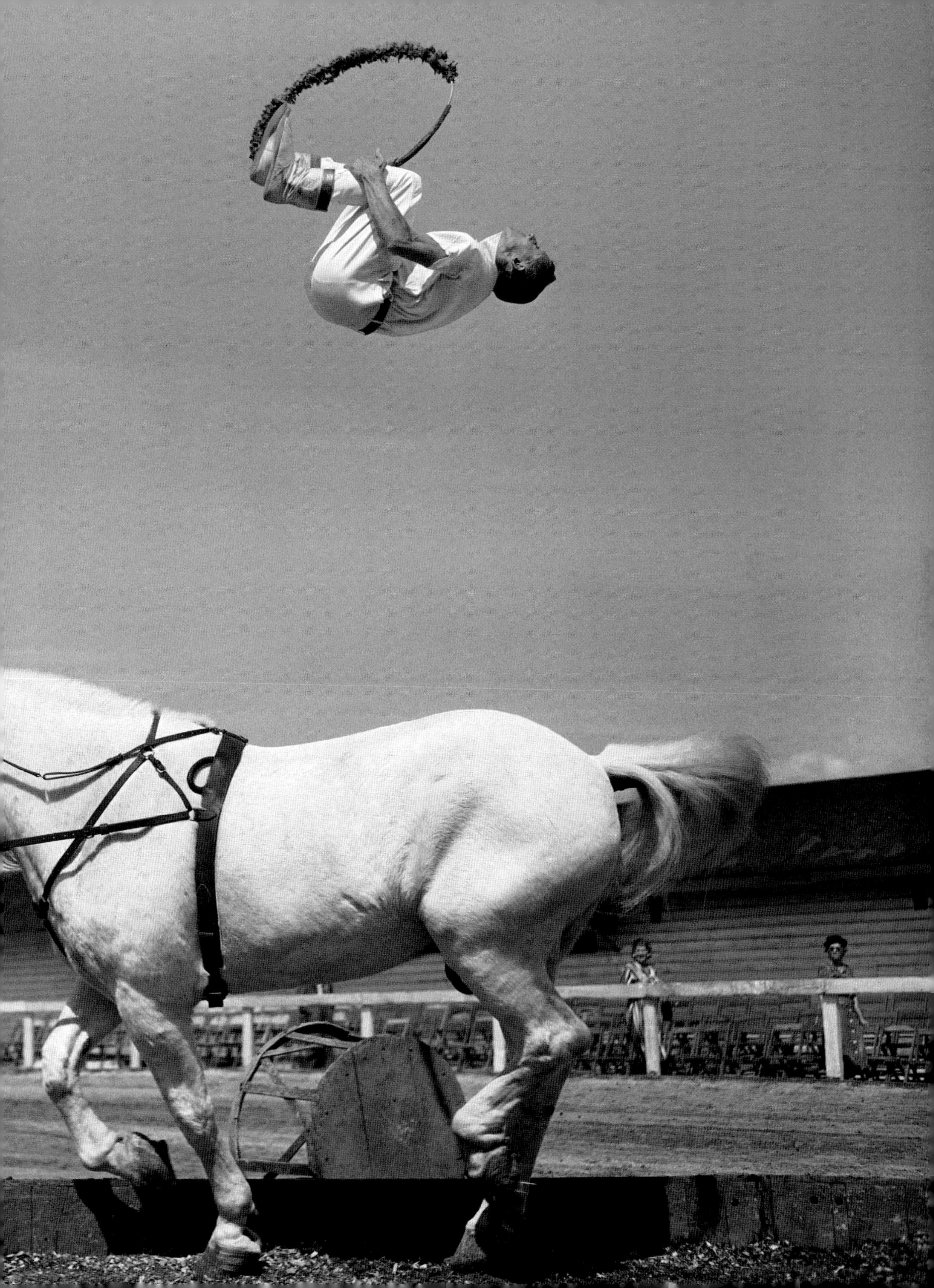

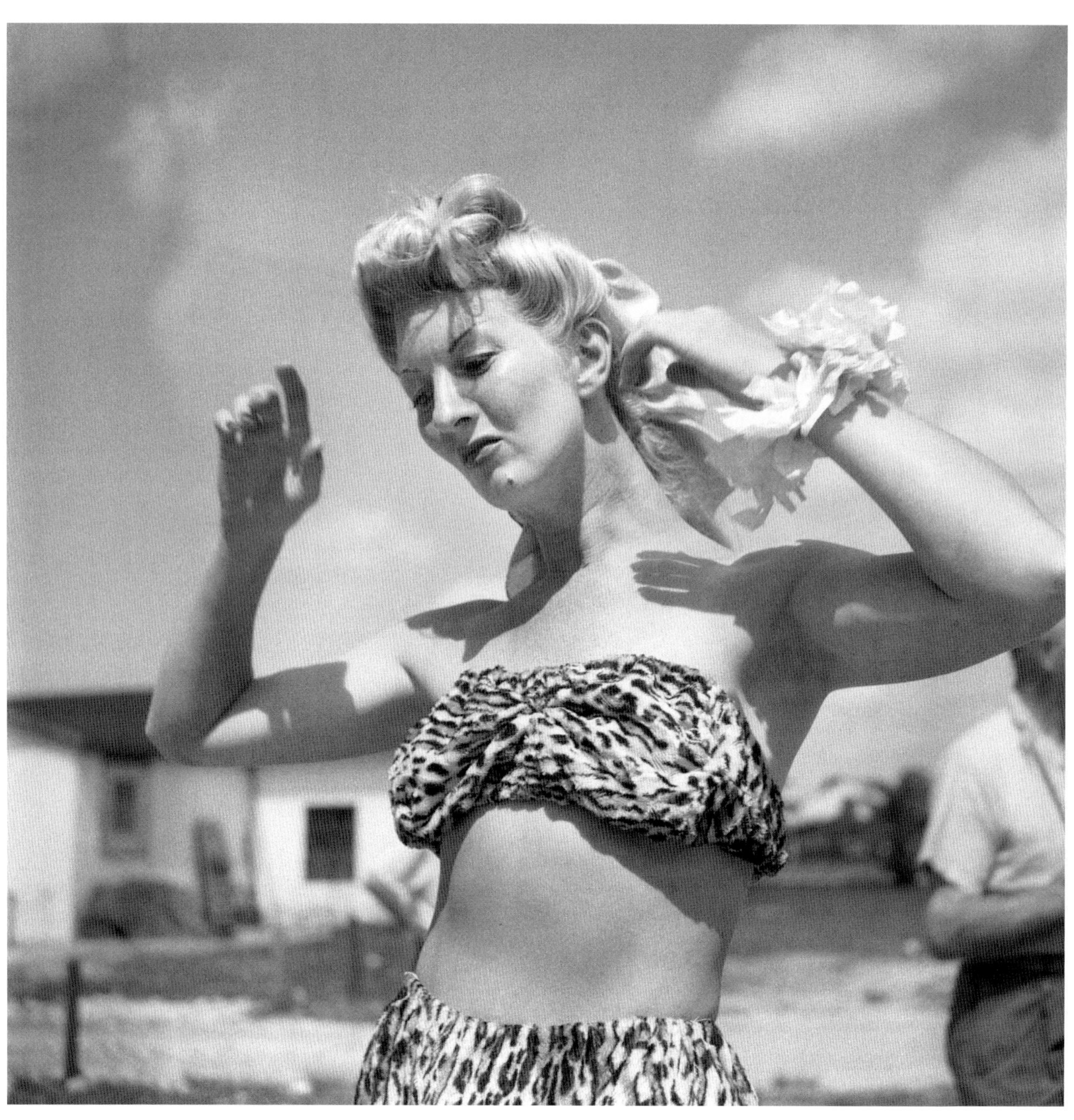

Beatrice Dante, formerly a performer with the Folies Bergère

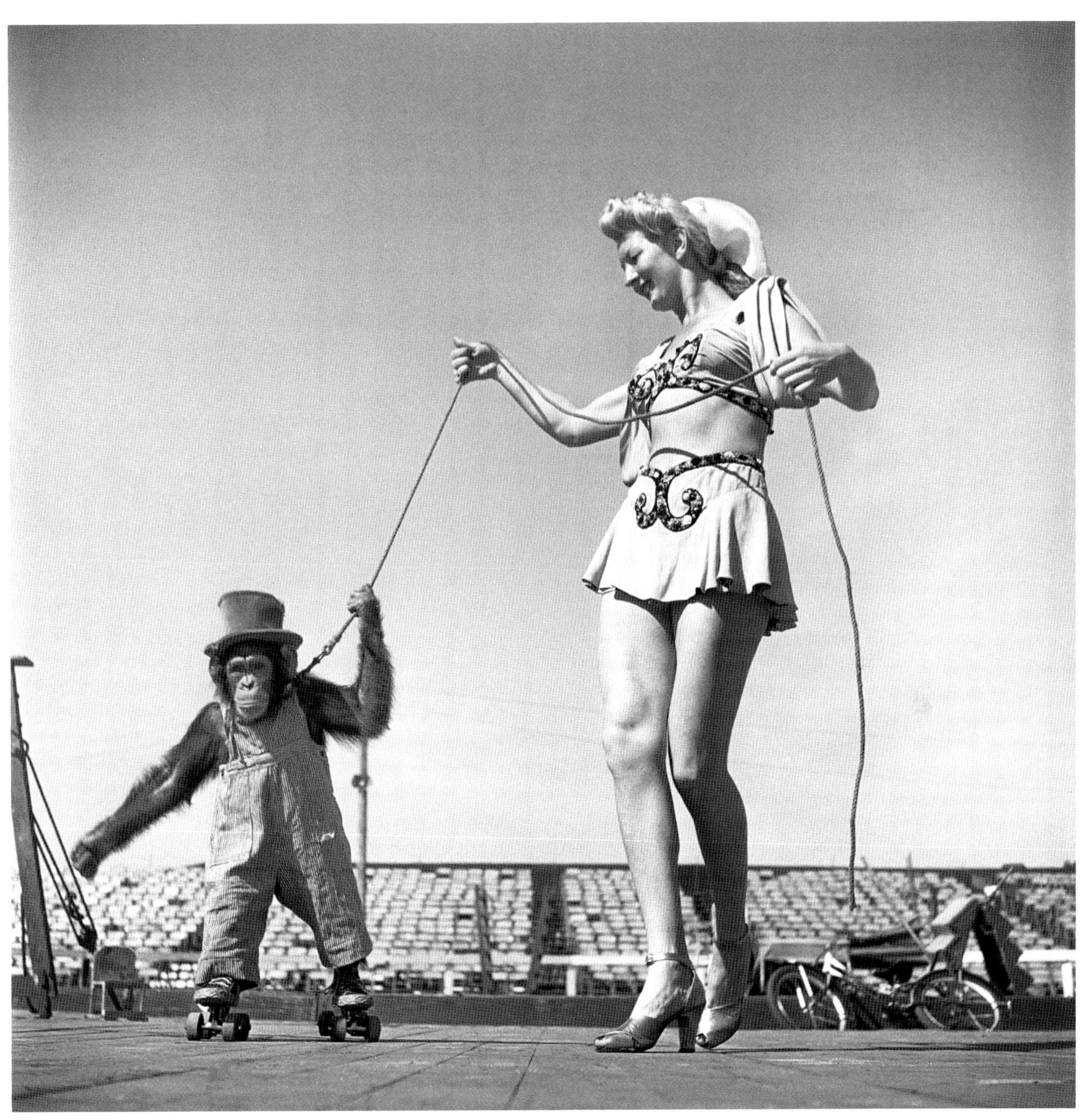

Dante with Buddy, a baby chimpanzee

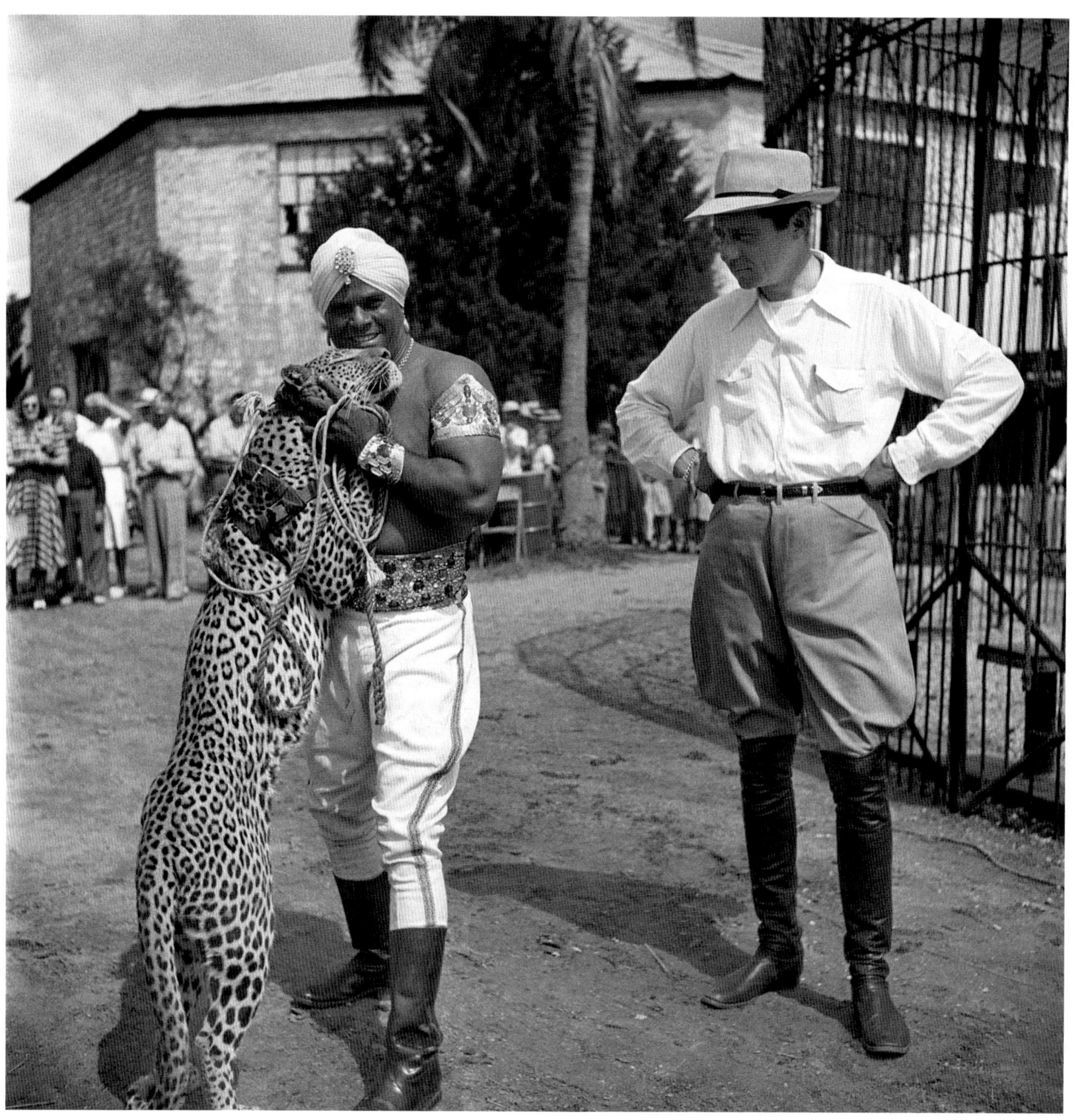

Leopards with their handlers

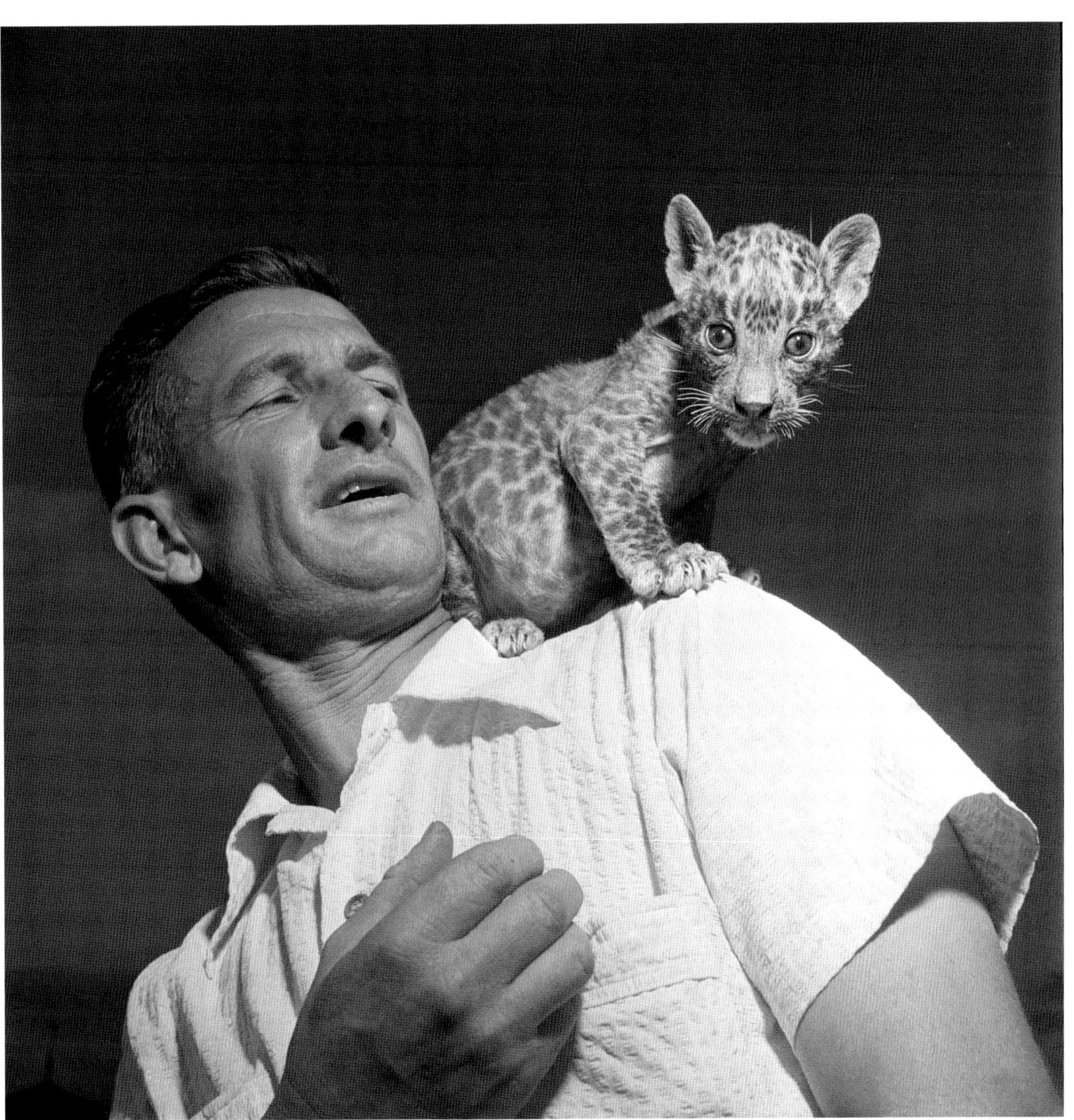

BELOW **A little boy with German-born clown Lou Jacobs**

OPPOSITE **Kubrick's portrait of Jacobs, featured on *Look*'s cover, represented one of his rare uses of color film.**

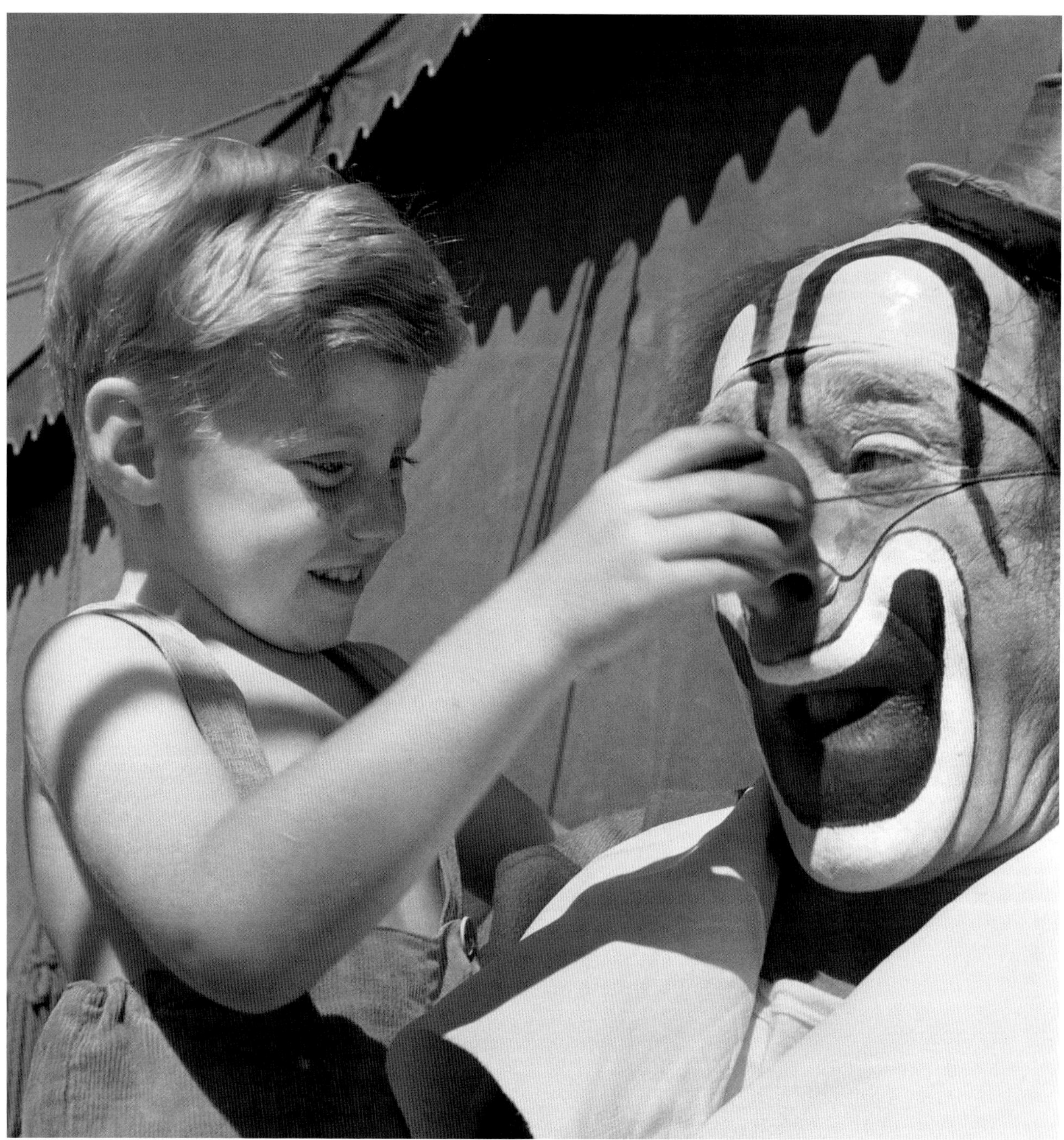

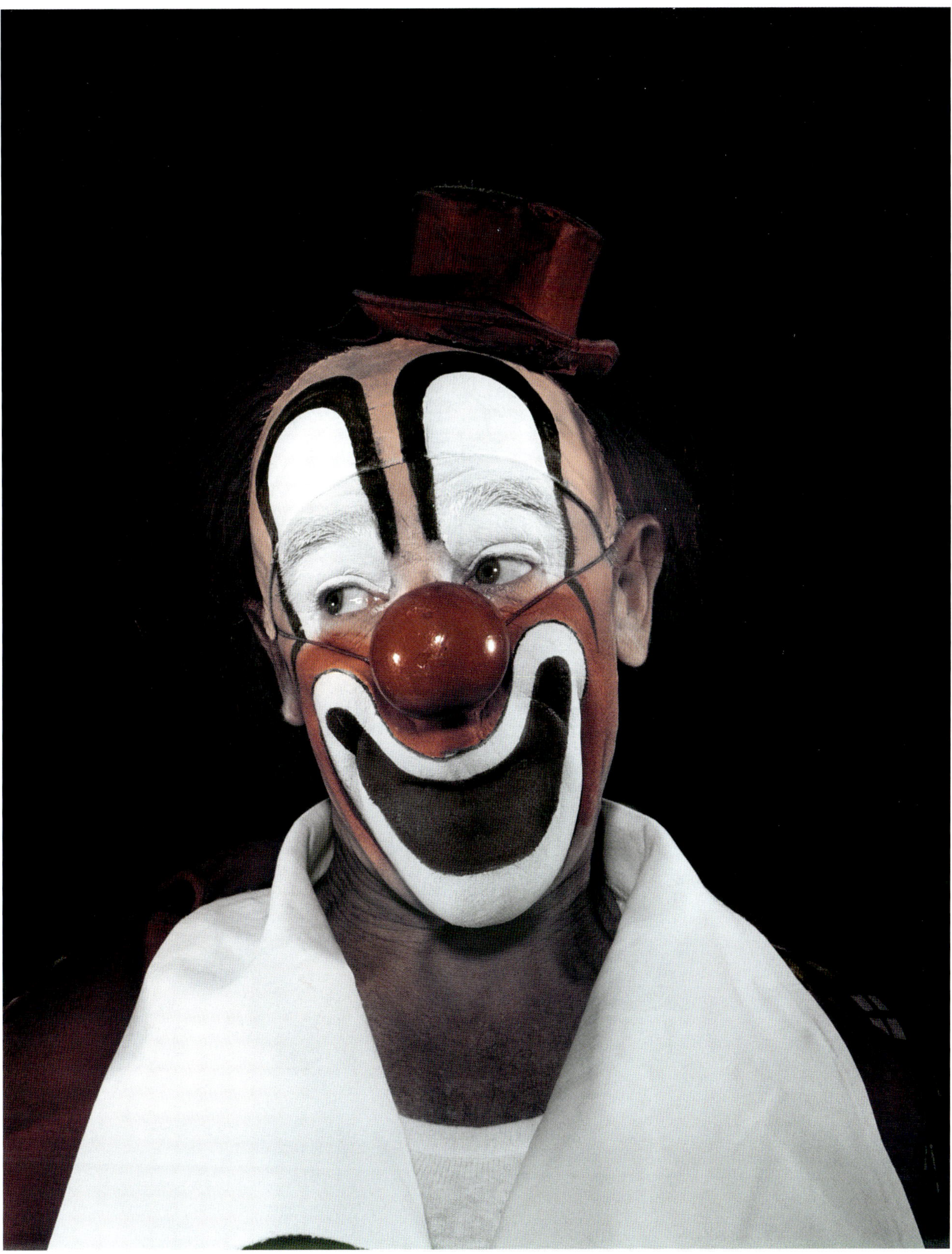

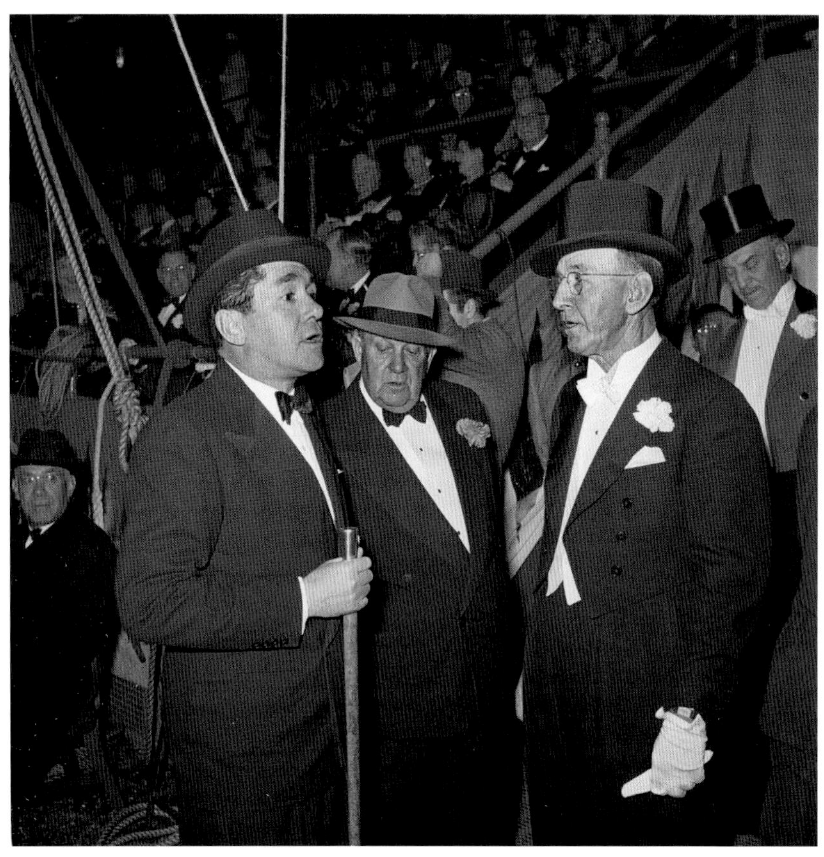

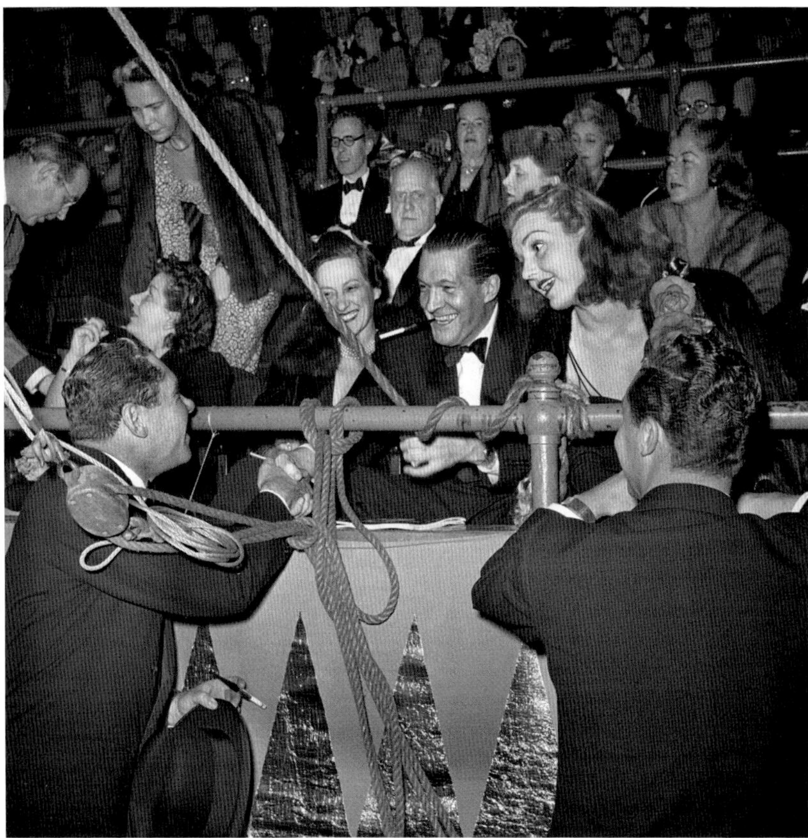

Well-heeled spectators at the circus. These included John Ringling North (top image, left) and cartoonist Peter Arno (bottom image, center), who was the subject of a celebrity profile shot by Kubrick.

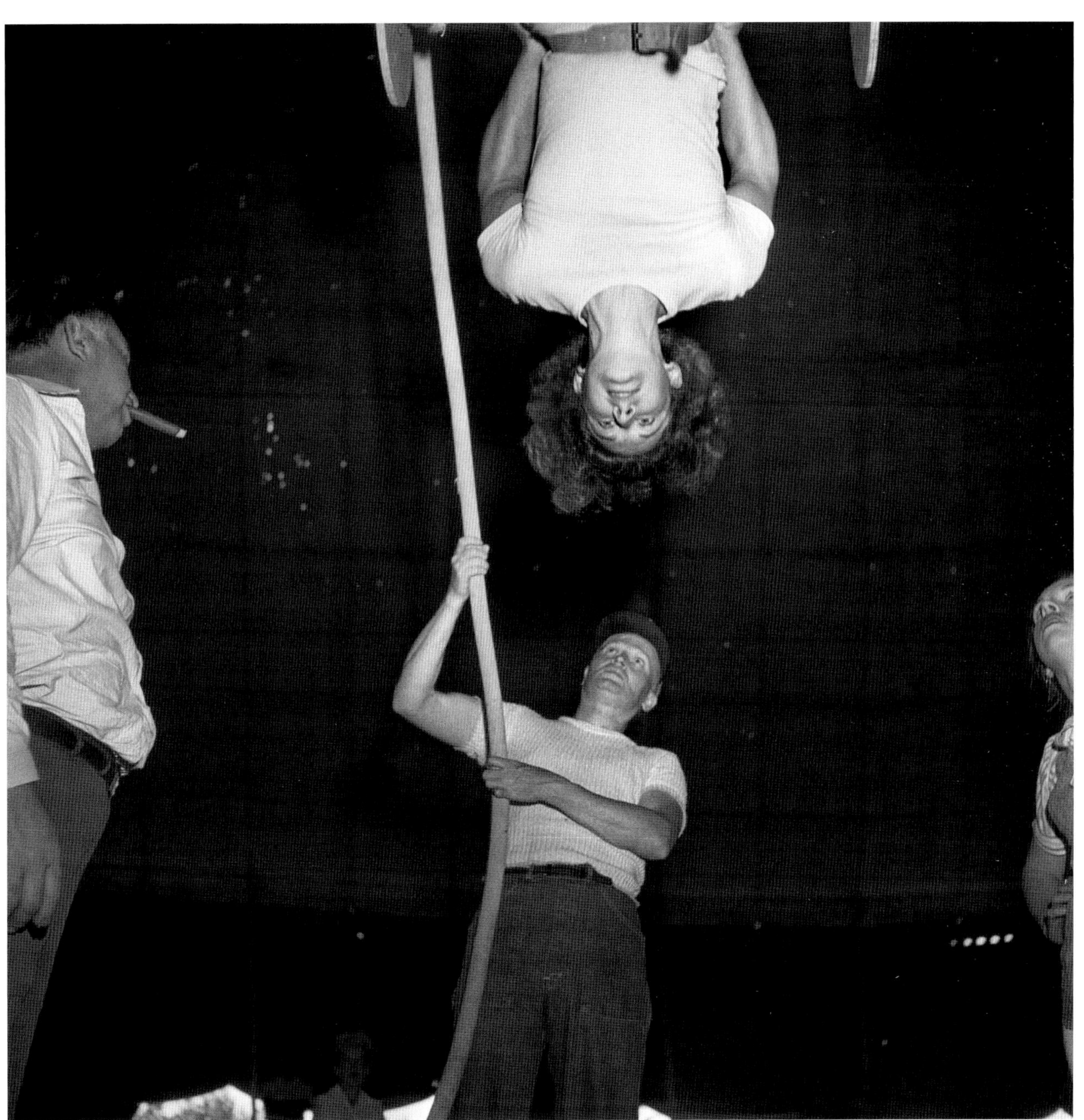

An acrobat rehearsing

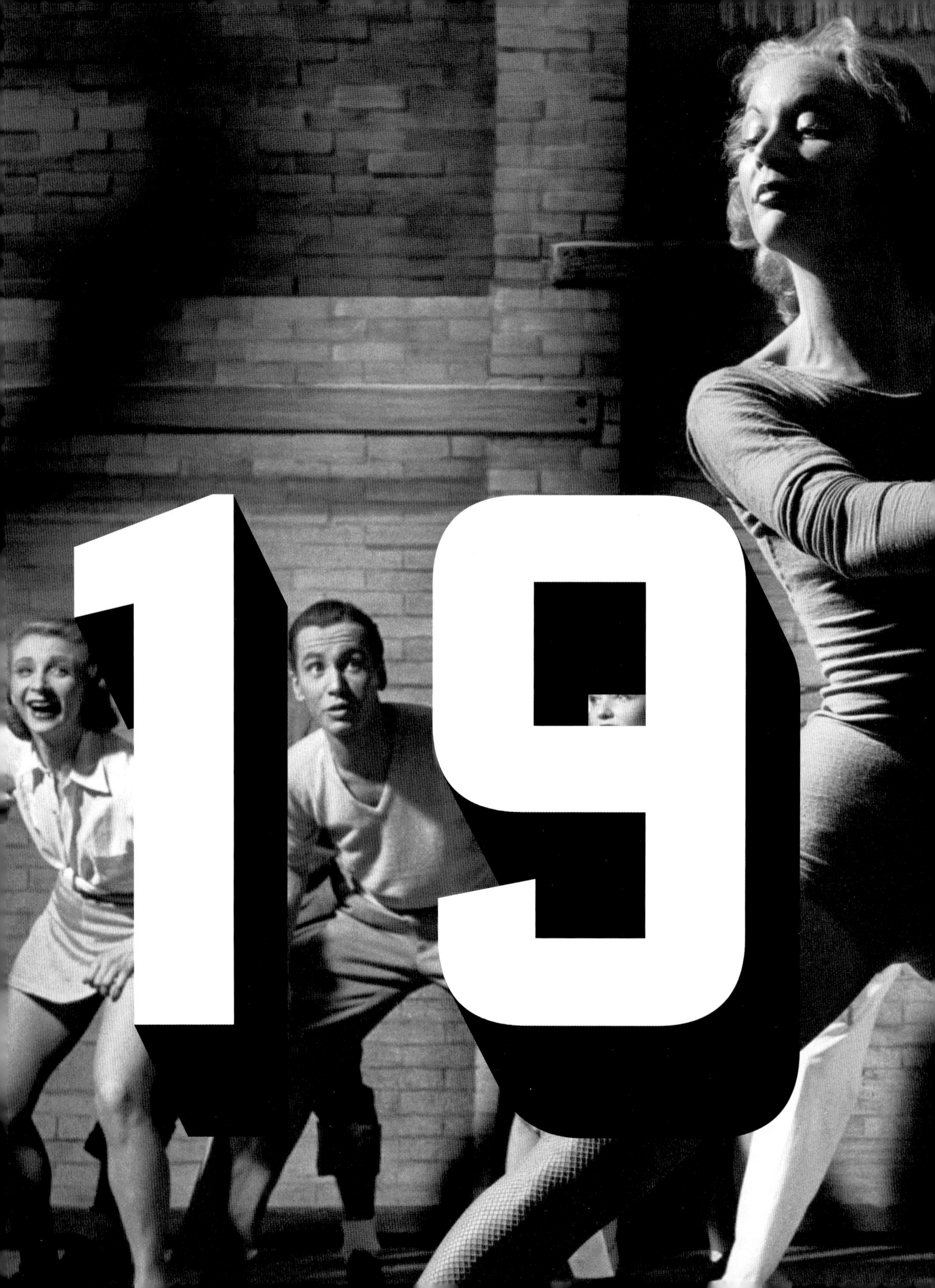
19

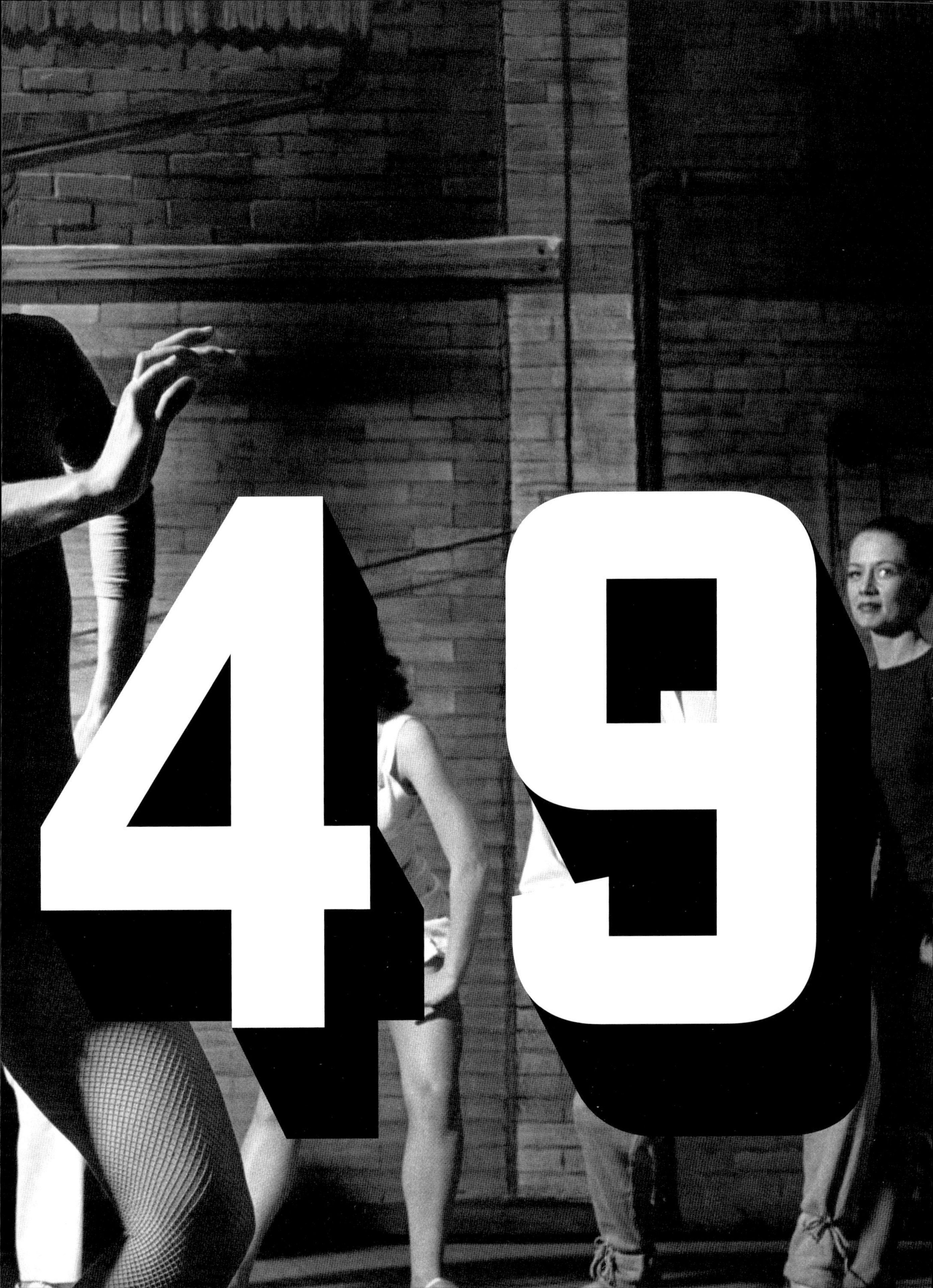
49

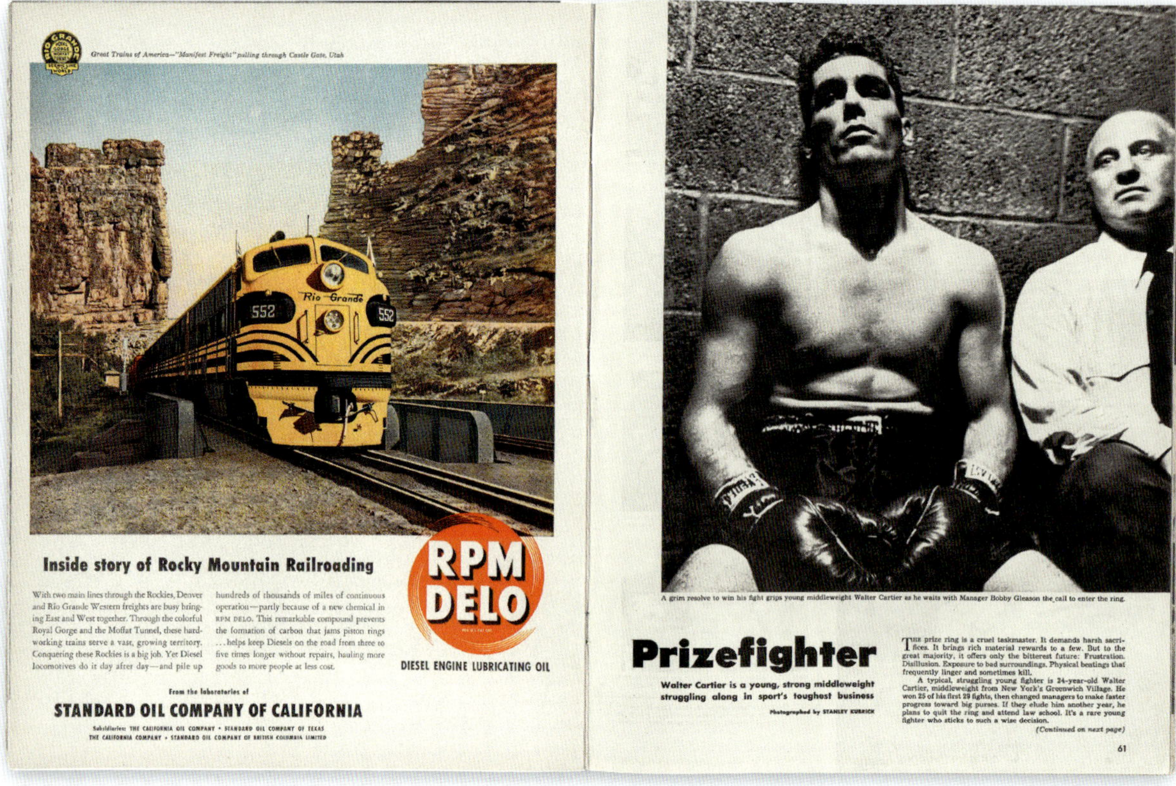

A grim resolve to win his fight grips young middleweight Walter Cartier as he waits with Manager Bobby Gleason the call to enter the ring.

Prizefighter

Walter Cartier is a young, strong middleweight struggling along in sport's toughest business

Photographed by STANLEY KUBRICK

The prize ring is a cruel taskmaster. It demands harsh sacrifices. It brings rich material rewards to a few. But to the great majority, it offers only the bitterest future: Frustration. Disillusion. Exposure to bad surroundings. Physical beatings that frequently linger and sometimes kill.

A typical, struggling young fighter is 24-year-old Walter Cartier, middleweight from New York's Greenwich Village. He won 25 of his first 29 fights, then changed managers to make faster progress toward big purses. If they elude him another year, he plans to quit the ring and attend law school. It's a rare young fighter who sticks to such a wise decision.

(Continued on next page)

61

PUBLISHED AS

PRIZEFIGHTER: WALTER CARTIER IS A YOUNG, STRONG MIDDLEWEIGHT STRUGGLING ALONG IN SPORT'S TOUGHEST BUSINESS

DATE

JANUARY 18, 1949

Following the personal and professional lives of 24-year-old middleweight boxer Walter Cartier, this seven-page article, for which Kubrick shot more than 1,200 images, was one of his largest and most significant assignments for *Look*. The photographs were visually stunning, with dramatic compositions and chiaroscuro lighting. Graphic design by *Look*'s art director Merle Armitage, which juxtaposed small and full-page images in asymmetrical page layouts, made Kubrick's photographs even more compelling. The essay's themes of struggle and violence against the backdrop of a harsh and uncaring world continued into Kubrick's films. Cartier himself was the subject of Kubrick's first film, the short newsreel *Day of the Fight*, while a brutal boxing match like those illustrated in the article opened the director's 1955 film *Killer's Kiss*. "The prize ring is a cruel taskmaster," the uncredited essay began. "It demands harsh sacrifices. It brings rich material rewards to a few. But to the great majority, it offers only the bitterest future: Frustration. Disillusion. Exposure to bad surroundings. Physical beatings that frequently linger and sometimes kill." After this ominous warning, the article juxtaposed brutal images of Cartier in the ring with pictures of his daily life: the routine he followed on the day of a fight, the "simple pleasures" he enjoyed between matches, and close interactions with his manager, Bobby Gleason, as they struggled together to advance his career. "Ability alone cannot carry a fighter into the big money and a chance at the championship," the article admonished. "His manager must be able to cope with the intrigues and connivings of the ring—a business in which no blows are barred."

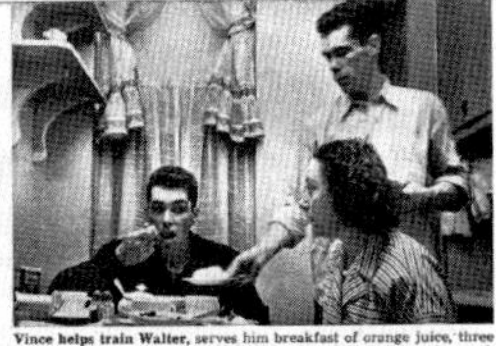

Walter sleeps until 9:30 on a day he's going to fight. In training, he gets up at 5:30, runs four miles. Twin brother Vincent sleeps on.

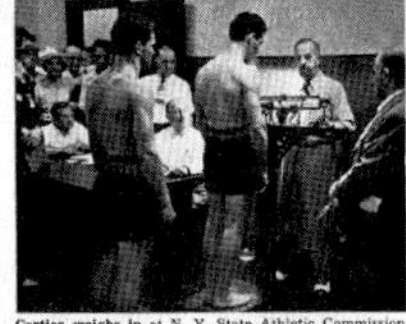

Vince helps train Walter, serves him breakfast of orange juice, three soft-boiled eggs, toast and coffee. Their Aunt Eva oversees the meal.

THE DAY OF A FIGHT

Cartier sleeps late, eats carefully, gets a physical check-up —and goes to church.

On way to fight, Walter stops at church, prays that he escape serious injury.

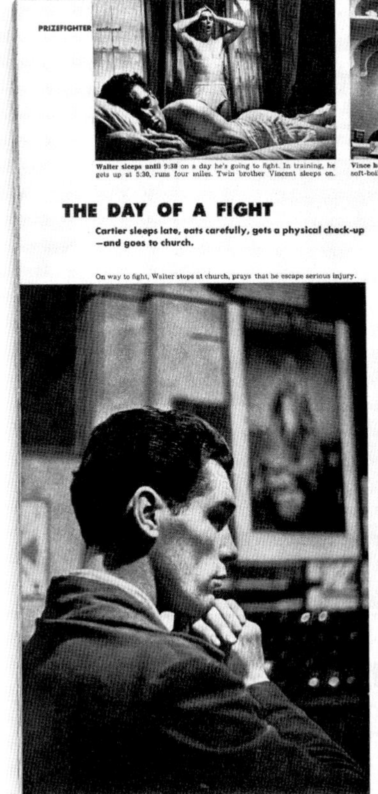

Cartier weighs in at N. Y. State Athletic Commission around noon. An official checks him on the scales.

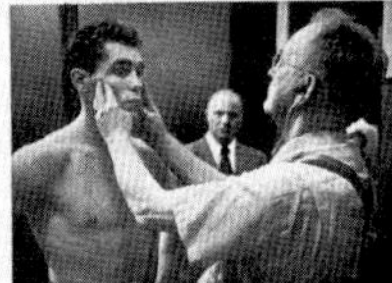

Doctor carefully examines eyes. Eye cuts, an occupational hazard, often impair vision, sometimes bring blindness.

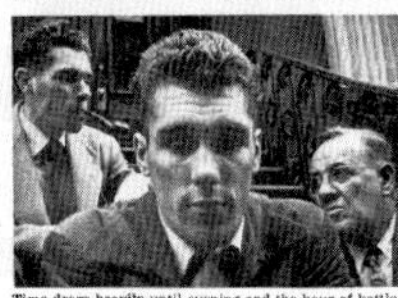

Time drags heavily until evening and the hour of battle. Walter sits it out on front steps with brother, neighbor.

The fight: Walter carries attack to Tony D'Amico at Jerome Stadium, drives spittle from Tony's mouth. He led until head butt cut his right eye, gave Tony technical KO.

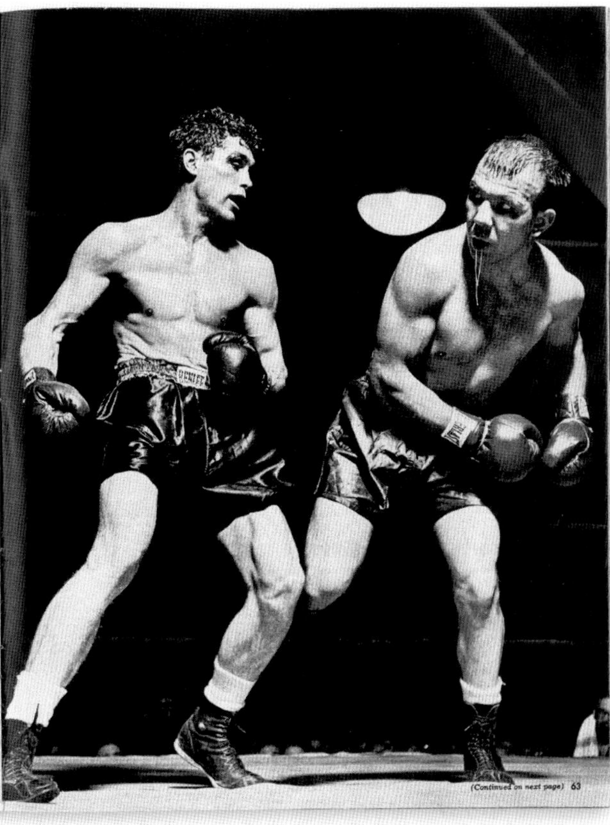

(Continued on next page) 63

SKILL IS NOT ENOUGH

Ability alone cannot carry a fighter into the big money and a chance at the championship. His manager must be able to cope with the intrigues and connivings of the ring—a business in which no blows are barred

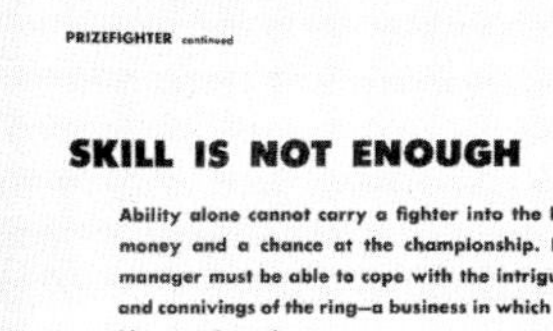

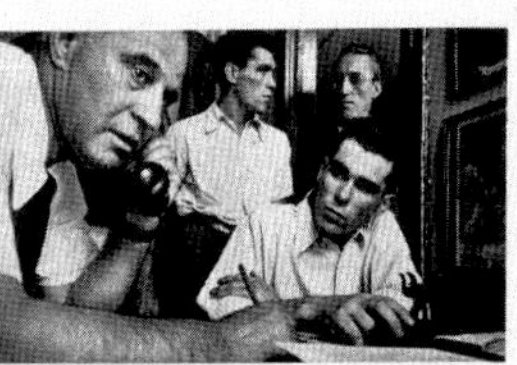

Cartier looks on anxiously as Gleason palavers over the telephone about an important match. Getting the right kind of fight is a manager's big job.

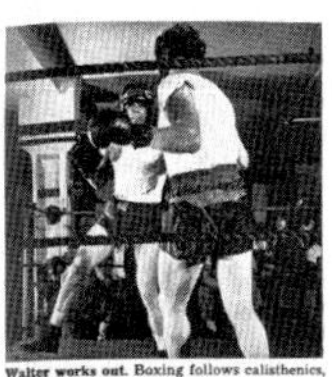

Walter works out. Boxing follows calisthenics, rope-skipping, shadow-boxing, bag-punching.

He gets a break. At Jersey City's Roosevelt Stadium, in prelim to Zale-Cerdan championship, he knocks out Jimmy Mangia in first round with right to the jaw.

This fight earned Walter biggest net purse: $700.

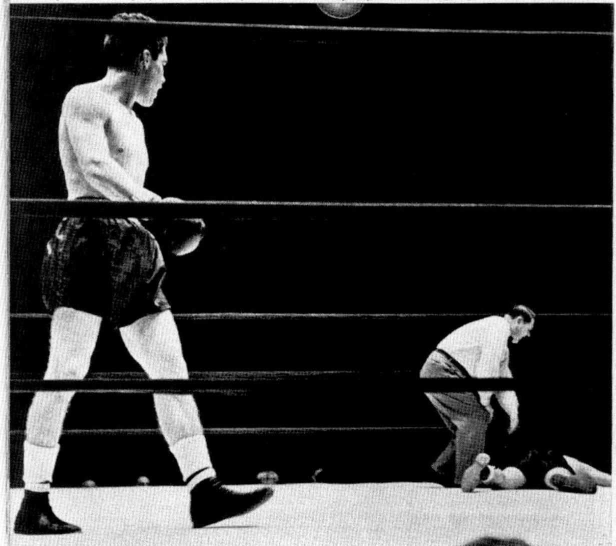

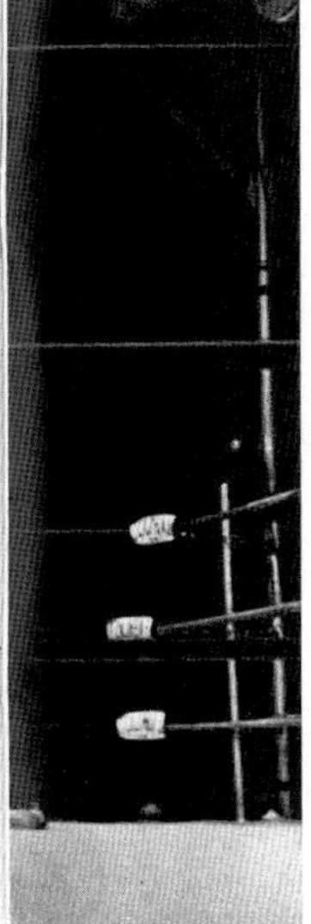

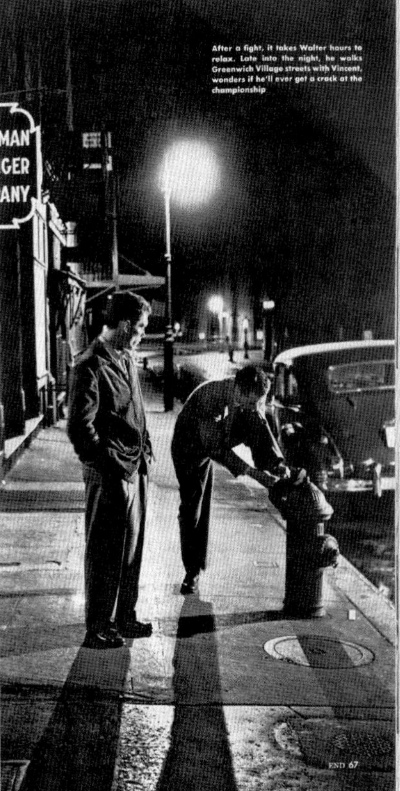

After a fight, it takes Walter hours to relax. Late into the night, he walks Greenwich Village streets with Vincent, wonders if he'll ever get a crack at the championship

END 67

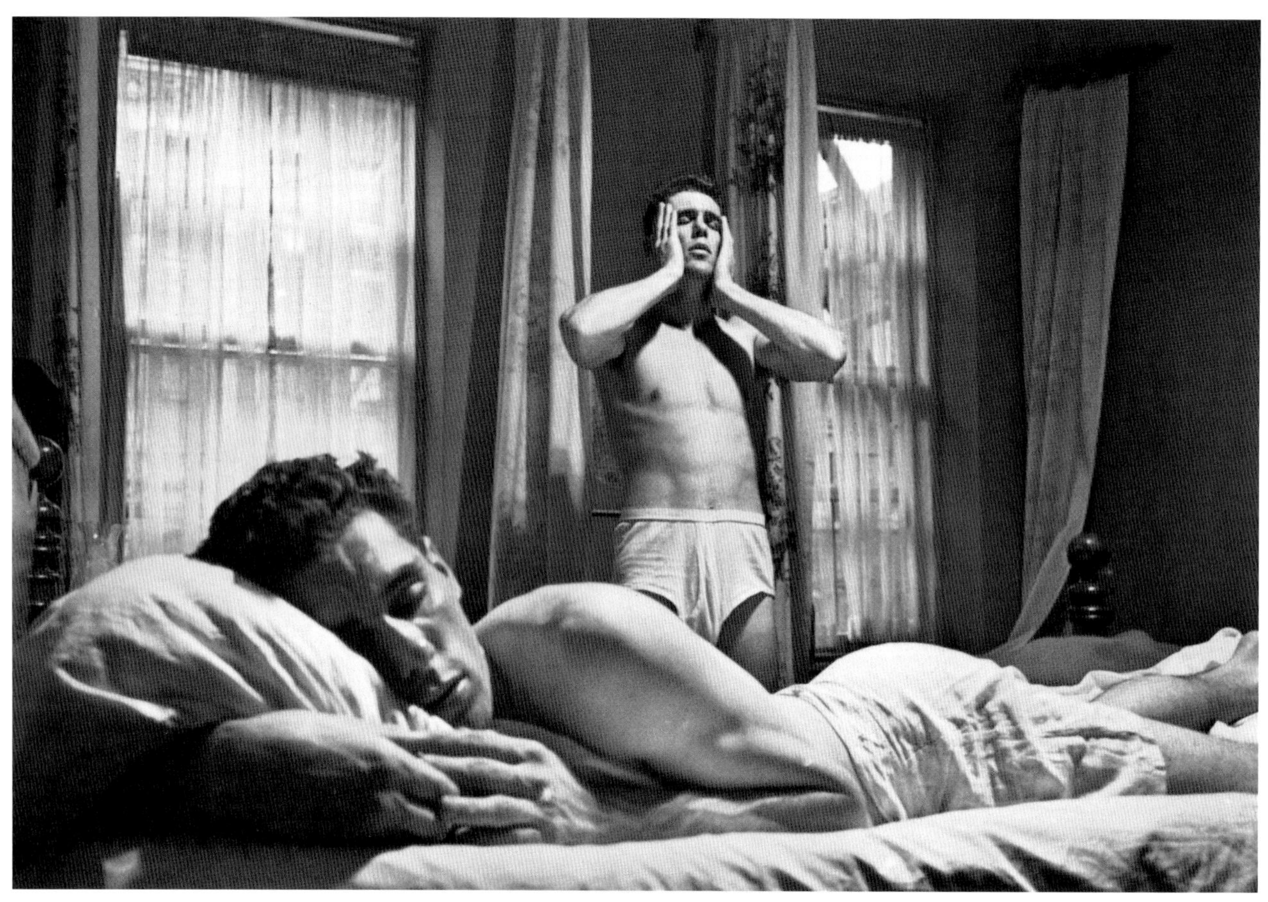

Cartier rose at 5:30 a.m. on training days, while his twin brother, Vincent, slept in

OPPOSITE **Cartier in Washington Square Park on his four-mile morning run**

FOLLOWING SPREAD **Cartier and his girlfriend relaxing at the beach**

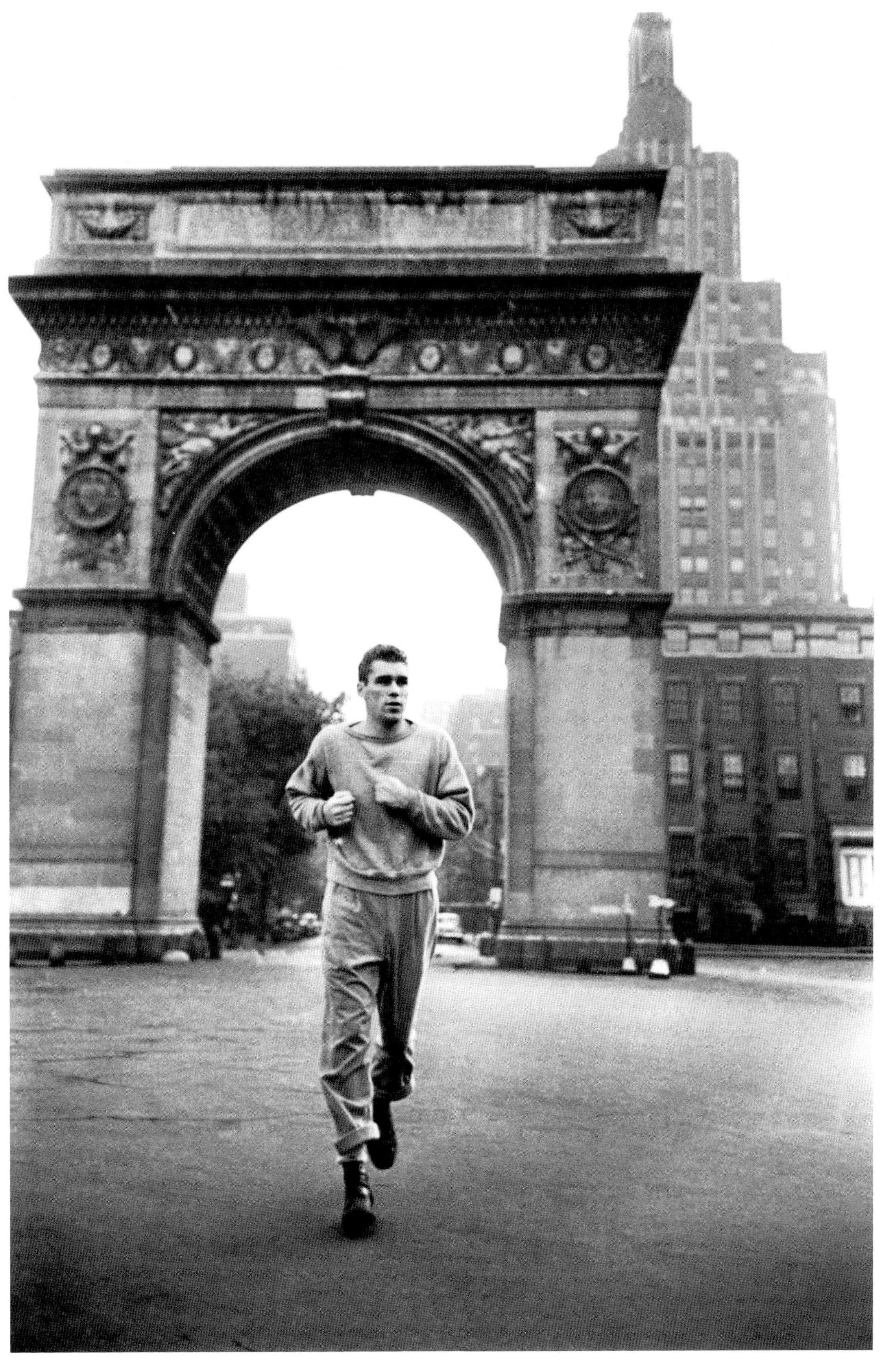

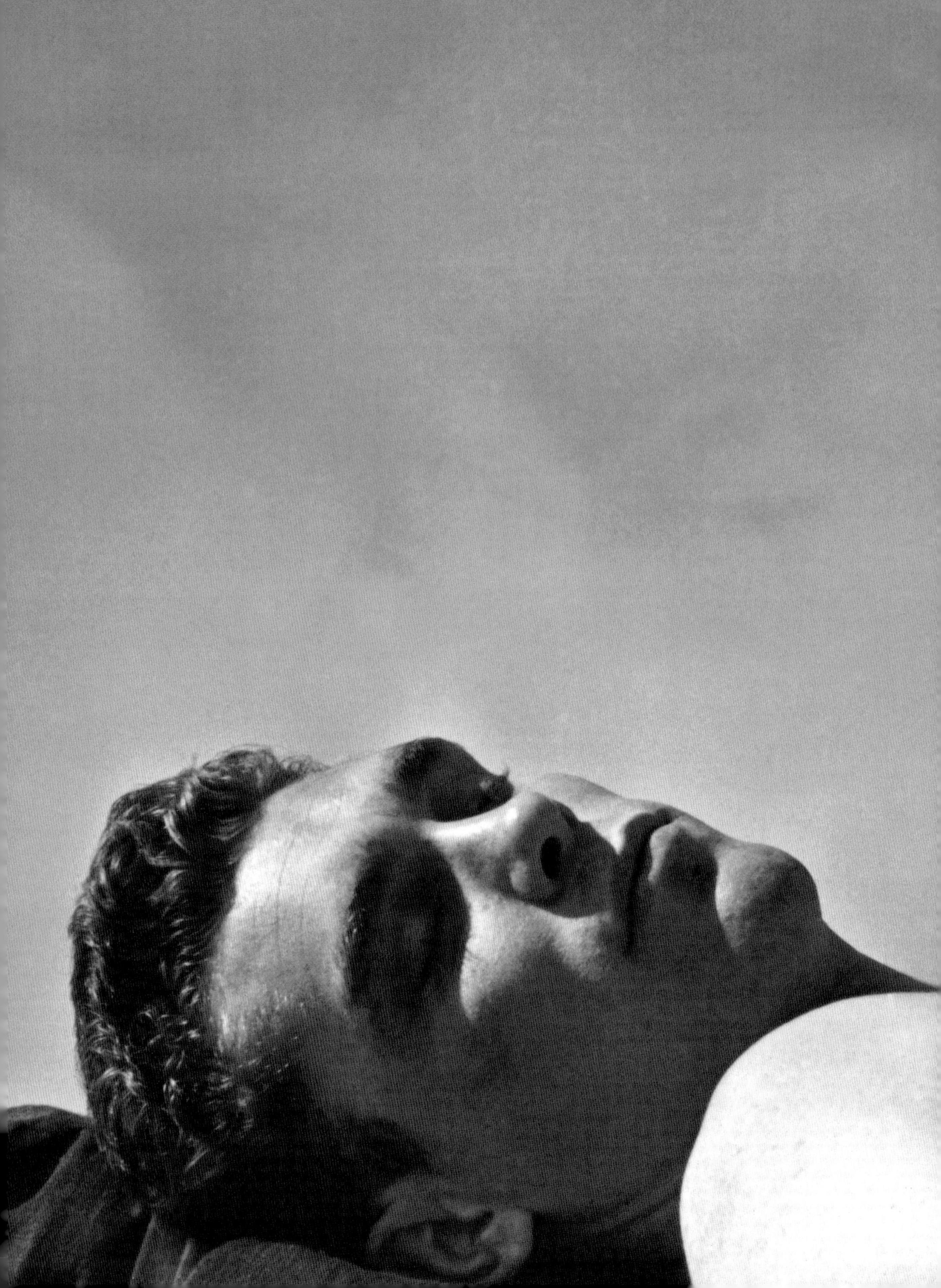

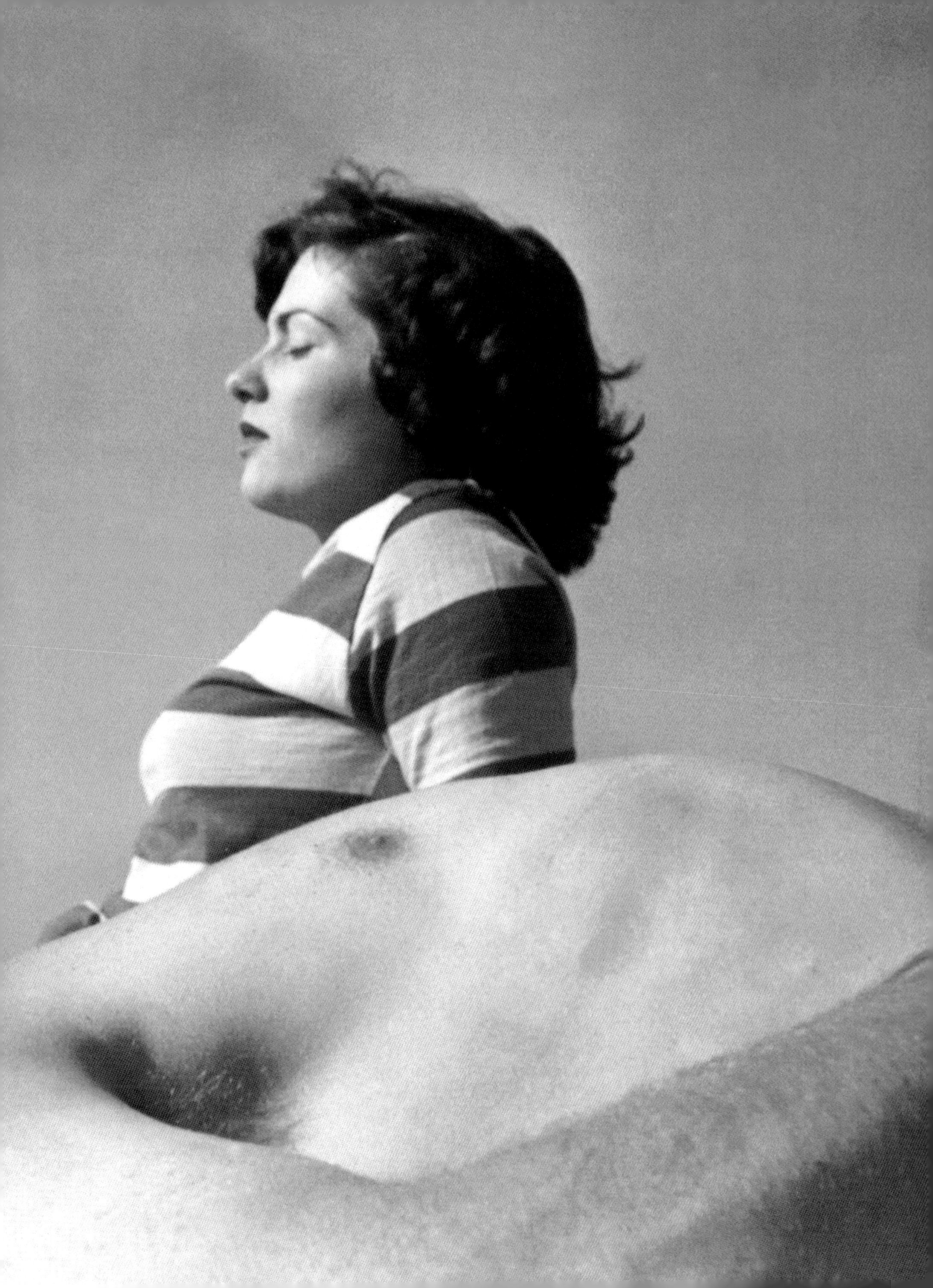

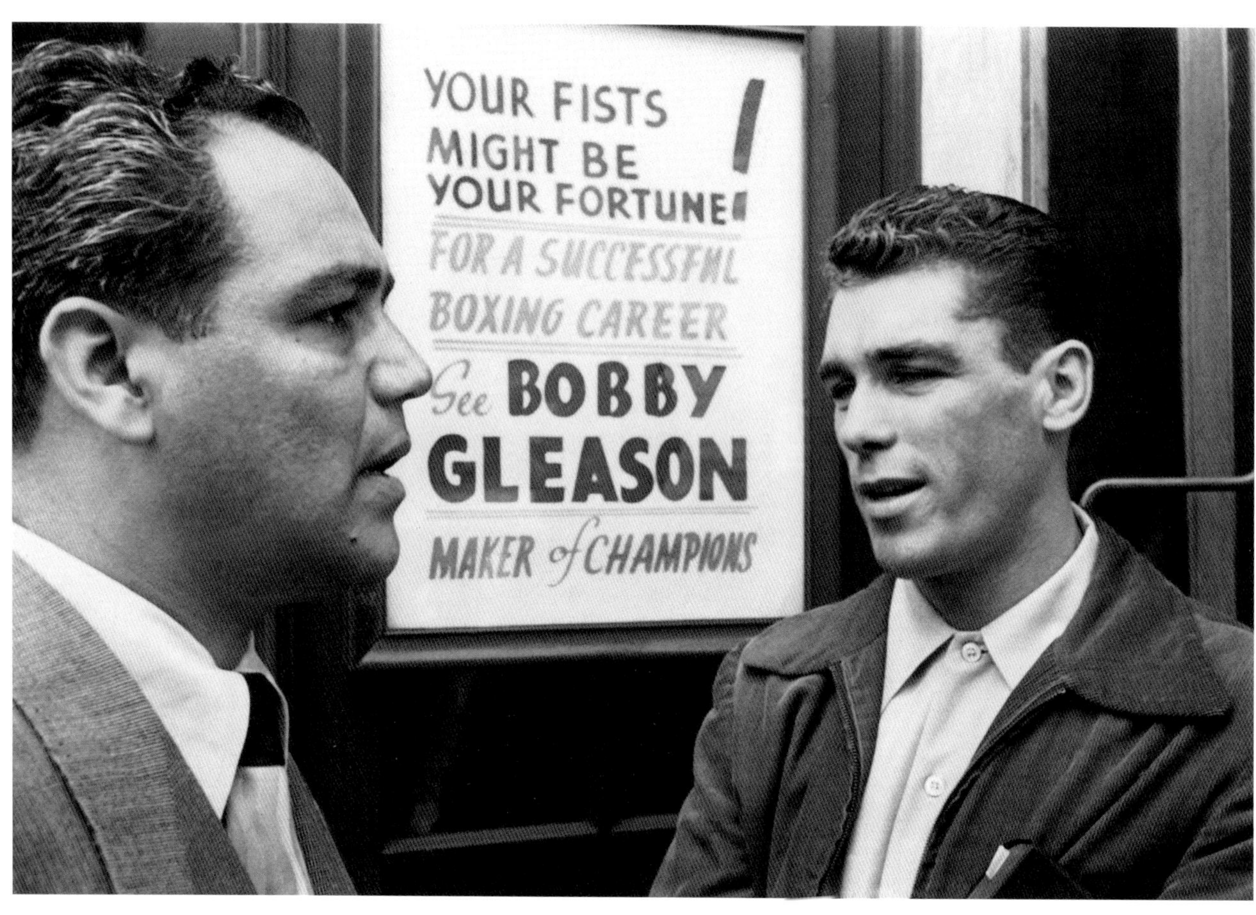

Cartier and an unidentified man in front of a sign touting his manager, Bobby Gleason

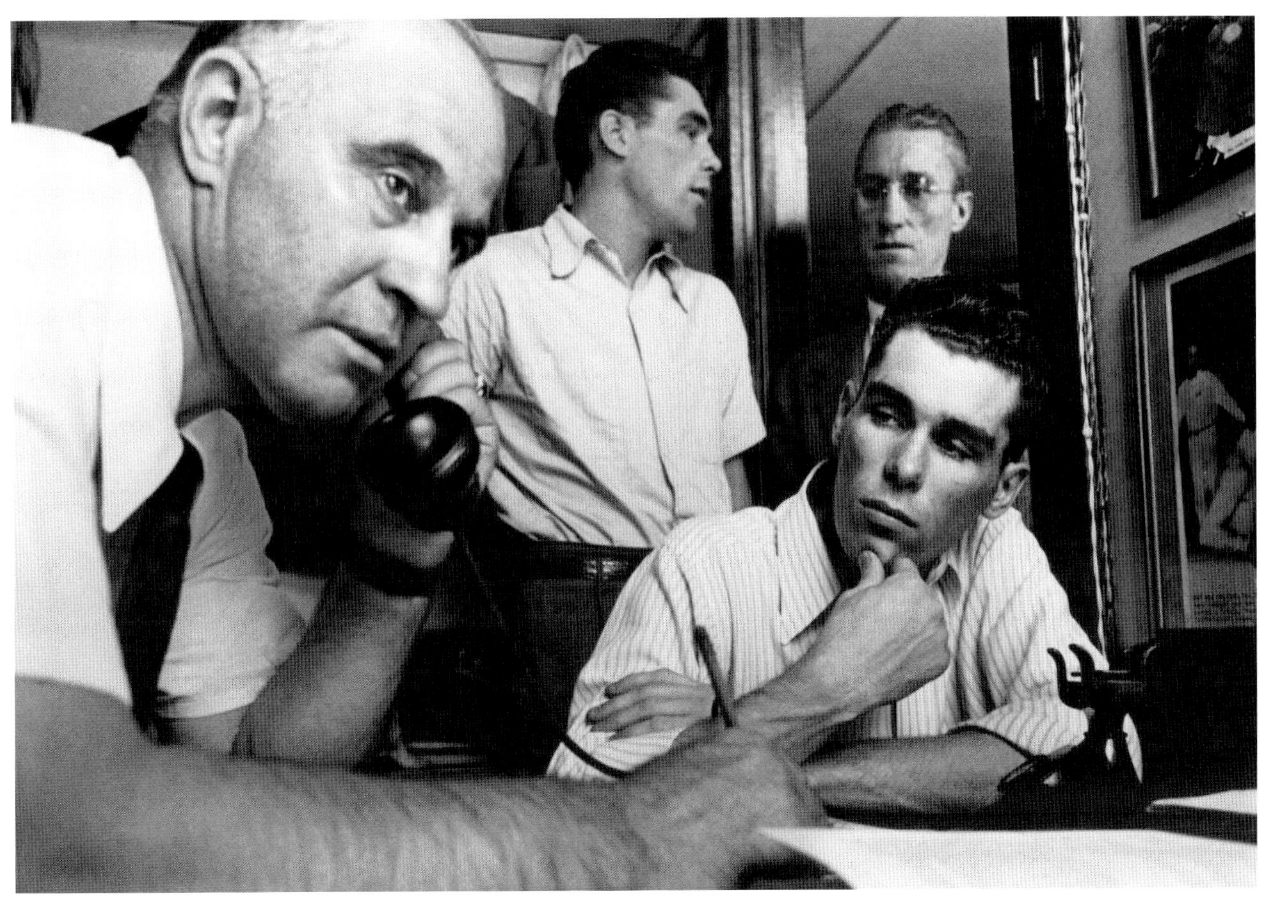

Cartier (right) looking on as his manager discusses a match

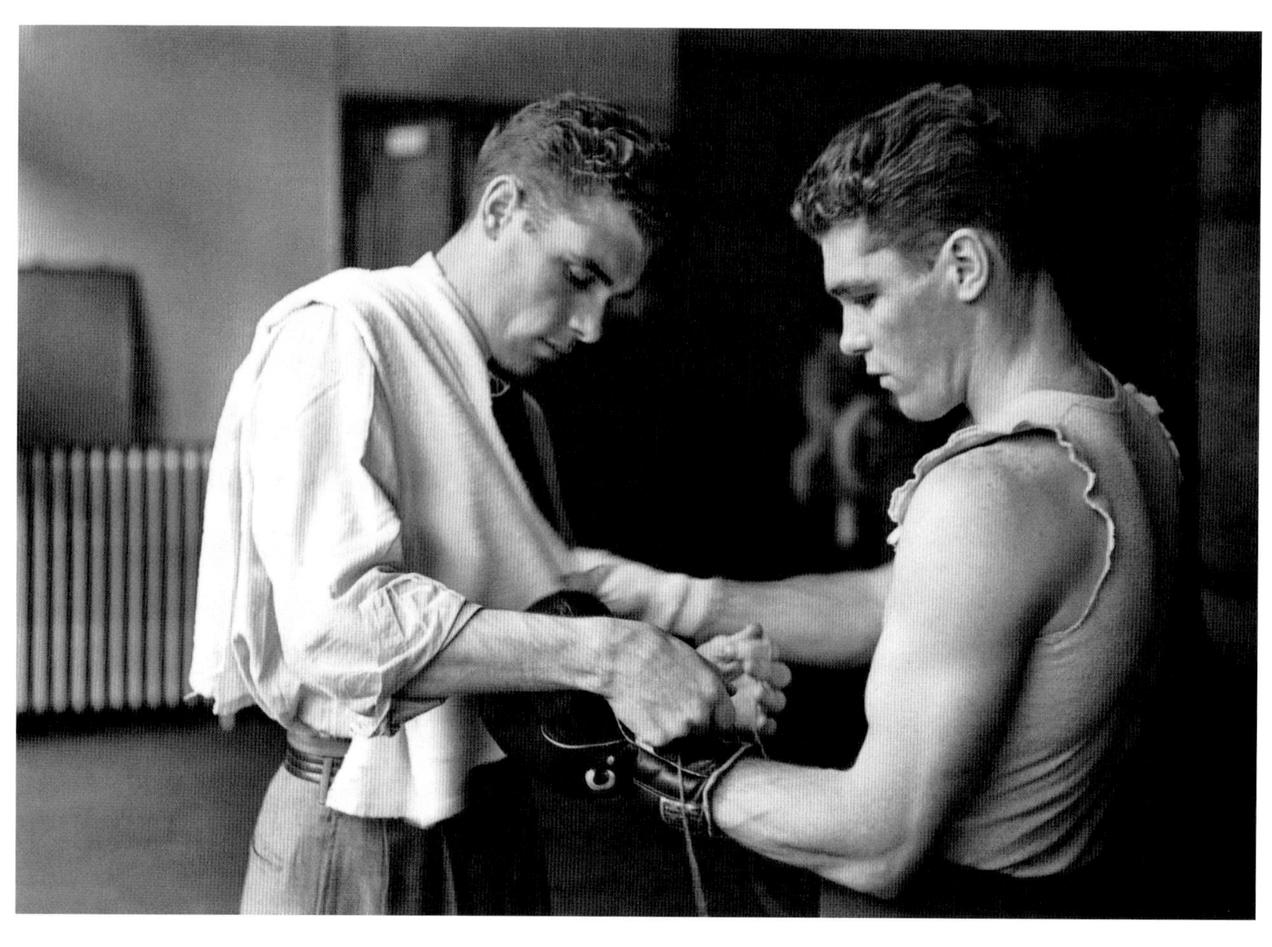

Walter's twin brother, Vincent, lacing his gloves

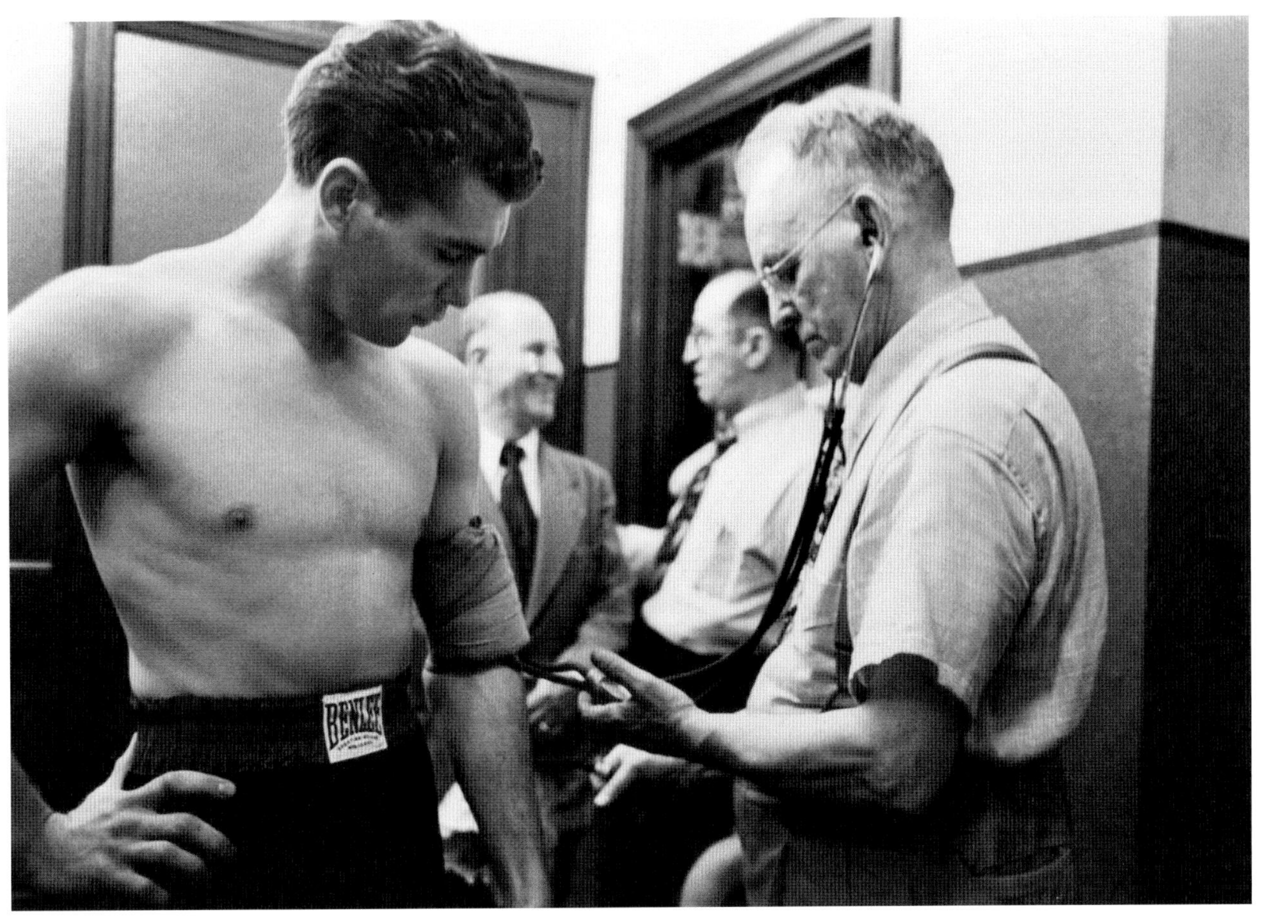

A doctor at the New York State Athletic Commission examining Cartier before the fight

FOLLOWING SPREAD **Cartier training with a heavy punching bag while his brother watches**

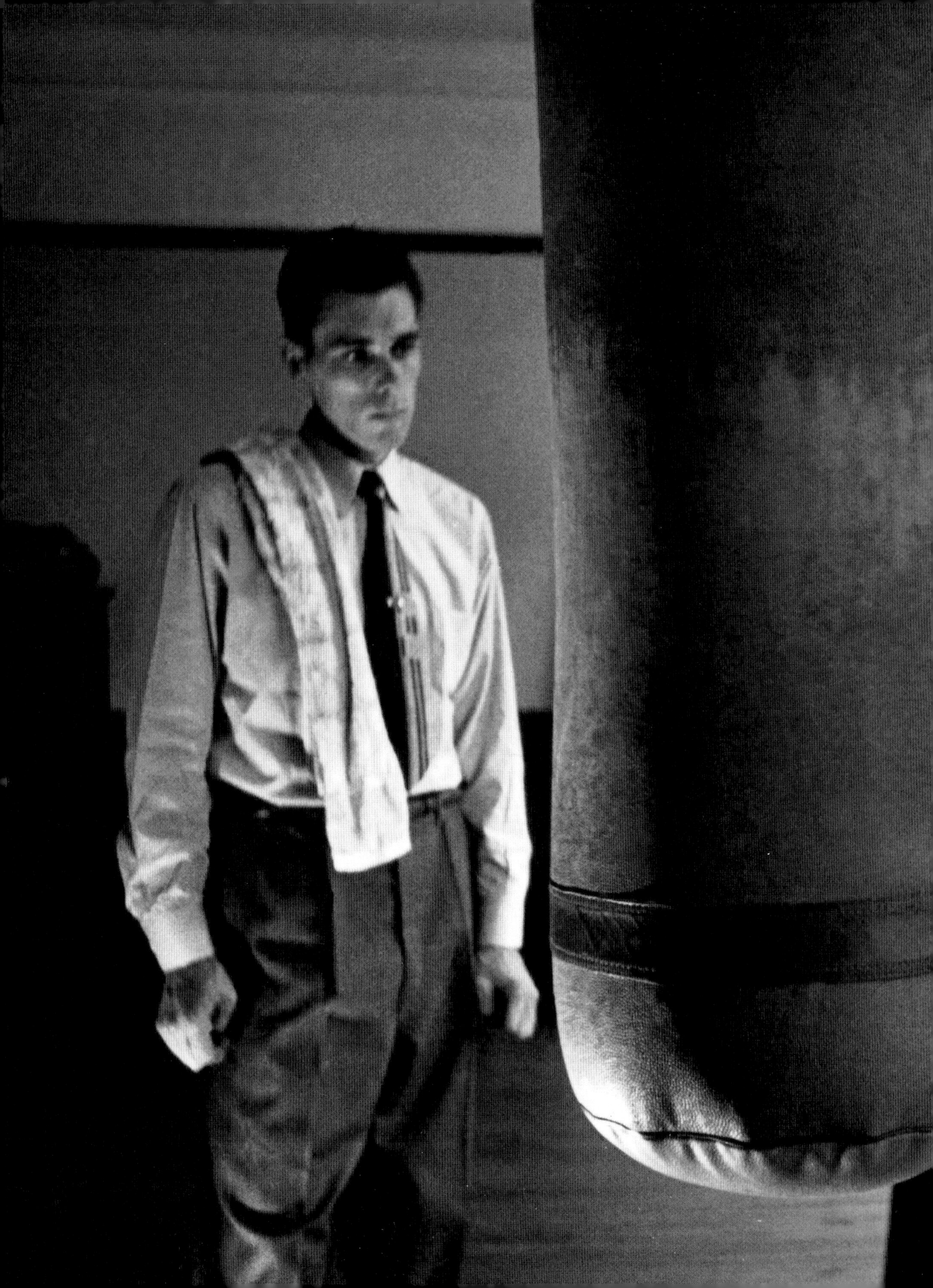

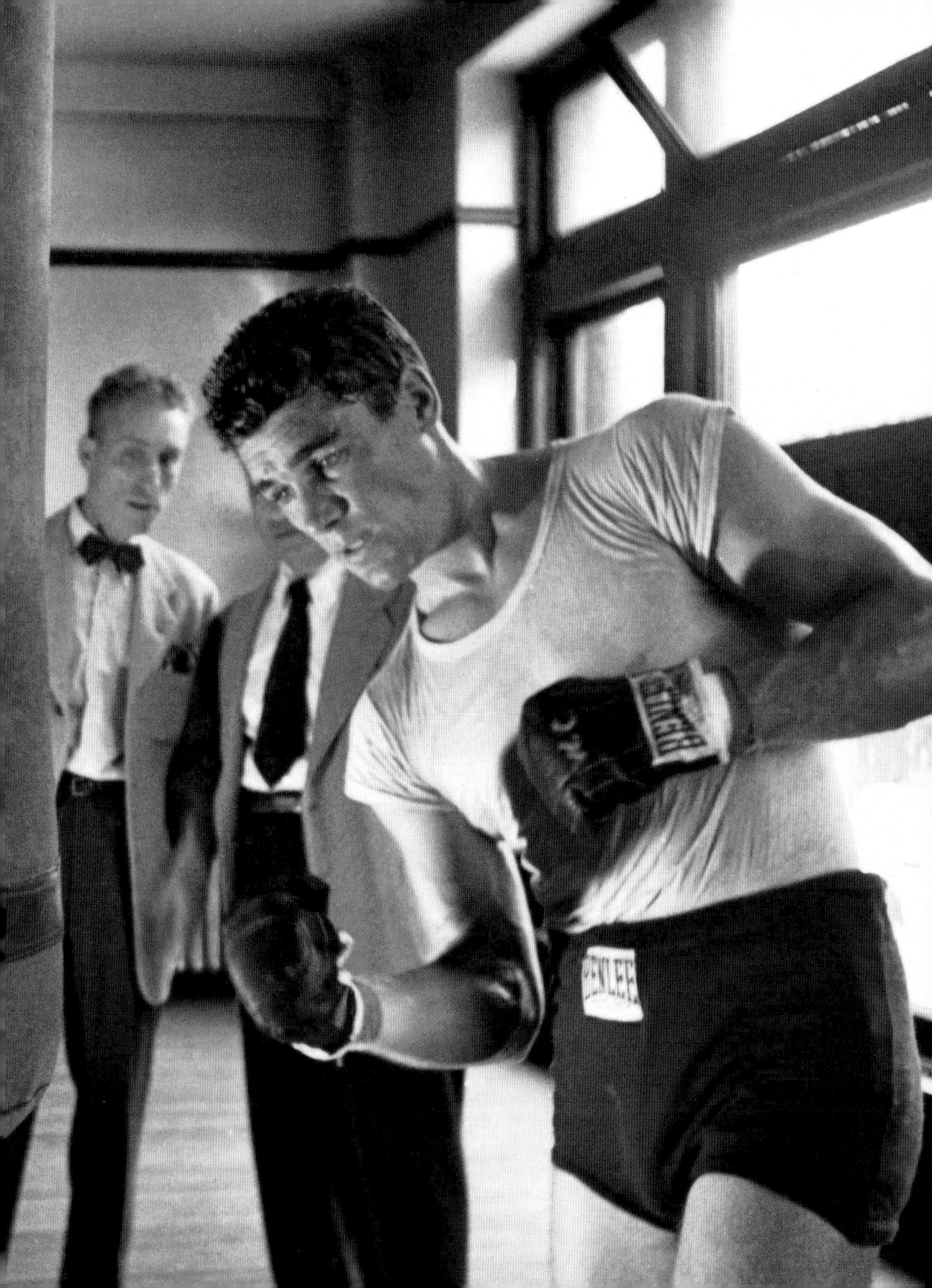

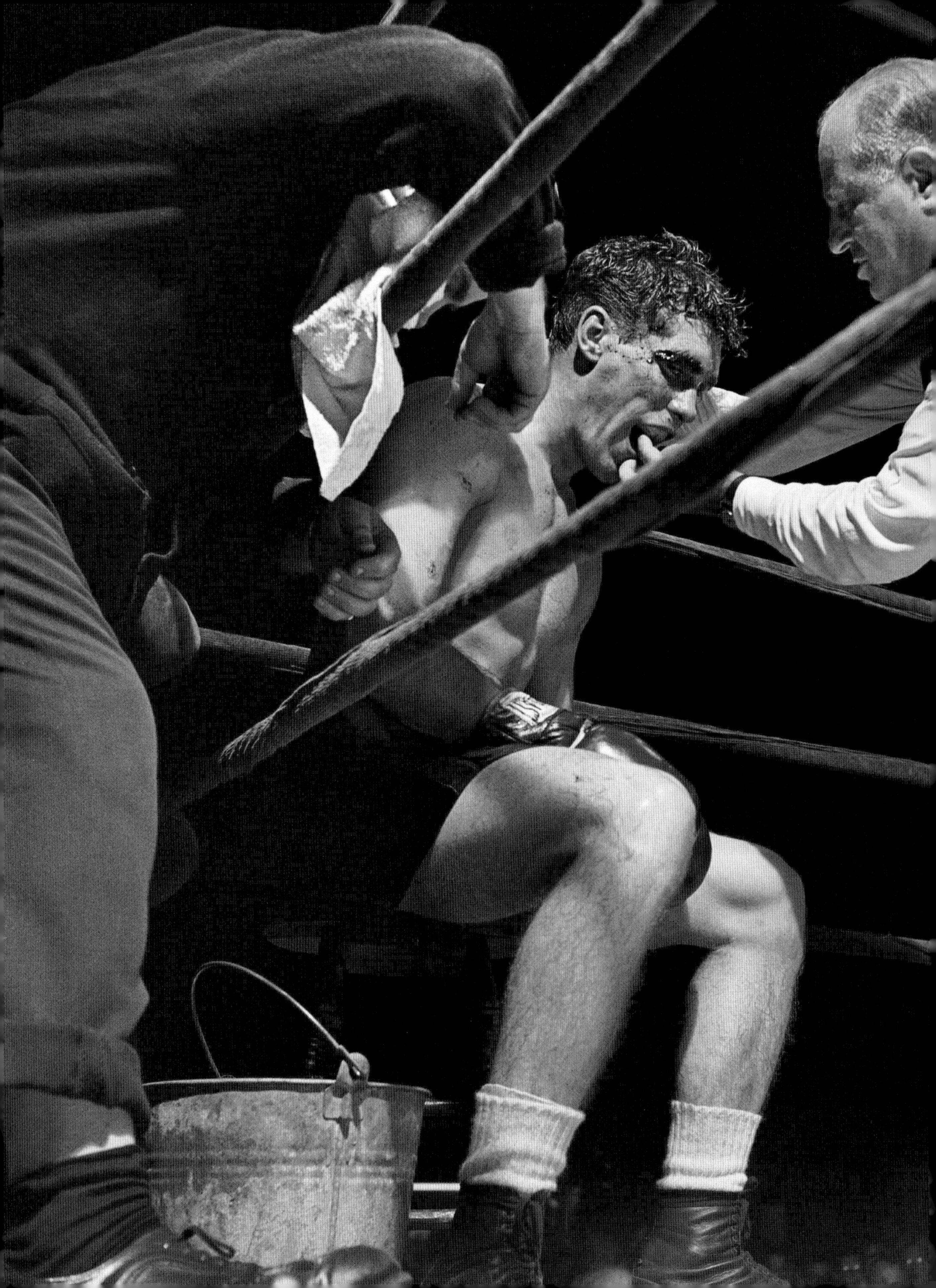

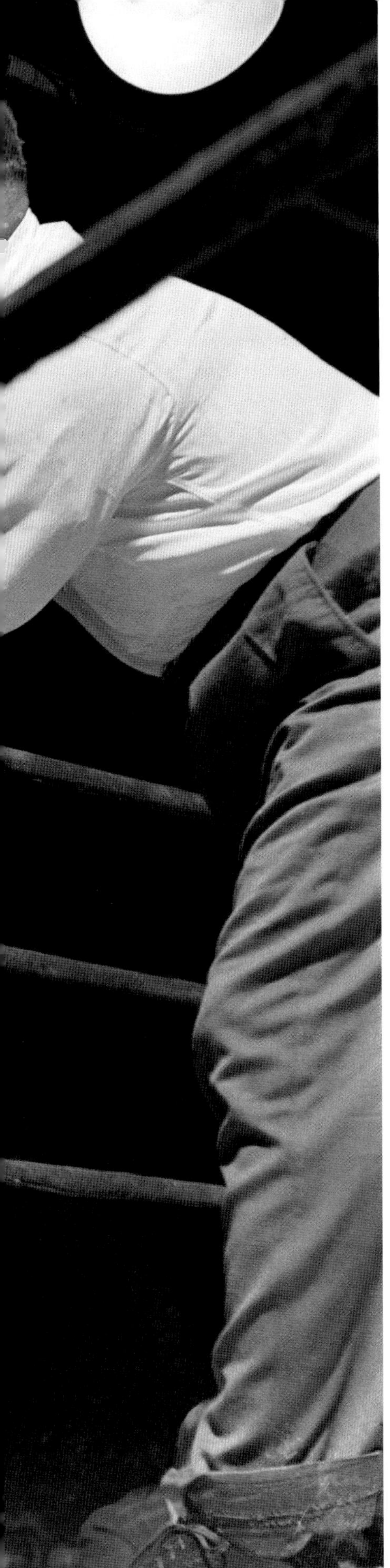

Cartier in the boxing ring

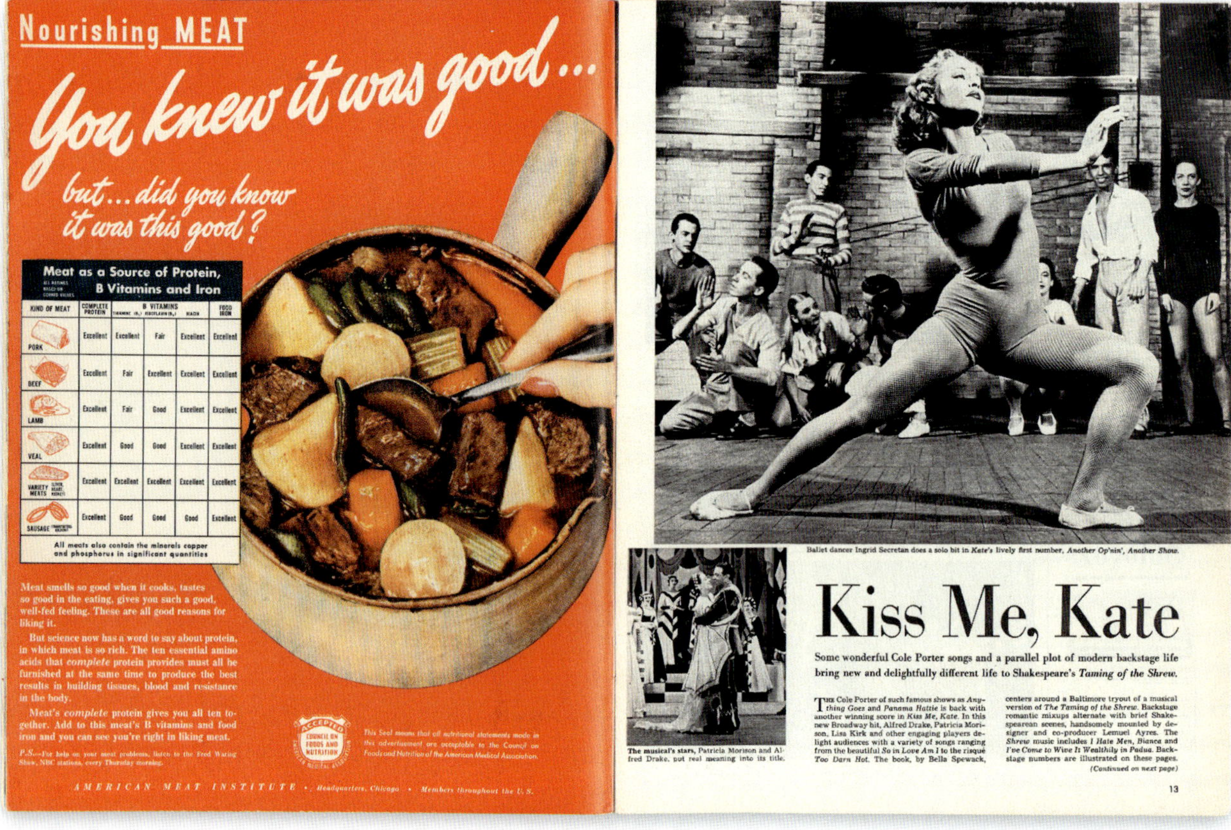

Nourishing MEAT

You knew it was good...

but... did you know it was this good?

Meat as a Source of Protein, B Vitamins and Iron

KIND OF MEAT	COMPLETE PROTEIN	B VITAMINS: THIAMINE (B1)	RIBOFLAVIN (B2)	NIACIN	FOOD IRON
PORK	Excellent	Excellent	Fair	Excellent	Excellent
BEEF	Excellent	Fair	Excellent	Excellent	Excellent
LAMB	Excellent	Fair	Good	Excellent	Excellent
VEAL	Excellent	Good	Good	Excellent	Excellent
VARIETY MEATS	Excellent	Excellent	Excellent	Excellent	Excellent
SAUSAGE	Excellent	Good	Good	Good	Excellent

All meats also contain the minerals copper and phosphorus in significant quantities

Meat smells so good when it cooks, tastes so good in the eating, gives you such a good, well-fed feeling. These are all good reasons for liking it.

But science now has a word to say about protein, in which meat is so rich. The ten essential amino acids that *complete* protein provides must all be furnished at the same time to produce the best results in building tissues, blood and resistance in the body.

Meat's *complete* protein gives you all ten together. Add to this meat's B vitamins and food iron and you can see you're right in liking meat.

P.S.—For help on your meat problems, listen to the Fred Waring Show, NBC stations, every Thursday morning.

ACCEPTED COUNCIL ON FOODS AND NUTRITION AMERICAN MEDICAL ASSOCIATION

This Seal means that all nutritional statements made in this advertisement are acceptable to the Council on Foods and Nutrition of the American Medical Association.

AMERICAN MEAT INSTITUTE • Headquarters, Chicago • Members throughout the U. S.

Ballet dancer Ingrid Secretan does a solo bit in *Kate's* lively first number, *Another Op'nin', Another Show.*

Kiss Me, Kate

Some wonderful Cole Porter songs and a parallel plot of modern backstage life bring new and delightfully different life to Shakespeare's *Taming of the Shrew.*

The Cole Porter of such famous shows as *Anything Goes* and *Panama Hattie* is back with another winning score in *Kiss Me, Kate*. In this new Broadway hit, Alfred Drake, Patricia Morison, Lisa Kirk and other engaging players delight audiences with a variety of songs ranging from the beautiful *So in Love Am I* to the risqué *Too Darn Hot*. The book, by Bella Spewack, centers around a Baltimore tryout of a musical version of *The Taming of the Shrew*. Backstage romantic mixups alternate with brief Shakespearean scenes, handsomely mounted by designer and co-producer Lemuel Ayres. The *Shrew* music includes *I Hate Men*, *Bianca* and *I've Come to Wive It Wealthily in Padua*. Backstage numbers are illustrated on these pages.

(Continued on next page)

The musical's stars, Patricia Morison and Alfred Drake, put real meaning into its title.

13

PUBLISHED AS

KISS ME, KATE: COLE PORTER AND SHAKESPEARE COMBINE TALENTS IN MUSICAL

DATE

JANUARY 18, 1949

Opening in late December 1948, *Kiss Me, Kate*, with music and lyrics by Cole Porter, was the composer's only musical to run for more than 1,000 performances on Broadway. A photograph from this assignment was included in the article "Midsummer Nights in New York" (July 19, 1949), which mentioned the popularity of the show despite the recent slowdown in the city's tourism.

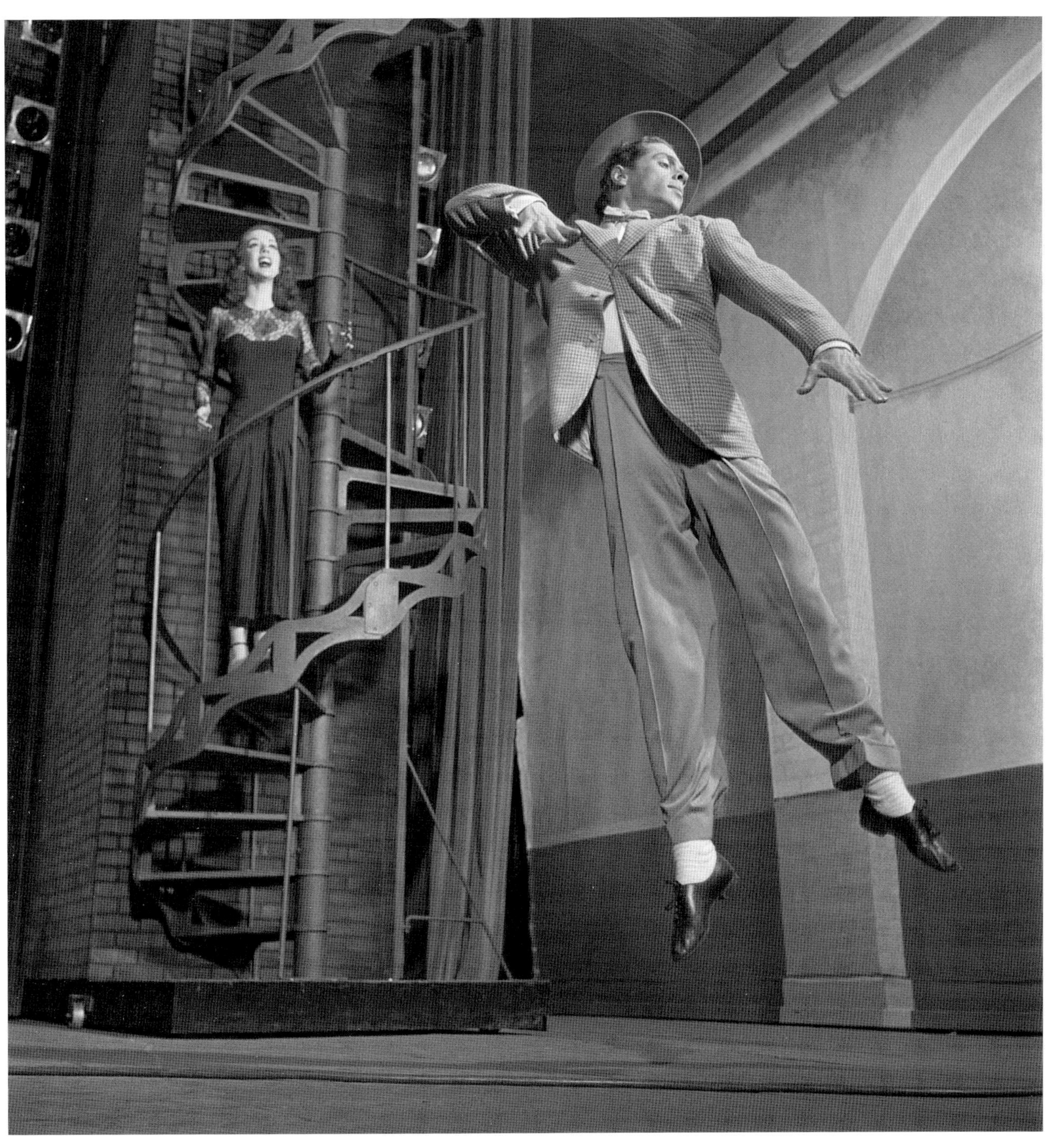

Lisa Kirk and Harold Lang performing the song "Why Can't You Behave?"

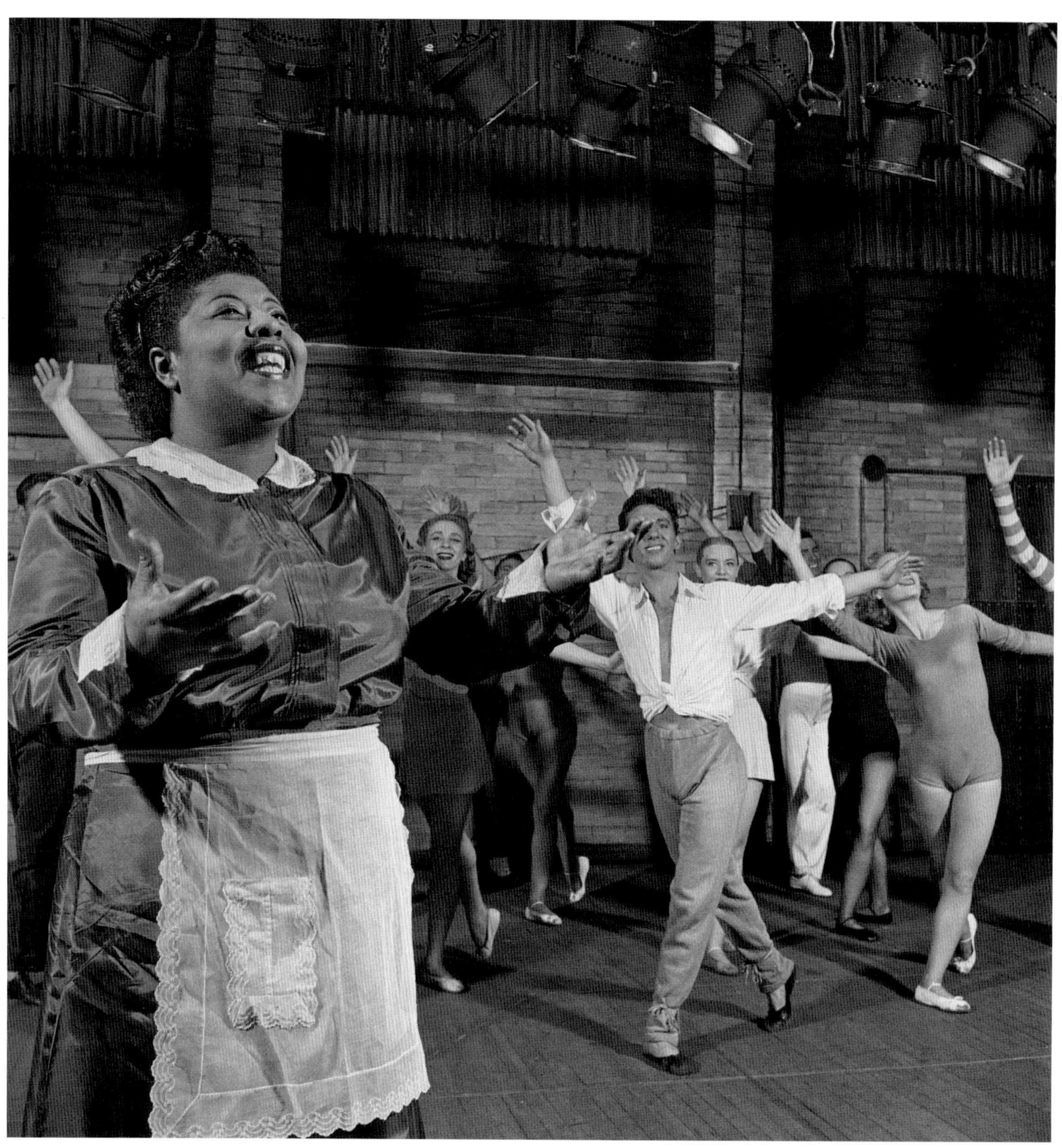

Cast rehearsing a musical number

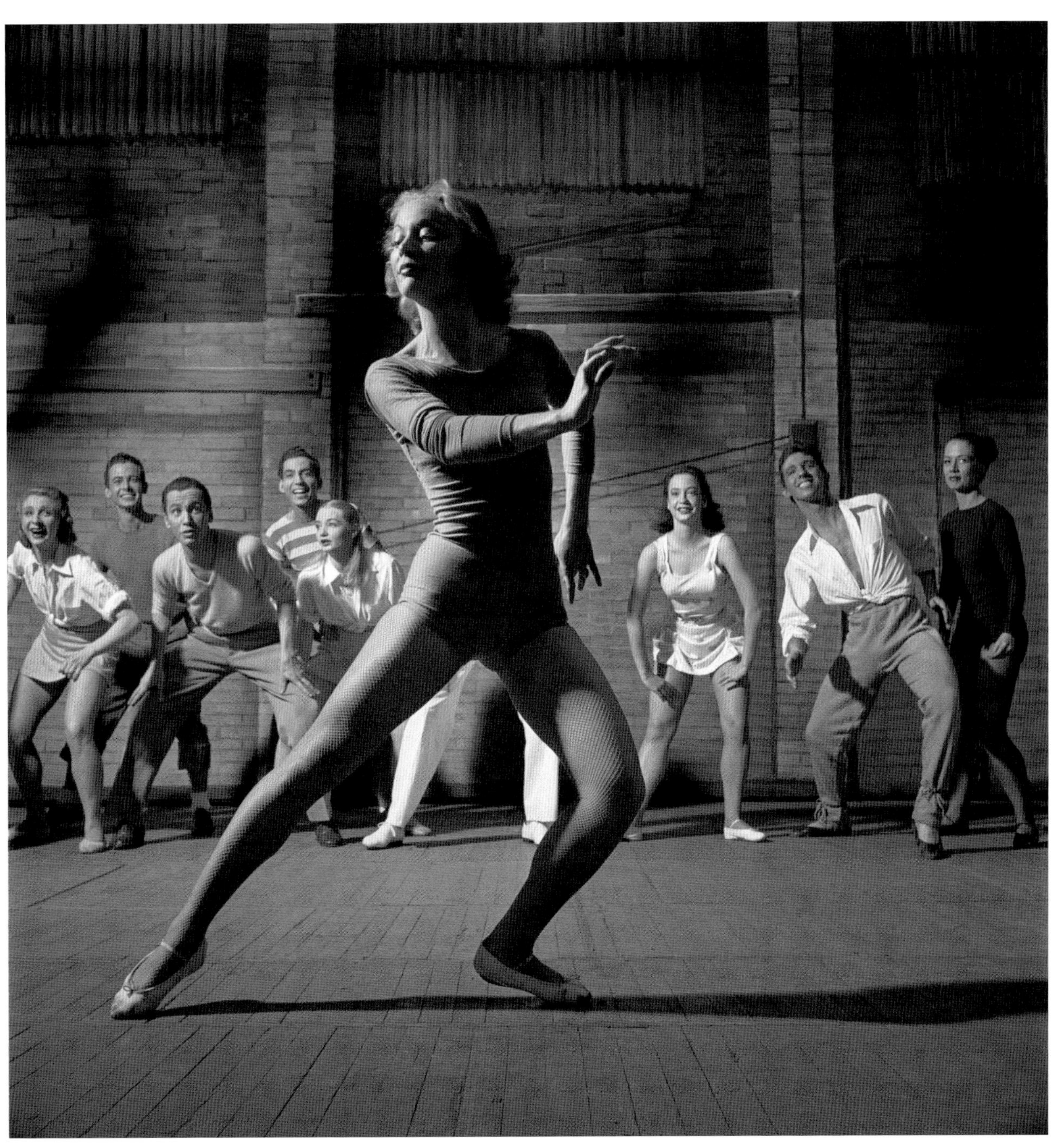

Ballet dancer Ingrid Secretan in the opening number, "Another Op'nin', Another Show"

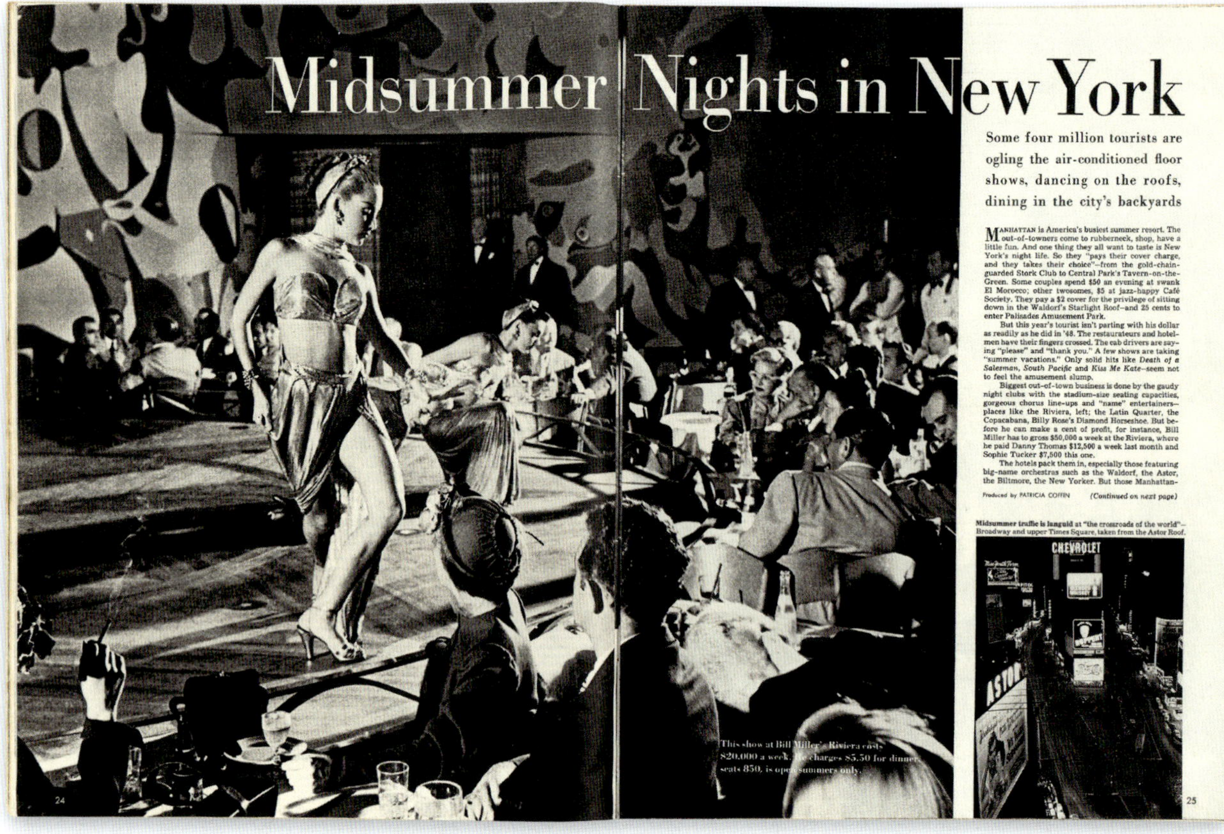

Midsummer Nights in New York

Some four million tourists are ogling the air-conditioned floor shows, dancing on the roofs, dining in the city's backyards

MANHATTAN is America's busiest summer resort. The out-of-towners come to rubberneck, shop, have a little fun. And one thing they all want to taste is New York's night life. So they "pays their cover charge, and they takes their choice"—from the gold-chain-guarded Stork Club to Central Park's Tavern-on-the-Green. Some couples spend $50 an evening at swank El Morocco; other twosomes, $5 at jazz-happy Café Society. They pay a $2 cover for the privilege of sitting down in the Waldorf's Starlight Roof—and 25 cents to enter Palisades Amusement Park.

But this year's tourist isn't parting with his dollar as readily as he did in '48. The restaurateurs and hotelmen have their fingers crossed. The cab drivers are saying "please" and "thank you." A few shows are taking "summer vacations." Only solid hits like *Death of a Salesman*, *South Pacific* and *Kiss Me Kate*—seem not to feel the amusement slump.

Biggest out-of-town business is done by the gaudy night clubs with the stadium-size seating capacities, gorgeous chorus line-ups and "name" entertainers—places like the Riviera, left; the Latin Quarter, the Copacabana, Billy Rose's Diamond Horseshoe. But before he can make a cent of profit, for instance, Bill Miller has to gross $50,000 a week at the Riviera, where he paid Danny Thomas $12,500 a week last month and Sophie Tucker $7,500 this one.

The hotels pack them in, especially those featuring big-name orchestras such as the Waldorf, the Astor, the Biltmore, the New Yorker. But those Manhattan-

Produced by PATRICIA COFFIN

(Continued on next page)

This show at Bill Miller's Riviera costs $20,000 a week. He charges $5.50 for dinner, seats 850, is open summers only.

Midsummer traffic is languid at "the crossroads of the world"—Broadway and upper Times Square, taken from the Astor Roof.

24 25

PUBLISHED AS

MIDSUMMER NIGHTS IN NEW YORK

Focusing on summer nightlife and tourism's impact on New York City, this story detailed the recent difficulty of such establishments as the Stork Club, El Morocco, and the "gaudy night clubs with stadium-size seating capacity" like the Riviera, the Latin Quarter, and Copacabana to get tourists to "part with their dollars." The author, a longtime *Look* editor who specialized in culture and entertainment, mentioned tourists' growing preference for Broadway theaters and smaller out-of-the-way spots in places like Greenwich Village. As sometimes happened with the work of *Look*'s photographers, this article recycled photographs Kubrick had shot for previous assignments, including an image of actress Beatrice Pearson he had taken for an unpublished story about her.

DATE

JULY 19, 1949

AUTHOR

PATRICIA COFFIN

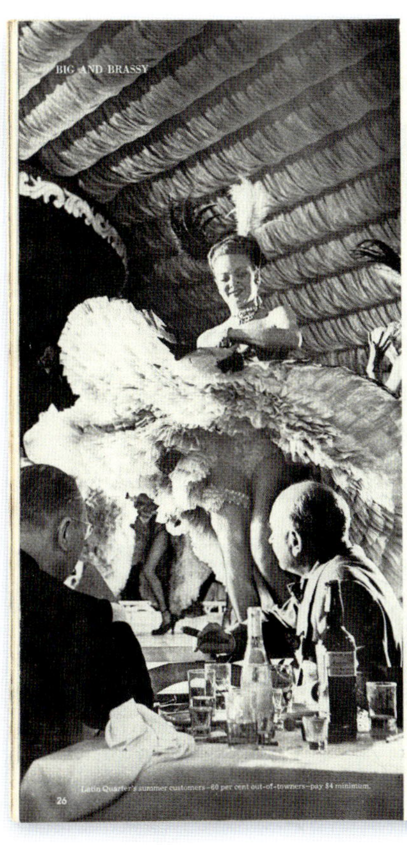

MIDSUMMER NIGHTS IN NEW YORK *continued*

ites who stay in town for the summer prefer more intimate haunts, less crowded rooms; places like the Plaza, the St. Regis, the Blue Angel, the Versailles or backyard restaurants like Ricky's in Greenwich Village.

The current No. 1 tune request is *Some Enchanted Evening* from the top musical of the season, *South Pacific*. Dancers favor the foxtrot and the rumba, in the order named. The dinner dish most ordered is roast beef. The most popular drink is Scotch. Naturally, summer drinks are in vogue. Says the Stork's Sherman Billingsley: "I make my biggest profit on the summer customer because he drinks the cheapest liquor—gin, rum and Dubonnet." Drinks at his place start at $1 after dark.

But most summer customers from out of town feel they are getting their money's worth—in air-cooled entertainment and, for free, the glamour of New York's Great White Way.

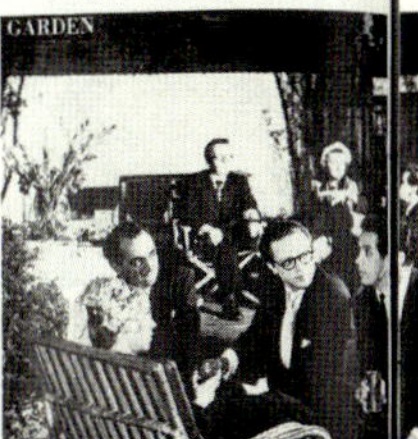

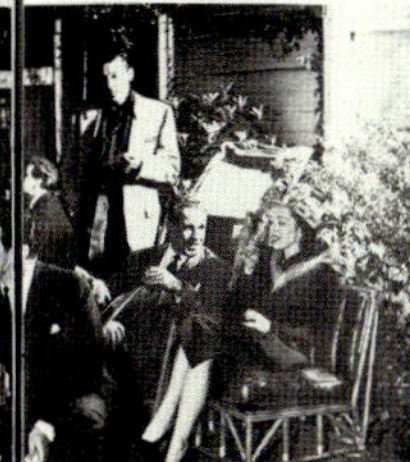

New Yorkers like to play in their own backyards. At this spaghetti party given by infants-wear designer Carlo Borgia are the Alfred Drakes, left, talking to John Conte, center. At right is Lisa Kirk and her new husband.

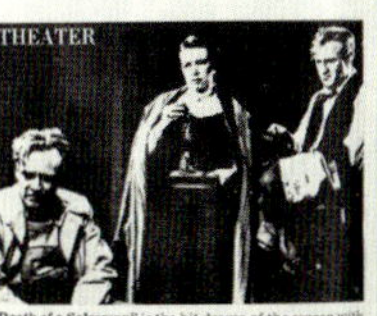

"Death of a Salesman" is the hit drama of the season with tickets—$4.80 tops—still as scarce as N. Y.'s parking space.

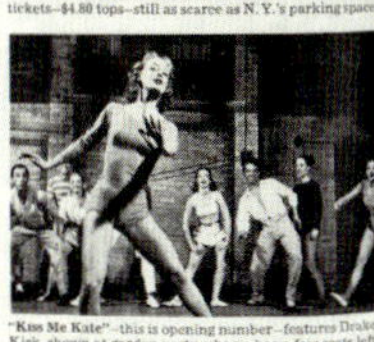

"Kiss Me Kate"—this is opening number—features Drake. Kirk, shown at garden party, above, has a few seats left.

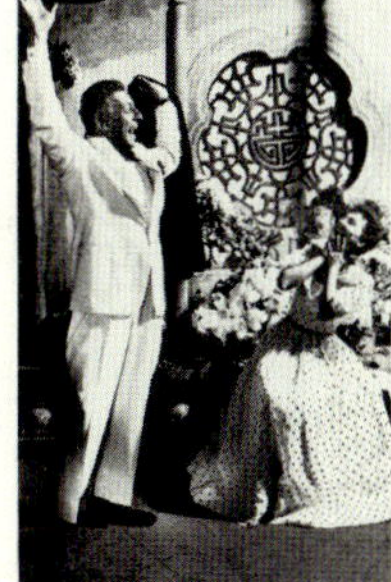

In "South Pacific," sold out, Ezio Pinza takes off Mary Martin's *I'm Gonna Wash That Man Right Outa My Hair*.

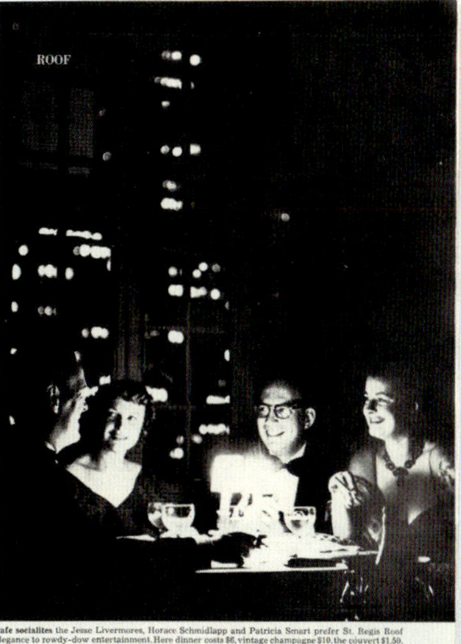

Cafe socialites the Jesse Livermores, Horace Schmidlapp and Patricia Smart prefer St. Regis Roof elegance to rowdy-dow entertainment. Here dinner costs $6, vintage champagne $10, the couvert $1.50.

At Palisades Park, which draws 60,000 a week end, 1949 spending fell from $1.25 to $1 per person.

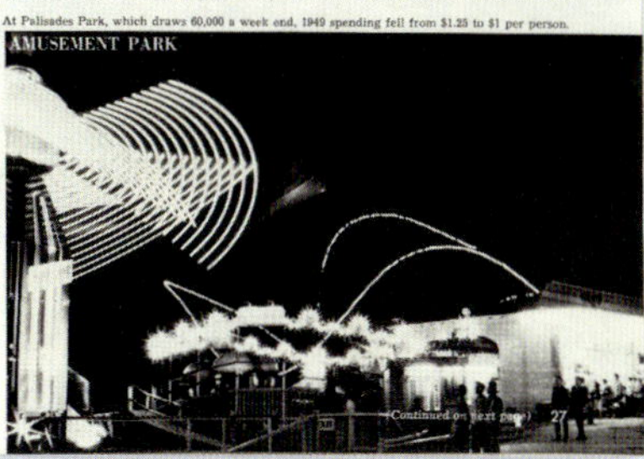

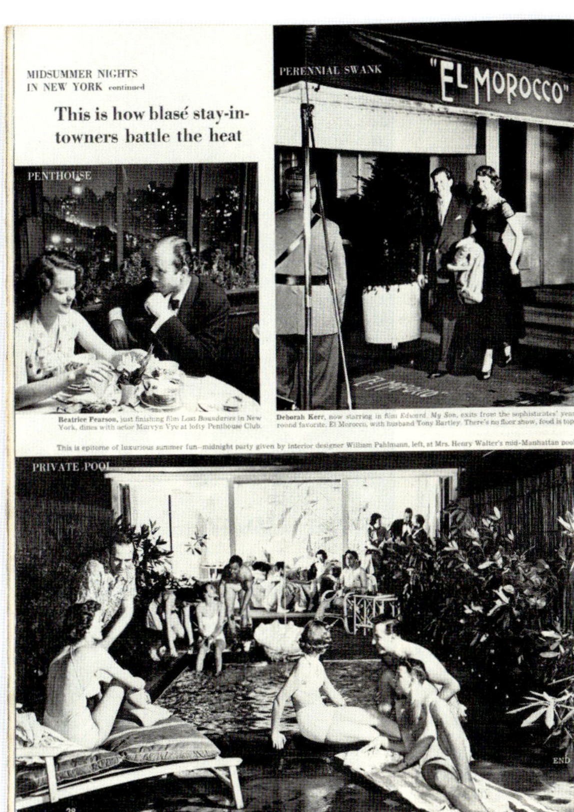

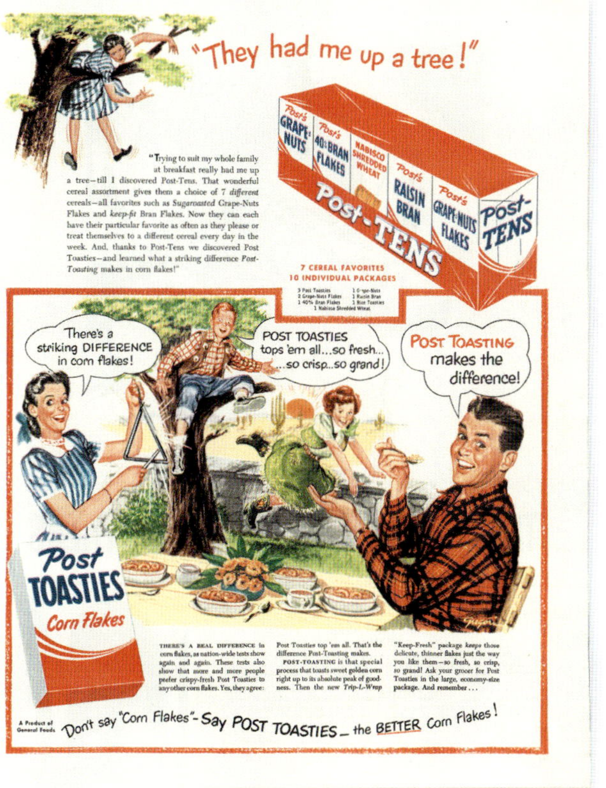

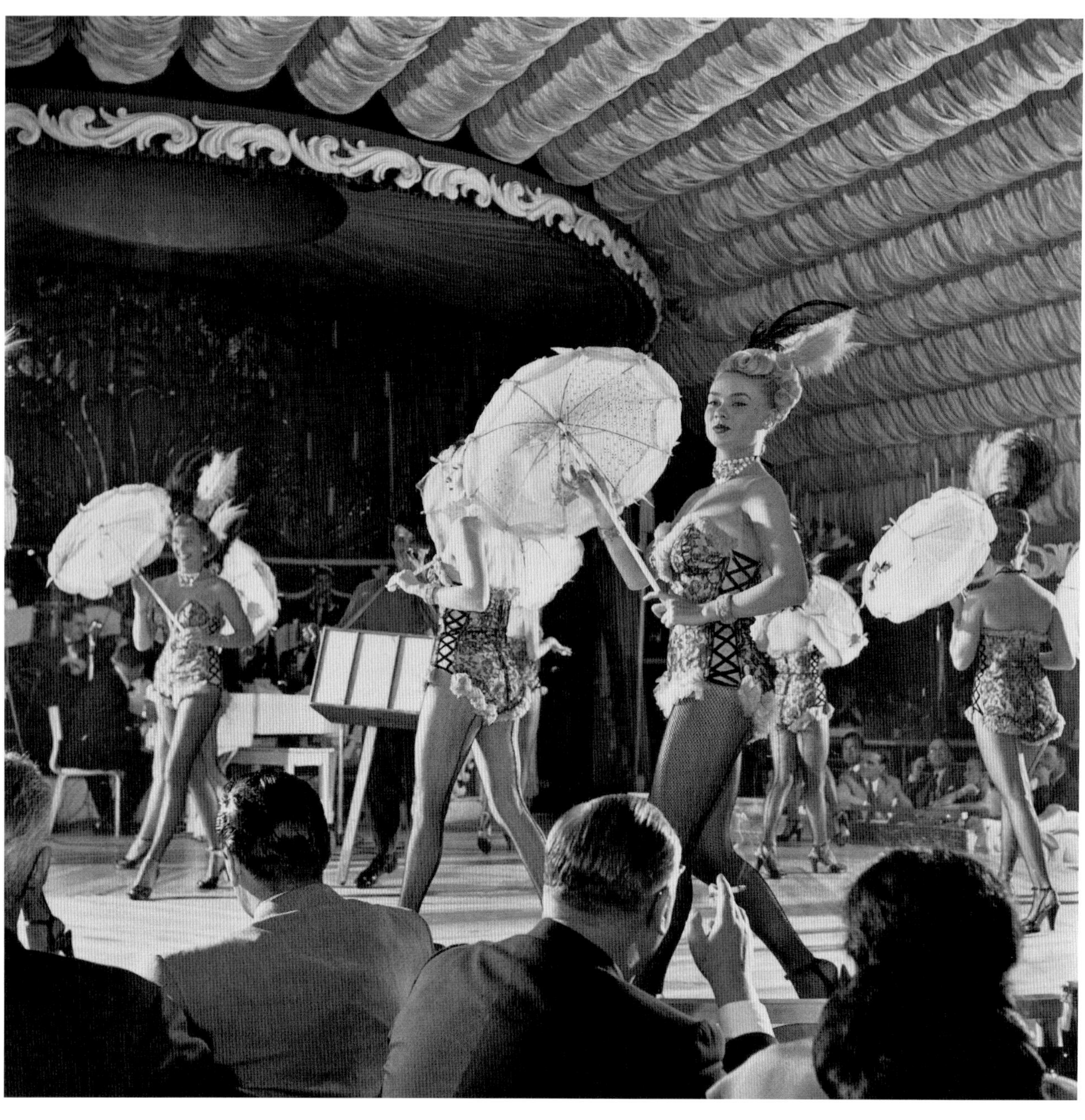

Club-goers taking in shows at the Latin Quarter

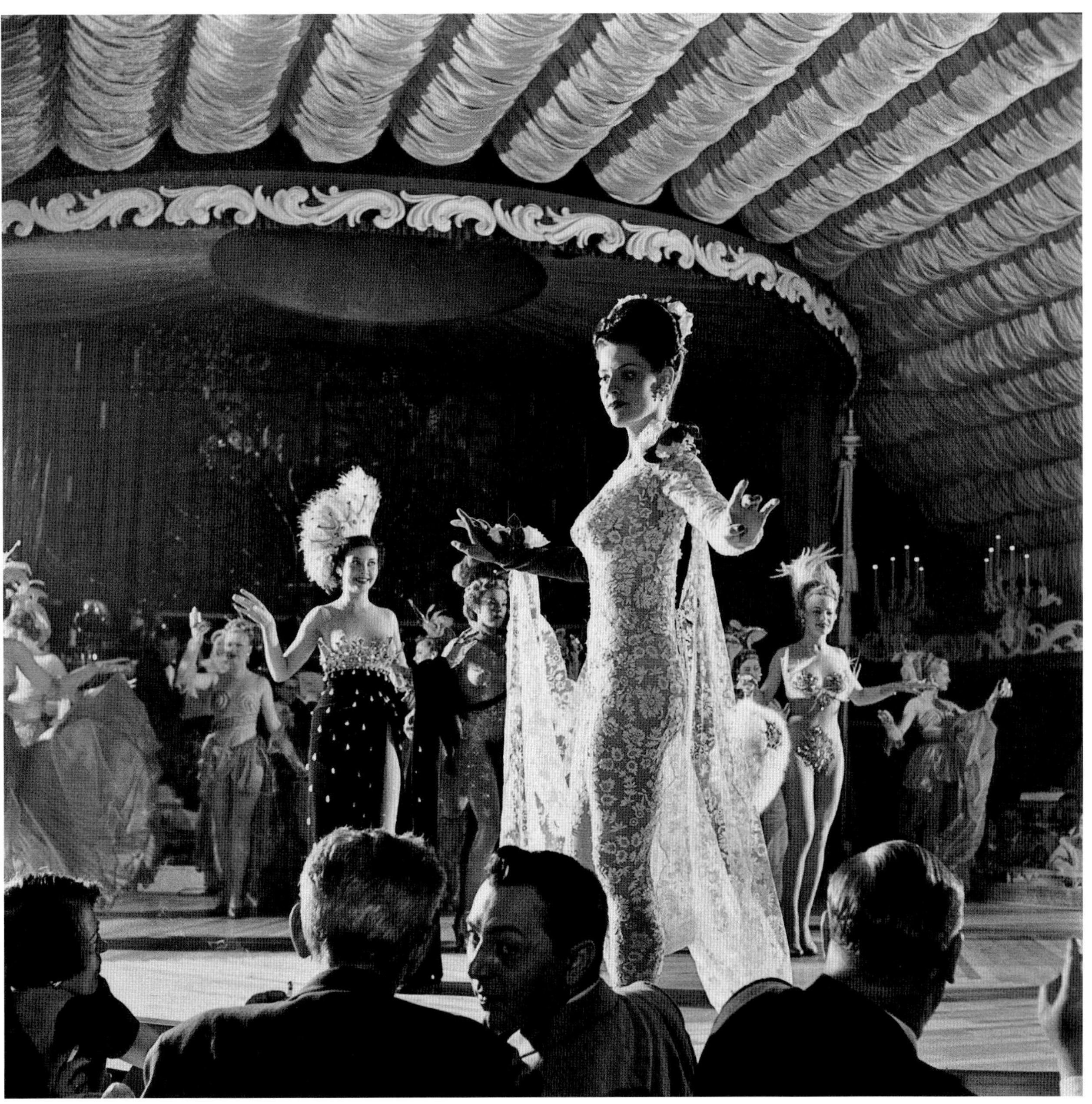

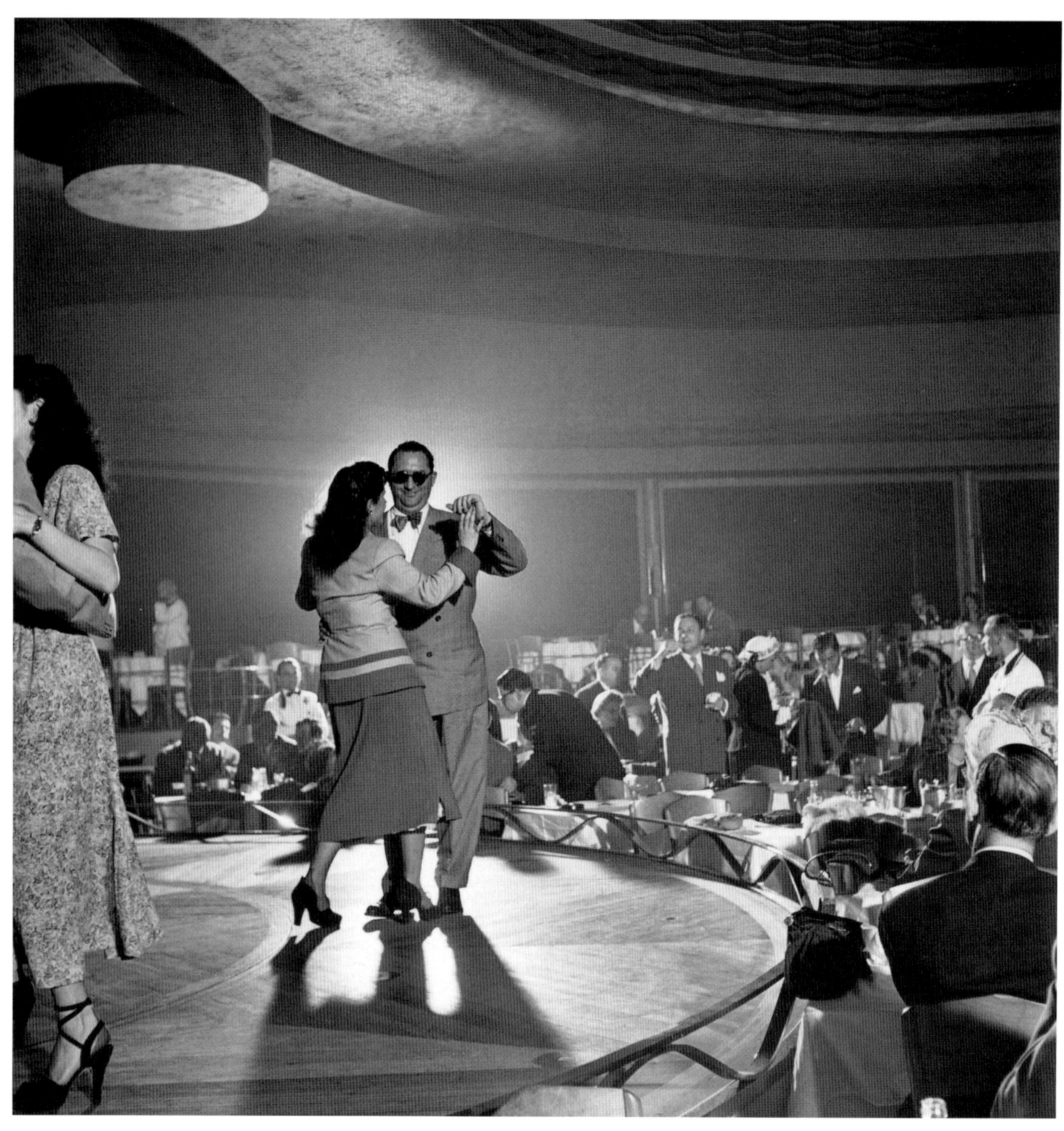

Dancers at the Copacabana

OPPOSITE **Showgirls primping backstage**

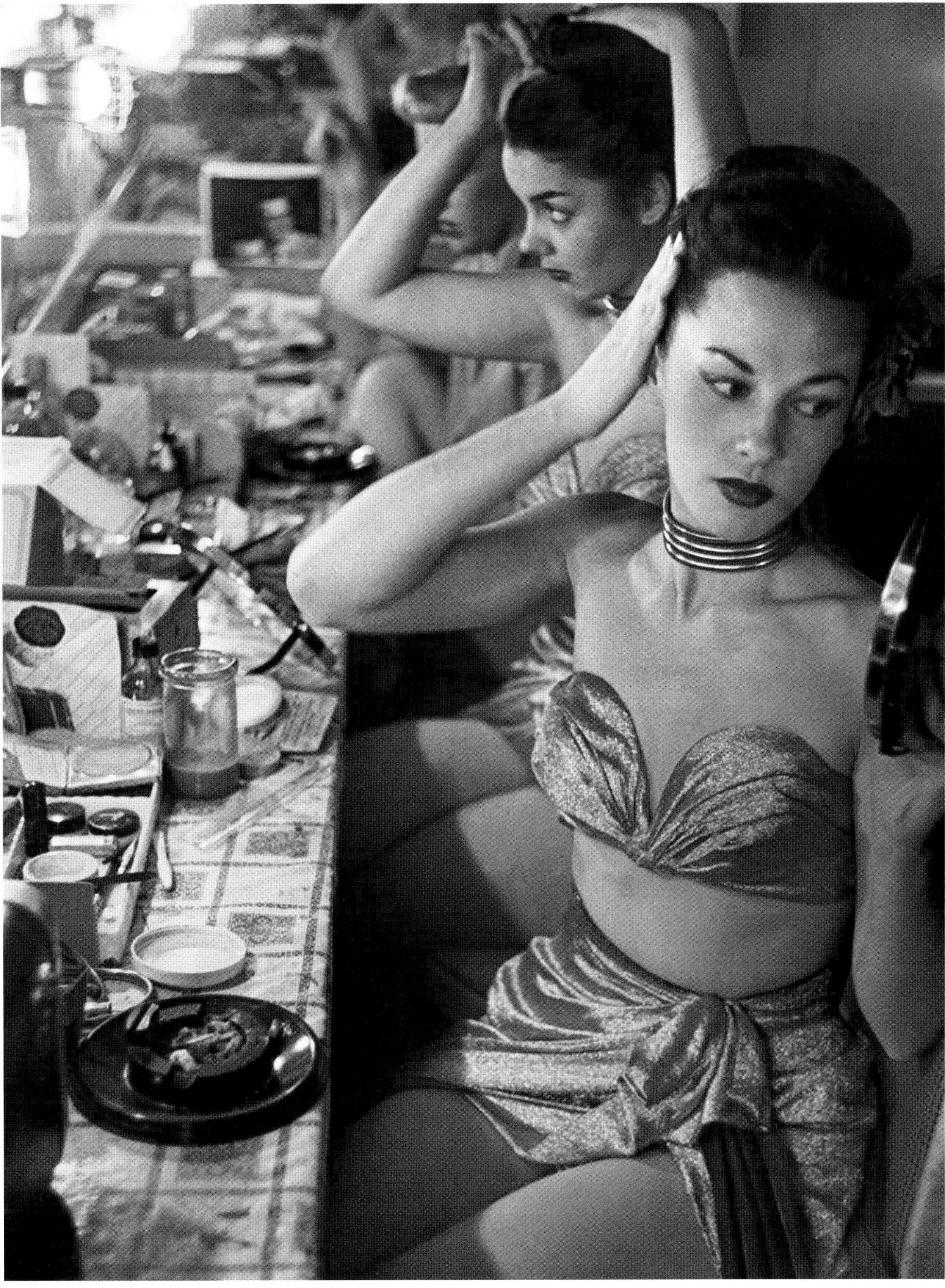

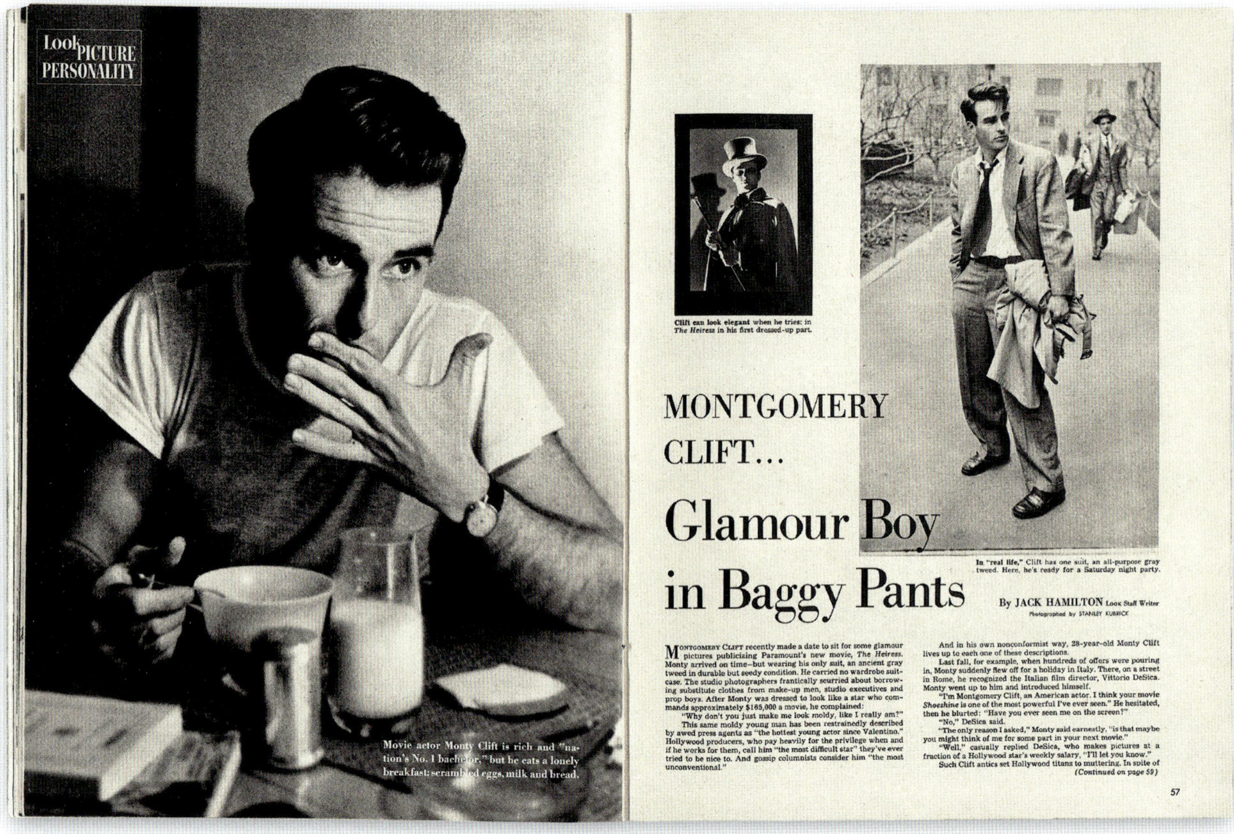

Look PICTURE PERSONALITY

Movie actor Monty Clift is rich and "nation's No. 1 bachelor," but he eats a lonely breakfast: scrambled eggs, milk and bread.

Clift can look elegant when he tries: in *The Heiress* in his first dressed-up part.

MONTGOMERY CLIFT...

Glamour Boy in Baggy Pants

In "real life," Clift has one suit, an all-purpose gray tweed. Here, he's ready for a Saturday night party.

By JACK HAMILTON Look Staff Writer

Photographed by STANLEY KUBRICK

Montgomery Clift recently made a date to sit for some glamour pictures publicizing Paramount's new movie, *The Heiress*. Monty arrived on time—but wearing his only suit, an ancient gray tweed in durable but seedy condition. He carried no wardrobe suitcase. The studio photographers frantically scurried about borrowing substitute clothes from make-up men, studio executives and prop boys. After Monty was dressed to look like a star who commands approximately $165,000 a movie, he complained:

"Why don't you just make me look moldy, like I really am?"

This same moldy young man has been restrainedly described by awed press agents as "the hottest young actor since Valentino." Hollywood producers, who pay heavily for the privilege when and if he works for them, call him "the most difficult star" they've ever tried to be nice to. And gossip columnists consider him "the most unconventional."

And in his own nonconformist way, 28-year-old Monty Clift lives up to each one of these descriptions.

Last fall, for example, when hundreds of offers were pouring in, Monty suddenly flew off for a holiday in Italy. There, on a street in Rome, he recognized the Italian film director, Vittorio DeSica. Monty went up to him and introduced himself.

"I'm Montgomery Clift, an American actor. I think your movie *Shoeshine* is one of the most powerful I've ever seen." He hesitated, then he blurted: "Have you ever seen me on the screen?"

"No," DeSica said.

"The only reason I asked," Monty said earnestly, "is that maybe you might think of me for some part in your next movie."

"Well," casually replied DeSica, who makes pictures at a fraction of a Hollywood star's weekly salary, "I'll let you know."

Such Clift antics set Hollywood titans to muttering. In spite of

(Continued on page 59)

57

PUBLISHED AS

MONTGOMERY CLIFT: GLAMOUR BOY IN BAGGY PANTS

DATE

JULY 19, 1949

AUTHOR

JACK HAMILTON

Published shortly before the release of *The Heiress*, the film that clinched Montgomery Clift's status as a huge Hollywood star, this article chronicled the actor's unstarlike behavior in New York City. There he lived in a fifth-floor walk-up apartment with peeling plaster, owned only one suit—"an ancient gray tweed in durable but seedy condition," and ate "a lonely breakfast." While *Look* profiles regularly included scenes of celebrities with their families, Kubrick here provided the requisite dose of domesticity by photographing Clift at the home of his good friend, fellow actor Kevin McCarthy. The September 1950 "New York Issue" of *Flair*, a short-lived cultural magazine created by *Look*'s parent company, Cowles Magazine, published Kubrick's portrait of Clift from this assignment.

PAGE 188 **Clift having breakfast in his apartment**

PAGE 189 **Clift wearing his only suit, an all-purpose gray tweed**

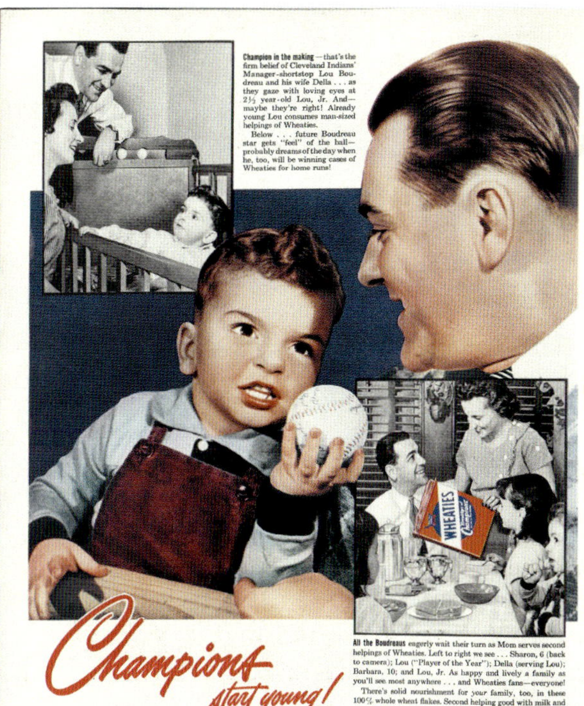

Clift loves children, "blue steaks"—and traveling alone

all this evidence, they know that Monty has such a shrewd business head that he gives Hollywood contract lawyers a headache.

Clift protests that he's not so eccentric. "An actor is like a tightrope walker in front of a crowd," he says. "One slip—and he's done for. Now, I'm an average guy. And I like average things. If a part in a movie doesn't mean or say anything to me, I figure it won't interest an audience."

He'll Play a Cad

So far, Clift has been seen in only two widely separate roles—as the skinny, taciturn cowhand who slugs it out with brawny John Wayne in *Red River*, and as the serious young GI who loves children in *The Search*. His next will be as a cad—a fortune-hunter who tampers with Olivia de Havilland's affections in William Wyler's *The Heiress*. This range suggests an actor of more than usual versatility. But it doesn't entirely explain the prompt world-wide adoption of Montgomery Clift by movie fans—or the reason why New York's top models, with much hullabaloo, selected him as "the nation's No. 1 bachelor."

To some, Clift's chief charm may possibly be his unaffected warmth and earthiness. He seems to look like the boy next door. But, he has a mobile, almost classic, photogenic quality about him that sets him apart, and helps to make him a forceful screen personality who appeals to men, women and children. He's 6 feet, weighs 155 pounds, has black hair and blue eyes, and hair on his chest that pokes out of his shirt collar. His whipcord energy keeps him moving 18 hours a day.

You Can't Just Coast

"Everything he does has fierce purpose," one of his girl friends says. "If you go bicycling with him—you never just coast. You have to pedal good and hard. If you even just talk with him, you have to give out with stimulating ideas or be scorned. And he's so excitable that once, in criticizing a steak I was broiling, he knocked my Frigidaire to one side."

In spite of all the curiosity about his private life, Monty tries to live as anonymously as possible. He's a relaxed bachelor who says it's nobody's business what girl he happens to be dating. One of his friends predicts, though, that he'll marry and have at least ten children of his own, because he can't go on loving all his friends' kids forever.

In New York, where he stays in his spare time between jobs and travel, Monty lives alone in a fifth-floor, walk-up, sublet apartment overlooking an alley filled with garbage cans. He pays $45 a month rent. The apartment has no rugs in any of its three tiny rooms and doesn't feature a comfortable chair. It does have handy coffee-makers everywhere, because Monty drinks coffee all day long. His clothes closet is a roomy, desolate place.

Clift, one of the three children of a New York stockbroker, has been a working actor since he was 14, in 1935. He made his New York stage debut in a play called *Fly Away Home*. "It was all an accident," says Clift. "My father

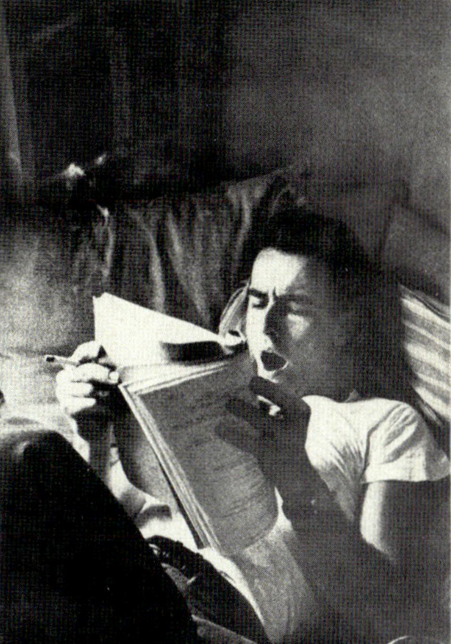

Clift, resting on day bed, yawns over one of the many hundred scripts eager producers have sent him since his spectacular debut in the movies. Monty's idea of heaven is a place with no scripts.

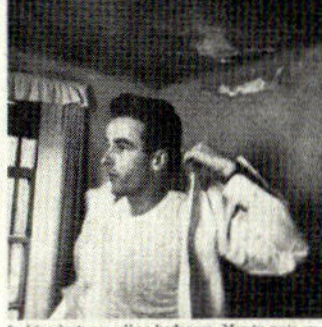

In his plaster-peeling bedroom, Monty puts on a white shirt, a reluctant sacrifice to convention.

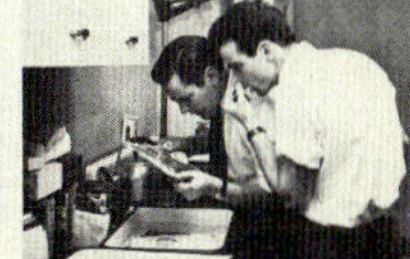

Friend Kevin McCarthy. Clift criticize their photo prints in Kevin's kitchen dark room.

(Continued on next page)

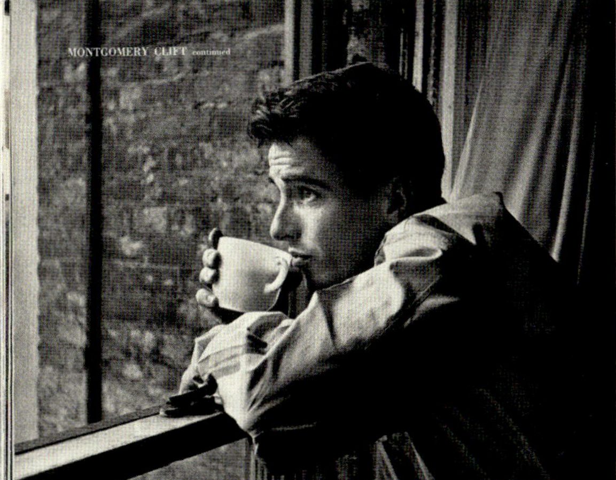

Bachelor Monty Clift, with morning coffee, looks out upon a gloomy day from his mid-Manhattan apartment. He pays $45 a month for it, walks up five flights.

Monty's as "strong as an ox" and eats like a stevedore

happened to know the play's producer. From then on, I was stuck."

In the next ten years, he appeared in a succession of Broadway plays, some hits—such as *There Shall Be No Night* with the Lunts—and others that went whfft in a day or so. His over-all average salary was about $4 a week.

At the beginning of his career, Monty was a nuisance who put ice down actors' backs as they made their entrances. But gradually he grew into a serious-minded juvenile who gave carefully thought-out—and colorful—performances. Other actors didn't understand him because he kept pretty much to himself. Tallulah Bankhead, who played with him in *The Skin of Our Teeth* in 1943, says, with a slight edge to her words, "He was very polite." She adds: "I hear he's changed."

In one of his many travel-lust jaunts—to Mexico in 1939—he got amoebic dysentery, which kept him out of the Army. To build himself up, he began eating stevedore's meals that are notorious among his friends. He stows away such fare as "blue steaks with blood that hasn't stopped flowing," strawberries, cream cheese, asparagus, creme brûlée—"and more steak." He's still a paid-up member of a Broadway gym, where he goes in for weight-lifting. "He looks like a skinny kid," says the gym owner, "but he's made himself strong as an ox."

So far, Clift hasn't spent much time in Hollywood. His first two movies were shot in Arizona and Europe. He stayed in the movie capital about two months during the filming of *The Heiress*. He lived alone in a cheap and convenient hotel where "the Murphy bed squeaked like hell."

Besides acting, Clift would sometime like to direct movies. He and his best friend, stage actor Kevin McCarthy, write out sample scripts and map them out photographically as a director might. "When my actor's body wears out," says Monty, "I want to know how to do something else."

Augusta McCarthy, Kevin's wife, says that Monty's first interest in life is not acting, directing, eating, or travel—but children. "We've known Monty seven years," she says. "My most vivid picture of him is the day he arrived at La Guardia Field on his return from Europe. He struggled from the plane with an armful of unwrapped toys for all the kids he knows. His own luggage was in a beach bag. . . .

"And don't for a minute think that Monty *really* believes he's a moldy character. He'll still be fascinating at 90."

Clift suggested this gag pose

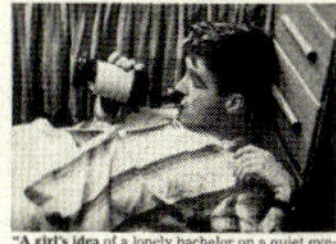

"A girl's idea of a lonely bachelor on a quiet evening at home. . . . Actually, I sublet this bottle."

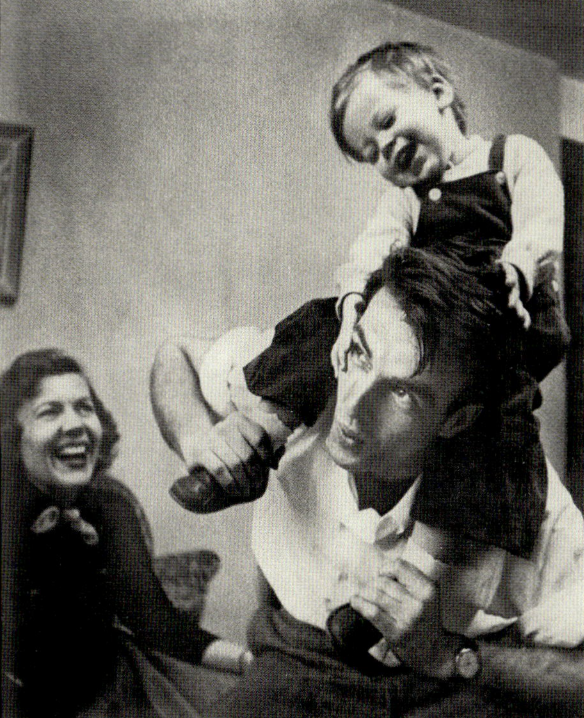

"Flip" McCarthy gets teetering ride from "Uncle" Monty as Flip's mother enjoys it too. Mrs. McCarthy: "Monty's our best friend even if he is hard on the furniture."

END

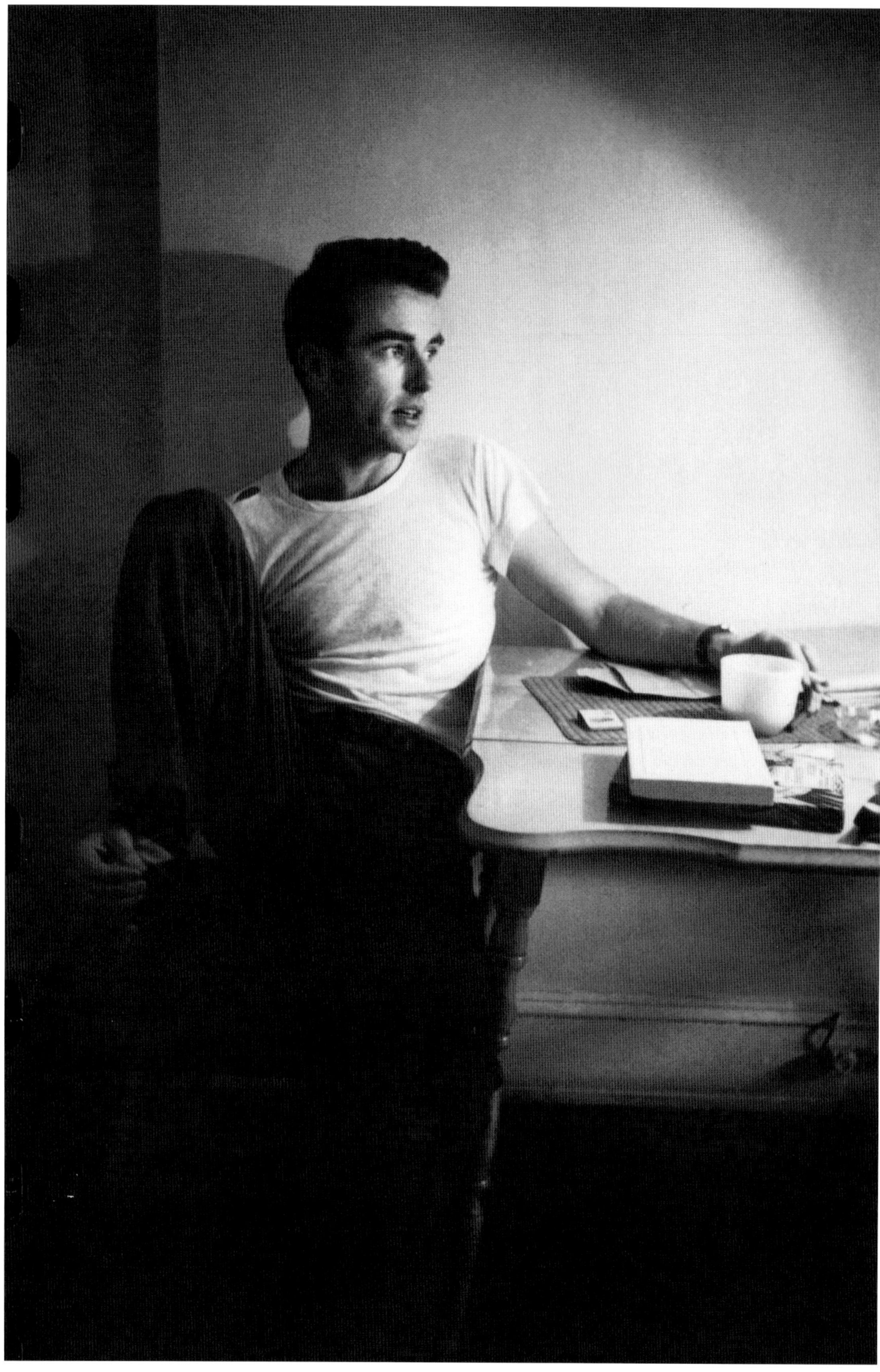

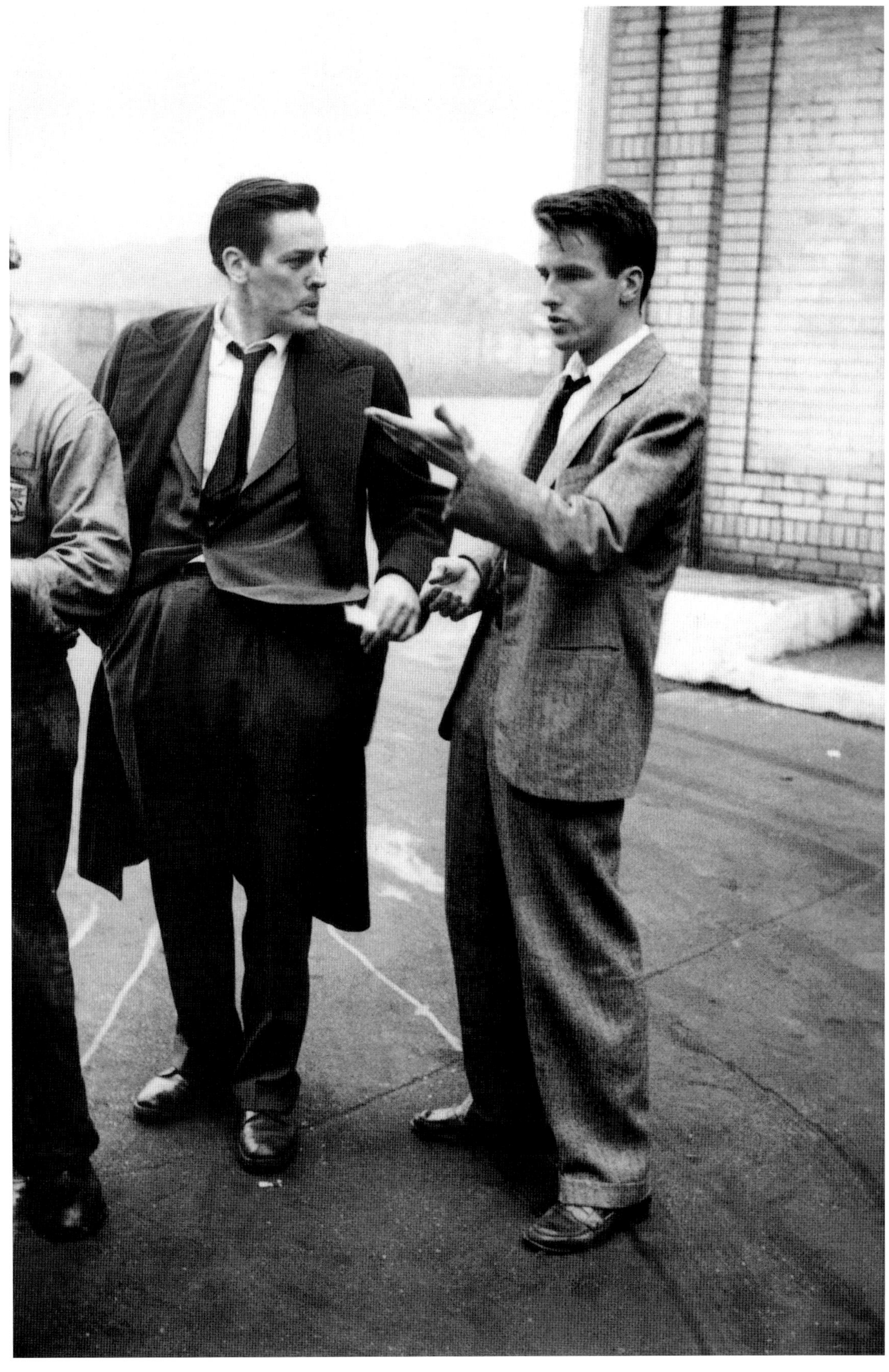

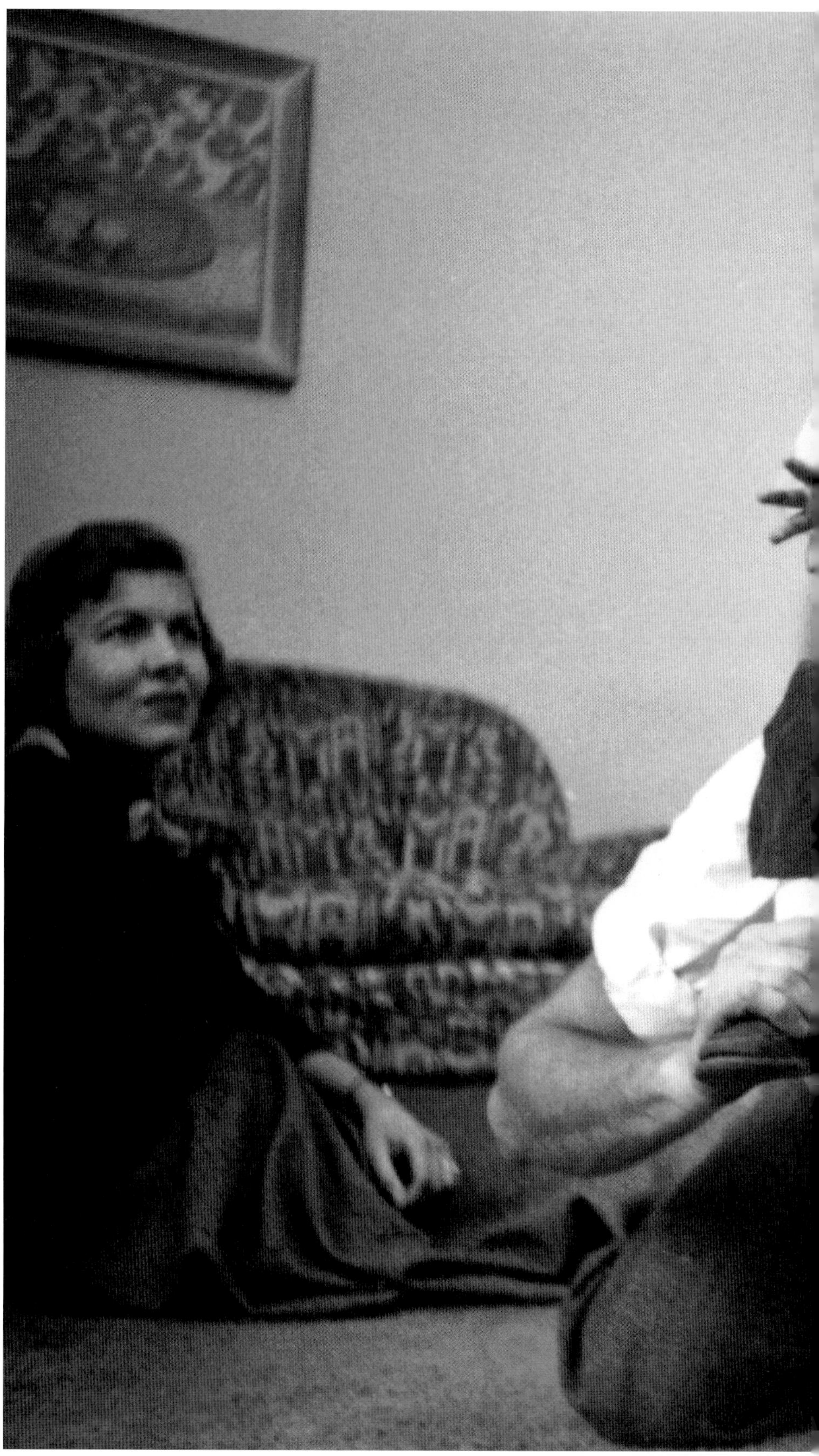

Clift at the home of his best friends, Kevin and Augusta McCarthy, with the couple's child, Flip

PAGE 192 **The actor on his daybed taking a break from reading a script**

PAGE 193 **"I'm an average guy," Clift told *Look*.**

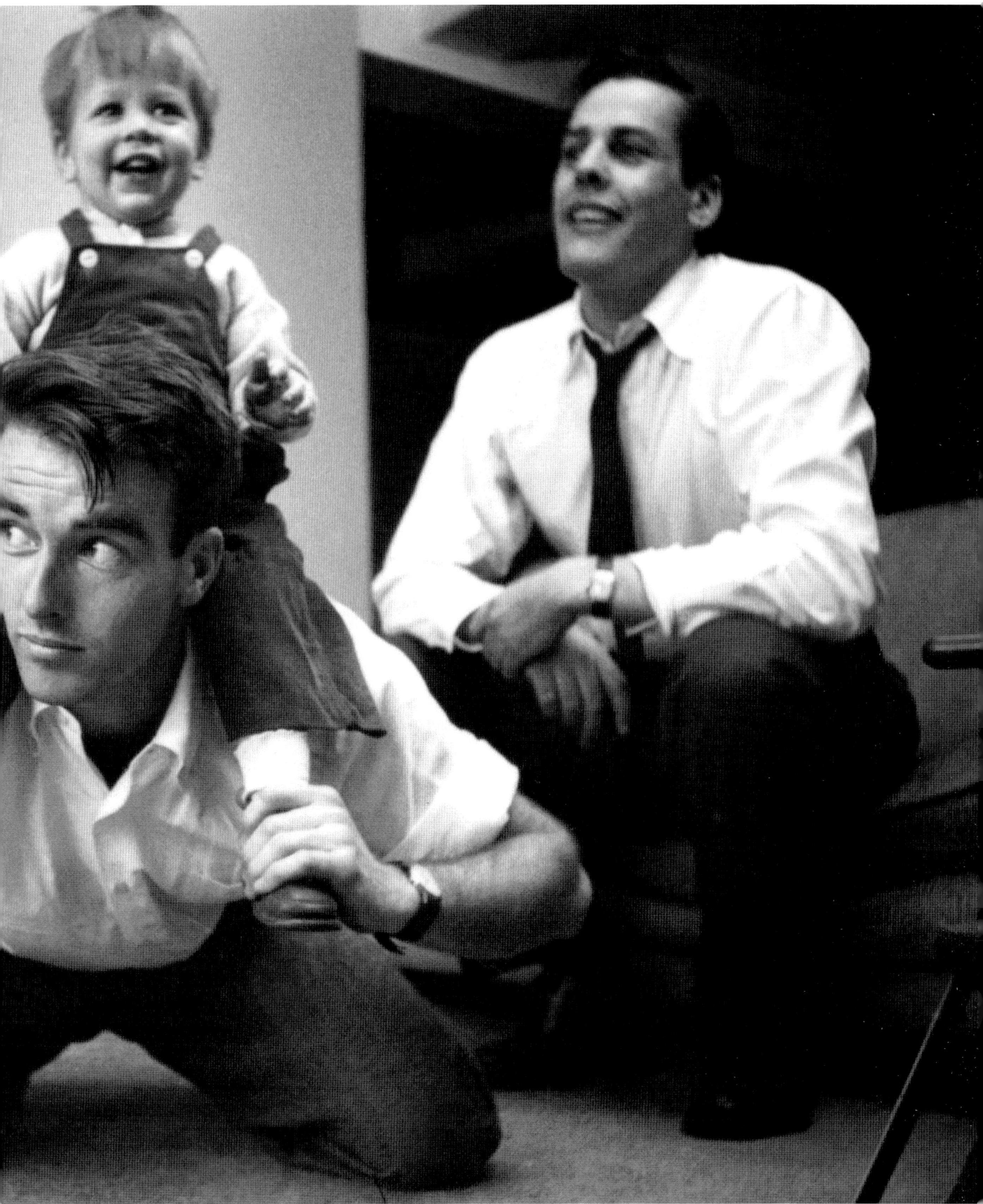

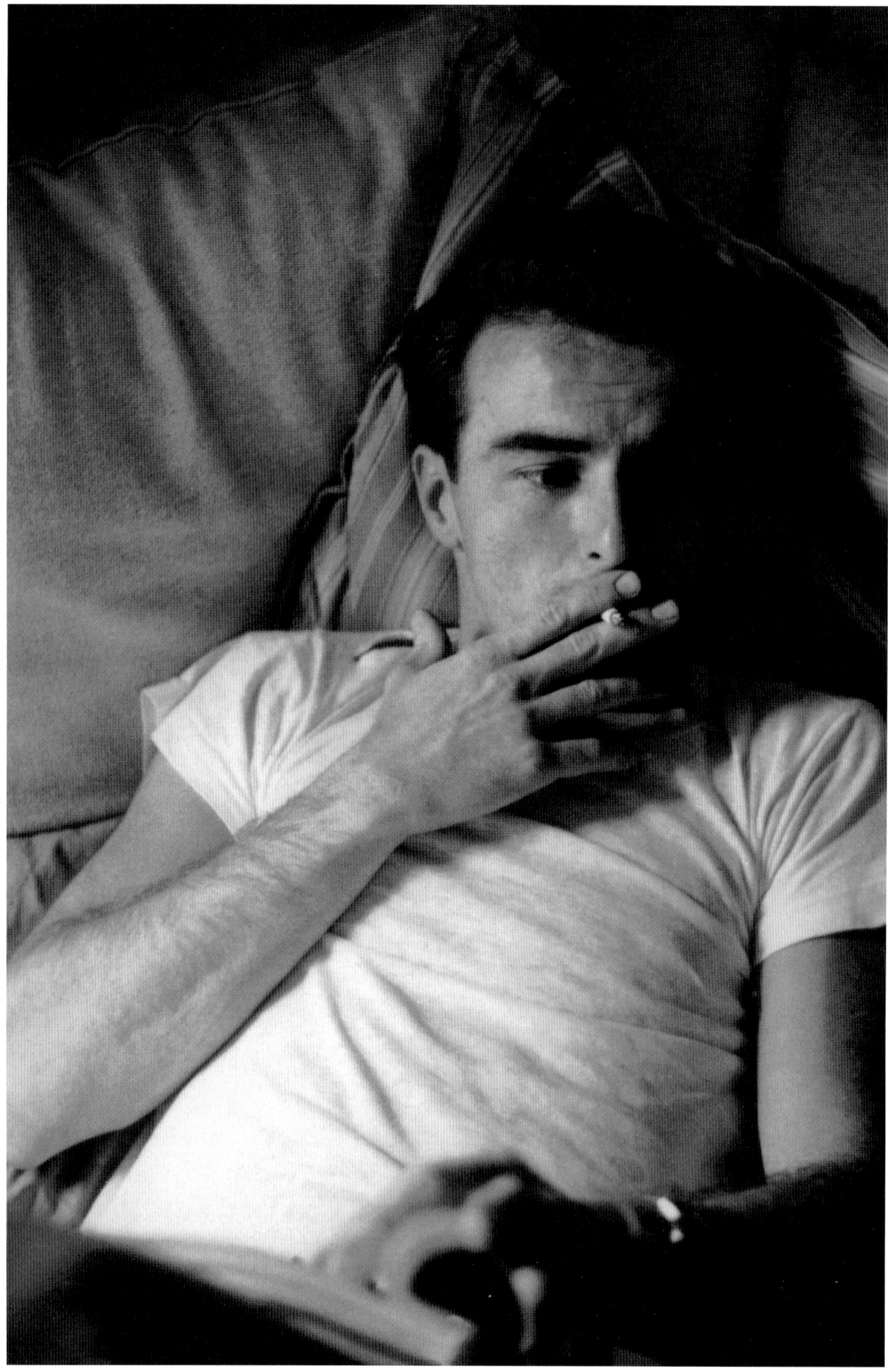

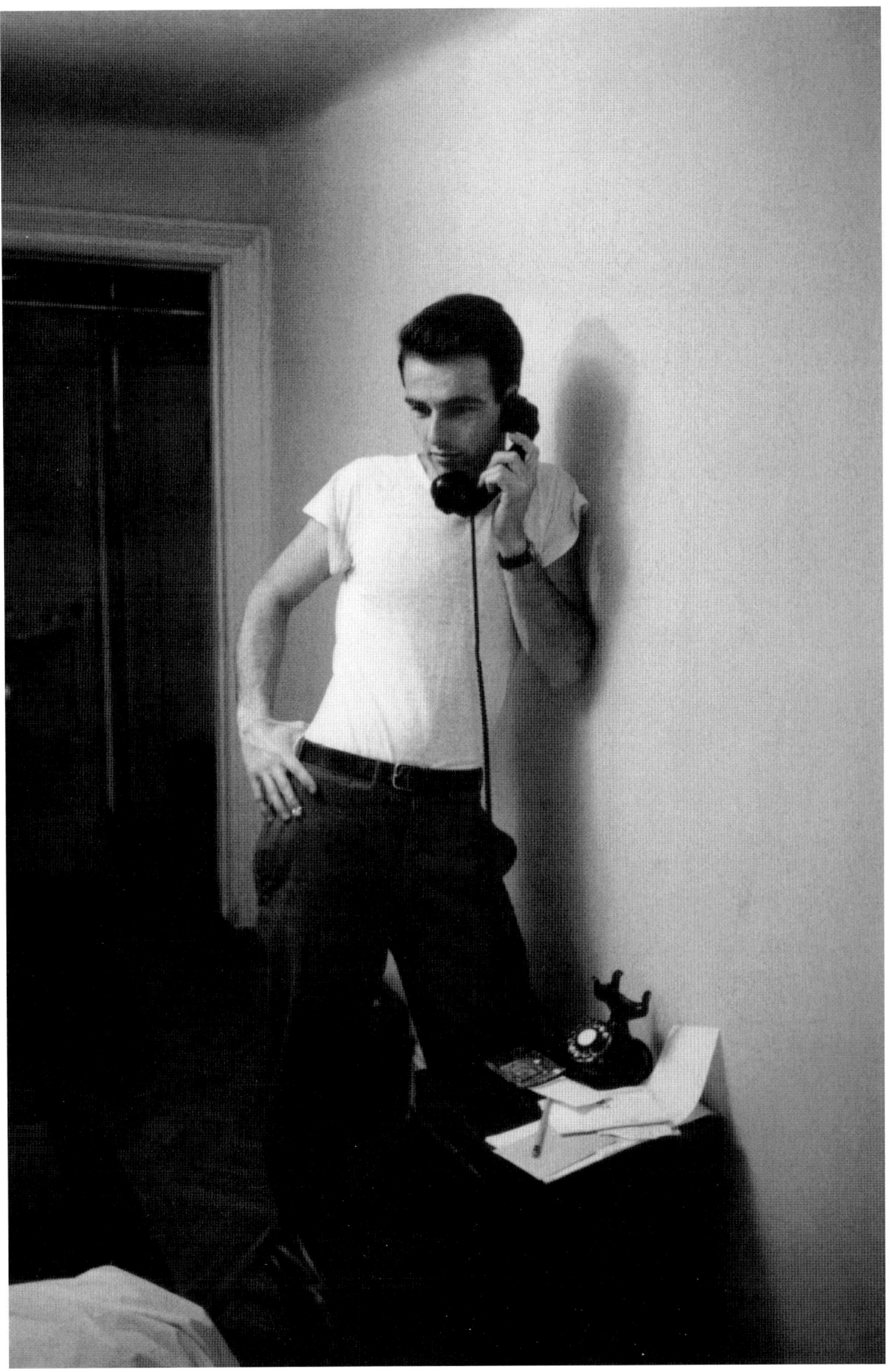

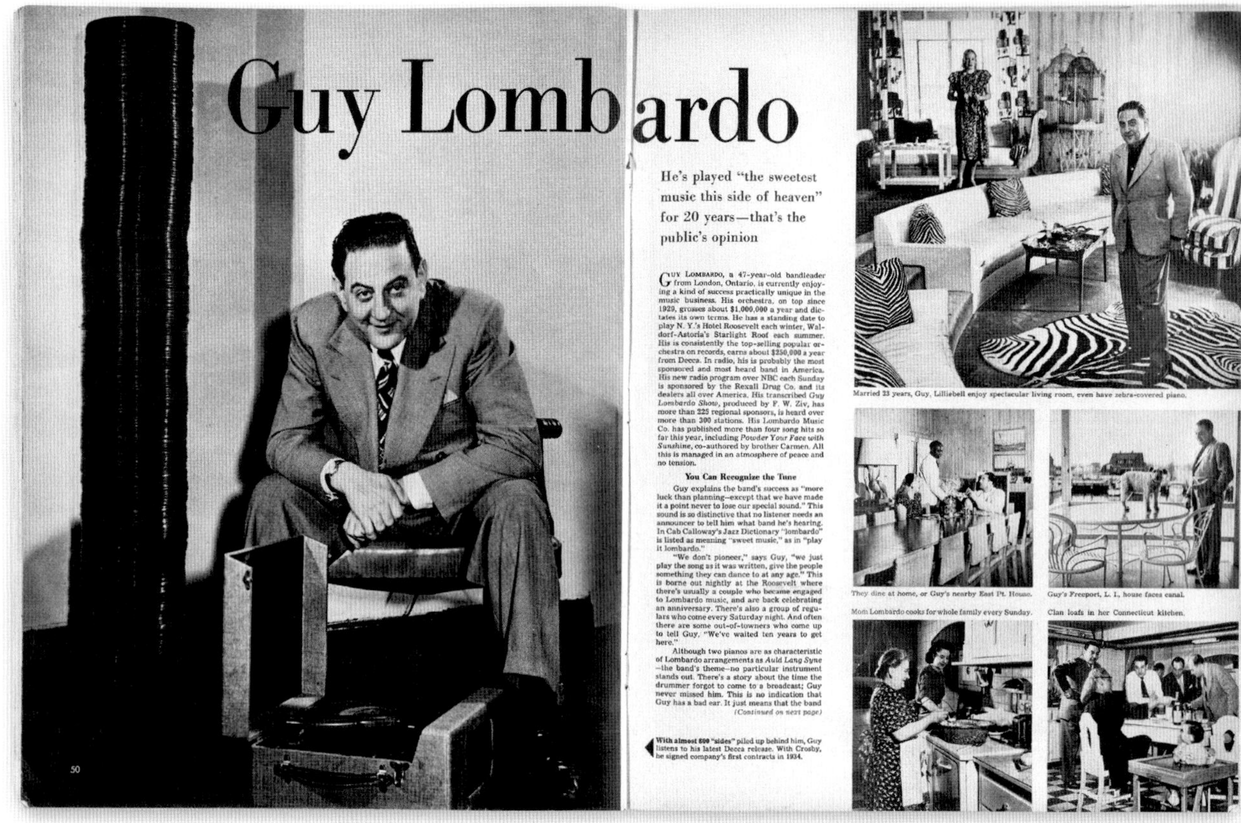

Guy Lombardo

He's played "the sweetest music this side of heaven" for 20 years—that's the public's opinion

GUY LOMBARDO, a 47-year-old bandleader from London, Ontario, is currently enjoying a kind of success practically unique in the music business. His orchestra, on top since 1929, grosses about $1,000,000 a year and dictates its own terms. He has a standing date to play N. Y.'s Hotel Roosevelt each winter, Waldorf-Astoria's Starlight Roof each summer. His is consistently the top-selling popular orchestra on records, earns about $250,000 a year from Decca. In radio, his is probably the most sponsored and most heard band in America. His new radio program over NBC each Sunday is sponsored by the Rexall Drug Co. and its dealers all over America. His transcribed *Guy Lombardo Show*, produced by F. W. Ziv, has more than 225 regional sponsors, is heard over more than 300 stations. His Lombardo Music Co. has published more than four song hits so far this year, including *Powder Your Face with Sunshine*, co-authored by brother Carmen. All this is managed in an atmosphere of peace and no tension.

You Can Recognize the Tune

Guy explains the band's success as "more luck than planning—except that we have made it a point never to lose our special sound." This sound is so distinctive that no listener needs an announcer to tell him what band he's hearing. In Cab Calloway's Jazz Dictionary "lombardo" is listed as meaning "sweet music," as in "play it lombardo."

"We don't pioneer," says Guy, "we just play the song as it was written, give the people something they can dance to at any age." This is borne out nightly at the Roosevelt where there's usually a couple who became engaged to Lombardo music, and are back celebrating an anniversary. There's also a group of regulars who come every Saturday night. And often there are some out-of-towners who come up to tell Guy, "We've waited ten years to get here."

Although two pianos are as characteristic of Lombardo arrangements as *Auld Lang Syne*—the band's theme—no particular instrument stands out. There's a story about the time the drummer forgot to come to a broadcast; Guy never missed him. This is no indication that Guy has a bad ear. It just means that the band

(Continued on next page)

With almost 800 "sides" piled up behind him, Guy listens to his latest Decca release. With Crosby, he signed company's first contracts in 1934.

Married 23 years, Guy, Lilliebell enjoy spectacular living room, even have zebra-covered piano.

They dine at home, or Guy's nearby East Pt. House.

Guy's Freeport, L. I., house faces canal.

Mom Lombardo cooks for whole family every Sunday.

Clan loafs in her Connecticut kitchen.

50

PUBLISHED AS

GUY LOMBARDO

DATE

AUGUST 2, 1949

Described in this article as playing "the sweetest music this side of heaven," 47-year-old Canadian-born bandleader Guy Lombardo led his own successful orchestra—"on top since 1929"—that grossed around a million dollars per year. Lombardo's band was ubiquitous in late-1940s America, recording popular records and performing on the radio and in nightclubs. Typical of *Look*'s celebrity profiles, the article combined photographs of Lombardo and his band with images of Lombardo and his family.

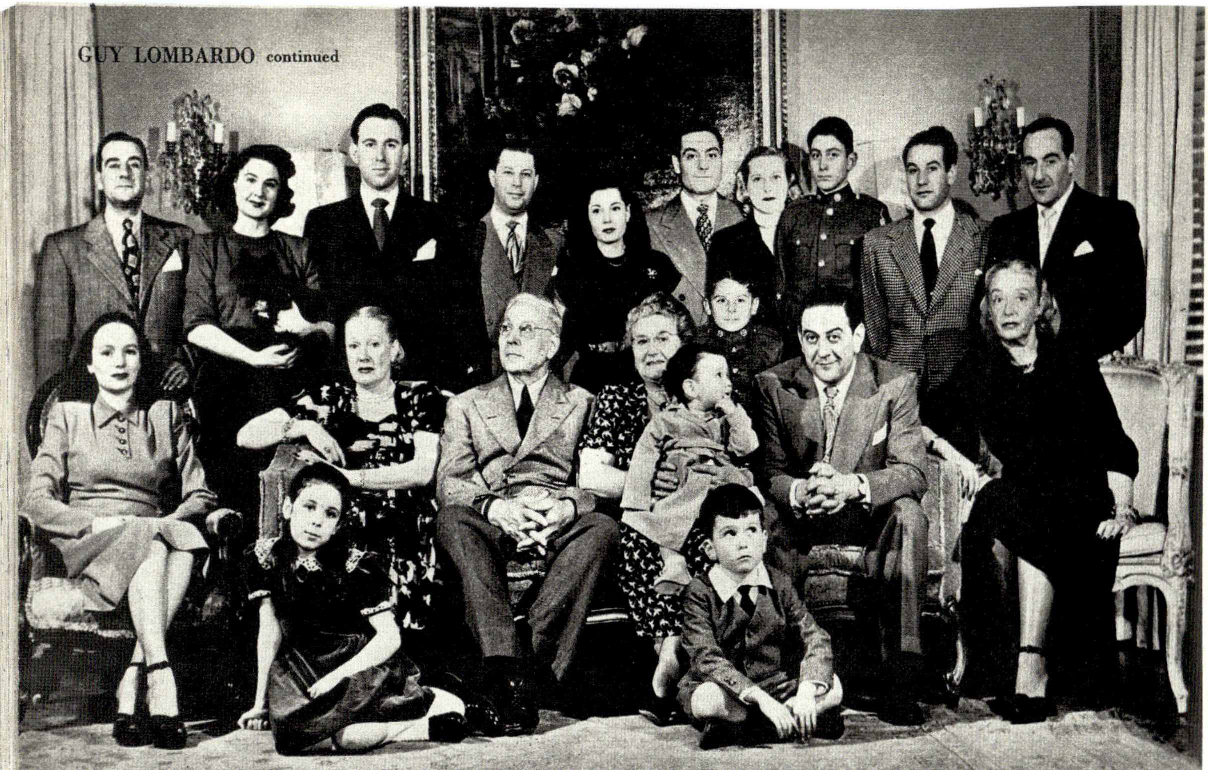

The Lombardos make it a rule to gather at Mom and Pop's for Christmas. With seven brothers and sisters; wives, husbands and children, they make even 20.

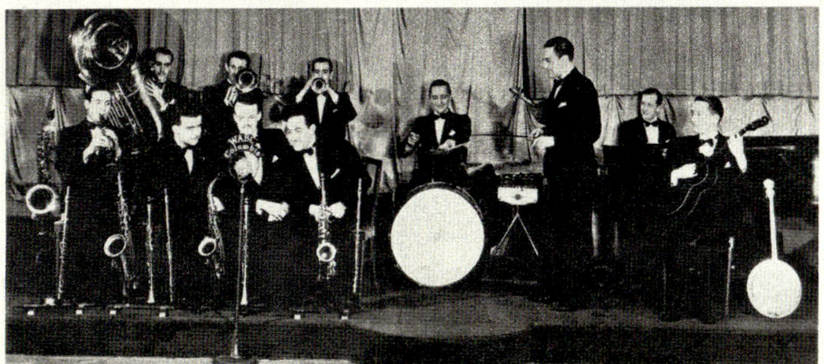

Royal Canadians came to Hotel Roosevelt in '29, along with market crash, play there every winter.

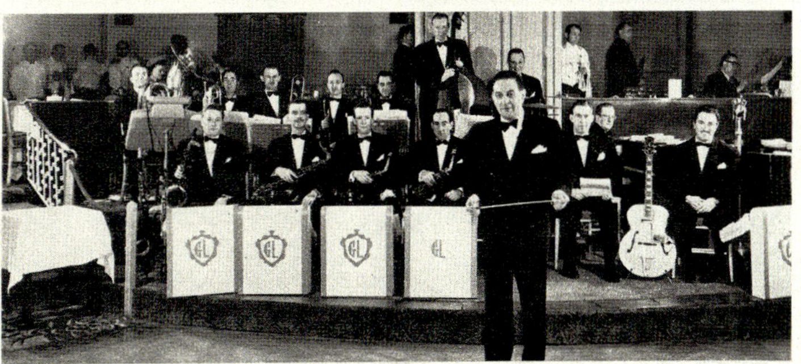

Today's band includes original eight musicians from London, Ontario, has 16 members, two pianos.

Guy likes his music slow and his motorboats fast

gets its beat from all sections.

The Lombardo band always has been a family affair. There's Guy, Carmen and Lebert. Sister Rosemarie used to sing with them. Sister Elaine married Kenny Gardner, the band's vocalist. Brother Vic left to form a band of his own. Brother Joe, an interior decorator, got into the act by designing the Roosevelt Grill. And though it's many years since the boys had to practice in their father's tailor shop so he could hear them, Pop Lombardo still takes a critical interest in their activities.

Guy has been voted one of the country's ten best-dressed men and laughingly says that he gave up playing the fiddle because it wore out his dinner jackets. But he is never as happy as when, covered with grease, he is fooling around with a motorboat. And he has done just as well on the water as on the bandstand. He's one of the country's top speedboat racers, has broken numerous speed marks, and hopes to set new records this summer. "If anyone should ask," says Guy, "just tell them I'm a speedboat racer who also leads a band."

Lom

In T

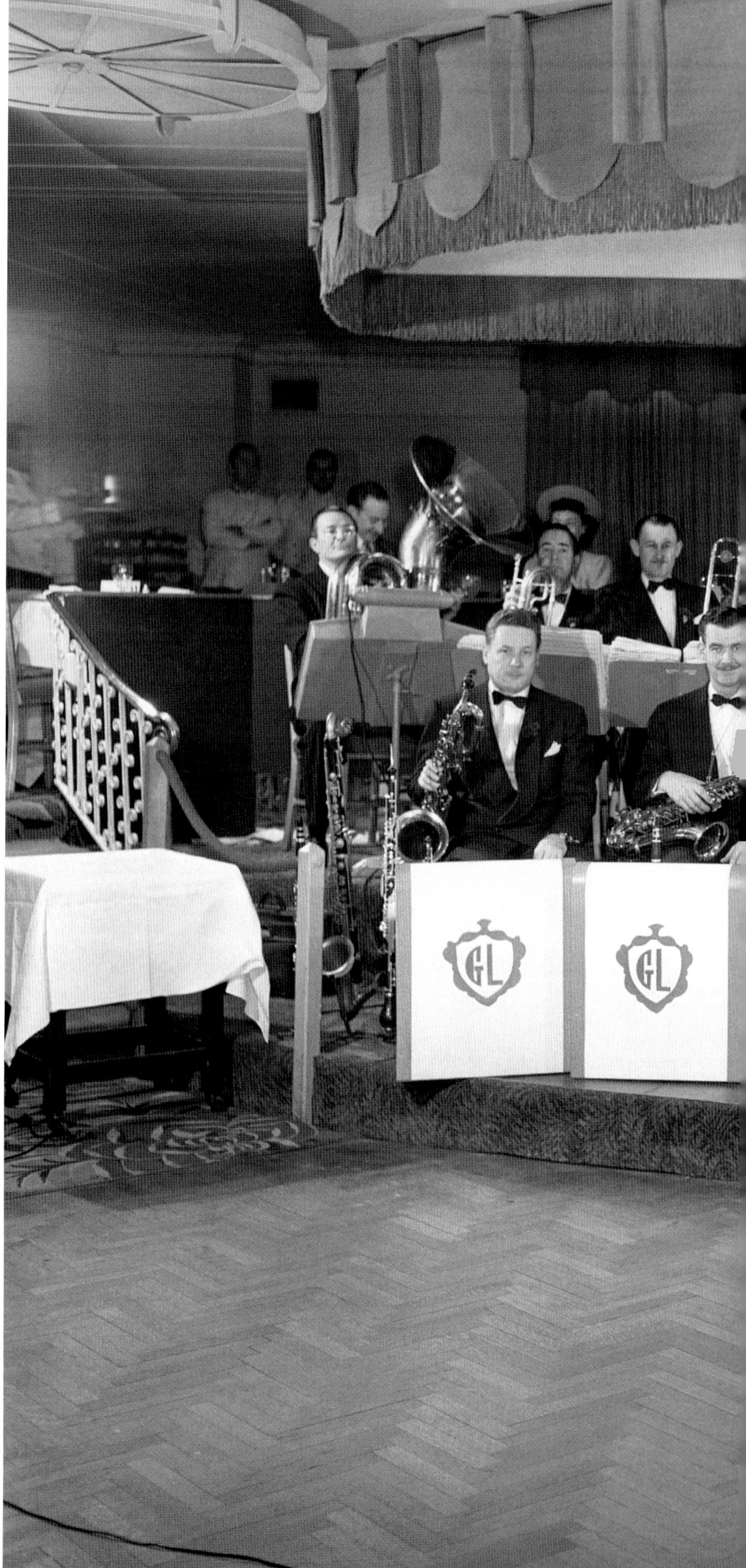

Guy Lombardo with his 16-member orchestra

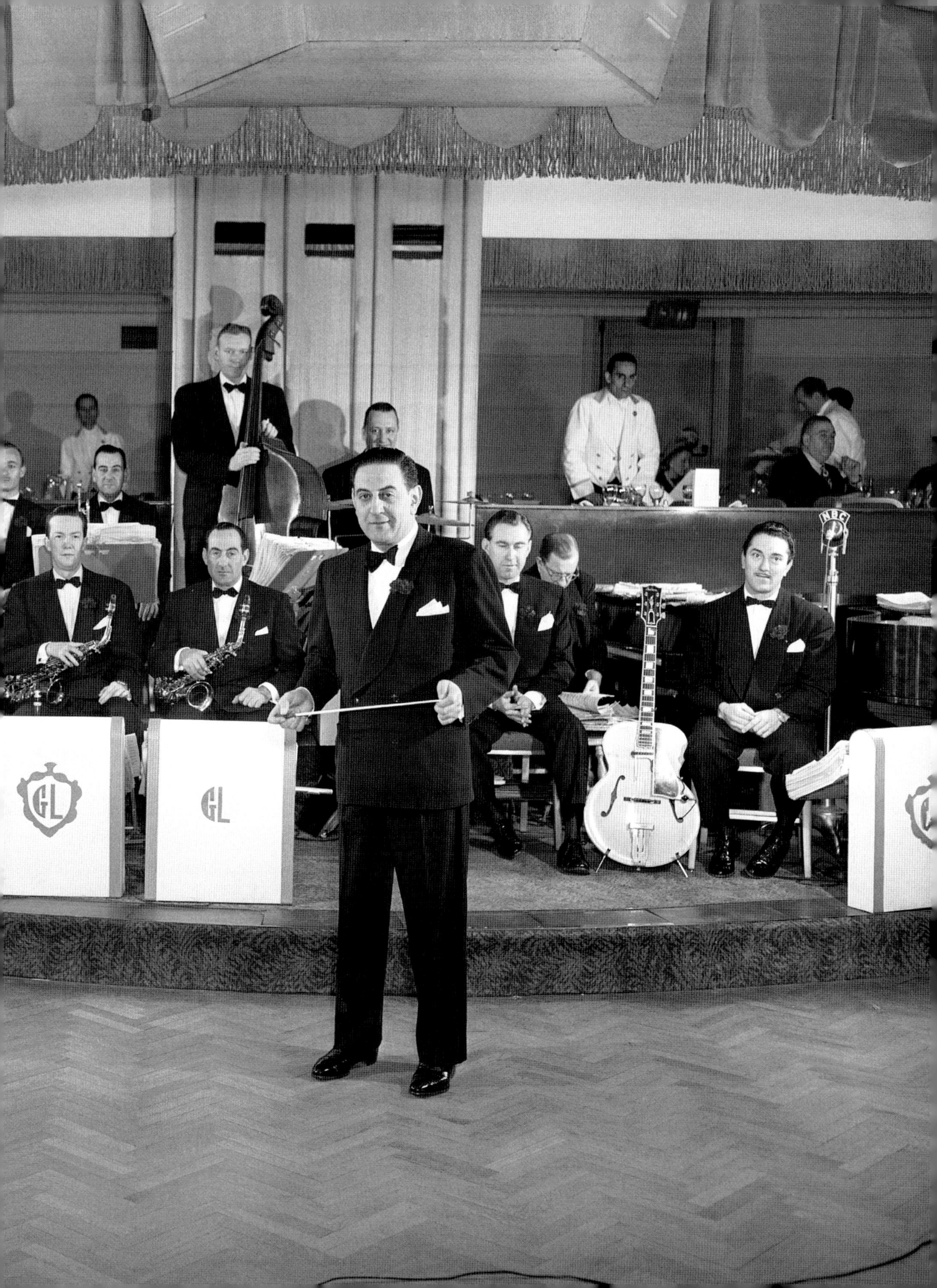
GL
GL
NBC

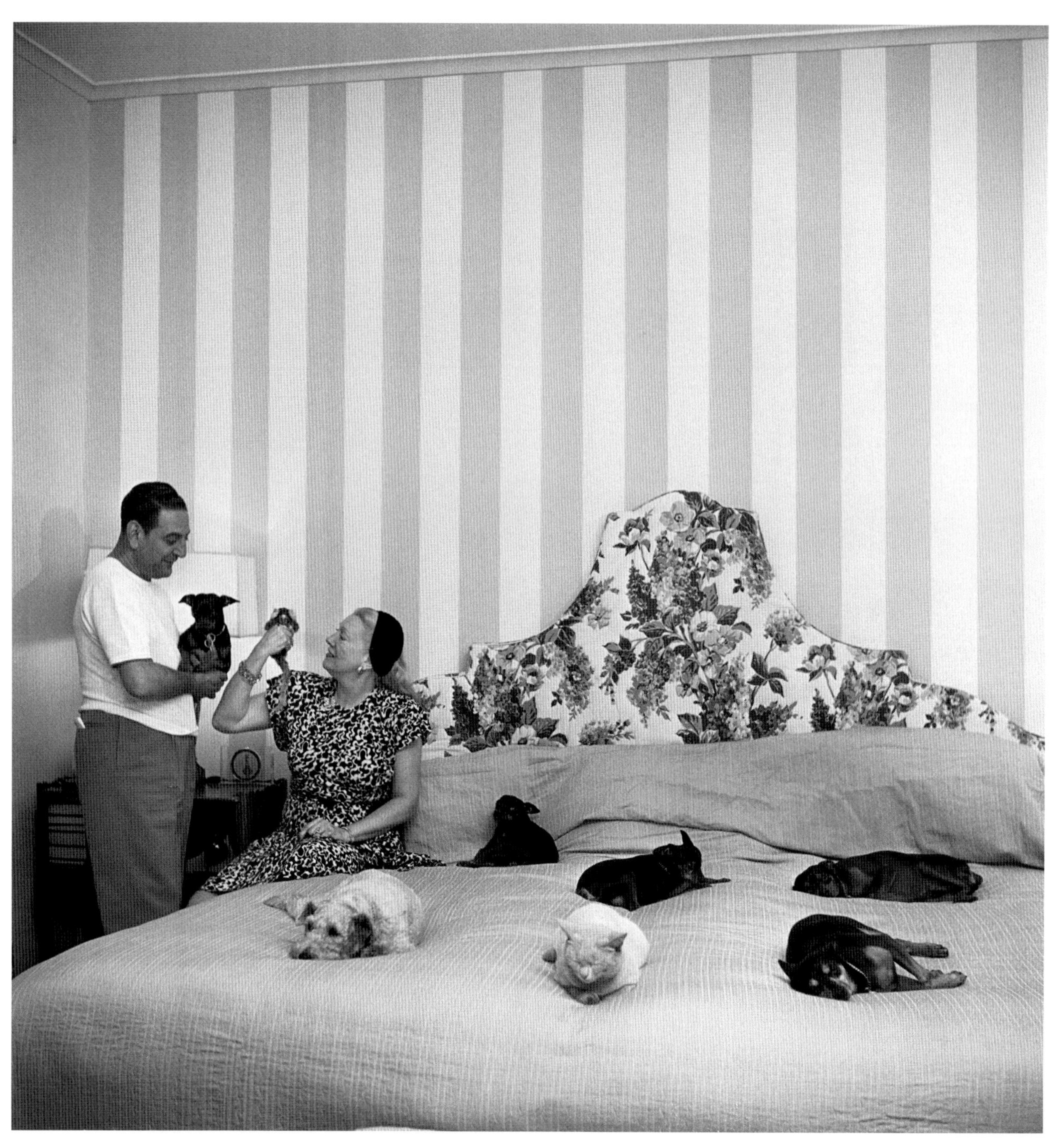

Lombardo and his wife, Lilliebell, owned six dogs, four birds, one cat, and a monkey.

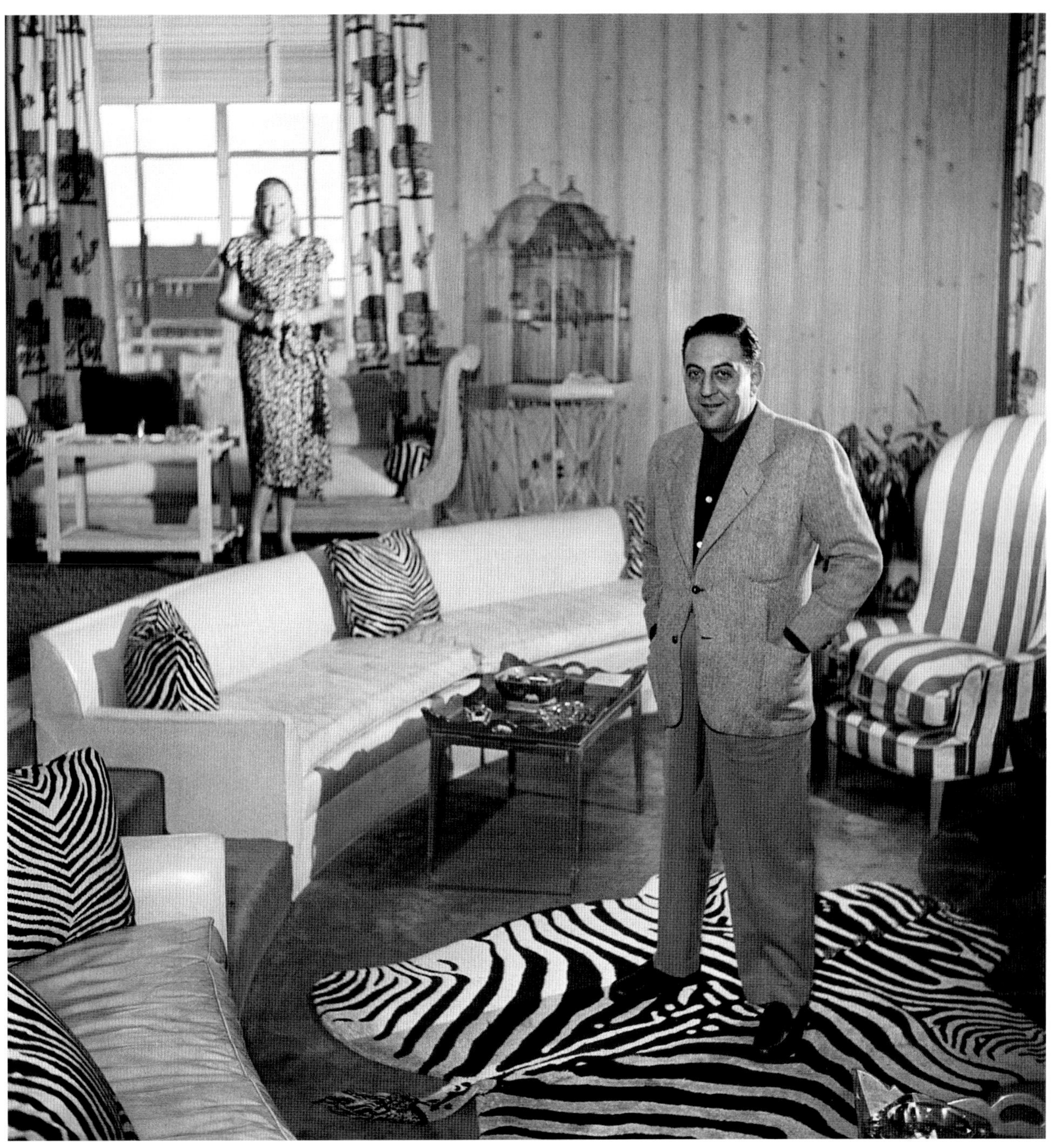

The Lombardos in their living room

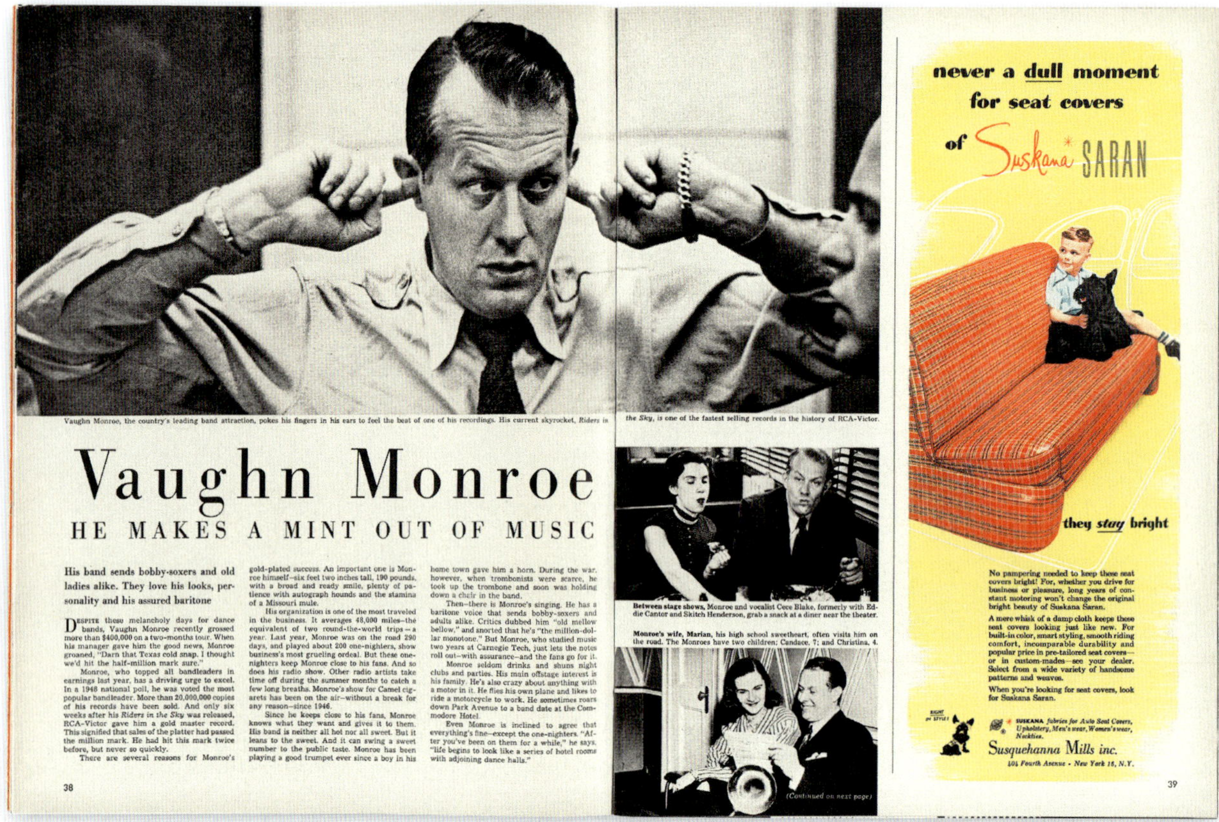

Vaughn Monroe, the country's leading band attraction, pokes his fingers in his ears to feel the beat of one of his recordings. His current skyrocket, *Riders in the Sky*, is one of the fastest selling records in the history of RCA-Victor.

Vaughn Monroe

HE MAKES A MINT OUT OF MUSIC

His band sends bobby-soxers and old ladies alike. They love his looks, personality and his assured baritone

DESPITE these melancholy days for dance bands, Vaughn Monroe recently grossed more than $400,000 on a two-months tour. When his manager gave him the good news, Monroe groaned, "Darn that Texas cold snap. I thought we'd hit the half-million mark sure."

Monroe, who topped all bandleaders in earnings last year, has a driving urge to excel. In a 1948 national poll, he was voted the most popular bandleader. More than 20,000,000 copies of his records have been sold. And only six weeks after his *Riders in the Sky* was released, RCA-Victor gave him a gold master record. This signified that sales of the platter had passed the million mark. He had hit this mark twice before, but never so quickly.

There are several reasons for Monroe's gold-plated success. An important one is Monroe himself—six feet two inches tall, 190 pounds, with a broad and ready smile, plenty of patience with autograph hounds and the stamina of a Missouri mule.

His organization is one of the most traveled in the business. It averages 48,000 miles—the equivalent of two round-the-world trips—a year. Last year, Monroe was on the road 290 days, and played about 200 one-nighters, show business's most grueling ordeal. But these one-nighters keep Monroe close to his fans. And so does his radio show. Other radio artists take time off during the summer months to catch a few long breaths. Monroe's show for Camel cigarets has been on the air—without a break for any reason—since 1946.

Since he keeps close to his fans, Monroe knows what they want and gives it to them. His band is neither all hot nor all sweet. But it leans to the sweet. And it can swing a sweet number to the public taste. Monroe has been playing a good trumpet ever since a boy in his home town gave him a horn. During the war, however, when trombonists were scarce, he took up the trombone and soon was holding down a chair in the band.

Then—there is Monroe's singing. He has a baritone voice that sends bobby-soxers and adults alike. Critics dubbed him "old mellow bellow," and snorted that he's "the million-dollar monotone." But Monroe, who studied music two years at Carnegie Tech, just lets the notes roll out—with assurance—and the fans go for it.

Monroe seldom drinks and shuns night clubs and parties. His main offstage interest is his family. He's also crazy about anything with a motor in it. He flies his own plane and likes to ride a motorcycle to work. He sometimes roars down Park Avenue to a band date at the Commodore Hotel.

Even Monroe is inclined to agree that everything's fine—except the one-nighters. "After you've been on them for a while," he says, "life begins to look like a series of hotel rooms with adjoining dance halls."

38

Between stage shows, Monroe and vocalist Cece Blake, formerly with Eddie Cantor and Skitch Henderson, grab a snack at a diner near the theater.

Monroe's wife, Marian, his high school sweetheart, often visits him on the road. The Monroes have two children: Candace, 7; and Christina, 4.

(Continued on next page)

39

PUBLISHED AS

VAUGHN MONROE: HE MAKES A MINT OUT OF MUSIC

DATE

AUGUST 16, 1949

The multitalented musician Vaughn Monroe was depicted in this story at the height of his popularity with the American public. The article touted the success of Monroe as a bandleader, making hefty profits on a cross-country tour that was simultaneously broadcast on the *Camel Caravan* radio program on CBS. In the accompanying images Monroe was shown on stage performing with his band, on the road, and in the studio. The six-foot-two "baritone with muscles" was a crowd-pleaser among "bobbysoxers and old ladies alike." He appeared in more than six motion pictures and hosted his own television shows during the 1950s.

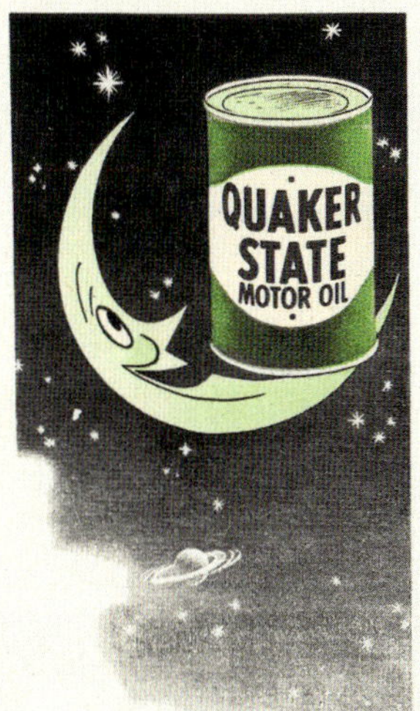

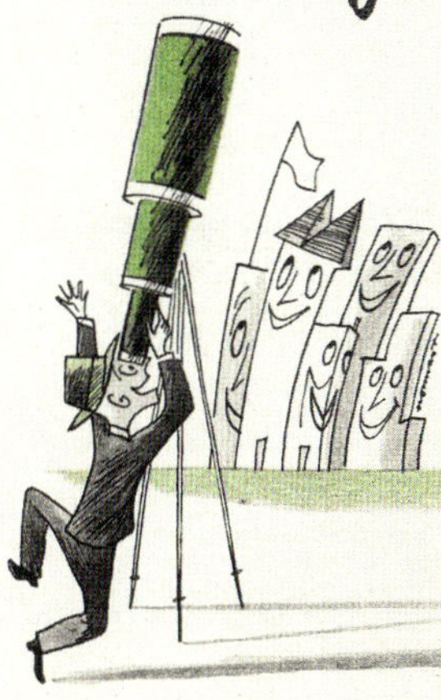

In the dance halls and recording studios, on the

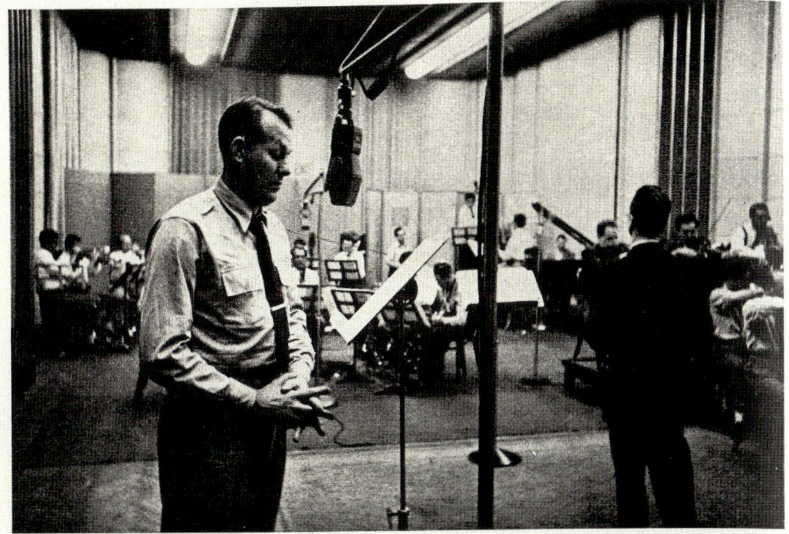

Recording date: Vaughn takes it easy after cutting a new platter. RCA-Victor has sold more than 20,000,000 of his records. His biggest recording hits include *Riders in the Sky, There! I've Said It Again* and *Ballerina.*

Stage show: Monroe climbs into a cowboy outfit for the closing production number on theater date. The band plays same songs but costumed acts give a fillip to the tunes. One nighters net Monroe an average of $2.750.

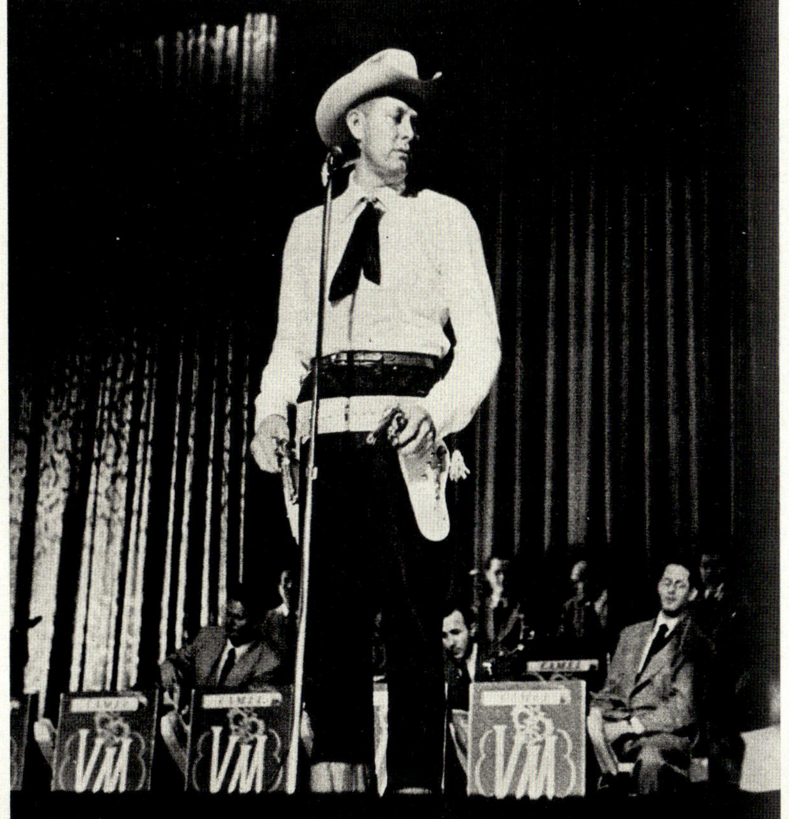

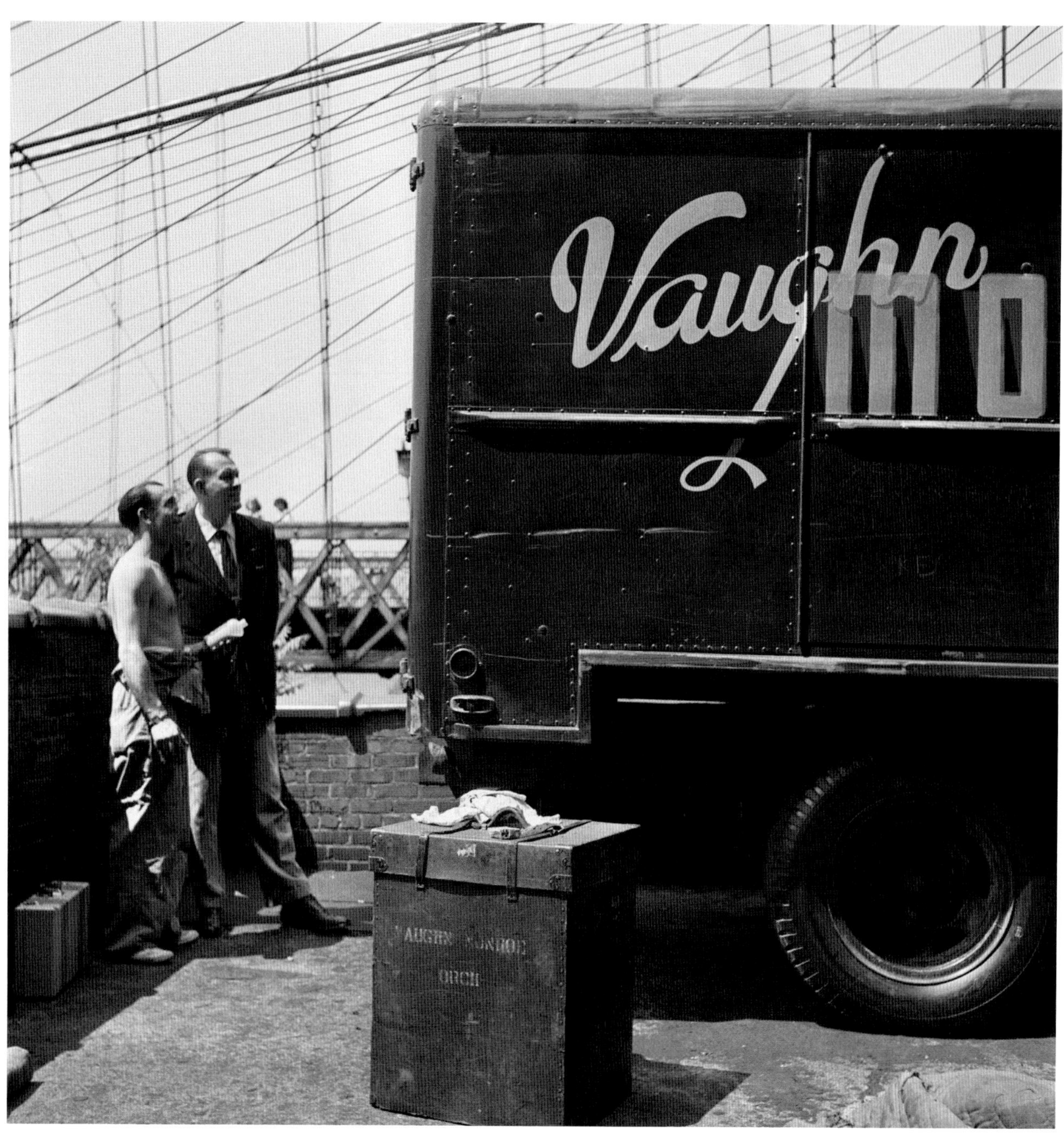

Monroe on and off the bus. He and his orchestra averaged 48,000 miles per year on the road.

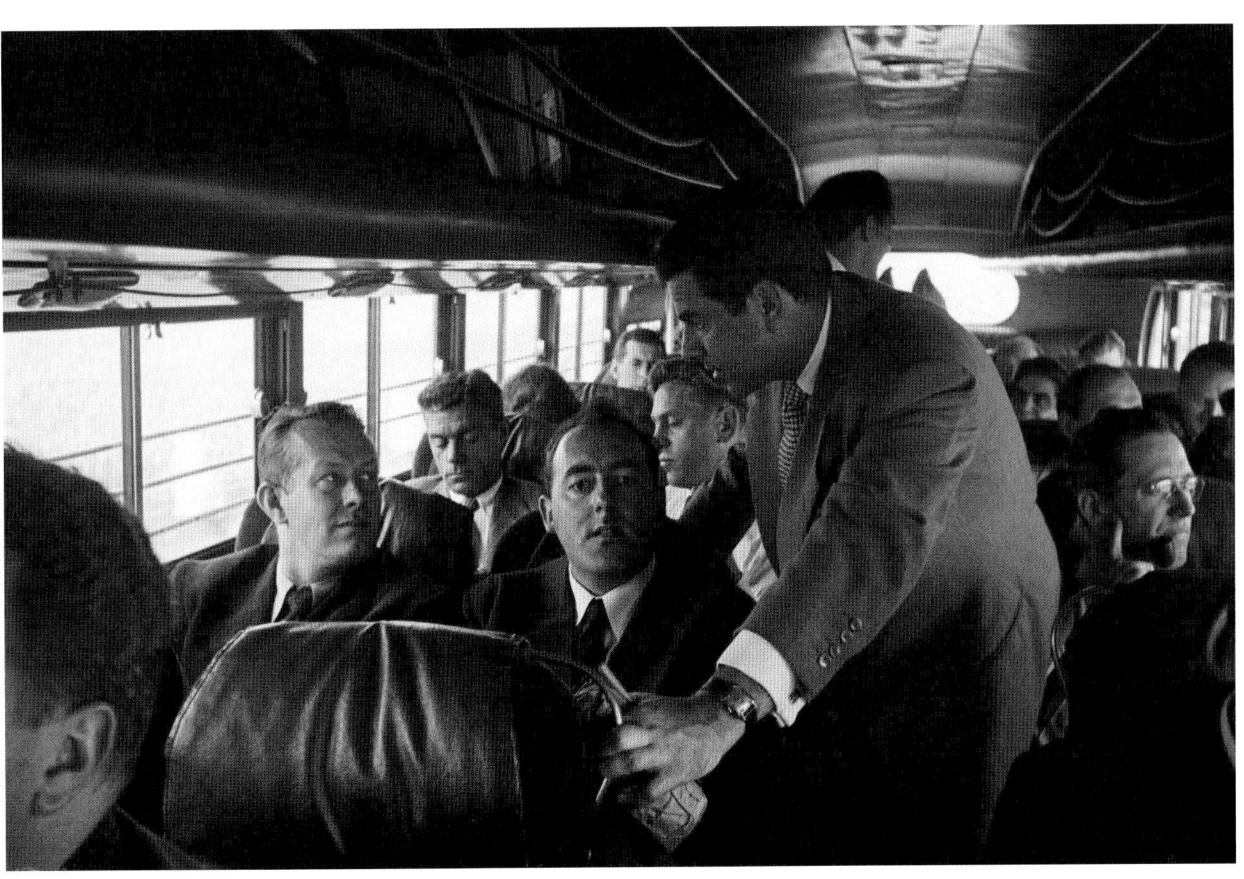

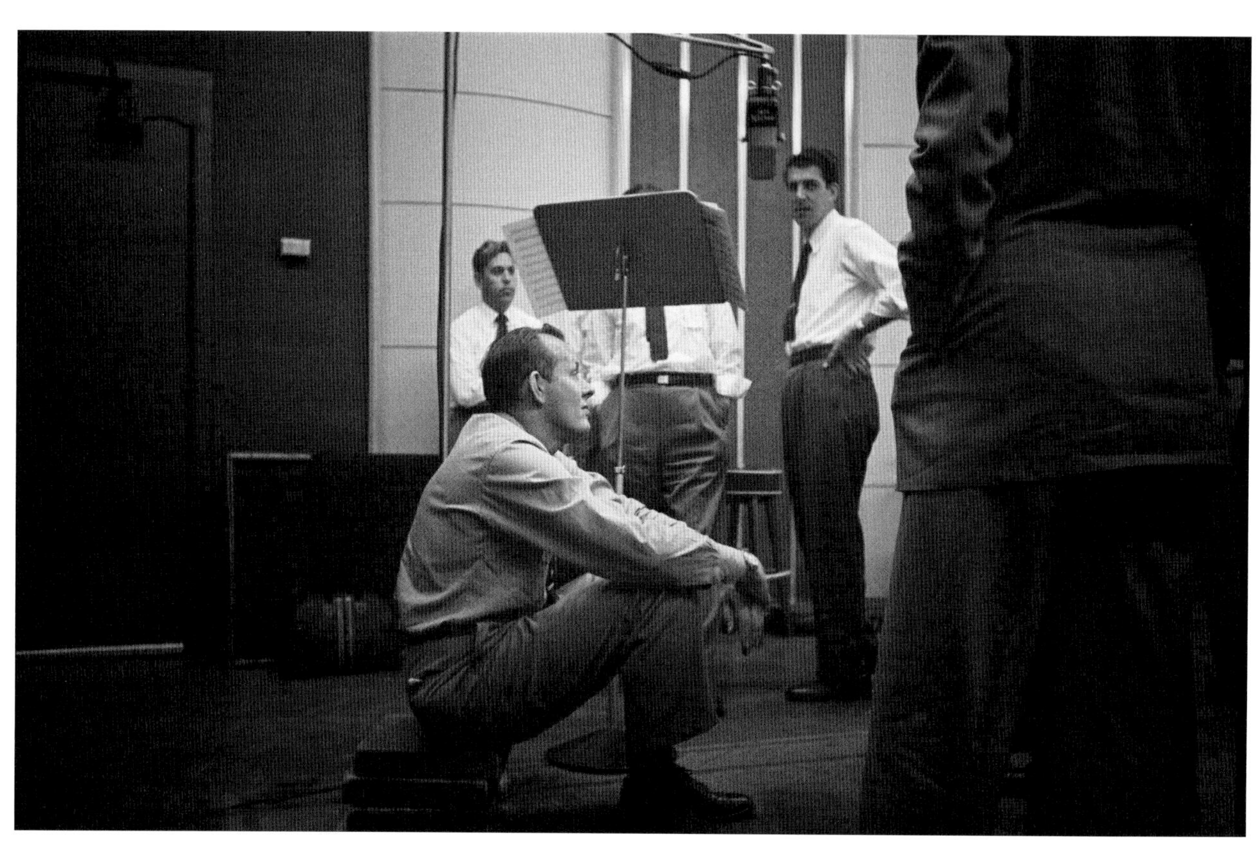

Monroe in the studio

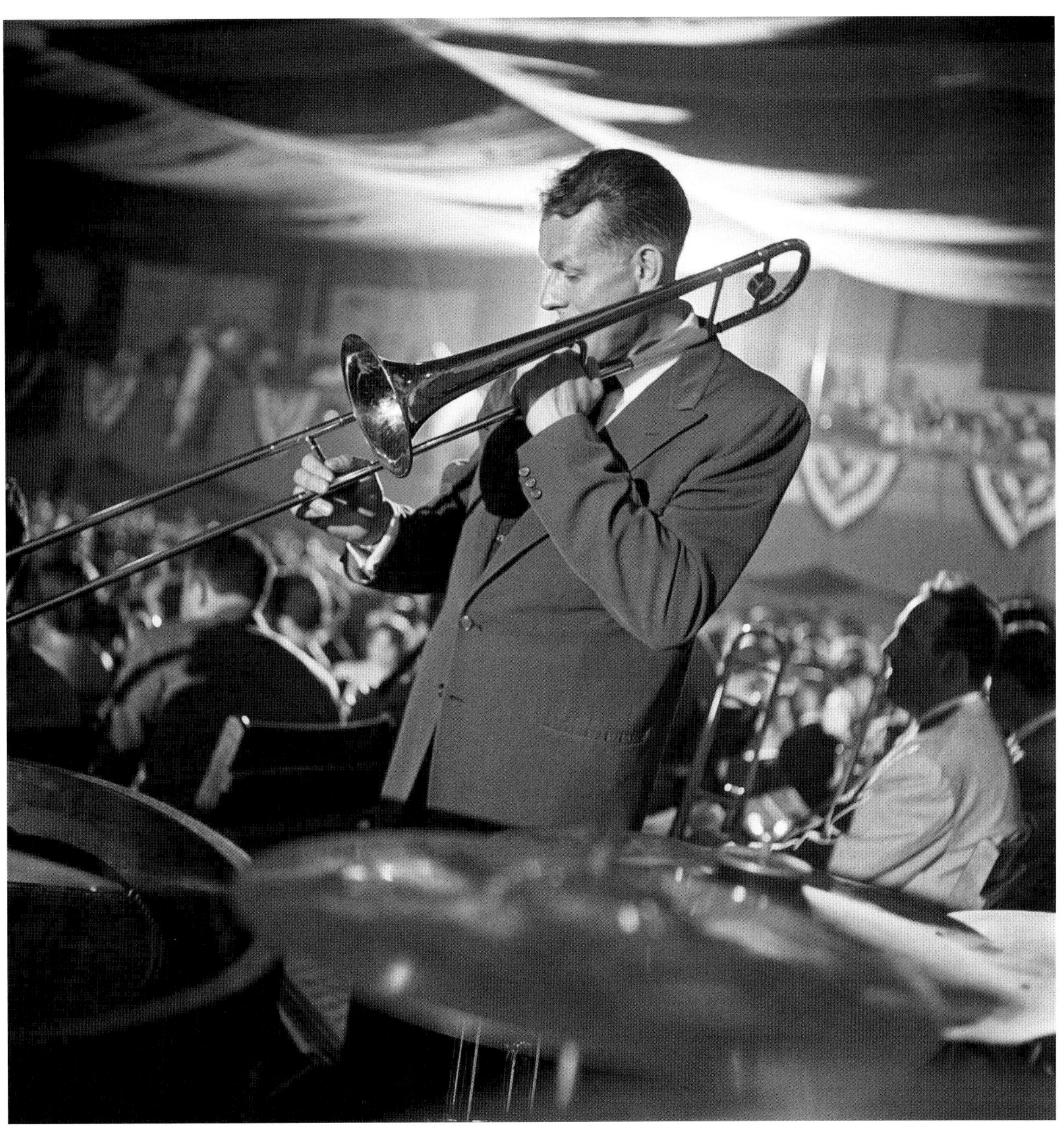

Monroe playing the trombone

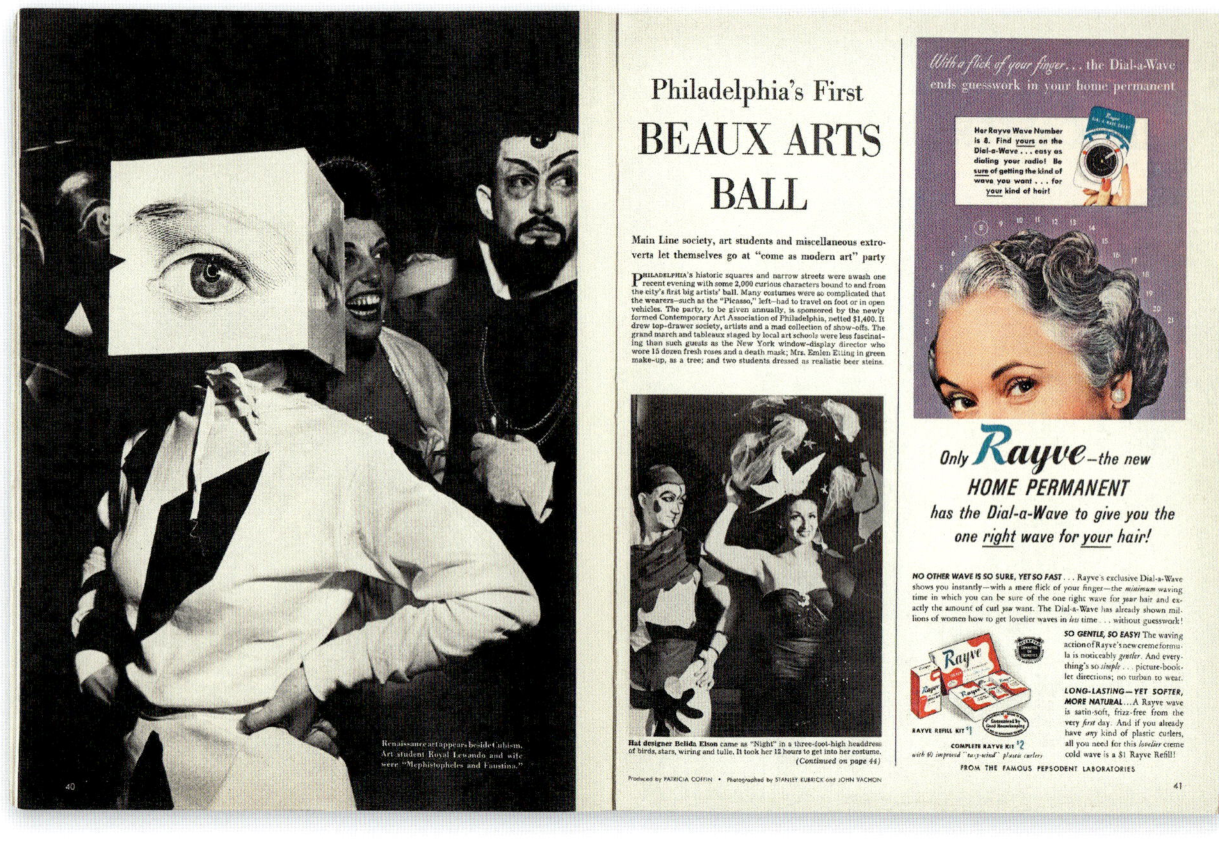

Renaissance art appears beside Cubism. Art student Royal Lewando and wife were "Mephistopheles and Faustina."

40

Philadelphia's First

BEAUX ARTS BALL

Main Line society, art students and miscellaneous extroverts let themselves go at "come as modern art" party

PHILADELPHIA'S historic squares and narrow streets were awash one recent evening with some 2,000 curious characters bound to and from the city's first big artists' ball. Many costumes were so complicated that the wearers—such as the "Picasso," left—had to travel on foot or in open vehicles. The party, to be given annually, is sponsored by the newly formed Contemporary Art Association of Philadelphia, netted $1,400. It drew top-drawer society, artists and a mad collection of show-offs. The grand march and tableaux staged by local art schools were less fascinating than such guests as the New York window-display director who wore 15 dozen fresh roses and a death mask; Mrs. Emlen Etting in green make-up, as a tree; and two students dressed as realistic beer steins.

Hat designer Belida Elson came as "Night" in a three-foot-high headdress of birds, stars, wiring and tulle. It took her 12 hours to get into her costume.

(Continued on page 44)

Produced by PATRICIA COFFIN • Photographed by STANLEY KUBRICK and JOHN VACHON

41

PUBLISHED AS

PHILADELPHIA'S FIRST BEAUX ARTS BALL

DATE

SEPTEMBER 13, 1949

AUTHOR

PATRICIA COFFIN

Kubrick photographed the lead image of this story about a "come as modern art" party held at the Hotel Broadwood by the newly created Contemporary Art Association of Philadelphia. Depicting a partygoer wearing a Cubist headdress decorated with an enormous eye—juxtaposed with a grinning woman in the article's printed version—the image was a bold, surrealistic expression of Kubrick's fascination with voyeurism. The event mixed "Main Line society, art students and miscellaneous extroverts" where the "most original" prize went to an artist who came as a two-headed Picasso. *Look* staffer John Vachon also took photographs for the article.

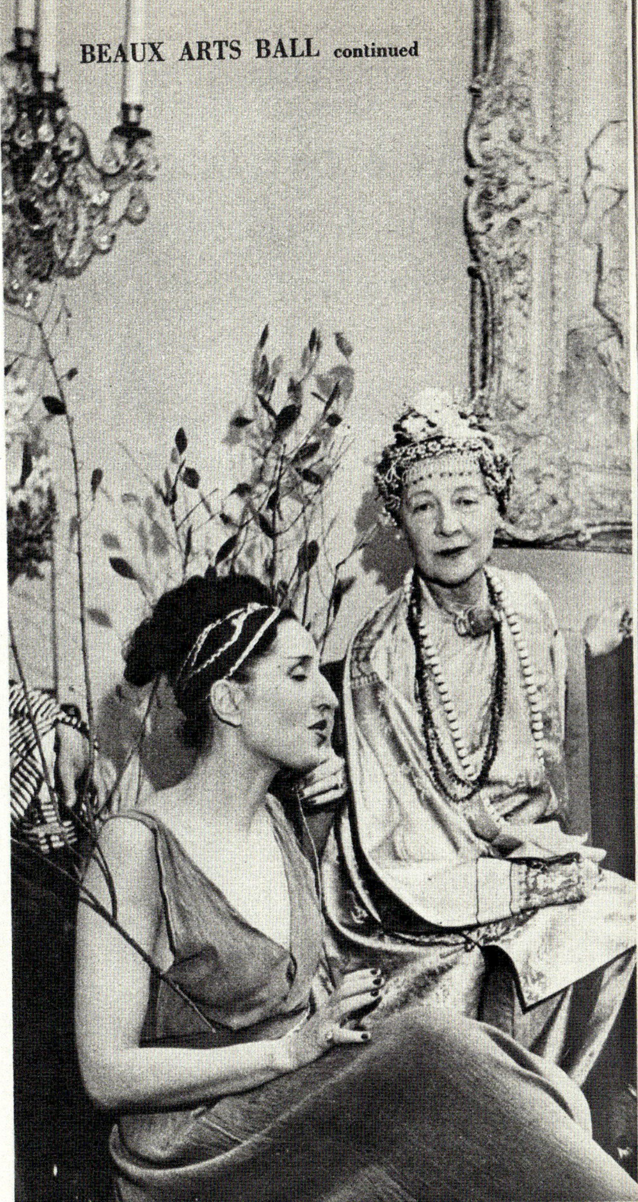

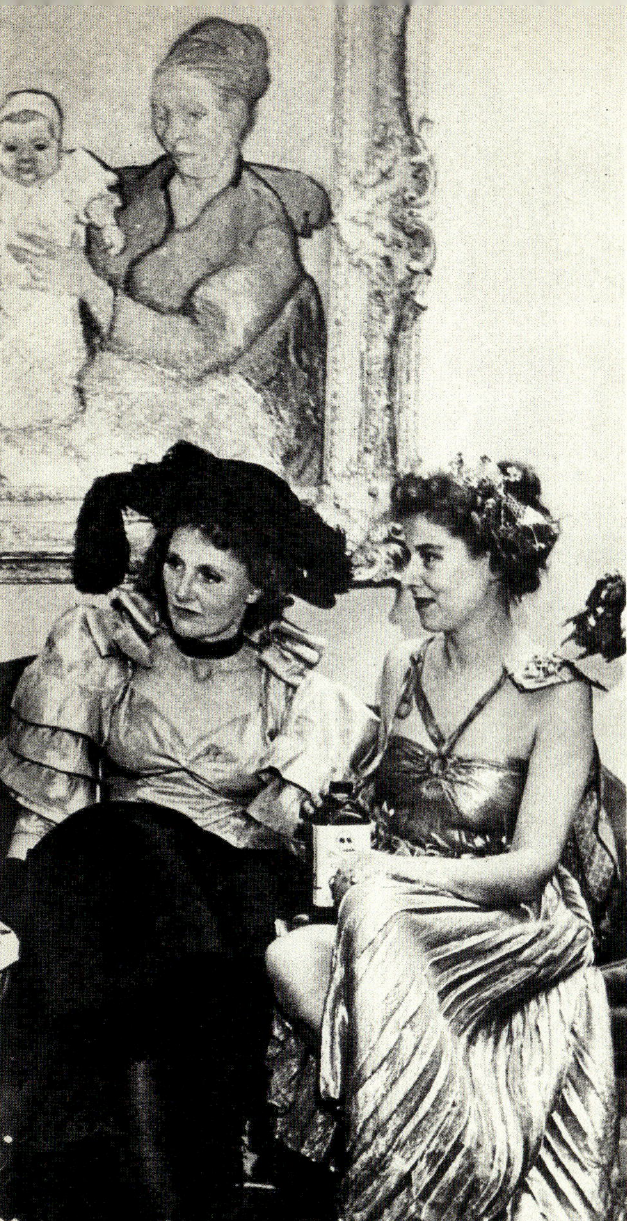

At pre-ball party, socialites chat seated under original Van Gogh in Mrs. William Elkins' Rittenhouse Square home. They are Gloria Braggiotti Etting; Mrs. Samis White, 3rd, wealthy modern art collector; art patron Mrs. Charles B. Grace of the steel family; Mrs. Franklin Watkins, wife of the painter.

Philadelphia society and Negro models mingled at party

Negro model Robert Newman won first prize as lighted candelabra.

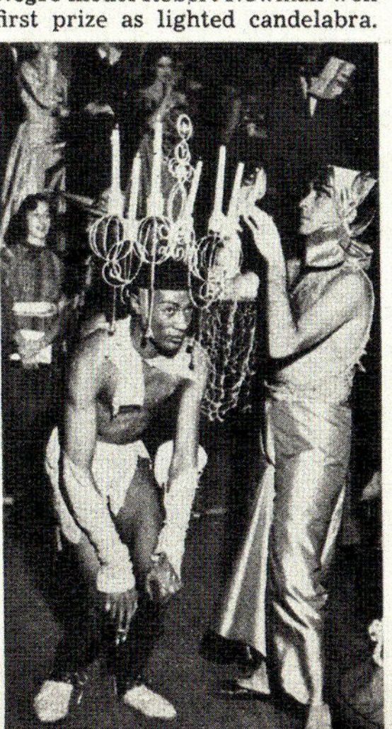

The "girl" at right, a man, broke into an impromptu Balinese dance.

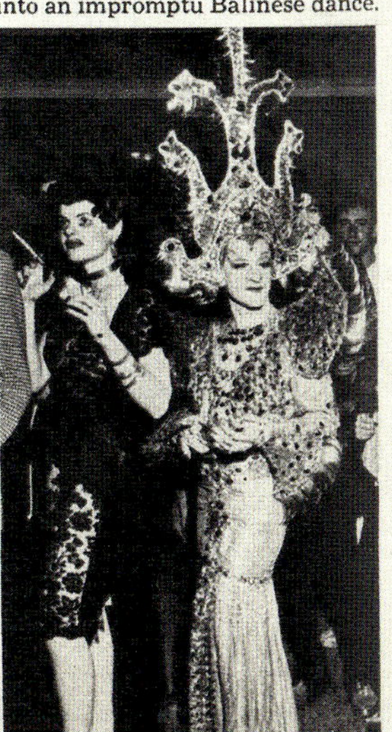

"Most original" prize went to artist Harold Diehl who came as a two-headed "Picasso," carried a drink in each hand, for each head.

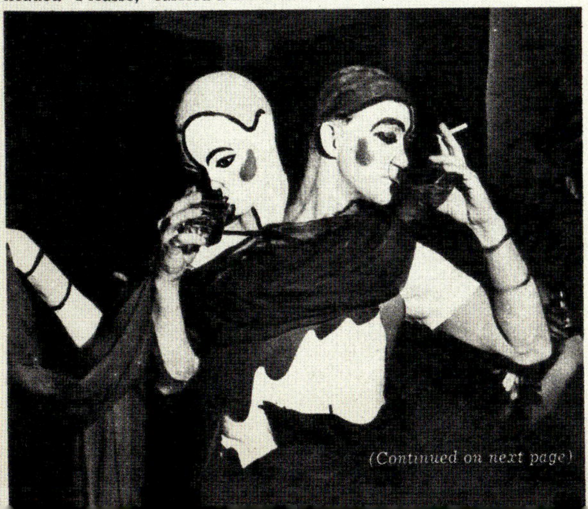

(Continued on next page)

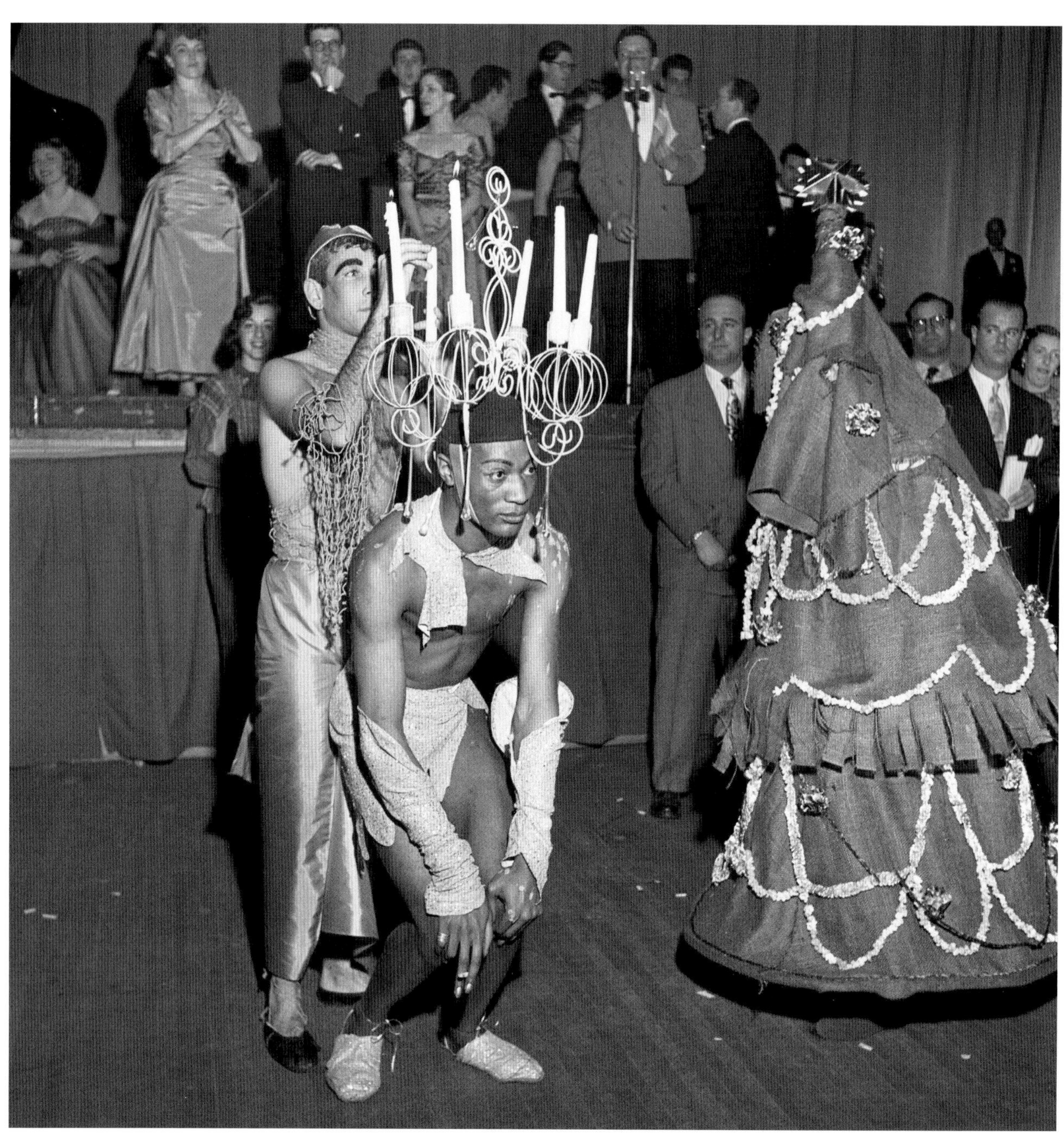

A partygoer lighting a human candelabra

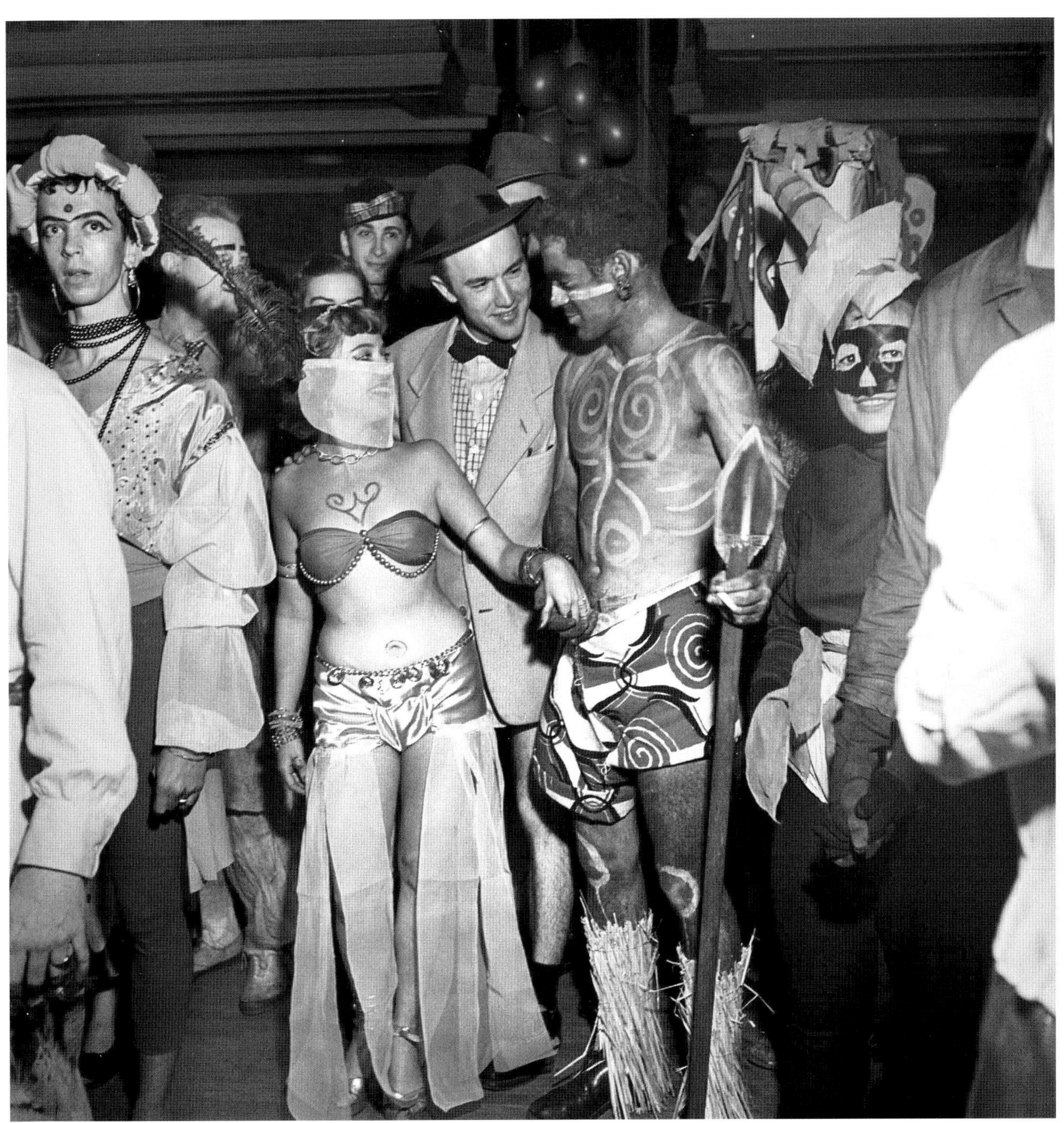

Revelers mixing at the ball

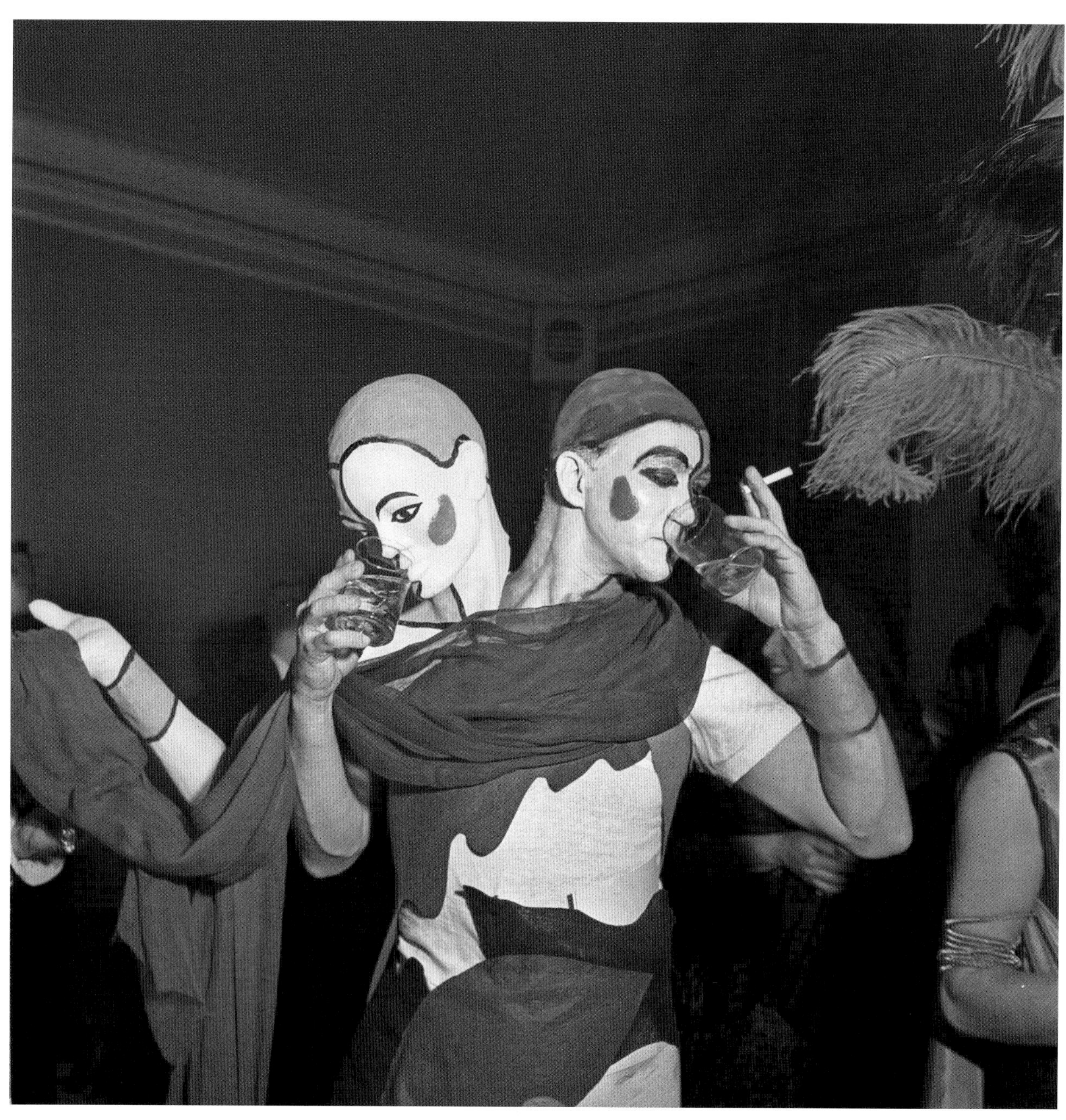

"Most original" prize winner, artist Harold Diehl, posing as a two-headed "Picasso"

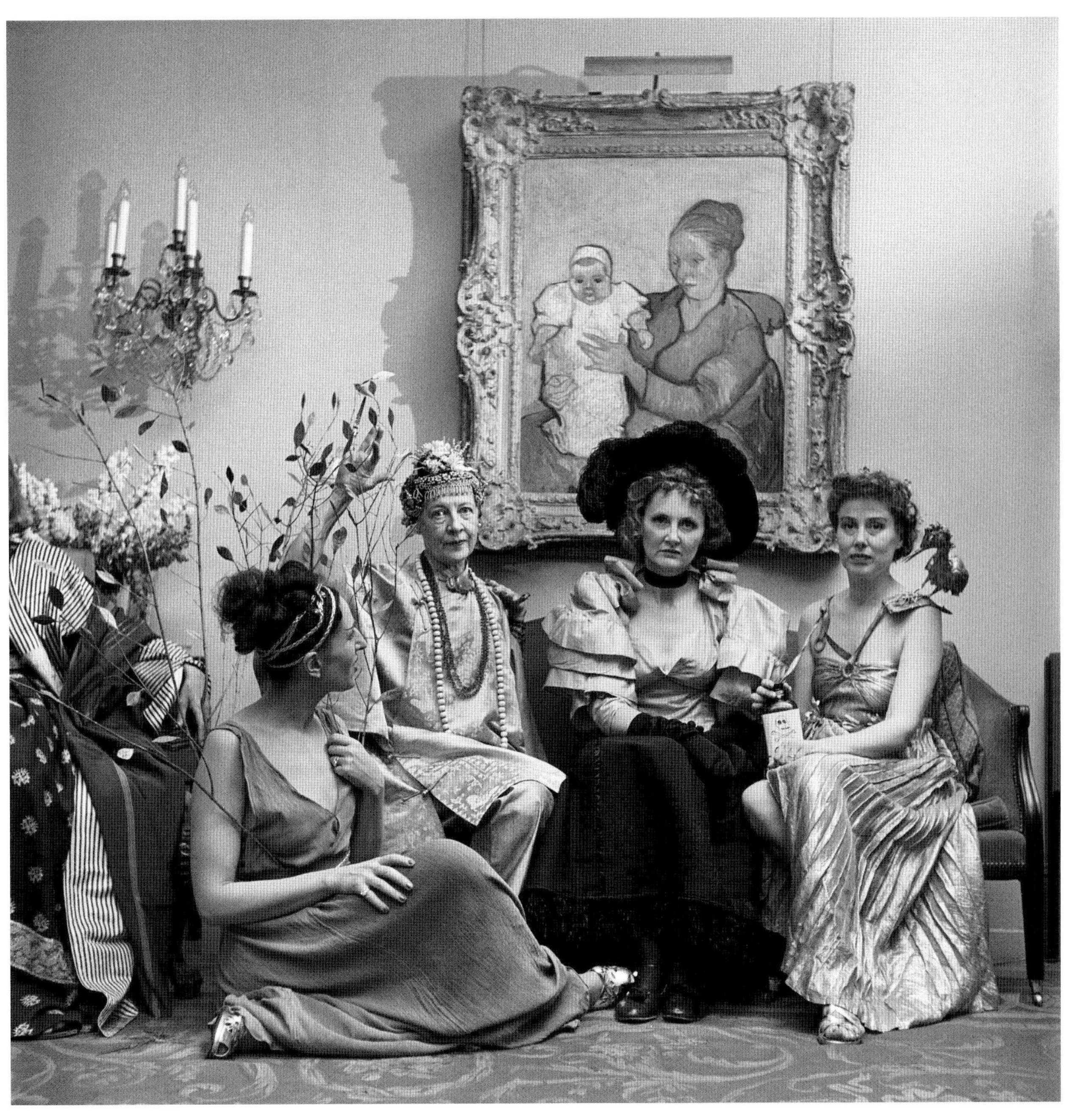

Socialites meeting for a pre-ball party at a home on Rittenhouse Square, with a painting by Vincent van Gogh in the background

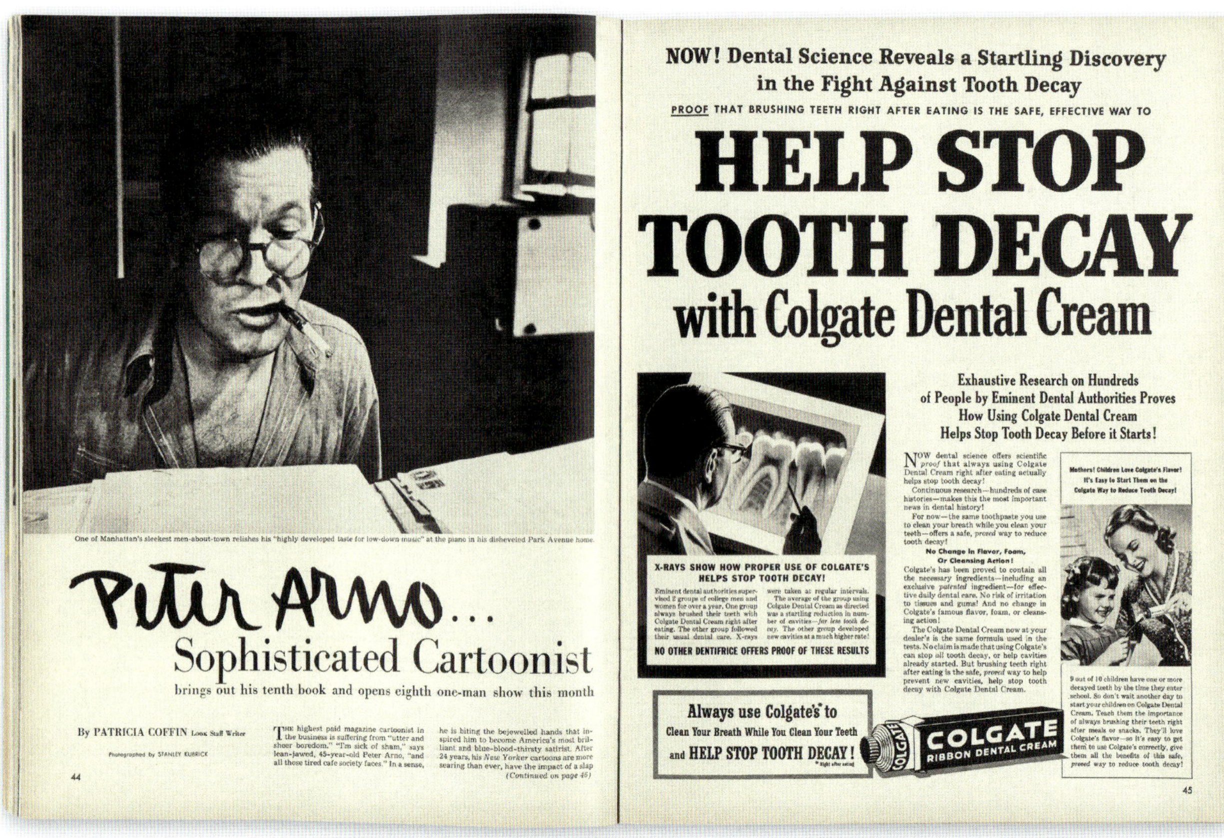

One of Manhattan's sleekest men-about-town relishes his "highly developed taste for low-down music" at the piano in his disheveled Park Avenue home.

Peter Arno…
Sophisticated Cartoonist
brings out his tenth book and opens eighth one-man show this month

By PATRICIA COFFIN Look Staff Writer

Photographed by STANLEY KUBRICK

The highest paid magazine cartoonist in the business is suffering from "utter and sheer boredom." "I'm sick of sham," says lean-jawed, 45-year-old Peter Arno, "and all those tired cafe society faces." In a sense, he is biting the bejewelled hands that inspired him to become America's most brilliant and blue-blood-thirsty satirist. After 24 years, his *New Yorker* cartoons are more searing than ever, have the impact of a slap

(Continued on page 46)

44

45

PUBLISHED AS

PETER ARNO . . . SOPHISTICATED CARTOONIST

Peter Arno was most famous for his sexually provocative cartoons for *The New Yorker* magazine, which first published one of his drawings the year it was launched in 1925. Written almost 25 years later, *Look*'s article on Arno, 45 years old at the time, illustrated the life of Manhattan's most celebrated man-about-town. Photographed at his Park Avenue apartment—"a shambles of unframed pictures, sketch-littered floors and furniture that needs recovering"—Arno drew a nude model, caught up on the day's news in bed, and entertained friends over food he cooked in his kitchen. On the town, Arno dated "fresh, unspoiled girls" half his age in "lowdown" bars and fancy restaurants.

DATE

SEPTEMBER 27, 1949

AUTHOR

PATRICIA COFFIN

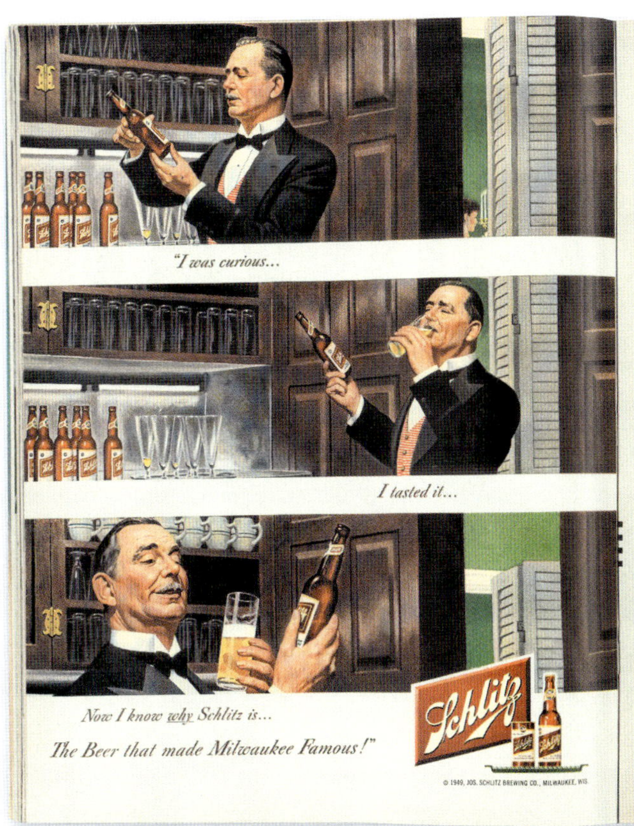

"I was curious...
I tasted it...
Schlitz
Now I know why Schlitz is...
The Beer that made Milwaukee Famous!"
© 1949, JOS. SCHLITZ BREWING CO., MILWAUKEE, WIS.

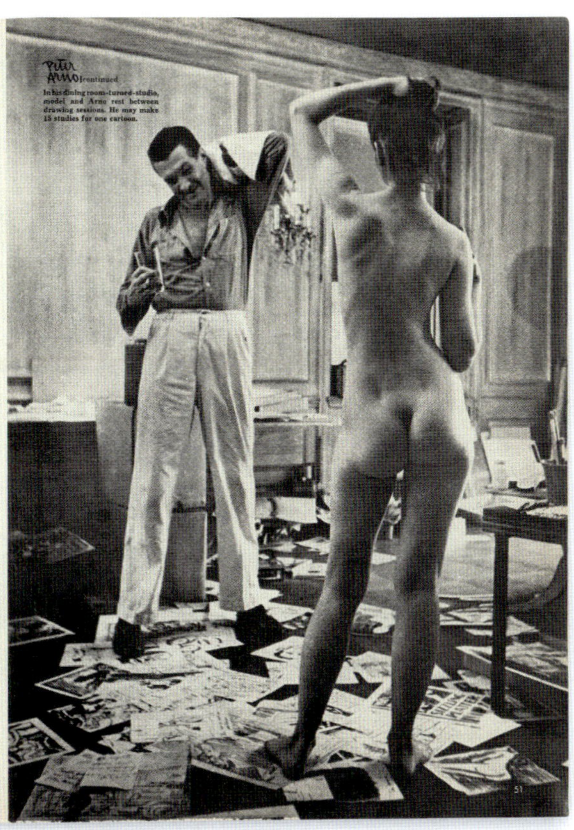

Peter Arno continued
In his dining room-turned-studio, model and Arno rest between drawing sessions. He may make 15 studies for one cartoon.
51

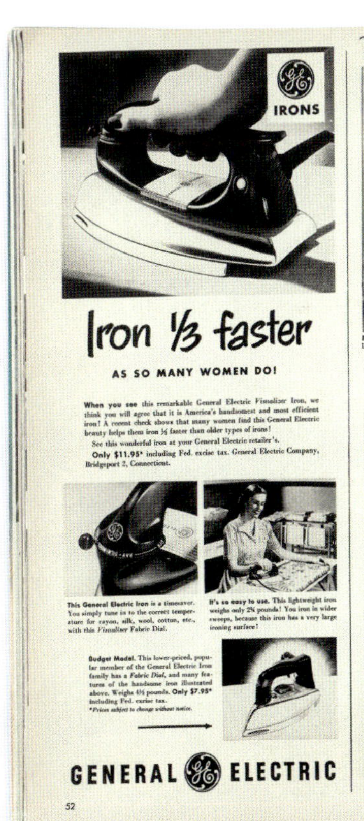

GE
IRONS
Iron 1/3 faster
AS SO MANY WOMEN DO!
When you see this remarkable General Electric Visualizer Iron, we think you will agree that it is America's handsomest and most efficient iron! A recent check shows that many women find this General Electric beauty helps them iron 1/3 faster than older types of irons!
See this wonderful iron at your General Electric retailer's.
Only $11.95* including Fed. excise tax. General Electric Company, Bridgeport 2, Connecticut.
This General Electric Iron is a timesaver. You simply tune in to the correct temperature for rayon, silk, wool, cotton, etc., with this Visualizer Fabric Dial.
It's so easy to use. This lightweight iron weighs only 2¾ pounds! You iron in wider sweeps, because this iron has a very large ironing surface!
Budget Model. This lower-priced, popular member of the General Electric Iron family has a Fabric Dial, and many features of the handsome iron illustrated above. Weighs 4½ pounds. Only $7.95* including Fed. excise tax.
*Prices subject to change without notice.
GENERAL ELECTRIC
52

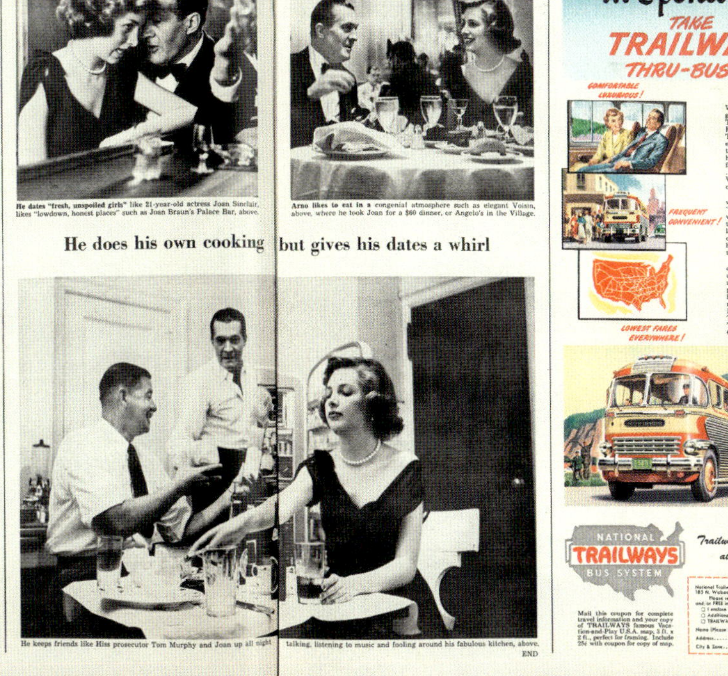

Peter Arno continued
He dates "fresh, unspoiled girls" like 21-year-old actress Joan Sinclair, likes "lowdown, honest places" such as Joan Braun's Palace Bar, above.
Arno likes to eat in a congenial atmosphere such as elegant Voisin, above, where he took Joan for a $60 dinner, or Angelo's in the Village.
He does his own cooking but gives his dates a whirl
He keeps friends like Hiss prosecutor Tom Murphy and Joan up all night talking, listening to music and fooling around his fabulous kitchen, above.
END

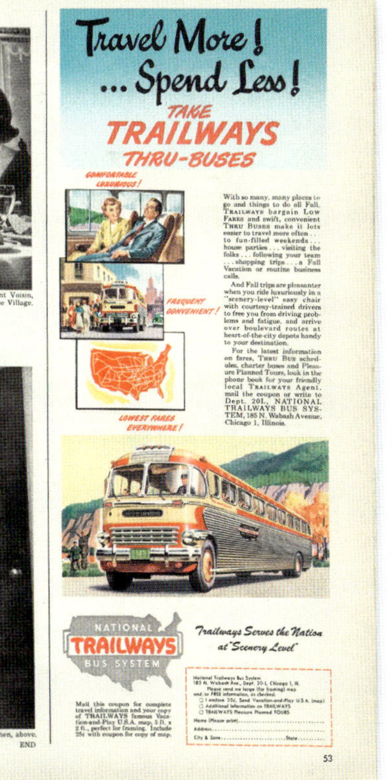

Travel More! ... Spend Less!
TAKE TRAILWAYS THRU-BUSES
COMFORTABLE LUXURIOUS!
FREQUENT CONVENIENT!
LOWEST FARES EVERYWHERE!
With so many, many places to go and things to do all Fall, TRAILWAYS bargain LOW FARES and swift, convenient THRU BUSES make it lots easier to travel more often . . to fun-filled weekends . . . house parties . . . visiting the folks . . . following your team . . . shopping trips . . . a Fall Vacation or routine business calls.
And Fall trips are pleasanter when you ride luxuriously in a "scenery-level" easy chair with courtesy-trained drivers to free you from driving problems and fatigue, and arrive over boulevard routes at heart-of-the-city depots handy to your destination.
For the latest information on fares, THRU BUS schedules, charter buses and Pleasure Planned Tours, look in the phone book for your friendly local TRAILWAYS Agent, mail the coupon or write to Dept. 20L, NATIONAL TRAILWAYS BUS SYSTEM, 185 N. Wabash Avenue, Chicago 1, Illinois.
NATIONAL TRAILWAYS BUS SYSTEM
Trailways Serves the Nation at "Scenery Level"
Mail this coupon for complete travel information and your copy of TRAILWAYS famous Vacation-and-Play U.S.A. map, 3 ft. x 2 ft., perfect for framing. Include 25¢ with coupon for copy of map.
National Trailways Bus System
185 N. Wabash Ave., Dept. 20-L, Chicago 1, Ill.
Please send me large (for framing) map and, or FREE information, as checked.
I enclose 25¢. Send Vacation-and-Play U.S.A. (map)
Additional information on TRAILWAYS
TRAILWAYS Pleasure Planned TOURS
Name (Please print)
Address
City & Zone
State
53

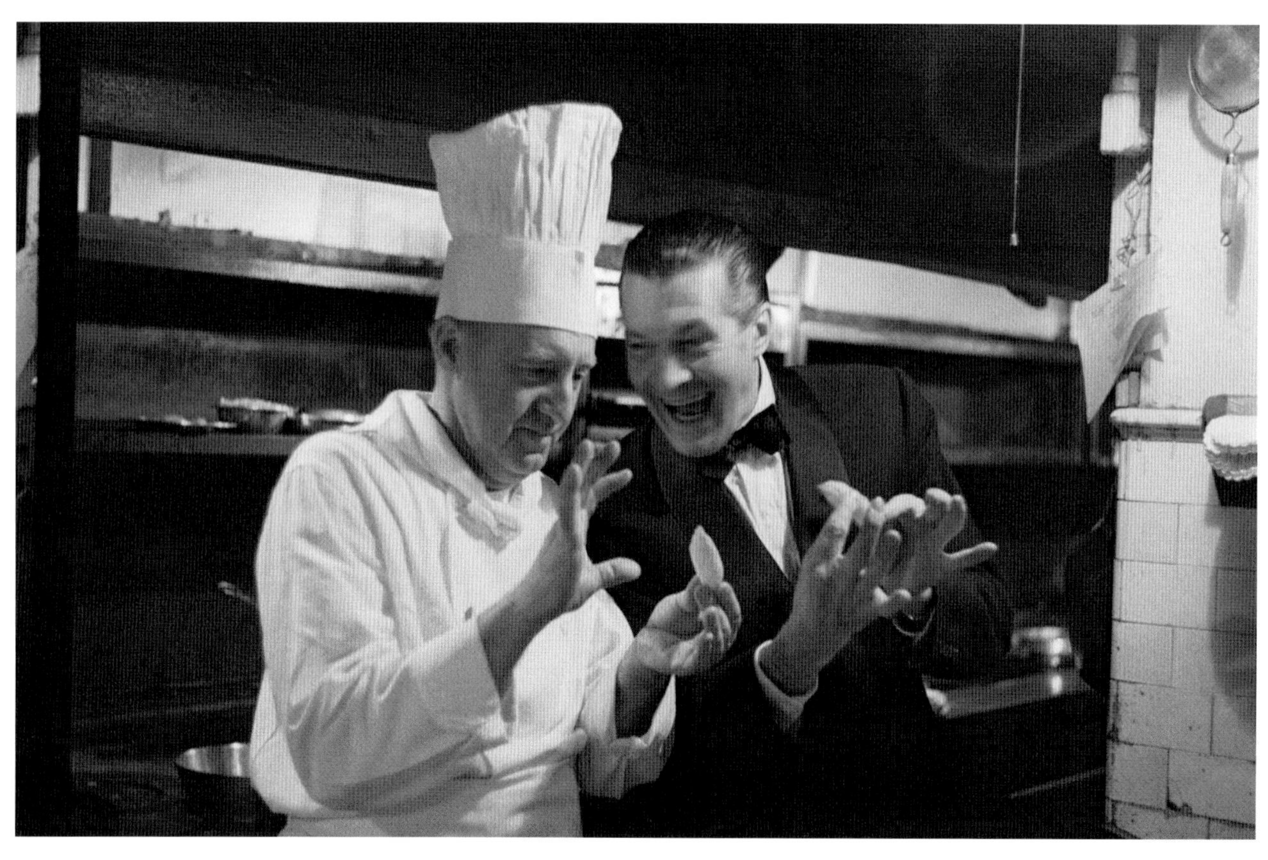

Arno, celebrated as a gourmet, in conversation with a restaurant chef

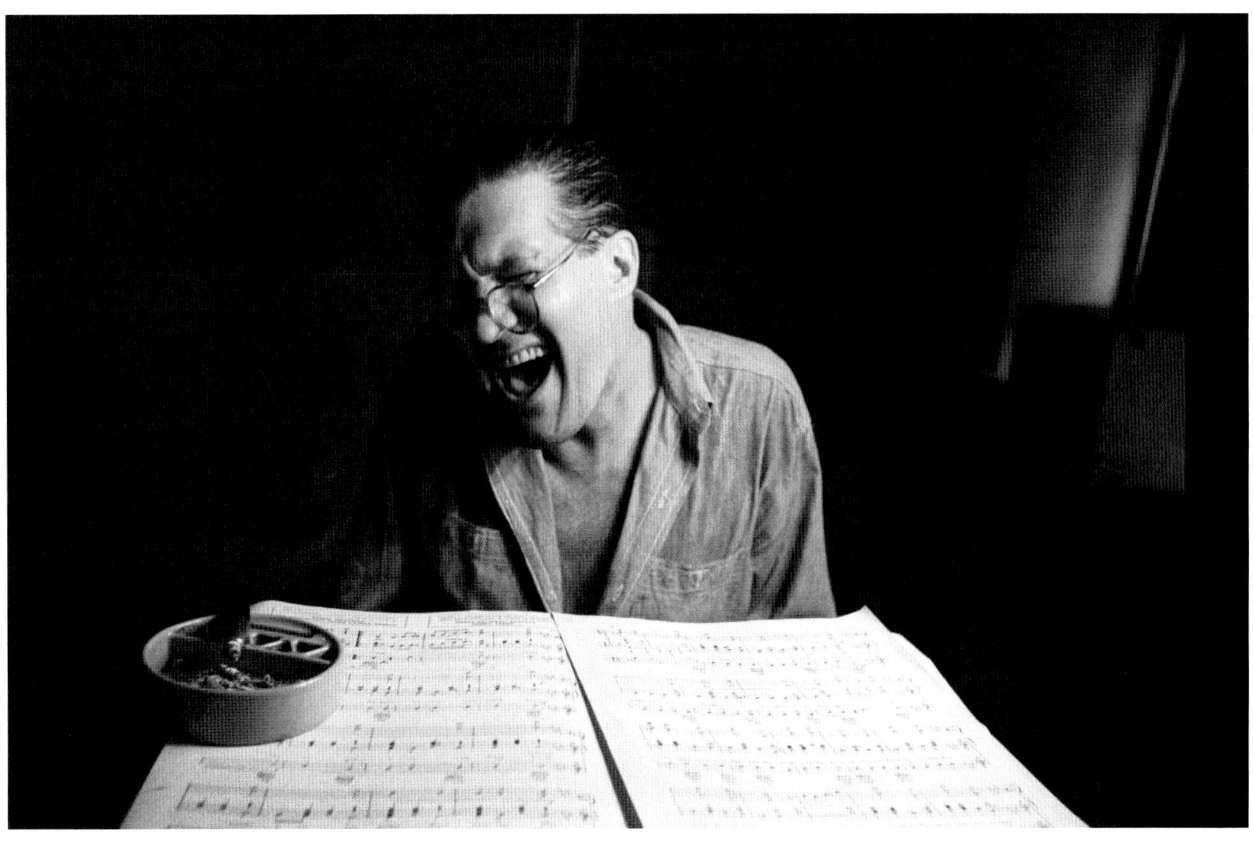

Arno playing the piano in his Park Avenue apartment

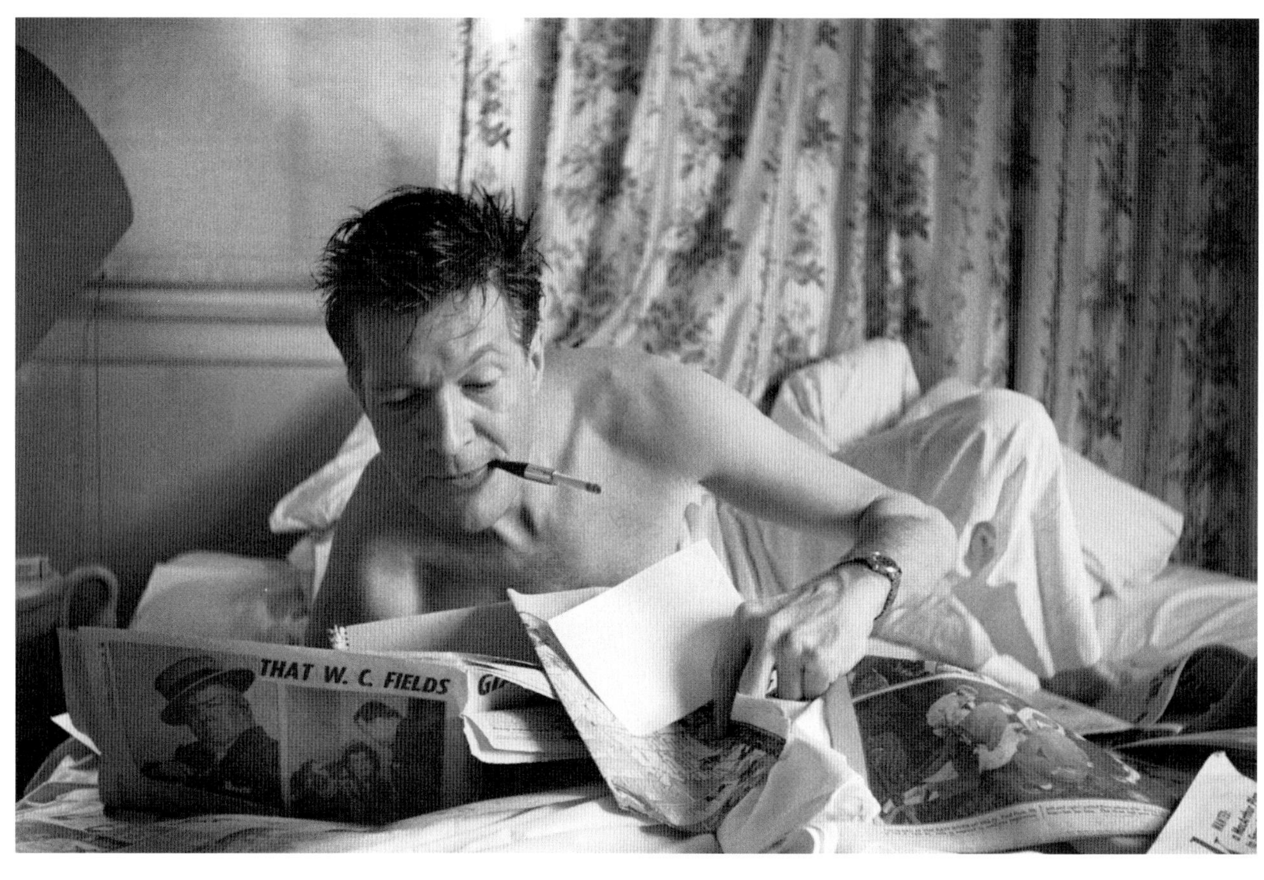

Arno catching up on the day's news in bed

OPPOSITE AND FOLLOWING SPREAD
Arno working with a model in his dining-room-turned-studio

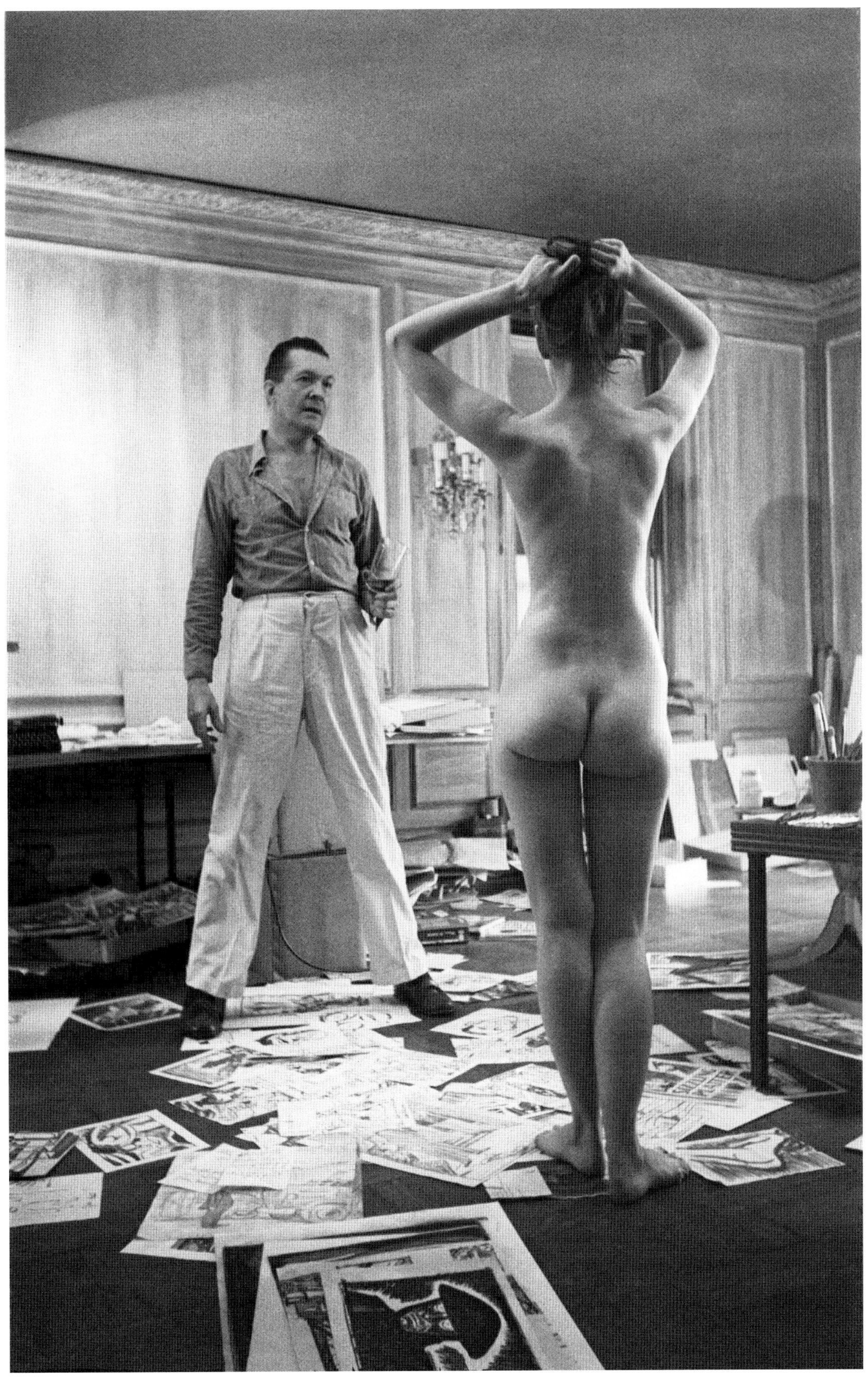

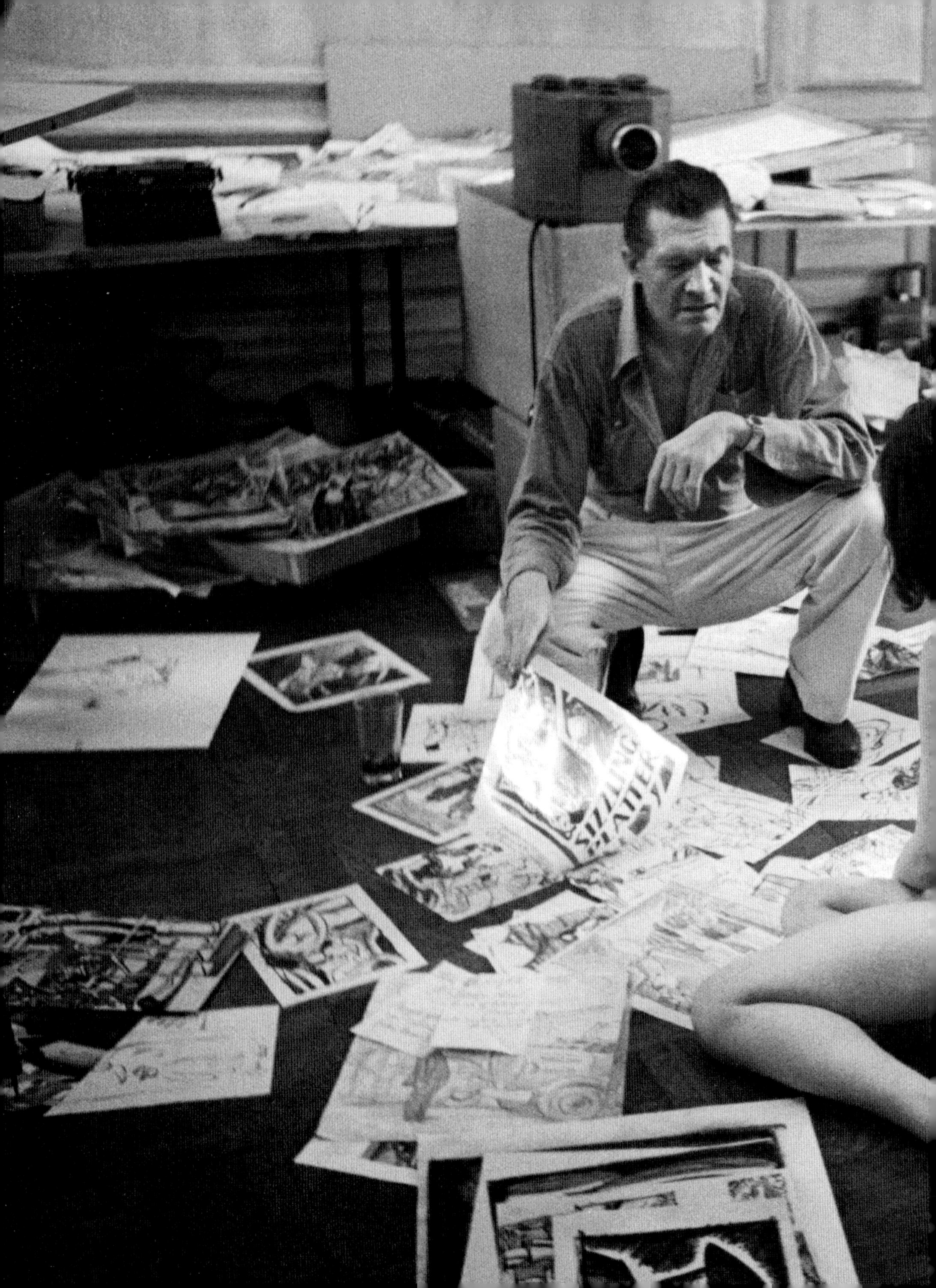

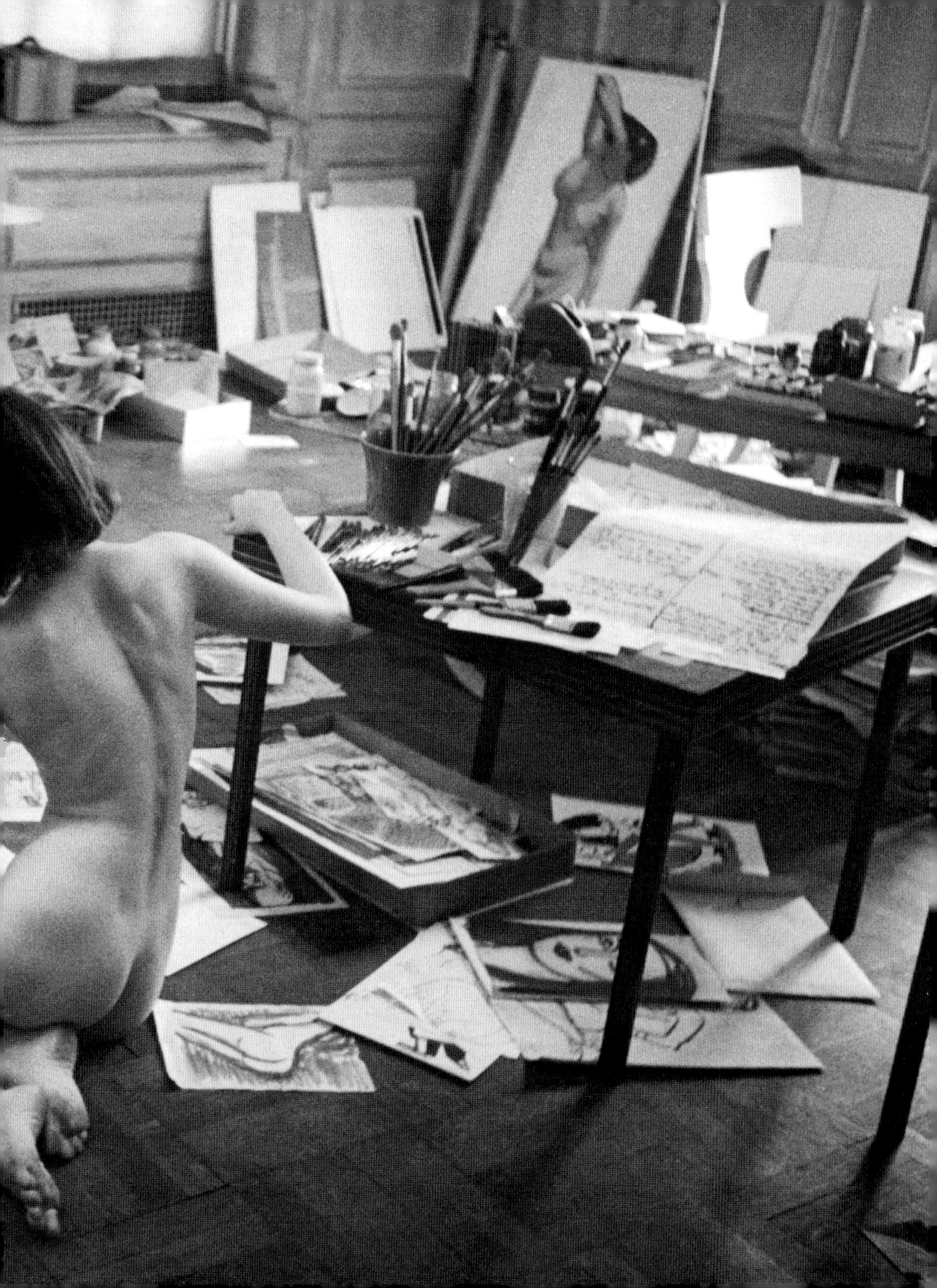

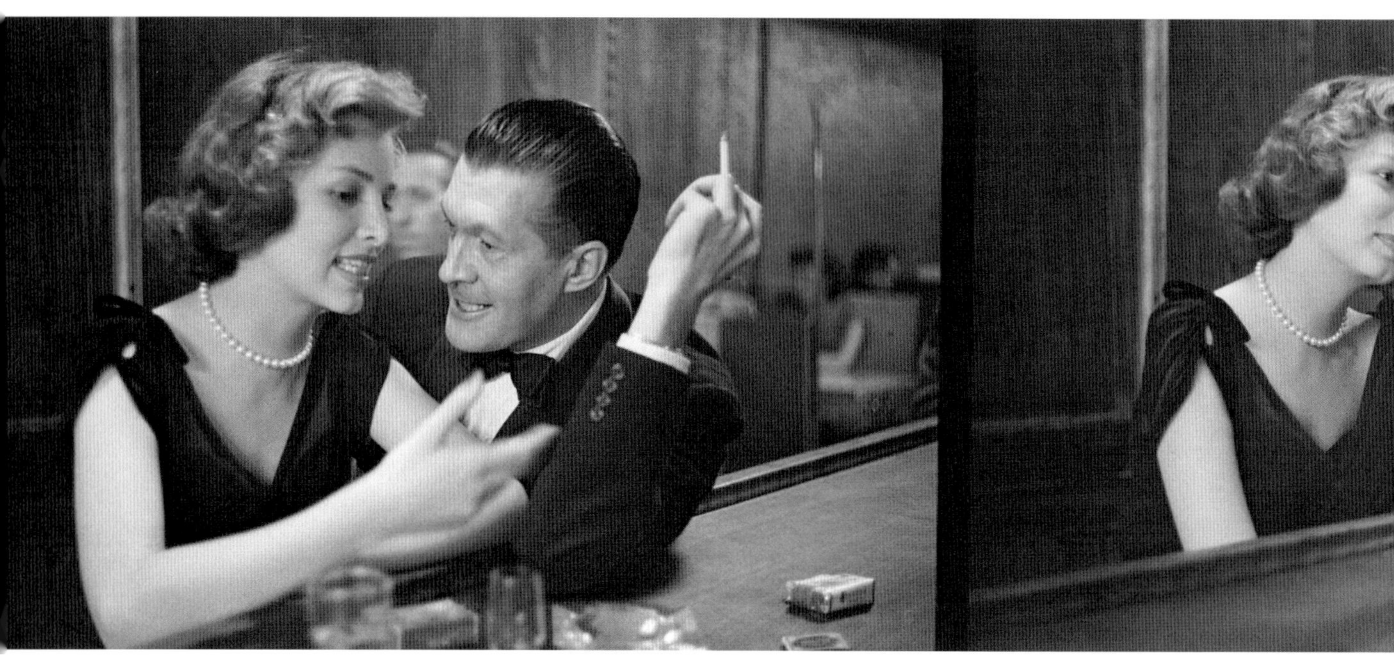

Arno on a date with 21-year-old actress Joan Sinclair

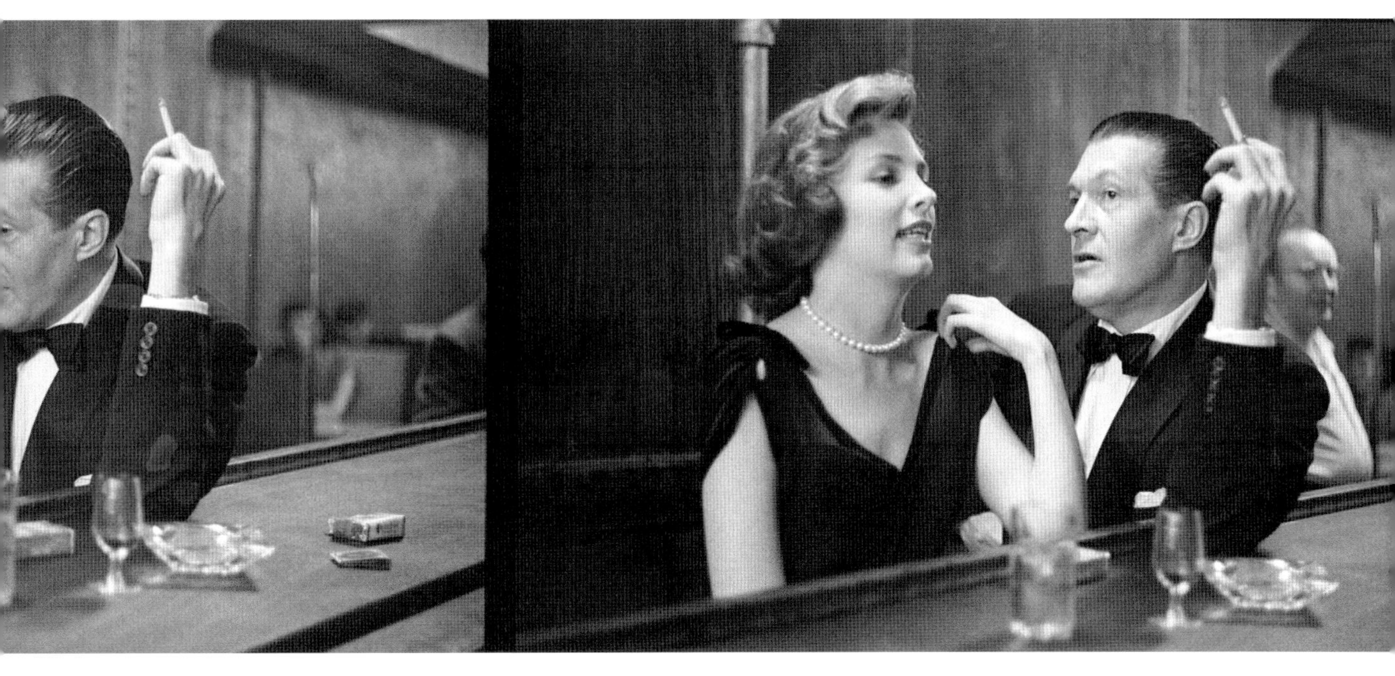

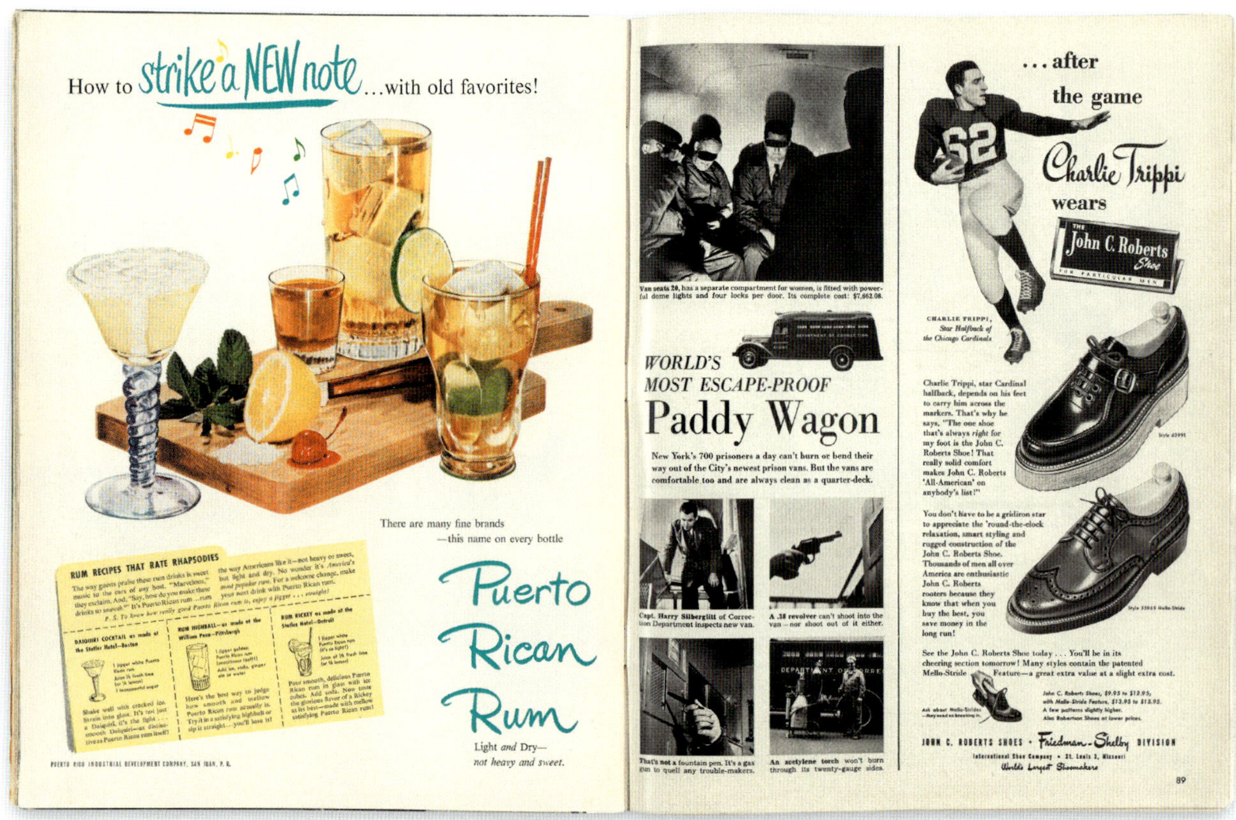

Van seats 20, has a separate compartment for women, is fitted with powerful dome lights and four locks per door. Its complete cost: $7,662.08.

WORLD'S MOST ESCAPE-PROOF

Paddy Wagon

New York's 700 prisoners a day can't burn or bend their way out of the City's newest prison vans. But the vans are comfortable too and are always clean as a quarter-deck.

Capt. Harry Silberglitt of Correction Department inspects new van.

A .38 revolver can't shoot into the van—nor shoot out of it either.

That's not a fountain pen. It's a gas gun to quell any trouble-makers.

An acetylene torch won't burn through its twenty-gauge sides.

PUBLISHED AS

PADDY WAGON

DATE

SEPTEMBER 27, 1949

Part Weegee, part film noir, Kubrick's photographs illustrated a short article describing the distinctive features of New York's newest escape-proof prison van. An acetylene torch and a .38 revolver could not penetrate its thick metal sides. Four locks per door sealed in as many as 20 prisoners. "But the vans are comfortable too," the article noted, "and are always clean as a quarter-deck."

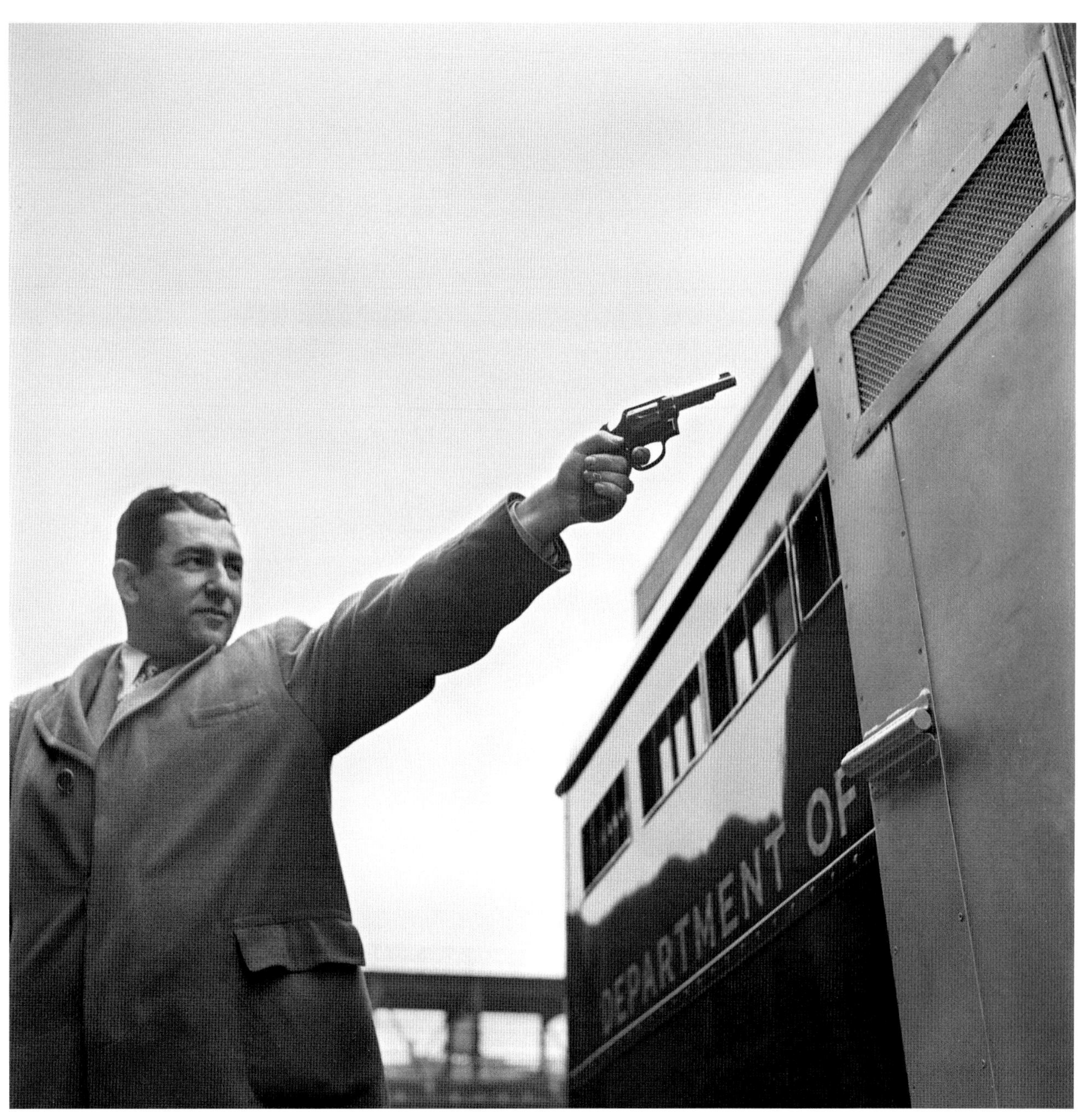

Captain Harry Silberglitt of the Department of Correction testing the armor of the new bulletproof wagon

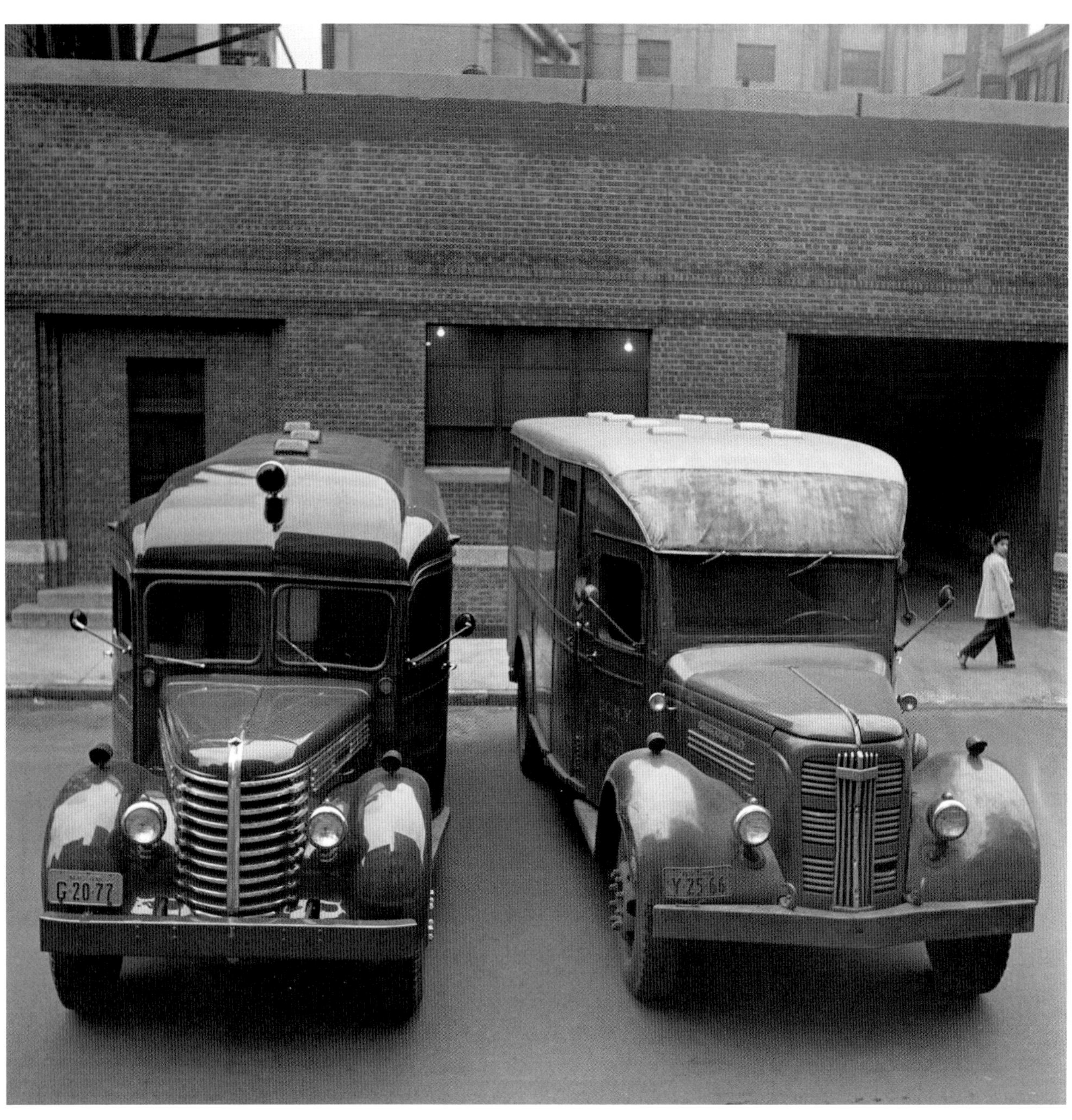

An old paddy wagon (right) parked next to a new model

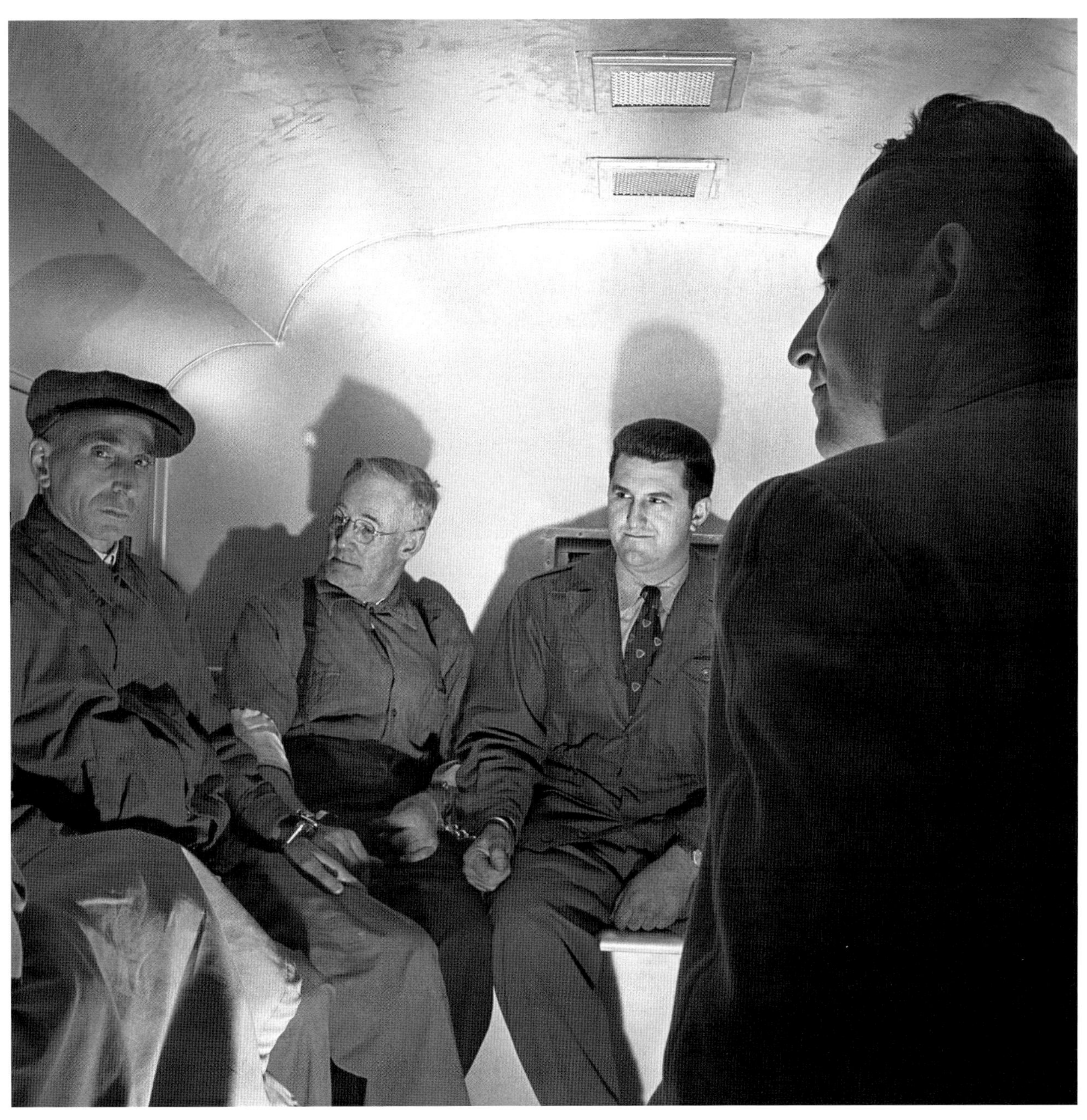

Inside the van, which seated 20 people

FOLLOWING SPREAD **An acetylene torch could not burn through the van's 20-gauge metal sides.**

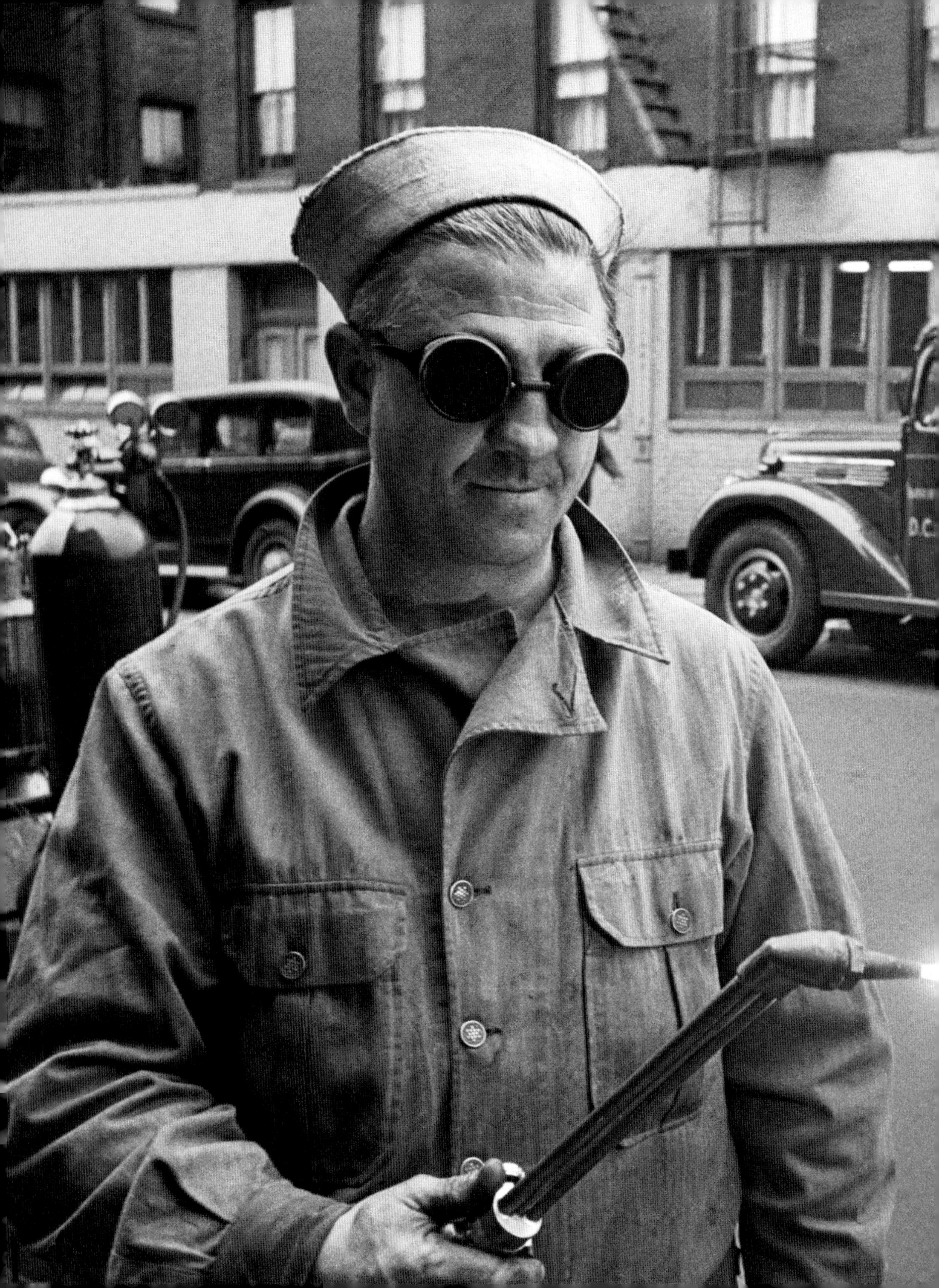
D.C.

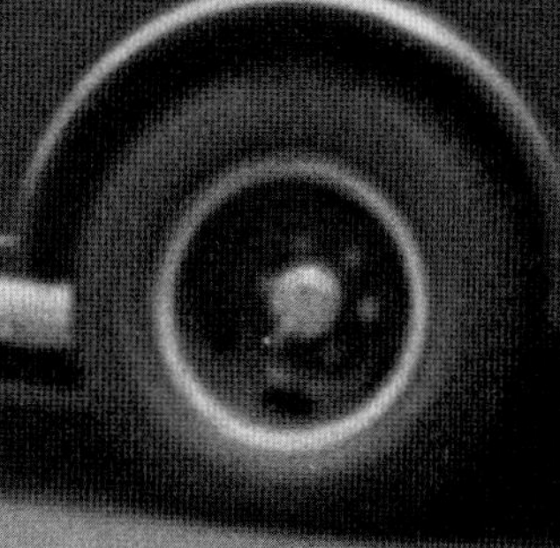
DEPARTMENT OF CORRECTION

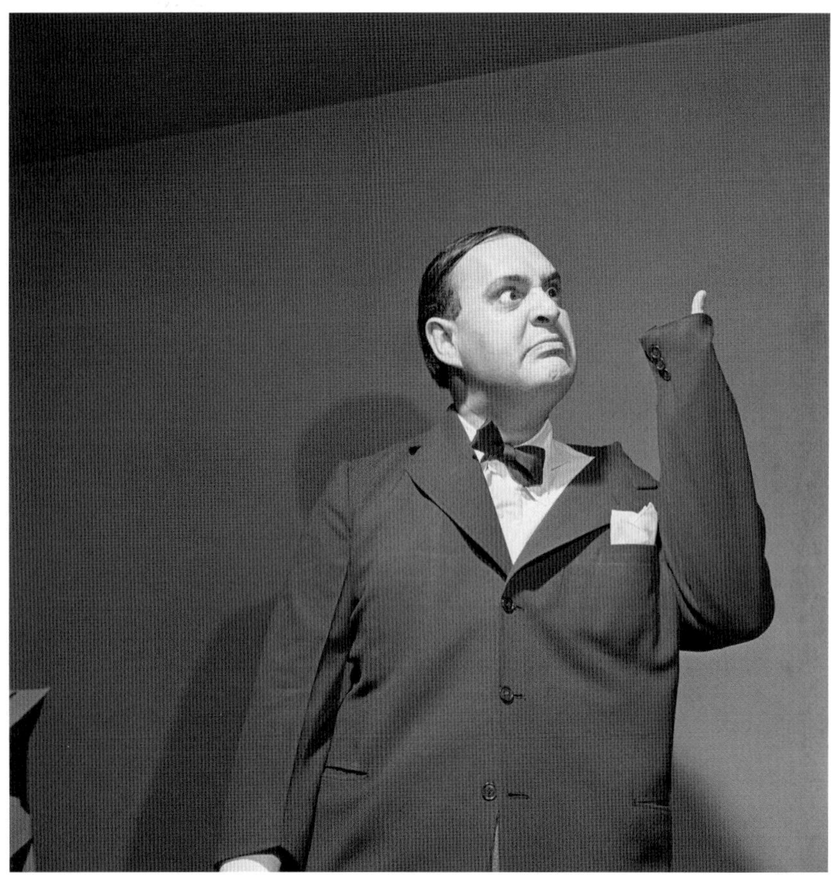

[UNPUBLISHED]

ZERO MOSTEL

[FILED DATE]

DECEMBER 12, 1949

This unpublished series of photographs of actor and comedian Zero Mostel comprised almost 30 photographs featuring Mostel emoting for the camera against a studio backdrop.The genesis for this series may have been Kubrick's photographs of a party given by Leonard Bernstein in the summer of 1949 (for an article published in March 1950) where Mostel was a guest.

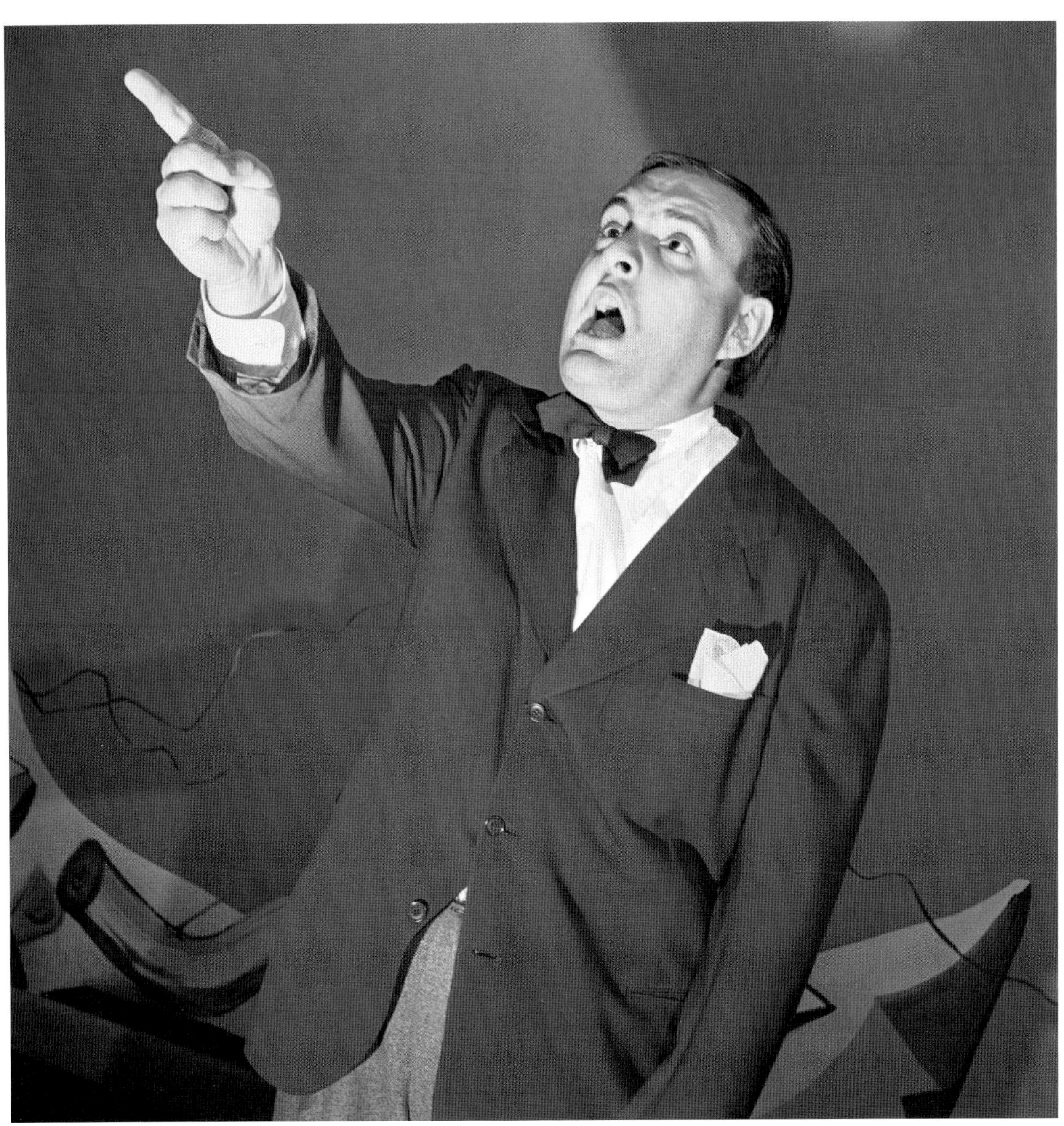

Mostel mugging for the camera

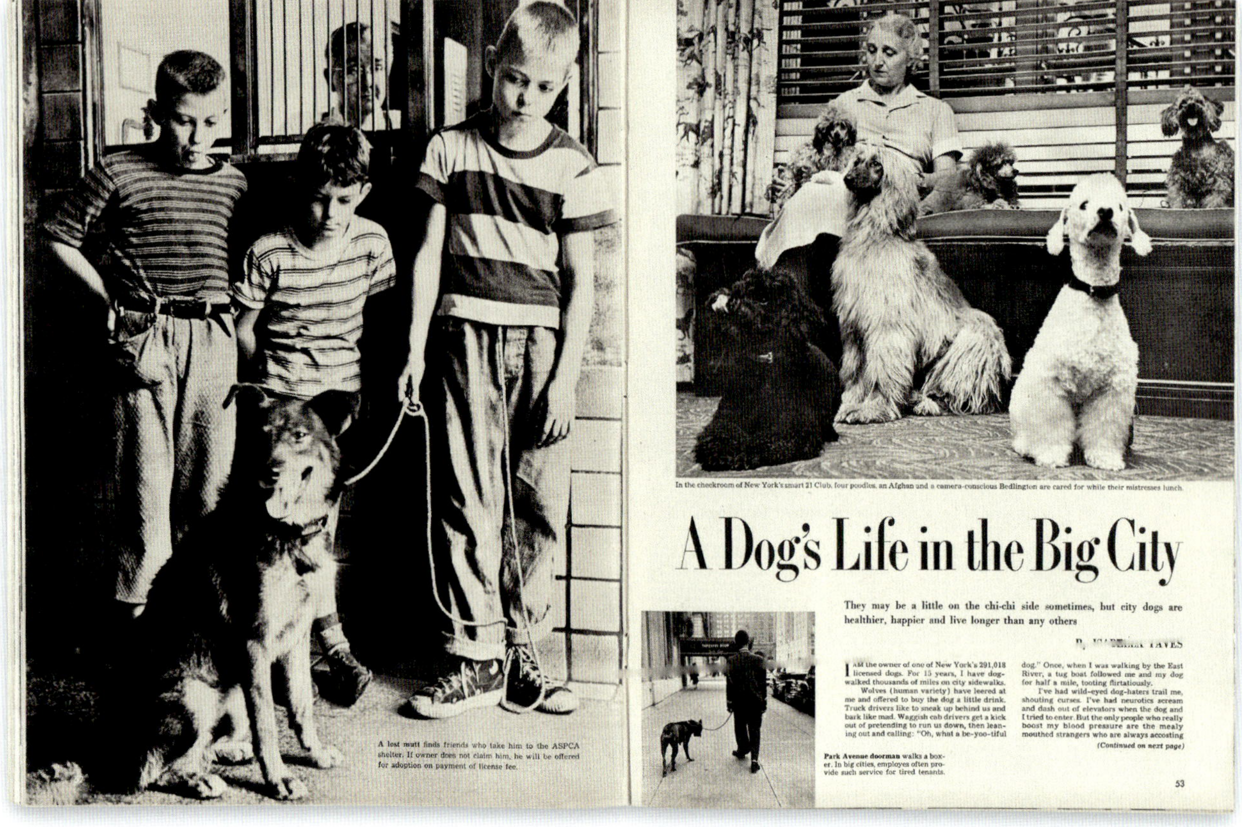

A lost mutt finds friends who take him to the ASPCA shelter. If owner does not claim him, he will be offered for adoption on payment of license fee.

In the checkroom of New York's smart 21 Club, four poodles, an Afghan and a camera-conscious Bedlington are cared for while their mistresses lunch.

A Dog's Life in the Big City

They may be a little on the chi-chi side sometimes, but city dogs are healthier, happier and live longer than any others

I AM the owner of one of New York's 291,018 licensed dogs. For 15 years, I have dog-walked thousands of miles on city sidewalks.

Wolves (human variety) have leered at me and offered to buy the dog a little drink. Truck drivers like to sneak up behind us and bark like mad. Waggish cab drivers get a kick out of pretending to run us down, then leaning out and calling: "Oh, what a be-yoo-tiful dog." Once, when I was walking by the East River, a tug boat followed me and my dog for half a mile, tooting flirtatiously.

I've had wild-eyed dog-haters trail me, shouting curses. I've had neurotics scream and dash out of elevators when the dog and I tried to enter. But the only people who really boost my blood pressure are the mealy mouthed strangers who are always accosting

(Continued on next page)

Park Avenue doorman walks a boxer. In big cities, employes often provide such service for tired tenants.

53

PUBLISHED AS

A DOG'S LIFE IN THE BIG CITY

DATE

NOVEMBER 8, 1949

AUTHOR

ISABELLA TAVES

Exploring the pampered lives of New York's 291,018 licensed dogs, this story extolled an "only in New York" quirkiness that *Look* often promoted in its coverage of the city. Kubrick's canine subjects ranged from a lost mutt to pedigreed dogs in the care of the chic 21 Club checkroom while their owners lunched. The article's author, a dog owner herself, rebutted the common belief that the city was too confining a place to raise dogs, asserting instead that "records show that big city dogs are healthier, happier and live longer than dogs in small towns or the country."

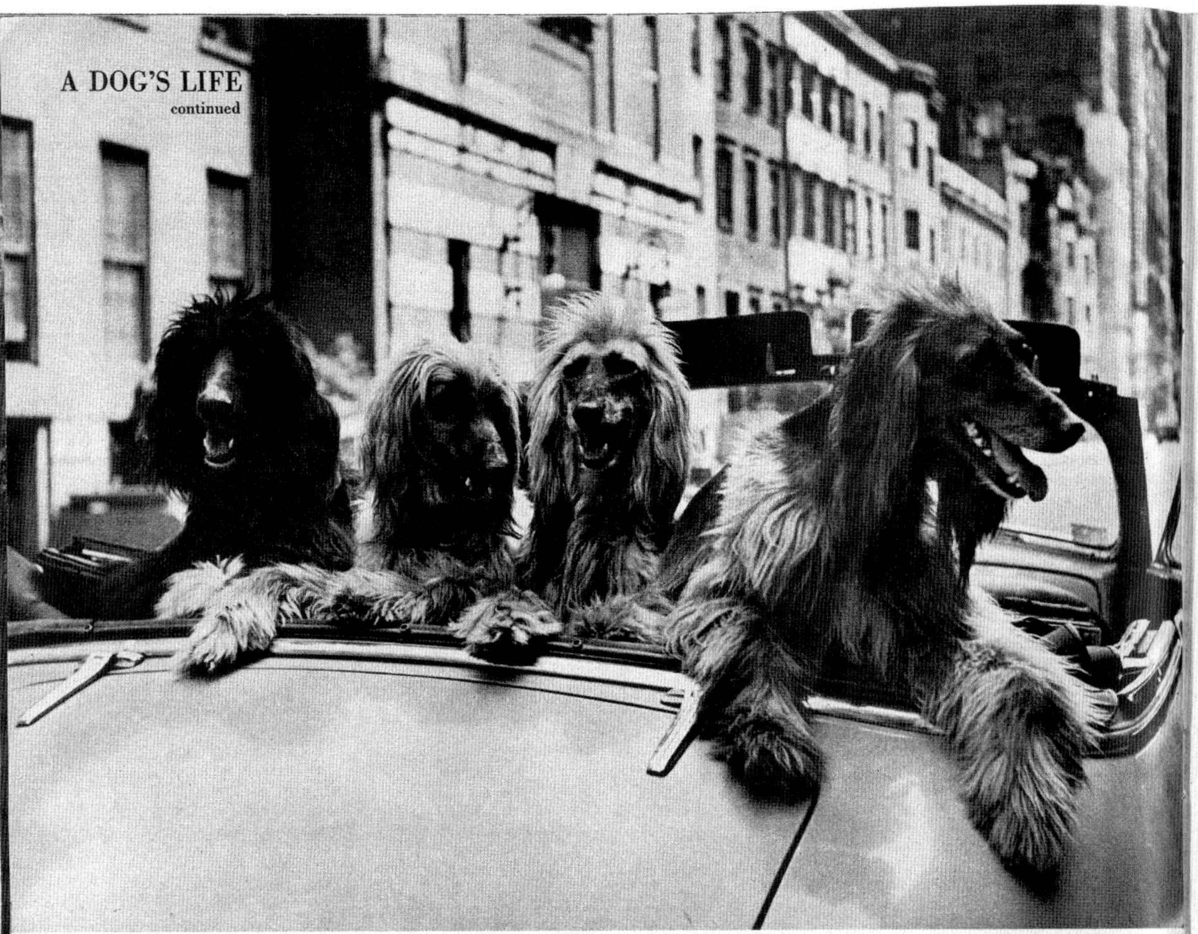

Like all city dogs, these prize-winning Afghans owned by Sunny Shay love to see Manhattan sights from a convertible but will settle for a taxicab.

City streets are always full of excitement for dogs

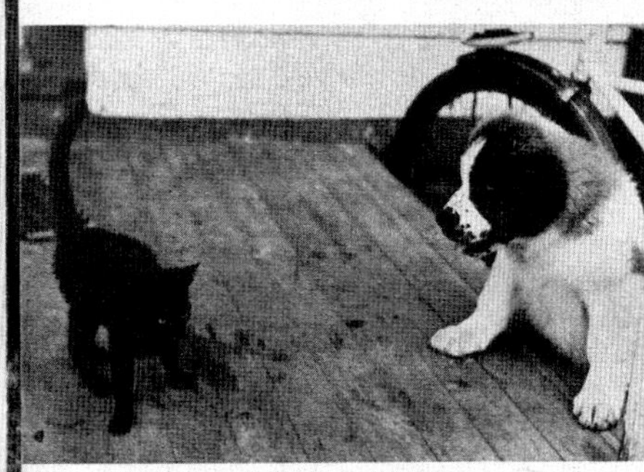

The cat is the enemy

In the country, dogs and cats sometimes learn to live together. But the city cat is tough. Even as a kitten, she stands her ground and aims claws at dogs' eyes.

me and announcing:

"I love dogs but I wouldn't be cruel enough to keep one in the city."

Actually, records show that big city dogs are healthier, happier and live longer than dogs in small towns or the country.

Dr. Raymond Garbutt, chief veterinarian of the ASPCA (American Society for the Prevention of Cruelty to Animals), has been treating city dogs for 30 years. He says: "In the country or suburbs, unless there is an outbreak of communicable disease, dogs always run loose. They get into dog fights and are killed by cars. They rummage in garbage cans, eating chicken bones and other dangerous matter. They lick up poisonous weed killers and insecticides. A New York dog, always on a leash and under supervision, has a far greater life expectancy than the same type and breed in the country."

Owning a dog in New York City is a lot of trouble—for the owner. The law says the animal must be on a leash at all times when he goes out. Nature forces you to take him out at least three times a day; four trips are kinder; and wily dogs can coerce easy-mark owners like me into six and seven trips. (This rule is for grown dogs. Puppies, even after they are house-broken, need more frequent trips.) You can never go out in the evening without climaxing it with a dog-walk; and a fairly long one, for the dog has been sleeping all evening and is now wide-awake and ready for fun. If you must go away for more than a few hours, you have to arrange to have the dog exercised – by your doorman, a friend or a professional dog walker. And, if you own a dog, you can never go off impetuously on trips.

When the dog travels with you, you must find out beforehand which hotels and inns will welcome him—or what trains will accept him and under what conditions. If you leave him at home, heart-broken, you must find a boarding place you can trust. Dog hospitals are reluctant to fill their

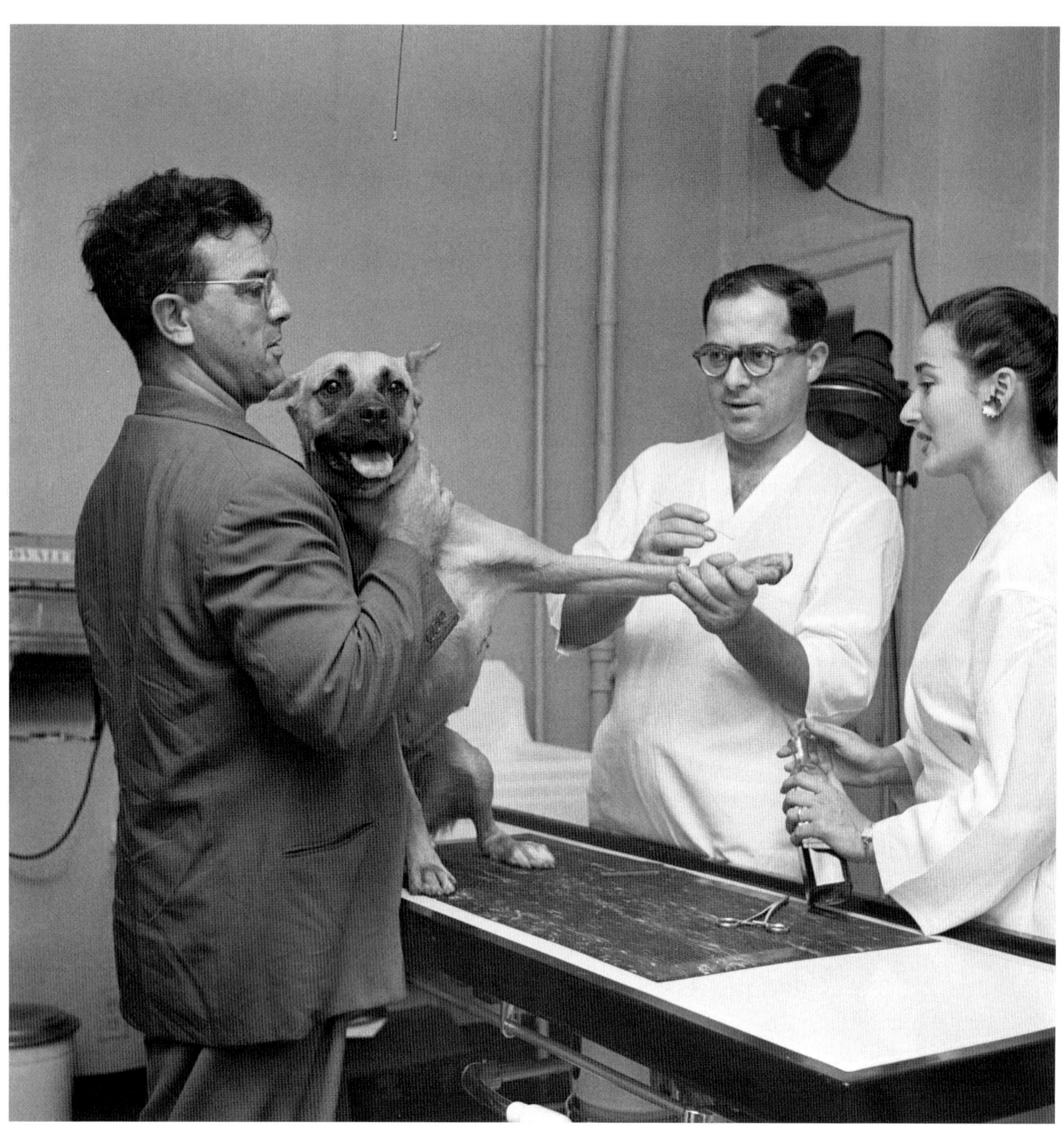

A city dog examined by a veterinarian

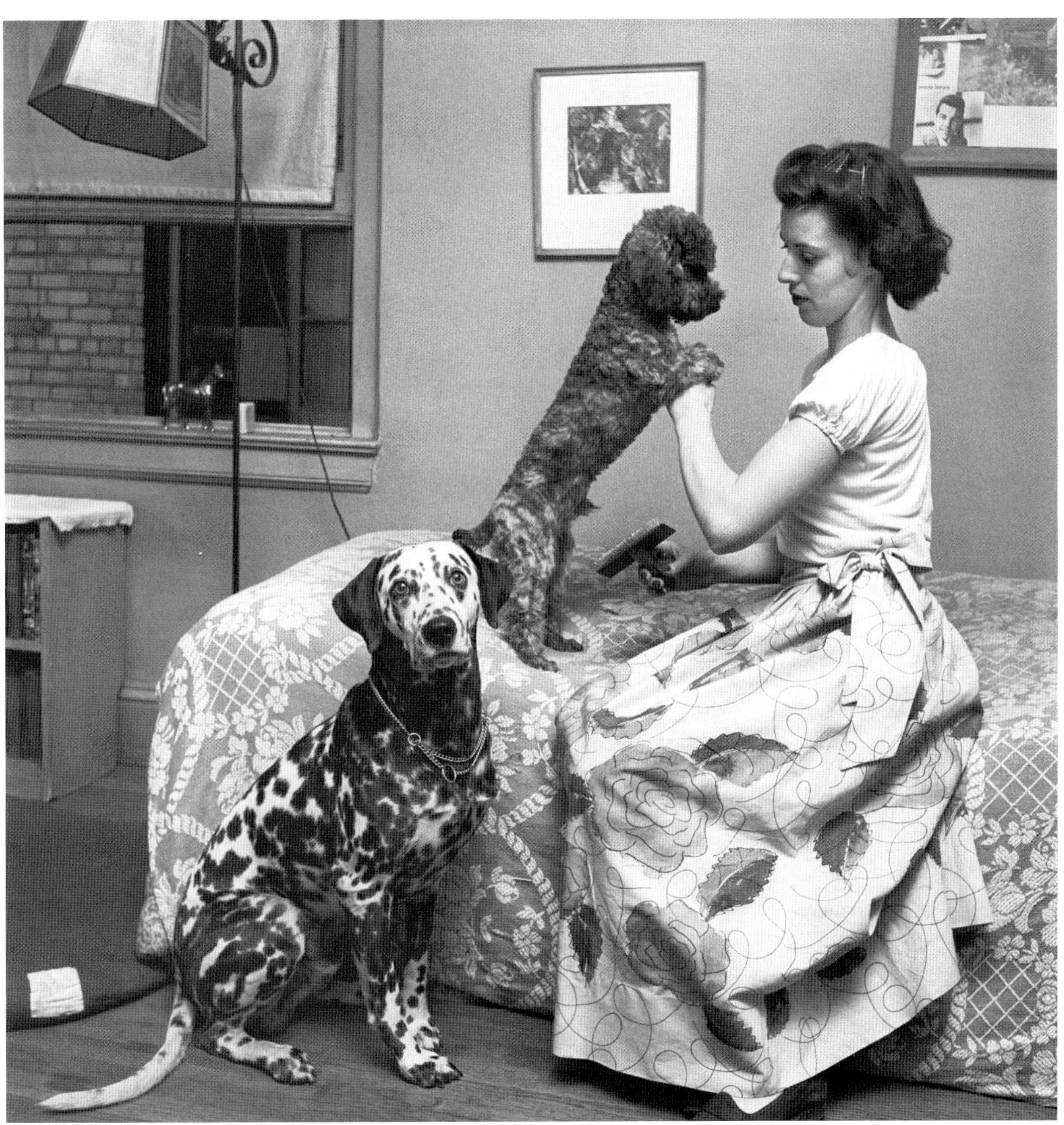

A camera-conscious Dalmatian

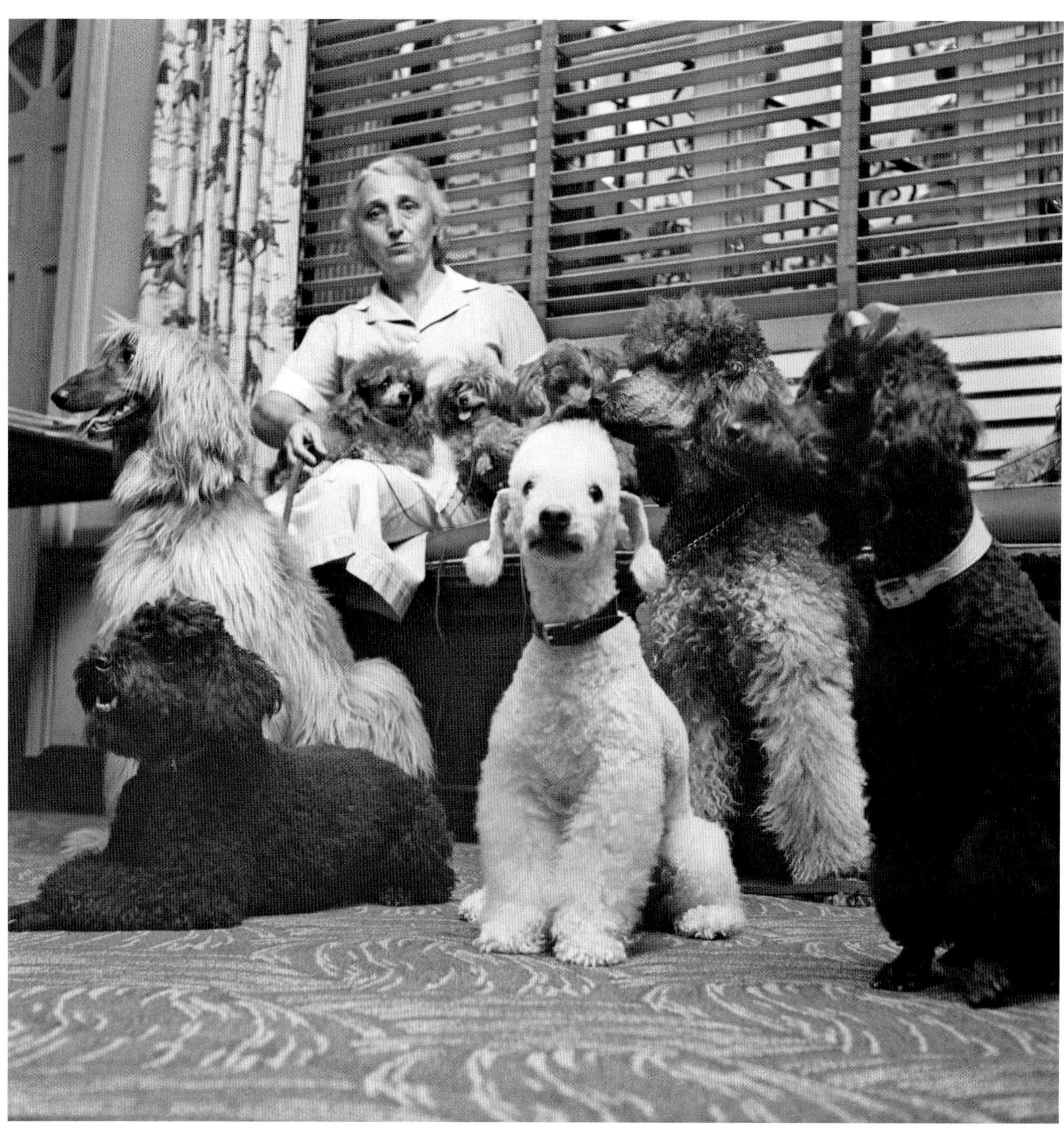

Pets being cared for in the checkroom of the 21 Club, while their owners lunch

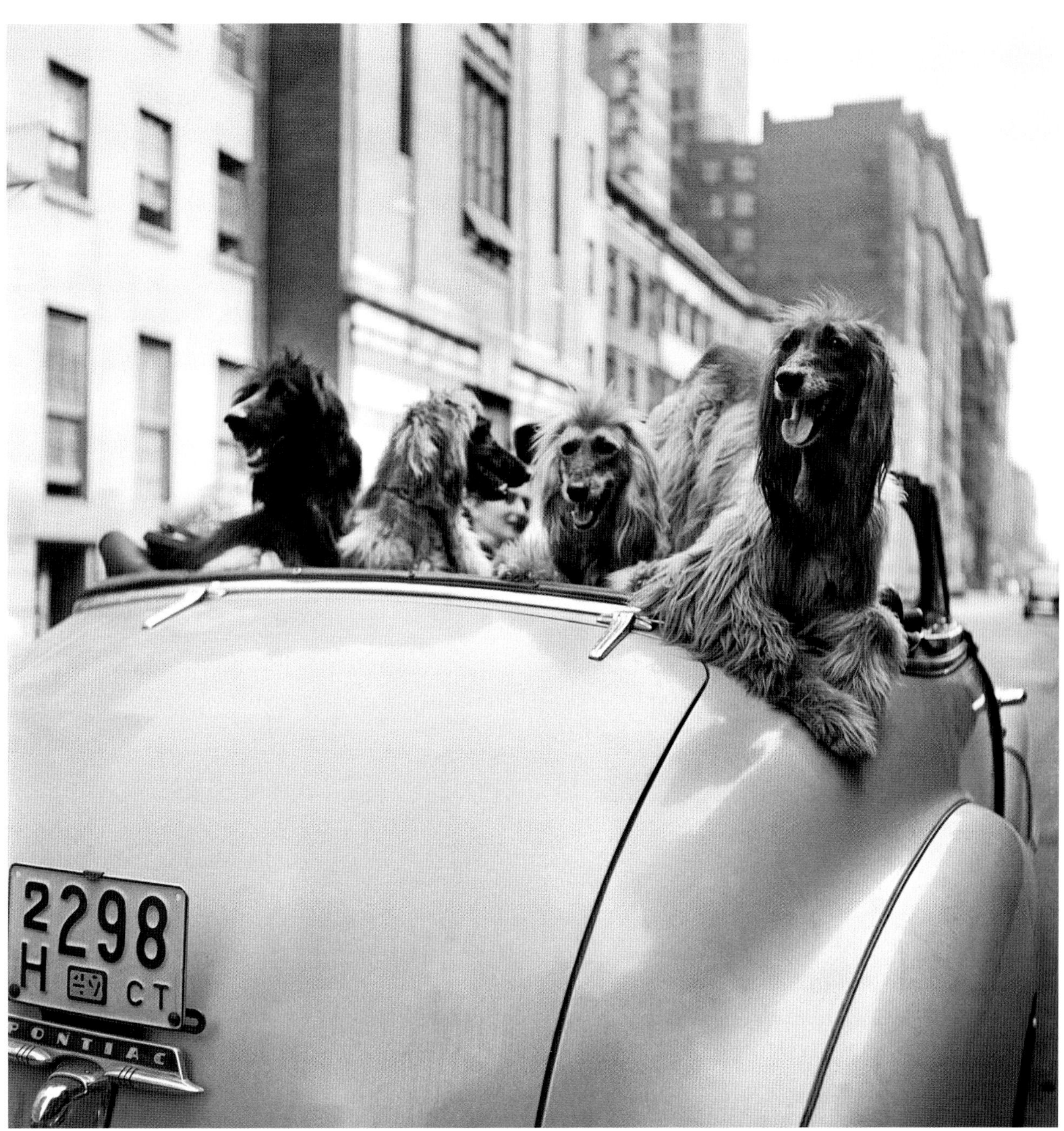

Prize-winning Afghan hounds out for an automobile ride in the streets of Manhattan

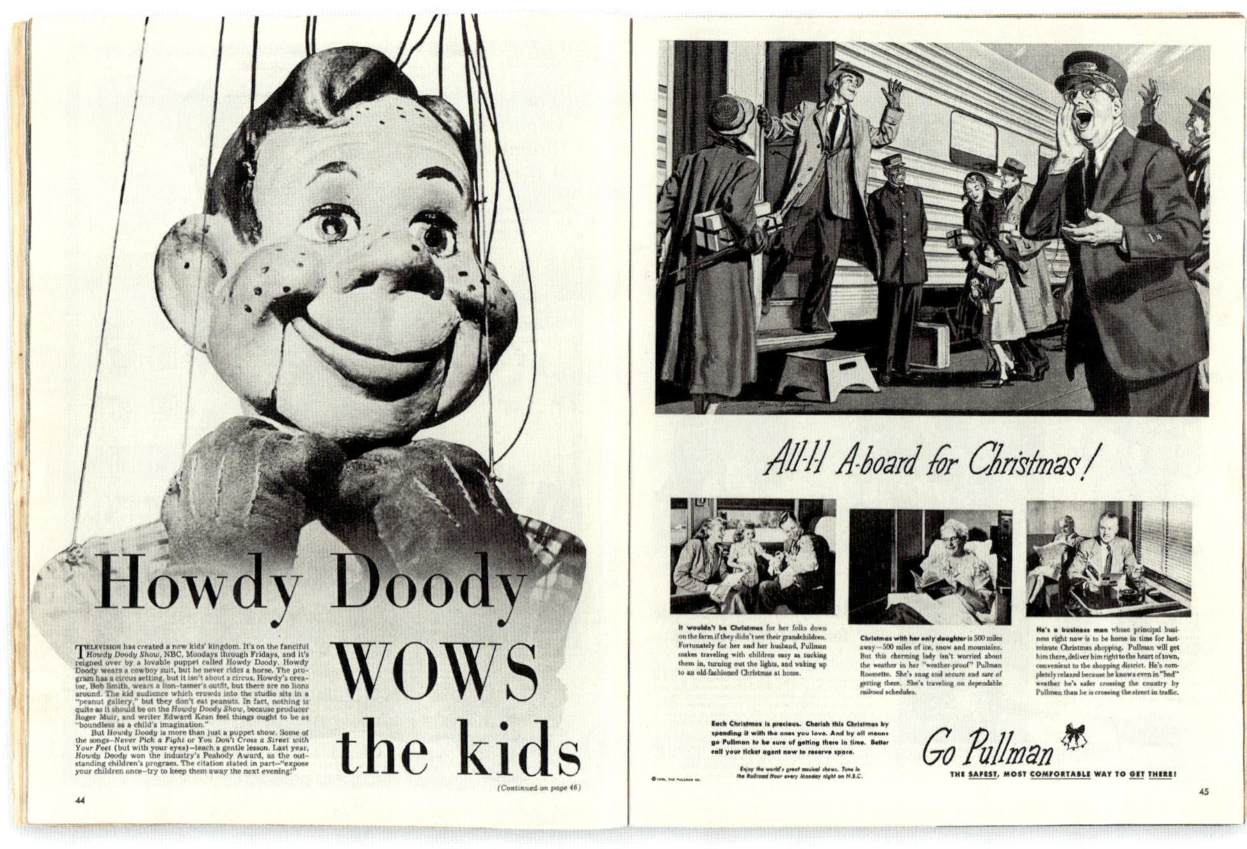

Howdy Doody WOWS the kids

TELEVISION has created a new kids' kingdom. It's on the fanciful *Howdy Doody Show*, NBC, Mondays through Fridays, and it's reigned over by a lovable puppet called Howdy Doody. Howdy Doody wears a cowboy suit, but he never rides a horse. The program has a circus setting, but it isn't about a circus. Howdy's creator, Bob Smith, wears a lion-tamer's outfit, but there are no lions around. The kid audience which crowds into the studio sits in a "peanut gallery," but they don't eat peanuts. In fact, nothing is quite as it should be on the *Howdy Doody Show*, because producer Roger Muir, and writer Edward Kean feel things ought to be as "boundless as a child's imagination."

But *Howdy Doody* is more than just a puppet show. Some of the songs–*Never Pick a Fight* or *You Don't Cross a Street with Your Feet* (but with your eyes)–teach a gentle lesson. Last year, *Howdy Doody* won the industry's Peabody Award, as the outstanding children's program. The citation stated in part–"expose your children once–try to keep them away the next evening!"

(Continued on page 46)

44

45

PUBLISHED AS

HOWDY DOODY WOWS THE KIDS

DATE

DECEMBER 20, 1949

Kubrick's photograph of television puppet Howdy Doody and his "voice," Bob Smith, accompanied by two young fans amid Howdy Doody merchandise—then valued at $10 million—stressed not only the rising viewership of the new medium, but also its capacity to influence consumers' buying habits.

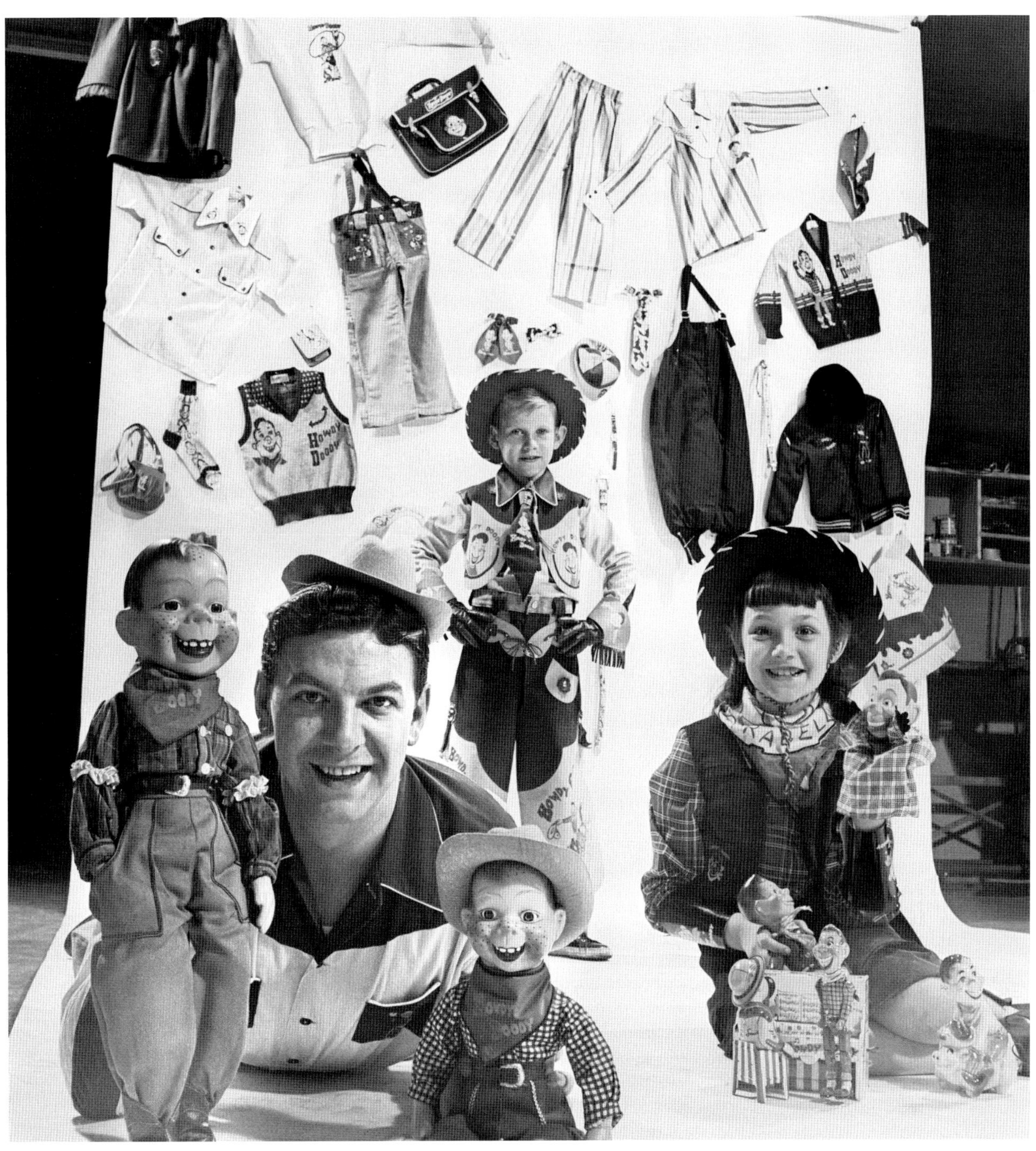

Howdy Doody with his on-screen companion, Bob Smith, posing with two fans amid licensed toys, clothes, and other products

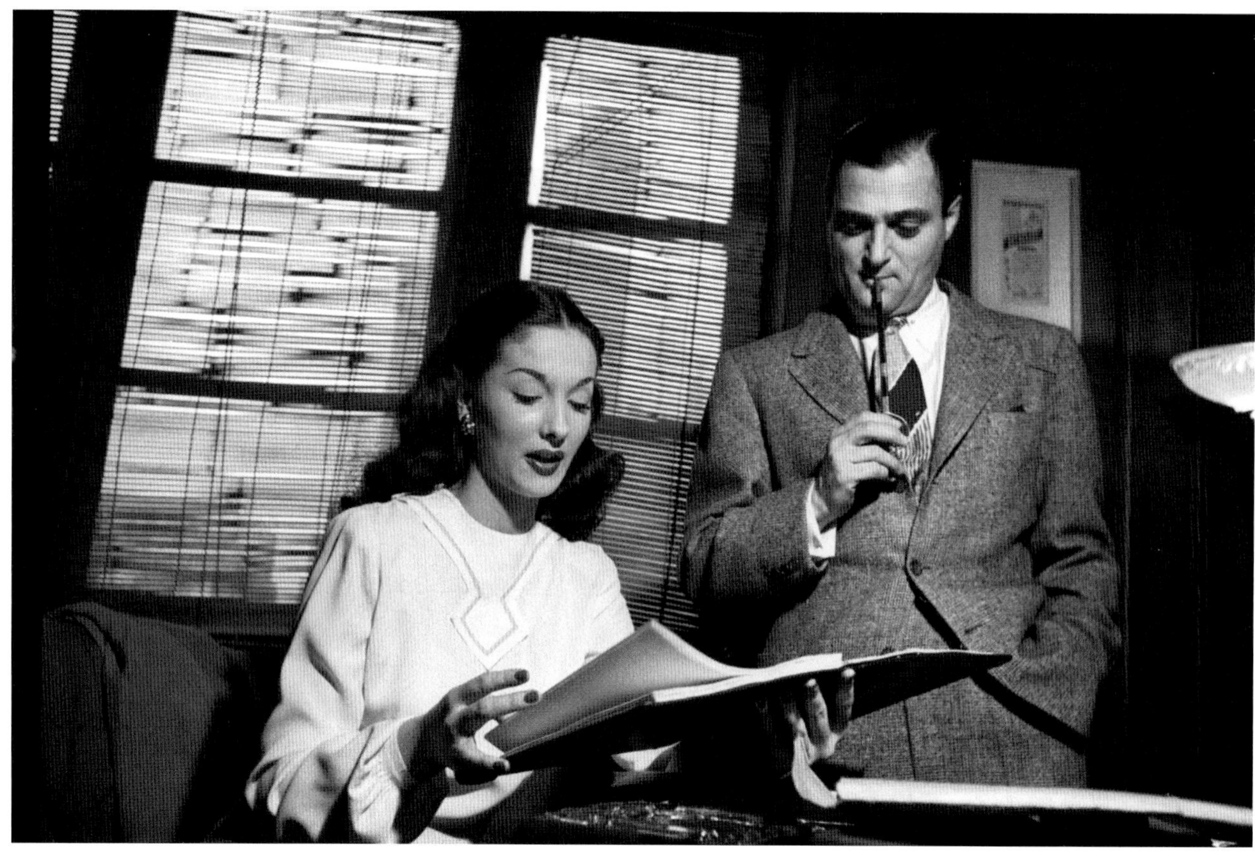

[UNPUBLISHED]

ROSEMARY WILLIAMS—SHOWGIRL

[FILED DATE]

MARCH 1949

One of Kubrick's largest unpublished profiles, numbering approximately 700 images, this portrait of aspiring model and actress Rosemary Williams would likely have been edited into a day-in-the-life piece contrasting her onstage persona and her backstage real life. At the time of the assignment, Williams was performing in the chorus of the Broadway production *As the Girls Go* and preparing for an appearance in producer Michael Todd's upcoming musical revue *Peep Show*. In addition to being one of Kubrick's largest assignments, it was also one of his most visually and technically varied. He photographed Williams indoors and out, in candid and consciously staged poses, using both small- (35 mm) and medium- (2¼ inch) format cameras.

Williams reviewing a script with theater and film producer Mike Todd

OPPOSITE **Williams window-shopping in Manhattan**

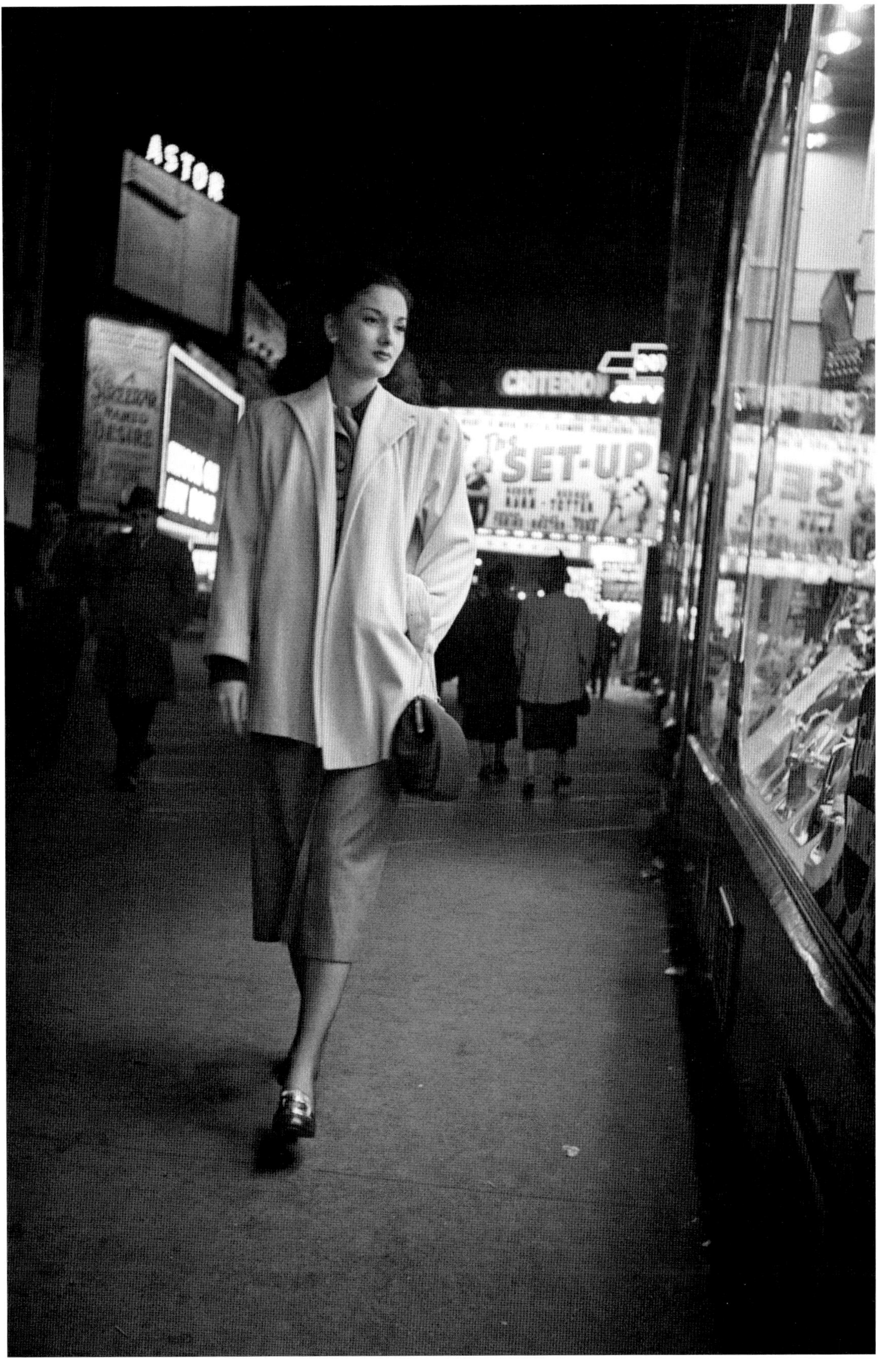
ASTOR
SET-UP

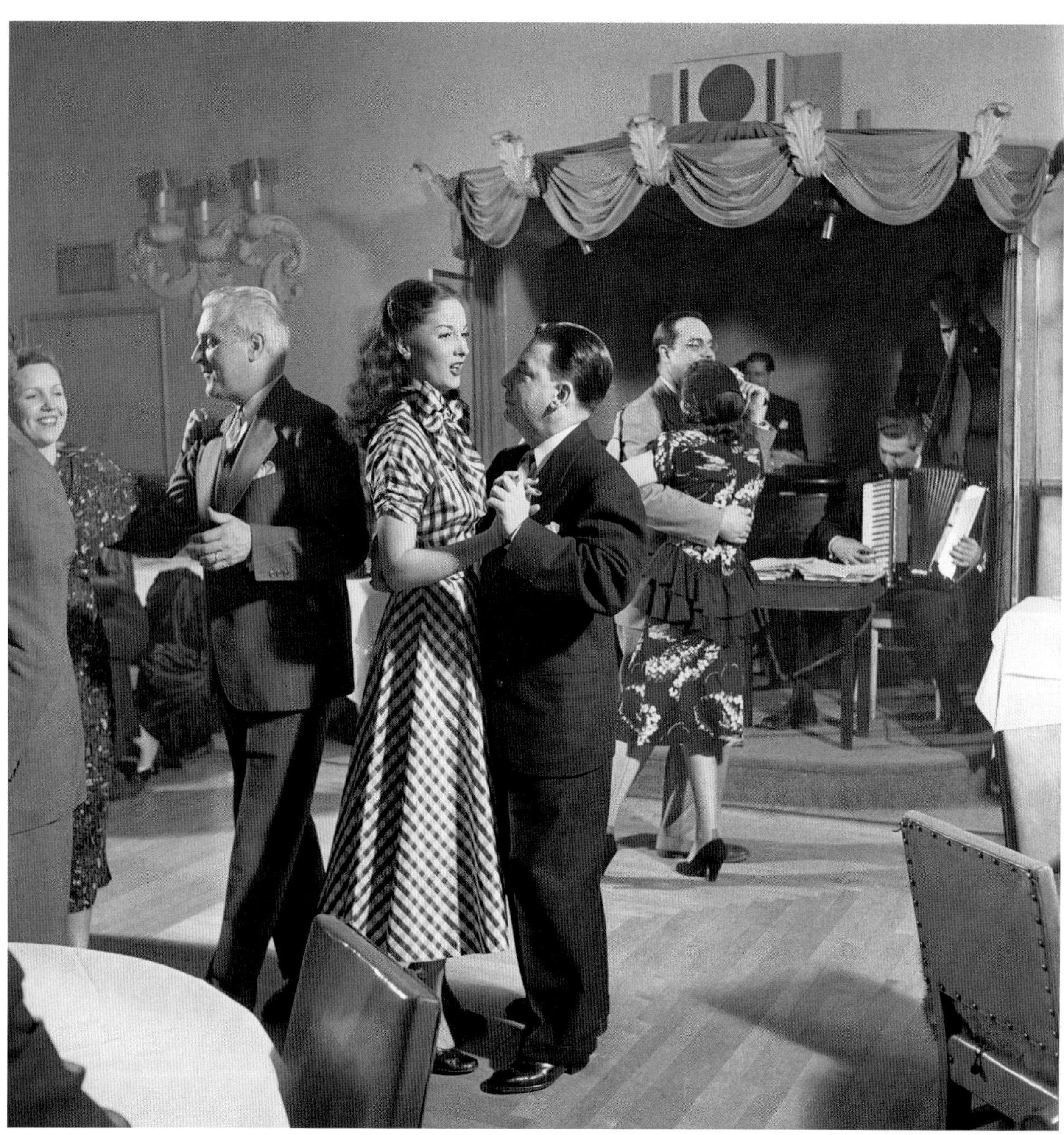

The actress out on the town

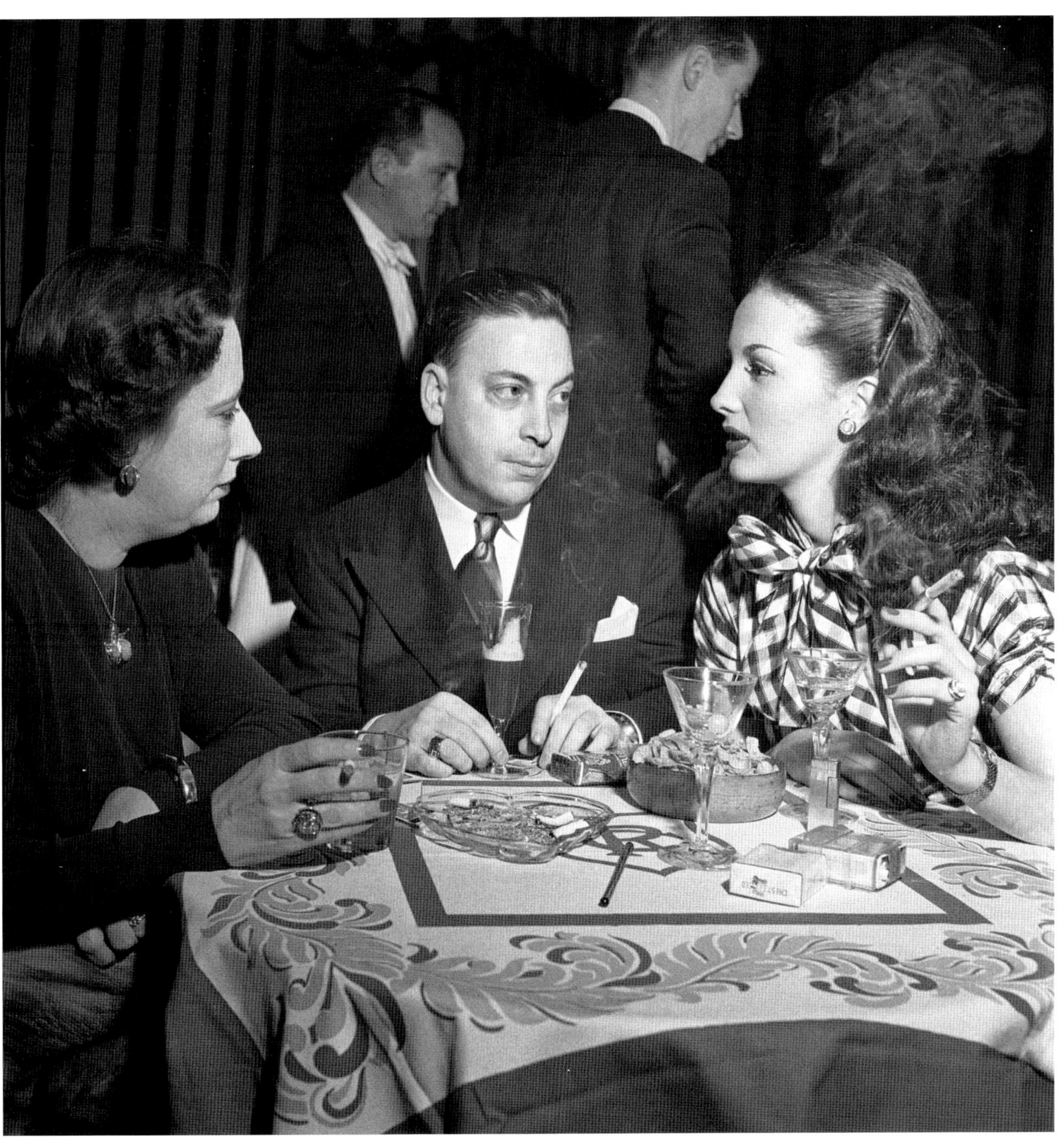

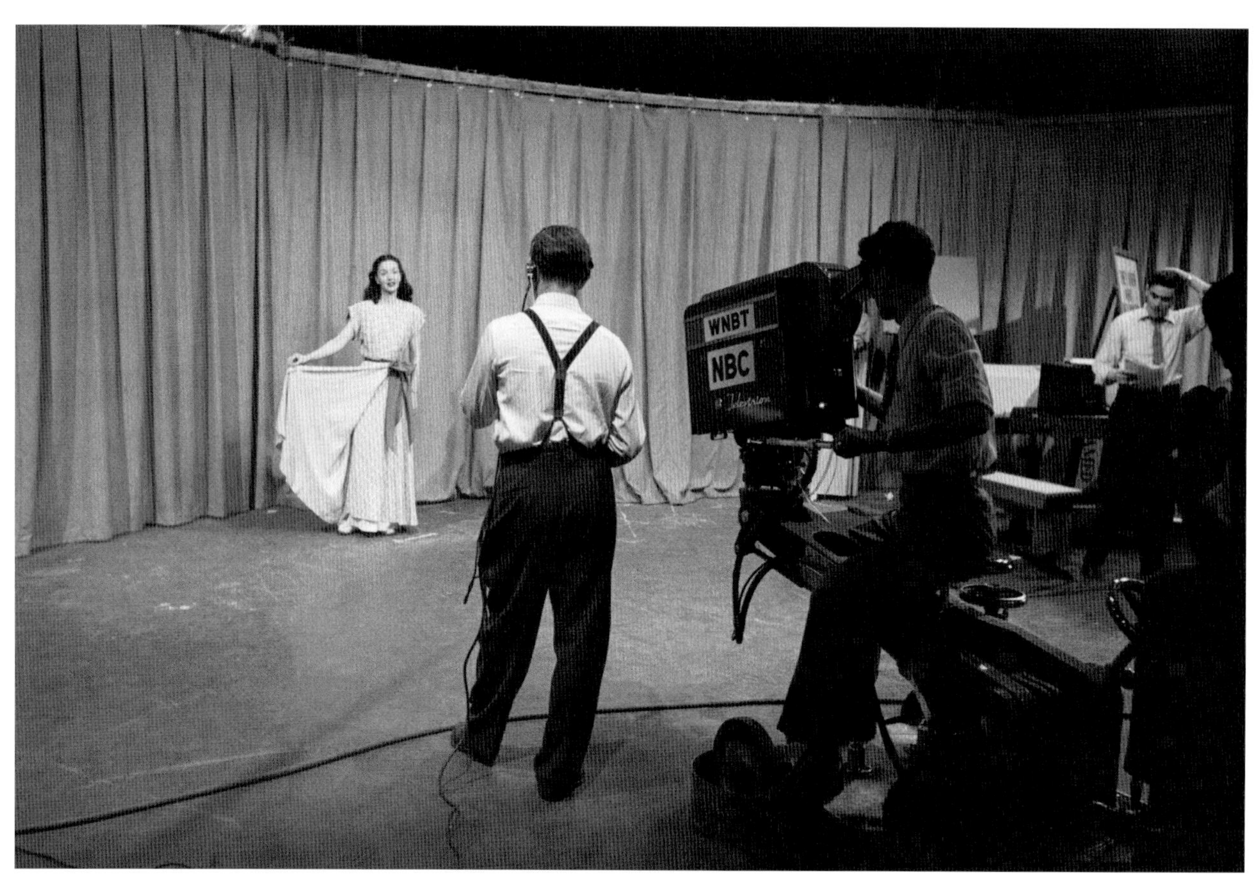

Williams recording a TV show

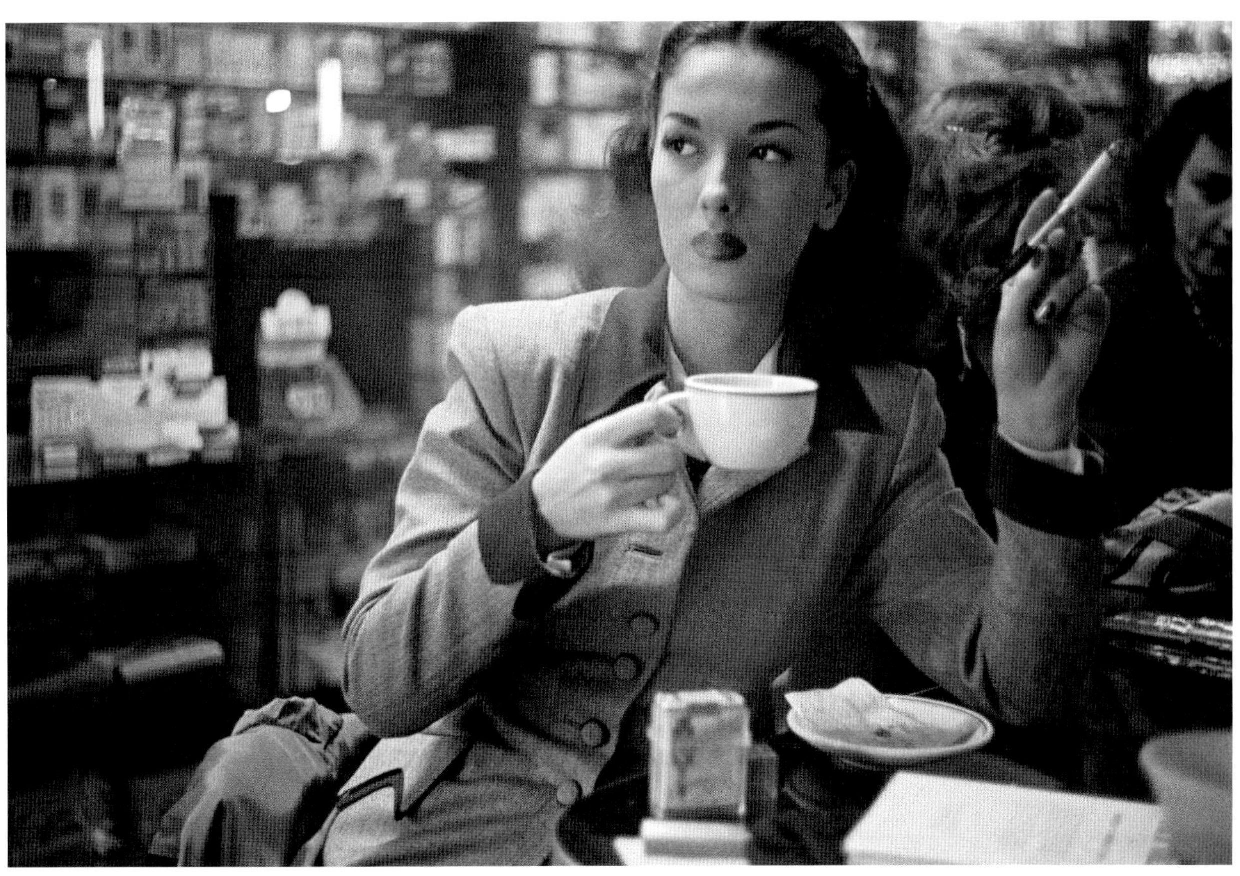

Williams enjoying a coffee break

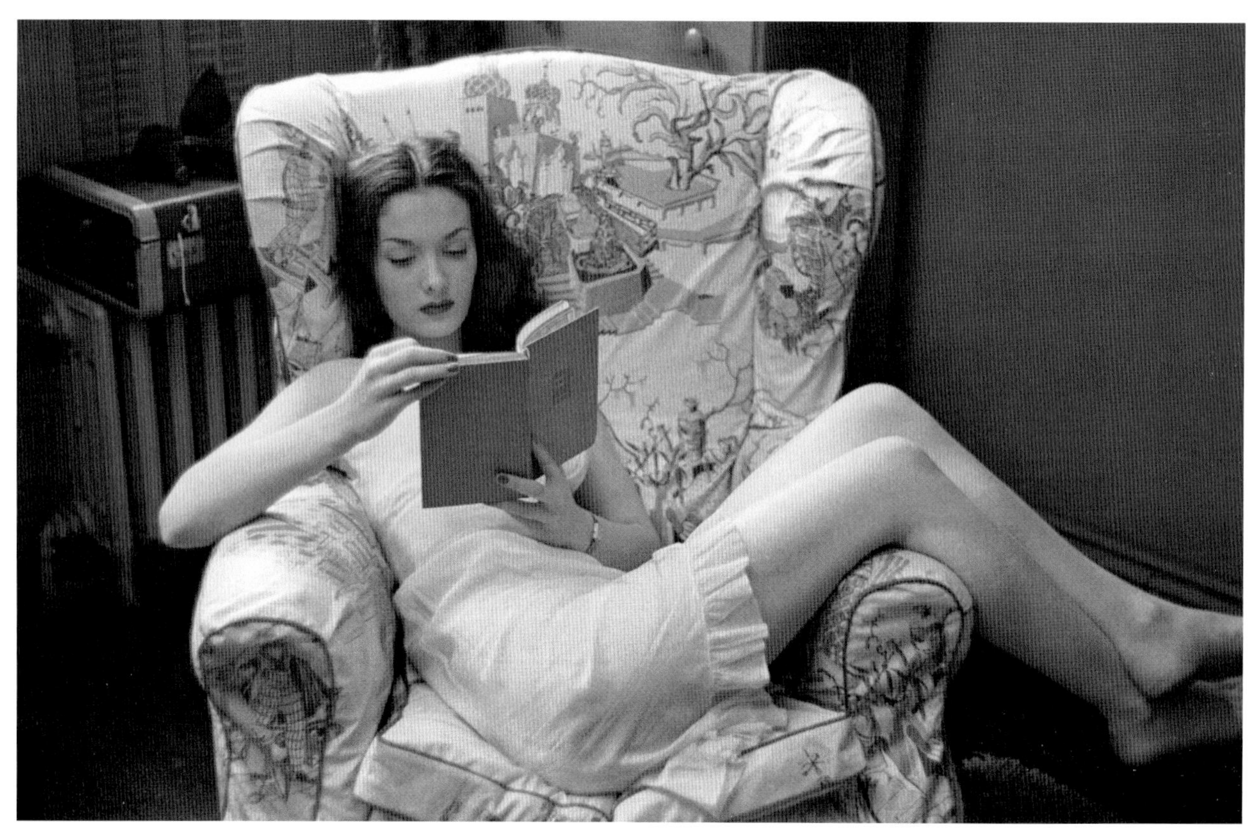

Williams relaxing in her living room

OPPOSITE **Williams making breakfast in her small kitchen**

FOLLOWING SPREAD **Williams being observed by Stanley Kubrick**

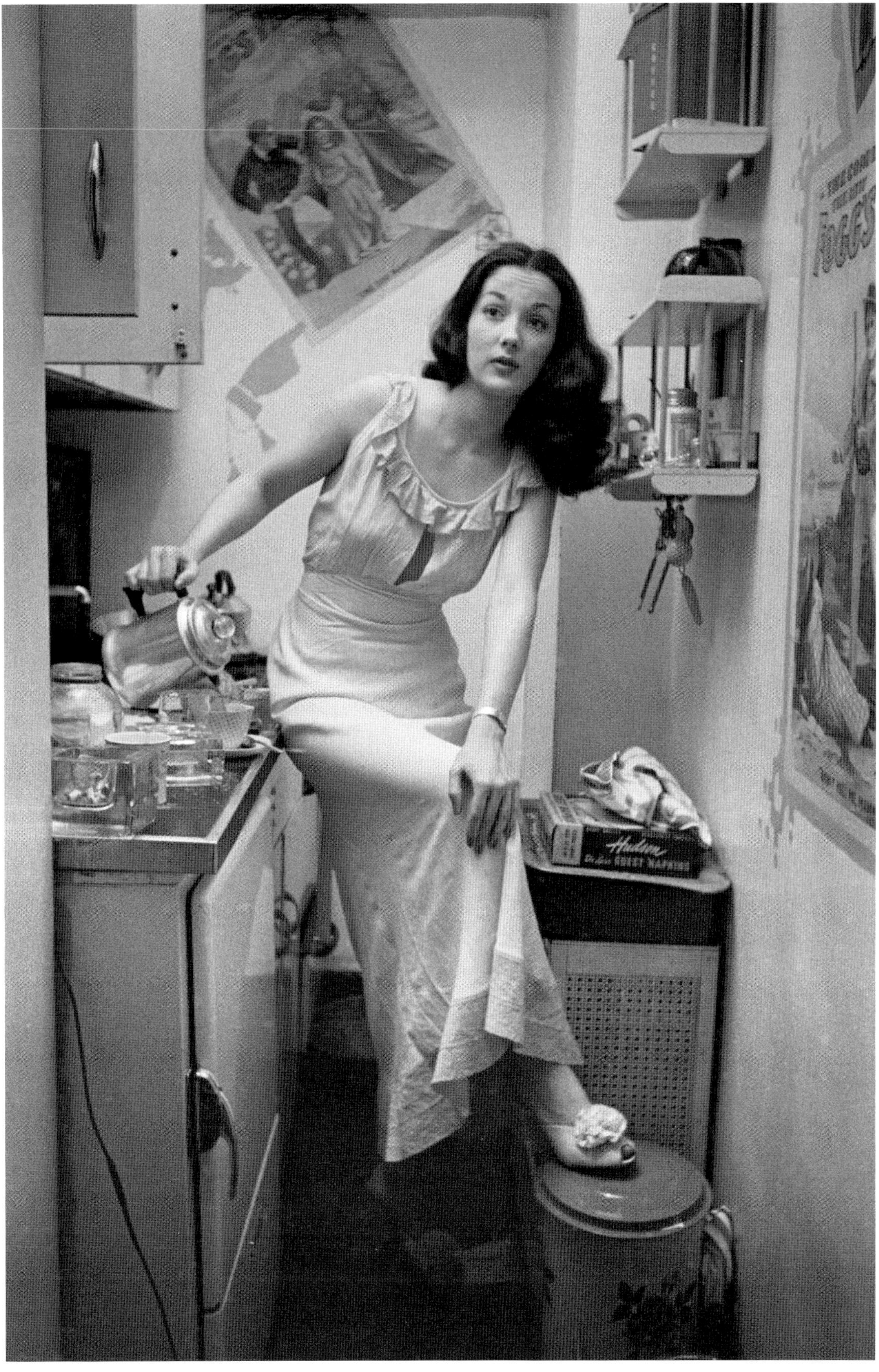
Hudson

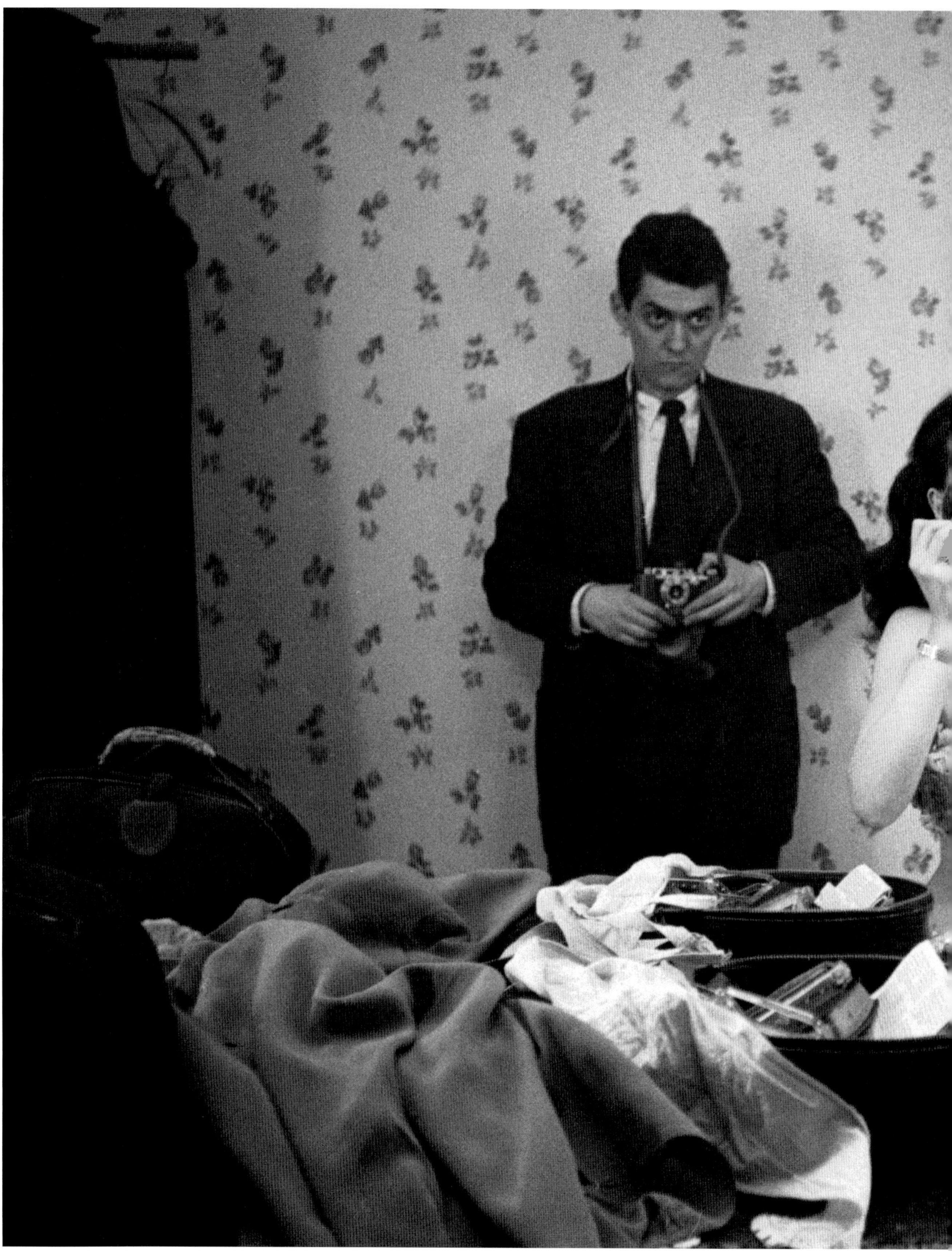

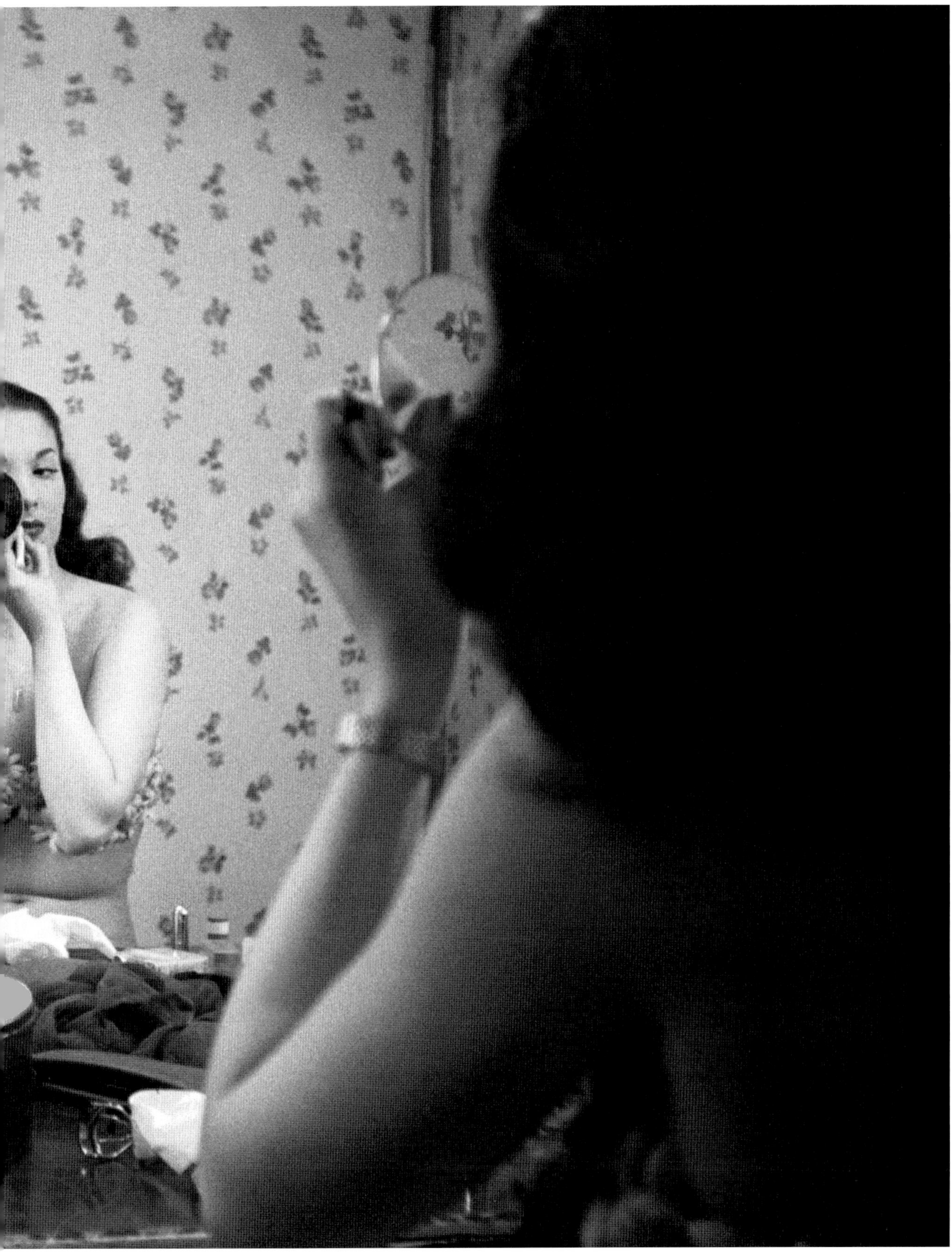

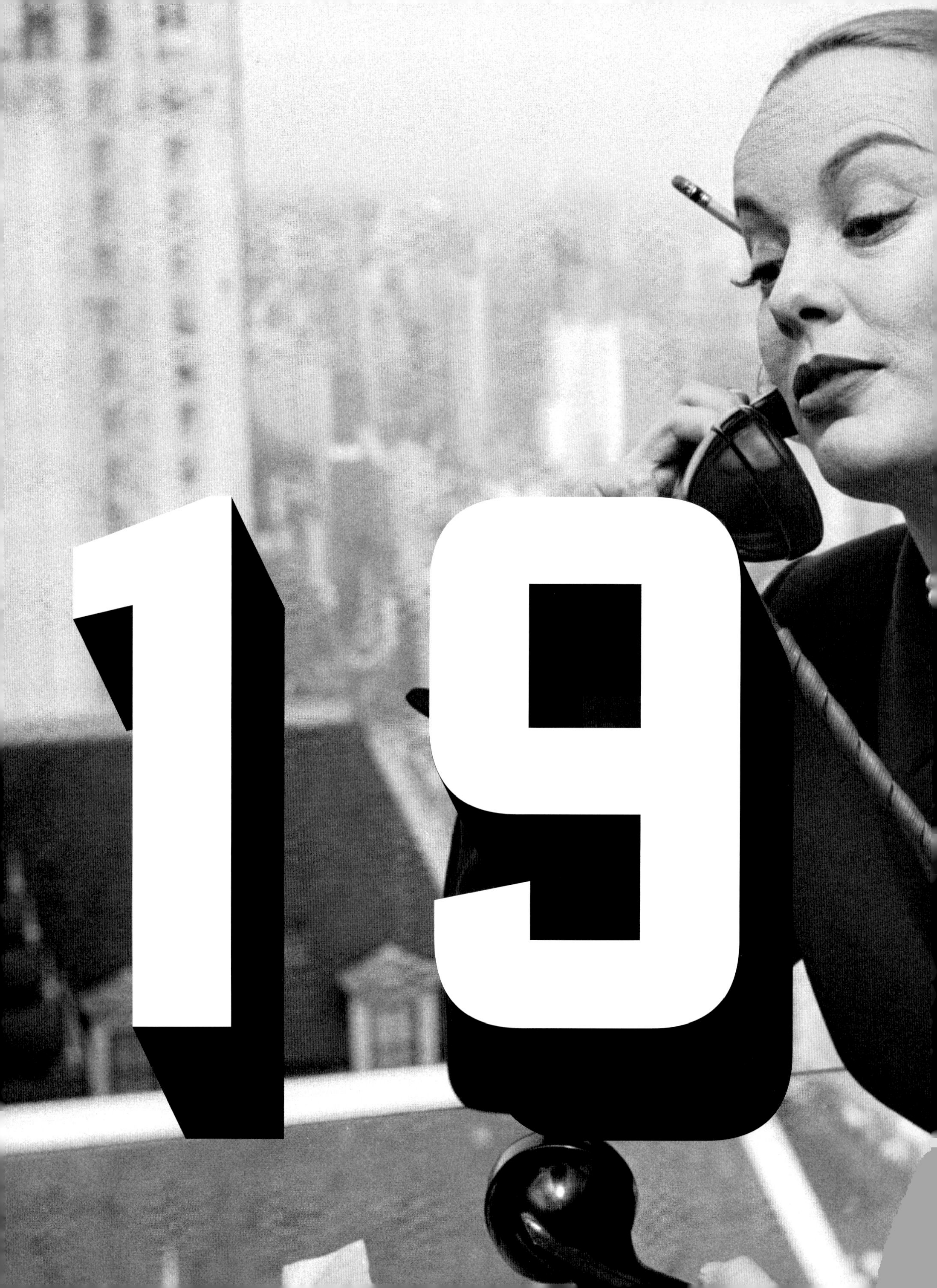
19

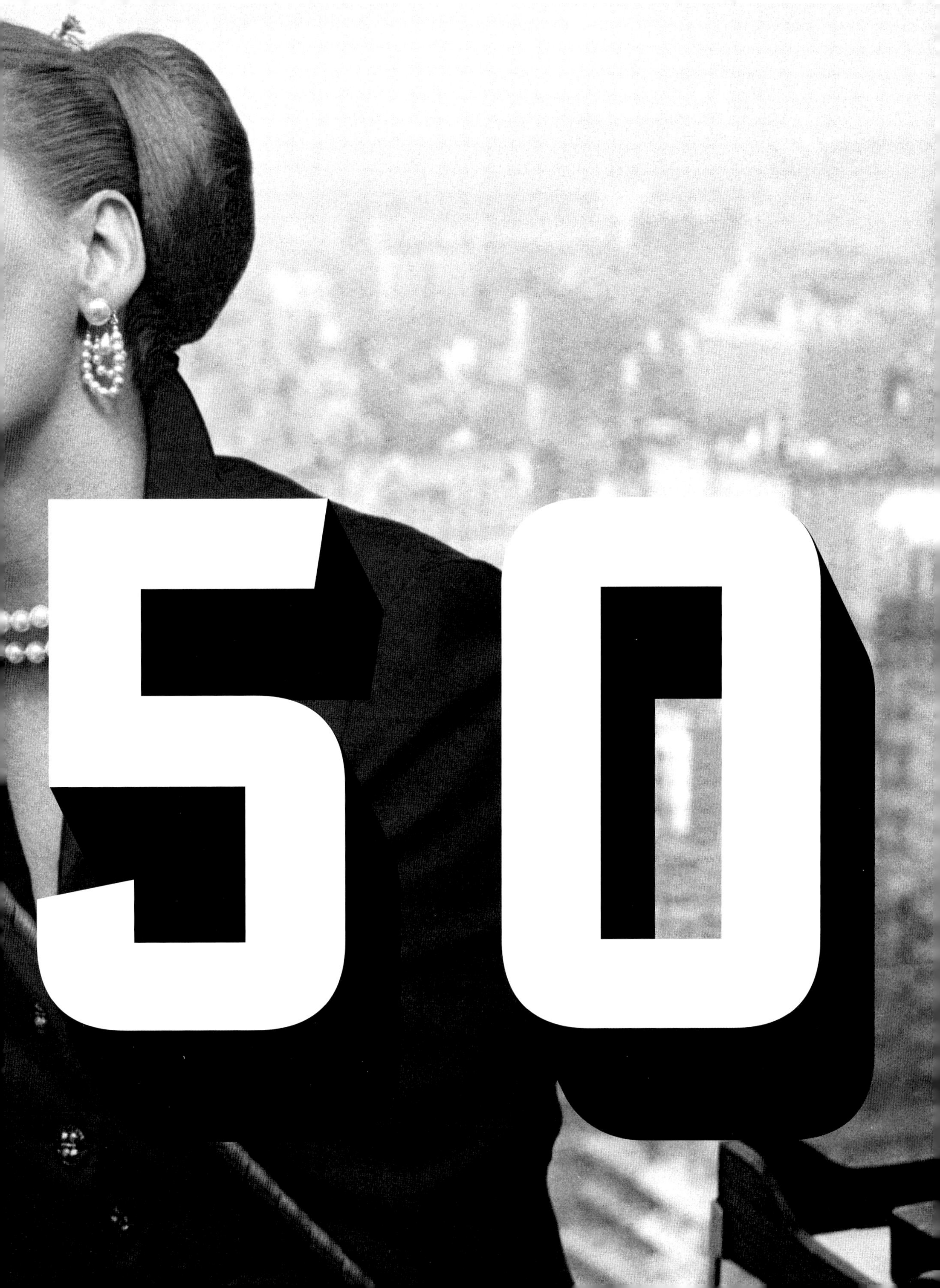
50

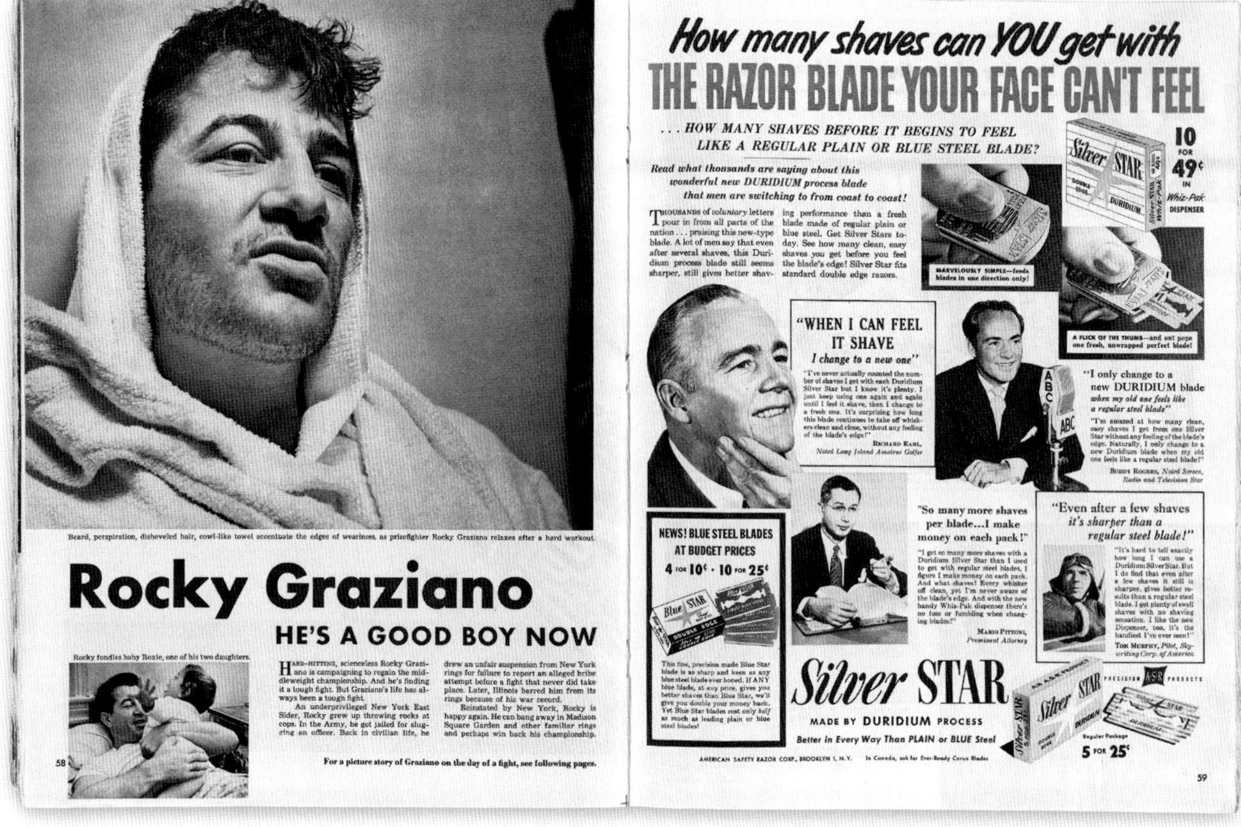

Beard, perspiration, disheveled hair, cowl-like towel accentuate the edges of weariness, as prizefighter Rocky Graziano relaxes after a hard workout.

Rocky Graziano

HE'S A GOOD BOY NOW

Rocky fondles baby Roxie, one of his two daughters.

HARD-HITTING, scienceless Rocky Graziano is campaigning to regain the middleweight championship. And he's finding it a tough fight. But Graziano's life has always been a tough fight.

An underprivileged New York East Sider, Rocky grew up throwing rocks at cops. In the Army, he got jailed for slugging an officer. Back in civilian life, he drew an unfair suspension from New York rings for failure to report an alleged bribe attempt before a fight that never did take place. Later, Illinois barred him from its rings because of his war record.

Reinstated by New York, Rocky is happy again. He can bang away in Madison Square Garden and other familiar rings and perhaps win back his championship.

58

For a picture story of Graziano on the day of a fight, see following pages.

PUBLISHED AS

ROCKY GRAZIANO: HE'S A GOOD BOY NOW

DATE

FEBRUARY 14, 1950

Although photographed in a similar style to Kubrick's earlier profile of Walter Cartier in "Prizefighter" (published January 18, 1949), this piece focused on Rocky Graziano's redemption from his troubled past. Here Graziano was presented as a both a professional businessman and a happy family man. Kubrick's photographs captured the boxer at home, with his manager, and at the gym preparing for a fight to regain his middleweight championship. The essay ended with an image of Graziano in the ring lunging towards his opponent.

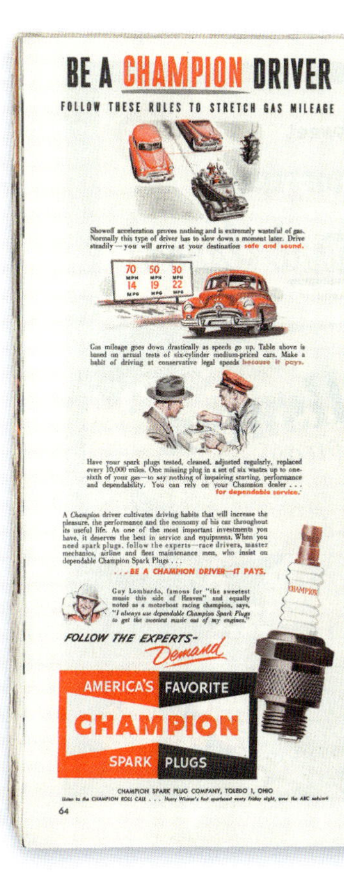

Rocky Graziano continued

Still ring rusty, Rocky gets off to a slow start against Horne

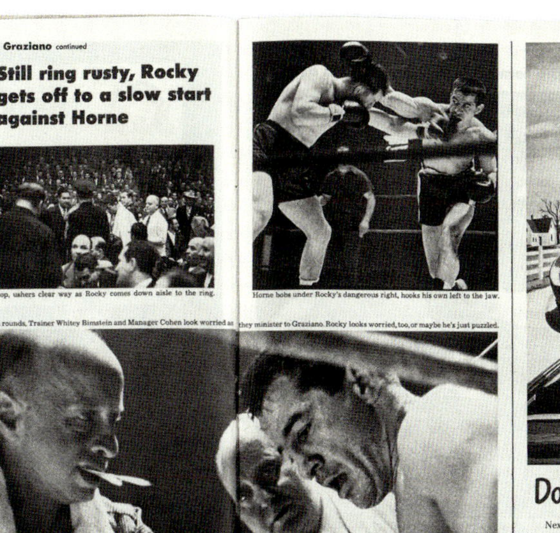

Cop, ushers clear way as Rocky comes down aisle to the ring.

Horne bobs under Rocky's dangerous right, hooks his own left to the jaw.

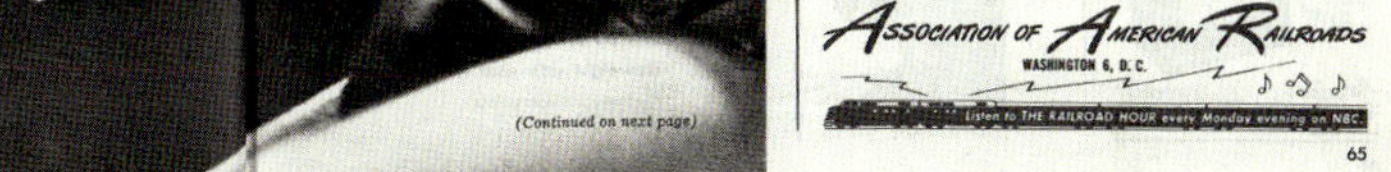

Between rounds, Trainer Whitey Bimstein and Manager Cohen look worried as they minister to Graziano. Rocky looks worried, too, or maybe he's just puzzled.

(Continued on next page)

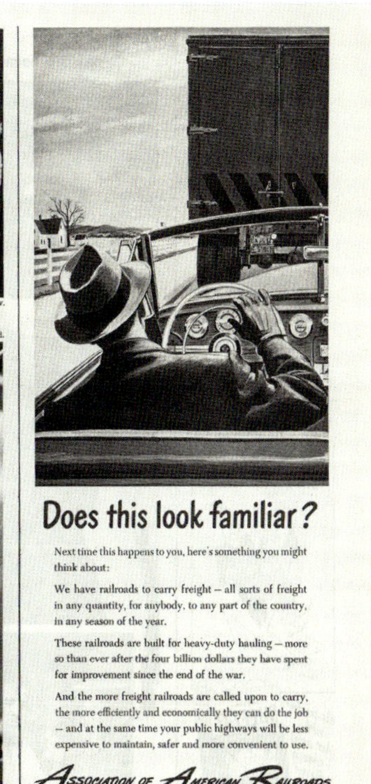

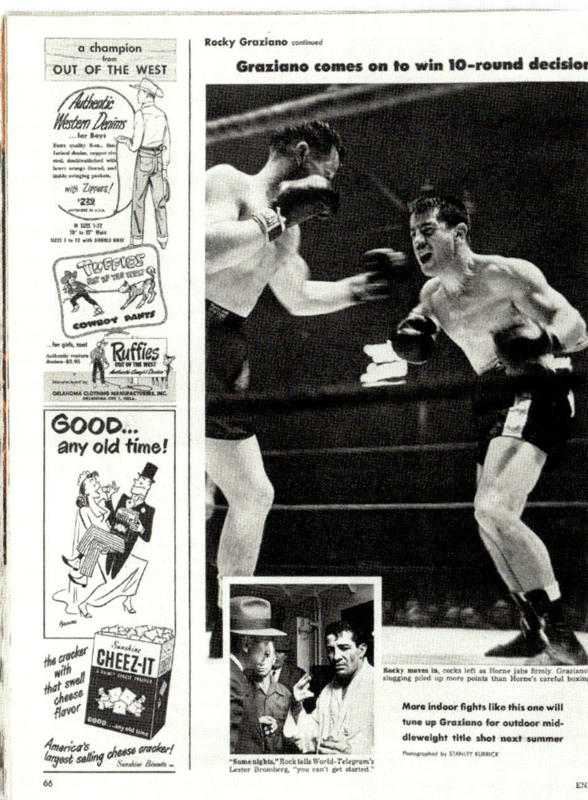

Rocky Graziano continued

Graziano comes on to win 10-round decision

Rocky moves in, cocks left as Horne jabs firmly. Graziano's slugging piled up more points than Horne's careful boxing.

"Somenights," Rock tells *World-Telegram's* Lester Bromberg, "you can't get started."

More indoor fights like this one will tune up Graziano for outdoor middleweight title shot next summer

Photographed by STANLEY KUBRICK

66

END

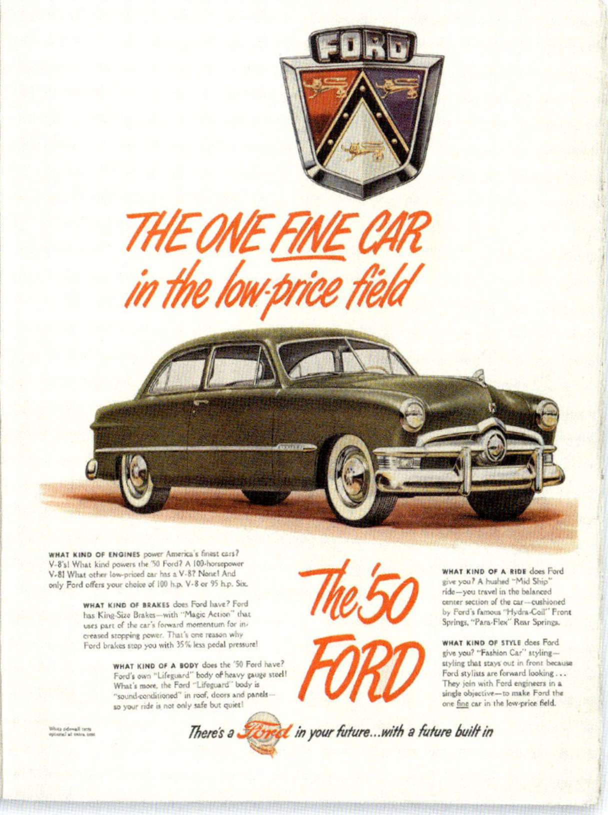

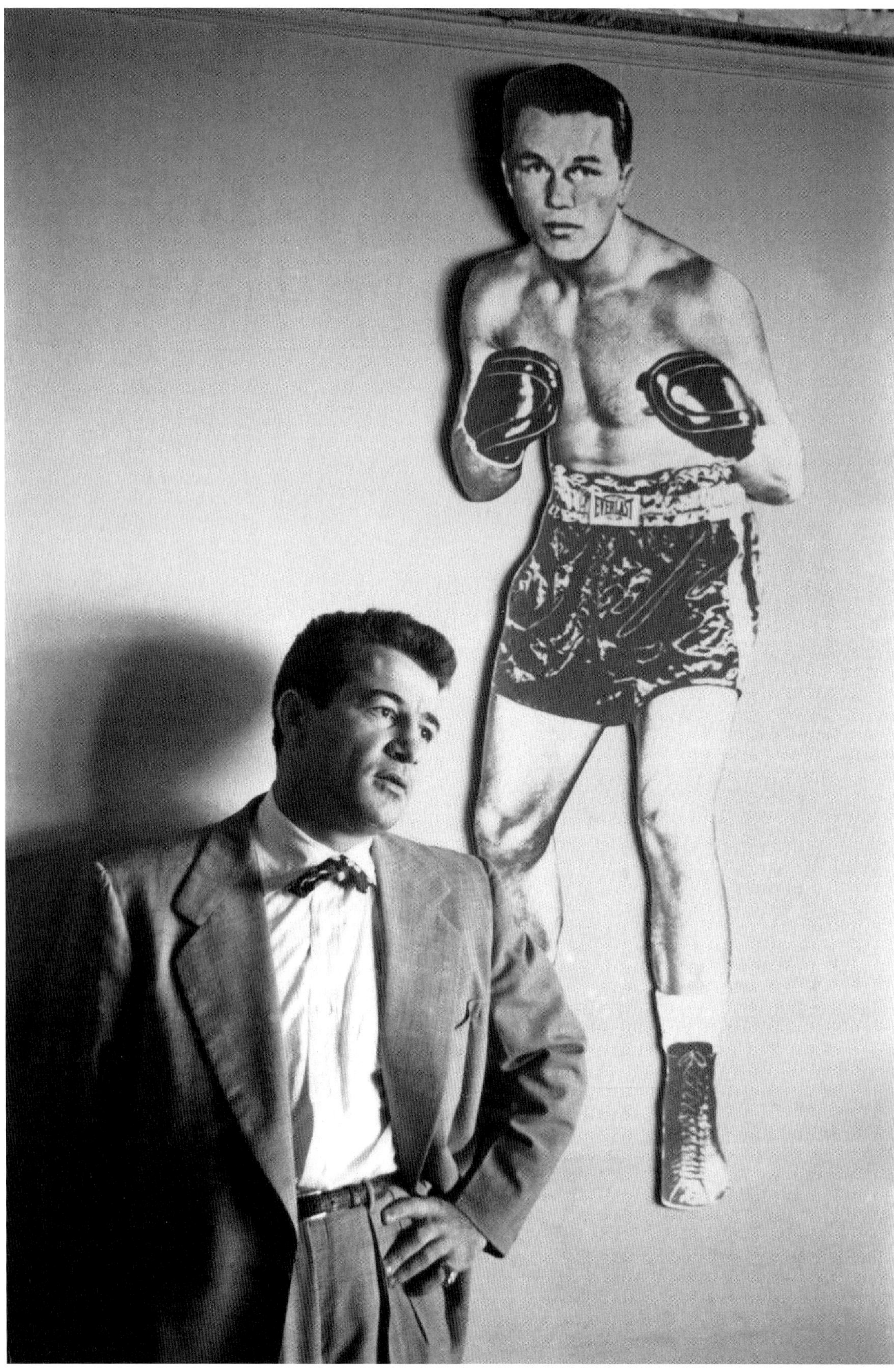
EVERLAST

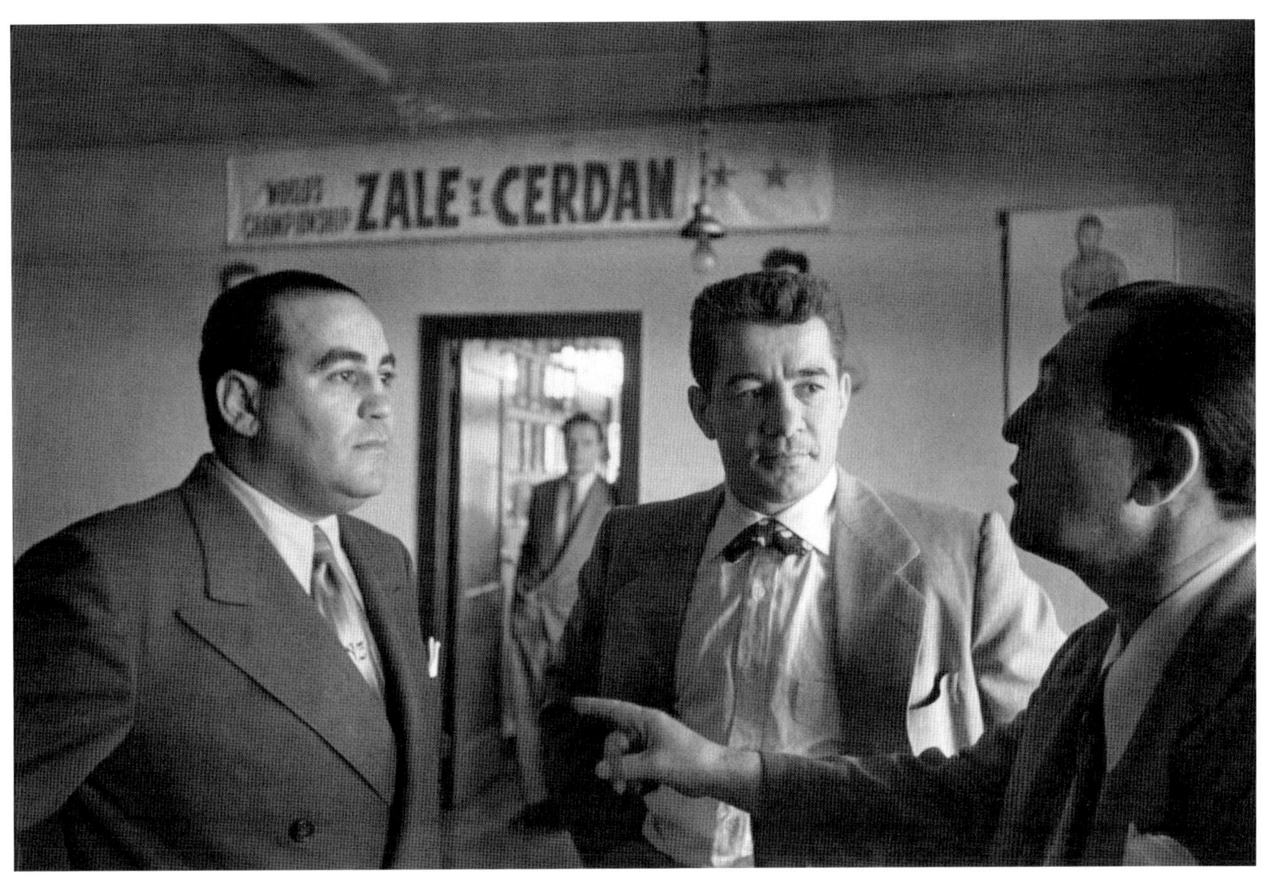

OPPOSITE **Graziano in front of a cardboard cutout of boxer Tony Zale**

ABOVE **Graziano doing business at a gym**

FOLLOWING SPREAD **Graziano having breakfast with his family**

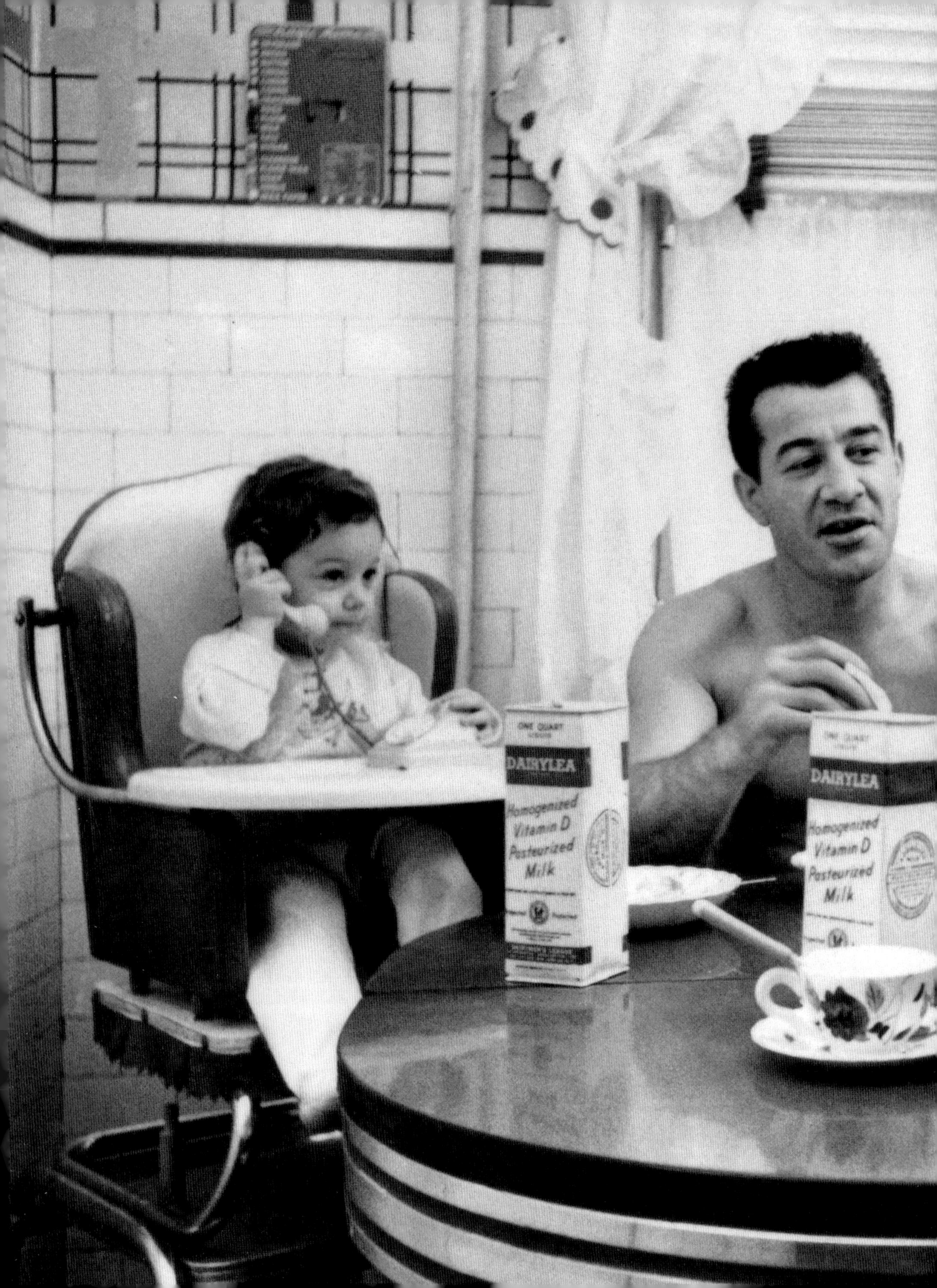
ONE QUART
DAIRYLEA
Homogenized
Vitamin D
Pasteurized
Milk
ONE QUART
DAIRYLEA
Homogenized
Vitamin D
Pasteurized
Milk

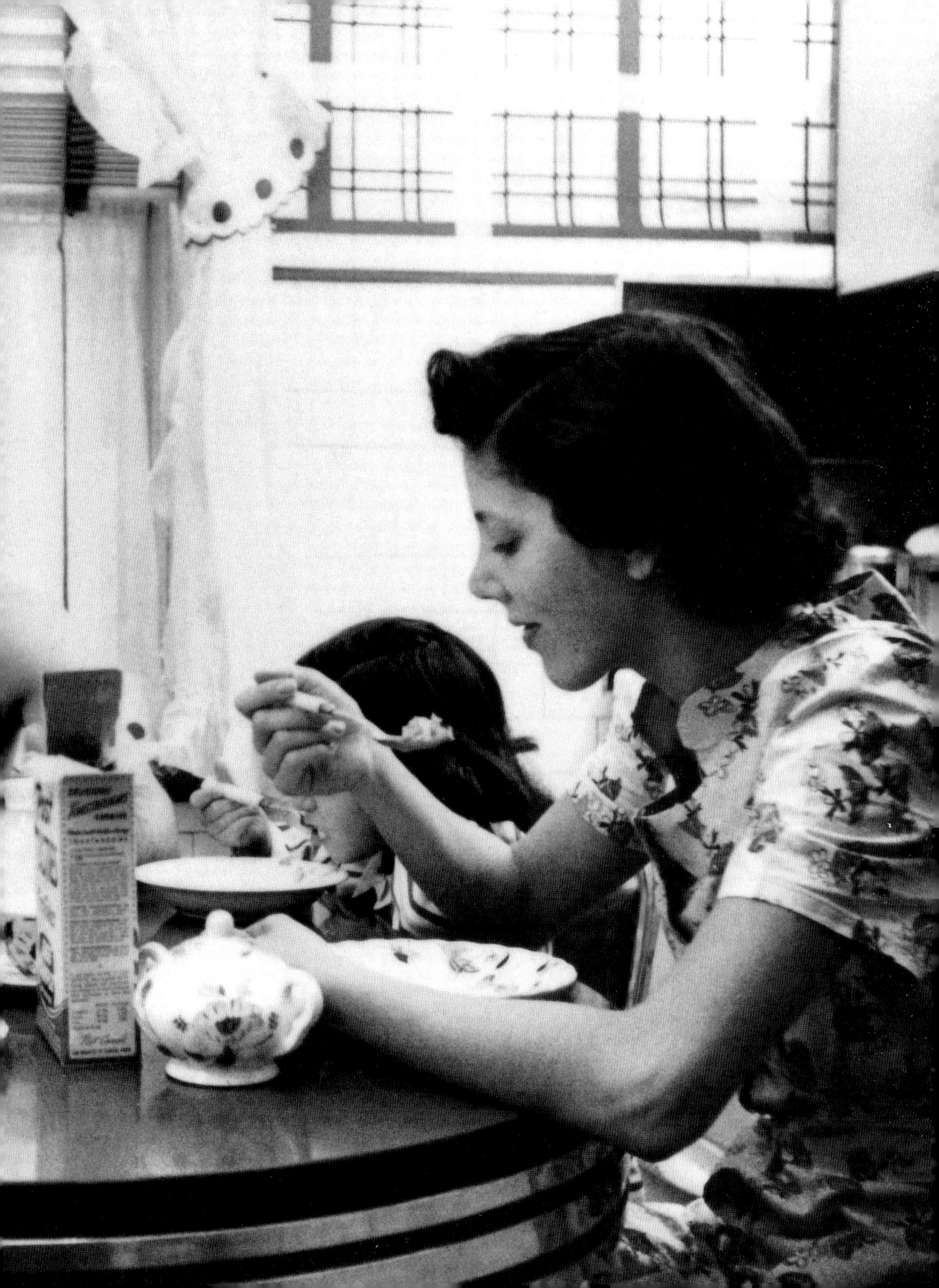

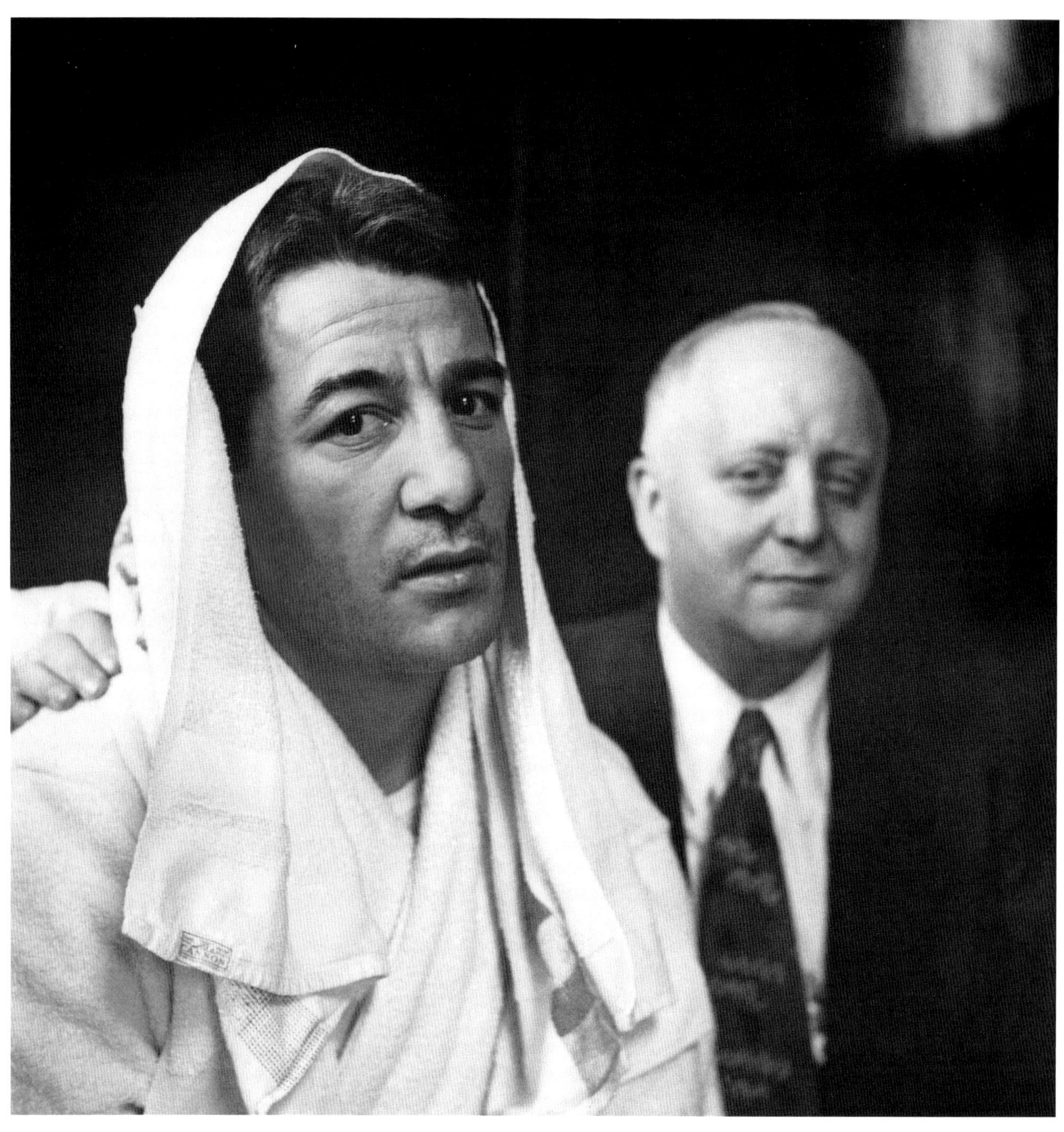

Graziano with his manager, Irving Cohen,
before the big fight (left) and relaxing (right)

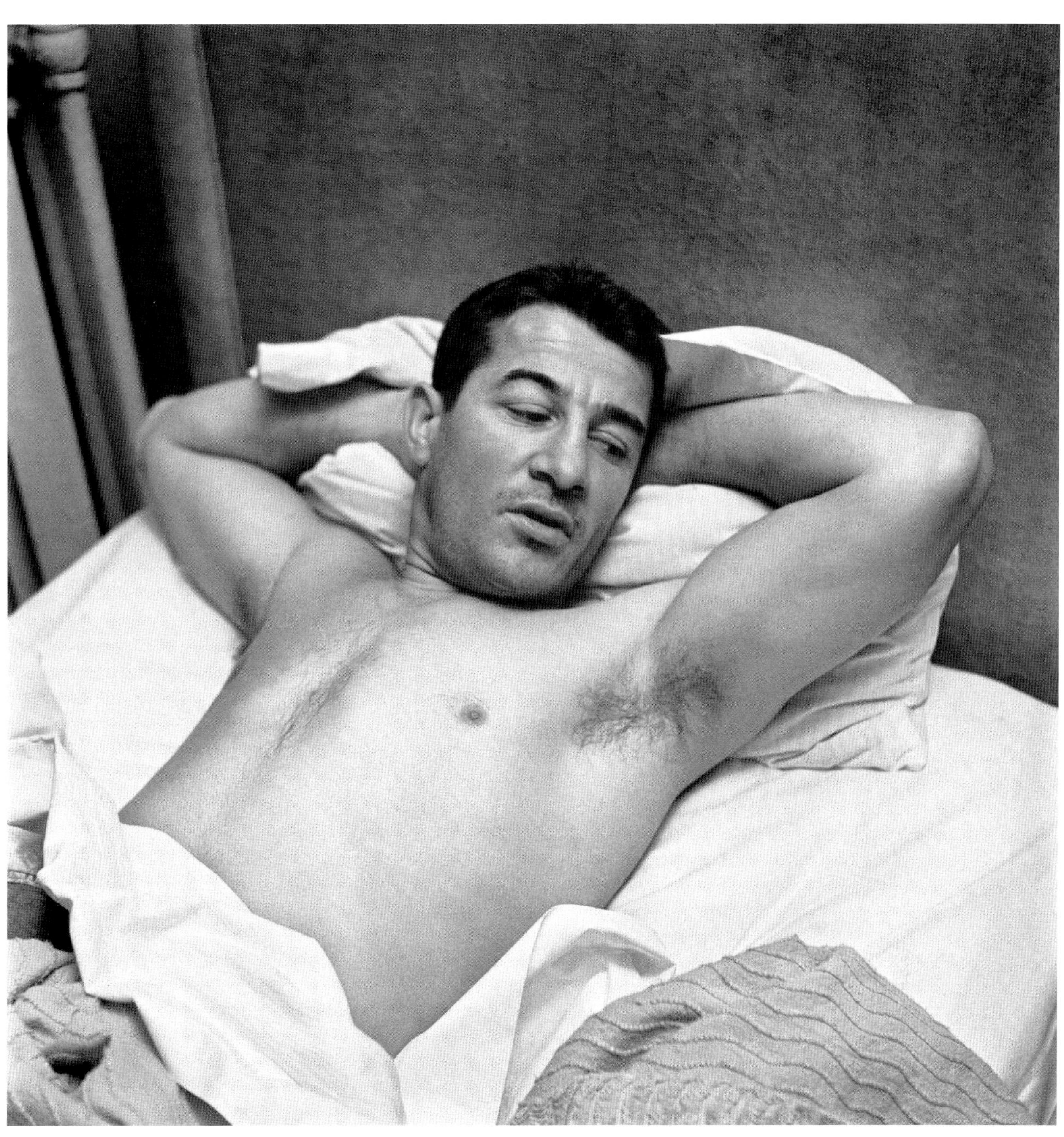

FOLLOWING SPREAD **Graziano going through his paces before the fight**

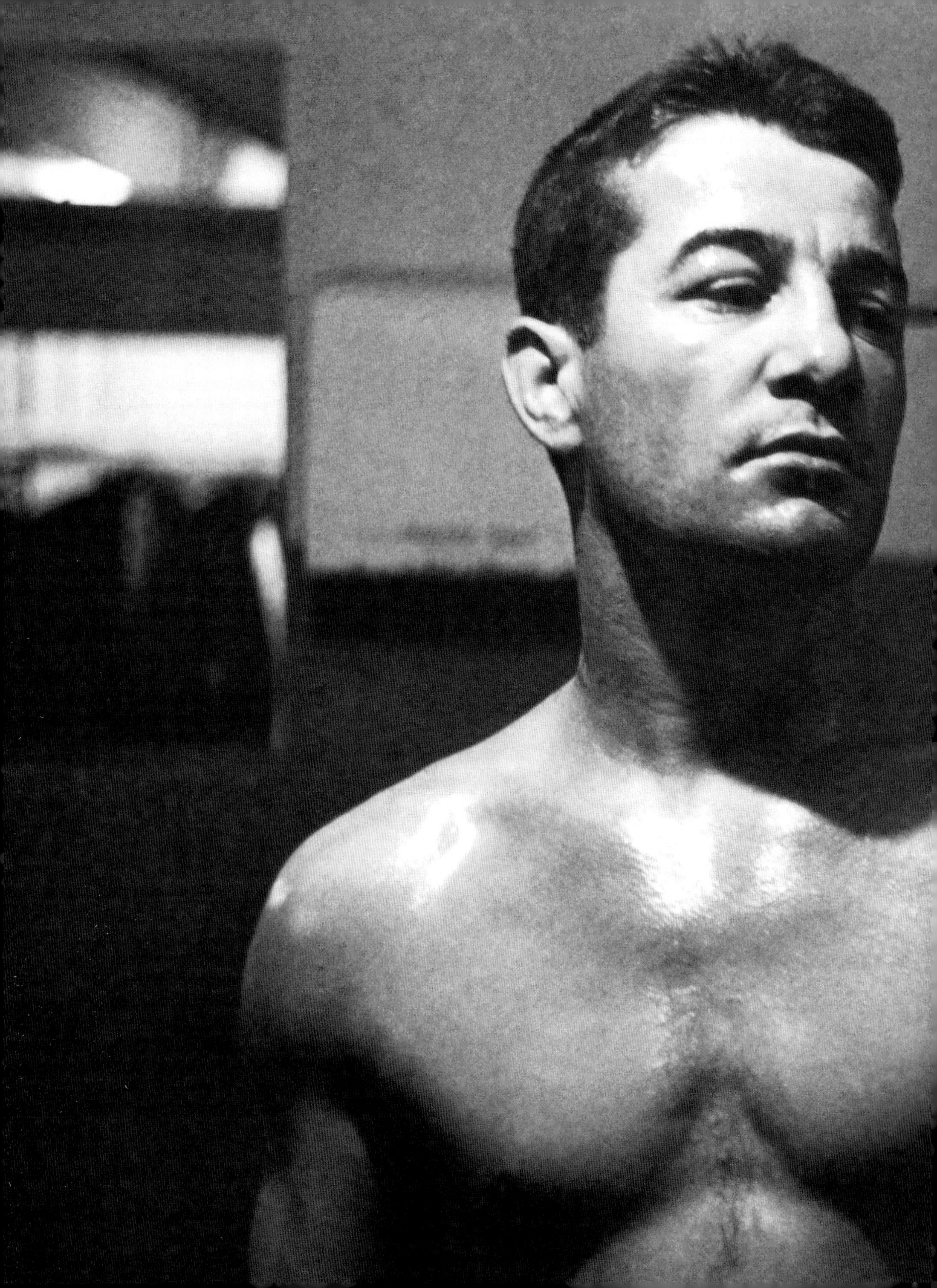

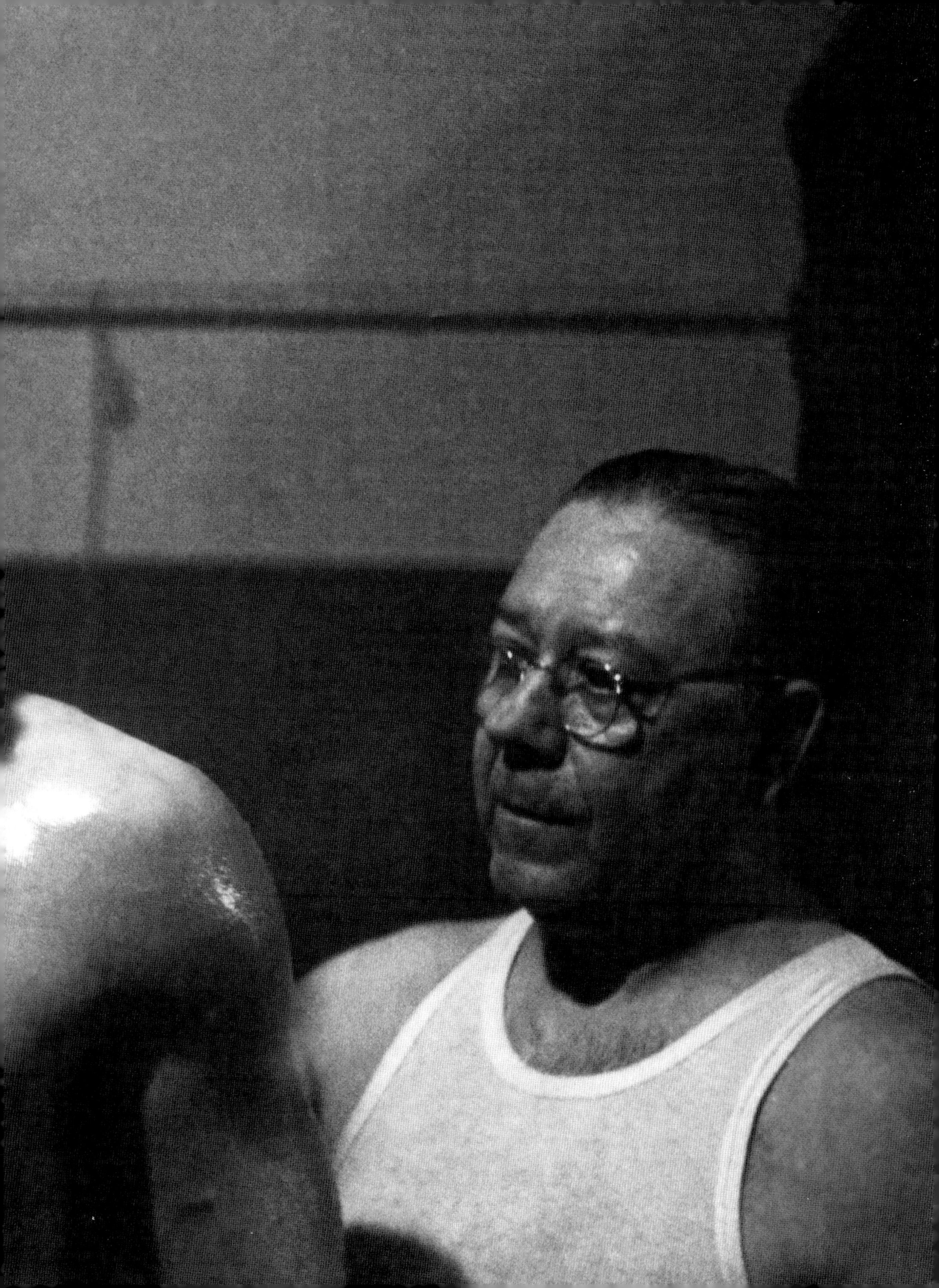

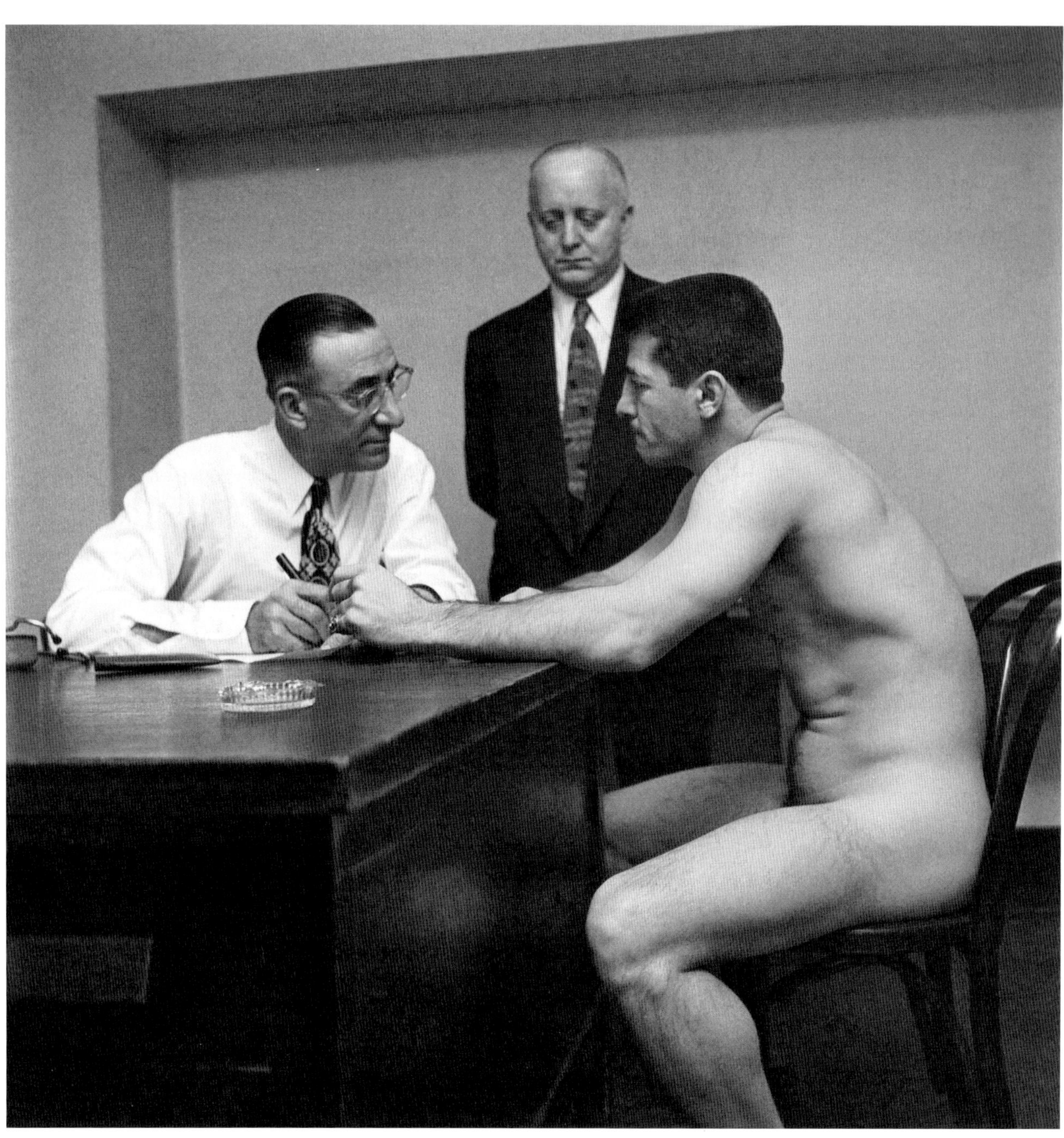

Graziano, his manager, and a doctor

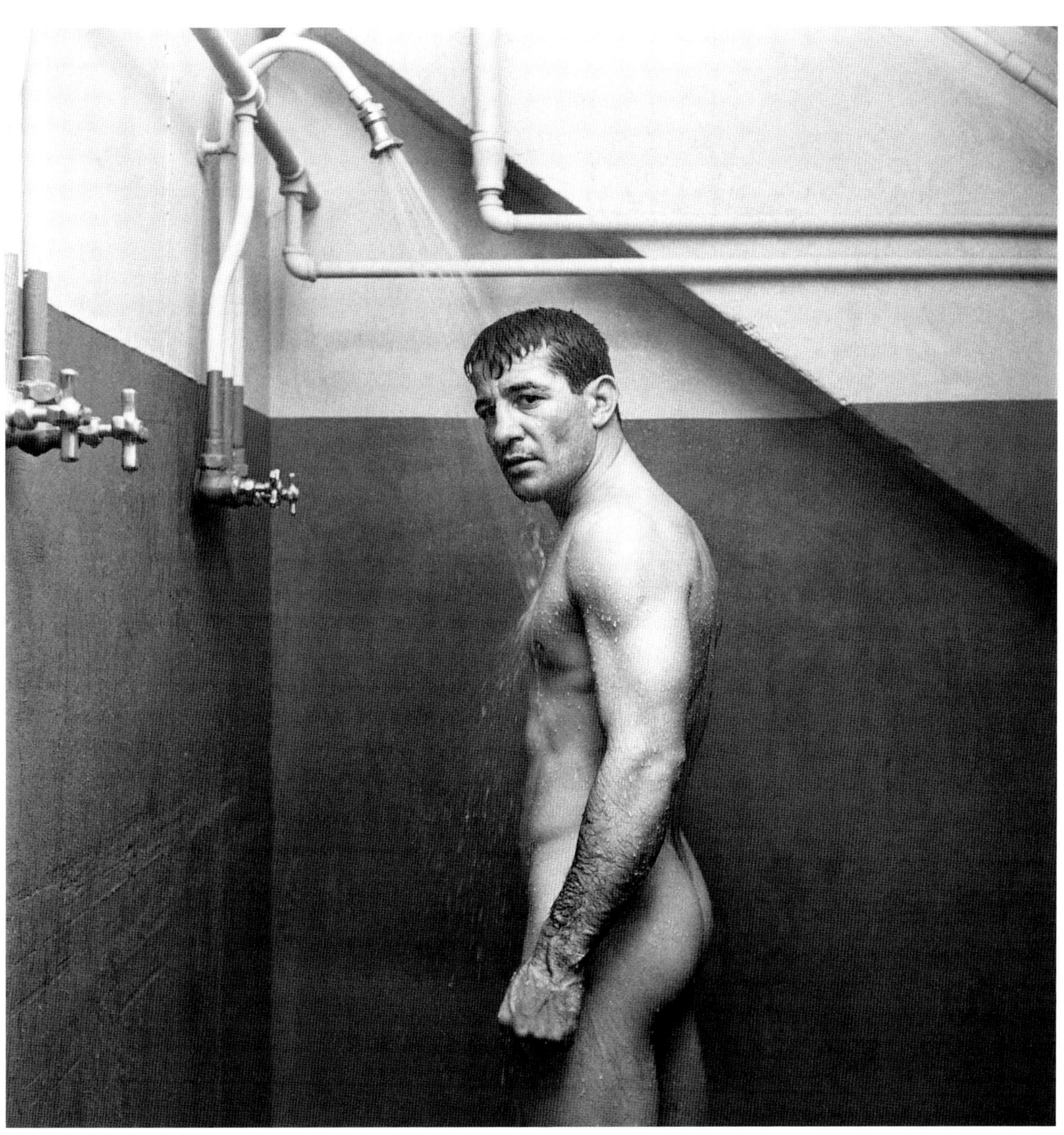

Graziano in the shower

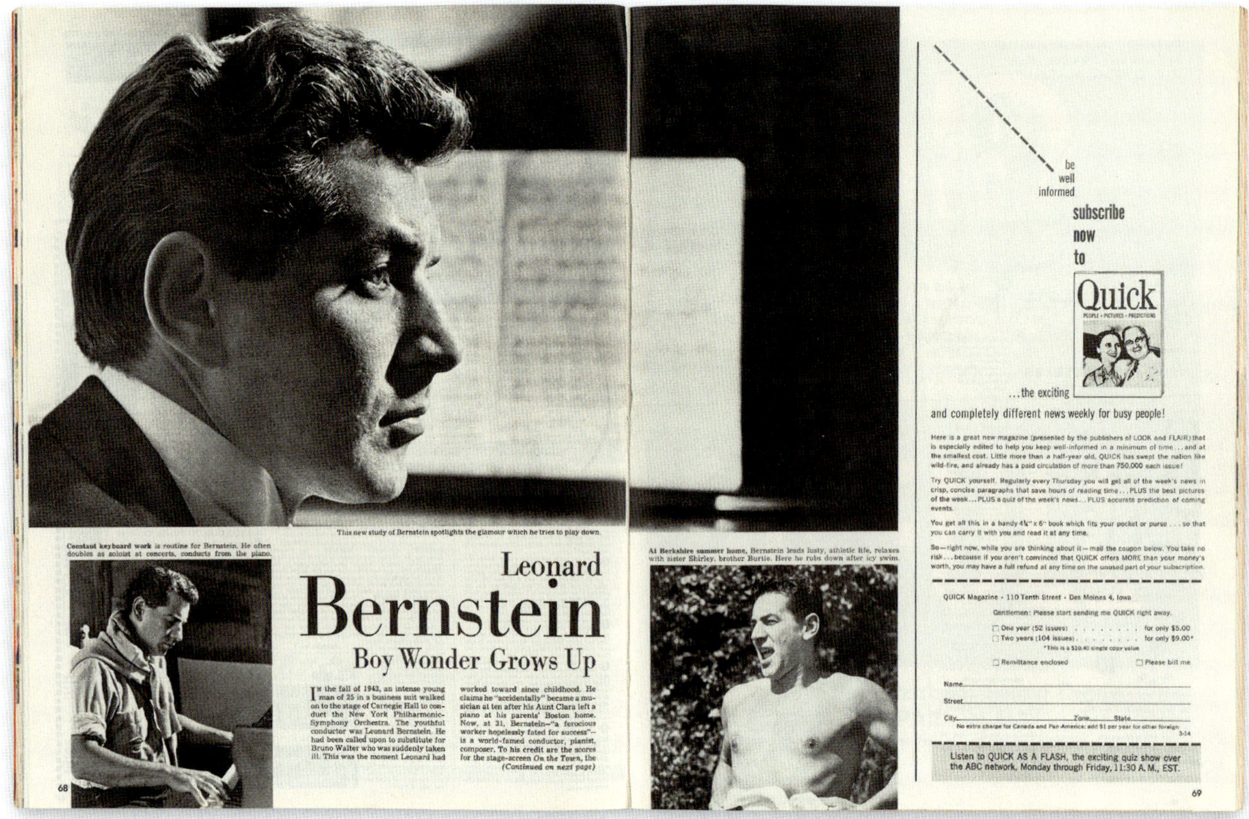

This new study of Bernstein spotlights the glamour which he tries to play down.

Constant keyboard work is routine for Bernstein. He often doubles as soloist at concerts, conducts from the piano.

Leonard

Bernstein

Boy Wonder Grows Up

In the fall of 1943, an intense young man of 25 in a business suit walked on to the stage of Carnegie Hall to conduct the New York Philharmonic-Symphony Orchestra. The youthful conductor was Leonard Bernstein. He had been called upon to substitute for Bruno Walter who was suddenly taken ill. This was the moment Leonard had worked toward since childhood. He claims he "accidentally" became a musician at ten after his Aunt Clara left a piano at his parents' Boston home. Now, at 31, Bernstein—"a ferocious worker hopelessly fated for success"—is a world-famed conductor, pianist, composer. To his credit are the scores for the stage-screen *On the Town*, the

(Continued on next page)

68

At Berkshire summer home, Bernstein leads lusty, athletic life, relaxes with sister Shirley, brother Burtie. Here he rubs down after icy swim.

69

PUBLISHED AS

LEONARD BERNSTEIN

DATE

MARCH 14, 1950

This article updated *Look*'s readers on the prolific career of conductor and composer Leonard Bernstein since he had made his sensational debut in 1943, at 25 years old, as a last-minute stand-in conductor for the New York Philharmonic Symphony Orchestra. Since then, in addition to composing the scores for the ballet *Fancy Free* and its popular Broadway adaptation, *On the Town*, Bernstein had also completed the symphonies *Jeremiah* and *The Age of Anxiety*.

LOOK EXECUTIVE OFFICES

511 Fifth Avenue, New York 17, New York

Gardner Cowles, *President and Editor*
John Cowles, *Chairman of the Board*
Marvin C. Whatmore, *Business Manager*
Vernon Myers, *Ass't to the President*
S. O. Shapiro, *Vice President*
James S. Milloy, *Vice President*
John F. Harding, *General Counsel*
Don Huber, *Treasurer*
Abner Sideman, *Newsstand Manager*
Lester Suhler, *Subscription Manager*
Felix Jager, *Promotion Director*
Charles C. Moffat, *Production Manager*

ADVERTISING OFFICES

Donald Perkins, *Advertising Manager*
511 Fifth Avenue, New York 17, New York
also
715 Locust Street, Des Moines 4, Iowa

Branch Offices:

Statler Building, Boston 16, Massachusetts
333 North Michigan Ave., Chicago 1, Ill.
Union Commerce Bldg., Cleveland 14, Ohio
General Motors Building, Detroit 2, Mich.
7046 Hollywood Blvd., Hollywood 28, Cal.
Bank of America Building,
300 Montgomery St., San Francisco 4, Cal.
12 South 12th Street, Philadelphia 7, Pa.

ADDRESS ALL SUBSCRIPTION MAIL

Subscription Office:

110 Tenth Street, Des Moines 4, Iowa
Les Suhler, *Subscription Manager*

When sending change of address, please give both old and new address and allow three weeks for first copy to arrive.

SUBSCRIPTION RATES

1 year (26 issues), $3.50; 2 years (52 issues), $6.00; 3 years (78 issues), $8.00—in United States and possessions. Pan-America and Canada: 1 year, $4.50—Other foreign: 1 year, $6.00.

ADDRESS ALL EDITORIAL MAIL

511 Fifth Avenue, New York 17, New York

Manuscripts or art submitted to LOOK should be accompanied by addressed envelopes and return postage. The Publisher assumes no responsibility for the return of unsolicited manuscripts or art.

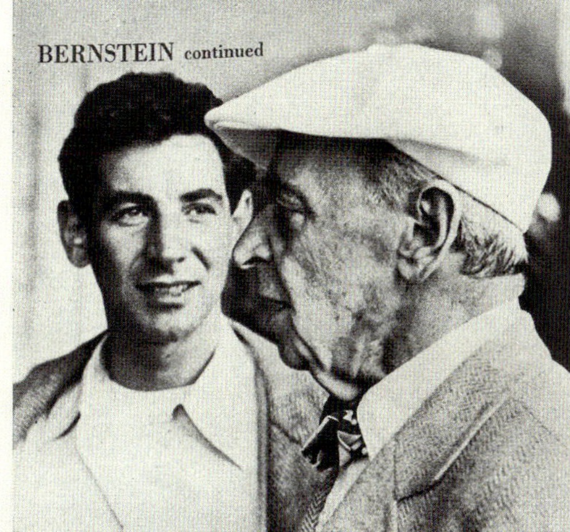

Bernstein and Serge Koussevitzky, former conductor of Boston Symphony, have worked together since he was a promising unknown out of Harvard.

Bachelor Bernstein loves people and parties

ballet *Fancy Free*, the *Jeremiah* and *The Age of Anxiety* symphonies. This season in New York, Bernstein had the unique honor to conduct three of the world's greatest symphony orchestras—New York, Boston, Philadelphia. He's soon off to Rome to conduct The Academy of Saint Cecilia Orchestra during Holy Week. Afterwards he'll repeat "the most thrilling experience of my life"—conducting the new Israeli Philharmonic in Israel and on its proposed tour here.

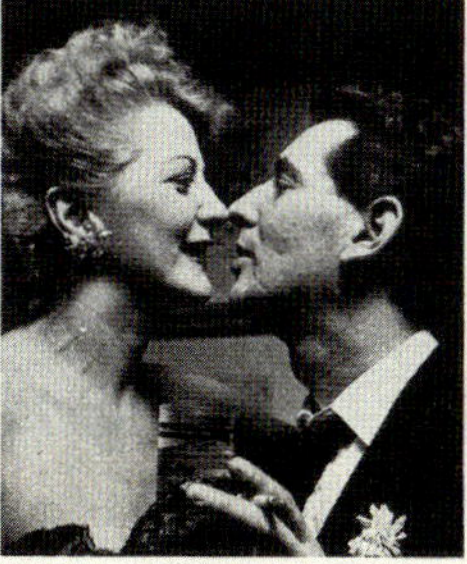

At after-concert party Leonard and actress Stella Adler kid around, perform mock romantic love scene.

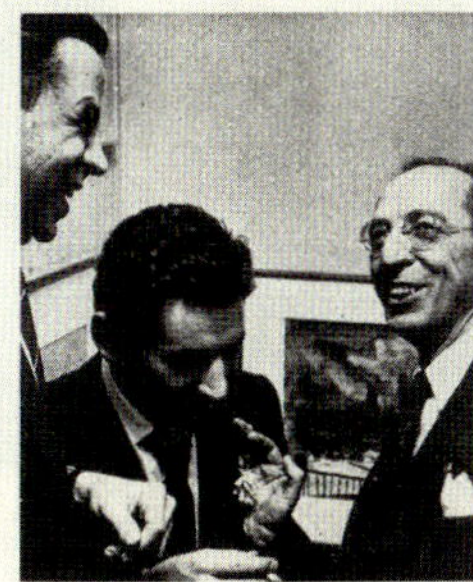

With musician friends Oscar Levant, Aaron Copland, he discusses score for forthcoming *Peter Pan.*

With William Kapell at the piano, Bernstein rehearses for an outdoor concert at Tanglewood. Here he introduced his *Age of Anxiety* symphony.

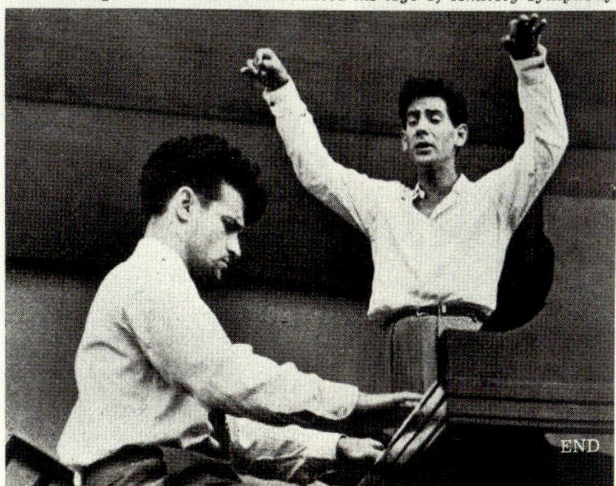

END

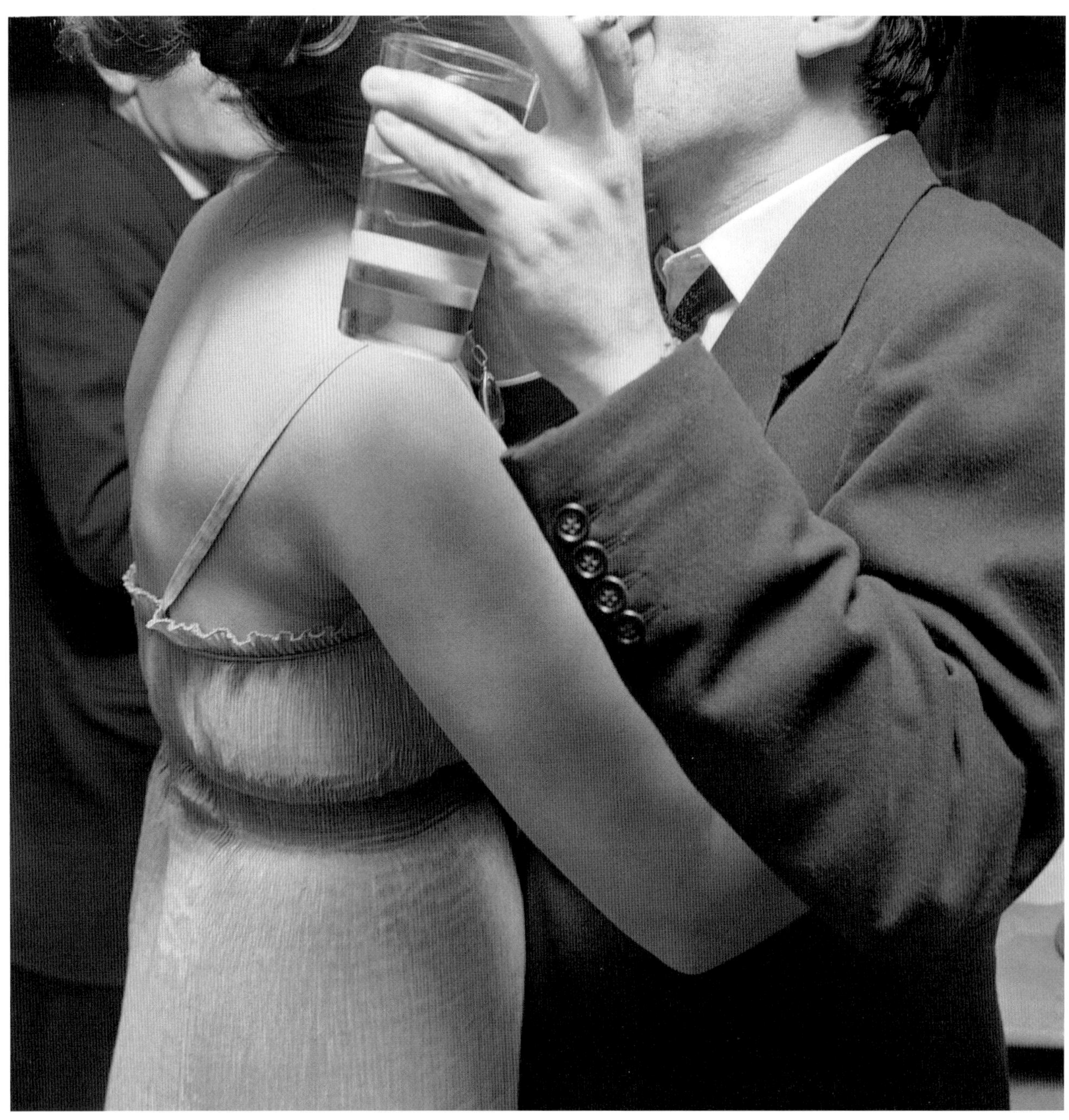

Guests at an after-concert party for Bernstein

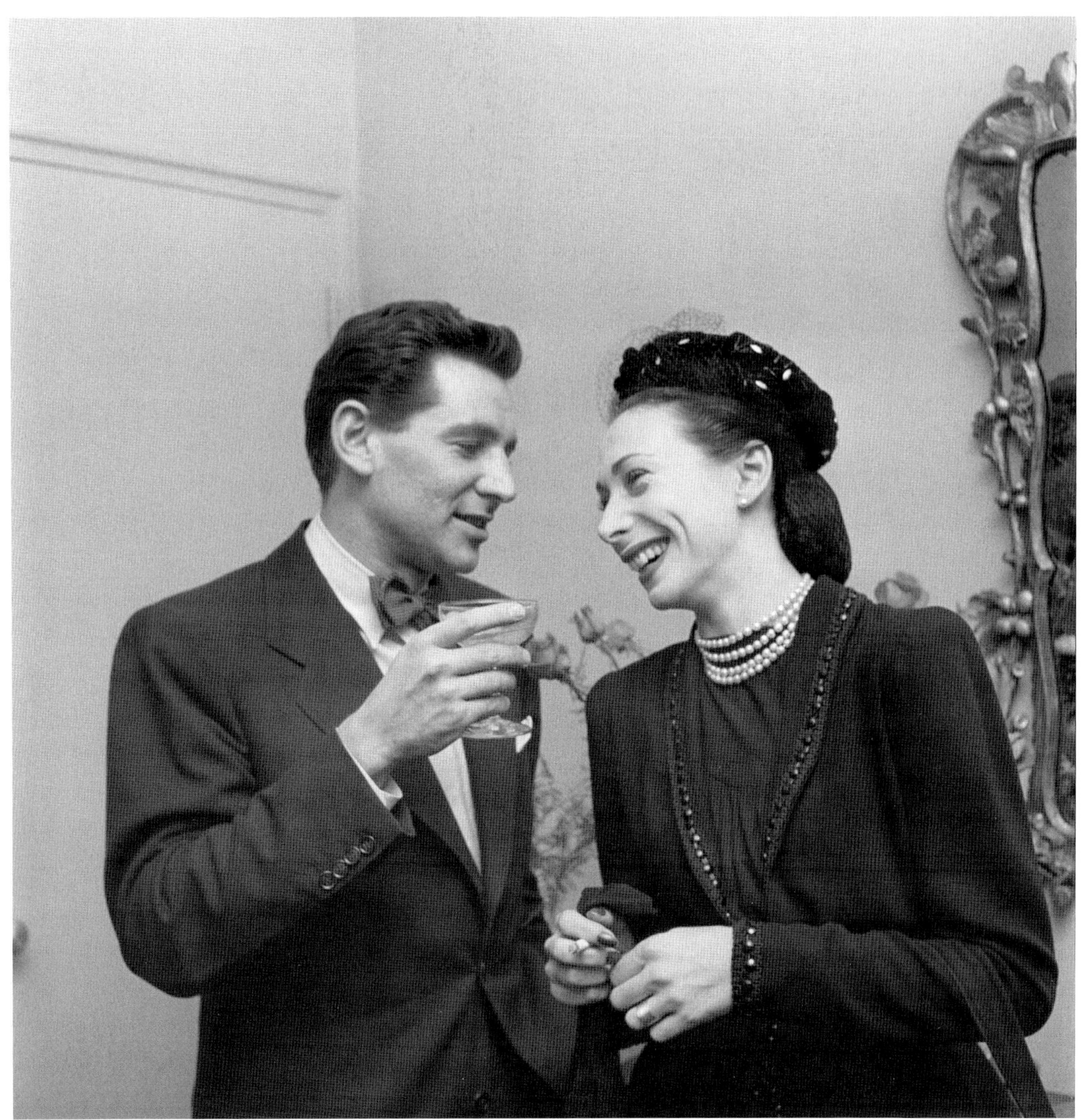

Bernstein at a party with dancer Nora Kaye

FOLLOWING SPREAD **Bernstein (left) with lyricists Betty Comden and Adolph Green, his collaborators on the musical *On the Town***

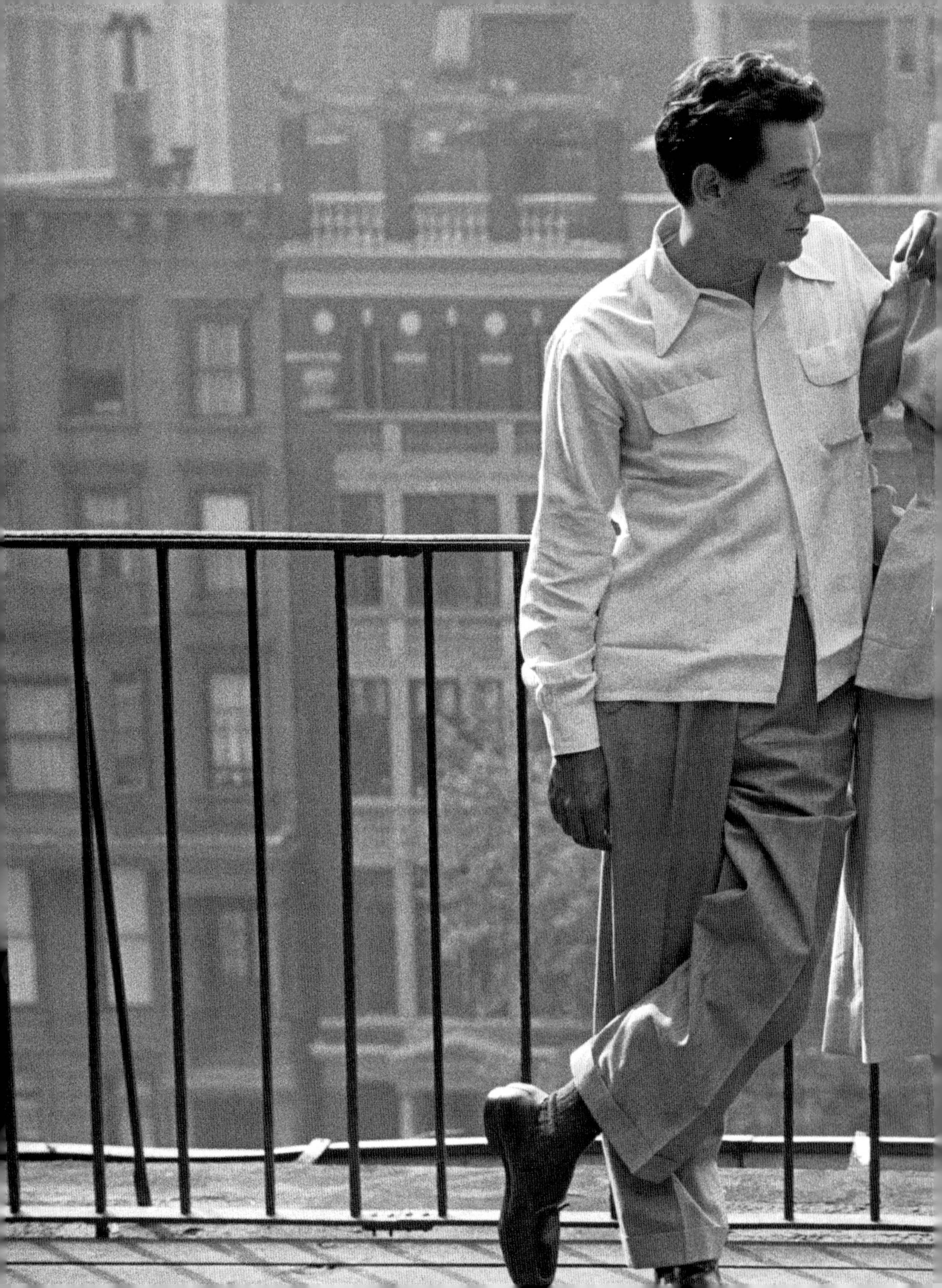

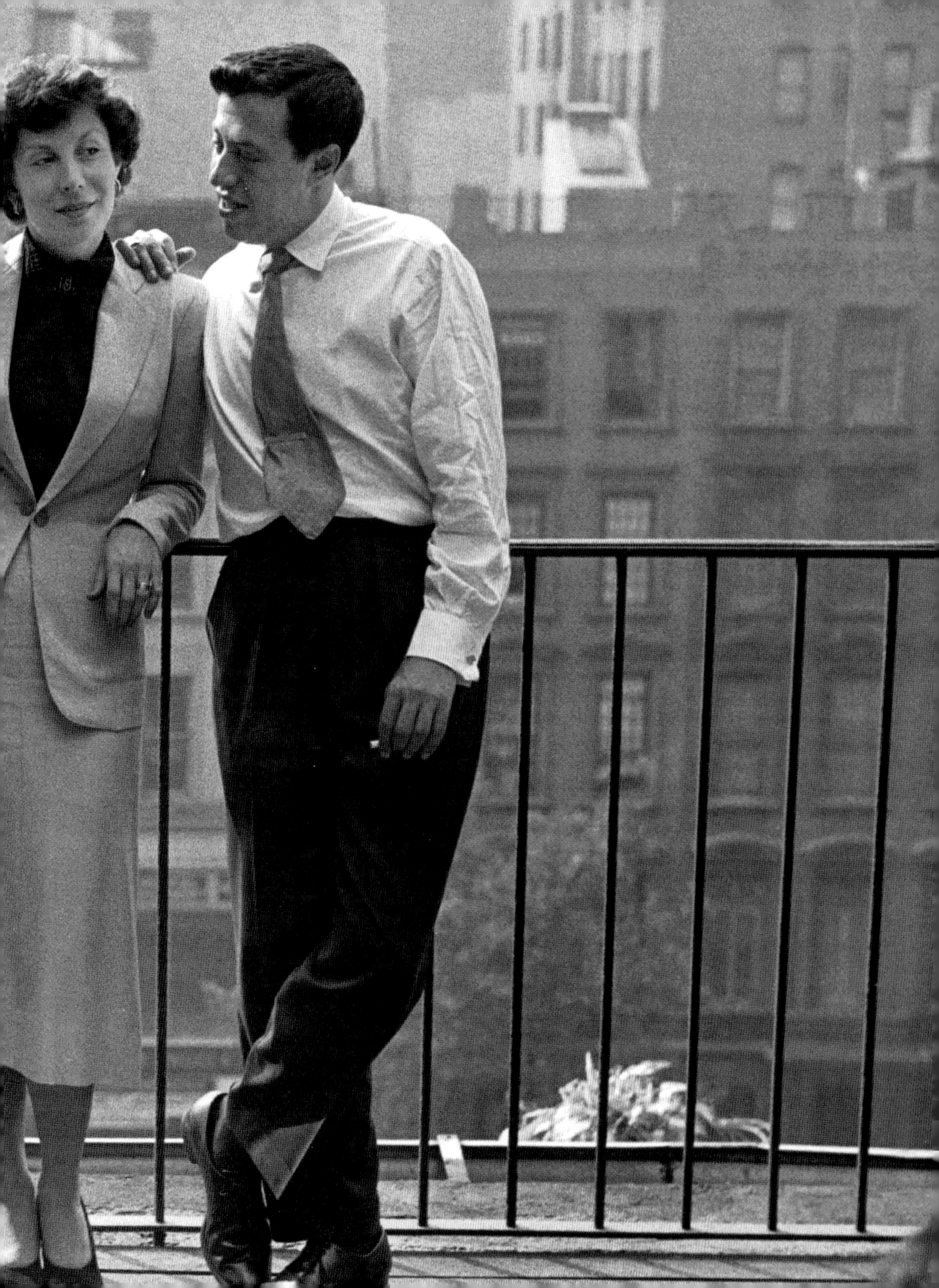

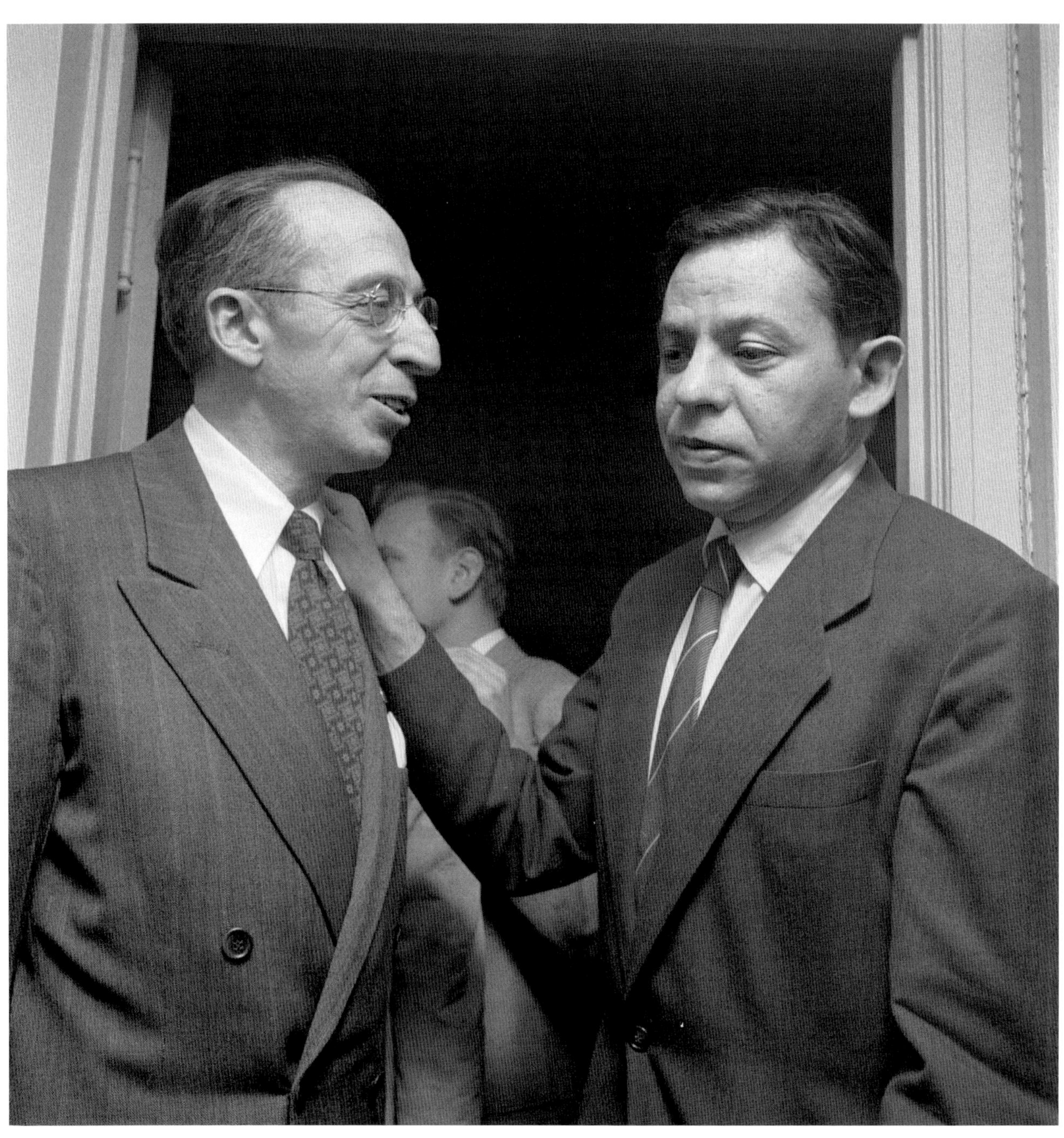

Composers Aaron Copland and Oscar Levant

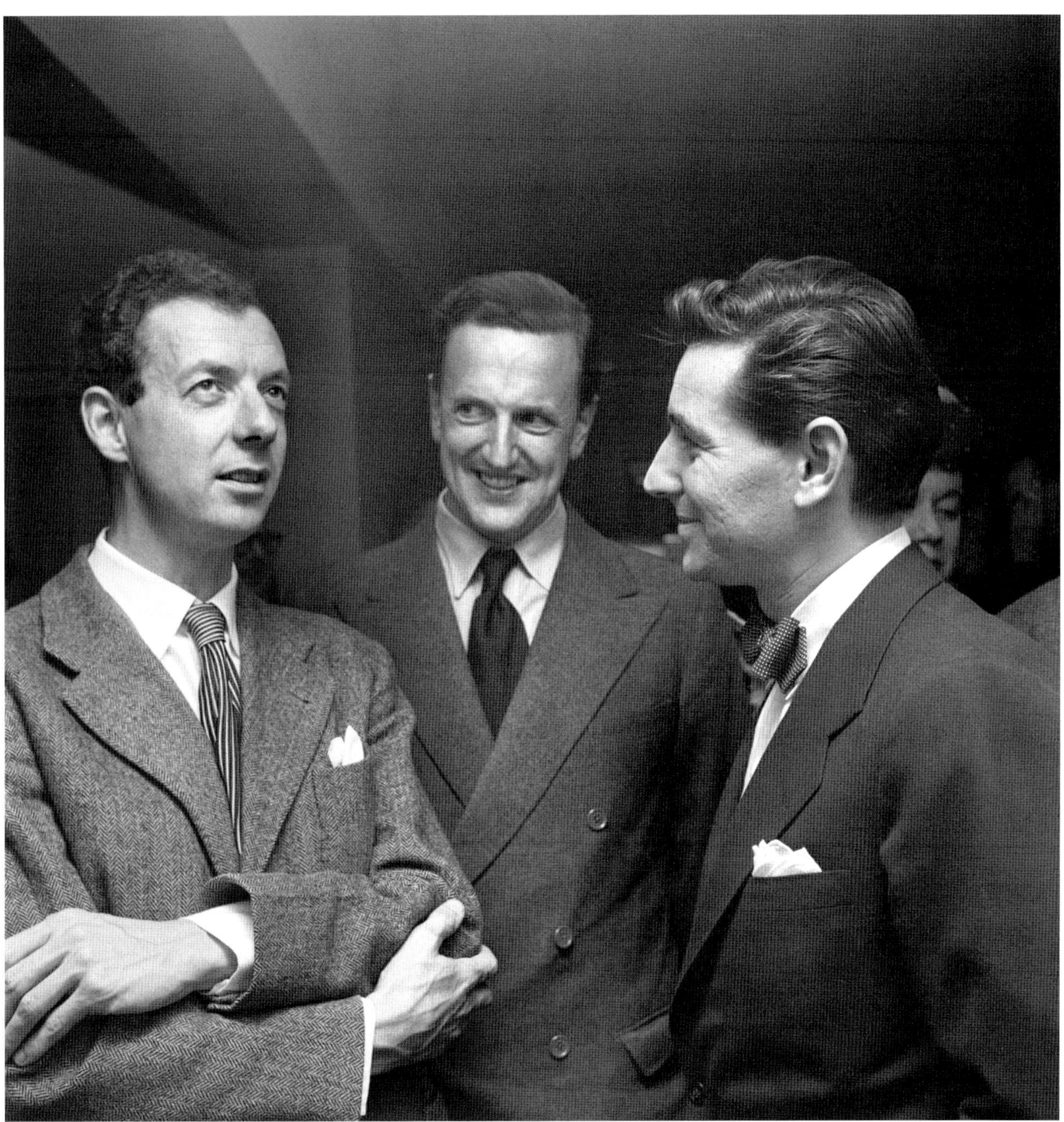

Bernstein with composer Benjamin Britten (left) and tenor Peter Pears (center)

FOLLOWING SPREAD **Bernstein relaxing at his summer home in the Berkshires**

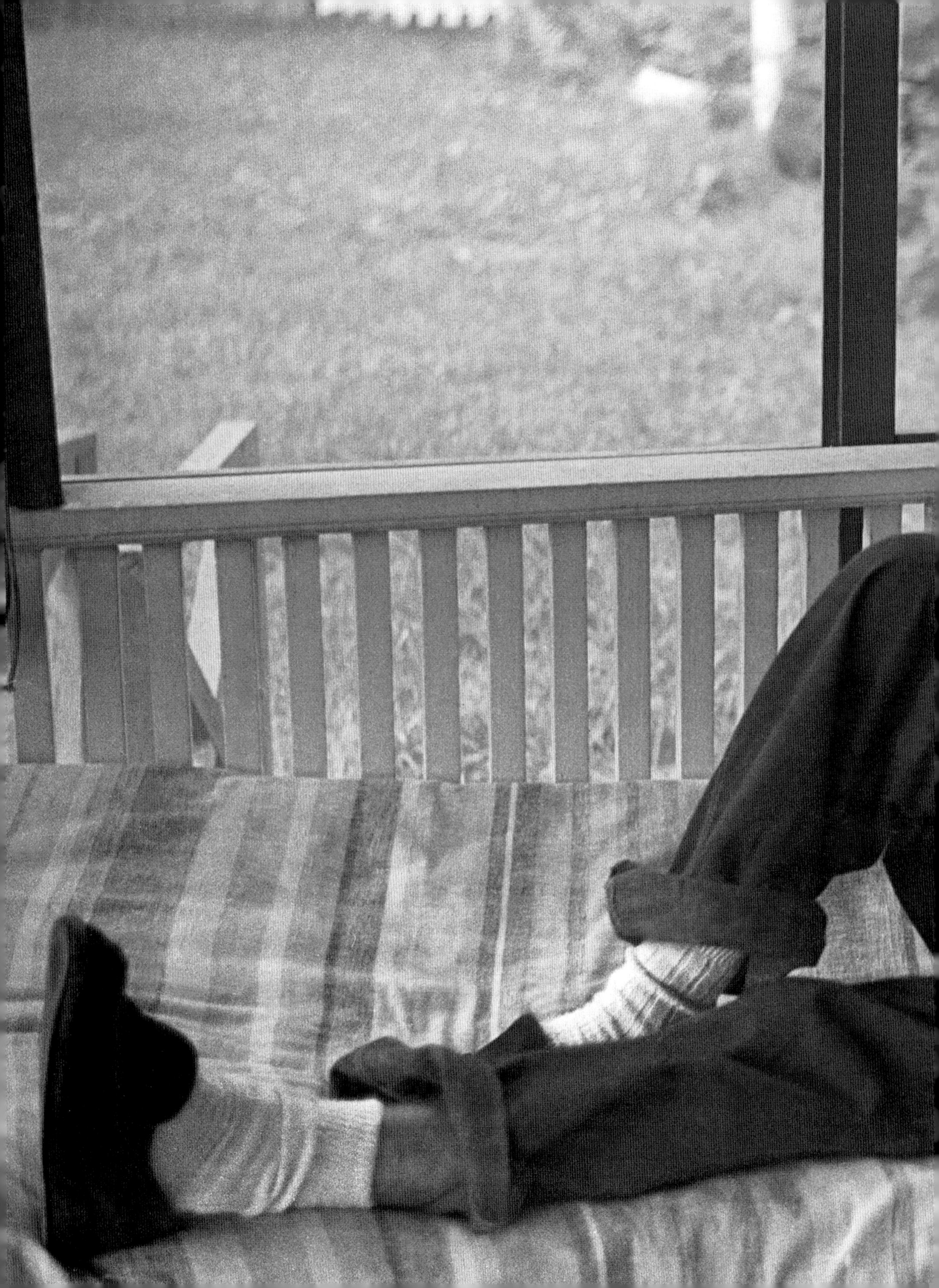

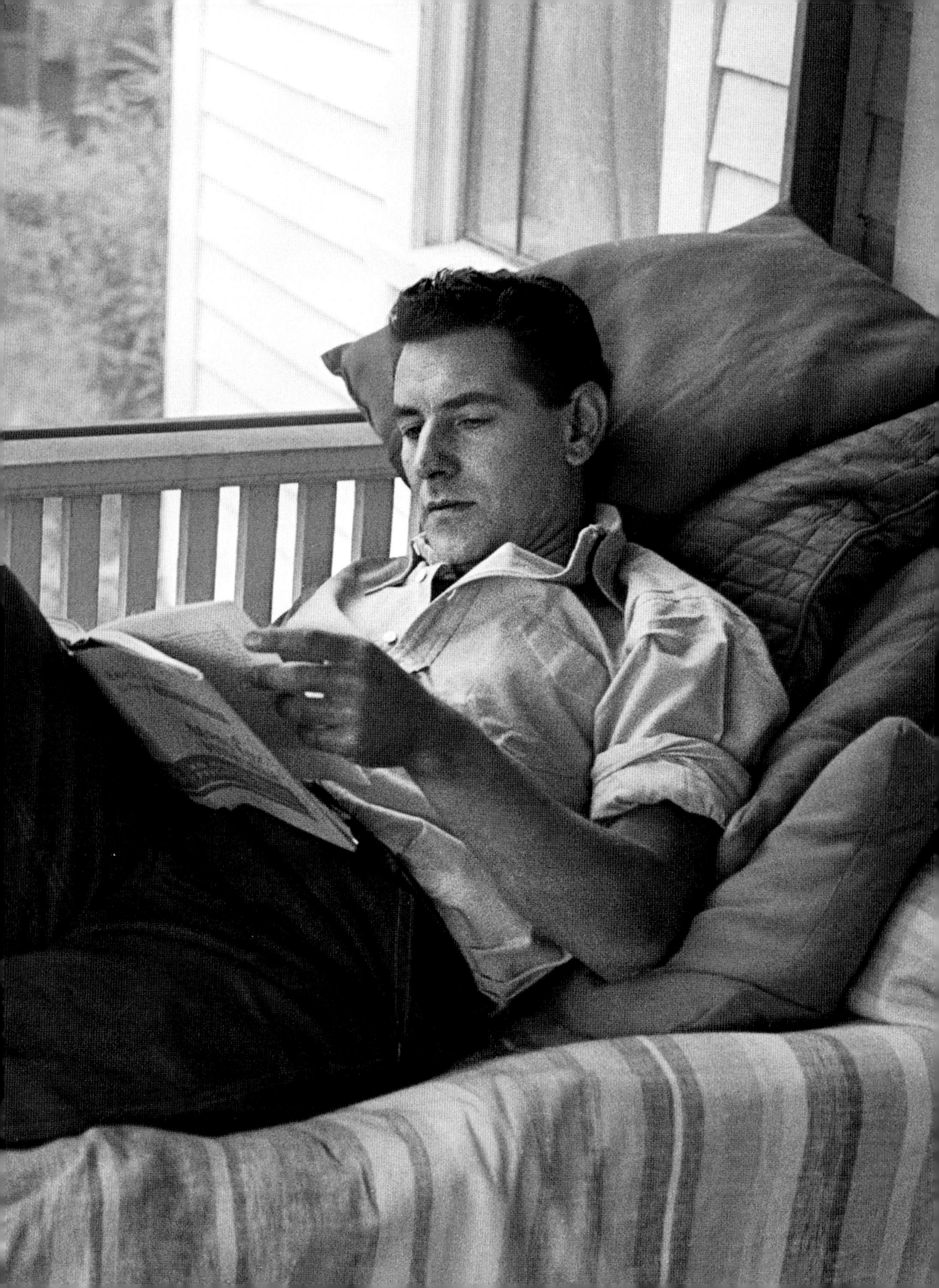

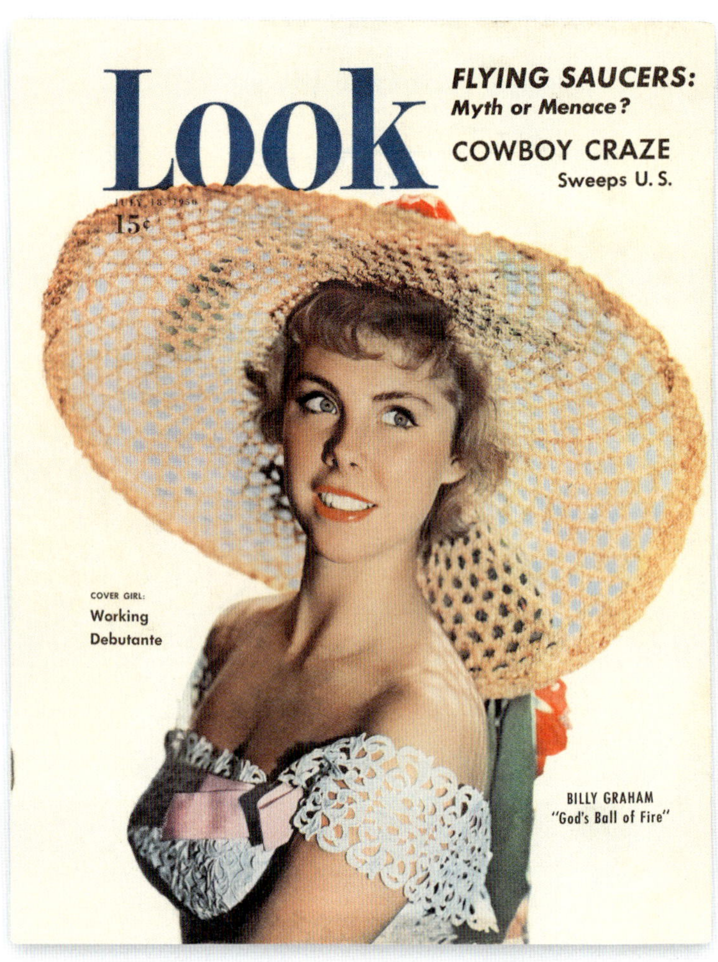

PUBLISHED AS

THE DEBUTANTE WHO WENT TO WORK

DATE

JULY 18, 1950

AUTHOR

PATRICIA COFFIN

Eighteen-year-old Betsy von Furstenberg, the subject of this five-page article, was the European-born daughter of an aristocratic German father and an American mother. Kubrick's photographs illustrated the surprisingly young von Furstenberg's split personality (a debutante who worked) by picturing the high-society milieu in which she spent her leisure time and the high-pressure theater and film worlds she inhabited as an aspiring actress. Kubrick's sunny photograph of von Furstenberg in a broad-brimmed hat appeared on the issue's cover, one of three images by Kubrick that were featured on *Look*'s covers.

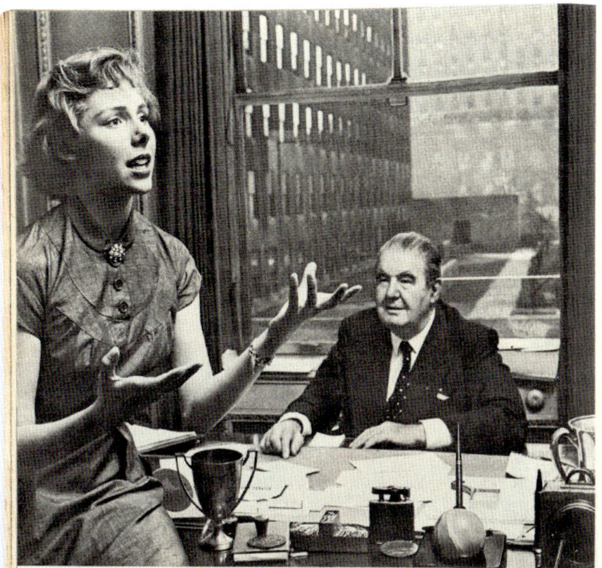

Betsy emotes for producer Gilbert Miller in his Radio City office. He agrees with producers in Italy, France, England that she has real promise as an actress.

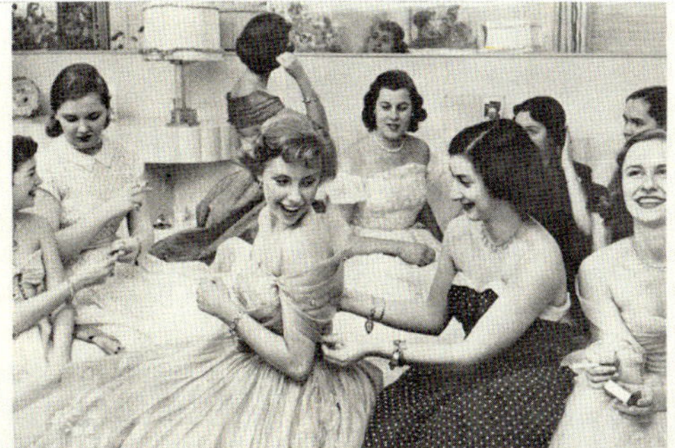

Gossiping with group of current debutantes—including her hostess, Sandra Stralem in polka dots—she catches up on social life she missed.

Discovered by publisher Mme. Pierre Lazareff, Betsy has appeared on 11 French magazine covers.

She strikes typical fashion pose. Betsy's been modeling since 14, started buying her own clothes at 15.

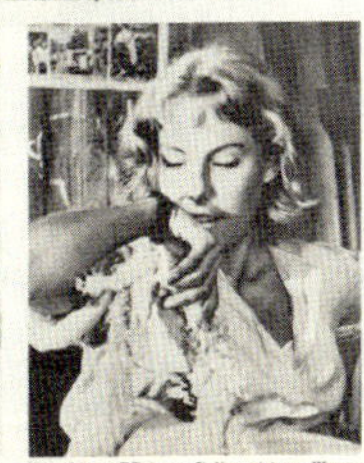

She plays a DP in an Italian picture, *Women Without Names*, due to be released this fall.

the Debutante who went to Work

Eighteen-year-old Betsy von Furstenberg made a movie in Italy instead of a debut in New York

BY PATRICIA COFFIN
LOOK Staff Writer

BECAUSE coming out seemed silly to Betsy von Furstenberg, she signed with a movie company in Rome last winter. While her former private schoolmates attended parties, proms and committee meetings in New York, Betsy was busy before the cameras. She was on location in an Italian DP camp with Simone Simon and Valentina Cortese. Before that, she'd made a hit as a fashion model in Paris, attracting the attention of several film producers. Now back to try Broadway or Hollywood, she has had offers from Broadway producers Gilbert Miller, Alfred de Liagre, Jr., George Abbott and two movie companies.

Betsy appeals because of her piquant, fly-away personality. Her face is fresh and expressive. Her wide amber eyes don't betray her tenacity or her sophistication. Betsy's been around.

She was born in a castle in Westphalia, Germany, the daughter of a count. Her mother—an American—was out boar hunting the night before Betsy arrived. Her parents were divorced when she was a baby and Betsy, who is an American citizen, has been commuting to Europe ever since. At seven, she studied ballet with Anton Dolin and appeared with him at the Center Theater. At eight, she won a N. Y. Skating Club competition. She studied acting under Sanford Meisner, appeared in stock with Dean Jagger, decided that acting was her true love. She finds the prospect of marriage versus a career "too complicated to think about," although she has a best beau who is a son of Mrs. George Vanderbilt, a grandson of the late Charles Howard, owner of race horses Seabiscuit and Noor.

"Peter's just my best friend," says Betsy. "We've known each other since childhood. I used to guard the bathroom door when Pete went in to sneak a smoke." Peter Howard's friendship for Betsy extends to sending her hats when she was in Europe, leaving school at 1 a.m. to meet her boat, arranging press interviews and introducing her to as many producers as he can spot during luncheons at "21." Due to enter Yale this fall, Peter wants to be a producer himself.

She's helped support herself modeling and acting although she says she is supposed to have five million dollars tied up in German marks. "The war mixed everything up. Things like the French taking the body of our town car and the Russians the wheels."

Betsy's grown beyond her sister debutantes—is a definite personality. She likes F. Scott Fitzgerald, Andre Gide, Armenian pastry and Dixieland clarinetist Sidney Bechet. She wears either bluejeans or Hattie Carnegie gowns—"no junior miss clothes for me! And I can't stand hypocrites, turnips, conventions, licorice candy or women—especially in groups."

(Continued on next page)

Photographed by STANLEY KUBRICK

40 41

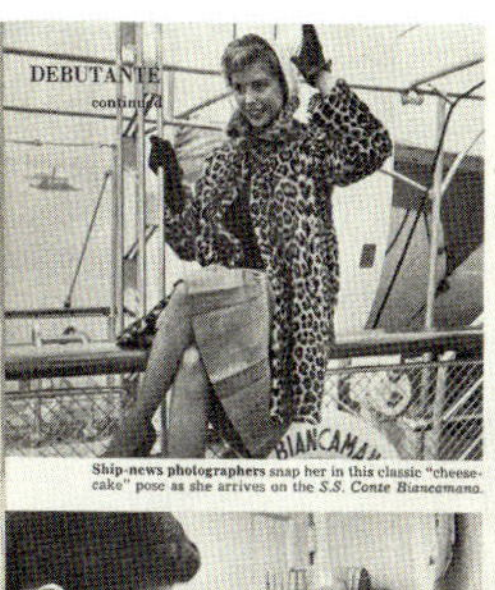

Ship-news photographers snap her in this classic "cheese-cake" pose as she arrives on the *S.S. Conte Biancamano.*

Her best beau, Peter Stewart Howard, center, son of Mrs. George Vanderbilt, takes her to Mr. John's for some new hats. He met the boat.

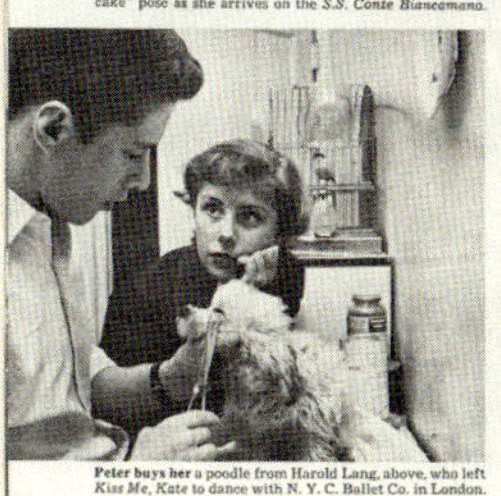

Peter buys her a poodle from Harold Lang, above, who left *Kiss Me, Kate* to dance with N. Y. C. Ballet Co. in London.

Betsy's shopping spree includes toying with a diamond lapel pin at Van Cleef and Arpels. She settled for gold bracelet charm from Peter.

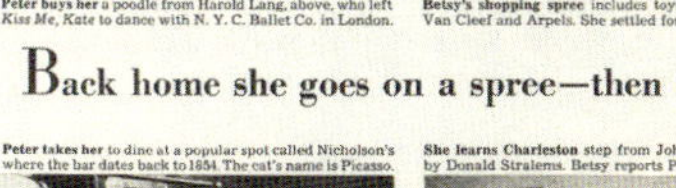

Back home she goes on a spree—then to work again

Peter takes her to dine at a popular spot called Nicholson's where the bar dates back to 1854. The cat's name is Picasso.

She learns Charleston step from John Hamlin at party given for her by Donald Stralems. Betsy reports Paris jitterbugs better than we do.

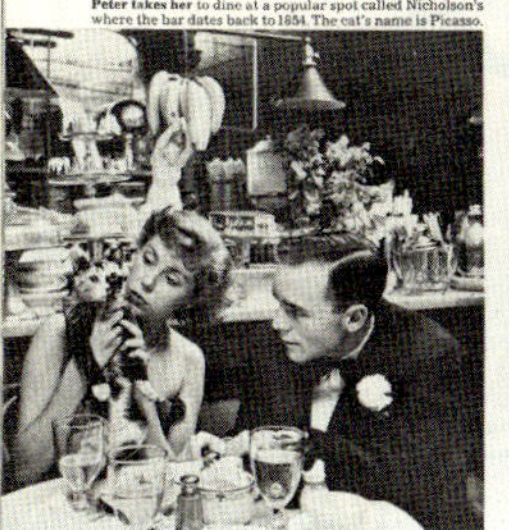

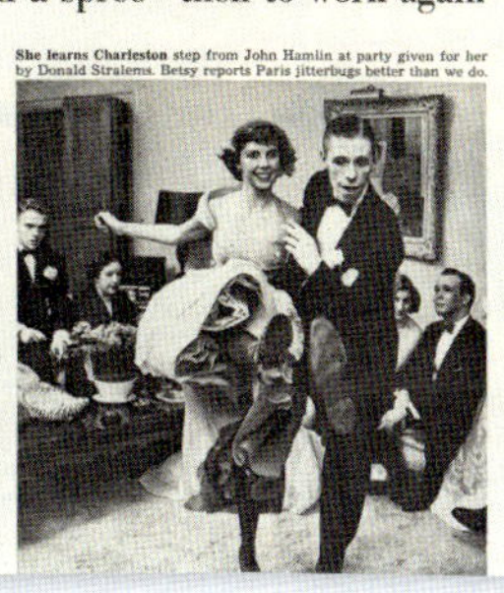

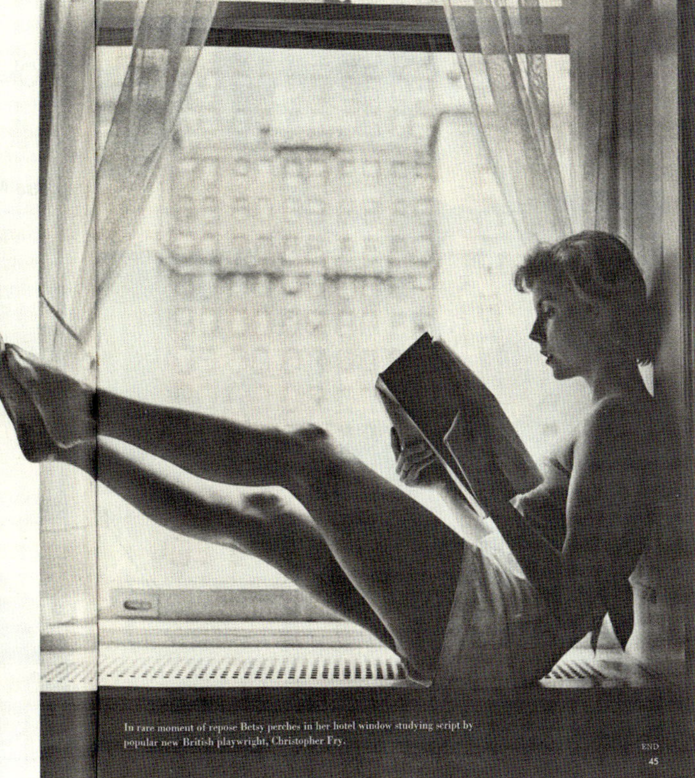

In rare moment of repose Betsy perches in her hotel window studying script by popular new British playwright, Christopher Fry.

END
45

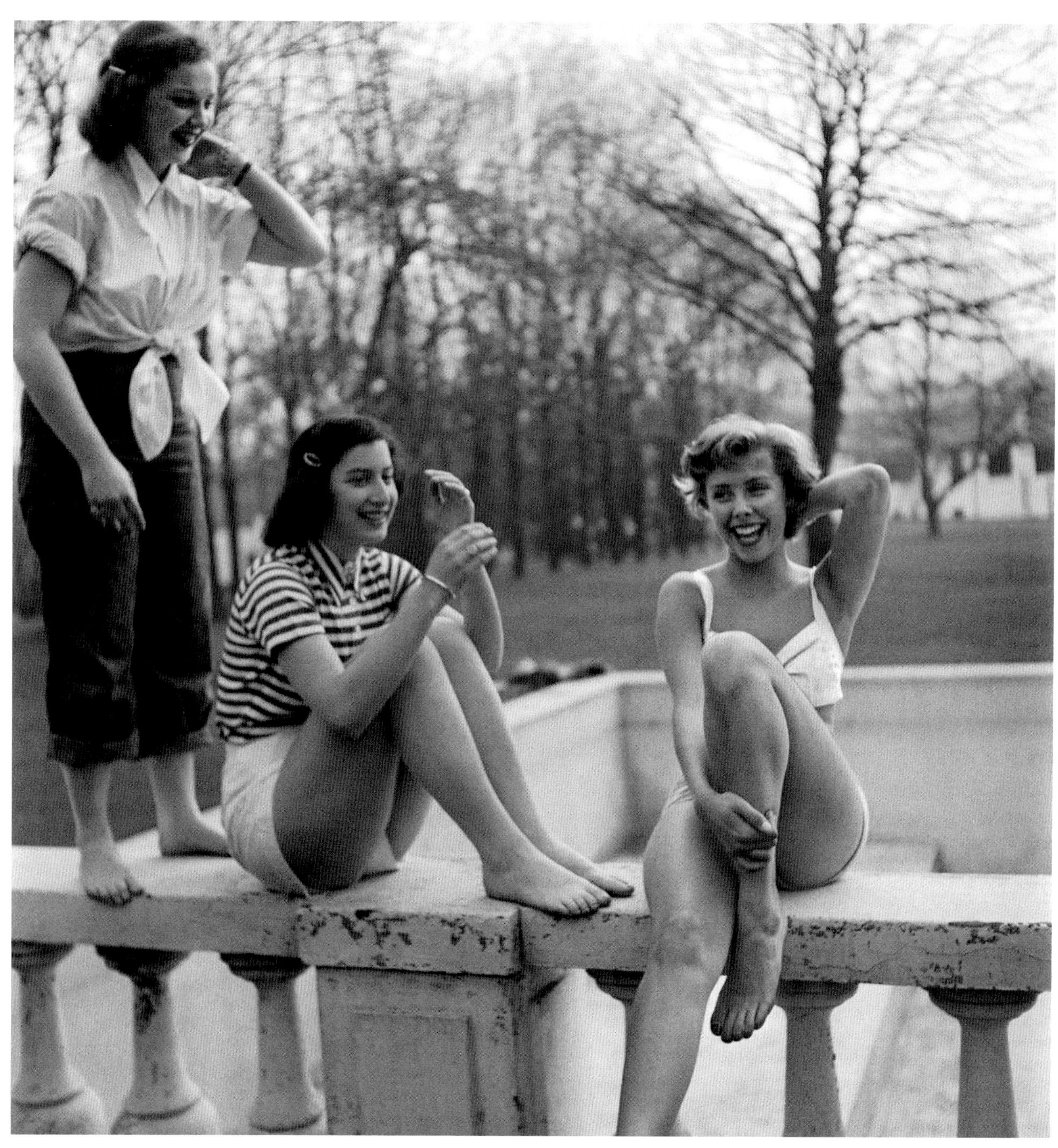

Von Furstenberg with classmates from the prestigious Hewitt School

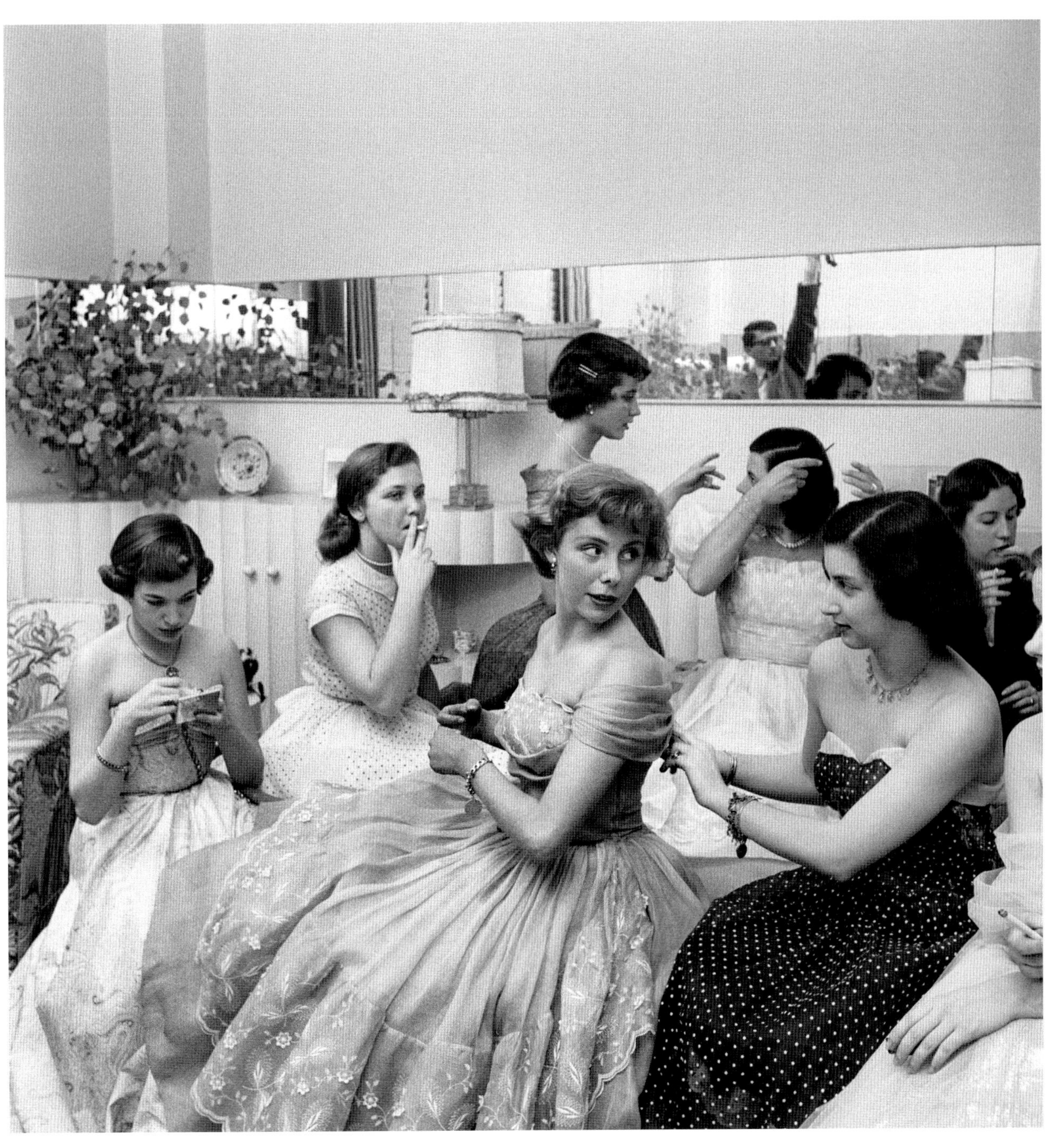

A friend adjusting von Furstenberg's gown at a party given in her honor

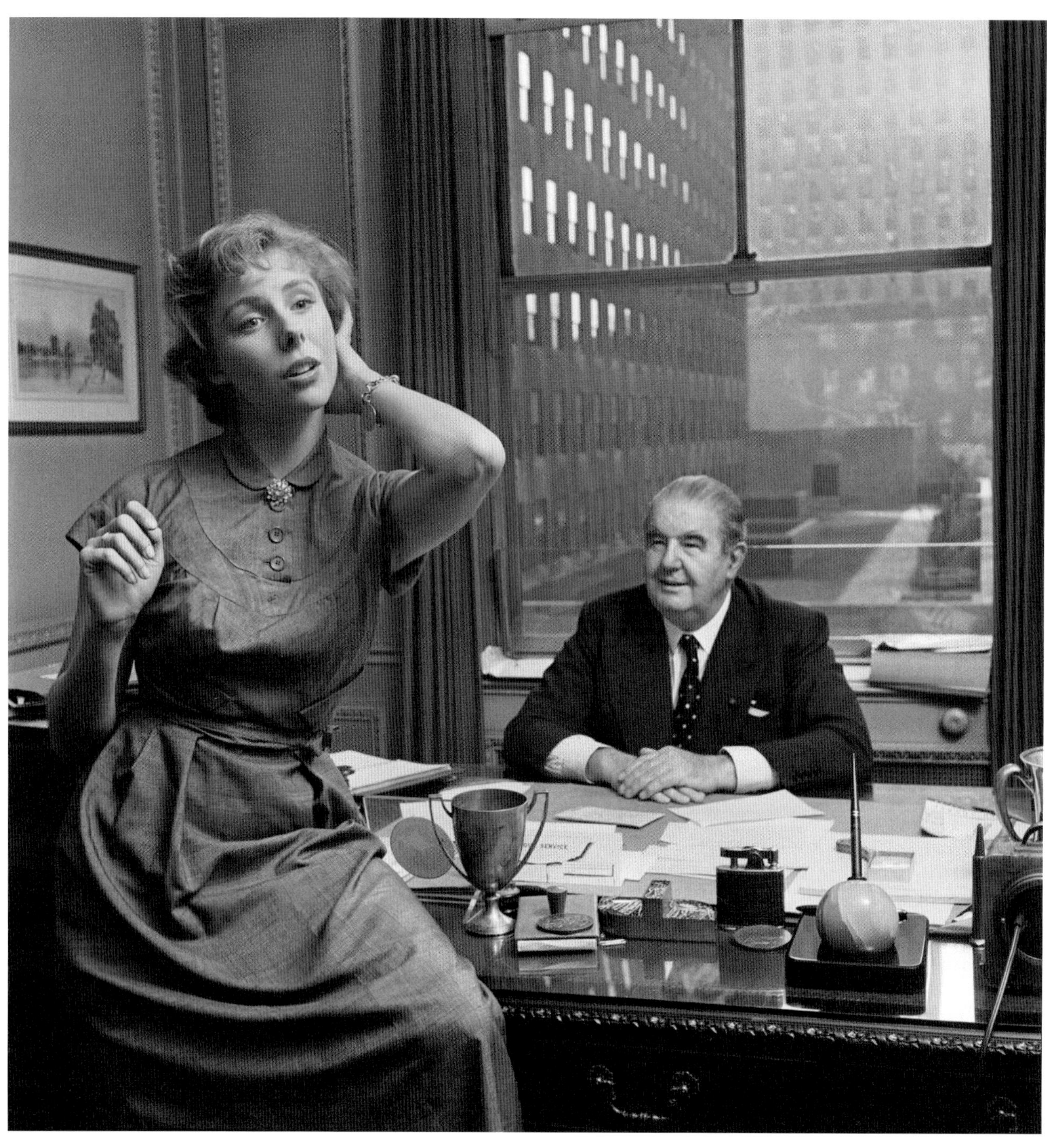

Von Furstenberg emoting for producer
Gilbert Miller in his office at the "Radio City"
section of Rockefeller Center

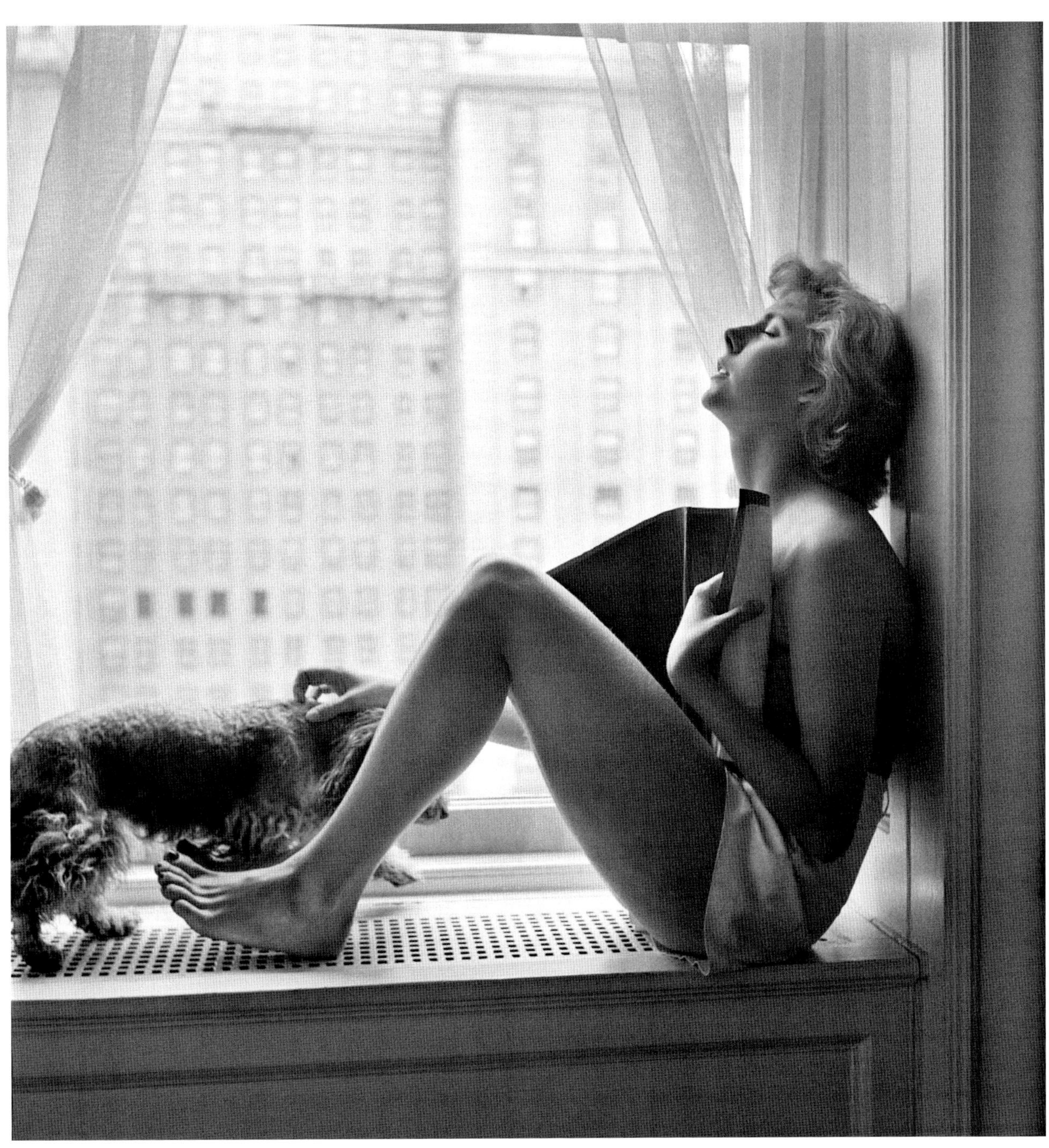

Von Furstenberg in her hotel room, reading
a script by British playwright Christopher Fry

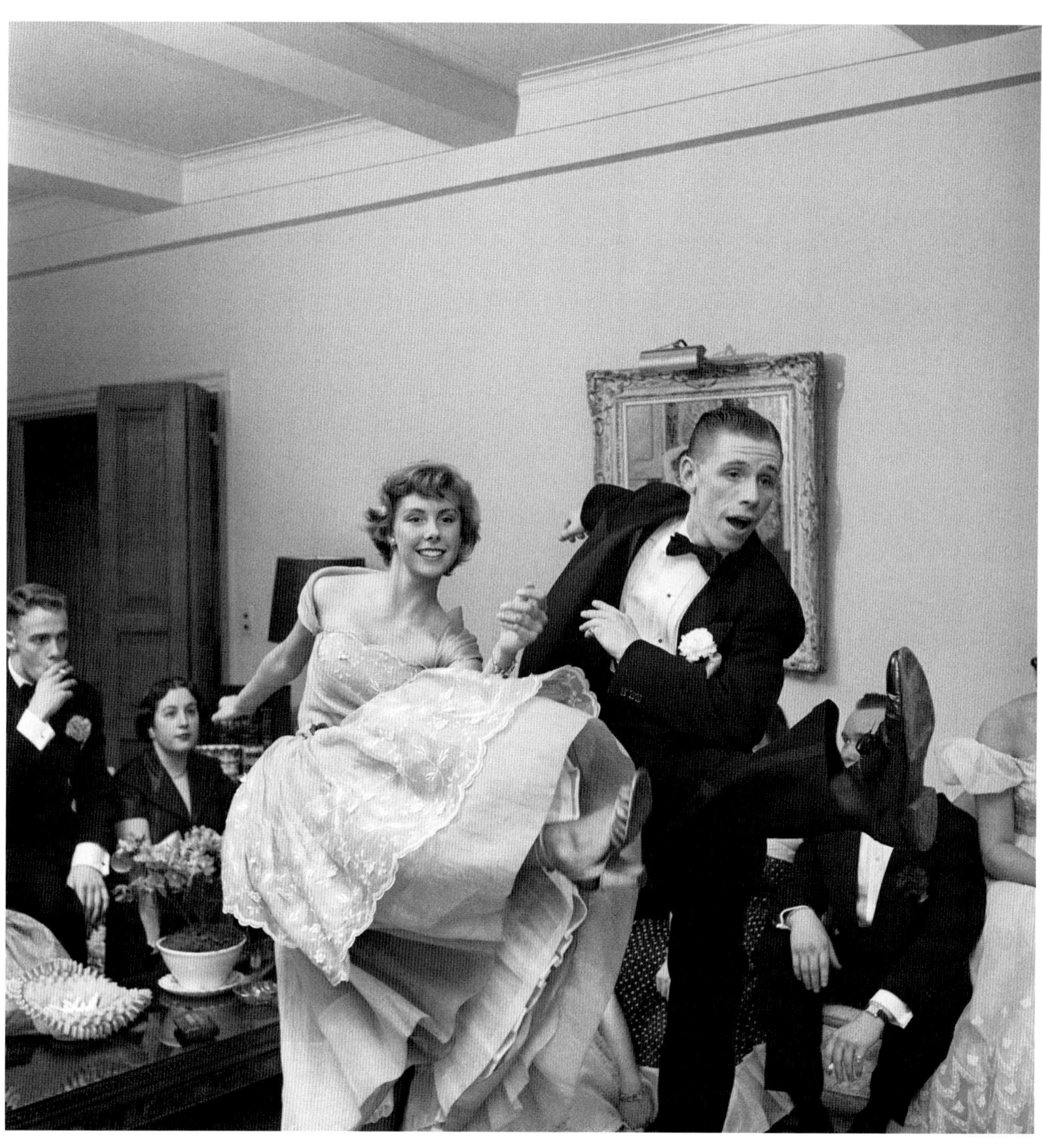

Von Furstenberg doing the Charleston
with friend John Hamlin

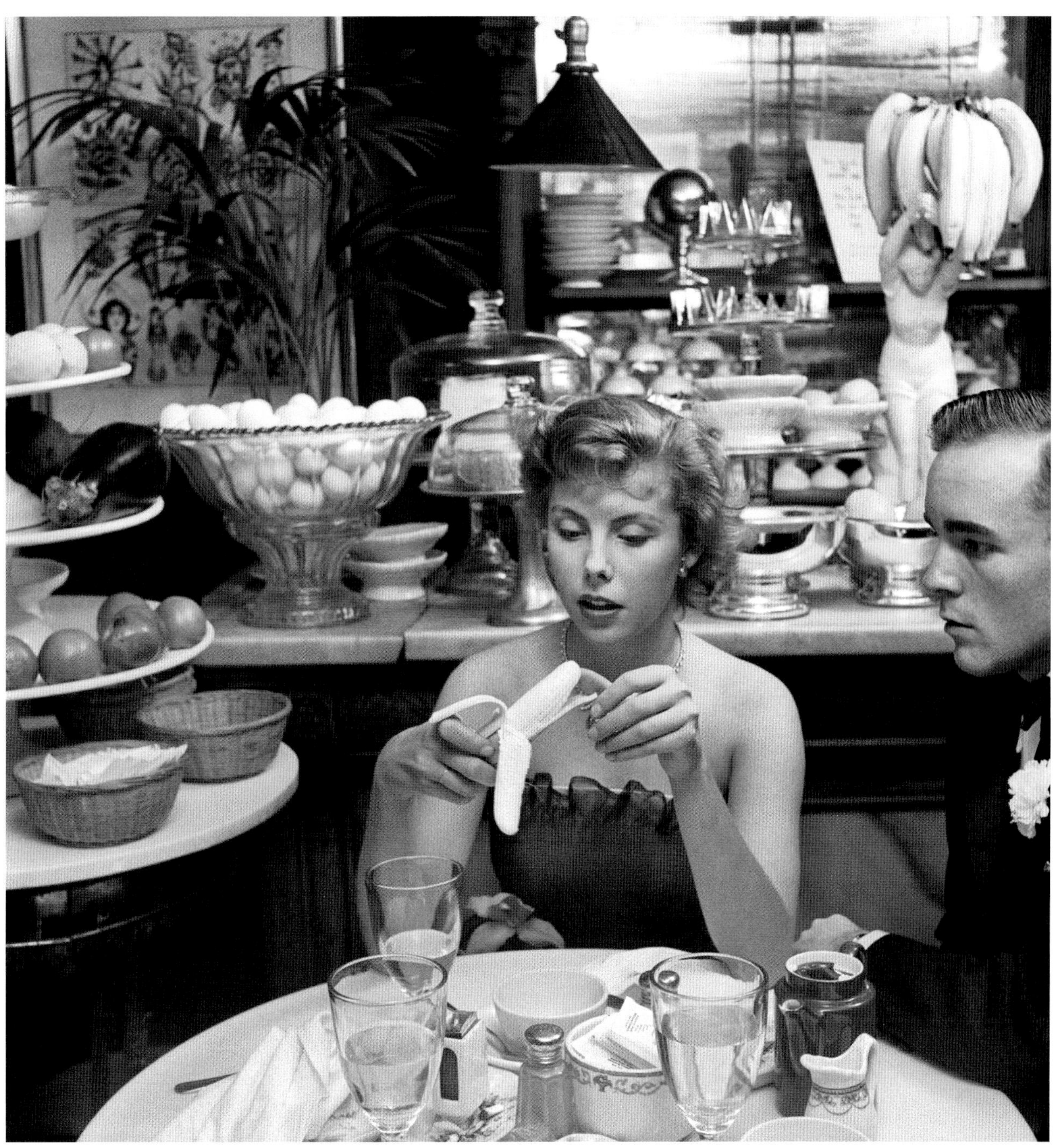

Von Furstenberg dining at Nicholson's with beau Peter Stewart Howard

FOLLOWING SPREAD **Von Furstenberg on the steps of the Plaza Hotel with Peter Stewart Howard**

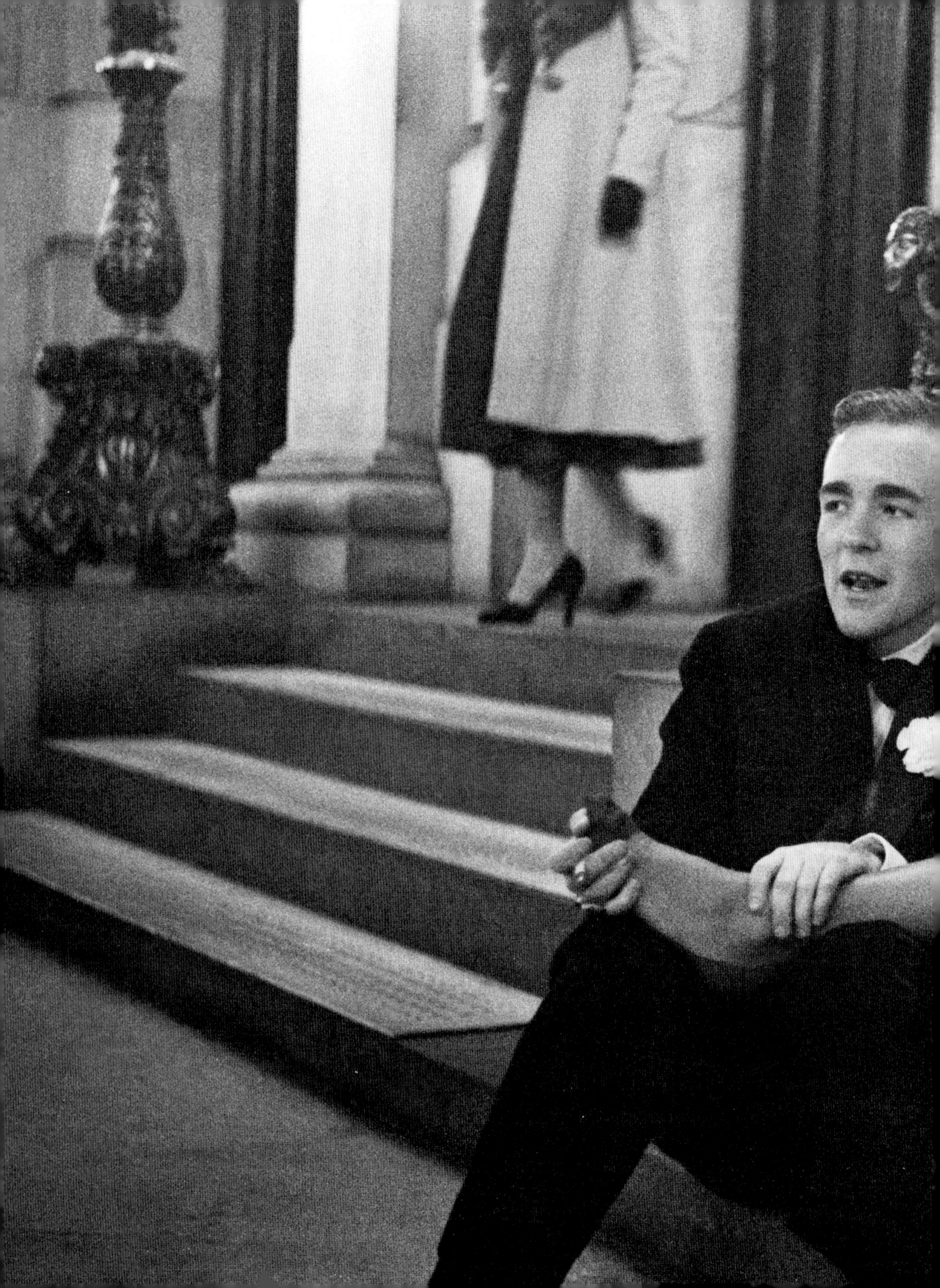

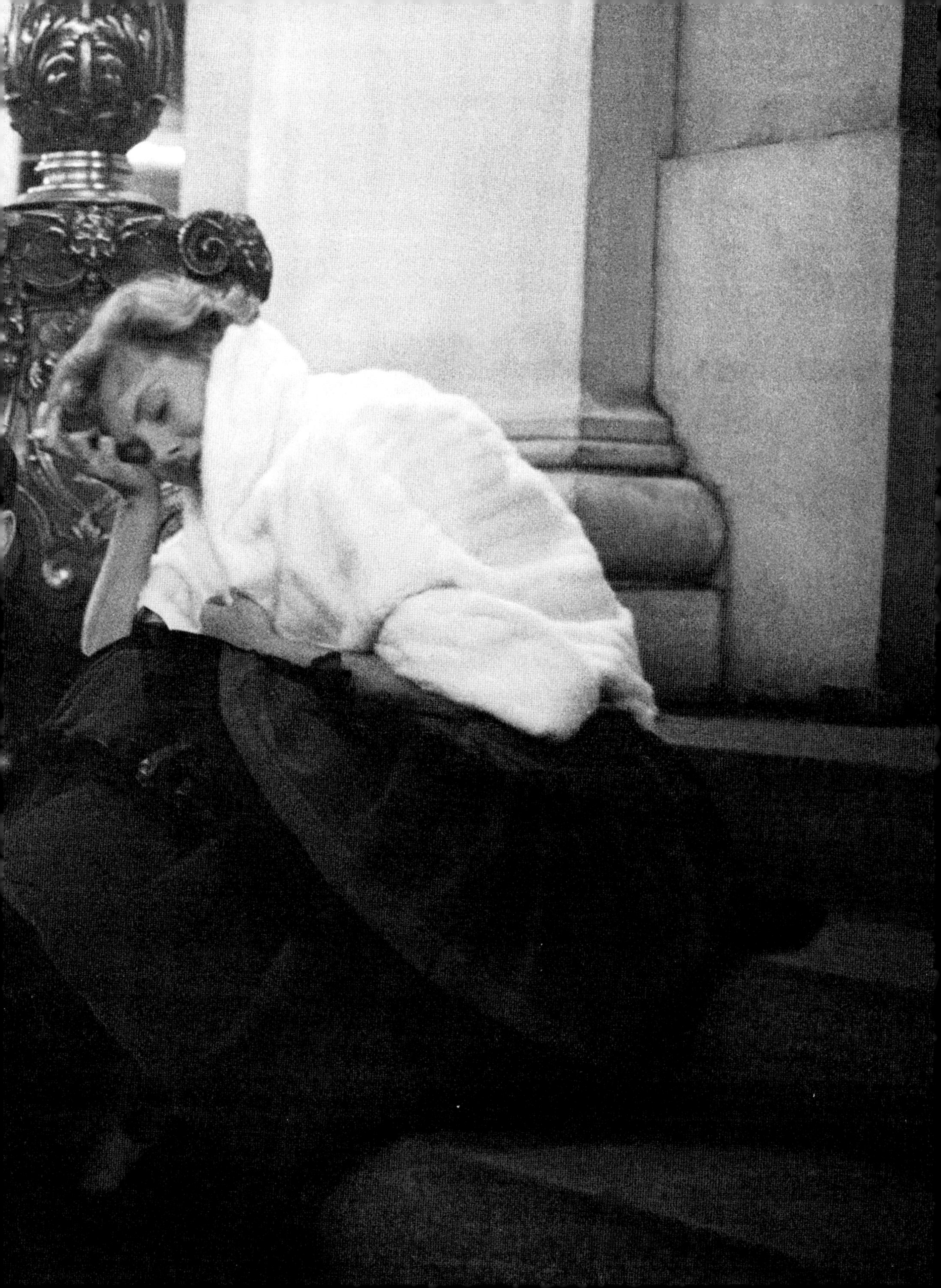

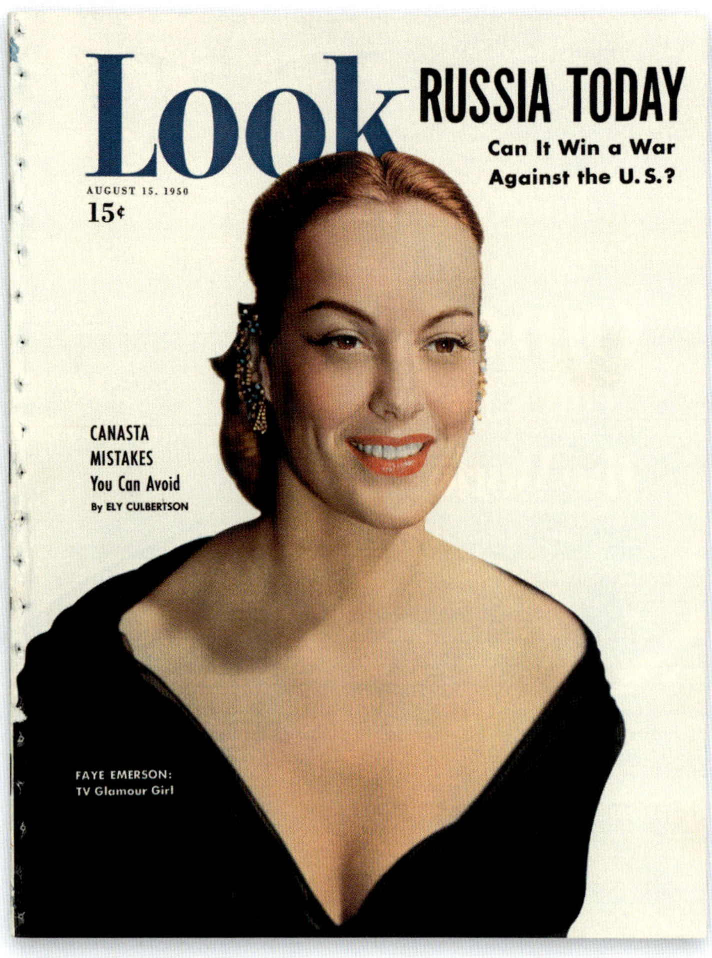

PUBLISHED AS

FAYE EMERSON: YOUNG LADY IN A HURRY

DATE

AUGUST 15, 1950

AUTHOR

ELEANOR HARRIS

For this story Kubrick photographed 32-year-old Faye Emerson, former Hollywood star and recently divorced wife of Franklin D. Roosevelt's son Elliott. While those credentials alone might have prompted a story on Emerson, it was probably her recent transition from film to television that merited this article's 10 photographs plus a cover image by Kubrick. Noting that Emerson was voted "Top Female Discovery of 1949" and was one of the nation's leading television personalities, the article followed her hectic personal and professional lives. "In two busy weeks," the article noted, "she made some 60 personal appearances, launched a new TV show, gave a party, changed apartments—an ordinary schedule for Faye." Even Faye's blond hairstyles warranted an additional story in the same issue, which also featured Kubrick's photographs.

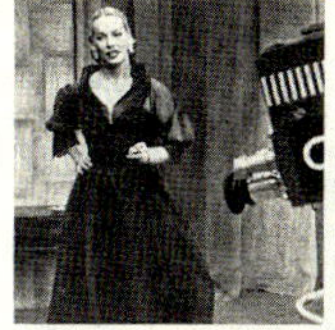

She ad libs smoothly on television but says it is like "mentally juggling 20 balls at once."

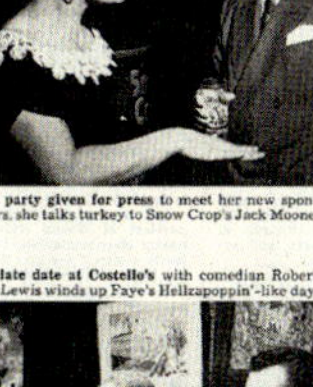

She rehearses *Parisienne* with Sam Wanamaker for his current Broadway repertory experiment.

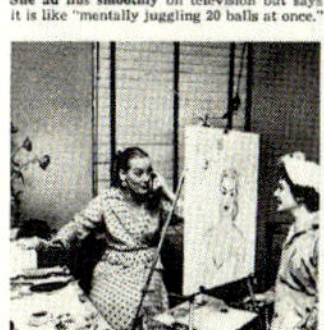

She sits for her portrait by Mildred Atkins, makes phone calls between shows at the Roxy.

She introduces Sid Caesar on the Roxy stage. For two weeks, she emceed four shows daily.

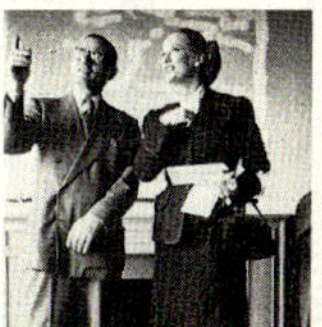

She takes time out to check the color scheme in her $500-a-month Park Avenue apartment.

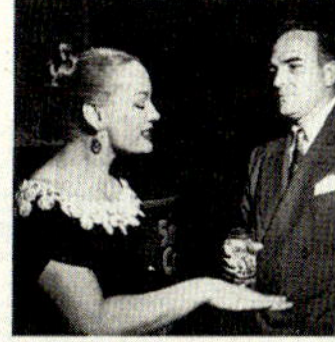

At party given for press to meet her new sponsors, she talks turkey to Snow Crop's Jack Moone.

Always in a hurry. Faye is interviewed on run by Social Registerite writer Eleanor Harris.

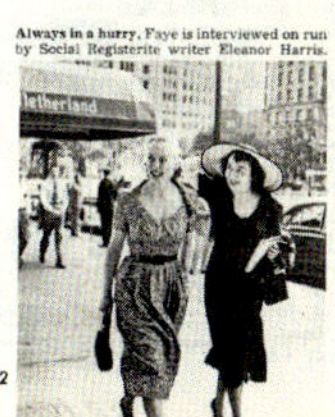

A late date at Costello's with comedian Robert Q. Lewis winds up Faye's Hellzapoppin'-like day.

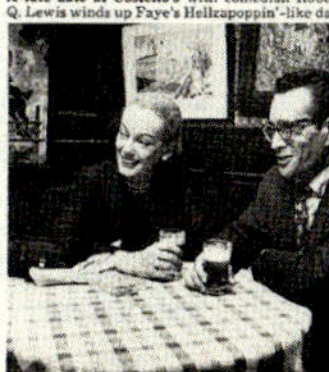

72

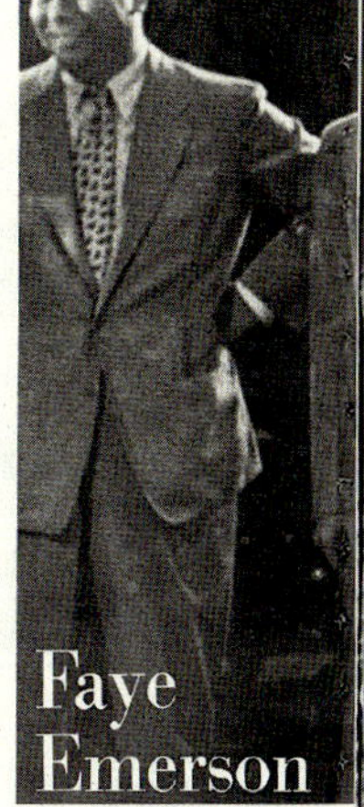

Look PICTURE PERSONALITY

Faye Emerson

TV's queen directs rehearsal of her new show, *Fifteen with Faye*. With 30 people in NBC studio at the time, Faye blew her top over a bungled bit of scenery, got what she wanted, reverted to her sweet sparkling self.

YOUNG LADY IN A HURRY

In two busy weeks, she made some 60 personal appearances, launched a new TV show, gave a party, changed apartments—an ordinary schedule for Faye

By ELEANOR HARRIS

In the 10 months she has been on television, Faye Emerson and her low-cut dresses have been the subject of much cheerful uproar. Faye herself has been named "Top Female Discovery of 1949" and is listed among the country's top favorite TV personalities.

In these same 10 months, the nation's press has debated the question: "Should Faye's dresses be cut so low?" Critical radio columnist John Crosby purred: "Men . . . are helplessly fascinated." Earl Wilson suggested: "You should buy a V-shaped screen on which to watch Miss Emerson." Columnist Frank Conniff tipped his hat to what lies above her collar bone: "It isn't every day that you see a high IQ in a low-cut gown." Then the conservative Fashion Academy suddenly dignified the discussion by naming her "Best Dressed Woman on Television."

Faye is a little bewildered by all the excitement. Except for one Broadway show, some scattered radio and TV appearances, the 32-year-old actress spent the past five years concentrating on her marriage to Elliott Roosevelt. After their separation, she said: "I wasn't sure anyone would remember Faye Emerson—or whether I'd sink or swim."

Her swimming ability was proved on her opening show—in which Faye had substituted for Diana Barrymore on a day's notice. When she leaned forward, her brown eyes straight into the camera, and said in her low and faintly Southern voice: "Hello everybody—I'm Faye Emerson—" TV producer Hardie Frieberg relaxed: "Our worries are over."

Suddenly, she was being discussed all over New York. Sponsors began shouting for her. TV experts studied her TV personality, reported: "She's charm personified. She's as gracious as your grandmother and never catty. She's as alluring as a lace brassiere. On top of that—she's bright!"

These qualities have made her the most overworked guest in radio and TV. In one week, she may act the leading role in an hour-long dramatic show and also pop up on three or four ad lib quiz programs. Faye often gives thought-provoking answers. Asked on TV's *Who Said That?*, who was the man of the century, she said: "Churchill was the man of the 19th century—but the man of the 20th century is Eleanor Roosevelt."

Faye's quickness is one of her greatest assets. She does charity-benefit speeches at the nudge of an elbow. Fellow actors claim she "sparks" them. After working with her on some 50 shows, Abe Burrows quips: "Faye Emerson is the guest star I would most like to be stranded with on a deserted TV program."

Away from the TV screen, she is full of TNT. She needs only three hours sleep. Her normal day includes 14 hours of hard work followed by seven hours of dancing. Here's a stand-out Emerson day: At 9 a.m., she did a two-hour fashion sitting for a magazine. By 11 a.m., she was deep in a seven-hour TV dramatic rehearsal. At 8 p.m., dressed in royal robes, she arrived at a packed ballroom to be crowned Queen of the Bock Beer Festival. At 10 p.m., dressed in a leopard skin, she was welcoming 50 guests to a costume party at her own home. To bed at 5 a.m. and up again for an early morning TV rehearsal. How did she feel? "Fine!"

"She's got more energy than a herd of

(Continued on next page)

Photographed by STANLEY KUBRICK

73

FAYE EMERSON continued

F.D.R. to Faye: "we've lots to talk about"

tigers," says her personal maid, Ruth Anderson. "Just keeping that girl's clothes in order is a full-time job. She races out looking elegant, and she rushes home looking like she'd been in a fight. I've seen her rip a dress to rags just wearing it on one television show. She's a high-powered girl."

"Certainly, I wear those fancy dresses," says Faye. "But, really, I'm a white-collar-and-cuffs girl. Till a year ago, I never wore make-up!" She's often unself-conscious as a puppy. Recently, she cut her hair. Until it grows, the sophisticated bun at the nape of her neck is not genuine Emerson. But if engrossed in a party game, she casually removes her hair piece, parks it on the piano. (For more about Faye's hair see page 77.)

Faye was born in Elizabeth, La. She spent her childhood in Texas and California, wound up acting in the San Diego Civic Theater. At 21, she married auto salesman William Wallace Crawford, Jr., had a son the following year. They nicknamed the baby Scoop.

"Until Scoop was born," says a close friend, "Faye was a thin, bony, brown-haired girl without a curve to her name. She's been curvacious ever since."

In 1941, Faye advanced to Hollywood via a seven-year Warner Brothers contract. There, her hair became blonde, her roles exotic and, for the next five years, she wove her way through some 20 pictures, among them *The Desert Song, Hotel Berlin, Danger Signal*. In '42, she divorced Crawford. A year later, she went to a party given by Howard Hughes for President Roosevelt's son, Elliott, then a colonel in the U. S. Army Air Force.

She Shelved Politics for Cupid

"Faye was asked because she is a ferocious Democrat," says a friend. "But the minute she and Elliott met, Cupid took the place of politics." Fourteen months later, they were married on the rim of Colorado's Grand Canyon in one of the country's most publicized weddings. Their 23-day honeymoon included Faye's first visit to the White House, where she met F.D.R. over the breakfast table. "She was so excited," says Elliott, "that, for once, she was dressed early. My father put his arm around Faye, pulled her down to kiss her, and said: 'You sit right here beside me—we've got a lot to talk about, you and I.'" They spent Christmas at Hyde Park with the family. She saw her father-in-law only one other time—at the inaugural ceremony. The following April, with John's and James' wives, she traveled East to attend the President's funeral.

When the war ended, Faye came East with Scoop. She and Elliott went on a seven-week trip through Russia as special correspondents for LOOK, talked to Stalin for an hour. Back home, they divided their time between a New York apartment and the Hyde Park cottage built by F.D.R. for his retirement. Here, they entertained swarms of important visitors, including Winston Churchill, "Ike" Eisenhower, Mme. Chiang Kai-shek. Sometimes, Eleanor Roosevelt came over from her house with a crowd of U.N. delegates in tow.

Publicity dogged Faye and Elliott. Faye sat beside her husband during the five Congressional investigations in which he was involved. She still says loyally: "He was cleared of everything." Other headlines dealt with his Christmas-tree venture during which Faye helped him hawk trees. Then came headlines announcing that Faye had slashed her wrists. Says Elliott: "This was pure accident, but again publicity distorted everything."

Behind the headlines, they seemed devoted. Elliott and Faye exchanged jewelry. He gave her a mink coat and a green convertible she still drives. When Faye came out of retirement in '48 to star in *The Play's the Thing*, Elliott was her stage-door Johnny. Faye was equally interested in his real-estate business and his writing. He says now: "Faye helped me edit my books—the first two volumes of my father's personal letters. *As He Saw It* and the novel I'm writing about John Paul Jones. She gave me the title for it: *Star Spangled Jones*."

But the two separated the summer of 1949. In New York Faye made the movie *Guilty Bystander*. Last January, she flew to Mexico for a divorce. Now, she and Scoop live in a Park Avenue terrace apartment.

She Makes Big Money, Spends Big Money

Faye's day-to-day living costs her $1,500 a month, not including clothes. She pays $500 a month rent, sends Scoop to private school, pays a maid and secretary. She receives no alimony from Elliott nor did he make a settlement. Her money is self-earned. She got around $1,000 a week for the *Faye Emerson Show* on CBS-TV, gets from $500 to $1,000 per guest appearance. This summer, she began earning another weekly $1,000 for her new TV show *Fifteen with Faye*—Wednesdays at 8 P.M., EDT, over NBC-TV, sponsored by Snow Crop frozen foods. "By the end of the year, I should easily make around $75,000," says Faye. TV experts predict that in 1951 she will earn $200,000 from television alone—a conservative estimate in view of her five-year, Pepsi-Cola contract for a tri-weekly 15 minute show over CBS-TV at 7:45 P.M., starting next month.

Her future plans include movies and a Broadway play. The pressure of offers has necessitated her opening a Fifth Avenue office called Penthouse Productions. With Hardie Frieberg, she plans to co-produce her own and other TV shows. Her super-selling power was proved when the Philadelphia Chapter of the American Marketing Association named her "TV's Number 1 Saleswoman."

Meanwhile, she continues to star in *Fifteen with Faye*, tossing banter with newscaster Kenneth Banghart against a beautiful summer terrace set. Its Manhattan audience, estimated at 556,000, is half made up of tired housewives who crave "glamour after a dull day." Backstage, Faye is in command. Her generalship is brilliant and inefficiency infuriates her. Her rages are volcanic, violent and brief. One night, during the run of *The Play's the Thing*, an acid-tongued press agent made the mistake of dropping into her dressing room and criticizing Elliott Roosevelt. Faye's loyalty went to her fists. Five-foot-four-inch Faye delivered a haymaker and chased the agent out of her room.

Faye has fought hard to be First Lady of Television. If she were worried that the public would remember her as Mrs. Roosevelt and not as Miss Emerson—she can relax.

END

Faye juggles two telephones and a dozen projects in her new 5th Ave. Penthouse Productions office.

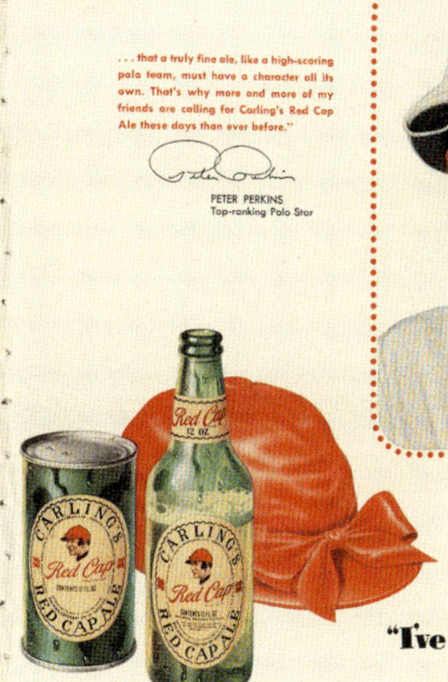

74

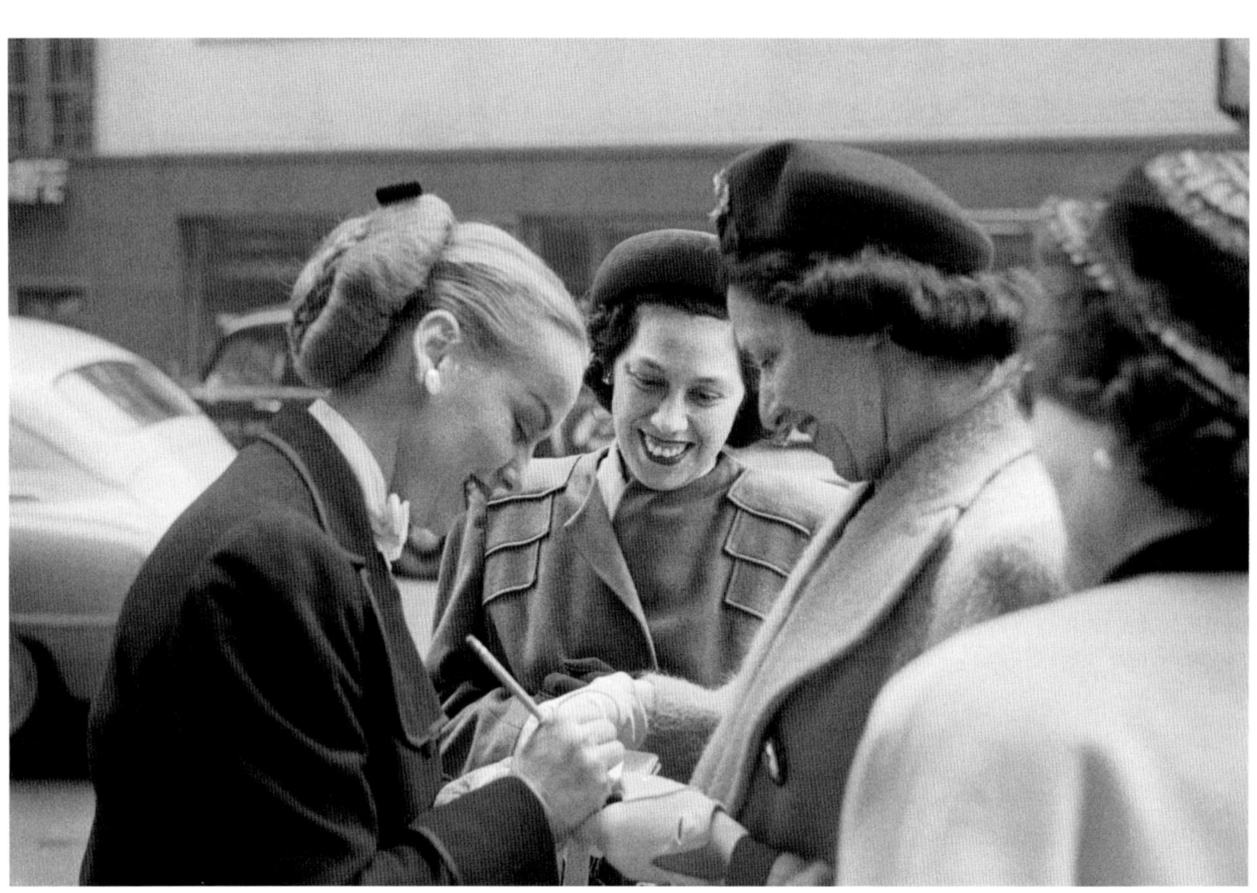

Emerson signing autographs for smiling fans

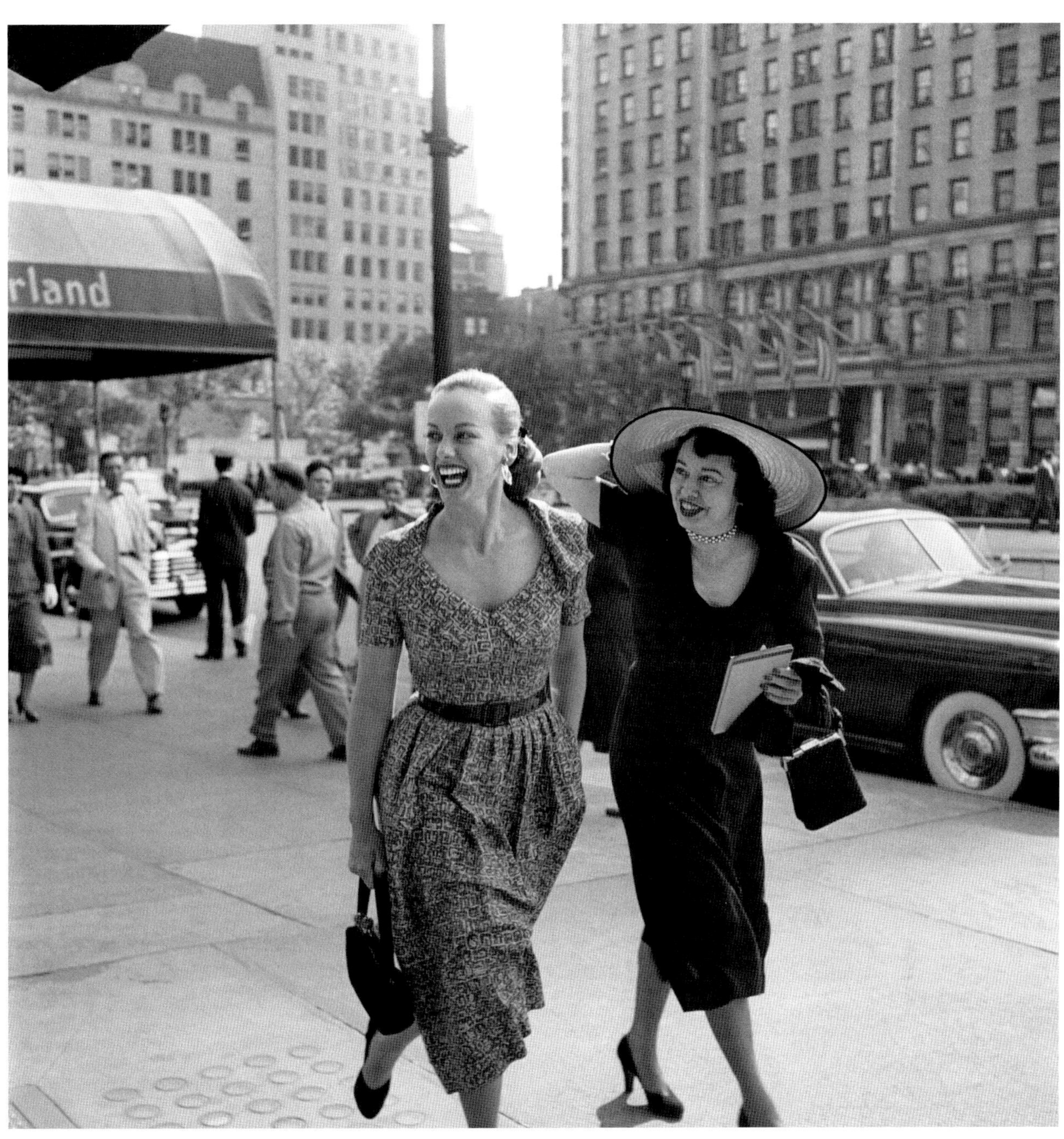

Emerson being interviewed near the Plaza Hotel by the article's author, society columnist Eleanor Harris

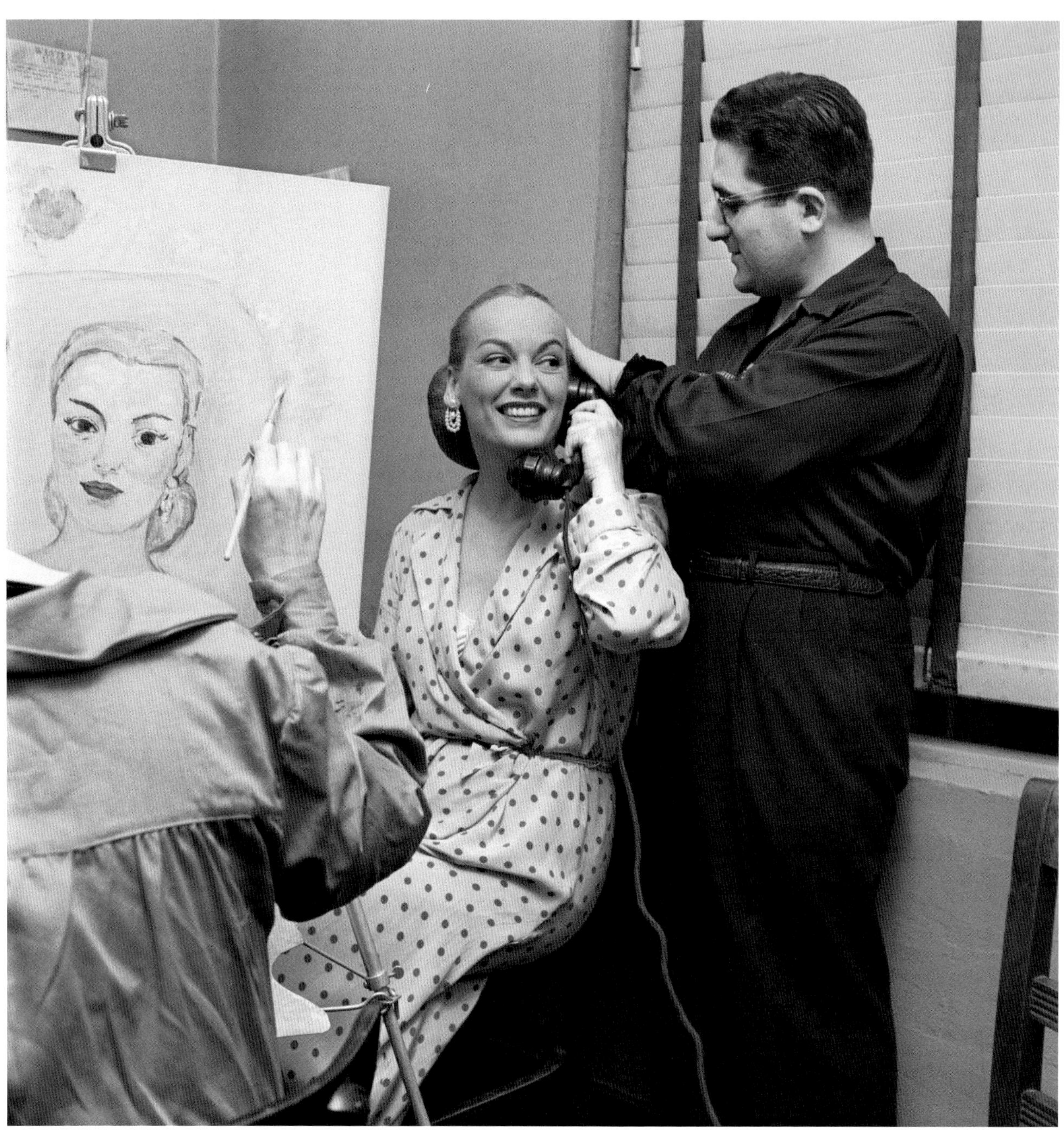

Emerson sitting for a portrait, having her hair done and making calls between shows at the Roxy Theater

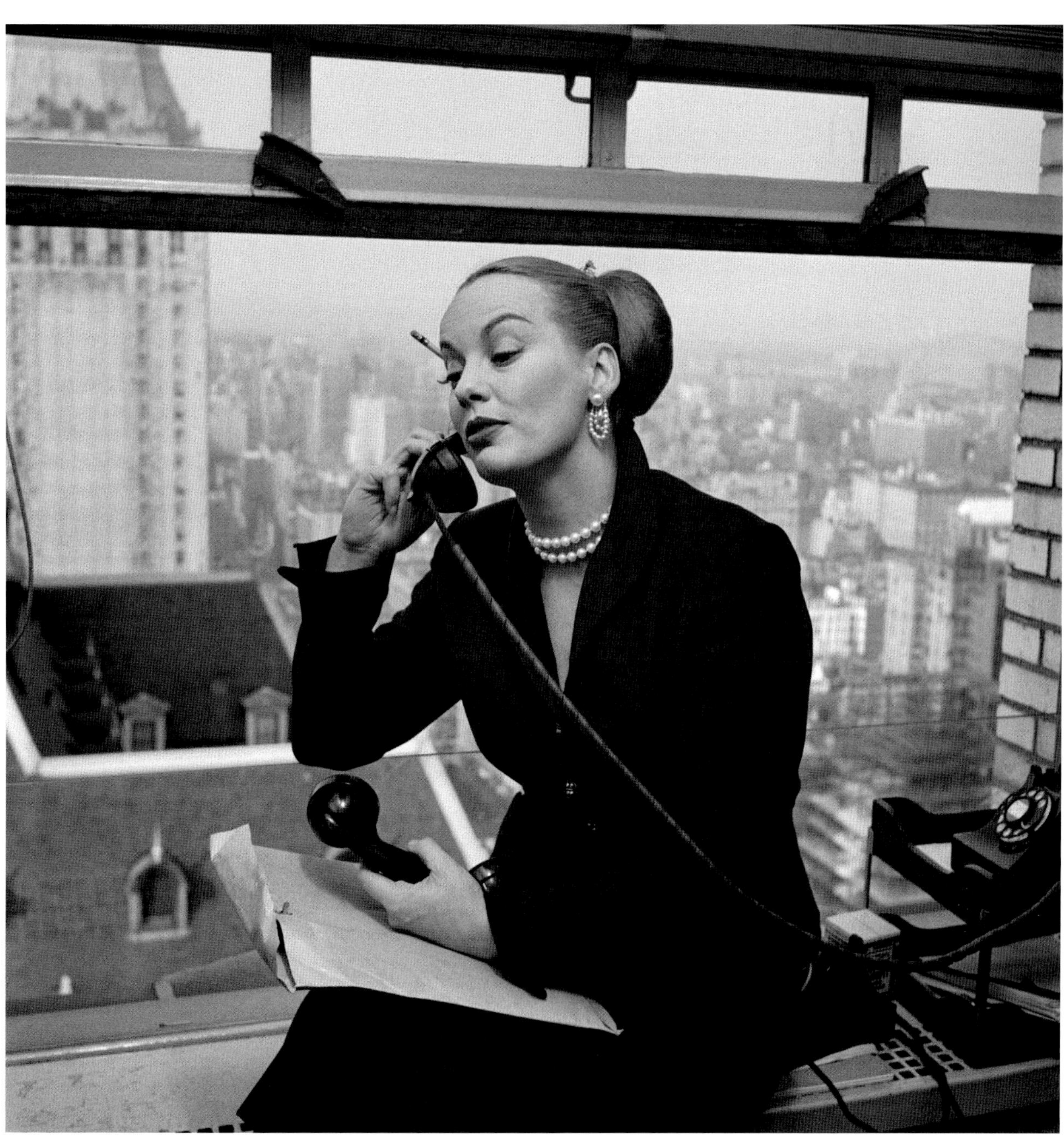

Emerson juggling two telephones at her
Fifth Avenue Penthouse Productions office

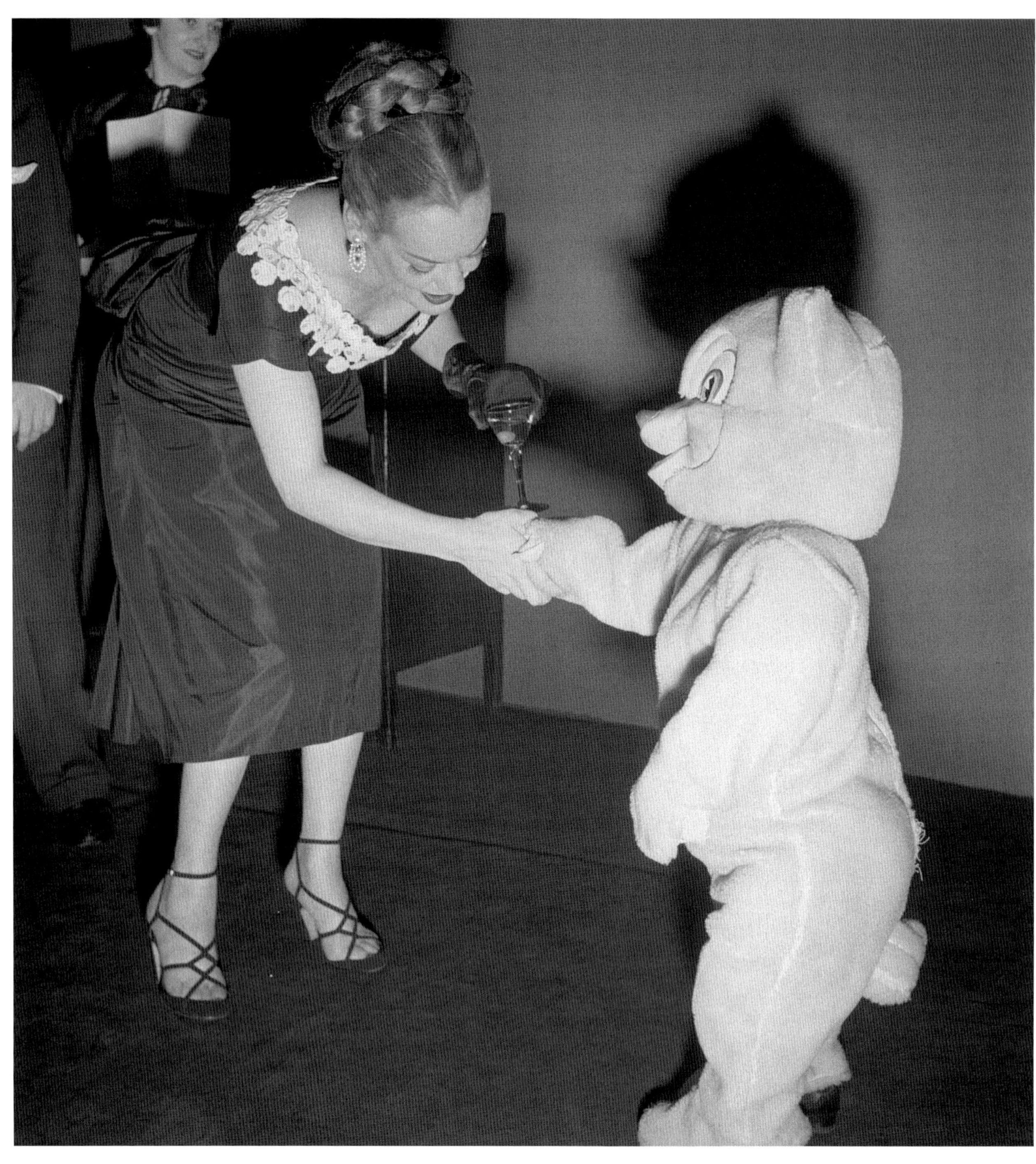

Emerson at a party given for her TV show's sponsors, Snow Crop frozen orange juice, and with the sponsor's mascot, Teddy

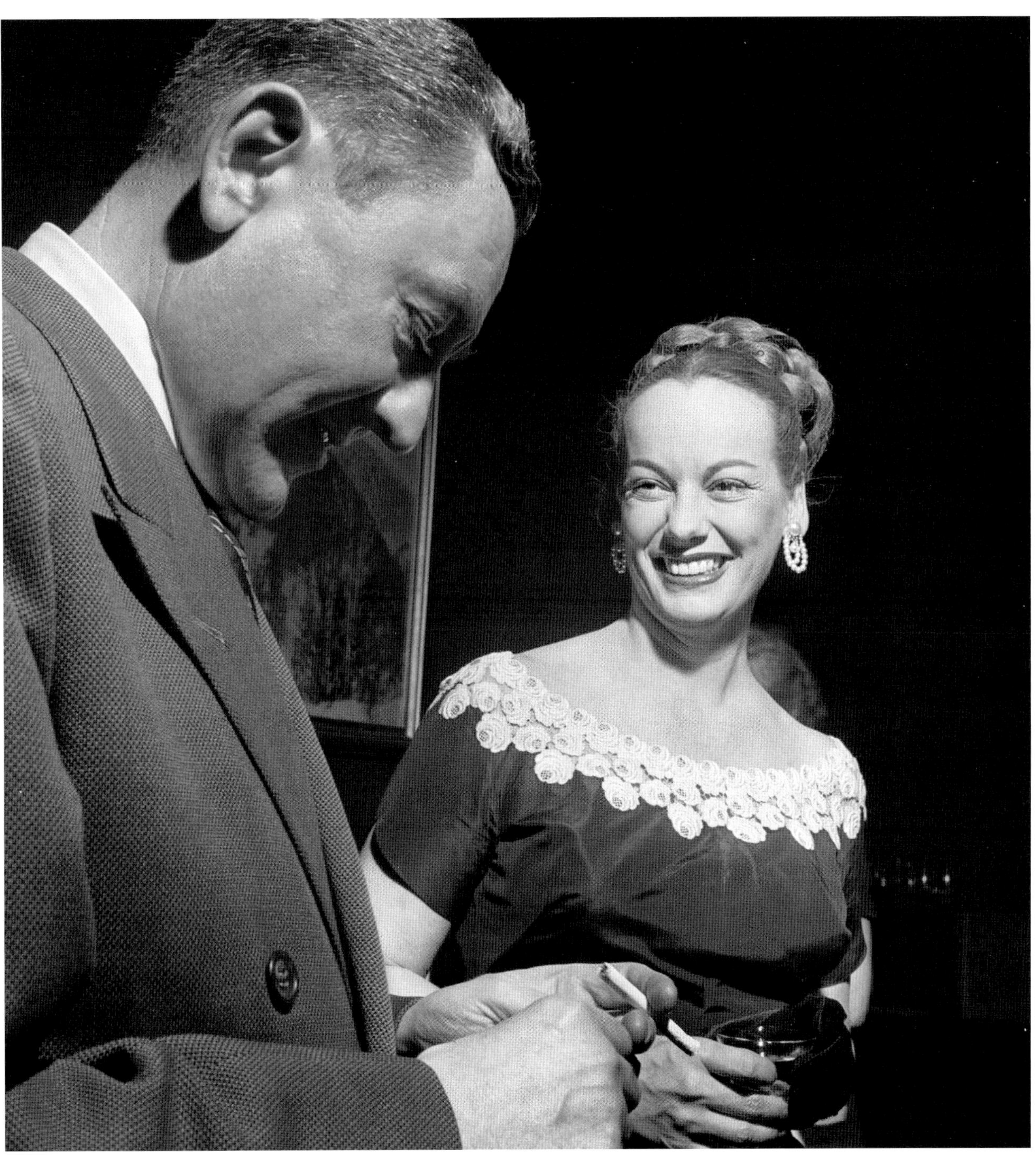

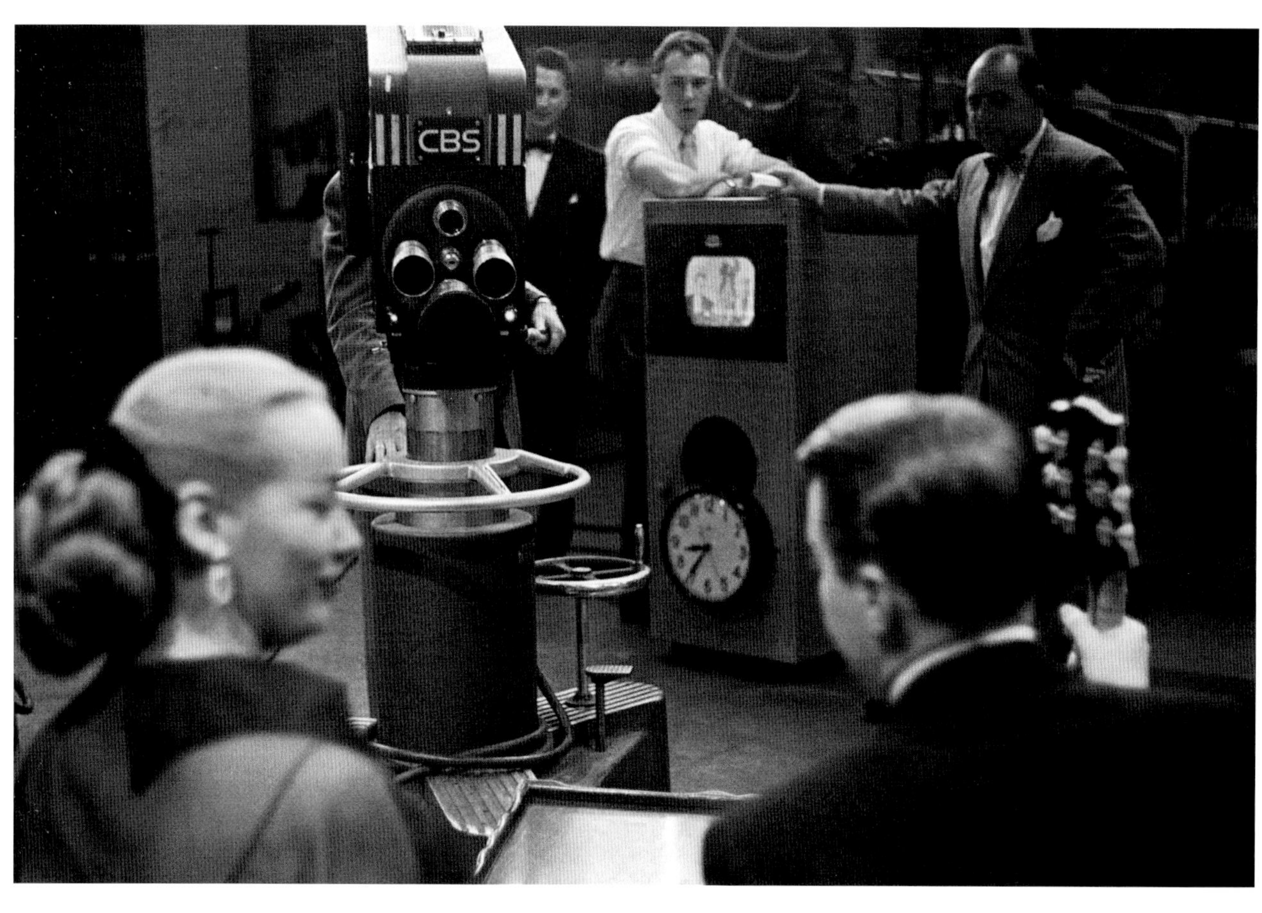

Emerson on the set of her new television show *Fifteen with Faye*

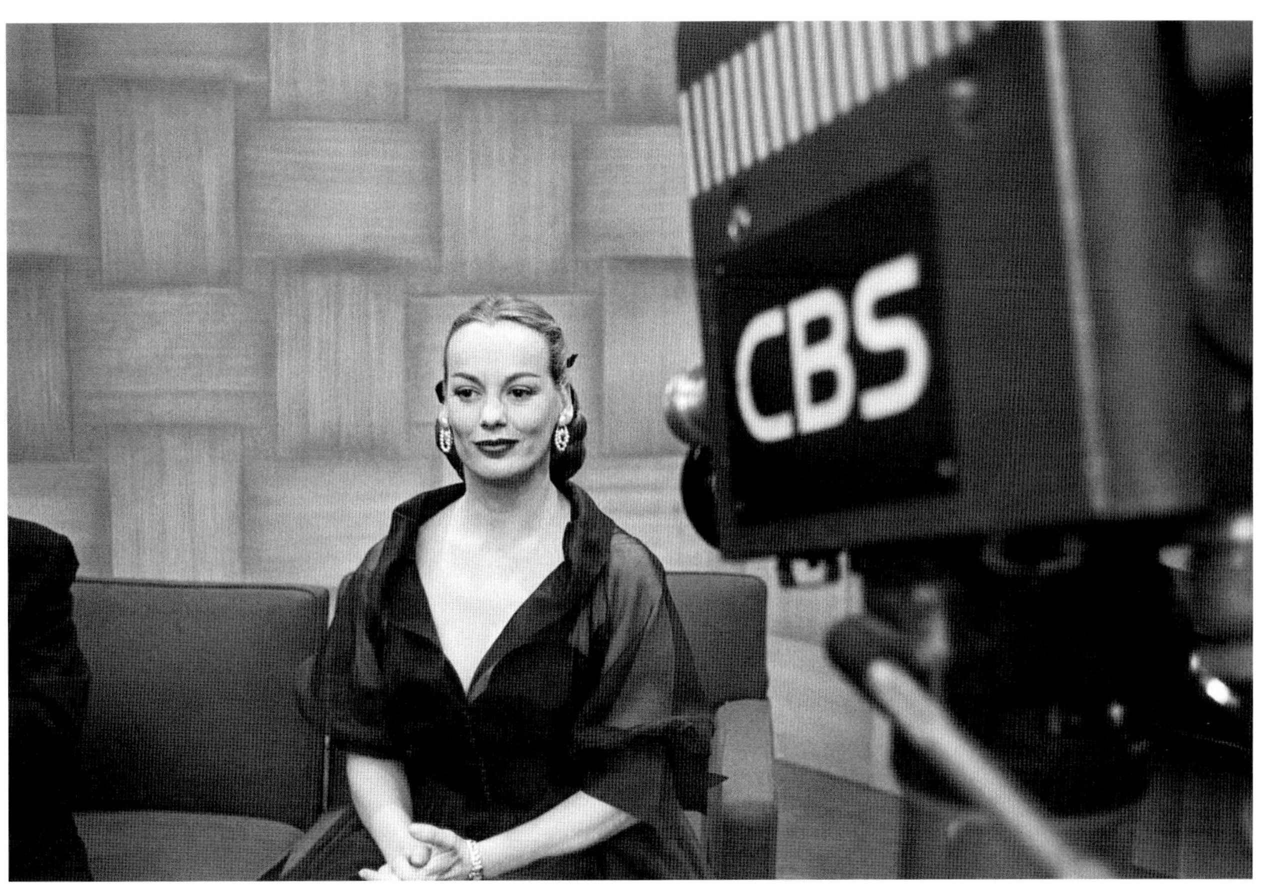
CBS

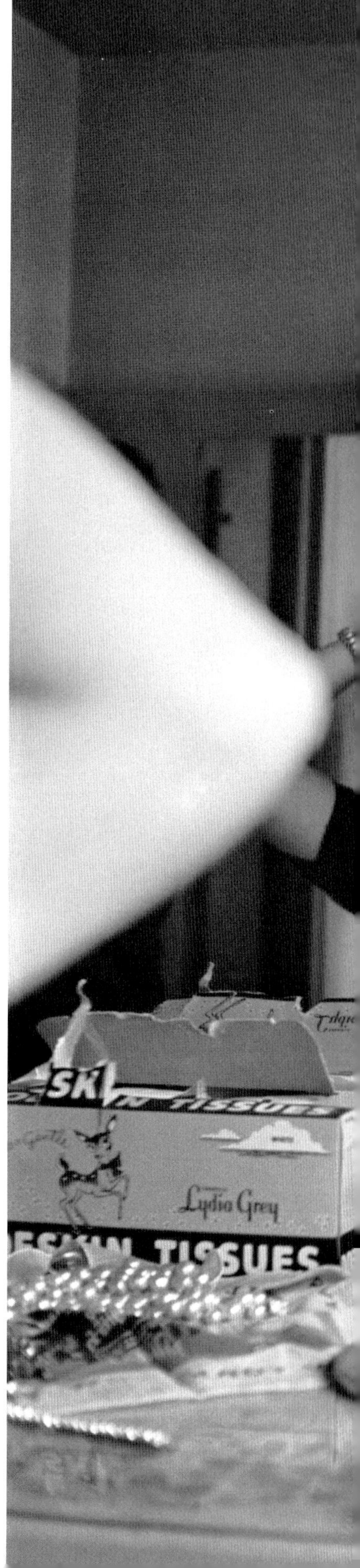

Emerson in her dressing room, having her portrait taken by Kubrick

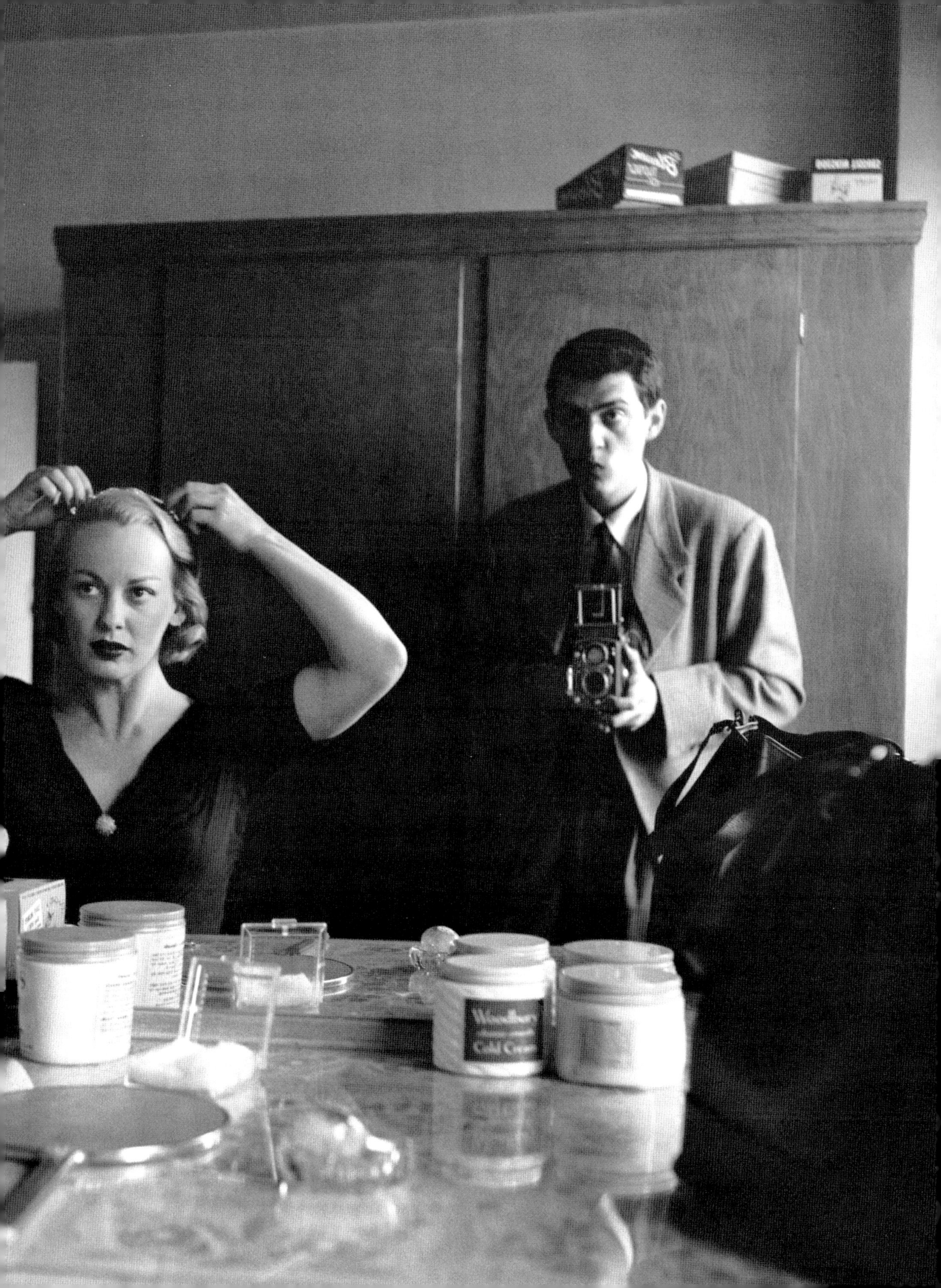

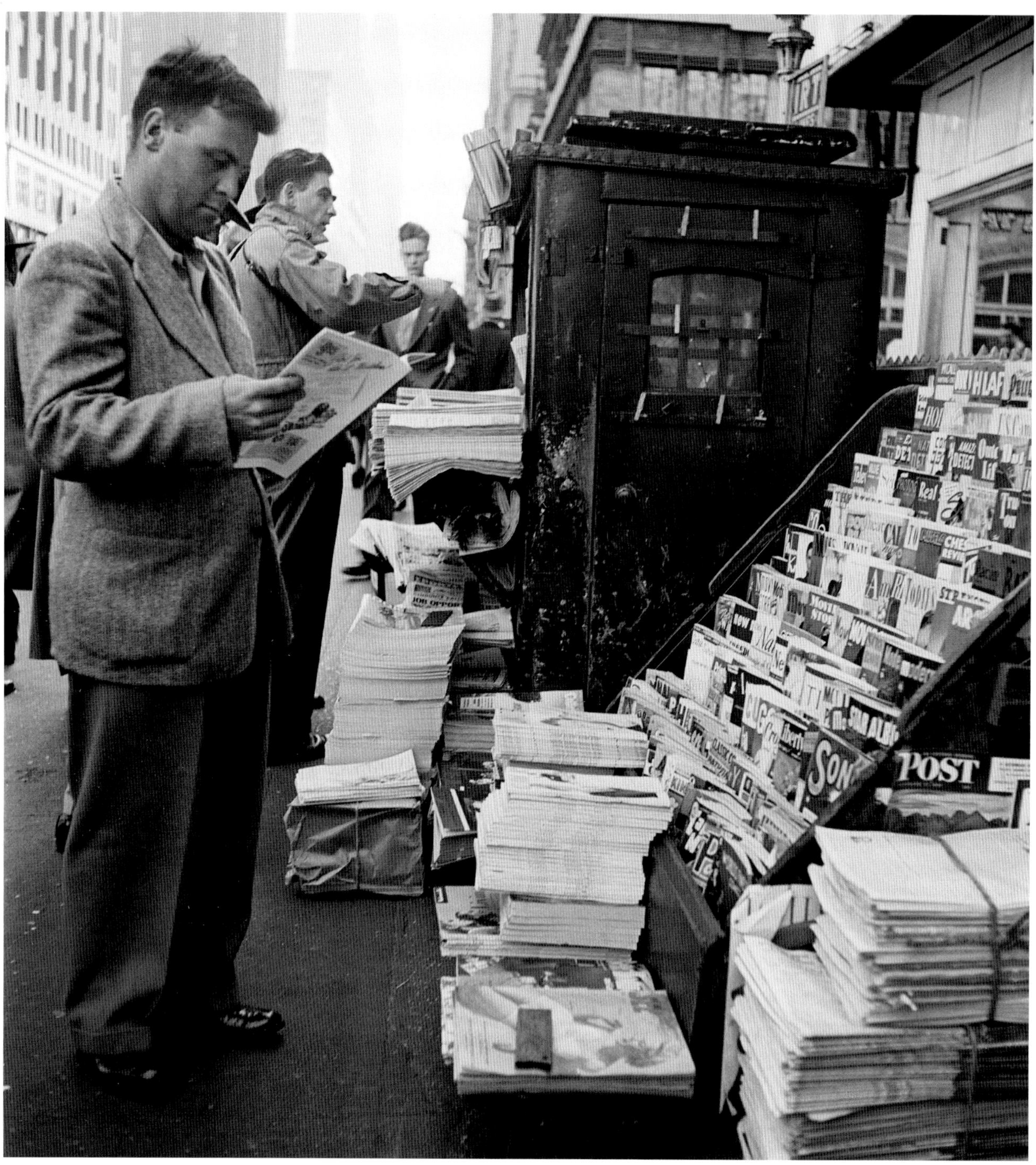
POST

ADDITIONAL ASSIGNMENTS 1946–1950

This appendix of Kubrick's additional assignments for *Look* magazine complements the work featured in the body of this book. Together, they represent all of Kubrick's assignments for *Look* that are held in the collections of the Museum of the City of New York. The editors considered various factors when deciding where in the book to place an assignment. Those in the appendix often comprised just a few photographs, sometimes planned for recurring short features. Most were unpublished, so little, if anything, is known about the story they were meant to illustrate. A few reiterated subject matter that the editors found more compellingly explored in other assignments. While the assignments here have neither the quantitative nor the qualitative heft of those in the body of the book, they provide a more complete picture of Kubrick's work for *Look*.

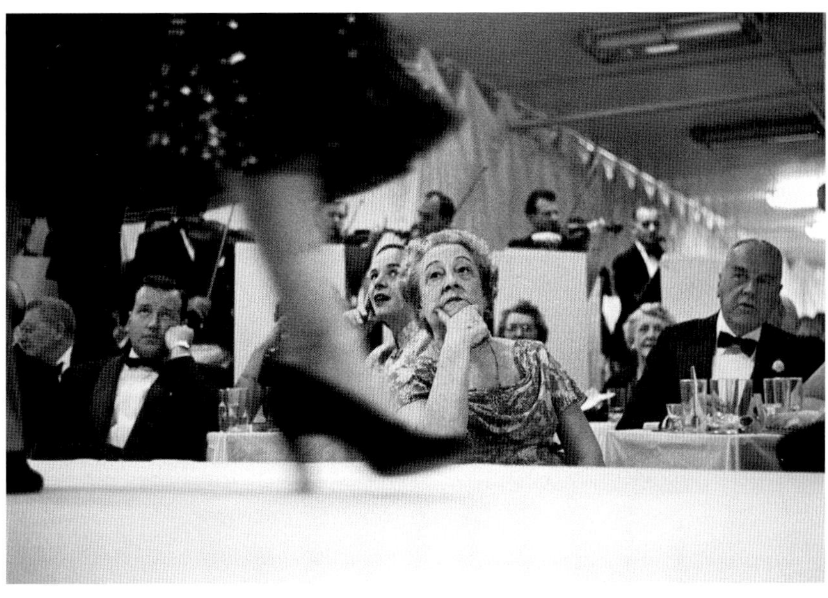

OPPOSITE
DATE: **OCTOBER 7, 1947**
TITLE: **NEWSSTAND**

ABOVE
DATE: **SEPTEMBER 12, 1949**
TITLE: **GIMBELS FASHION SHOW**

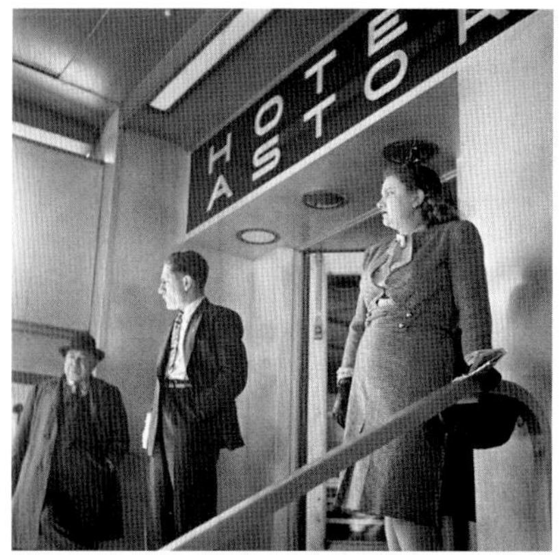

DATE: **APRIL 16, 1946**
TITLE: **ASTOR HOTEL**

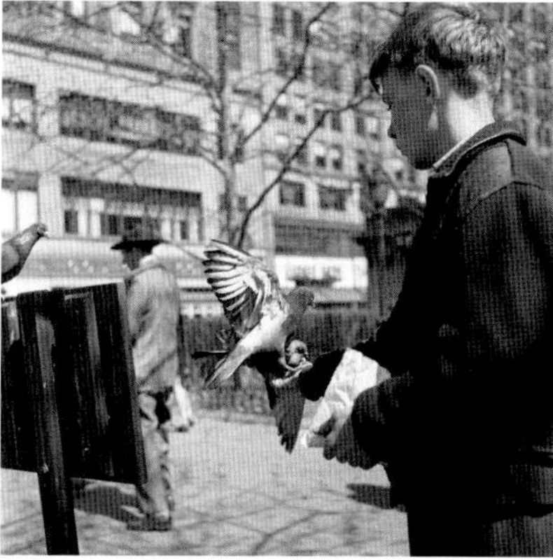

DATE: **APRIL 17, 1946**
TITLE: **PIGEONS**

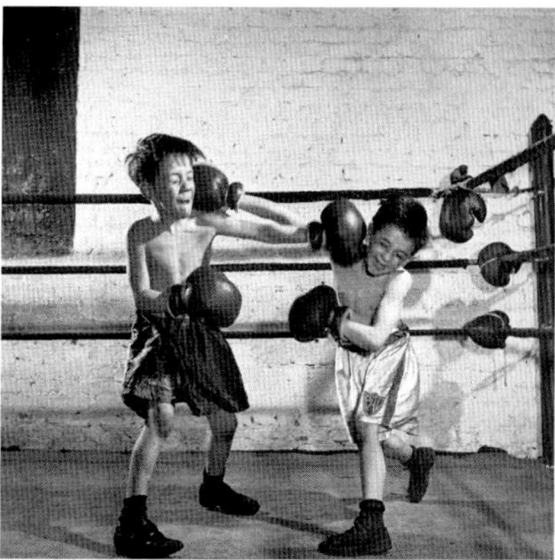

DATE: **MAY 13, 1946**
TITLE: **POLICE ATHLETIC LEAGUE**

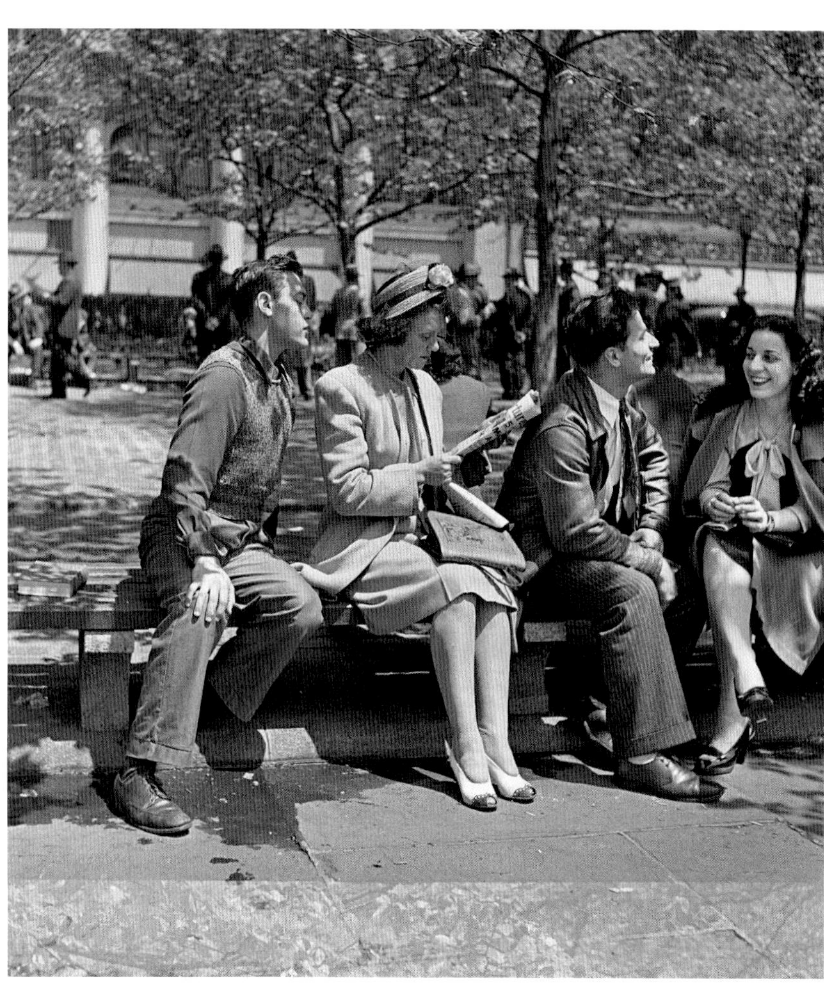

DATE: **APRIL 17, 1946**
TITLE: **PARK BENCH NUISANCE**

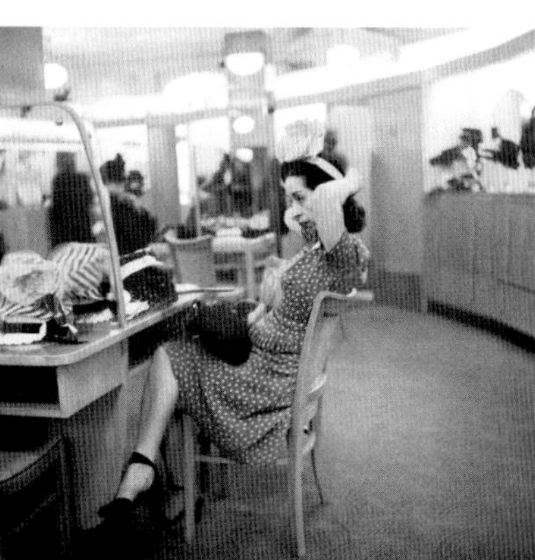

DATE: **JUNE 11, 1946**
TITLE: **A WOMAN BUYS A HAT**

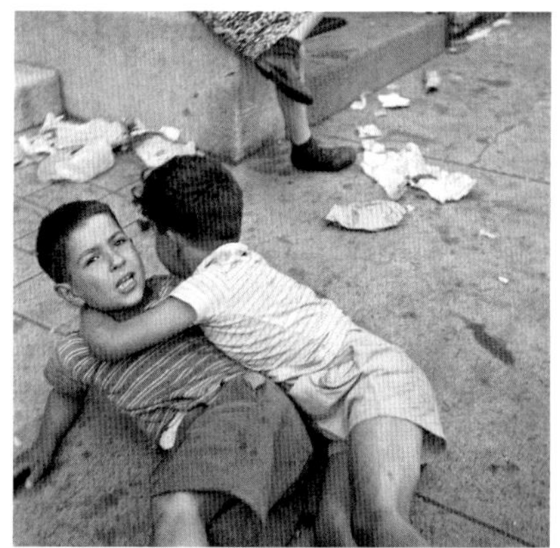

DATE: **JULY 16, 1946**
TITLE: **STREET FIGHTER**

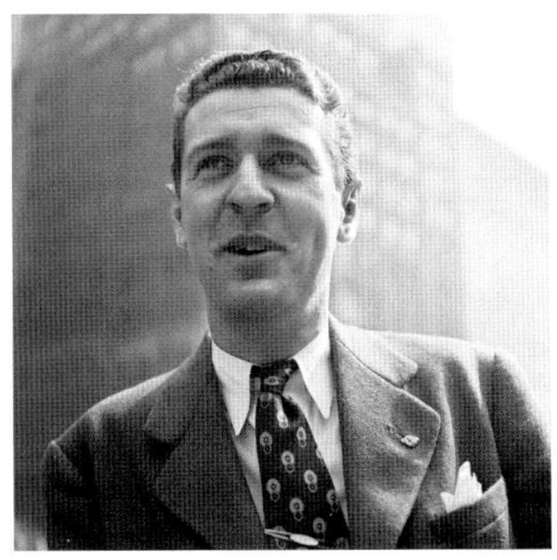

DATE: **DECEMBER 10, 1946**
TITLE: **MEET THE PEOPLE: WHAT'S YOUR IDEA OF A GOOD TIME?**

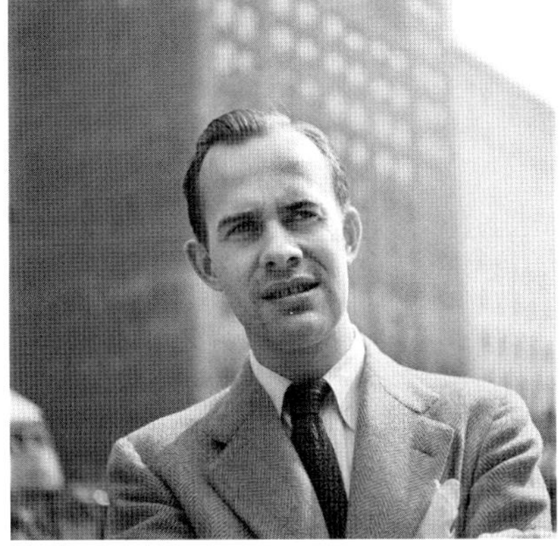

DATE: **DECEMBER 10, 1946**
TITLE: **HAROLD SHAW, PRODUCER**

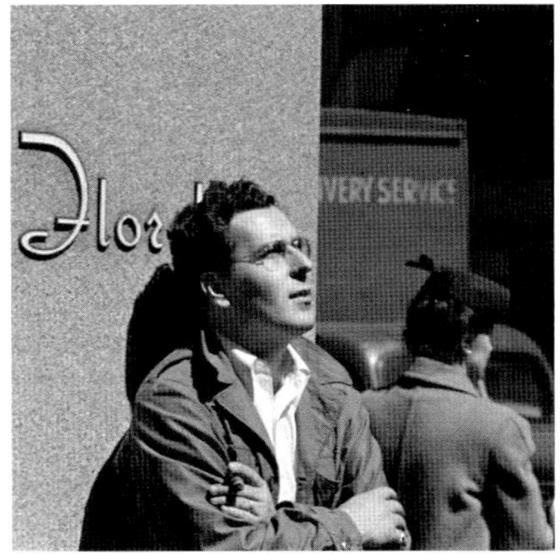

DATE: **APRIL 15, 1947**
TITLE: **PEOPLE WAITING**

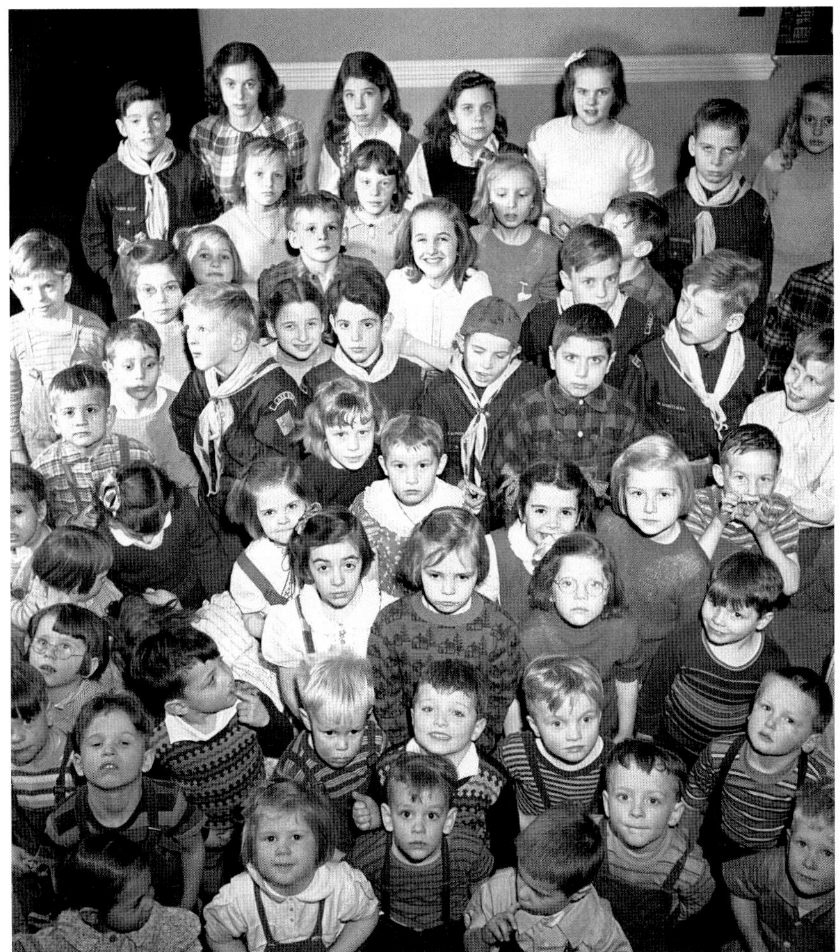

DATE: **JANUARY 20, 1947**
TITLE: **ORPHANAGE STORY/LAKE BLUFF, ILLINOIS**

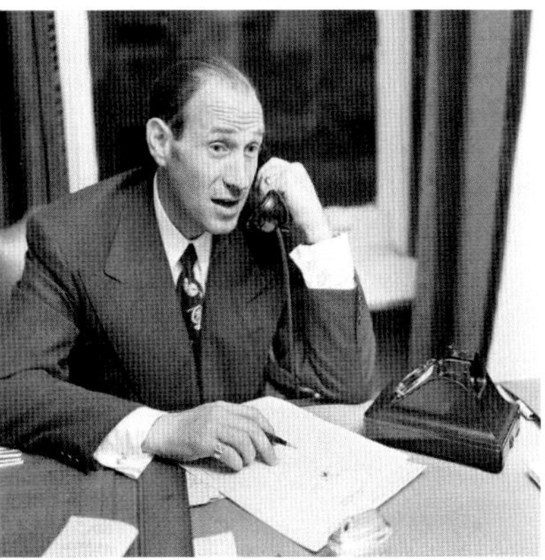

DATE: **JUNE 25, 1947**
TITLE: **BUDDY CLARK, SINGER**

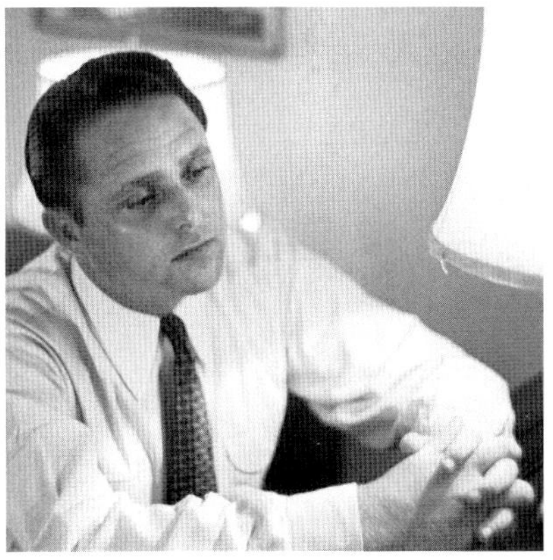

DATE: **SEPTEMBER 4, 1947**
TITLE: **CHRISTOPHER LYNCH**

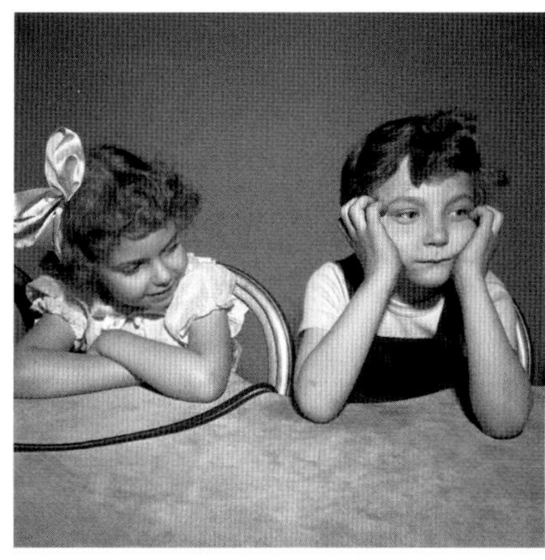

DATE: **SEPTEMBER 16, 1947**
TITLE: **MEET THE PEOPLE: IF YOU'RE BAD HOW SHOULD YOU BE PUNISHED?**

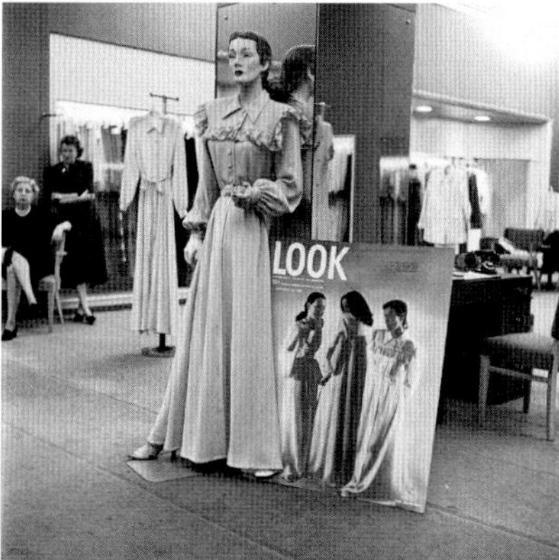

DATE: **OCTOBER 14, 1947**
TITLE: **LORD & TAYLOR DISPLAY**

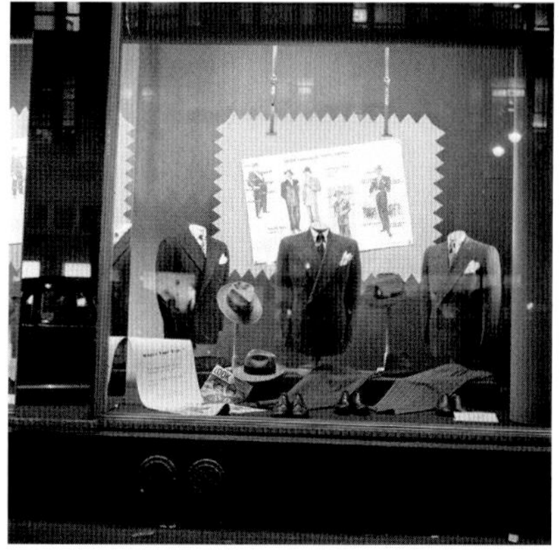

DATE: **OCTOBER 21, 1947**
TITLE: **ABRAHAM STRAUS**

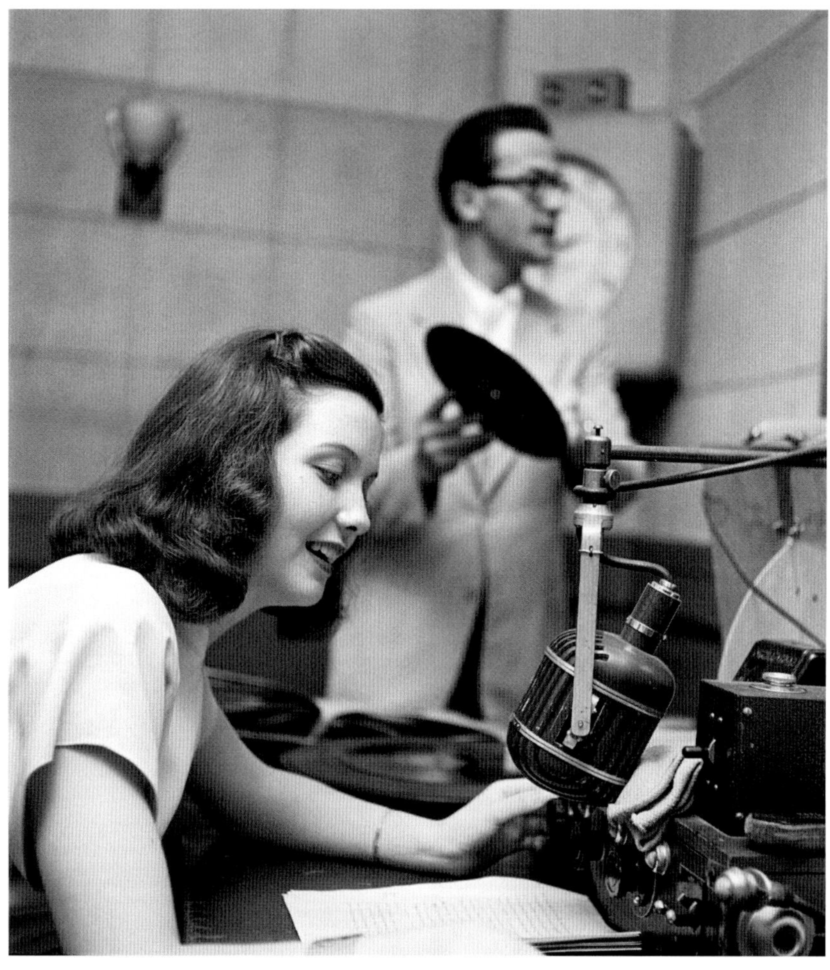

DATE: **OCTOBER 14, 1947**
TITLE: **TEENAGERS TAKE OVER A RADIO STATION**

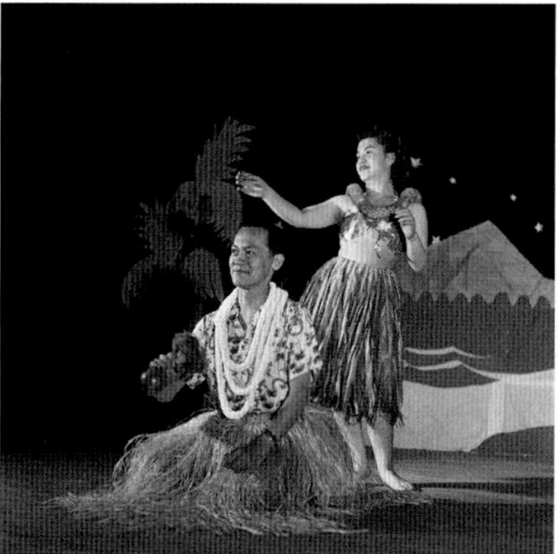

DATE: **OCTOBER 27, 1947**
TITLE: **INTERNATIONAL HOUSE**

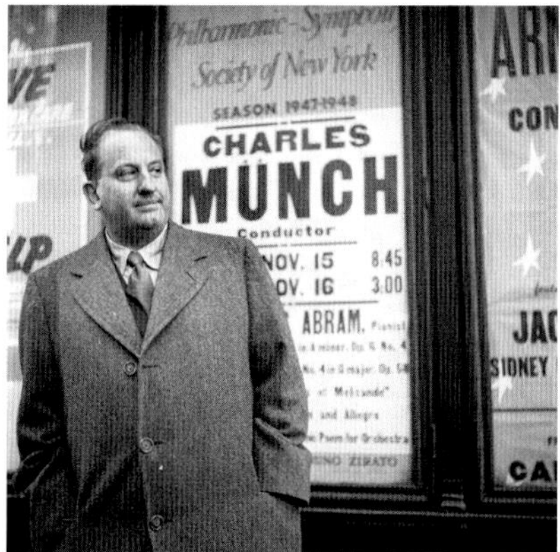

DATE: **NOVEMBER 14, 1947**
TITLE: **SOL HUROK, IMPRESARIO**

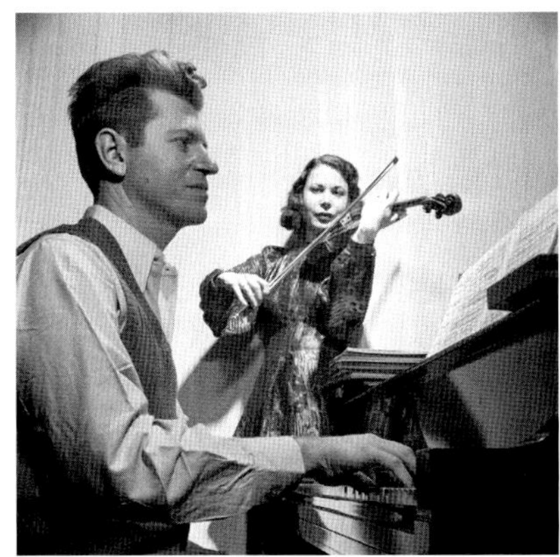

DATE: **DECEMBER 1, 1947**
TITLE: **EUGENE LITZ AND WIFE**

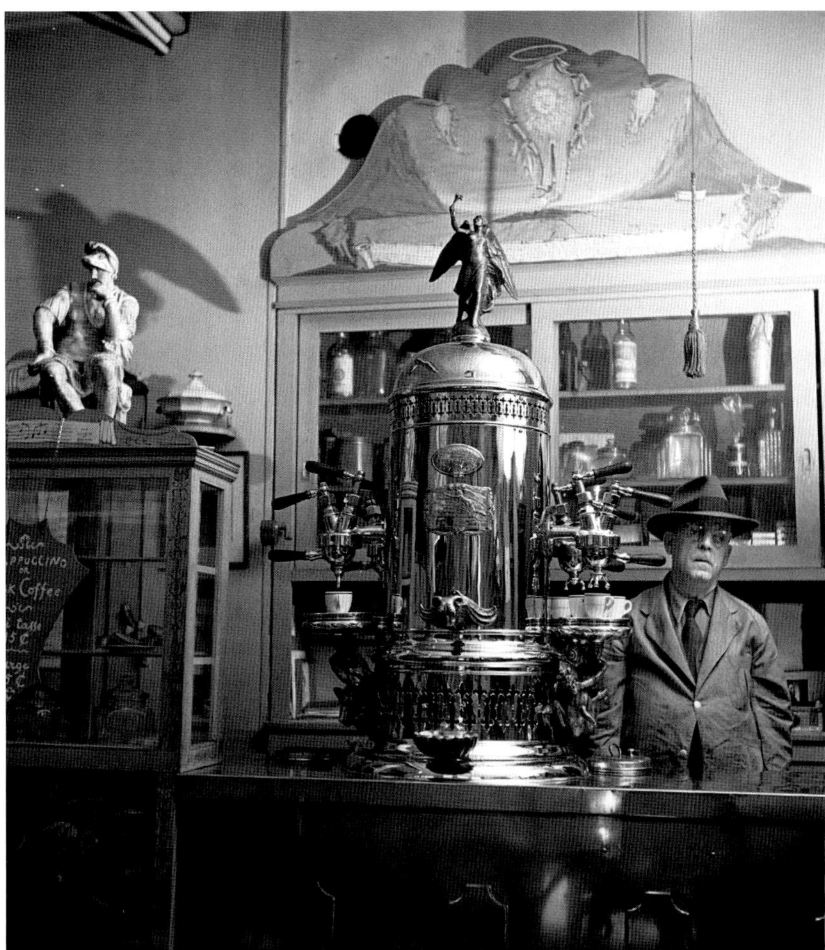

DATE: **DECEMBER 9, 1947**
TITLE: **COFFEE: AMERICA LOVES IT AND MAKES IT IN MANY WAYS**

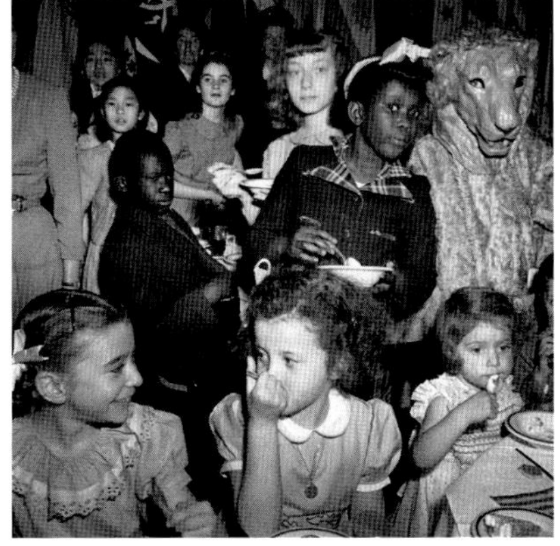

DATE: **DECEMBER 1, 1947**
TITLE: **UNITED NATIONS CHILDREN'S PARTY**

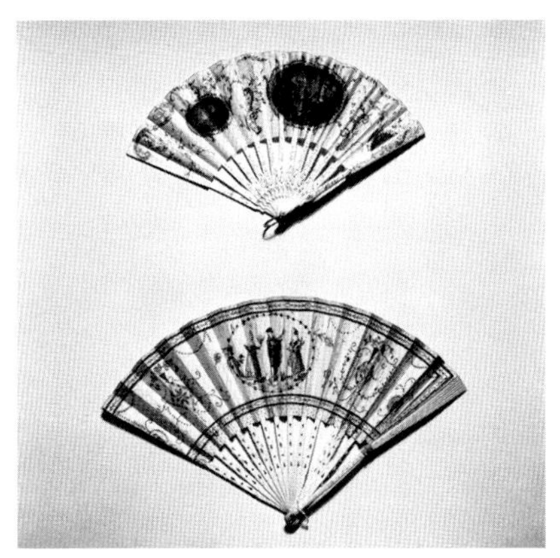

DATE: **DECEMBER 9, 1947**
TITLE: **FANS WILL FLUTTER AGAIN**

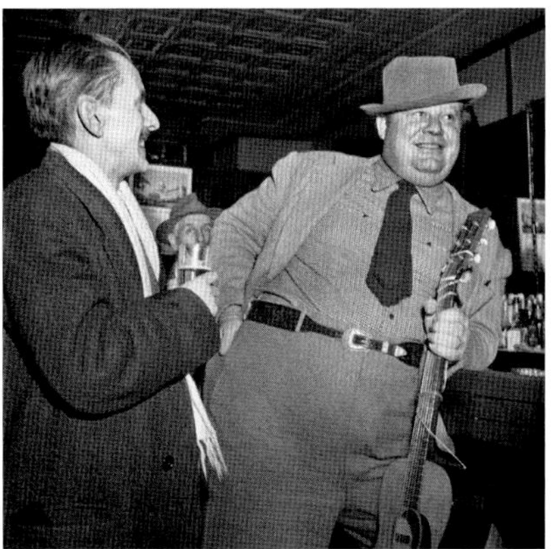

DATE: **DECEMBER 15, 1947**
TITLE: **BURL IVES**

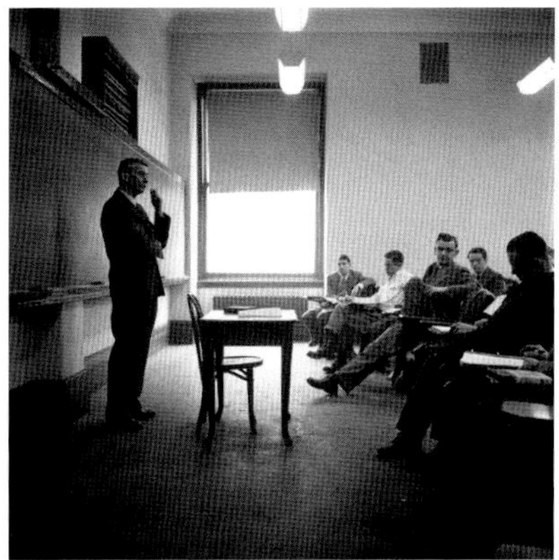

DATE: **FEBRUARY 9, 1948**
TITLE: **MARK VAN DOREN**

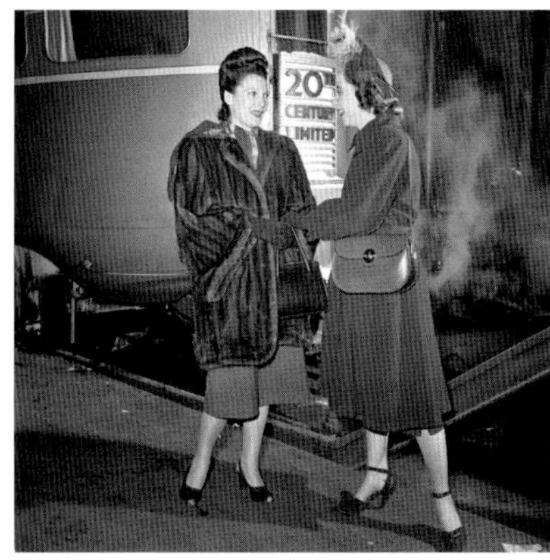

DATE: **APRIL 1, 1948**
TITLE: **NEW YORK CENTRAL—20TH CENTURY LIMITED**

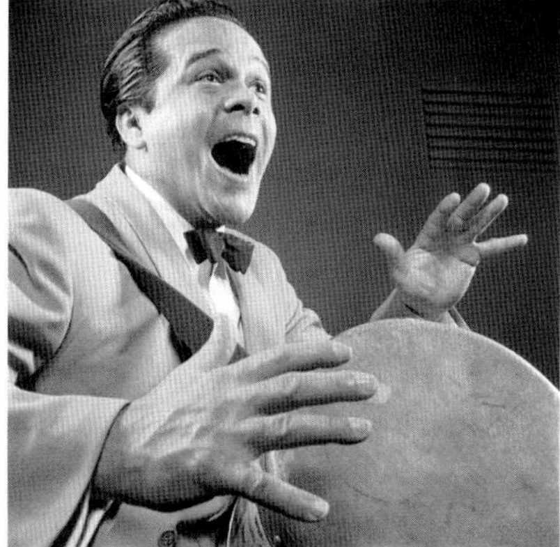

DATE: **APRIL 13, 1948**
TITLE: **MIGUELITO VALDÉS**

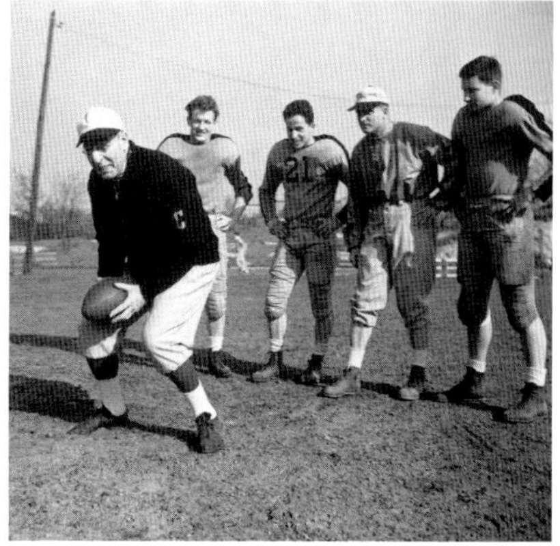

DATE: **APRIL 1948**
TITLE: **LOU LITTLE**

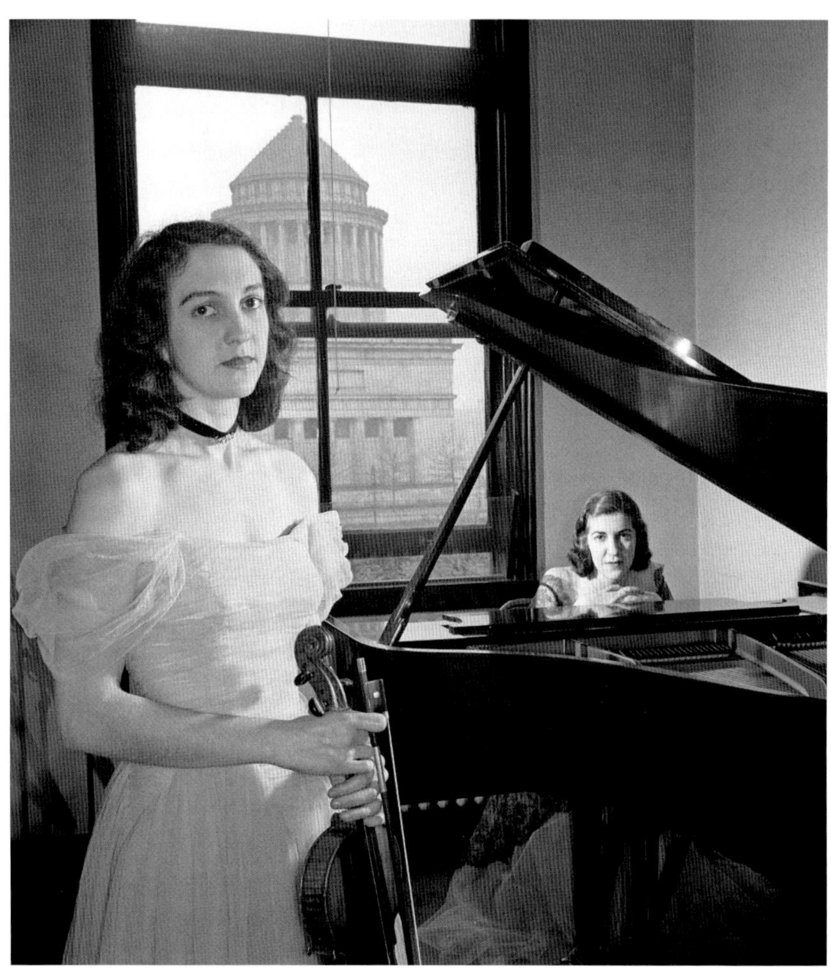

DATE: **APRIL 29, 1948**
TITLE: **TWO SISTERS**

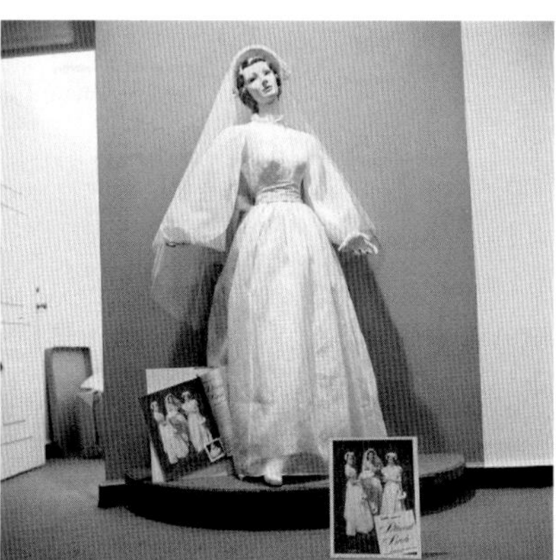

DATE: **MAY 20, 1948**
TITLE: **FRANKLIN SIMON & CO.**

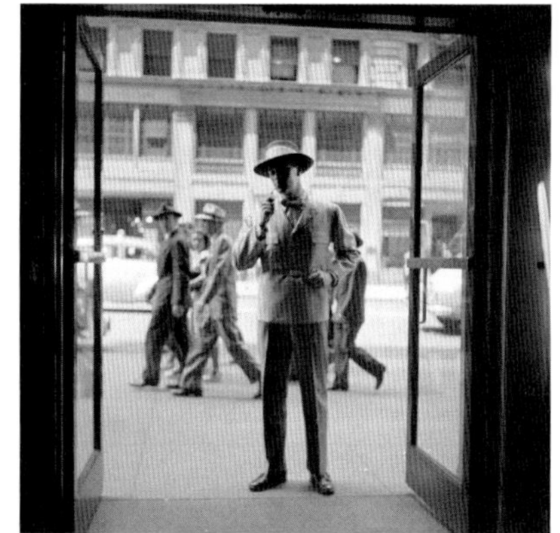

DATE: **AUGUST 17, 1948**
TITLE: **NEW LOOK FOR MEN**

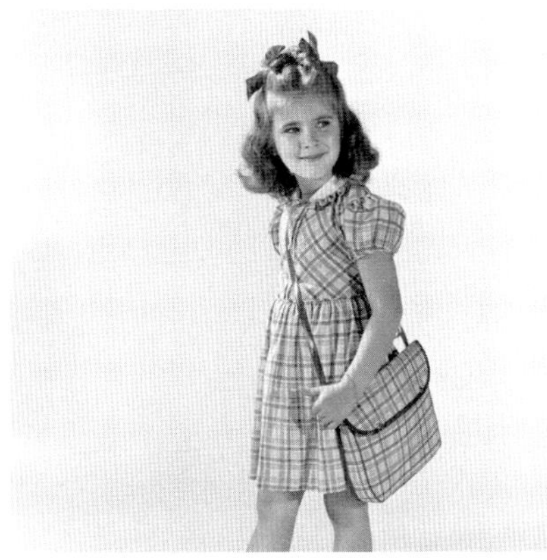

DATE: **AUGUST 17, 1948**
TITLE: **BUMPER BABY CROP STARTS SCHOOL**

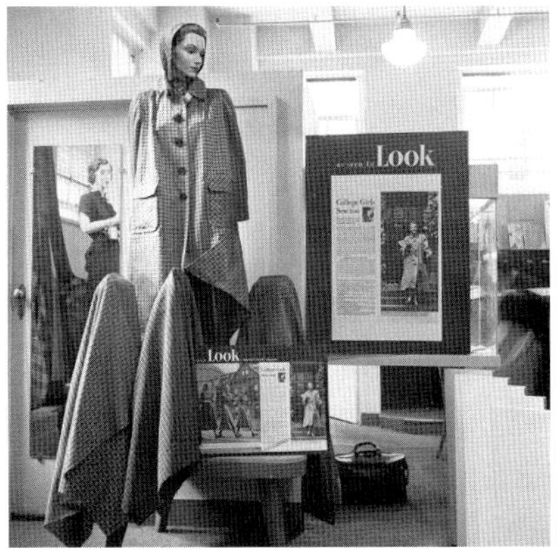

DATE: **SEPTEMBER 2, 1948**
TITLE: **BLOOMINGDALE'S**

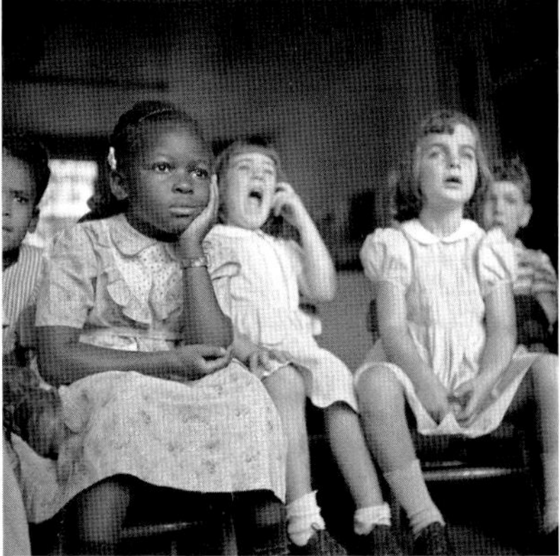

DATE: **OCTOBER 1, 1948**
TITLE: **CHILDREN'S BOOK TRYOUTS**

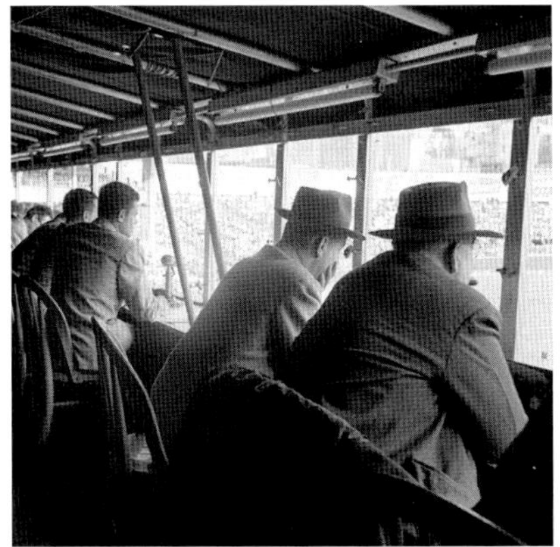

DATE: **OCTOBER 18, 1948**
TITLE: **FOOTBALL WRITERS**

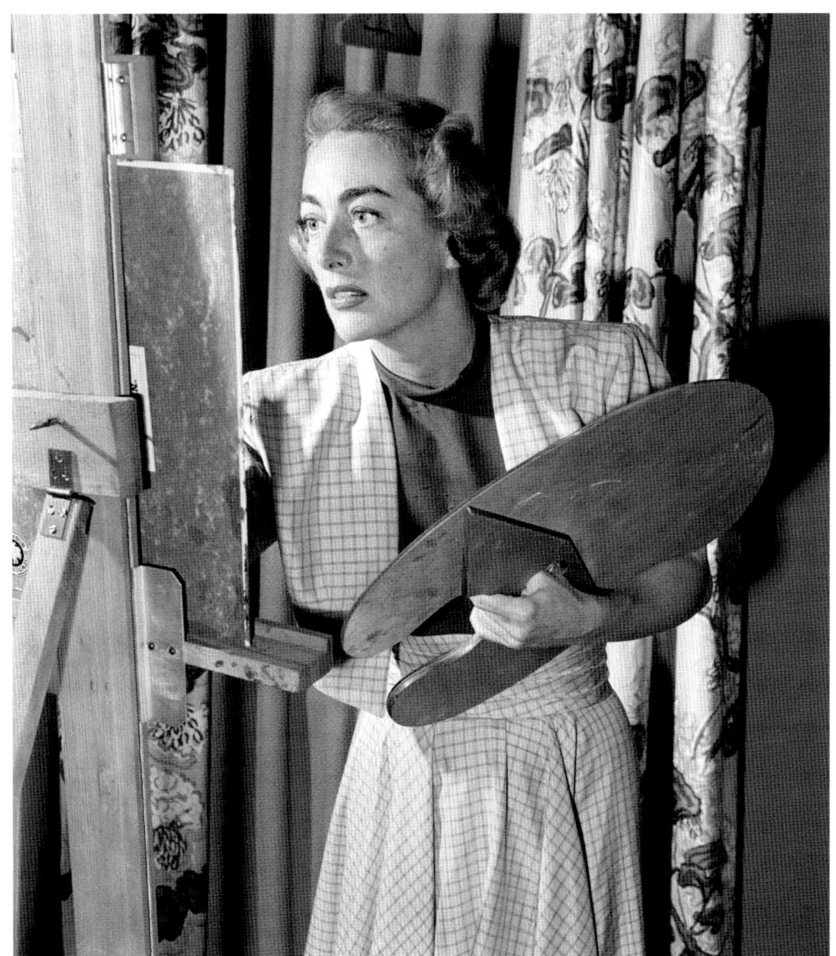

DATE: **OCTOBER 12, 1948**
TITLE: **CELEBRITIES PAINT FOR A CAUSE**

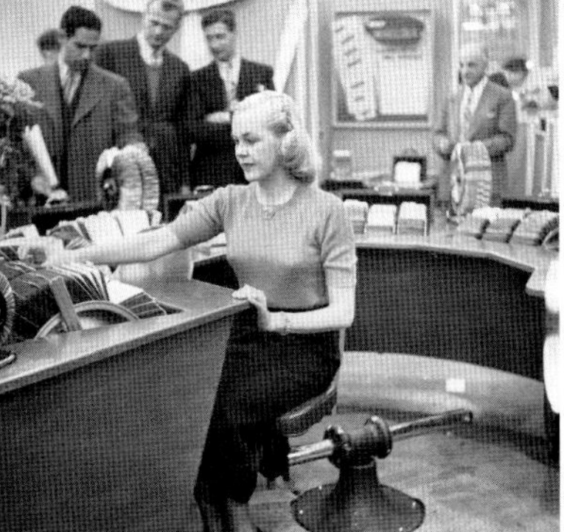

DATE: **OCTOBER 28, 1948**
TITLE: **NATIONAL BUSINESS SHOW**

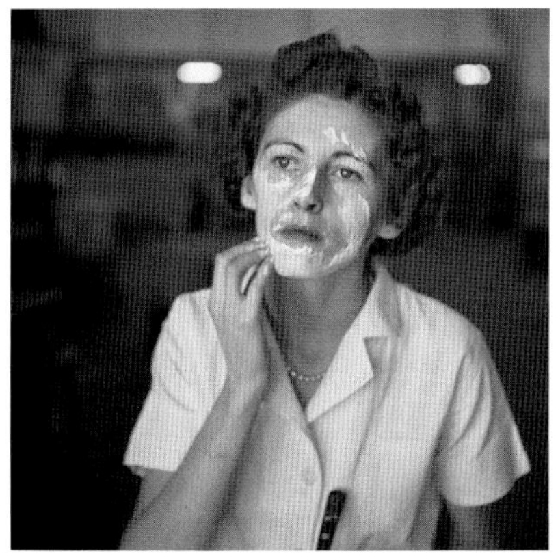

DATE: **OCTOBER 28, 1948**
TITLE: **CHEMIST (BOTANY)**

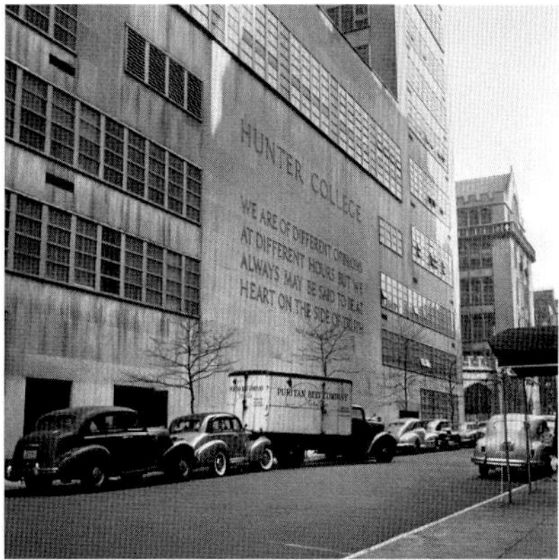

DATE: **NOVEMBER 23, 1948**
TITLE: **HUNTER COLLEGE**

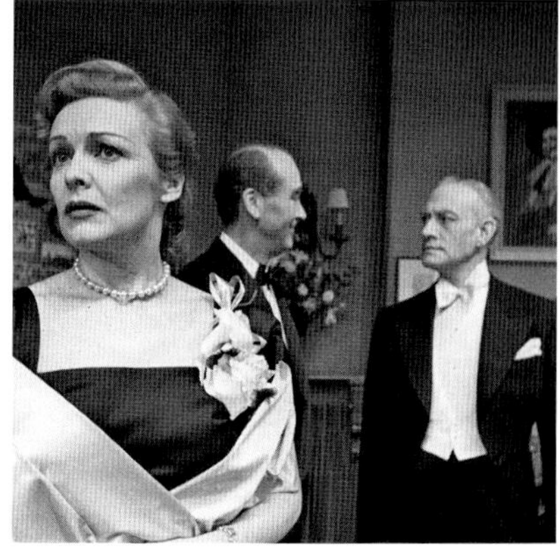

DATE: **DECEMBER 9, 1948**
TITLE: ***GOODBYE MR. FANCY***

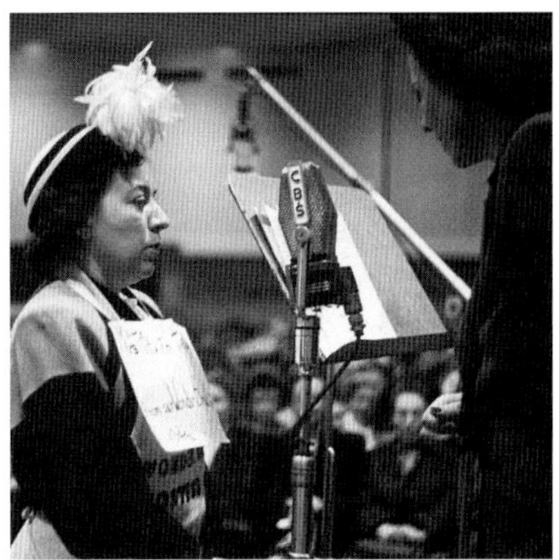

DATE: **JANUARY 7, 1949**
TITLE: **RADIO GRAND SLAM SHOW**

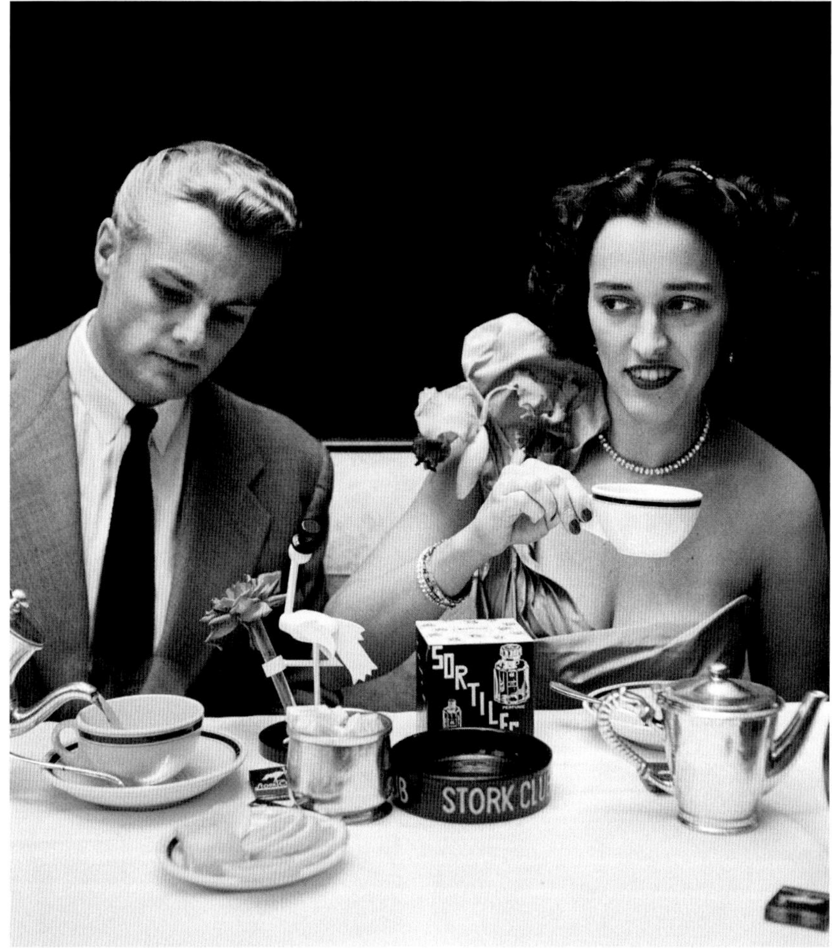

DATE: **FEBRUARY 1, 1949**
TITLE: **AMERICA'S MAN GODFREY: ONE OF THE HIGHEST-PAID AND MOST-LISTENED-TO ENTERTAINERS IN THE NATION**

DATE: **CA. 1949**
TITLE: **NIGHTCLUBS—STORK CLUB**

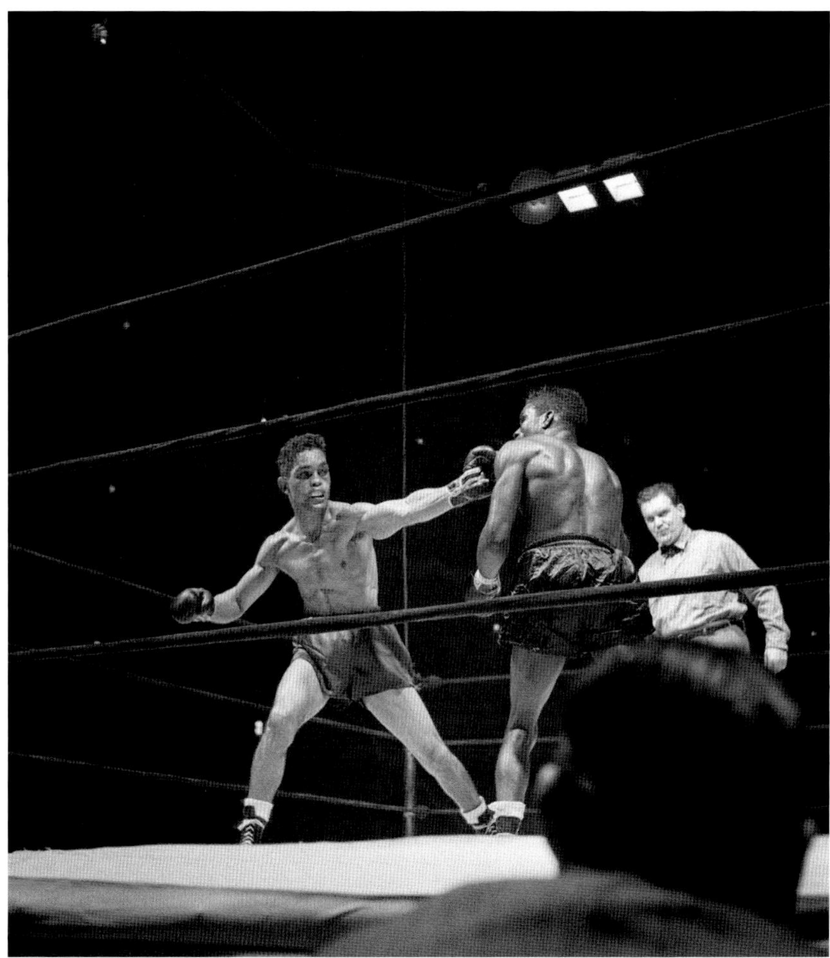

DATE: **FEBRUARY 15, 1949**
TITLE: **FIGHT NIGHT AT THE GARDEN**

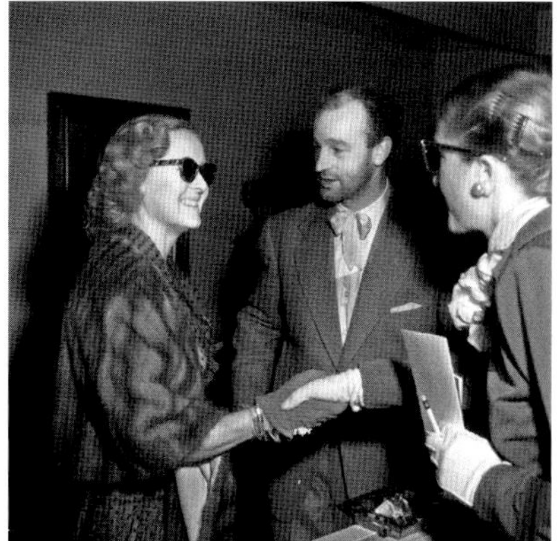

DATE: **JANUARY 20, 1947**
TITLE: **ORPHANAGE STORY/LAKE BLUFF, ILLINOIS**

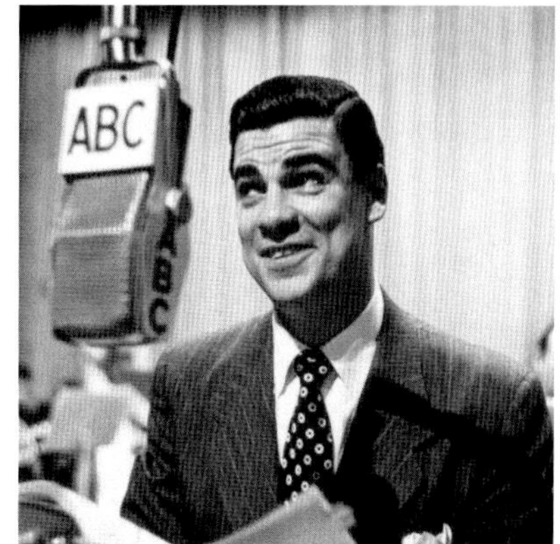

DATE: **APRIL 26, 1949**
TITLE: **RADIO—*STOP THE MUSIC* / BERT PARKS**

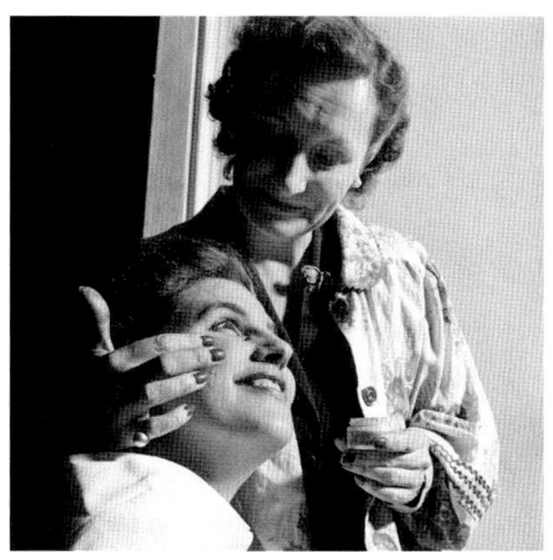

DATE: **APRIL 27, 1949**
TITLE: **LIGHTHOUSE FOR THE BLIND**

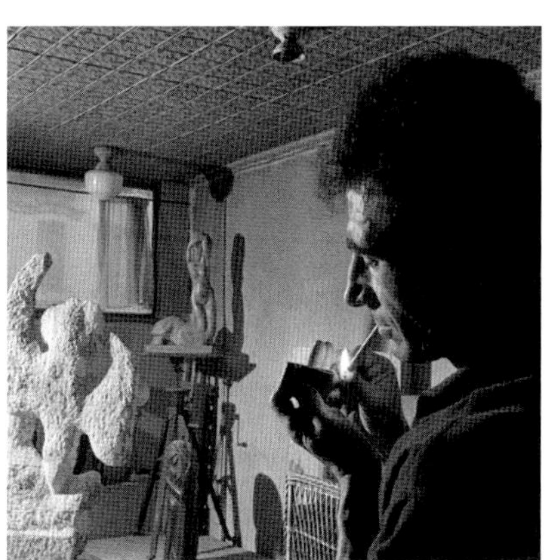

DATE: **MAY 10, 1949**
TITLE: **PINT-SIZE SCULPTOR WITH BIG IDEAS**

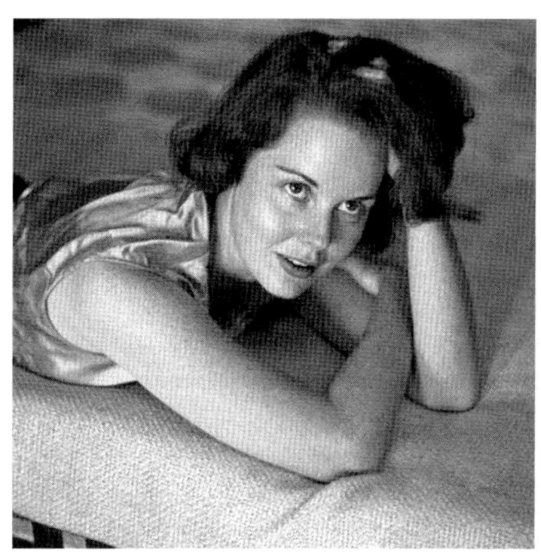

DATE: **AUGUST 18, 1949**
TITLE: **BEATRICE PEARSON**

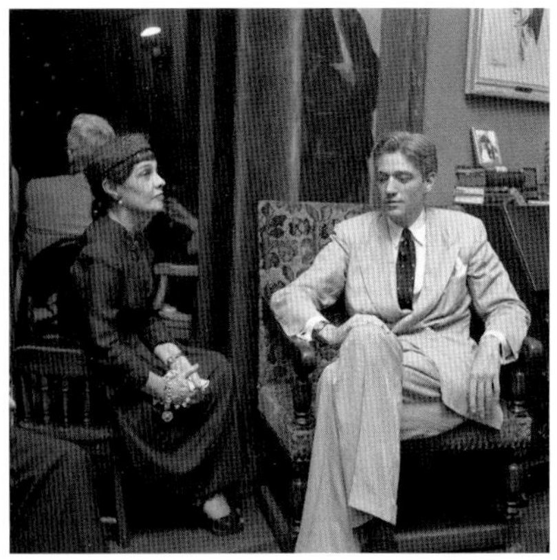

DATE: **SEPTEMBER 27, 1949**
TITLE: **ANGELS WANTED**

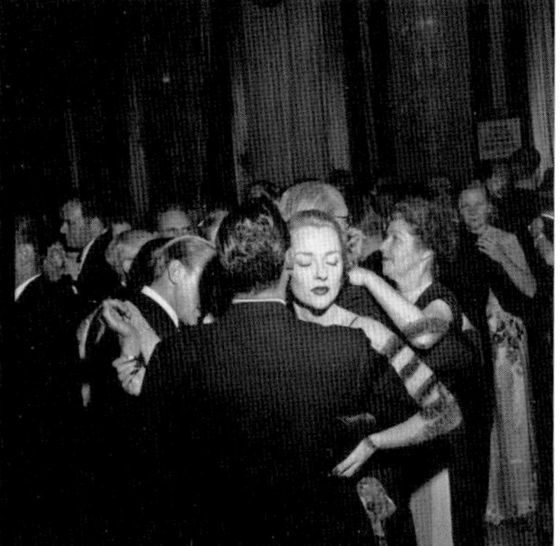

DATE: **DECEMBER 6, 1949**
TITLE: **NEW YORK SOCIETY BALL**

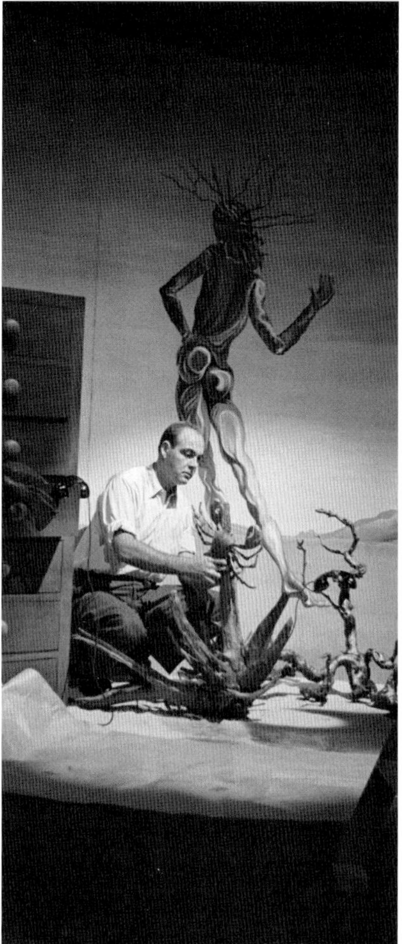

DATE: **DECEMBER 20, 1949**
TITLE: **MUSEUM FIRST NIGHTS**

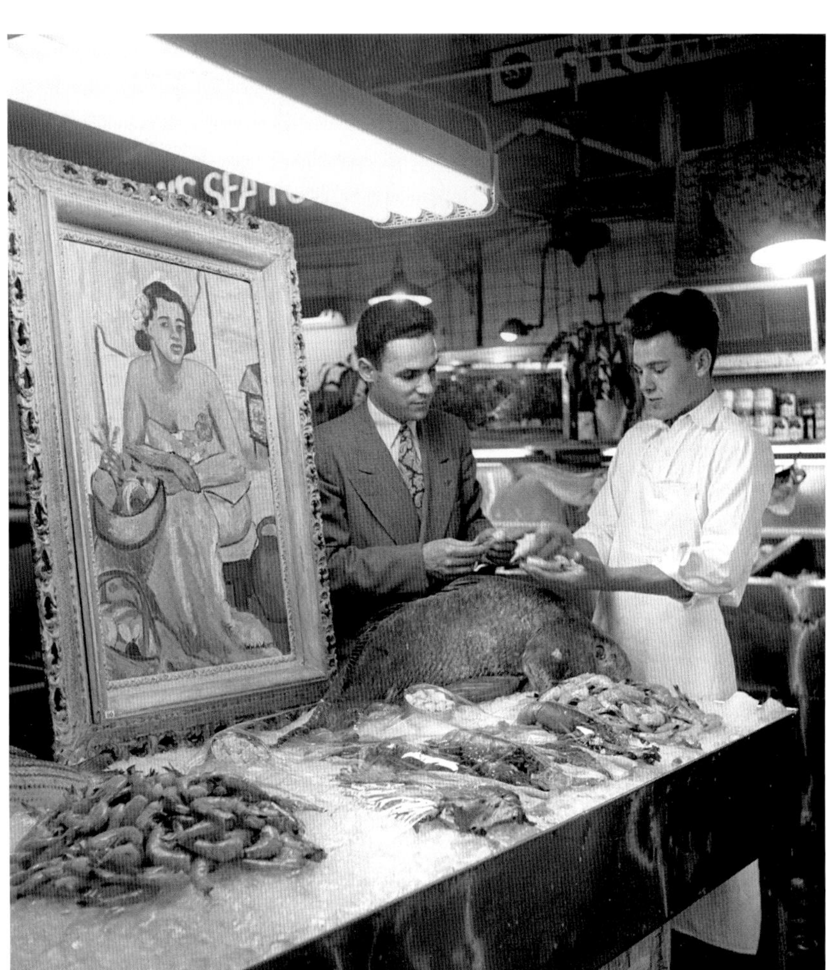

DATE: **MAY 23, 1949**
TITLE: **ART IN THE MARKETPLACE**

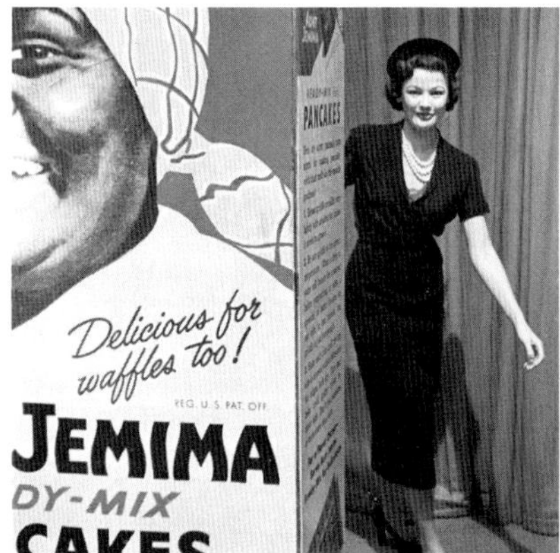

DATE: **MARCH 28, 1950**
TITLE: ***QUICK AS A FLASH***

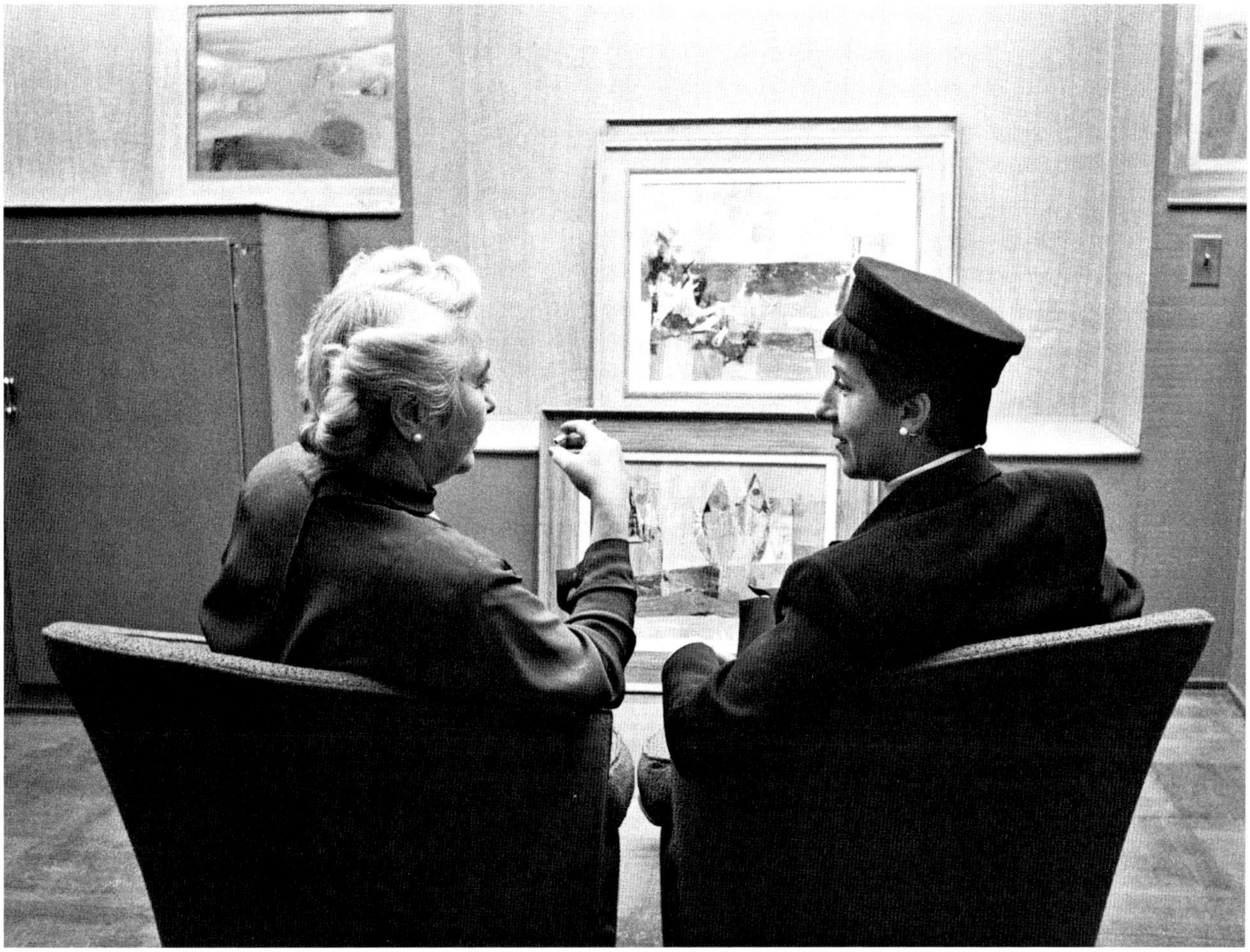

DATE: **FEBRUARY 28, 1950**
TITLE: **BIG LITTLE ART COLLECTION**

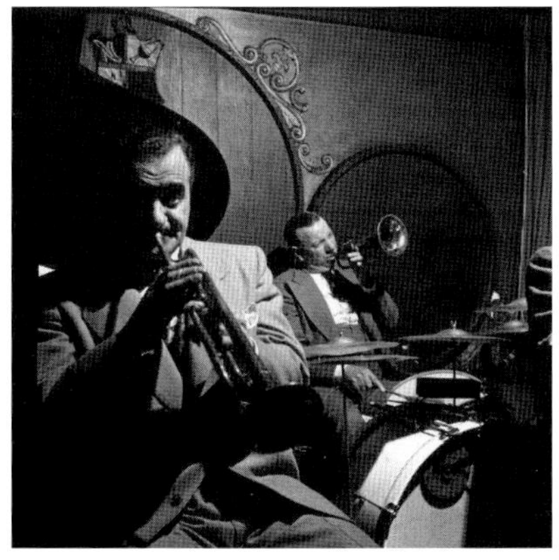

DATE: **JUNE 6, 1950**
TITLE: **PHIL NAPOLEON**

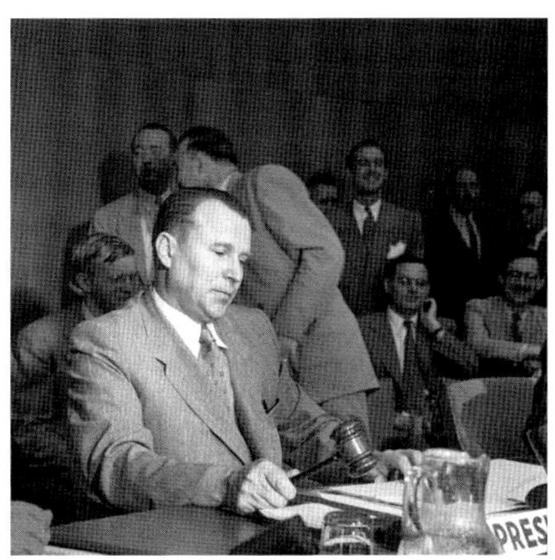

DATE: **AUGUST 3, 1950**
TITLE: **UNITED NATIONS**

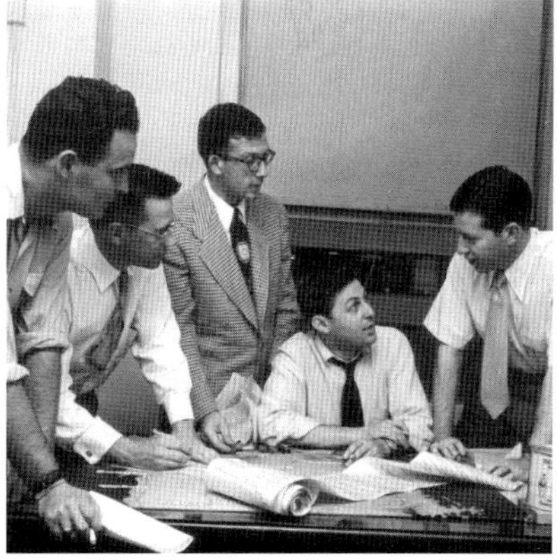

DATE: **DECEMBER 5, 1950**
TITLE: **HOW RADIO'S NEWS TEAM COVERS THE NEWS**

DONALD ALBRECHT & SEAN CORCORAN

DURCH EIN ANDERES OBJEKTIV: STANLEY KUBRICKS FOTOGRAFIEN

Stanley Kubricks frühe Karriere als Fotojournalist bei der Zeitschrift *Look* ist für die meisten Menschen, die ihn als Filmemacher kennen, eine Offenbarung. Zwischen 1940 und 1950, bevor er Stanley Kubrick, der international berühmte Regisseur solcher Filme wie *Dr. Seltsam*, *2001: Odyssee im Weltraum* und *Uhrwerk Orange* wurde, war er nur Stanley, ein Teenager aus New York mit einer frappierenden fotografischen Sensibilität, der für *Look* Human-Interest-Geschichten hinterherjagte.

1928 in der Bronx geboren, war Kubrick weniger an einer akademischen Ausbildung interessiert – er war ein schwacher Schüler, der gerade mal die Highschool absolviert hatte – als an den Lektionen des wahren Lebens. Für Kubrick wurden die Büros von *Look* in Manhattan zum College, die Redakteure und Fotografen zu seinen Professoren und die Stadt New York zu seinem Studienfach. „Als ich 21 war, hatte ich schon vier Jahre lang erlebt, wie es in der Welt zuging", sagte Kubrick später über seine Zeit bei *Look*. „Ich glaube, wäre ich aufs College gegangen, wäre ich nie ein Filmregisseur geworden."[1] Als er seine Fotokamera auf seine Geburtsstadt und gelegentlich auch darüber hinaus richtete, inspirierte ihn deren dramatisches Personal. Ihn fesselten die Berühmtheiten, Exzentriker und jungen Schuhputzer in ihren Straßen ebenso wie ihre Nachtklubs und Sportarenen. Er hielt die New Yorker in erinnerungswürdigen Bildern fest, die dem Pathos des Alltagslebens Ausdruck verliehen und dabei über seine Jugend hinwegtäuschten – sie wiesen bereits voraus auf seine Zukunft als einer der großen Künstler des 20. Jahrhunderts.[2]

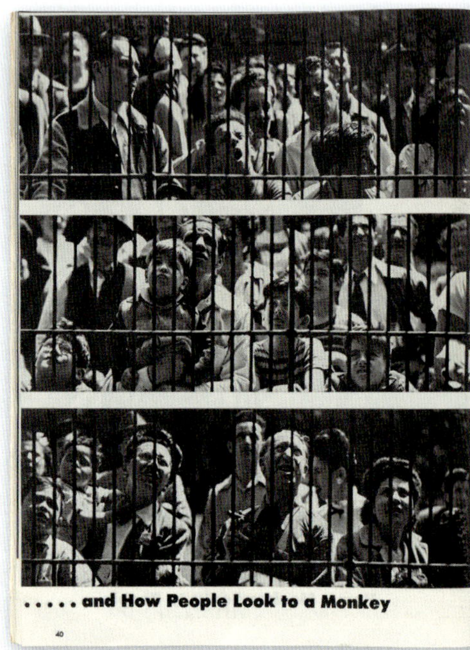

Die Leidenschaft für die Fotografie (und das Schachspiel) hatte Kubrick von seinem Vater, einem Arzt und engagierten Amateurfotografen, geerbt, der Stanley zu seinem 13. Geburtstag eine Graflex-Kamera schenkte und ihm damit unwiderruflich den Weg zu seiner Karriere wies. In den 1940er-Jahren gab es für einen aufstrebenden Fotografen keinen besseren Ort als *Look*. Die Zeitschrift war Anfang 1937 von Gardner Cowles Jr. gegründet worden mit dem Ziel, „den Leser ebenso zu interessieren wie seine Frau, seinen Privatsekretär und seinen Laufburschen".[3] Während die Autoren und Fotografen der Zeitschrift auf der Suche nach ganz unterschiedlichen Geschichten durch die Welt reisten, stellte sich heraus, dass es auch vor der Tür von *Look* spannende Themen gab. Die Zeitschrift porträtierte New York dramatisch, humorvoll und witzig, hob dabei das Menschliche und Zwischenmenschliche hervor und berichtete über Einzelne als Beispiele für die Gesellschaft als Ganzes.

Look und *Life* wetteiferten als berühmte Rivalen um die Gunst der Leser, doch jede der beiden Zeitschriften stellte das zeitgenössische Leben in ihrem eigenen Stil dar, wobei *Look* Cowles' Ansicht nach „eine breitere und bodenständigere Perspektive" einnahm als ihre Konkurrentin.[4] *Life*, 1936 von Henry Luce gegründet, hatte sich Größeres vorgenommen als *Look*: „Das Leben anschauen, die Welt sehen, Augenzeuge großer Ereignisse sein; die Gesichter der Armen und die Gesten der Stolzen beobachten."[5] Da *Look* nur alle zwei Wochen erschien, mussten die Mitarbeiter bei ihren Themen nicht so aktuell sein und waren bei der Suche nach Human-Interest-Geschichten freier als das Team von *Life*, das durch die wöchentliche Erscheinungsweise seiner Zeitschrift anders eingespannt war. Die Artikel von *Look* schienen, so die Historikerin Mary Panzer, „eine irgendwie fremde Zivilisation darzustellen, ein eigenartiges, anderes Universum ... *Look* erforschte oft, was seine vornehmen Kritiker als ‚Schattenseite Amerikas' verachteten. In der Tat war *Look* voll von dunklen Geschichten über Arbeitslosigkeit, Alkoholismus, Jugendkriminalität und Scheidungen – Themen, die die Leser von *Life* anscheinend seltener zu Gesicht bekamen, und wenn, dann wurden sie oft mit einer Prise Hoffnung serviert."[6]

Panzer schrieb auch, dass *Life* wie ein gut geöltes, hierarchisch organisiertes Fließband arbeitete, wogegen *Look* mit Teams operierte, die sich je nach Aufgabe neu zusammensetzten: „Sie dachten darüber nach, wie sie eine Geschichte am besten erzählen konnten. Das brachte eine Zeitschrift hervor, die immer wieder anders war und ihre Leser oft überraschte."[7] Die offene Arbeitsweise geht wahrscheinlich auf den Herausgeber Daniel D. Mich zurück, der von der Gründung von *Look* 1937 bis zu seinem Tod 1965 dort in einer Vielzahl verantwortlicher Positionen tätig war. Mich förderte ein Arbeitsumfeld, in dem sowohl die Redaktion als auch die freien Mitarbeiter eine Fülle an Ideen hervorbrachten. Das letzte Wort bei der Veröffentlichung eines Artikels hatte stets Mich, der den richtigen Erscheinungszeitpunkt und seine Bedeutung für die *Look*-Leser abschätzte. (Viele Artikel wurden seinen Kriterien nicht gerecht und daher nie veröffentlicht.) Daraus lernten erfolgreiche Fotografen, dass es von Vorteil war, immer viele Aufnahmen zu machen, damit die Bildredaktion eine große Auswahl an Fotos für das Layout von Geschichten zur Verfügung hatte.

Kubricks Arbeit für *Look* begann 1945, als die Zeitschrift sein Foto eines niedergeschlagenen Zeitungsverkäufers am Tag nach dem Tod von Franklin Delano Roosevelt veröffentlichte. Später gab Kubrick zu, er habe den Verkäufer um der dramatischen Wirkung willen gedrängt, deprimierter dreinzuschauen, als er in Wirklichkeit war – ein frühes Beispiel für seine Fähigkeit, sich eine Performance auszudenken und sie zu inszenieren. Diese Gelegenheit machte aus dem Amateurfotografen Kubrick einen Profi. Im Frühjahr 1946 schlug Helen O'Brian, die Bildredakteurin von *Look* – sie hatte bereits mehrere von Kubricks Fotos angekauft (einschließlich des Zeitungsverkäufers) –, der Zeitschrift vor, ihn als Auszubildenden einzustellen. Das war bei *Look* nicht üblich, aber Kubrick machte gerade seinen Abschluss an der William Howard Taft High School, und die Redaktion hatte das Talent und die Ambitionen des jungen Mannes bereits erkannt. Kubrick war der bei Weitem jüngste Fotograf der Zeitschrift (gerade einmal 17 Jahre alt), aber bei einem Gehalt von damals 50 Dollar die Woche konnte man sich auf das Risiko einer Festanstellung bedenkenlos einlassen.

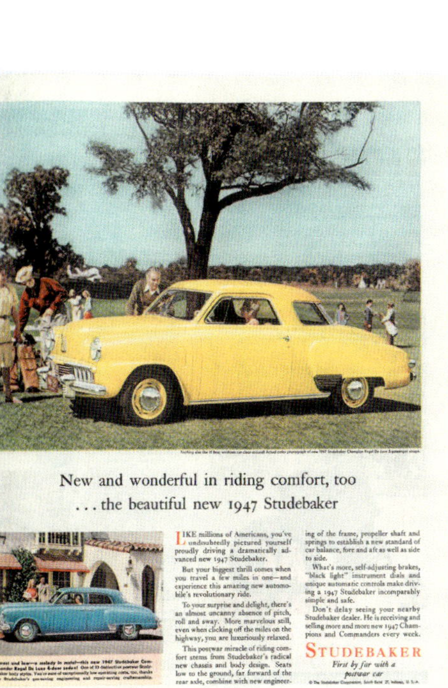

HOW A MONKEY LOOKS TO PEOPLE…
HOW PEOPLE LOOK TO A MONKEY
PUBLISHED: **AUGUST 20, 1946**

In seinen ersten Jahren bei *Look* wurde Kubrick mit kleinen Geschichten beauftragt. Sie bestanden aus einer Handvoll von Aufnahmen und kurzen Begleittexten. „How a Monkey Looks to People ... And How People Look to a Monkey" (Wie ein Affe für Menschen aussieht ... und wie die Menschen für einen Affen aussehen; veröffentlicht am 20. August 1946) und „Bronx Street Scene" (Eine Straßenszene aus der Bronx; veröffentlicht am 26. August 1946) zeigen Kubricks scharfe Beobachtungsgabe und wie ihn menschliche Beziehungen faszinieren. Seine Bilder fangen in aller Öffentlichkeit intime Momente zwischen New Yorkern ein, von zwei Familien, die den Zoo in der Bronx genießen, bis hin zu Freunden, die tief ins Gespräch versunken sind. Seine dramatischen Kompositionen laden diese gewöhnlichen und alltäglichen Situationen mit Spannung und Humor auf. Kubrick übernahm oft konkrete Aufträge, legte dem Redakteur aber auch eigene Fotogeschichten vor. „Teacher Puts the ‚Ham' in Hamlet" (Ein Lehrer lässt den Hamlet lebendig werden; veröffentlicht am 2. April 1946) besteht aus einer Bilderserie über seinen Englischlehrer an der Highschool, Aaron Traister, der mit Begeisterung Szenen aus *Hamlet* vorspielt. Für jeden seiner Aufträge fand Kubrick eine ebenso eingängige wie kraftvolle Erzählweise. Seine Arbeitgeber hatten sein Talent erkannt, und im Oktober 1946 wurde er als Fotograf fest angestellt.

Der jugendliche Novize war nun Mitglied einer illustren Gruppe von Fotojournalisten, unter ihnen Arthur Rothstein, der technische Direktor der Zeitschrift, und John Vachon. Beide waren Fotografen der Farm Security Administration gewesen, die Franklin Delano Roosevelt eingerichtet hatte, um die Lebensbedingungen der armen Landbevölkerung während der Weltwirtschaftskrise zu dokumentieren. Ihre Sensibilität prägte auch ihre Arbeit für *Look* und beeinflusste den jungen Kubrick, der gelegentlich mit ihnen oder auch mit freien Fotojournalisten zusammenarbeitete, so bei „Fight Night at the Garden" (Kampfnacht im Madison Square Garden; veröffentlicht am 15. Februar 1949) mit Rothstein und Vachon und bei dem unveröffentlichten Auftrag „Advertising Sign Painters at Work" (Werbemaler bei der Arbeit; mit Frank Bauman und Tom Weber; eingereicht am 3. September 1947). Die älteren Fotografen bei *Look* machten sich auch in Kubricks Privatleben zu seinen Mentoren. Sie gründeten den Bringing Up Stanley Club (Klub für Stanleys Erziehung) und halfen dem Teenager, sich an seinem Arbeitsplatz und in der Welt zurechtzufinden. Zum Beispiel erwies sich seine Garderobe als ein Hindernis, das erfolgreich überwunden werden konnte: „Nachdem er zuerst Teenagerklamotten – Sportschuhe, Freizeitjackett und Sporthemd – trug, bevorzugt er nun Glencheckanzüge und weiße Hemden."[8]

Schließlich wurde Kubricks Name am 7. Januar 1947 im Impressum der Zeitschrift genannt. Sein erster größerer Auftrag „Love and Life on the New York Subway" (Leben und Liebe in der New Yorker U-Bahn) wurde zwei Monate später in der Ausgabe vom 4. März veröffentlicht. Um sich auf die Geschichte vorzubereiten, war er zwei Monate lang U-Bahn gefahren, eine Kamera um den Hals mit einem Draht, der unter seinem Ärmel zu einem Auslöser in seiner Tasche führte und so verbarg, dass er die Leute in der U-Bahn fotografierte. Manchmal setzte er auch einen Mitarbeiter ein, um Bilder zu inszenieren, die er für seine Geschichte brauchte – eine ganz normale Praxis im Fotojournalismus der damaligen Zeit. In den 29 Fotos des Artikels konnte Kubrick zeigen, was der Autor „eine der größten und neugierigsten Reisen, die die Welt für fünf Cent zu bieten hat", nannte.[9] Kubrick fotografierte müde Pendler, Betrunkene, Liebende und Einsame in ihrem alltäglichen Leben.

Im Herbst 1947 begann Kubrick, an größeren Aufträgen zu arbeiten, die mit Texten einhergingen. Eine der frühesten Geschichten, „Shoeshine Boy" (Schuhputzjunge; eingereicht am 6. Oktober 1947), zeigte einen Tag im Leben eines Heranwachsenden aus New York, wie er zur Schule ging, Sport trieb, mit seinen Freunden spielte, seinen Taubenschlag pflegte und für seine Familie Geld verdiente, indem er in den Straßen von New York Schuhe putzte. In dem unveröffentlichten Artikel beleuchtete Kubrick, der ungefähr sieben Jahre älter war als sein Protagonist, den Kontrast zwischen der erwachsenen Arbeitsethik von Mickey und seinen fröhlichen, kindlichen Späßen. Im Frühling 1948 war dank einer raschen Folge umfangreicher Aufträge Kubricks Fähigkeit gereift, lange, narrative Fotoessays zu fertigen. In „Columbia University" (veröffentlicht am 11. Mai 1948) untersuchte er das damals allgemein herrschende Vertrauen in den Fortschritt Amerikas und seiner Wissenschaft, repräsentiert von einer amerikanischen Elite-Universität. „How the Circus Gets Set" (Wie der Zirkus sich bereitmacht; veröffentlicht am 25. Mai 1948), ein Porträt des Ringling Brothers Circus, gewann der skurrilen Zirkusumgebung humorvolle Gegenüberstellungen ab und akzentuierte Kubricks Interesse an exzentrischen und absurden Themen. Diesen Fotoessays folgten rasch zwei Aufträge außerhalb von New York. „Mooseheart – the Child City" (Mooseheart – die Kinderstadt; veröffentlicht am 8. Juni 1948) hat ein Waisenhaus knapp 65 Kilometer westlich von Chicago zum Thema, und „Holiday in Portugal" (Ferien in Portugal; veröffentlicht am 3. August 1948) folgte einem jungen amerikanischen Ehepaar auf seiner Europareise.

Von allen Themen, die Kubrick für *Look* bearbeitete, verbinden sich keine enger mit seinem erwachenden Interesse am Film als seine Erkundung der Unterhaltungs- und Medienindustrie, die bereits zu seiner Zeit wichtige Facetten von New Yorks Ökonomie und Identität waren. Geschichten über Persönlichkeiten des Radios und Fernsehens demonstrieren, wie Kubrick den Übergang vollzog von einem Novizen, der sein Handwerk lernte, zu einem reifen Künstler, der mit seinem kraftvollen und humanistisch geprägten Fotojournalismus neue Maßstäbe setzte. Seine Fähigkeit, die komplexe Psyche eines Menschen in eine visuelle Form zu übersetzen, wird in seinen späteren Porträts des Komponisten und Dirigenten Leonard Bernstein, des Boxers Walter Cartier, des Fernsehstars Faye Emerson, der Theaterschauspielerin Betsy von Furstenberg und des Showgirls Rosemary Williams offenbar. In jedem dieser Porträts erforscht Kubrick das private und öffentliche Leben dieser Menschen. In einigen – zum Beispiel denen von Emerson und von Furstenberg – suggerieren Kubricks Bilder, dass die öffentliche und private Persona identisch sind, während andere wie die von Williams den Bruch zwischen der glamourösen Bühnenpersona und der harten Wirklichkeit hinter der Bühne betonen.

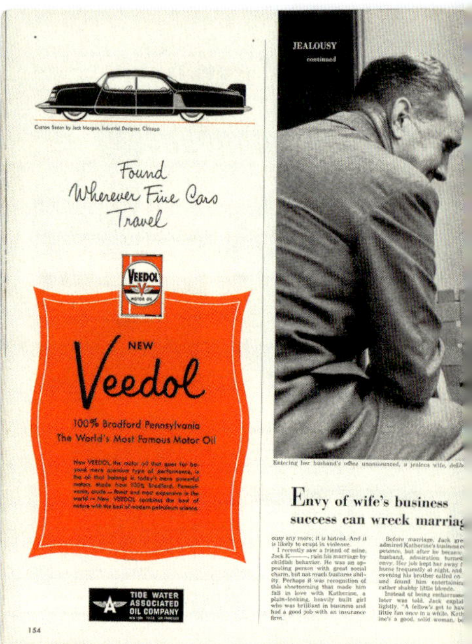

Das Radio war zu der Zeit immer noch die vorherrschende Form der Heimunterhaltung, und Kubrick arbeitete mit an *Looks* Porträts populärer Radiopersönlichkeiten wie Vaughn Monroe (veröffentlicht am 16. August 1949) und Arthur Godfrey (veröffentlicht am 1. Februar 1949). Das Fernsehen steckte zu jener Zeit noch in den Kinderschuhen, und *Look* konzentrierte sich darauf, seine Leser mit dem Medium vertraut zu machen. (Ironischerweise verdrängte der kleine Bildschirm innerhalb des nächsten Jahrzehnts die Zeitschriften als populärste Form der Kommunikation, was 1971 schließlich zum Ende von *Look* führte.) In der Ausgabe vom 7. Januar 1947 veröffentlichte *Look* zum Beispiel als Teil einer Serie neuer Trends in der Unterhaltungsindustrie Kubricks Foto eines typischen Fernsehstudios zusammen mit Beschreibungen aller Produktionskomponenten, um der Leserschaft dabei zu helfen, das neue Medium zu verstehen. Einige Jahre später wurde Kubrick beauftragt, Fotos vom Set der *The Howdy Doody Show* mit Bob Smith in der Rolle des Buffalo Bob und der Marionette Howdy Doody (veröffentlicht am 20. Dezember 1949) und ein ausführliches Porträt von Faye Emerson zu machen, einer Hollywoodschauspielerin, die in den späten 1940er-Jahren Talkshow-Moderatorin im Fernsehen wurde (veröffentlicht am 15. August 1950). Kubrick sah dabei ganz unmittelbar, wie Berühmtheiten ihr öffentliches Image gestalteten; er war regelmäßig hinter der Bühne und am Set, ganz nah am Produktionsprozess.

Das deutlichste Vorzeichen für Kubricks Filmkarriere sind seine unveröffentlichten Fotografien, die er am Set von *Stadt ohne Maske* (1948) machte, einem Film, der einen Academy Award gewinnen sollte und eine der ersten Hollywoodproduktionen war, die wieder an Originalschauplätzen gedreht wurden. Das muss für den Liebhaber des populären Film noir, den Kubrick in den kommerziellen Kinos der Stadt ebenso leidenschaftlich konsumierte wie Kunstfilme im Museum of Modern Art, eine aufregende Erfahrung gewesen sein. Er verbrachte viele Stunden am Set und sah dem Regisseur Jules Dassin und dem Kameramann

William H. Daniels dabei zu, wie sie die dunklen Machenschaften der Polizei auf den Straßen von New York filmten. Auch wenn man nicht weiß, ob ihn diese inspirierende Erfahrung zum Film gebracht hat, ist doch klar, dass sie ihn sehr beeindruckt haben muss. „In seiner Freizeit experimentiert Stanley als Kameramann", beobachtete man bei *Look* im Mai 1948, „und er träumt von dem Tag, an dem er Dokumentarfilme drehen kann."[10]

1950, gegen Ende seiner Anstellung bei *Look*, untersuchte Kubrick in drei Aufträgen Liebe unter Teenagern, ihr Dating-Verhalten und Eifersucht unter Eheleuten, wobei er die Teenager-Geschichten effektvoll mit Highschoolschülern inszenierte und die Rollen der Eheleute mit Schauspielern. Wie wichtig diese Aufträge für ihn auch waren, so ist es doch die Geschichte „Prizefighter" (Preiskämpfer; veröffentlicht am 18. Januar 1949) über Walter Cartier, die dann tatsächlich Kubricks Karriere als Filmemacher einleitete. Kubrick ließ ihn als Protagonisten seines ersten unabhängig produzierten Dokumentarfilms *Day of The Fight* auftreten, ein 16-Minuten-Film, der 1951 Premiere hatte und auf der ganzen Welt gezeigt wurde.

Nachdem er einige Kurzfilme fertiggestellt hatte, ohne mit ihnen Gewinn zu machen, erkannte Kubrick, dass er Spielfilme drehen musste, wenn er im Kino Karriere machen wollte. Er kündigte im August 1950 bei *Look* und begann mit der Arbeit an seinem ersten Spielfilm *Fear and Desire* (1953), einer abstrakten Untersuchung der Beziehungen zwischen Soldaten und einem namenlosen Mädchen, die in einen Krieg zwischen nicht näher benannten Ländern verwickelt sind. Die zwei folgenden Filme von Kubrick, *Der Tiger von New York* (1955) und *Die Rechnung ging nicht auf* (1956), hatten die Film-noir-Ästhetik seiner besten Arbeiten bei *Look*, vor allem der Aufträge, in denen er das Halbweltleben von Boxern und Showgirls in der Stadt darstellte.

Für Kubrick sollten sich die fünf Jahre bei *Look* als prägend erweisen. Er lernte dort, im Team mit anderen zu arbeiten, wie es beim Film ganz ähnlich ist. Er lernte, wie man Geschichten in dynamischen Bildfolgen erzählt und sich dabei auf subtile Interaktionen unter Menschen konzentriert. Er lernte in meisterhafter Weise das Framing, die Komposition und die Beleuchtung mitreißender Bilder, von denen viele so leidenschaftslos auf das Leben schauen, wie er das auch in seinen Filmen tut. Wenn man auf Kubricks frühe Karriere bei *Look* zurückblickt, kann man seine Erfahrungen dort als Beginn seiner gefeierten Karriere als Künstler und Filmemacher betrachten: Es war eine Zeit, in der er seine Talente als Geschichtenerzähler und Bildermacher ausbildete, auch wenn er dabei durch ein anderes Objektiv schaute.

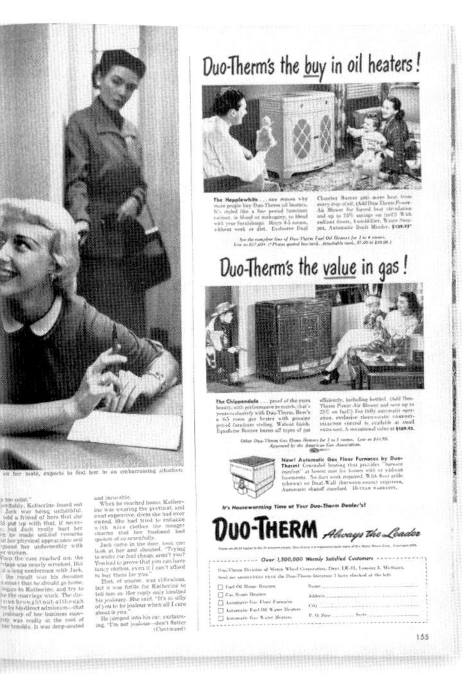

JEALOUSY: A THREAT TO MARRIAGE
PUBLISHED: **OCTOBER 24, 1950**

ANMERKUNGEN

1 Stanley Kubrick, zitiert nach Paul D. Zimmerman, „Kubrick's Brillant Vision", *Newsweek*, 3. Januar 1972, S. 3.
2 Einige der Informationen über die Zeitschrift *Look*, die in den Text eingeflossen sind, stammen aus dem Essay „Only in New York" von Donald Albrecht und Thomas Mellins, erschienen in ihrem Buch *Only in New York: Photographs from* Look *Magazine*, Hrsg. Museum of the City of New York und The Monacelli Press, 2009. Zu Kubricks Anstellung bei der Zeitschrift *Look* lieferte der Text von Philippe Mather, *Stanley Kubrick at* Look *Magazine: Authorship and Genre in Photojournalism and Film*, erschienen bei Intellect, 2013, wertvolle Hinweise.
3 Gardner Cowles Jr., zitiert in „Look Out", *Time*, 11. Januar 1935, S. 25.
4 Gardner Cowles Jr., ebd.
5 *Life*, Statement zum Selbstverständnis der Zeitschrift, zitiert nach der Website von Beinecke Rare Book & Manuscript Library, https://brbl-dl.library.yale.edu/vufind/Author?author=Life+magazine&type=Author&page=2, abgerufen am 4. Dezember 2017.
6 Mary Panzer, „Eyes Wide Open", *Vanity Fair*, März 2005, S. 410–442.
7 Mary Panzer, „Eyes Wide Open", *Vanity Fair*, März 2005, S. 410–442.
8 „A veteran photographer at 19, Stanley makes up for youth with zeal" (Mit 19 ist Stanley als Fotograf schon ein alter Hase und kompensiert seine Jugend durch Arbeitseifer), *Look*, 11. Mai 1948, S. 2.
9 „Life and Love on The New York Subway", *Look*, 4. März 1947, S. 60.
10 „A veteran photographer at 19, Stanley Kubrick makes up for youth with zeal", *Look*, 11. Mai 1948, S. 2.

LUCY SANTE

STANLEY KUBRICK: SEHEN LERNEN

„Stanley verhielt sich immer so, als wisse er etwas, was man selbst nicht wusste", schrieb der Autor und Journalist Michael Herr und zitierte dabei eine Jugendbekanntschaft von Kubrick.[1] Es wird niemanden erstaunen, dass Stanley Kubrick, der unvergleichliche Regisseur von *Dr. Seltsam, oder wie ich lernte, die Bombe zu lieben, 2001: Odyssee im Weltraum, Barry Lyndon* und zehn weiteren unvergänglichen und von ihm fanatisch kontrollierten Spielfilmen so etwas wie ein Wunder war. Kein Wunderkind, wohlgemerkt, aber beinahe. Noch bevor er die Highschool verließ, hatte er schon zwei Fotos an die Zeitschrift *Look* verkauft, und sehr bald nach seinem Schulabschluss wurde er dort fest angestellter Fotograf und blieb es, bis er 22 war. Er machte Aufnahmen zu allen möglichen Sujets in New York City und darüber hinaus; er fotografierte Berühmtheiten, längere Bildessays, Human-Interest-Geschichten, machte Schnappschüsse von Menschen auf der Straße, Bilder mit versteckter Kamera und schoss Sequenzen in streng horizontalem Bildformat, die auf seine zukünftige Filmkarriere vorauswiesen.

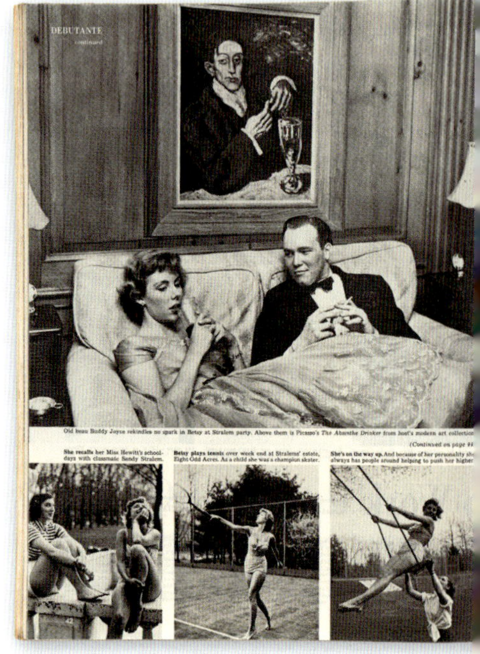

Die späten 1940er-Jahre waren eine gute Zeit, um Fotograf zu werden. Der Krieg war vorbei, die Leute hatten mehr Geld als in den 15 Jahren davor und gaben es aus, und jeder Zeitungskiosk quoll über von Illustrierten. Sie folgten dem Weg, den *Life* und *Look* in den späten 1930er-Jahren vorgegeben hatten, gar nicht zu reden von *Fortune, Vogue* und *Harper's Bazaar*, und es gab nun Dutzende von themenübergreifenden Fotoillustrierten für unterschiedliche Geldbörsen und Bildungsniveaus. Fachzeitschriften, die sich zuvor mit Line Art, monochromen Zeichnungen, begnügt hatten, füllten nun ihre Seiten ebenfalls mit Fotografien. Und New York war der beste Ort auf der Welt, um dieses Handwerk auszuüben. Die Stadt war nicht nur der Mittelpunkt des Zeitschriftengeschäfts, sondern auch der Jahrmarkt der Gegensätze. An jeder Ecke bot sich zu jeder Stunde ein Tableau, ein menschliches Schauspiel, ein zufälliger Zusammenprall unterschiedlichster Elemente. Was Paris in den 1920er-Jahren gewesen war – als dort Dutzende wichtiger Fotokarrieren ihren Anfang nahmen –, das beanspruchte nun New York zu sein, und unternehmungslustige junge Leute aus allen fünf Stadtteilen und darüber hinaus zögerten nicht, die Möglichkeiten zu ergreifen, welche die Stadt bot.

Zeitlich steht Kubrick in der Mitte der folgenden Reihe New Yorker Straßenfotografen: Ted Croner und Louis Stettner, Jahrgang 1922; Diane Arbus und Saul Leiter, Jahrgang 1923; Robert Frank und Jerome Liebling, Jahrgang 1924; Simpson Kalisher, Jahrgang 1926; Garry Winogrand, William Klein und Elliott Erwitt, Jahrgang 1928; Bruce Davidson, Jahrgang 1933, und Lee Friedlander, 1934. Es ist aufschlussreich, Kubrick mit dem im selben Jahr geborenen Winogrand zu vergleichen, der wie er in der Bronx aufwuchs und ebenfalls auf eine Collegeausbildung verzichtete, um Fotograf zu werden. Winogrand hatte es viel schwerer als Kubrick; er arbeitete viele Jahre als freier Mitarbeiter, und es gelang ihm nur sehr selten, eine Aufnahme in einer renommierten Zeitschrift unterzubringen; die meisten seiner frühen Bilder erschienen in *Collier's, Pageant* und *Redbook*. Aber die freie Mitarbeit hatte auch Vorteile. Zwar sehen sich die frühen Zeitschriftenarbeiten der beiden Männer zum Verwechseln ähnlich – zum Beispiel ist Winogrands Porträtstudie eines jungen Boxers, „What Makes Nick Run?" (Was hält Nick am Laufen?, *Pageant*, Mai 1955),[2] atmosphärisch dem Werk von Kubrick sehr nah –, aber Winogrand hatte ausreichend viele Auszeiten, um einen radikal eigenen Stil zu entwickeln mit den für ihn typischen gekippten Horizonten und dem chaotischen Reichtum an visuellen Informationen, die bereits sehr früh in seinen Bildern auftauchen. Kubrick dagegen lernte all seine Fähigkeiten, während er zugleich an die Ausführung bestimmter Aufträge gebunden war. Klarheit und Thema hatten Vorrang, erst dann kam, wenn überhaupt, der persönliche Ausdruck.

Er begann seine Karriere bei *Look* mit Themen, die ihm nahe waren – örtlich, emotional und ganz buchstäblich. Der einzige Lehrer in der Taft High School, dem er sich eng verbunden fühlte, war Aaron Traister, der bekannt war für seinen begeisternden Englischunterricht; 1948 veröffentlichte *Look* eine Story mit vier Fotos von Kubrick, die zeigen, wie sein Lehrer in der Klasse Szenen aus *Hamlet* vorspielt. Im selben Jahr präsentierte die Zeitschrift eine Doppelseite mit 18 Bilder von Menschen, die in der Praxis eines Zahnarztes in allen möglichen Befindlichkeiten warten, von Langeweile bis hin zu heftigem Schmerz. Kubrick hatte jedes dieser Bilder fotografiert, und der Zahnarzt war sein eigener. Er nahm auch Bildserien von Menschen in der Bronx auf, wie sie schwatzen und gestikulieren und einander abschätzig mustern. Zu der Zeit war Kubrick noch ein Anfänger. Seine Bilder waren klar und effektiv, aber ihnen fehlte noch das gewisse Etwas. Vielleicht ist das der Grund, weshalb sie sehr oft in Bildreihen gezeigt wurden. Je mehr von ihnen nebeneinanderstanden, desto stärker war ihr Eindruck. Man könnte auch sagen, dass Kubrick bereits damals anfing, in kinematografischen Kategorien zu denken. Und dass er so viele Aufnahmen machte, weil es ihn mehr interessierte, den Verlauf einer Handlung zu präsentieren als ein einziges, bedeutungsschweres Bild.

Kubricks Fotos vermitteln einen starken Eindruck davon, wie New York City in den 1940er-Jahren war: rowdyhaft, heruntergekommen, optimistisch, eigensinnig, launisch, theatralisch und demokratisch. Es war die Hauptstadt dieser Zeit und bedeutender als jemals zuvor. In Kunst und Werbung wurden dort die meisten Bilder der ganzen Welt produziert, und die neuen Hochhäuser aus Glas und Stahl veränderten das Gesicht von Midtown Manhattan (darunter das Bürogebäude von *Look* in der Madison Avenue 488, das 1950 vollendet wurde). Zugleich war es noch eine von allen Schichten bevölkerte, heterogene Hafenstadt, durchzogen von vitalen ethnischen Arbeitervierteln, aus denen erst wenige Einwohner den Exodus in die Vorstädte angetreten hatten.

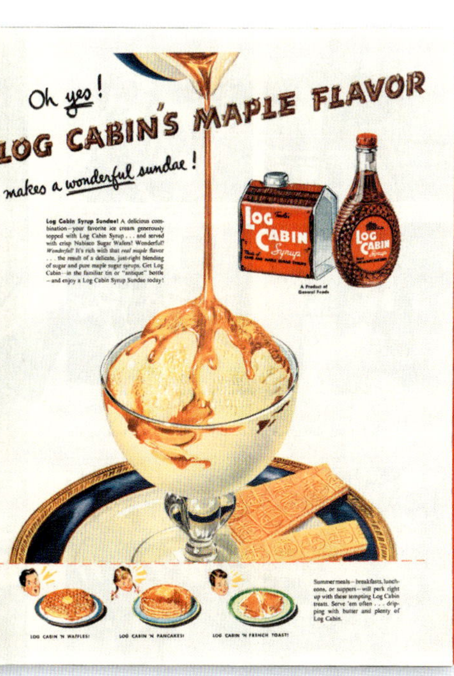

THE DEBUTANTE WHO WENT TO WORK
PUBLISHED: **JULY 18, 1950**

Es gab Klassenunterschiede, aber alle wohnten in denselben Straßen, tranken in denselben Kneipen und aßen ihr Mittagessen in denselben Snackbars. Sogar ein Prominenter wie Peter Arno, ein Cartoonist des *New Yorker*, der ein Mädchen, das halb so alt war wie er selbst, zu einer Abendunterhaltung ausführte, kehrte auf ein Bier in einem völlig unscheinbaren Lokal ein, das man heute als „Spelunke" bezeichnen würde. Den großen deutschen Künstler George Grosz, einen Emigranten, hat Kubrick porträtiert, wie er mitten auf dem Bürgersteig der Fifth Avenue rittlings auf einem Stuhl sitzt und dabei aussieht wie der Chef eines Reisebüros – das Bild war für eine Doppelseite über New York als Hauptstadt der Künste bestimmt, auf der ansonsten konventionellere Bilder von anderen Fotografen abgedruckt waren. Anders als *Life*, eher so wie *People*, eine Zeitschrift, die später im selben Verlag erschien, liebte *Look* es, Berühmtheiten bei der Arbeit und in der Freizeit zu porträtieren, bei gestellten Telefonaten und bei der Küchenarbeit. So sieht man die mädchenhafte Schauspielerin Betsy von Furstenberg, wie sie gefilmt wird, wie für ihre Kleider Maß genommen wird, wie sie ihr Make-up richtet, in ihrem Apartment ein Drehbuch studiert, sich im Büro ihres Agenten produziert, mit dem Fahrrad einen Ausflug macht, sich auf einer langweiligen Party mit einem nervösen jungen Mann im Abendanzug amüsiert und neben ihm in einem schicken Restaurant eine Banane schält. Solche Porträts waren glamouröse Lifestyle-Fantasien, die nur entfernt mit den tatsächlichen Aktivitäten ihrer Protagonisten zu tun hatten, aber als eindrucksvolle Posen in Form kleiner, fotoromanartiger Biopics zusammengestellt wurden, die Kubrick, wie man wohl sagen darf, ebenso sehr inszeniert wie fotografiert hat.

Er musste sich ein Skript ausdenken, das für einen nicht abreißenden Wirbel von Aktionen im Leben des Stars sorgte, die sich idealerweise alle im Lauf eines einzigen Tages voller Elan zutrugen. Von einigen Menschen bekam er dabei mehr Unterstützung als von anderen. Leonard Bernstein scheint darauf bestanden zu haben, vor unterschiedlichen Kulissen wie eine Gottheit in die Ferne schauend fotografiert zu werden, während Guy Lombardo kaum mehr zu tun gewillt war, als seine verschiedenen Besitztümer vorzuführen, einschließlich einer Schar kleiner Hunde. Und dann ist da Montgomery Clift, den Kubrick fotografierte, als Clifts dritter Film in die Kinos kam; an der Schwelle zum Ruhm, der ihm aber schon sicher zu sein scheint. Er trägt ein zerrissenes T-Shirt, sieht melancholisch aus, trinkt Kaffee und raucht. Er ist ein Homosexueller, der sich notwendigerweise versteckt, allein lebt und seine sozialen Kontakte aus dem Scheinwerferlicht heraushält. Es war quasi unmöglich, um ihn herum eine romantische Lifestyle-Fantasie zu erschaffen, ohne dabei zu Erfindungen zu greifen. So besuchten Kubrick und er die Familie seines Freundes Kevin McCarthy, wo Clift brav für deren kleinen Sohn Pferdchen spielt. Man betrachte im Gegensatz dazu Arnos offen zur Schau gestellte Verhältnisse mit sehr jungen Frauen, die ohne Kommentar und einfach als etwas, was einem älteren Lebemann zusteht, gezeigt werden.

Ein Showgirl namens Rosemary Williams sorgte für eine besonders lebhafte und unkonventionelle New Yorker Geschichte voller Kontraste und Charaktere, die schon fast wie ein Film noir wirkt. Interessanterweise war das, was an ihrem Leben so ideal für diese Art von Geschichte war, auch der Grund dafür, dass sie nie veröffentlicht wurde. Williams kam nach

New York, um Theater zu spielen, aber da die Jobs an „richtigen" Bühnen rar waren, bezahlte sie ihre Miete, indem sie als Showgirl arbeitete, was heißt, dass sie bei dieser Arbeit eine Menge nackte Haut zeigte – vielleicht zu viel für eine Familienzeitschrift. Ihr Leben kann nicht einfach gewesen sein – trotz ihrer aufwendigen Garderobe lebte sie wie viele Künstler am Rande der Gesellschaft –, aber wir sehen sie durch den Filter männlichen Entzückens. Dazu passt, dass Kubrick selbst in ihrem Make-up-Spiegel auftaucht, dünn und hoch konzentriert. Außer im Theater, wo sie hinter der Bühne leicht bekleidet mit ihren Kolleginnen Karten spielt, sieht man Williams immer nur dann, wenn sie den Männern schöne Augen macht: ihrem Manager, einer Verabredung beim Mittagessen, einem Schauspielerkollegen auf der Bühne, dem Mann eines älteren Paares, das sie in einen deprimierenden Nachtklub begleitet. Passend porträtierte Kubrick sie unter einem Theatervordach am Times Square, wo für *Ein abgekartetes Spiel* geworben wird.

Alle Menschen, die Kubrick porträtierte, gleichgültig, wie sehr ihre Existenz nach Schickeria aussieht, lebten doch deutlich spürbar in derselben Stadt wie sein „Shoeshine Boy", der direkt aus einem Buch von Horatio Alger stammen könnte. Er trägt einen Hut wie Huntz Hall von den Bowery Boys, er schleppt seinen Kasten durch die Stadt und macht Reklame für sein Geschäft, er spielt mit seinen Freunden um Flaschenverschlüsse und studiert die Kinoreklame – aber er geht auch zur Schule, holt die Wäsche der Familie aus der Wäscherei, sieht nach seinen Tauben auf dem Hausdach und posiert mit vielen Brüdern und Schwestern vor ihrer Hauswand, die mit Kreide beschmiert ist. Aus der Ferne betrachtet, sieht die Fotoserie fast zu gut aus, um wahr zu sein; sie könnte perfekt in eine Bildauswahl der Photo League passen, einer Fotografenkooperative mit sozialem Bewusstsein, die von 1936 bis 1951 bestand, als sie während der Kommunistenjagd der McCarthy-Ära verboten wurde. In ihr war die Mehrzahl der New Yorker Straßenfotografen aus der Generation vor Kubrick tätig. Aber mit ihrer ausführlichen Dokumentation der Straßenspiele von Kindern und ihren rauflustigen, unbeugsamen Protagonisten, darunter ein Bursche so blond wie ein Farmjunge im Mittleren Westen, dessen Familie *Look* abonniert haben könnte, unterscheidet die Geschichte sich doch grundlegend von der typischen Photo-League-Kost.

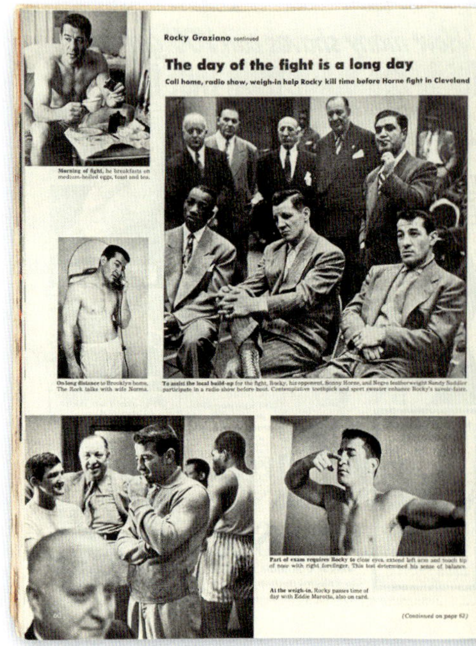

Rocky Graziano continued

The day of the fight is a long day

Call home, radio show, weigh-in help Rocky kill time before Horne fight in Cleveland

Morning of fight, he breakfasts on medium-boiled eggs, toast and tea.

On long distance to Brooklyn home, The Rock talks with wife Norma.

To assist the local build-up for the fight, Rocky, his opponent, Sonny Horne, and Negro featherweight Sandy Saddler participate in a radio show before bout. Contemplative toothpick and sport sweater enhance Rocky's savoir-faire.

Part of exam requires Rocky to close eyes, extend left arm and touch tip of nose with right forefinger. This test determined his sense of balance.

At the weigh-in, Rocky passes time of day with Eddie Marotta, also on card.

(Continued on page 62)

Am Wochenende erholten sich die Bürger in Kubricks demokratischer Stadt, indem sie die Fähre über den Hudson zum Vergnügungspark in Palisades nahmen. Dort machte Kubrick 1946, als er noch ein Neuling war, eine Fotoserie, und der Auftrag erlaubte ihm, sich auf einen Aspekt seines Handwerks zu konzentrieren, den zu erforschen er bisher noch keine Möglichkeit gehabt hatte. Dabei stellte sich heraus, dass er es wirklich liebte, seine Aufnahmen zu komponieren, und während Manhattan und die Bronx nicht so viele Gelegenheiten dafür boten, war der Vergnügungspark wirklich ideal – nicht zu überfüllt und mit viel offenem Raum um die dramatisch hohen Fahrgeschäfte herum. Er bot Kubrick die Chance für Aufnahmen von unten, in denen er Jugendliche im Kontrast zu den hoch aufragenden Attraktionen zeigte – eine Variation der sich gegen den Himmel abhebenden Posen der Arbeiterhelden, die Dorothea Lange, Robert Capa und Alexander Rodtschenko in den 1930er-Jahren fotografierten. Er konnte dieser Neigung aufs Neue nachgeben, als er 1948 den Zirkus der Ringling Brothers aufnahm. *Look* eröffnete die Doppelseite mit der raffiniert komponierten Aufnahme des Eigentümers John Ringling North, den Kubrick zu drei Vierteln von unten fotografierte, als er wie für einen Schrei die Hand an den Mund legt, während links über ihm Akrobaten auf einem Drahtseil Fahrrad fahren – die Nachkriegs- und Freizeitversion eines konstruktivistischen Plakats.

Dass die Menschen und besonders die Kinder in der Stadt anscheinend ständig draußen waren, demonstriert eine Bilderserie, die Kubrick 1947 beim Filmdreh von *Stadt ohne Maske* für einen nicht veröffentlichten Beitrag fotografierte. Es war zu der Zeit sehr selten, dass ein Hollywoodfilm zum Teil an Originalschauplätzen gedreht wurde, in der Delancey Street und auf der Manhattan Bridge in der Lower East Side, und wenn die Leute sich auf Autos räkeln, um den Kamerawagen drängen und sich an jedem Set so weit wie möglich nach vorne drängeln, sieht es so aus, als sei die ganze Nachbarschaft dabei gewesen. Kubricks Bilder erinnern an die Menschenmengen bei Weegee, und er hat ihn sogar ein- oder zweimal selbst fotografieren können, denn Weegee, der die Rechte am Titel seines gleichnamigen Fotobands verkauft hatte, war als technischer Berater am Set. Zu der Zeit war er schon eine Berühmtheit und nicht mehr Fotograf bei der Tagespresse, aber er übte noch jahrzehntelang großen Einfluss auf jeden Straßenfotografen der Stadt und darüber hinaus aus. Was in Kubricks Werk am offensichtlichsten auf Weegee hinweist, ist eine Reihe voyeuristischer Ultraviolettfotos von Freunden und Klassenkameraden, die sich im Dunkeln verliebt in den Armen liegen, obwohl der Einfluss des Meisterfotografen von Menschenmengen und Radau sich auch in Kubricks Bildern von Gaffern und Kunststücken zeigt wie in der Aufnahme einer Frau mit einer Reklametafel. 15 Jahre später engagierte Kubrick Weegee als Berater für Spezialeffekte und als Standbildfotografen für *Dr. Seltsam*; seine Fotos sind alles, was von der Tortenschlacht übrig geblieben ist, die ursprünglich die letzte Szene des Films hätte sein sollen.

Weegees Einfluss wird auch in Kubricks U-Bahn-Geschichte sichtbar, seinem ersten mehrseitigen Fotofeature. Kubrick verbrachte ganze Tage und Nächte in der U-Bahn und porträtierte die Stadt abwechselnd als romantisch, entfremdet, geheimnisvoll und alltäglich. Seine Porträts der einzelnen Fahrgäste gleichen in unheimlicher Weise denen von Walker Evans, obwohl er die keinesfalls kennen konnte (Evans nahm seine Bilder 1941 auf, die meisten von ihnen erschienen aber erst 1966 in dem Buch *Many Are Called*). Kubricks Fotos schließen romantische Intermezzi mit ein, die einerseits offensichtlich inszeniert (das Paar in der U-Bahn-Station an der 81. Straße, hinter dem ein hilfloses Wrack ausgestreckt auf dem Boden liegt) und andererseits offenbar authentisch sind (das ineinander verschlungene Paar auf den Rattansitzen). Ein Mann im Abendanzug mit einem Menjoubärtchen, der seinen schlafenden Sohn im Arm hält, lässt an einen Bauchredner mit seiner Puppe denken. In der Grand Central Station nimmt Kubrick die Rolltreppen mit der niedrigen, geneigten Decke von oben auf, sodass es aussieht, als wiesen ihre beiden Dreiecke auf einen weit entfernten Strudel hin, was an die Weltraumeffekte in *2001: Odyssey im Weltraum* erinnert.

Sein Porträt der Pferderennbahn Aqueduct aus dem Jahr 1947 ist wahrscheinlich das Werk, in dem der Filmregisseur Kubrick allmählich zu erkennen ist. Zum Teil, weil die Bilder uns an die Pferderennszenen in *Die Rechnung ging nicht auf* (1956) erinnern, seinen dritten Spielfilm, aber auch weil die Wettenden bei dem Rennen wie typische Kubrick-Protagonisten aussehen. Jede Figur ist unverwechselbar, ob sie nun allein gezeigt wird oder vor dem Hintergrund einer Menschenmenge, und jede lässt auf eine komplexe Lebensgeschichte schließen: die ehrwürdige alte Dame mit ihrem 20er-Jahre-Hut und ihrem Haarknoten, die ihren Wettschein ausfüllt; der junge Mann mit Fedora und Fliegersonnenbrille, dessen Lippen sich verächtlich verziehen und der aussieht wie ein Auftragskiller; der harte Typ im Ruhestand, möglicherweise ein Hafenarbeiter oder Cutman aus dem Boxsport, der noch einmal auf seinen Wettzettel schaut, bevor er ihn in den Mülleimer schnippt. Diese Menschen haben spürbar Kubricks Sympathie und seine Fantasie in einer Weise angeregt wie wenige Sujets zuvor. Sie sind ganz sicher keine Berühmtheiten, aber sie weigern sich, in der Menge unterzugehen – und werden dabei zu Darstellern auf einer Bühne. Kubrick ist sich zu dieser Zeit bereits bewusst, dass seine Kamera nicht einfach nur ein mechanischer Aufnahmeapparat ist, sondern ein sensibles Instrument, das auch noch auf die flüchtigsten Gefühle seines Bedieners reagiert.

Damals war das Boxen ein Teil des Lebens in der Stadt, ein Sport, bei dem Tausende zusahen, der armen Jungs eine dramatische Möglichkeit bot, den Slum zu verlassen und zum Star zu werden. Kubrick veröffentlichte vier Boxgeschichten in *Look*, einschließlich zweier Features über Preiskämpfe und eines Porträts des problembeladenen, aber charismatischen Rocky Graziano, der später eine kleine Karriere im Showbusiness machte. Die emblematischste Geschichte aber war die über Walter Cartier, einen bescheidenen und nachdenklichen Mann mit dem Aussehen eines Matinee-Stars, der zudem irritierenderweise einen Zwillingsbruder hatte, Vincent, einen Rechtsanwalt. Kubrick folgte Walter den ganzen Tag vor seinem Kampf mit der Kamera, einschließlich eines Kirchenbesuchs, einer Übungseinheit mit seinem Trainer und ruhiger Selbstbesinnung im Massageraum, bevor er in den Ring stieg. Die Kampfszenen sind dunkel und explosiv, die Handlung entfaltet sich in dramatischen Schüben. Ein Jahr später wählte Kubrick Cartier zum Protagonisten seines ersten 16 Minuten dauernden Dokumentarfilms *Day of the Fight* (1951) mit demselben Szenario wie die Fotogeschichte in *Look*. RKO Pictures kaufte den Film für 100 Dollar mehr oder auch weniger, als er gekostet hatte (die Angaben variieren), aber das war der Beginn seiner zukünftigen Karriere. Einige Monate später drehte er einen weiteren Dokumentarfilm, *Flying Padre* (1951), über einen Priester im Südwesten des Landes, der zu seinen weit verstreuten indianischen Gemeinden im eigenen kleinen Flugzeug reiste. Danach verließ Kubrick *Look* und fing an, seinen ersten Spielfilm zu planen.

Kubricks Arbeit bei *Look* hat ihren eigenen Wert als Porträt von New York zu einem wichtigen Zeitpunkt – kurz nach dem Krieg und kurz bevor alle Menschen einen Fernseher hatten –, als die Stadt ihren bunt gemischten und zugleich unschuldigen Höhepunkt erreicht hatte. Und als erstklassige Sammlung von Aufnahmen eines aufstrebenden Dokumentarfotografen, der sich vielleicht noch nicht ganz auf der Höhe seiner Kunst befand, aber fest entschlossen war, seinen eigenen, höchst individuellen Weg einzuschlagen, der bereits schemenhaft erkennbar ist. Als noch unausgereiftes Werk eines bedeutenden Filmregisseurs bieten die Bilder fast zu viele Hinweise, sowohl ästhetischer als auch psychologischer Art, auf das Kommende. Man kann die Anfänge von Kubricks Chiaroscuro-Stimmungen ausmachen, seine Weltraumkompositionen, sein schnelles Hin- und Herschalten zwischen dem Kleinen und dem Großen. Der Betrachter erkennt hier auch, wie fanatisch Kubrick auf jedes Detail achtete und wie er die Welt als großes Studio nutzte, in dem keine Nuance übersehen und nichts dem Zufall überlassen wird. Stanley Kubrick hatte Glück mit seiner ersten Anstellung; dort lernte er zu sehen.

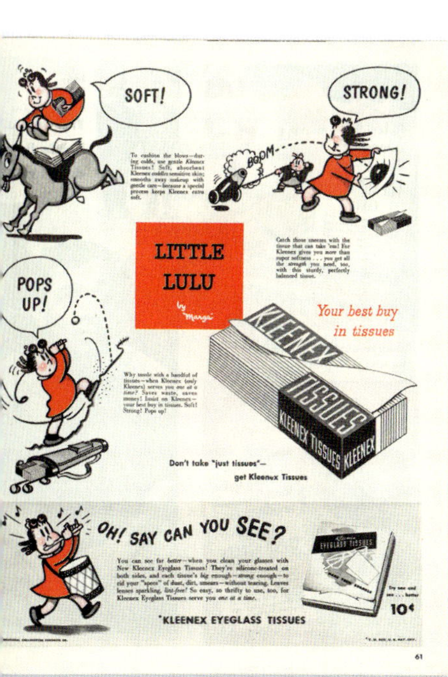

ROCKY GRAZIANO: HE'S A GOOD BOY NOW
PUBLISHED: **FEBRUARY 14, 1950**

FOLLOWING SPREAD **Backstage at the Riviera, from the 1949 article "Midsummer Nights in New York"**

ANMERKUNGEN

1 Michael Herr, *Kubrick*, New York: Grove Press, 2000, S. 4.

2 Leo Rubifien, *Garry Winogrand*, New Haven: Yale University Press, 2013, S. 18.

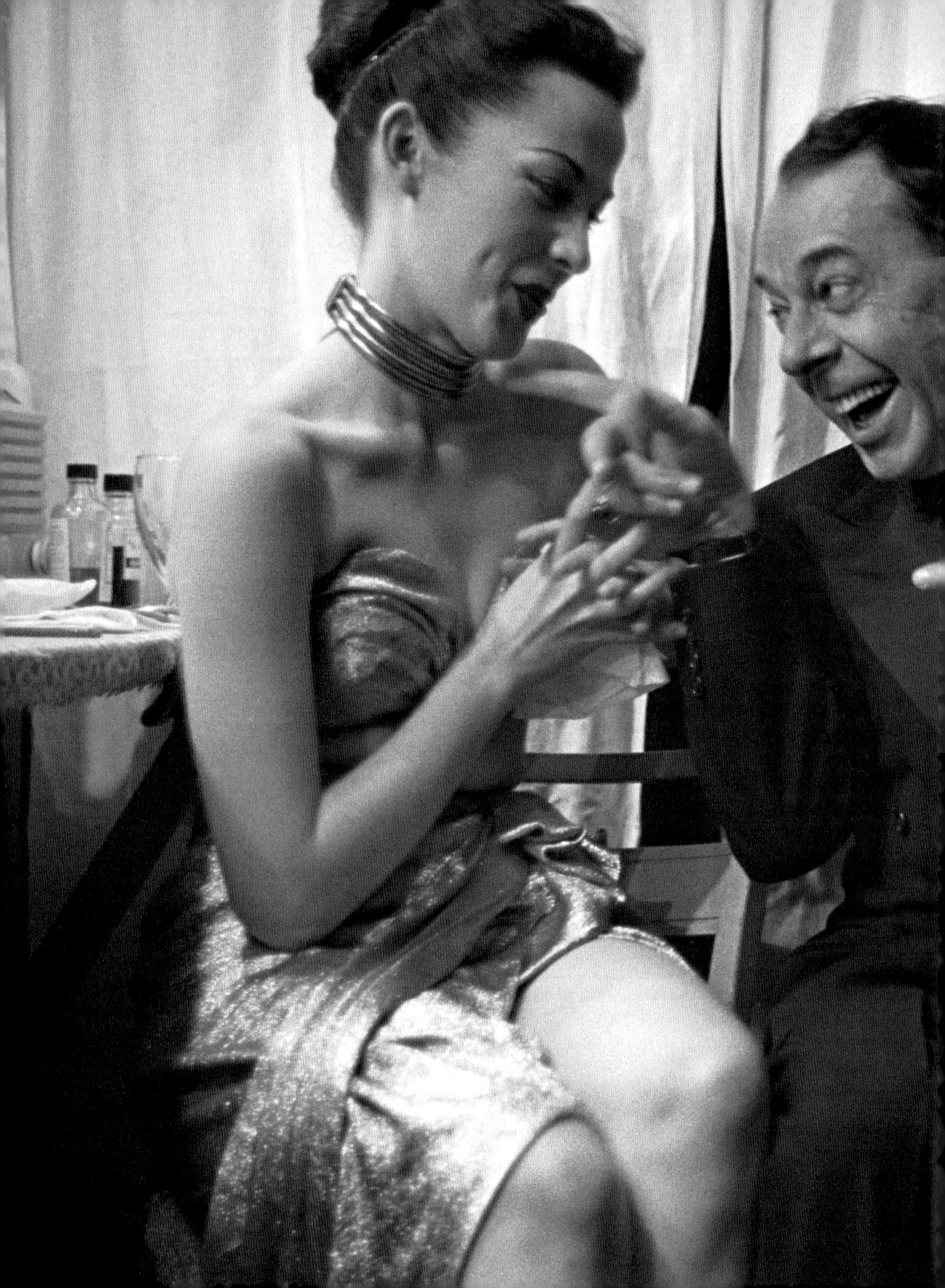

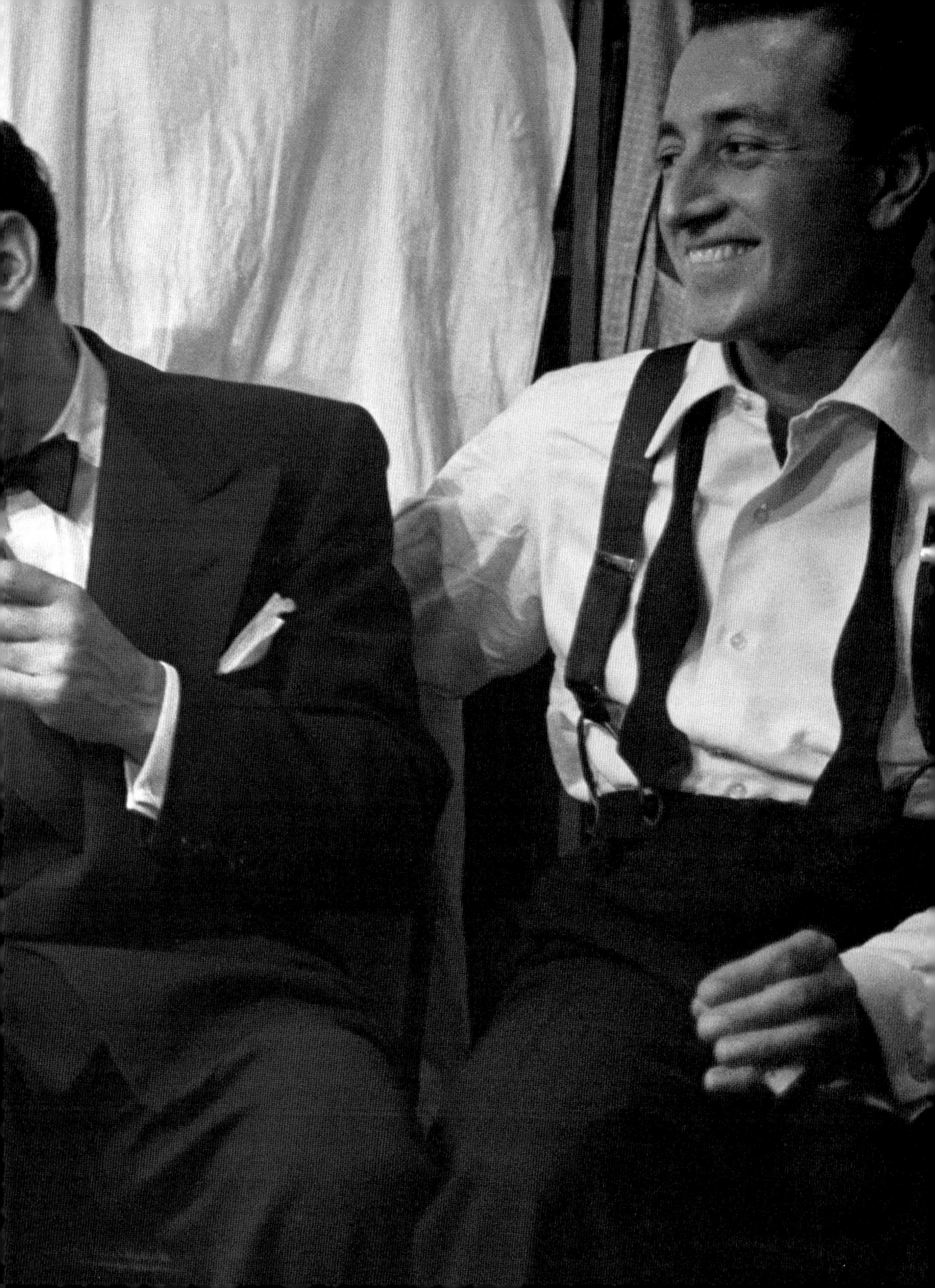

DONALD ALBRECHT & SEAN CORCORAN

À TRAVERS UN AUTRE OBJECTIF : LES PHOTOS DE STANLEY KUBRICK

Pour la plupart de ceux qui ne le connaissent que comme cinéaste, la carrière de photojournaliste de Stanley Kubrick est une révélation. Entre 1945 et 1950, avant d'être le réalisateur mondialement connu, auteur de films comme *Docteur Folamour, 2001 : l'Odyssée de l'espace* et *Orange mécanique*, il était simplement Stanley, un adolescent de New York doté d'une remarquable sensibilité photographique, arpentant les rues à la recherche de reportages à résonance humaine pour le magazine *Look*.

Né dans le Bronx en 1928, élève médiocre ayant peiné à finir le lycée, Kubrick recherchait moins une éducation formelle que les leçons du monde réel. Les bureaux de *Look* à Manhattan deviendraient son université; ses rédacteurs et ses collègues photographes seraient ses professeurs, et la ville de Manhattan son champ d'études. Plus tard, il a déclaré à propos de ses années chez *Look* : « À 21 ans, j'avais déjà derrière moi quatre années passées à comprendre comment fonctionnait le monde. Si j'étais allé à l'université, je ne serais jamais devenu réalisateur[1]. » Braquant son objectif sur sa ville natale, et parfois un peu au-delà, Kubrick était inspiré par la personnalité haute en couleur de New York. Les célébrités, les excentriques et les cireurs de chaussures qui peuplaient les rues attiraient son regard. Les night-clubs et les salles de sport le fascinaient. Il rendait hommage aux New-Yorkais dans des images qui reflétaient l'âpreté de la vie ordinaire, des images d'une maturité étonnante qui laissaient déjà entrevoir son avenir en tant que l'un des plus grands artistes du xxe siècle[2].

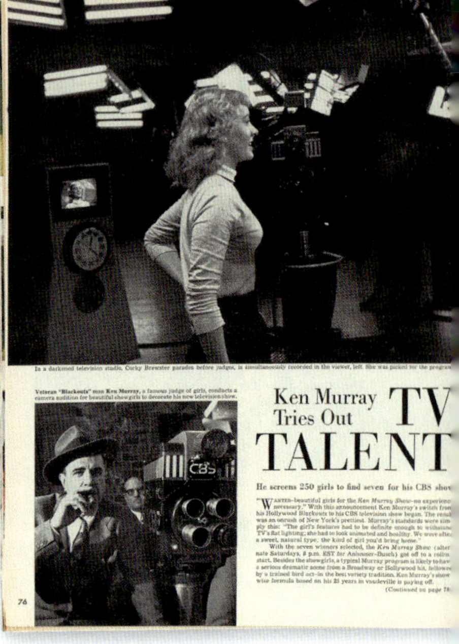
In a darkened television studio, Corky Brewster parades before judges, is simultaneously recorded in the viewer, left. She was picked for the progra

Veteran "Blackouts" man Ken Murray, a famous judge of girls, conducts a camera audition for beautiful showgirls to decorate his new television show.

Ken Murray Tries Out TV TALENT

He screens 250 girls to find seven for his CBS sho

"WANTED–beautiful girls for the *Ken Murray Show*–no experienc necessary." With this announcement Ken Murray's switch fro his Hollywood *Blackouts* to his CBS television show began. The resu was an onrush of New York's prettiest. Murray's standards were sim ply this: "The girl's features had to be definite enough to withstan TV's flat lighting; she had to look animated and healthy. We were afte a sweet, natural type, the kind of girl you'd bring home."

With the seven winners selected, the *Ken Murray Show* (alter nate Saturdays, 8 p.m. EST for Anheuser-Busch) got off to a rollin start. Besides the showgirls, a typical Murray program is likely to hav a serious dramatic scene from a Broadway or Hollywood hit, followe by a trained bird act–in the best variety tradition. Ken Murray's show wise formula based on his 25 years in vaudeville is paying off.

(Continued on page 7

76

Kubrick tenait sa passion de la photographie – et des échecs – de son père, cardiologue et photographe amateur lui-même, lequel offrit au jeune Stanley un Graflex professionnel pour ses 13 ans, déclenchant irrévocablement sa vocation. Dans les années 1940, il n'y avait pas meilleur endroit pour un photographe débutant que le magazine *Look*, fondé début 1937 par Gardner Cowles Jr. avec pour mission d'offrir « de la lecture intéressante pour [vous], [votre] épouse, [votre] secrétaire particulière, [votre] garçon de bureau[3] ». Si ses rédacteurs et photographes parcouraient le monde pour rapporter des reportages couvrant une large gamme de sujets, le terrain de prédilection de *Look* était juste devant sa porte. Le magazine dépeignait New York avec théâtralité, humour et esprit, mettant l'accent sur les interactions humaines et puisant des messages universels dans des récits individuels.

Si *Look* et *Life* rivalisaient pour attirer l'attention du public, les deux titres se distinguaient par leur ligne éditoriale pour rendre compte de la vie contemporaine et de l'actualité. Selon Cowles, *Look* visait un « champ plus large et terre à terre » que son concurrent[4]. *Life*, fondé en 1936 par Henry Luce, s'était fixé une mission plus grandiose : « Voir la vie, voir le monde, être le témoin des grands événements, observer les visages des pauvres et les gestes des orgueilleux[5]. » Parce qu'ils travaillaient pour un bimensuel, les journalistes de *Look* n'étaient pas tenus de couvrir les dernières nouvelles et avaient plus de liberté pour chercher des sujets sur des histoires vécues que leurs collègues de *Life*, contraints par des impératifs hebdomadaires. Selon l'historienne Mary Panzer, les articles de *Look* semblaient dépeindre « une civilisation un peu étrangère, un univers alternatif excentrique… *Look* explorait souvent ce que ses critiques distingués décrivaient avec mépris comme le "côté sordide de la vie américaine". De fait, *Look* abondait d'articles sombres sur le chômage, l'alcoolisme, la délinquance juvénile, le divorce… des sujets que les lecteurs de *Life* trouvaient plus rarement dans leur magazine et, lorsque cela était le cas, ils étaient souvent traités avec optimisme[6] ».

Panzer observa également que *Life* fonctionnait comme une chaîne de montage hiérarchisée et bien huilée alors que, chez *Look*, les équipes changeaient au gré des reportages : « Ils réfléchissaient à comment raconter l'histoire au mieux. Cela donnait un magazine irrégulier et souvent surprenant[7]. » Ce fonctionnement plus souple venait peut-être du rédacteur en chef Daniel D. Mich, lequel occupa une variété de postes de direction au sein du magazine entre 1937 et son décès en 1965. Mich avait instauré une atmosphère de travail qui engendrait une pléthore d'idées de reportages, proposés aussi bien par les journalistes maison que free-lance. La décision de publier un article revenait à Mich, qui jugeait de sa pertinence et de son à-propos. (De nombreux articles ne remplissaient pas ces critères et n'étaient jamais publiés.) Tout au long de ce processus, les bons photographes apprirent qu'il était préférable de mitrailler leur sujet afin de donner au département artistique un vaste choix d'images pour leur mise en page.

Kubrick entra chez *Look* en 1945 avec sa photo d'un crieur de journaux démoralisé le lendemain de la mort de Franklin D. Roosevelt. Kubrick avoua plus tard avoir demandé au vendeur de paraître plus déprimé qu'il ne l'était réellement pour obtenir un effet plus dramatique – il avait déjà cette capacité à mettre en scène ses sujets. Cette première publication fit passer Kubrick de photographe amateur à professionnel. Au printemps 1946, Helen O'Brian, directrice photo chez *Look*, qui avait déjà acheté plusieurs des photographies de Kubrick – dont celle du crieur de journaux –, proposa d'engager celui-ci comme apprenti. Certes, ce n'était pas là une pratique habituelle du magazine, mais Kubrick était en dernière année de lycée (William Howard Taft) et l'équipe avait reconnu le talent et l'ambition du jeune homme. À tout juste 17 ans, Kubrick était de loin le plus jeune photographe du magazine et, avec un salaire de 50 dollars par semaine, la direction ne prenait pas un grand risque.

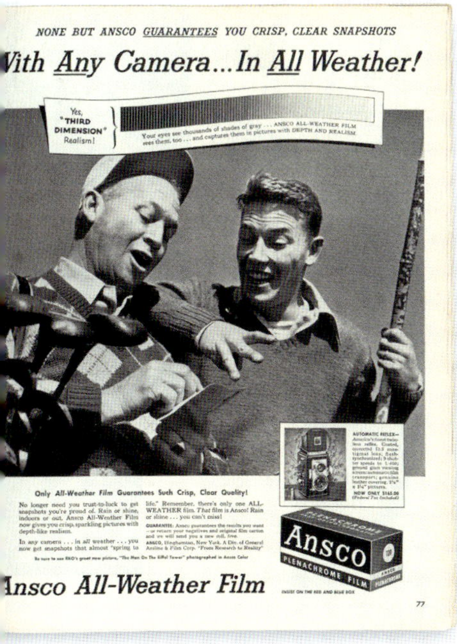

Au cours de ses premières années chez *Look*, Kubrick se vit confier de petits sujets consistant en quelques photographies accompagnées de textes brefs. « How a Monkey Looks to People… and How People Look to a Monkey », publié le 20 août 1946, et « Bronx Street Scene », publié le 26 novembre 1946, démontraient un sens aigu de l'observation et une fascination pour l'humain. Ces clichés capturaient des moments intimes entre New-Yorkais au milieu de la foule : deux familles s'extasiant devant les animaux du zoo du Bronx et un groupe d'amis plongés dans une conversation animée. Par ses choix de composition, il conférait à ces moments ordinaires de la tension et de l'humour. Outre ces commandes, Kubrick soumettait ses propres reportages aux chefs de rubriques du magazine. « Teacher Puts 'Ham' in Hamlet », publié le 2 avril 1946, était une série photographique ayant pour sujet son professeur de lycée, Aaron Traister, interprétant *Hamlet*. Son talent pour raconter des histoires fut vite reconnu par ses employeurs et il fut engagé dans l'équipe des photographes maison en octobre 1946.

L'adolescent intégra officiellement le groupe illustre de photoreporters, dont Arthur Rothstein, le directeur technique du magazine, et John Vachon. Tous deux avaient été photographes pour la Farm Security Administration (FSA) créée par Franklin D. Roosevelt pour documenter les conditions de vie des démunis dans les zones rurales durant la Grande Dépression. La sensibilité dont ils avaient fait preuve lors de cette mission caractérisait également leur travail pour *Look*. Celle-ci influença le jeune Kubrick tandis qu'il travaillait à leurs côtés ou auprès d'autres photoreporters aguerris sur divers reportages, tels que « Fight Night at the Garden », avec Rothstein et Vachon, publié le 15 février 1949, ou d'autres jamais parus comme « Advertising Sign Painters at Work », avec Franck Bauman et Tom Weber, classé dans les archives le 3 septembre 1947. Ses mentors l'encadrèrent également dans sa vie privée, allant jusqu'à créer un « Bringing Up Stanley Club » (littéralement « Éduquons Stanley ») pour aider l'adolescent à naviguer dans le monde du travail. Ils s'attaquèrent d'abord à son allure vestimentaire : « Autrefois porté sur la panoplie habituelle du teenager – chaussures bicolores, veste ample, chemise de sport –, Stanley penche désormais pour le costume en tweed et les chemises blanches[8]. »

Le 7 janvier 1947, le nom de Kubrick fait son entrée dans l'ours du magazine. Son premier grand reportage « Life and Love on the New York Subway » fut publié deux mois plus tard, dans le numéro du 4 mars. Afin de photographier les passagers à leur insu, il avait passé quinze jours dans le métropolitain new-yorkais avec un appareil photo autour du cou, ce dernier étant relié à un déclencheur caché dans sa poche par un fil passant dans sa manche. Il utilisait parfois un collaborateur pour mettre en scène des situations nécessaires pour illustrer l'article, une pratique commune à l'époque. Ses vingt-neuf photos, qui documentaient ce que l'auteur qualifiait de « mode de transport le plus long et le plus

KEN MURRAY TRIES OUT TV TALENT
PUBLISHED: **MAY 9, 1950**

bruyant du monde accessible pour cinq cents seulement[9] », montraient des banlieusards las, des ivrognes, des amoureux ou des âmes esseulées dans leur vie quotidienne.

À partir de l'automne 1947, Kubrick commença à réaliser des reportages plus longs. L'un d'eux, « Shoeshine Boy », archivé le 6 octobre 1947, racontait une journée dans la vie de Mickey, un adolescent de New York, qui allait à l'école, faisait du sport, pariait avec ses amis, élevait des pigeons sur les toits et rapportait un peu d'argent à sa famille en cirant des chaussures dans les rues de New York. Dans ce reportage non publié, Kubrick, seulement sept ans plus âgé que son sujet, faisait ressortir les contrastes entre la déontologie très adulte de Mickey au travail et l'exubérance de ses jeux d'enfants.

Au printemps 1948, la capacité de Kubrick à réaliser des longs reportages photographiques narratifs lui valut une série de commandes. « Columbia University », publié le 11 mai 1948, explore le culte du progrès américain, alors répandu, et la foi dans les avancées scientifiques incarnées par une université d'élite. « How the Circus Gets Set », publié le 25 mai 1948, brosse le portrait du cirque Ringling Bros, l'occasion pour Kubrick d'effectuer des juxtapositions humoristiques dans un décor hors norme, satisfaisant son goût pour l'absurde. Ces deux reportages furent rapidement suivis par deux autres, qui l'entraînèrent hors de New York : « Mooseheart – The Child City », publié le 8 juin 1948, dépeint un orphelinat situé à une soixantaine de kilomètres à l'ouest de Chicago, tandis que « Holiday in Portugal », publié le 3 août 1948, suit un jeune couple américain en vacances en Europe.

De tous les sujets que Kubrick couvrit pour *Look*, aucun n'est plus en phase avec son nouvel intérêt pour le cinéma que l'exploration du monde du divertissement et des médias, à cette époque déjà deux pans majeurs de l'économie et de l'identité de New York. À travers ses reportages sur des personnalités de la radio et de la télévision, le jeune novice apprenant les ficelles du métier évolue en un artiste plus mûr, repoussant les limites du photojournalisme puissant et humaniste. Son aptitude à traduire la vie psychologique complexe d'un individu en images est manifeste dans ses reportages sur le compositeur et chef d'orchestre Leonard Bernstein, le boxeur Walter Cartier, l'actrice Faye Emerson, la comédienne de théâtre Betsy von Furstenberg ou la danseuse de revue Rosemary Williams. Dans chacun de ces portraits, Kubrick explore la vie privée et publique de son sujet. Dans certains cas, ceux d'Emerson et de von Furstenberg par exemple, ses images laissent entendre que les personnalités privées et publiques ne font qu'une. Dans d'autres, comme dans son portrait de Williams, elles soulignent la dichotomie entre la personnalité glamour sur scène et la réalité plus crue des coulisses.

À l'époque, la radio était encore la forme de divertissement dominante dans les foyers. Kubrick réalisa plusieurs reportages sur des personnalités radiophoniques, comme Vaughn Monroe, publié le 6 août 1949, et Arthur Godfrey, publié le 1er février 1949. La télévision n'en était qu'à ses débuts, mais *Look* cherchait déjà à familiariser ses lecteurs avec ce nouveau médium – ironie de la vie, au cours de la décennie suivante, le petit écran supplanterait les magazines comme forme de communication la plus populaire, culminant avec la fermeture de *Look* en 1971. Par exemple, son numéro du 7 janvier 1947, dans le cadre d'une série sur les nouvelles tendances du divertissement, comportait une photo de Kubrick montrant un studio de télévision typique, avec des descriptifs de chaque élément de production. Plusieurs années plus tard, Kubrick fut envoyé en reportage sur le plateau de l'émission *The Howdy Doody Show*, où Bob Smith incarnait Buffalo Bob s'entretenant avec la marionnette Howdy Doody (publié le 20 décembre 1949), et il réalisa un portrait approfondi de Faye Emerson, une actrice hollywoodienne reconvertie en animatrice de talk-show à la fin des années 1940 (publié le 15 août 1950). Kubrick était donc aux premières loges pour observer comment les célébrités modelaient leur personnage public. Il se tenait régulièrement dans les coulisses et sur le plateau, suivant de près le processus de production.

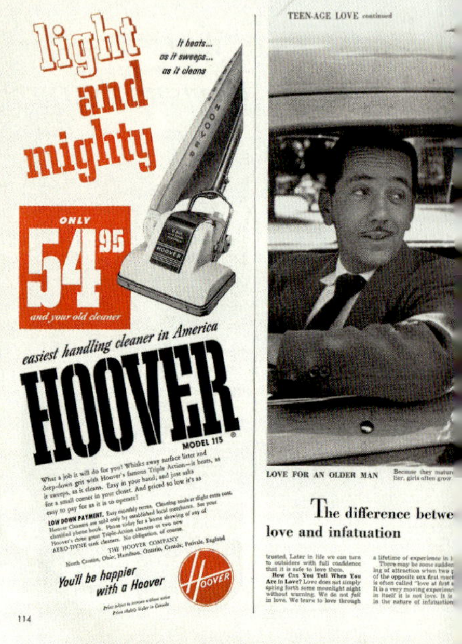

Les signes avant-coureurs les plus clairs de sa future carrière se lisent dans ses photos non publiées prises sur le tournage de *La Cité sans voiles* (1948), un film récompensé par plusieurs Oscars et l'une des premières productions hollywoodiennes à renouer avec les plans en décors naturels. On imagine la fascination du jeune homme qui dévorait les films noirs au cinéma ainsi qu'au musée d'Art moderne. Kubrick passa de longues heures à observer le cinéaste Jules Dassin et son chef opérateur William H. Daniels filmant les procédures policières dans les rues de New York. Bien qu'on ne sache si cette expérience déclencha en lui l'envie de faire des films, elle eut forcément un impact. En mai 1948, le magazine *Look* observait : « Pendant son temps libre, Stanley s'essaie à la caméra et rêve de pouvoir un jour réaliser des documentaires[10]. »

En 1950, Kubrick explora les thèmes de l'amour adolescent, des rendez-vous galants formels entre teenagers et de la jalousie conjugale dans trois reportages qu'il mit en scène, faisant poser des lycéens pour les histoires adolescentes et des acteurs pour les scènes de vie conjugale. Aussi fondamentaux ces trois articles furent-ils, ce fut son reportage « Prizefighter» sur le boxeur Walter Cartier, publié le 18 janvier 1949, qui lança formellement sa carrière de cinéaste. Kubrick choisira Cartier comme sujet de son premier documentaire de 16 minutes, *Day of the Fight*, qu'il produisit lui-même et présenta en 1951. Il fut ensuite distribué mondialement.

Après avoir réalisé plusieurs documentaires sans engranger de profits, Kubrick comprit que, s'il voulait faire carrière dans le cinéma, il devait passer à la fiction. Il présenta sa démission à *Look* en août 1950 et se mit au travail sur son premier long métrage, *Fear and Desire* (1953), une exploration abstraite des rapports entre des soldats et une jeune femme anonyme au cours d'une guerre entre des pays non identifiés. Ses deux films suivants, *Le Baiser du tueur* (1955) et *L'Ultime Razzia* (1956), partageaient la même esthétique noire que certains de ses reportages les plus marquants pour *Look*, notamment ceux explorant les vies sombres de personnages urbains tels que des boxeurs et des danseuses de revue.

Les cinq années passées chez *Look* s'avérèrent formatrices pour Kubrick. Au sein du magazine, il participa au processus créatif dans un environnement collaboratif qui n'était pas très différent de celui du cinéma. Il y apprit à raconter des histoires à travers des images dans des séquences narratives dynamiques et à se concentrer sur la subtilité des interactions humaines. Il y développa l'art du cadrage, de la composition et de l'éclairage afin de rendre ses images plus saisissantes. Bon nombre de ces dernières présentaient déjà cette vision froide et impartiale qu'il adopterait dans bon nombre de ses films. On peut aisément considérer ces premières années chez *Look* comme le début de sa remarquable carrière d'artiste et de cinéaste, comme l'époque où il peaufina ses talents de conteur et de créateur d'images, quoiqu'en utilisant un objectif différent.

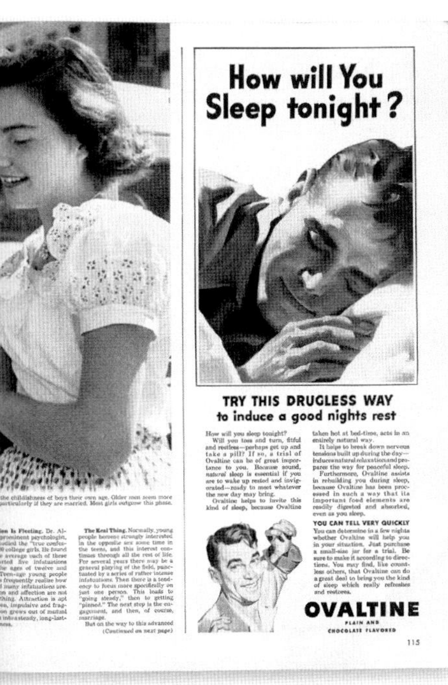

WHAT TEENAGERS SHOULD KNOW ABOUT LOVE
PUBLISHED: **OCTOBER 10, 1950**

NOTES

1 Stanley Kubrick, cité dans «Kubrick's Brilliant Vision» de Paul D. Zimmerman, *Newsweek*, 3 janvier 1972, 31.
2 Pour certaines des informations sur le magazine *Look*, nous avons puisé dans le texte «Only in New York» de Donald Albrecht et Thomas Mellins, figurant dans leur ouvrage *Only in New York: Photographs from Look Magazine*, coédité par le Museum of the City of New York et The Monacelli Press en 2009. Pour la période de Kubrick chez *Look*, notre source la plus précieuse fut *Stanley Kubrick's Tenure at Look Magazine: Autorship and Genre in Photojournalism and Film*, écrit par Philippe Mather et publié par Intellect en 2013.
3 Gardner Cowles Jr., cité dans «Look Out», *Time*, 11 janvier 1937, 25.
4 Gardner Cowles Jr., cité dans «Look Out», *Time*, 11 janvier 1937, 25.
5 Énoncé de mission du magazine *Life*, cité sur le site web de la Beinecke Rare Book & Manuscript Library, https://brbl-dl.library.yale.edu/vufind/Author?author=Life+magazine&type=Author&page=2, consulté le 4 décembre 2017.
6 Mary Panzer, «Eyes Wide Open», *Vanity Fair*, mars 2005, 410-442.
7 Mary Panzer, «Eyes Wide Open», *Vanity Fair*, mars 2005, 442.
8 «A veteran photographer at 19, Stanley Kubrick makes up for youth with zeal», *Look*, 11 mai 1948, 2.
9 «Life and Love on the New York Subway», *Look*, 4 mars 1947, 60.
10 «A veteran photographer at 19, Stanley Kubrick makes up for youth with zeal», *Look*, 11 mai 1948, 2.

LUCY SANTE

STANLEY KUBRICK : L'APPRENTISSAGE DU REGARD

Citant un ami d'enfance de Kubrick, l'auteur et journaliste Michael Herr a écrit : « Stanley se comportait toujours comme s'il savait quelque chose que vous ignoriez[1]. » On ne sera pas surpris d'apprendre que Stanley Kubrick, l'incomparable réalisateur de *Docteur Folamour*, *2001 : l'Odyssée de l'espace*, *Barry Lyndon* et de dix autres films cultes réalisés avec un soin fanatique était une sorte de prodige. Non pas un enfant prodige, mais presque. Avant même d'avoir terminé ses études secondaires, il avait déjà vendu deux photos à *Look*. Peu après le lycée, il fut engagé par le magazine comme photographe maison, un poste qu'il conserva jusqu'à ses 22 ans. Il couvrit toutes sortes de sujets, à New York et au-delà, réalisant des portraits de célébrités, des essais, des articles d'intérêt humain, des instantanés de rue, des clichés volés et de longues séquences présentées sous des formats horizontaux qui présageaient sa future carrière cinématographique.

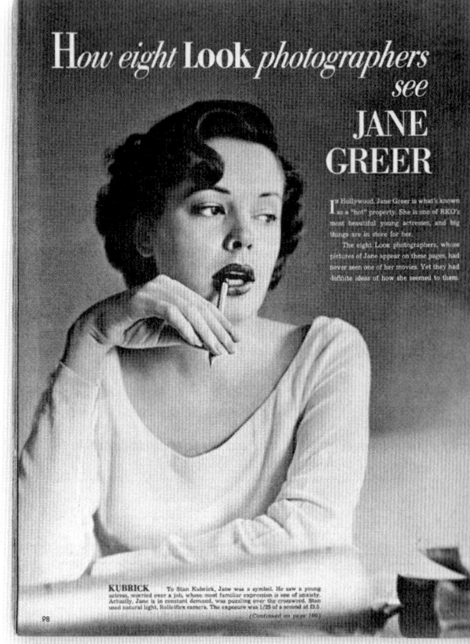

How eight Look photographers see JANE GREER

In Hollywood, Jane Greer is what's known as a "hot" property. She is one of RKO's most beautiful young actresses, and big things are in store for her.

The eight Look photographers, whose pictures of Jane appear on these pages, had never seen one of her movies. Yet they had definite ideas of how she seemed to them.

KUBRICK To Stan Kubrick, Jane was a symbol. He saw a young actress, worried over a job, whose most familiar expression is one of anxiety. Actually, Jane is in constant demand, was puzzling over the crossword. Stan used natural light, Rolleiflex camera. The exposure was 1/25 of a second at f3.5.

(Continued on page 100)

98

La fin des années 1940 était une bonne époque pour devenir photographe. La guerre était terminée, les gens n'avaient jamais eu autant d'argent à dépenser depuis quinze ans et tous les kiosques débordaient de magazines illustrés. S'engouffrant dans la voie ouverte à la fin des années 1930 par *Life* et *Look*, sans parler de *Fortune*, de *Vogue* ou d'*Harper's Bazaar*, il existait désormais des douzaines de revues d'intérêt général illustrées avec des photographies, ciblant toutes sortes de classes sociales et de niveaux culturels. Des journaux spécialisés qui dépendaient autrefois du dessin au trait se mirent également à remplir leurs pages de photographies. New York était le meilleur endroit au monde pour se lancer dans le métier. Outre le fait d'être le centre du secteur de l'édition de presse, la ville n'avait jamais été aussi contrastée. Ses artères fourmillaient de gens de toutes sortes ; n'importe quel coin de rue à n'importe quelle heure du jour ou de la nuit offrait un tableau de quelque sorte, un spectacle humain, une collision aléatoire d'éléments disparates. Ce que Paris avait été dans les années 1920, lorsqu'elle avait donné naissance à des douzaines de grandes carrières photographiques, New York pouvait à présent le revendiquer pour soi. De jeunes aspirants photographes entreprenants issus des cinq *boroughs* et d'au-delà surent profiter de l'occasion.

Chronologiquement, Kubrick se situe au milieu de la myriade de photographes new-yorkais ayant mitraillé les rues de cette époque : Ted Croner et Louis Stettner, nés en 1922 ; Diane Arbus et Saul Leiter, nés en 1923 ; Robert Frank et Jerome Liebling, nés en 1924 ; Simpson Kalisher, né en 1926 ; Garry Winogrand, William Klein et Elliott Erwitt, nés en 1928 ; Bruce Davidson, né en 1933 ; et Lee Friedlander, né en 1934. Il est intéressant de comparer Kubrick avec son contemporain Winogrand, né la même année que lui, originaire lui aussi du Bronx, et ayant, lui aussi, renoncé à des études universitaires pour se consacrer à la photographie. Winogrand eut beaucoup plus de mal à percer, travaillant en free-lance durant de longues années, parvenant rarement à placer une image dans une publication de prestige. Le plus gros de ses premières photographies parut dans des magazines comme *Collier's*, *Pageant* et *Redbook*. Toutefois, le travail en free-lance avait ses avantages. Si les premières publications des deux jeunes hommes se confondent parfois – par exemple, le portrait de Winogrand d'un jeune boxeur « What Makes Nick Run » (*Pageant*, mai 1955)[2] est, sur le plan tonal, très proche du travail de Kubrick sur des sujets similaires –, Winogrand avait plus de temps et de liberté pour développer un style radical propre : ses horizons typiquement inclinés et ses amoncellements chaotiques d'informations visuelles apparurent très rapidement dans son portfolio. En revanche, Kubrick apprenait les ficelles du métier tout en étant tenu par des critères spécifiques : la clarté et le traitement du sujet devaient primer ; l'expression personnelle était secondaire.

Kubrick commença sa carrière chez *Look* avec des sujets qui lui étaient proches, émotionnellement et littéralement. Le seul professeur de son lycée avec lequel il se sentait des affinités s'appelait Aaron Traister et était connu pour ses discours enflammés durant les cours d'anglais. En 1946, *Look* publia un article de Kubrick avec quatre photos montrant l'enseignant interprétant *Hamlet* en classe. La même année, le magazine publia une série de dix-huit clichés montrant des patients dans la salle d'attente d'un dentiste, avec des expressions allant de l'ennui à la profonde douleur. Toutes étaient de Kubrick, prises chez son propre dentiste. Il réalisa également plusieurs séries séquentielles avec des inconnus dans les rues du Bronx, papotant, gesticulant ou échangeant des regards torves. Kubrick n'était alors qu'un débutant, et ses photos, bien que claires et efficaces, manquaient un peu de personnalité. Sans doute est-ce pourquoi autant de ces premières images étaient publiées sous la forme d'un assemblage de vignettes ; plus il y en avait, plus l'impression était forte. Mais peut-être aussi Kubrick pensait-il déjà en termes cinématographiques et estimait-il que prendre autant de clichés en série revenait à saisir la continuité de l'action – et non pas à rechercher une image unique chargée de sens.

Les images de Kubrick traduisent bien l'atmosphère de New York à la fin des années 1940 : turbulente, opiniâtre, usée, optimiste, lunatique, théâtrale, démocratique. C'était la capitale de son temps, plus importante qu'elle ne l'avait jamais été, leader mondial en matière de production d'images via la publicité et l'art, avec ses nouvelles constructions en verre et en acier remodelant Midtown (y compris les nouveaux bureaux de *Look*, au 488 de l'avenue Madison, accomplis en 1950). Parallèlement, c'était encore une ville portuaire populeuse et hétérogène, avec ses nombreux quartiers ethniques et prolétaires dont les habitants n'avaient pas encore cédé à l'exode vers les banlieues.

S'il existait des différences de classes, tout le monde partageait les mêmes rues, buvait souvent dans les mêmes bars et déjeunait aux mêmes comptoirs. Même un dandy comme Peter Arno, dessinateur au *New Yorker*, entraînant une fille deux fois plus jeune que lui à une soirée, s'arrêtait boire une bière dans le genre d'établissement sans prétention qui, aujourd'hui, serait qualifié de « boui-boui ». Le grand artiste allemand expatrié George Grosz est photographié à califourchon sur une chaise à même le trottoir de la 5ᵉ Avenue – comme s'il était le président d'une agence de voyages –, pour illustrer un article sur New York, capitale des arts, qui, outre cette image, avait opté pour des photos plus conventionnelles d'autres photographes. Contrairement à *Life* et à l'instar de son autre concurrent *People*, *Look* aimait les portraits de célébrités au travail et au repos, mimant des conversations téléphoniques ou s'affairant dans leur cuisine. Ainsi, l'actrice ingénue Betsy von Furstenberg est montrée en tournage, durant des essayages, retouchant son maquillage, lisant un script dans son appartement, dans le bureau de son agent, se promenant à bicyclette, dans une réception guindée en compagnie d'un jeune homme nerveux en tenue de soirée, épluchant une banane dans un restaurant aux côtés du même jeune homme. Ces « portraits » étaient en réalité des fictions glamour vaguement inspirées des activités réelles des sujets. Ces dernières étaient reconstituées en poses soignées et assemblées en minibiographies que Kubrick mettait en scène avant de photographier.

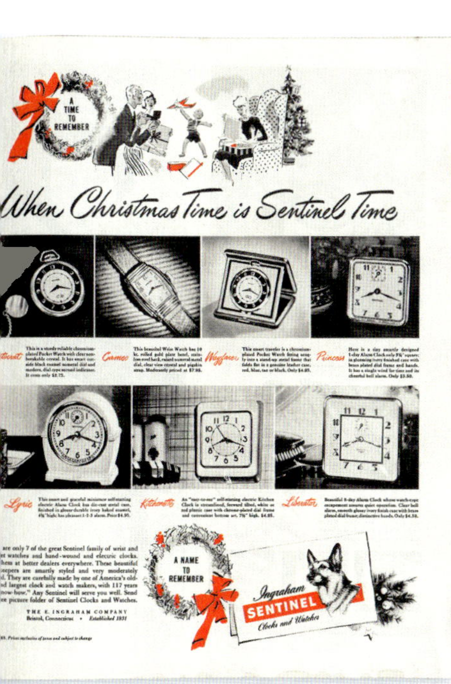

HOW EIGHT *LOOK* PHOTOGRAPHERS SEE JANE GREER
PUBLISHED: **DECEMBER 21, 1948**

Il débutait sûrement avec un scénario en tête, prévoyant suffisamment d'activités pour créer une impression de continuité, idéalement structurées autour d'une journée typique et chargée. Certaines personnalités étaient plus coopératives que d'autres. Leonard Bernstein semble avoir tenu à être photographié principalement le regard perdu au loin, tel un dieu, dans différents décors. Guy Lombardo n'accepta d'être montré qu'exhibant divers biens en sa possession, dont une meute de petits chiens. Puis il y a Montgomery Clift, dont le portrait devait coïncider avec la sortie de son troisième film, pas encore une star mais en bonne voie pour le devenir. Il porte un tee-shirt déchiré, paraît mélancolique et songeur, boit du café et fume. C'est un homosexuel qui se cache par nécessité, vit seul et maintient ses fréquentations loin des objectifs. Il est virtuellement impossible de construire une fiction romantique autour de lui sans recourir à des artifices, si bien que Kubrick et lui se rendent chez la famille d'un ami de Clift, Kevin McCarthy, où l'acteur joue vaillamment, quoiqu'un peu maladroitement, avec le plus jeune fils. On remarquera le contraste avec Arno, qui collectionne ouvertement les très jeunes femmes sans susciter le moindre commentaire, comme si c'était la chose la plus naturelle du monde de la part d'un homme du monde vieillissant.

Le portrait de Rosemary Williams, une danseuse de revue, offre une histoire new-yorkaise particulièrement éloquente et canaille, à la lisière du film noir, remplie de contrastes et de personnages secondaires. Détail intéressant, sa routine quotidienne, qui en faisait un sujet idéal, est probablement la raison pour laquelle le reportage ne fut jamais publié. Williams vint à New York avec des ambitions théâtrales et, à défaut de trouver suffisamment de travail sur la scène « traditionnelle », payait son loyer en dansant dans des revues, ce qui signifie que, au cours d'une journée, elle était souvent peu vêtue, sans doute pas assez pour un magazine familial. Sa vie ne devait pas être facile, même si nous la voyons toujours à travers le prisme du plaisir masculin. Kubrick lui-même apparaît dans le reflet du miroir de sa loge, le regard gourmand et concentré. Hormis dans les coulisses du théâtre, où on la voit jouant aux cartes avec ses collègues, Williams est montrée partout souriant à des hommes : à son manager, à un ami lors d'un déjeuner, à un autre acteur, au mari d'un couple plus âgé qu'elle accompagne dans un night-club déprimant. Elle est également photographiée sous la marquise d'un cinéma de Times Square annonçant *The Set-Up*[3], qui avait peut-être une signification particulière pour Kubrick.

Tous les sujets de portrait de Kubrick, aussi mondains soient-ils, cohabitent dans la même ville que le petit cireur de chaussures, qui semble tout droit sorti d'un roman d'Horatio Alger. Coiffé d'un chapeau à la Huntz Hall, des Bowery Boys, il traîne son matériel d'un lieu à l'autre, échange des capsules de bouteille avec ses amis, lorgne les affiches de cinéma, mais va également à l'école, rapporte le linge de la famille, s'occupe de ses pigeons sur le toit et pose avec ses nombreux frères et sœurs devant leur immeuble couvert de graffitis à la craie. Avec le recul, cette série paraît trop bonne pour être vraie, digne d'une sélection d'œuvres de la Photo League, une coopérative de photographes à vocation sociale, fondée en 1936 et tuée par le maccarthysme en 1951. Tous les photographes de rue de la génération ayant précédé celle de Kubrick y ont participé à un moment ou un autre. Son reportage ne diffère du travail typique de la Photo League, avec sa documentation extensive sur les gamins de la rue, leurs jeux et leurs bagarres, que parce que son sujet est aussi blond que n'importe quel garçon vivant dans une ferme du Midwest et dont les parents seraient abonnés à *Look*.

Les habitants de la ville démocratique de Kubrick se détendaient le week-end en traversant l'Hudson à bord du ferry pour se rendre dans le parc d'attractions de Palisades. Kubrick y réalisa un reportage en 1946, alors qu'il était encore un débutant, et l'expérience lui permit de se concentrer sur un aspect du métier qu'il n'avait pas encore exploré. Il y découvrit qu'il aimait composer ses plans, ce que Manhattan ou le Bronx ne lui permettaient pas vraiment de faire. Le parc, pas trop bondé et avec beaucoup d'espaces dégagés autour des attractions, s'avérait idéal. Il permit à Kubrick de réaliser des prises de vue en contre-plongée, opposant les adolescents aux manèges monumentaux, une variation sur les plans d'ouvriers héroïques se détachant sur le ciel, réalisés dans les années 1930 par Dorothea Lange, Robert Capa et Alexandre Rodtchenko. Il put développer à nouveau ce style quand il photographia le cirque Ringling Bros. en 1948. Le reportage dans *Look* s'ouvre sur son plan hautement travaillé du directeur John Ringling North, en contre-plongée de trois quarts, mettant sa main en porte-voix tandis que, en arrière-plan et sur la gauche, un funambule et des acrobates s'entraînent, version ludique d'après-guerre d'une affiche constructiviste.

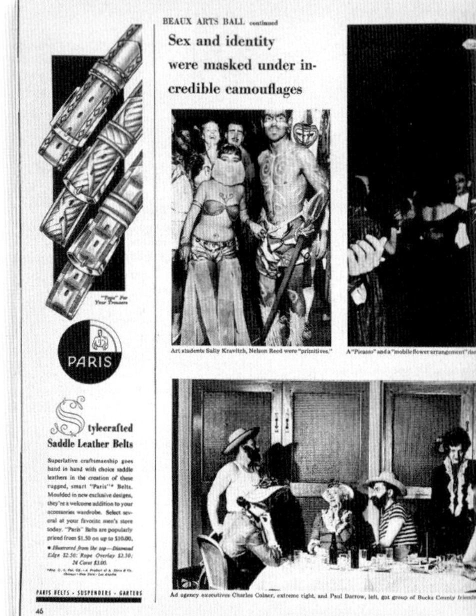

BEAUX ARTS BALL continued

Sex and identity were masked under incredible camouflages

Art students Sally Kravitch, Nelson Reed were "primitives."

A "Picasso" and a "mobile flower arrangement"

Ad agency executives Charles Coiner, extreme right, and Paul Darrow, left, got group of Bucks County friends

PARIS

Stylecrafted Saddle Leather Belts

Superlative craftsmanship goes hand in hand with choice saddle leathers in the creation of these rugged, smart "Paris"* Belts. Moulded in new exclusive designs, they're a welcome addition to your accessories wardrobe. Select several at your favorite men's store today. "Paris" Belts are popularly priced from $1.50 on up to $10.00.

PARIS BELTS · SUSPENDERS · GARTERS

46

Une série d'images prises par Kubrick lors du tournage de *La Cité sans voiles* en 1947, rassemblées en un reportage non publié, tend à prouver que les gens, surtout les enfants, vivaient dehors tout le temps. À l'époque, il était rare qu'une production hollywoodienne tourne dans des décors naturels, en l'occurrence dans Delancey Street et autour du Manhattan Bridge, dans le Lower East Side. Toute la population du quartier semble être venue assister au tournage, grimpant sur les voitures, entourant le camion de la caméra, se bousculant pour ne rien rater. Les images de Kubrick rappellent les foules de Weegee, qu'il parvint à capturer dans un ou deux plans car ce dernier avait vendu son titre au studio et travaillait comme conseiller technique sur le tournage. À l'époque, Weegee était déjà une célébrité et ne travaillait plus pour la presse quotidienne. Il demeura néanmoins une inspiration majeure pour tous les photographes de rue à New York et ailleurs durant des décennies. La trace la plus évidente de l'influence de Weegee sur le travail de Kubrick se trouve dans une série de clichés ultraviolets voyeuristes de ses amis et camarades de classe surpris dans des enlacements romantiques dans le noir. On retrouve également l'esprit du maître des foules et du tumulte dans ses images de badauds et de détails de rue, comme la femme-sandwich faisant la réclame pour un restaurant. Quinze ans plus tard, Kubrick engagea Weegee comme conseiller en effets spéciaux et photographe de plateau sur *Docteur Folamour* ; ses images nous fournissent la seule trace restante de la bagarre à la tarte à la crème initialement prévue pour la dernière séquence du film.

L'influence de Weegee se fait également sentir dans le reportage de Kubrick sur le métro, son premier article de plusieurs pages publié dans *Look*. Il constitue le portrait d'une ville tout à la fois romantique, aliénée, mystérieuse et quotidienne. Ses portraits individuels d'usagers évoquent ceux de Walker Evans, bien qu'il ne puisse les avoir vus – Evans prit les photos rassemblées dans *Many Are Called* en 1941, mais elles ne furent publiées que dans les années 1960. La série comporte des notes romantiques – un couple dans la station « 81rst Street IND », un sans-abri allongé en arrière-plan – et probablement authentiques : un couple enlacé sur l'une des banquettes en rotin. Un homme avec une fine moustache en tenue de soirée, le bras autour de son fils endormi, évoque un ventriloque et sa marionnette. Le long escalator de Grand Central, avec son plafond bas et incliné, est photographié d'en haut, si bien que ses deux triangles semblent pointer vers un vortex lointain, un plan qui nous rappelle les effets d'espace profond dans *2001 : l'Odyssée de l'espace*.

C'est avec son reportage sur l'hippodrome de l'Aqueduct, en 1947, que l'on voit poindre le futur cinéaste, en partie parce que les images évoquent les futures scènes de champ de courses de *L'Ultime Razzia* (1956), son troisième film, mais surtout parce que les turfistes ressemblent déjà à des personnages kubrickiens. Chacun est différent, photographié seul ou avec une foule en arrière-plan, et chacun évoque une histoire complexe : la vieille dame respectable avec son chapeau et son chignon à la Gibson Girl, qui remplit sa grille de paris ; un jeune homme en feutre et lunettes noires, la mine dégoûtée, qui ressemble à un tueur à gages ; un dur à cuir à la retraite, peut-être un ancien docker ou un ex-soigneur de ring de boxe, qui lance un dernier regard à sa grille perdante avant de la jeter à la poubelle. Toutes ces personnes ont vraisemblablement touché Kubrick et excité son imagination comme peu de sujets l'avaient fait auparavant. Bien que n'étant pas des célébrités, elles refusent de se fondre dans la foule et deviennent des acteurs sur une scène. Kubrick a pris conscience que son appareil photo n'était pas simplement un dispositif mécanique, mais un instrument étrangement sensible qui répond aux moindres émotions de son opérateur.

À cette époque, la boxe était une composante essentielle de la vie urbaine, un sport spectacle qui attirait les foules, un moyen pour des enfants pauvres de sortir des bidonvilles et de devenir des stars. Kubrick publia quatre reportages sur la boxe dans *Look*, dont deux matchs nocturnes et un portrait de Rocky Graziano, un boxeur perturbé mais charismatique qui ferait ensuite une petite carrière dans le show-biz. Toutefois, son reportage le plus emblématique est celui sur Walter Cartier, un homme humble et introspectif aux allures de jeune premier, possédant un frère jumeau avocat, Vincent. Kubrick le suivit durant toute une journée avant son combat du soir, l'accompagnant dans son église, lors d'une séance avec son entraîneur, puis lors d'une contemplation méditative de la salle de massage avant de monter sur le ring. Les scènes de combat sont sombres et explosives, l'action transmise par des mouvements fulgurants. Un an plus tard, Kubrick fit de Cartier l'objet de son premier film, un documentaire de 16 minutes intitulé *Day of the Fight* (1951) qui suit le même scénario que le reportage. Il fut acheté par RKO Pictures pour, selon les versions, 100 dollars de plus ou de moins que ce qu'il avait coûté. Quoi qu'il en soit, la nouvelle carrière de Kubrick était lancée. Quelques mois plus tard, il réalisa un second court métrage documentaire, *Flying Padre* (1951), sur un prêtre du Sud-Ouest qui visite ses paroisses amérindiennes éparpillées sur un vaste territoire à bord de son petit avion. Après ce dernier, Kubrick quitta *Look* et commença à travailler à son premier long métrage.

Le travail de Kubrick chez *Look* est précieux à plus d'un titre. Il constitue un portrait de New York à une période cruciale, juste après la guerre et juste avant que tout le monde possède un poste de télévision : la ville était alors hétéroclite et innocente. Il représente également un recueil exceptionnel de clichés par un jeune photographe documentaliste, peut-être encore pas tout à fait mûr mais déjà prêt à se tracer une voie très personnelle dont on peut entrevoir les prémices. En tant qu'œuvre embryonnaire d'un futur grand réalisateur, il nous offre presque trop d'indices, à la fois psychologiques et esthétiques, sur ce qui est à venir. On distingue les débuts de ses humeurs en clair-obscur, de ses compositions avec profondeur de champ, de ses allées et venues constantes entre le micro et le macro. On y remarque son sens du détail presque fanatique, sa volonté d'utiliser le monde comme un vaste studio où aucune nuance n'est négligée et où rien n'est laissé au hasard. Stanley Kubrick a eu de la chance avec son premier emploi : c'est là qu'il a appris à observer.

PHILADELPHIA'S FIRST BEAUX ARTS BALL
PUBLISHED: **SEPTEMBER 13, 1949**

FOLLOWING SPREAD **Rosemary Williams waiting while a companion changes a flat tire at night, from an unpublished 1949 assignment**

NOTES

1 Michael Herr, *Kubrick*, New York: Grove Press, 2000, 4.
2 Leo Rubinstein, *Garry Winogrand*, New Haven, Yale University Press, 2013, 18.
3 Littéralement « le piège », un film de boxe sorti en France sous le titre *Nous avons gagné ce soir*, 1949 (NdT).

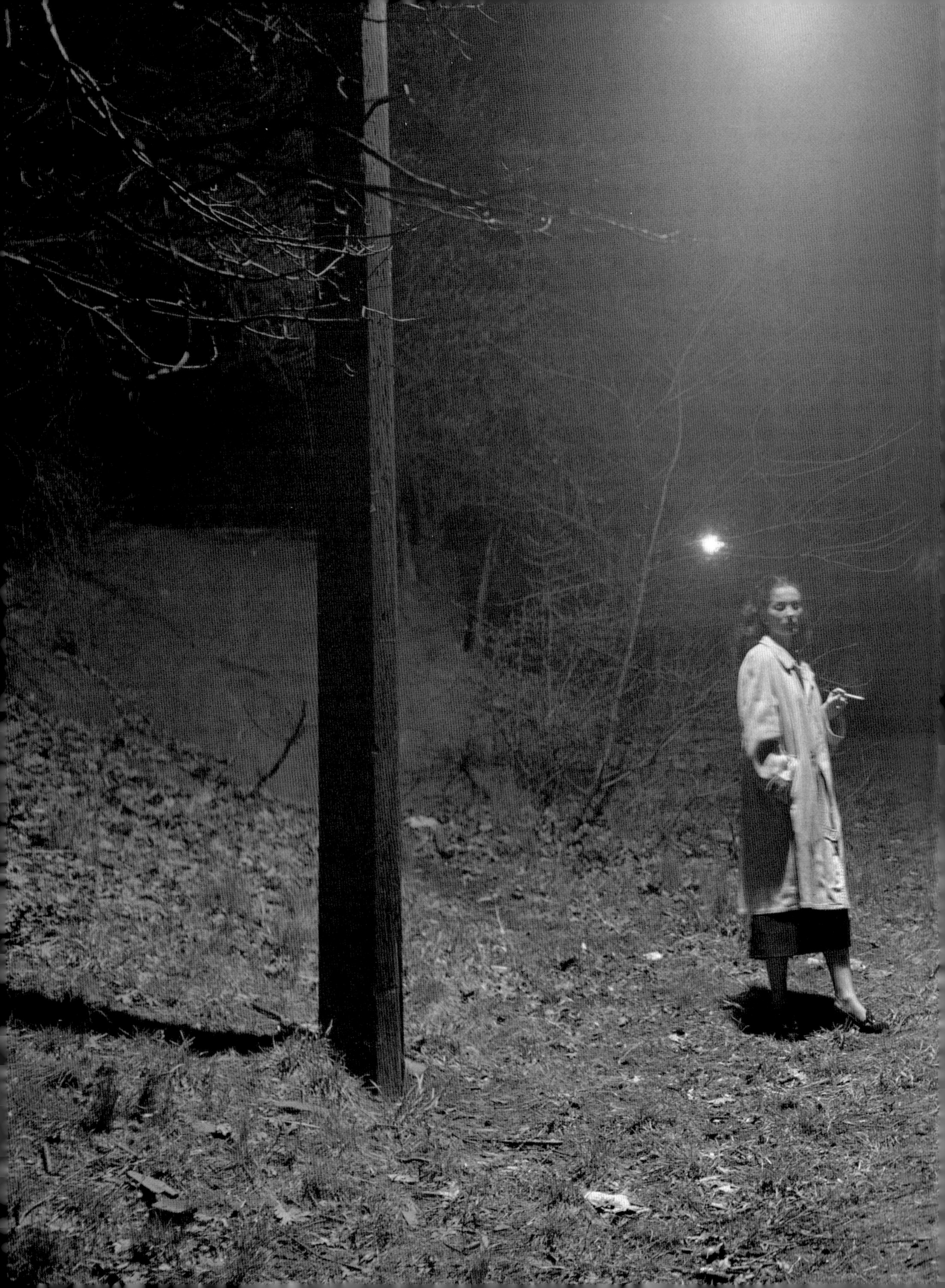

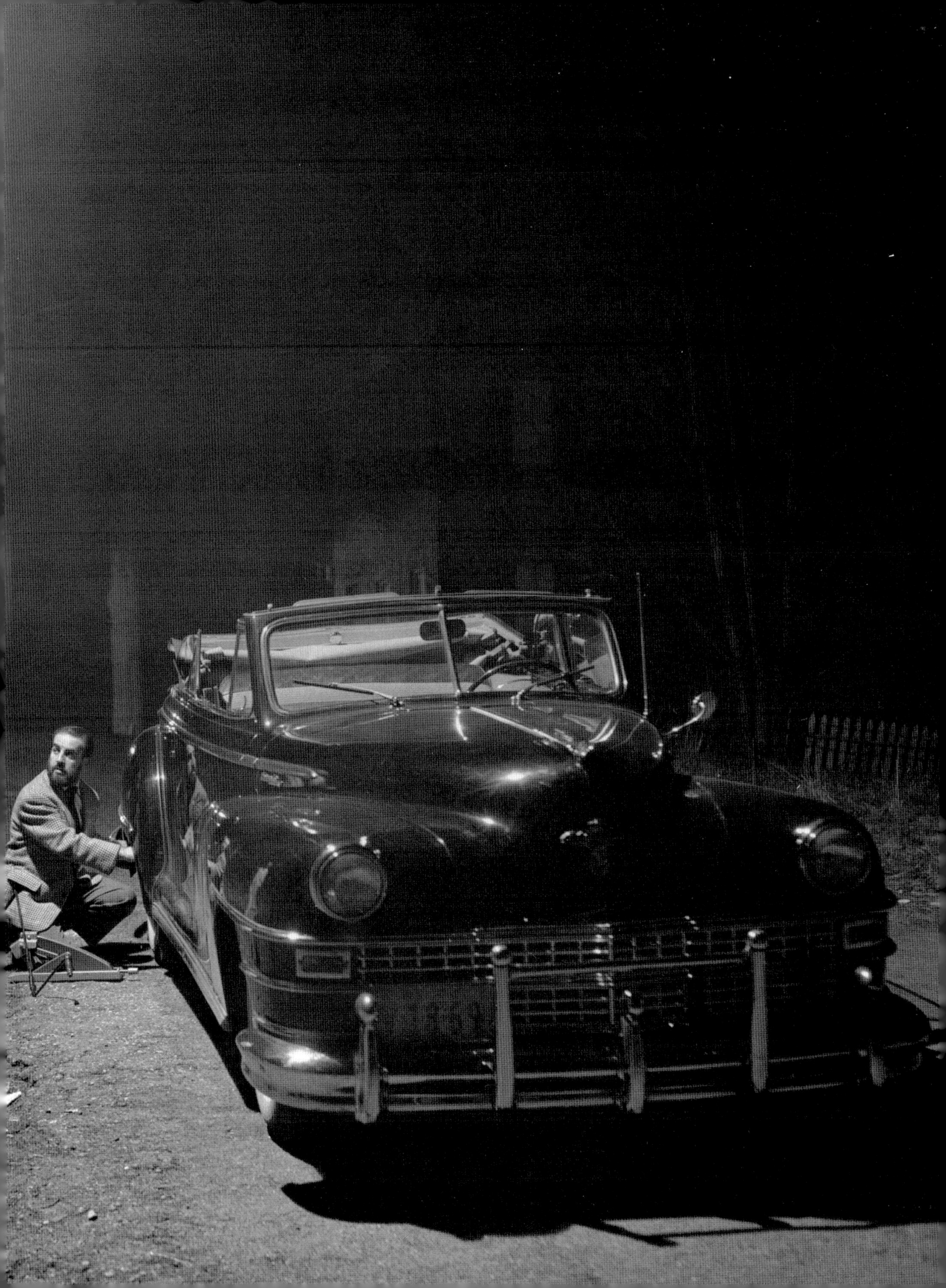

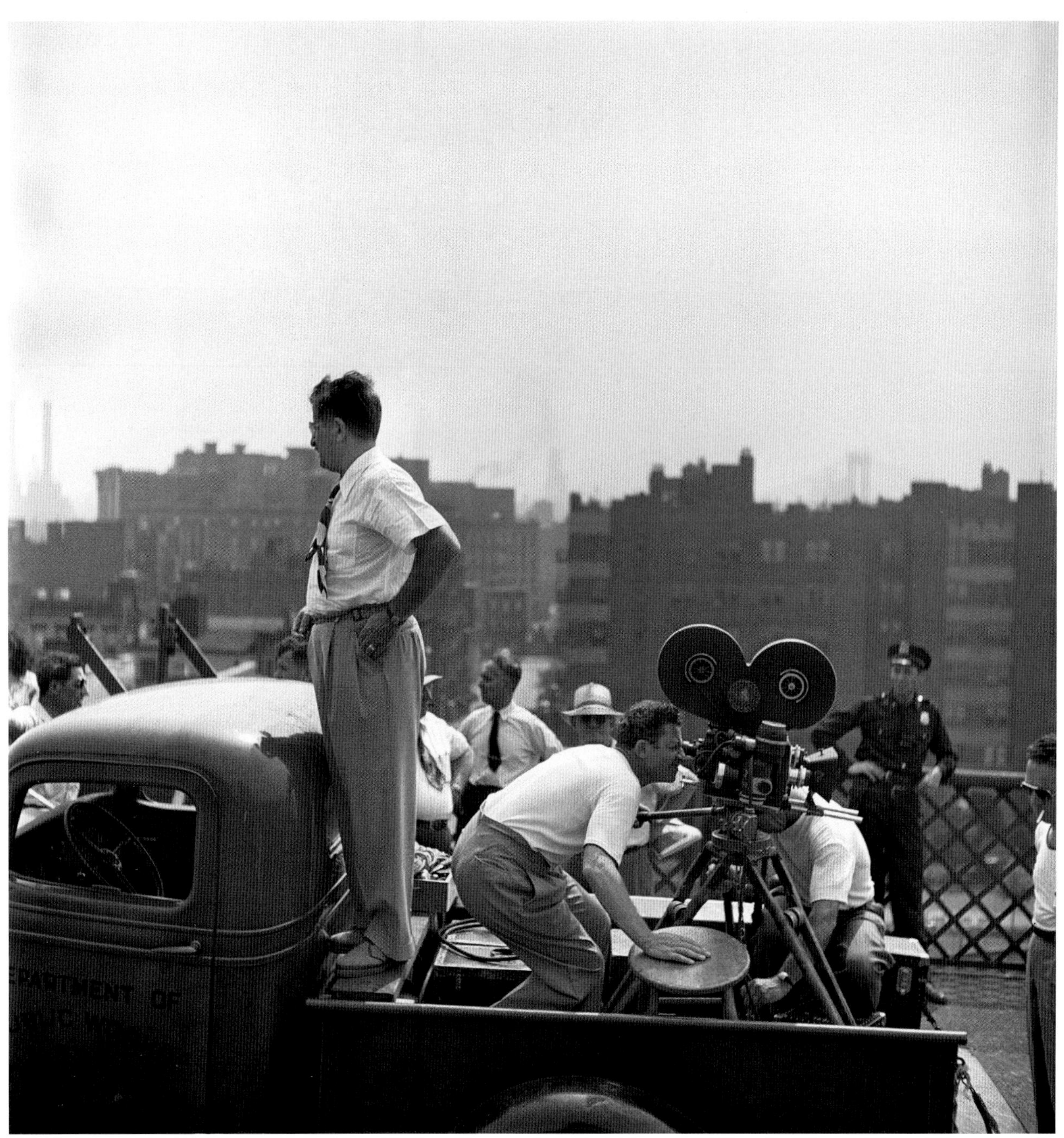

Cinematographer William H. Daniels (left) and director Jules Dassin (at camera) prepare to shoot a scene from *The Naked City* on the Williamsburg Bridge, from an unpublished 1947 assignment

FILMOGRAPHY

SHORT FILMS / DOCUMENTARIES

Day of the Fight **(1951)**
Flying Padre **(1951)**
The Seafarers **(1953)**

FEATURE FILMS

Fear and Desire **(1953)**
Killer's Kiss **(1955)**
The Killing **(1956)**
Paths of Glory **(1957)**
Spartacus **(1960)**
Lolita **(1962)**
Dr. Strangelove or: How I Learned to Stop Worrying and Love the Bomb **(1964)**
2001: A Space Odyssey **(1968)**
A Clockwork Orange **(1971)**
Barry Lyndon **(1975)**
The Shining **(1980)**
Full Metal Jacket **(1987)**
Eyes Wide Shut **(1999)**

BIBLIOGRAPHY

Albrecht, Donald, & Thomas Mellins. *Only in New York: Photographs from* Look *Magazine*. New York: Monacelli Press, 2009.

Bernstein, Jeremy. Interview with Stanley Kubrick, November 27, 1966. Audio CD in *The Stanley Kubrick Archives*, edited by Alison Castle. Cologne: TASCHEN, 2005.

Bizony, Piers. *The Making of Stanley Kubrick's* "2001: A Space Odyssey." Cologne: TASCHEN, 2015.

Castle, Alison, ed. *The Stanley Kubrick Archives*. Cologne: TASCHEN, 2005. Reprinted 2016.

__________, ed. *Napoleon: The Greatest Movie Never Made*. Cologne: TASCHEN, 2011.

Ciment, Michel. *Kubrick: The Definitive Edition*. New York: Faber & Faber, 1982 (first English edition). Reprinted 2003.

Crone, Rainer. *Stanley Kubrick: Drama and Shadows*. London: Phaidon Press, 2005.

Duncan, Paul. *Stanley Kubrick: The Complete Films*. Cologne: TASCHEN, 2011.

Kubrick, Christiane. *Stanley Kubrick: A Life in Pictures*. London: Little, Brown, 2002.

LoBrutto, Vincent. *Stanley Kubrick: A Biography*. New York: Da Capo Press, 1997.

Mather, Philippe. *Stanley Kubrick at* Look *Magazine: Authorship and Genre in Photojournalism and Film*. Bristol, UK, and Chicago: Intellect, 2013.

Panzer, Mary. "Eyes Wide Open." *Vanity Fair*, March 2005, 408–413, 442–444.

Pryor, Thomas M. "Young Man with Ideas and a Camera." *New York Times*, January 14, 1951.

Reynolds, Charles. "Interview with Kubrick." *Popular Photography*, December 1960, 144–149.

Rosten, Leo, ed. *The* Look *Book*. New York: Harry N. Abrams, 1975.

Rothstein, Arthur. *Photojournalism*. New York: AMPHOTO, 1979.

Stagg, Mildred. "Camera Quiz Kid... Stan Kubrick." *The Camera*, October 1948, 36–41, 152.

Zimmerman, Paul D. "Kubrick's Brilliant Vision." *Newsweek*, January 3, 1972, 28–33.

IMPRINT

Stanley Kubrick's photographs were donated to the Museum of the City of New York starting in 1956 by Cowles Magazines, Inc., the parent company of *Look* magazine.

All photographs are courtesy of Museum of the City of New York / SK Film Archives LLC.

Editor: Reuel Golden, New York
Design and layout: Pure+Applied, New York
German translation: Michael Stoeber, Hanover
French translation: Philippe Safavi, Paris

Hohenzollernring 53,
D-50672 Köln, Germany
www.taschen.com

Museum of the City of New York
1220 5th Avenue
New York, NY 10029
www.mcny.org

Printed in Germany
978–3–8365–9542–1

FRONT COVER
Stanley Kubrick and Rosemary Williams from an unpublished 1949 assignment

BACK COVER
Boxer Walter Cartier in Washington Square Park from the 1949 article titled "Prizefighter"

FRONTISPIECE
A partygoer wearing a Cubist headdress, from the 1949 article titled "Philadelphia's First Beaux Arts Ball"

TITLE-PAGE VERSO
New Yorkers watching the filming of the movie *The Naked City*, from an unpublished 1947 assignment

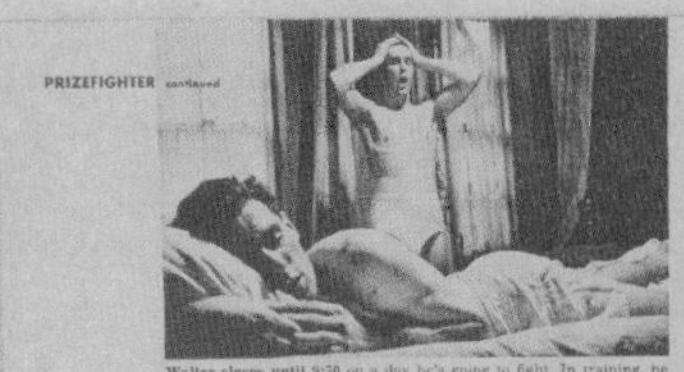

Walter sleeps until 9:30 on a day he's going to fight. In training, he gets up at 5:30, runs four miles. Twin brother Vincent sleeps on.

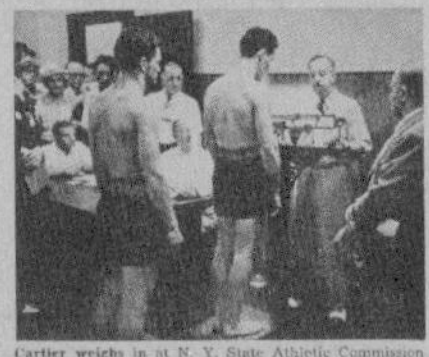

Vince helps train Walter, serves him breakfast of orange juice, three soft-boiled eggs, toast and coffee. Their Aunt Eva oversees the meal.

THE DAY OF A FIGHT

Cartier sleeps late, eats carefully, gets a physical check-up —and goes to church.

On way to fight, Walter stops at church, prays that he escape serious injury.

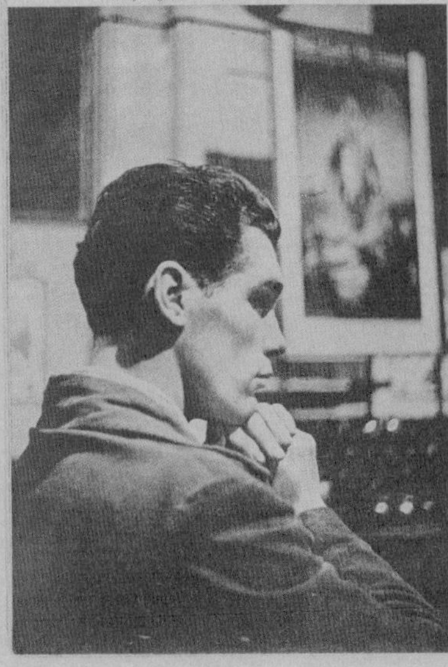

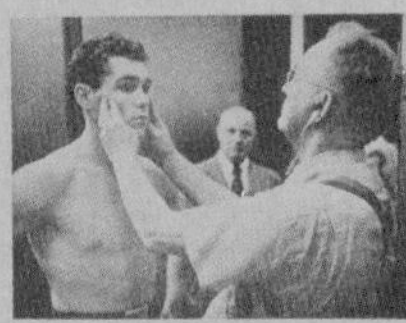

Cartier weighs in at N. Y. State Athletic Commission around noon. An official checks him on the scales.

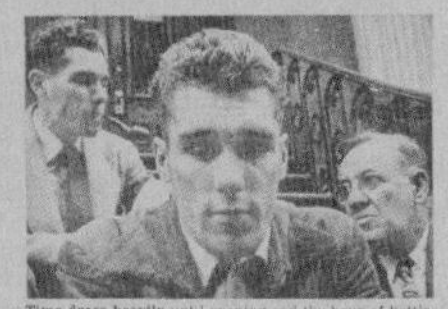

Doctor carefully examines eyes. Eye cuts, an occupational hazard, often impair vision, sometimes bring blindness.

Time drags heavily until evening and the hour of battle. Walter sits it out on front steps with brother, neighbor.

The fight: Walter carries attack to Tony D'Amico at Jerome Stadium, drives spittle from Tony's mouth. He led until head butt cut his right eye, gave Tony technical KO.

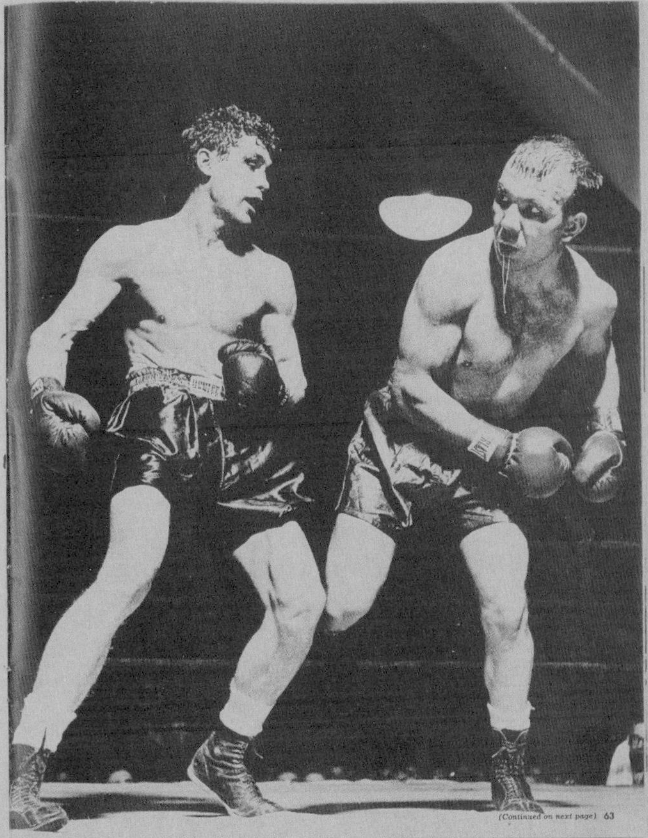

(Continued on next page)

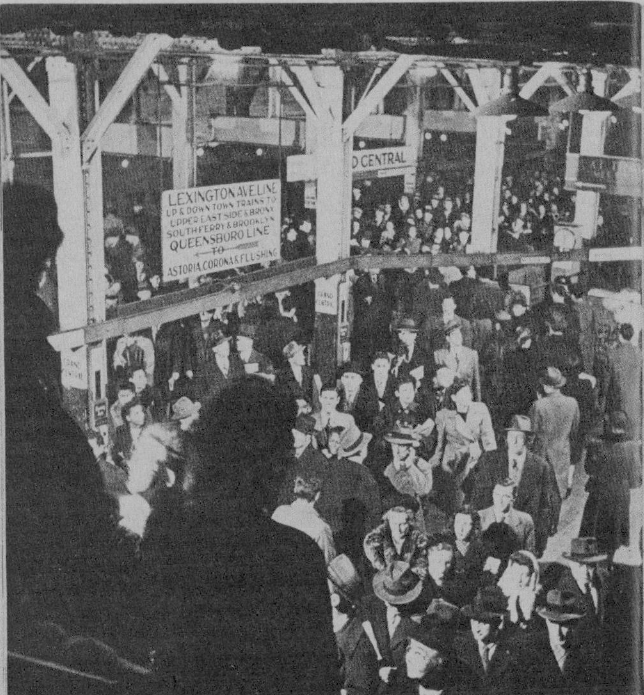

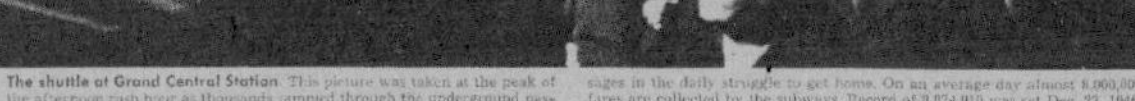

The shuttle at Grand Central Station. This picture was taken at the peak of the afternoon rush hour as thousands jammed through the underground passages in the daily struggle to get home. On an average day almost 8,000,000 fares are collected by the subways. Record of 8,874,910 was set Dec. 23, 1946.

Life and Love on the New York Subway

New York's subway trains are a reading room on wheels, a lover's lane and, after 11 p.m., a flophouse. And they give the city's 8,000,000 subway riders the noisiest and biggest nickel's worth of transportation in the world. The average New Yorker spends more than an hour a day packed into the subway. He's called a sardine – for obvious reasons. These pictures show that practically everything and anything can happen in a subway train. And subway riders are not surprised.

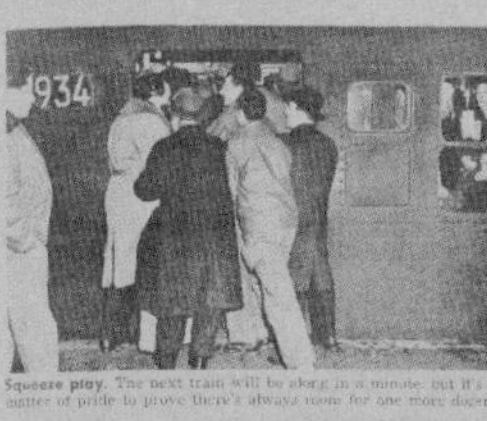

Squeeze play. The next train will be along in a minute, but it's a matter of pride to prove there's always room for one more dozen.

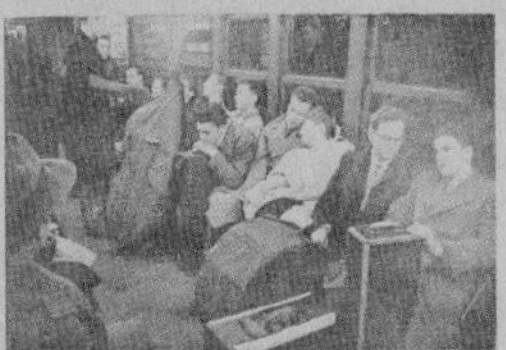

It's not so crowded later in day. So this 15-piece orchestra, complete with instruments and girl vocalist, travels by subway to a late show.

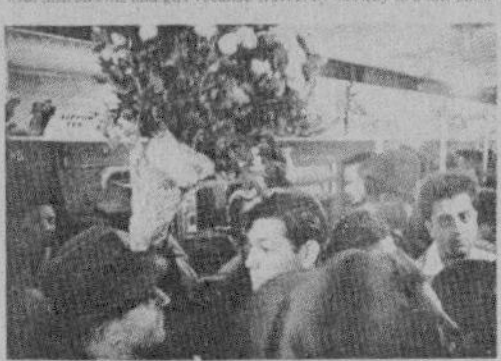

Flowers for my lady. They may be a bit battered by the time they reach her, but this lad's doing his best to keep them above the crowd.

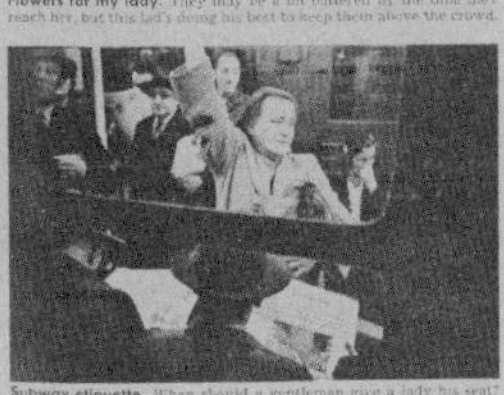

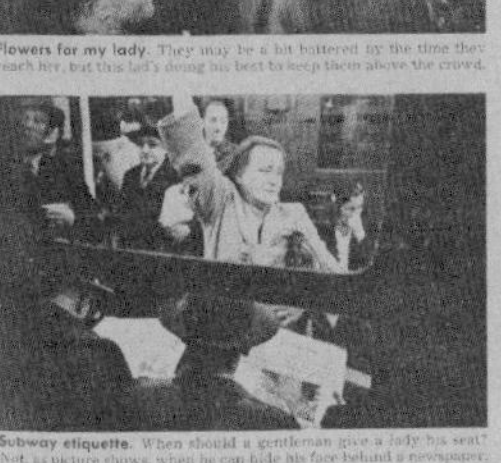

Subway etiquette. When should a gentleman give a lady his seat? Not, as picture shows, when he can hide his face behind a newspaper.

(Continued on page 62)

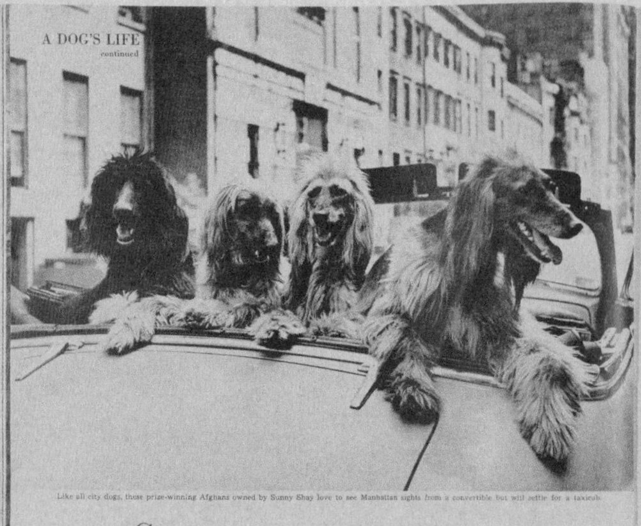

Like all city dogs, these prize-winning Afghans owned by Sunny Shay love to see Manhattan sights from a convertible but will settle for a taxicab.

City streets are always full of excitement for dogs

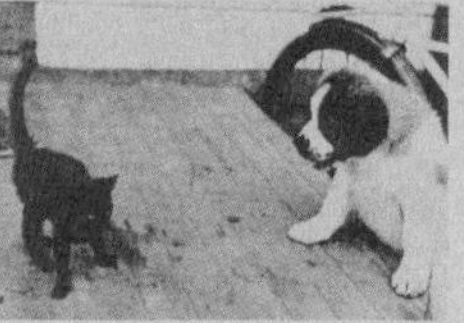

The cat is the enemy

In the country, dogs and cats sometimes learn to live together. But the city cat is tough. Even as a kitten, she stands her ground and aims claws at dogs' eyes.

me and announcing:

"I love dogs but I wouldn't be cruel enough to keep one in the city."

Actually, *records show that big city dogs are healthier, happier and live longer than dogs in small towns or the country.*

Dr. Raymond Garbutt, chief veterinarian of the ASPCA (American Society for the Prevention of Cruelty to Animals), has been treating city dogs for 30 years. He says: "In the country or suburbs, unless there is an outbreak of communicable disease, dogs always run loose. They get into dog fights and are killed by cars. They rummage in garbage cans, eating chicken bones and other dangerous matter. They lick up poisonous weed killers and insecticides. A New York dog, always on a leash and under supervision, has a far greater life expectancy than the same type and breed in the country."

Owning a dog in New York City is a lot of trouble—for the owner. The law says the animal must be on a leash at all times when he goes out. Nature forces you to take him out at least three times a day; four trips are kinder; and wily dogs can coerce easy-mark owners like me into six and seven trips. (This rule is for grown dogs. Puppies, even after they are house-broken, need more frequent trips.) You can never go out in the evening without climaxing it with a dog-walk; and a fairly long one, for the dog has been sleeping all evening and is now wide-awake and ready for fun. If you must go away for more than a few hours, you have to arrange to have the dog exercised—by your doorman, a friend or a professional dog walker. And, if you own a dog, you can never go off impetuously on trips.

When the dog travels with you, you must find out beforehand which hotels and inns will welcome him—or what trains will accept him and under what conditions. If you leave him at home, heart-broken, you must find a boarding place you can trust. Dog hospitals are reluctant to fill their cages with healthy animals. Boarding kennels in the city cost $2 to $3 a day, and most family pets are so unhappy penned up in kennels that they punish you afterwards by coming home thin, emotional wrecks. Kind friends can be imposed on to keep your dog just so often. So the dog owner has to resort to boarding the dog with professionals who charge from $15 to $25 a week, with extra charges for bathing, teeth cleaning, special diets to tempt poor eaters, delivery and pick-up and emergency trips to the vet.

Country dog-owners are sometimes aghast at the de luxe life a dog can lead in a big city—if his master or mistress will pay the freight. Sometimes, I am too.

Dogs Join Swank Club

On fashionable East 57th Street in New York, the Dog Bath Club (dues, $10 a year) has a swimming pool for its members and kennels air-cooled so that the temperature was never above 75 degrees on the days last summer when New York was sizzling in the heat wave. Professional dog-sitters and dog-walkers charge baby-sitting rates. Trainers do everything from house-breaking your puppy (at $5 a day) to teaching an old dog the new trick of going through a revolving door.

Country owners can get away with neglecting a dog's coat and personal hygiene by leaving him out of doors and making him sleep in the basement or barn. But in the city, an ungroomed dog sheds a nightmare of hairs over rugs and upholstery. And a city dog that needs a bath or a tooth-cleaning is as offensive as any other member of your family in the same condition.

If you have ever bathed a reluctant large dog in your bathtub, you recognize that the fee of $5 charged by professionals is not exorbitant. Owners of poodles and terriers which require tricky grooming pay more. Blanche Saunders' fashionable poodle-clipping shop does a rushing business in leg o' mutton and pom-pom trims at $7, $8 or $9 per job, depending upon the size of the dog.

Canine Psychiatrist on Call

For maladjusted dogs, there is a lady psychiatrist who lists among her clients the pets of men and women high up in the theater, society and government. Just outside the city, there are two large pet cemeteries. In Hartsdale, N.Y., 2 by 3-foot plots start at $35, with headstones, caskets and grave care extra. The Bide-A-Wee Home for Friendless Animals, an endowed institution, also operates a pet cemetery on Long Island, with plots running from $22 to $100 each.

Of the 15,000 veterinarians in the United States, only about 12 per cent specialize in the care of small animals. But, like M.D.'s, the vets with big ideas and big ambitions settle in areas of large population. And some of the New York City dog hospitals are as effete in their way as the elaborate sanitariums for human patients.

A friend of mine tells of a conversation she overheard in the clinic waiting room of one of these dog hospitals. A nervous dog-owner was inquiring about the condition of her dachshund. The answer came back, gravely, from the chart: 'Temperature, normal; respiration, good; ap-

(Continued on next page)

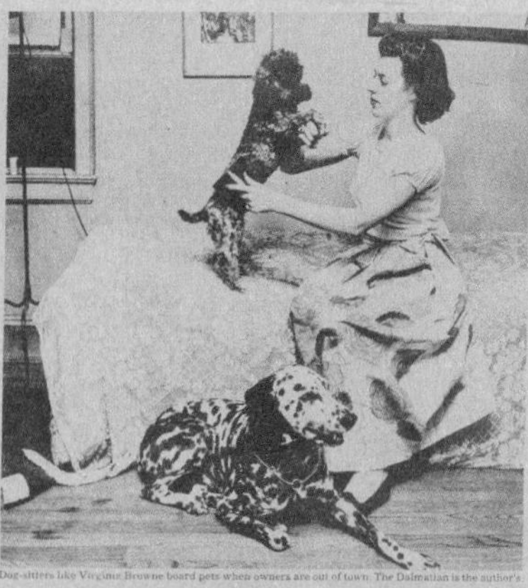

Dog-sitters like Virginia Browne board pets when owners are out of town. The Dalmatian is the author's.

The butcher is one of the city dog's best friends

Eager-eyed spaniels get hand-outs at MacNamara's butcher shop. Customers' dogs get ground sirloin.

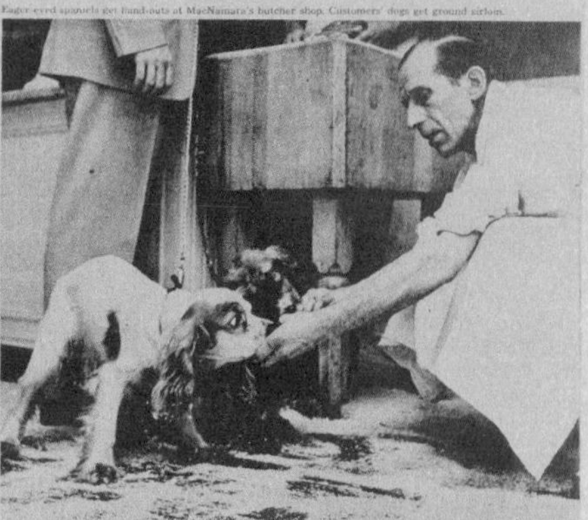

CELEBRITIES and unknowns rub elbows, all intent on selecting right horse in each race. Bets range from $2 to $100 for each ticket (though some bets run to the thousands). Faces, caught by LOOK cameraman, tell race results, indicate tenseness of spectators while horses are running, relief as they win, disgust as they lose.

"RACE-TRACK" wives worry husbands and creditors, spend household allowances on horses, can't meet bills at end of month. Women make up largest part of crowd, yell louder than men, react violently to results. Illogically, ladies bet because horses have pretty manes, familiar names, lucky numbers—win surprisingly often.

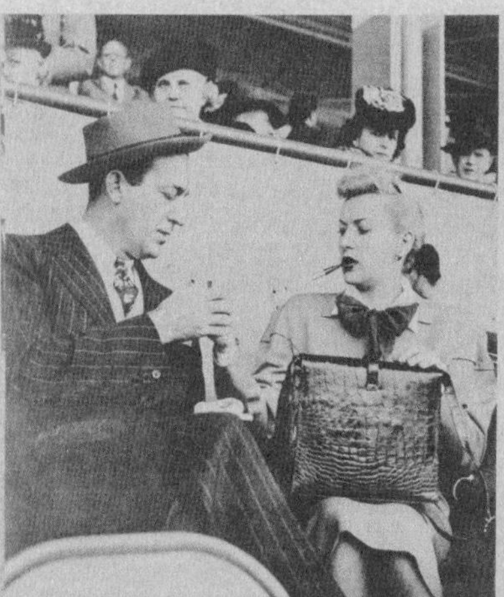

Bandleader Harry James, wife Betty Grable, are tense as they light cigarets; as horse owners, they are regulars at California's Santa Anita and Hollywood Park race tracks.

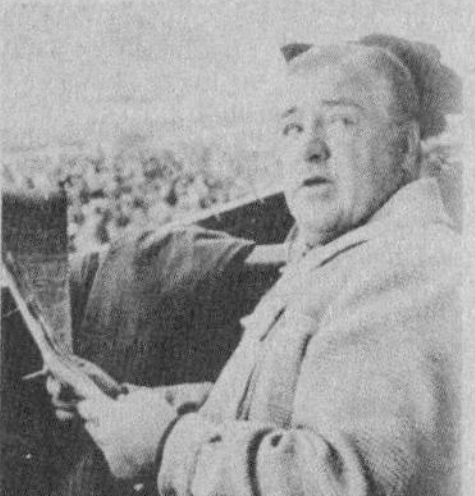

Lou Costello has speculative look. He, like so many fellow Californians, wears sport jacket of loud racing checks to race track.

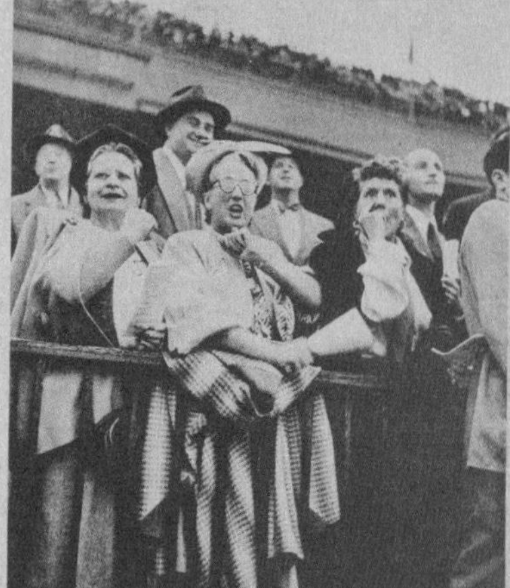

Middle-aged woman, with cinder in eye, typifies older matron who finds horse-racing a time-killer; seems to thrive on excitement.

Shouting women, encouraging their horses, end day almost as exhausted as regular jockeys; comfortable shoes are rule when standing all day at rail for closer view of horses.

CELEBRITIES' REACTIONS *are barometer of betting* . . PUBLIC REACTIONS *are more intense, money means more*

Bud Abbott chews cigaret holder until horses cross the finish line.

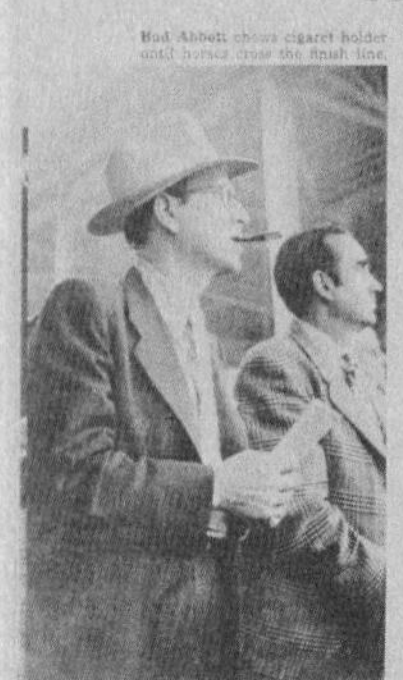

"Prince" Mike Romanoff, Hollywood restaurateur, checks tote-board for odds on next race.

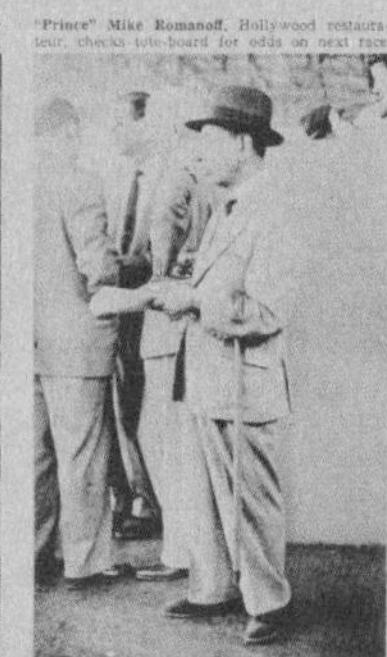

Two New Yorkers, dressed to the hilt, wear feathered hats, elaborate corsages and jewelry; one sports ubiquitous dark glasses.

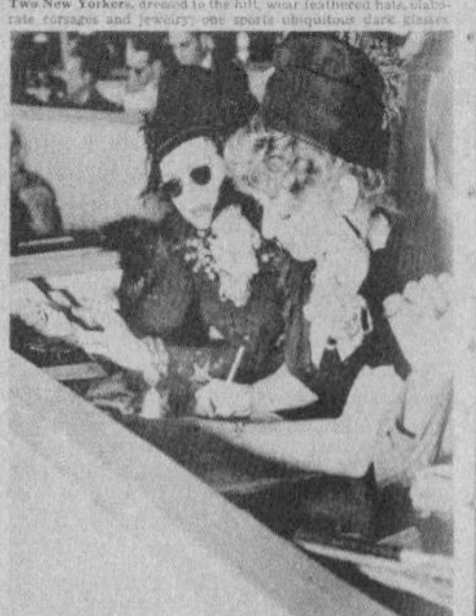

Surrounded by calm friends, lady who apparently bet on a lagging horse yells instructions to jockey, is dismayed when he loses.

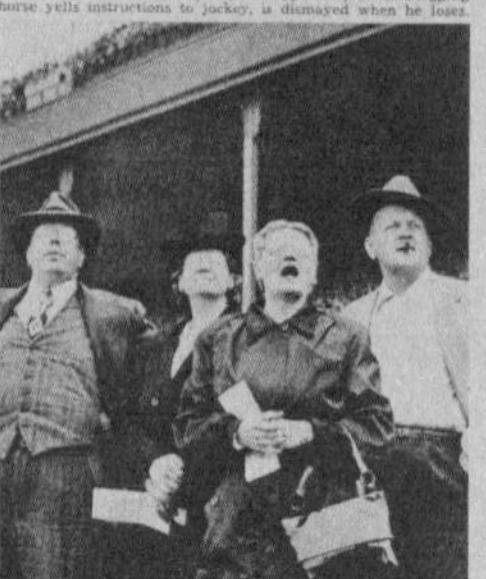

Three women, one disgruntled loser, watch race's end. One acts as if horse she bet on deliberately double-crossed her, friends obviously feel otherwise—must have won.

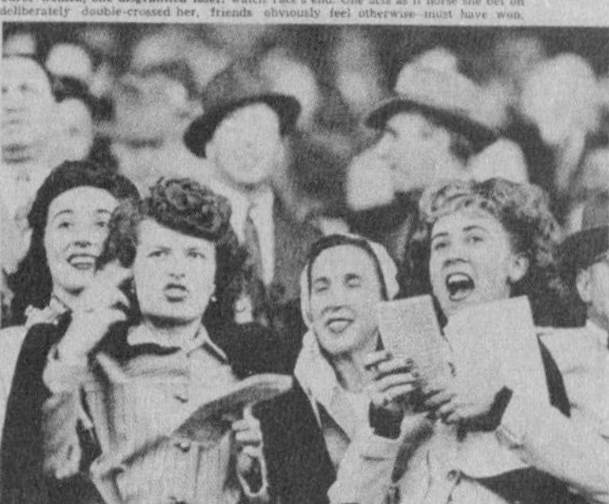